PERGAMON INTERNATIONAL LIBRARY
of Science, Technology, Engineering and Social Studies

*The 1000-volume original paperback library in aid of education,
industrial training and the enjoyment of leisure*

Publisher: Robert Maxwell, M.C.

International Population Assistance: The First Decade

*A Look at the Concepts and Policies
Which Have Guided the UNFPA in its First Ten Years*

To ▮

*In recognition of his
work on human values,*

THE PERGAMON TEXTBOOK
INSPECTION COPY SERVICE

An inspection copy of any book published in the Pergamon International Library will gladly be sent to academic staff without obligation for their consideration for course adoption or recommendation. Copies may be retained for a period of 60 days from receipt and returned if not suitable. When a particular title is adopted or recommended for adoption for class use and the recommendation results in a sale of 12 or more copies, the inspection copy may be retained with our compliments. The Publishers will be pleased to receive suggestions for revised editions and new titles to be published in this important International Library.

Other Titles of Interest

BALASSA, B.
Policy Reform in Developing Countries

BHALLA, A.
Towards Global Action for Appropriate Technology

CLARKE, J.
Population Geography and the Developing Countries

EPSTEIN, T. S. & JACKSON, D.
The Feasibility of Fertility Planning

LASZLO, E.
The Objectives of the New International Economic Order

MENON, B.
Global Dialogue: The New International Economic Order

SALAS, R.
People: An International Choice

SINHA, R. & DRABEK, A.
The World Food Problem: Consensus and Conflict

International Population Assistance: The First Decade

A Look at the Concepts and Policies Which Have Guided the UNFPA in its First Ten Years

by

RAFAEL M. SALAS

Executive Director, United Nations Fund for Population Activities

PERGAMON PRESS

OXFORD · NEW YORK · TORONTO · SYDNEY · PARIS · FRANKFURT

U.K.	Pergamon Press Ltd., Headington Hill Hall, Oxford OX3 0BW, England
U.S.A.	Pergamon Press Inc., Maxwell House, Fairview Park, Elmsford, New York 10523, U.S.A.
CANADA	Pergamon of Canada, Suite 104, 150 Consumers Road, Willowdale, Ontario M2J 1P9, Canada
AUSTRALIA	Pergamon Press (Aust.) Pty. Ltd., P.O. Box 544, Potts Point, N.S.W. 2011, Australia
FRANCE	Pergamon Press SARL, 24 rue des Ecoles, 75240 Paris, Cedex 05, France
FEDERAL REPUBLIC OF GERMANY	Pergamon Press GmbH, 6242 Kronberg-Taunus, Pferdstrasse 1, Federal Republic of Germany

Copyright © 1979 Rafael M. Salas

First edition 1979

British Library Cataloguing in Publication Data

Salas, Rafael M
International population assistance.
- (Pergamon international library).
1. United Nations Fund for Population Activities
- History
I. Title
301.32'1   HB848   79-40301
ISBN 0-08-024701-6 Hardcover
ISBN 0-08-024700-8 Flexicover

Printed in Great Britain by A. Wheaton & Co. Ltd., Exeter

CONTENTS

Appendixes continued on next page.

Appendixes

Preface

I first met Rafael Salas in 1969. He had just been appointed Executive Director of the United Nations Fund for Population Activities and at that time had little more than an office and a great deal of enthusiasm. It is a tribute to that enthusiasm and to his energetic leadership that the Fund is now such a firmly established and well-respected feature of the development scene and that this book, which marks the first ten years of its existence, has so much to tell.

The extent and nature of the Fund's activities have significantly broadened since it was first set up. It now not only provides a reputable source of population information and innovative programme ideas; it also funds and coordinates a wide range of projects in a number of developing countries. Its universal acceptance by the governments of both the developing and the developed world, as well as by non-governmental organisations, is due very much to its adherence to the three fundamental principles of neutrality, flexibility and innovation which Dr. Salas has stressed in his introduction. The increasing number of requests for help highlights the success which it has had in dealing with what still remains for some governments a sensitive subject.

The Fund's recognition that population activities must be an integral part of a country's development is, I am sure, also an important factor in its success. The problems of high population growth rates will not be solved simply through the provision of family planning services. Couples must actually want to reduce their family size and they will not do so until it is clear to them that their families will be healthier, better fed and generally better off. Population and family planning programmes must, therefore, be seen as part of the wider problem of economic and social development, and go hand in hand with development programmes which will promote income creation and improve the total quality of life for the poor.

This book provides a comprehensive source of information on the establishment, development and operation of the Fund throughout its life. It sets out the aims which have guided the Fund, traces the growth of its different policies from their inception to adoption, and looks forward to their possible further development. The layout is unusual; concepts and policies are presented alphabetically, enabling the reader quickly to locate topics of particular interest. It thus achieves a delicate balance of historical and sectoral analysis. Dr. Salas is to be commended for a book which will, I am sure, be of immense interest to a wide range of readers and of particular value to all who are concerned in any way with development issues and the problems posed by population growth.

The British Government, like many other governments, has provided substantial support to the Fund and the book provides ample justification, if any were needed, for our doing this. I look forward to the continued development and expansion of the Fund's activities. I will also look forward with interest to the publication of a similar volume in another ten years time.

London   JUDITH HART
March 1979   Minister for Overseas Development

INTRODUCTION

The year 1979 is significant for the United Nations Fund for Population Activities (UNFPA). It marks, for the organization, ten years of extending population assistance to developing countries. These were years of promoting, testing, demonstrating and enlarging the understanding of population activities globally. For those who have been managing the Fund's affairs, it has been the seminal period for clarifying and conceptualizing these activities.

Unlike most fledgling organizations in the United Nations, the UNFPA began its operations in 1969 without fixed operational guidelines. Population as a field for technical assistance was new and the countries which first contributed the funds were not explicit on the delivery of the assistance. Thus, the Fund was given the broad mandate to promote understanding of the population question and to extend assistance to developing countries in population. Within this wide authority, the Fund had to adopt and put forward policies and operational procedures which in its judgement best met the needs of the developing countries. Initially, this meant adapting what was workable among the operational procedures of the voluntary programmes of the United Nations, particularly the United Nations Development Programme. Population assistance was extended to countries as development assistance was, since this was the type of activity which was already understood by most developing countries.

In a few years, however, a pattern of requests began to emerge from the recipient countries that was distinctively "population". Requests were made and projects were delivered in various categories such as basic data collection, population dynamics, population policies, population communication and education, and family planning. Although links to development projects were maintained, these categories, taken as a whole, were considered eventually to be the field proper for population assistance.

To maintain the responsiveness of this assistance and continue the growth of the UNFPA, I have decided at this time to put together in one volume the concepts and policies that have governed the operation of the Fund in the past ten years. My statements about the UNFPA, which have been generally frugal of emotional expressions, are the basic materials in which these concepts and policies have been explained. Most of these statements have been printed and circulated and have become, in many instances, the bases on which the projects of the Fund have been validated and accepted by both donor and recipient countries.

It is obvious that, because the concepts and policies were thought of in relation to the Fund's activities, their meanings have become stable only as the Fund's activities have been accepted as valid by the countries. Comprehensively, they are products of solving problems while extending population assistance. They are thoughts that have been tested, modified and accepted by countries in the course of giving and receiving support to their population programmes. They are the result of the deliberations of various legislative and political bodies that have governed and influenced the workings of the Fund. They are the decisions that the officers of the organization have individually and collectively made to enable the Fund to reach its objectives. They are also the effects of the interaction of the Fund with institutions, media and action groups outside the United Nations system. All of them were conceived as much as it was possible, within the realistic appraisal by countries of their population problems and their solutions.

The concepts and policies are presented in alphabetical format to enable the reader to refer to them easily. The date beneath each quotation indicates when the statement was made and shows, if the sequence is followed, how the concept or policy evolved or continued after it was first stated. A selection of representative statements in chronological order has been reprinted at the end of the volume to give the reader an insight on how, when and to whom these statements were delivered.

I claim no finality for these concepts nor for their universal application. All that is claimed is that these concepts and policies have worked satisfactorily for the UNFPA in the delivery of assistance. Obviously, the concepts will change in the succeeding years as the countries and the Fund perceive population work differently. New concepts will have to be formulated to accommodate the changes. Some of these concepts will remain valid and workable, others will have to be dropped as irrelevant, and still others may become more important than they are today. One such concept that seems to indicate future prominence is that of population distribution. This was not an area for assistance in the early years of the UNFPA. Now, a number of countries have asked for assistance in this area and the signs are that more will be requested in the future.

This volume may be helpful primarily to those who wish to understand conceptually the workings of the United Nations Fund for Population Activities. It might also be useful to those who work in the ministries and missions of member countries of the United Nations; the different agencies, organs, offices and units of the system; the members of our legislative and governing bodies, councils and committees; to executing agencies and non-governmental organizations that have relationships with the UNFPA; to scholars, academicians and students who are interested in the work of the United Nations in population; to members of the media who may need a source book of information on the Fund's working policies. And perhaps, even more so, to the future officers of the UNFPA, who will be obviously interested in both the continuity and change of the Fund's concepts and policies.

Because, like individuals, organizations must have good memories to be effective, I have endeavoured in writing, editing, correcting and making these statements, to be as consistent as possible. The Fund has been guided from the very beginning by three principles in conceptualizing its work: neutrality towards the population policies of the countries, flexibility in rendering the assistance, and innovativeness in adapting procedures to changing population needs. This responsive stance has enabled the UNFPA to possess a consistent set of policies that has both continuity and stability.

In preparing and writing my statements, I have been helped by many people, mostly from the staff of the UNFPA.

I am particularly grateful to Alex Marshall, former editor of the UNFPA's publication, *Populi,* who helped me most in writing my statements, and to Michael Carder who helped on one or two occasions.

In several important conferences and meetings, the statements of the Fund were collective efforts of the senior staff. In these, Tarzie Vittachi, Stanley Johnson, Hart Schaaf and John Keppel had the primary role in drafting the statements.

Halvor Gille, Deputy Executive Director of the Fund, has contributed extensively in the formulation of the Fund's policies. I have, therefore, included in this volume under his own name policy statements that he has written which are essential for the complete understanding of the Fund's operation.

Finally, I am grateful to Jack Voelpel of the Executive Director's staff for suggesting the format of the book and editing the project, with the assistance of his researcher, Stephen Sanders.

The concepts and policies in this volume are just the first part of a series that must foreseeably come forth from a growing programme like the United Nations Fund for Population Activities. Other views and different directions must, in time, find expression in its sequel.

New York, 31 January 1979   RAFAEL M. SALAS
                                                                  Executive Director

CHRONOLOGY

Events Leading to the Establishment of Operational Activities of the United Nations Fund for Population Activities in 1969

1946

• United Nations Population Commission is established by the Economic and Social Council in October with the objectives of arranging for studies and advising the Council on the size, structure and changes in the world's population, and on the interplay of demographic factors and economic and social factors.

• Population Division is established within the United Nations Secretariat in the Department of Social Affairs to carry out the studies and administer the programmes recommended by the Population Commission and other United Nations bodies. A major task assigned to the Population Division is that of supplying and interpreting facts on population to United Nations agencies and to governments for use in planning their programmes of economic and social development.

1949

• United Nations Expanded Programme of Technical Assistance is established (General Assembly resolution 304 (IV)), the first concerted, large-scale effort by the United Nations system in the use of technical assistance for the economic and social development of the developing countries.

1952

• Technical assistance on family planning is provided for the first time. WHO sends Dr. Abraham Stone to India upon the request of the Government to advise for two months on the application of the "rhythm" method of family planning and the United Nations sends a Swedish statistician, Wahlund, to evaluate the effectiveness of the method. This leads, however, to an extensive debate in WHO with the result that the subject of family planning is disregarded for a number of years.

1954

- The first World Population Conference under United Nations auspices, co-sponsored by the International Union for the Scientific Study of Population, meets in Rome in August and September. It is a purely scientific gathering adopting no resolutions or recommendations to governments.

1962

- In the fall of 1962, the General Assembly holds its first full-scale debate on the question of whether the United Nations should be involved in helping Member States to solve their population problems. In a final resolution (1838, XVII, dated 18 December 1962), the General Assembly recognizes for the first time the close relationship which exists between economic development and population growth. The resolution requests the Secretary-General to conduct an inquiry among Member States and the Specialized Agencies, concerning the particular problems confronting them as a result of the reciprocal action of economic development and population changes, recommends that the Economic and Social Council (ECOSOC) should intensify its studies and research on the interrelationship of population growth and economic and social development, and notes that the United Nations should encourage and assist governments, especially those of the less developed countries, in obtaining basic data and in carrying out essential studies of the demographic aspects, as well as other aspects, of their economic and social development problems.

1963

- First Asian Population Conference is held in New Delhi, India, sponsored by the United Nations Regional Economic Commission for Asia and the Far East (name changed in 1974 to Economic and Social Commission for Asia and the Pacific). Over 200 participants from 14 Asian countries and five members of ECAFE from outside the region attend. A final resolution notes that "the efforts to find satisfactory and effective solutions to population problems are hampered in many countries in the region by lack of facilities and funds, of technical assistance, and of comprehensive and reliable demographic statistics, and by insufficient development of demographic and socio-biological research and shortage of personnel with appropriate training and experience". In its recommendations on "International Co-operation", the Conference specifically notes: "The United Nations and its Specialized Agencies should expand the scope of the technical assistance which they are prepared to give at the request of Governments in the development of statistics, research experimentation and action programmes relating to population problems".

[In an assessment of the first Asian Population Conference, nine years later at the second Asian Population Conference, Rafael M. Salas, Executive Director of the United Nations Fund for Population Activities, said: "The first Conference held in 1963 was of great significance, both for the United Nations system, and for the development of population programmes all over the Asian region. The decision to hold the first Conference was characteristically bold. It came at a time when the international community was deeply divided on population questions. During the 1950's and early 1960's the majority of Member States of the United Nations were reluctant to face up to the implications of rapid population growth. It was the Asian countries which kept population issues alive in international forums and which began an international laboratory for the formulation and implementation of strategies to deal with population problems."]

1964

- The Asian Population Conference leads to the decision of ECOSOC in August to adopt a resolution (1048 XXXVII, "Population growth and economic and social development", adopted unanimously), urging "the Secretary-General and the Specialized Agencies concerned to explore ways and means of strengthening and expanding their work in the field of population, including the possibilities of obtaining voluntary contributions". The resolution draws the Asian Population Conference resolution on this subject to "the attention of the General Assembly".

1965

- In February, the United Nations Technical Assistance Board (later incorporated into the United Nations Development Programme), responding to a request from the Indian Government, sends a five-member group, headed by Sir Colville Deverell, then Secretary-General of the International Planned Parenthood Federation, to India to review the Indian family planning programme and to make recommendations for its expansion. It is the first United Nations-sponsored mission of its kind.

- In March, Julia Henderson, Director of the Bureau of Social Affairs of the United Nations, in response to inquiries concerning the mission to India, noted above, states to the Population Commission that the United Nations, in accordance with relevant resolutions adopted by intergovernmental bodies, is ready to respond to requests from governments for technical assistance in the implementation of their population policies, including family planning.

- In March, the Commission on the Status of Women at its 18th Session adopts a resolution (Resolution 7, XVIII), requesting the Secretary-General to investigate the relationship between family planning and the status of women, and affirms that "married couples should have access to all relevant educational information concerning family planning".

- In March and April, the Under-Secretary-General for Economic and Social Affairs, Philippe de Seynes, at the Population Commission session refers to the rapid growth of population in developing countries, which, he says, is becoming an obstacle to economic progress, and points out that insufficient attention has been given in the past to the influence of population trends and says that this neglect must be rectified. He emphasizes that the United Nations must do its share in this regard by drawing up a constructive programme.

• B. R. Sen, Director-General of the Food and Agriculture Organization, also addresses the Population Commission and says: "The situation certainly calls for the adoption of population stabilization as an urgent social priority."

• At the Population Commission meeting, the report (E/CN.9/182) of an ad hoc Committee of Experts chaired by Miloš Macura (who later becomes Director of the United Nations Population Division) identifies five areas in which research and technical work should be intensified: fertility (to which it assigned top priority), mortality, internal migration and urbanization, demographic aspects of economic development, and demographic aspects of social development. The Committee also recommends that the United Nations should provide assistance on all aspects of population problems, "including inter alia the formulation and execution of family welfare planning programmes". The Population Commission recommends an expanded United Nations population programme for the period 1965-1980 for both the United Nations and the Specialized Agencies in order to meet the present and future needs of Member States. The 15-year programme includes a proposal for widening the scope and increasing the amount of technical assistance to be given to governments at their request on all aspects of population questions, including demographic training, data collection, research, gathering of information and experience, and action programmes—accompanied by a parallel expansion and intensification of research and technical work and other aspects of the population programme at Headquarters and at the regional level.

• In May, the Advisory Committee on the Application of Science and Technology to Development makes its second report to ECOSOC, listing eight problem areas which it believes to be of special significance to a large number of developing countries and which lend themselves to a large-scale attack in which the developed countries might co-operate with the developing countries. One of these eight problem areas is "a more complete understanding of population problems". The Committee says that "there is a strong case for research to be undertaken on a world-wide scale in the three following fields: (a) research on demographic, social and economic interrelationships; (b) research on human reproduction and means for its regulation; (c) communications research in relation to population problems".

• In May, the World Health Assembly, the governing body of the World Health Organization at its 18th session adopts a resolution (WHA 18.49, 21 May 1965) dealing with population activities, which is the first of its kind to be adopted by a United Nations Specialized Agency. The World Health Assembly asks its Director-General to develop further the programme proposed (a) in the fields of reference services, studies on medical aspects of sterility and fertility control methods, and health aspects of population dynamics, and (b) in the field of advisory services including technical advice on the health aspects of human reproduction, providing that such technical advice "should not involve operational activities".

• In May, the United Nations Social Commission meets and agrees that national family planning programmes are essential in strengthening family life and improving the status of women.

• In July, ECOSOC meets and unanimously adopts a resolution (1084, XXXIX, 30 July 1965) which endorses the expanded population programme recommended by the Population Commission, requests the Secretary-General to provide advisory services and training on action programmes in the field of population to governments re-questing assistance, and re-emphasizes the existing authority for providing such services. It invites the regional economic commissions and the interested Specialized Agencies to give consideration "to possibilities of modifying and expanding their programmes of activities in the population fields along the lines indicated by the recommendations of the Population Commission". The resolution requests the Secretary-General "to consider giving a position for the work in population in the United Nations Secretariat that would correspond to its importance".

• In August and September, the second World Population Conference is held in Belgrade, Yugoslavia, under the auspices of the United Nations and the International Union for the Scientific Study of Population. The Conference discusses not only the latest demographic phenomena and population projections, but also fertility and family planning. Because of the nature of the meeting, no resolutions or recommendations are adopted.

1966

• In March, the Commission on the Status of Women welcomes "the increasing recognition of the role of the United Nations organizations in providing assistance, upon the request of governments, in educational programmes concerned with the planning of families". (4, XIX).

• In May, the World Health Assembly reaffirms (WHA 19.43) its earlier decision that "the role of WHO is to give Members technical advice, upon request, in the development of activities in family planning, as part of an organized health service, without impairing its normal preventive and curative functions . . .".

• In October, the Executive Board of UNICEF asks a joint UNICEF/WHO Committee on Health Policy for advice on the best way in which UNICEF might participate in programmes of family planning (E/ICEF/CRP/66-43).

• In November, the General Conference of UNESCO authorizes the Director-General, "in co-operation with the competent international, regional and national governmental and non-governmental organizations, to stimulate and provide assistance towards scientific studies concerning the relations between the development of education and evolution of population . . ." (14. C3. 252).

• In December, Secretary-General U Thant issues a "Declaration on Population" signed by the Heads of State of Colombia, Finland, India, Malaysia, Morocco, Nepal, Republic of Korea, Singapore, Sweden, Tunisia, United Arab Republic and

Yugoslavia. The Declaration is eventually to be signed by the Heads of State of 30 countries. It says, in part:

> "As heads of governments actively concerned with the population problem, we share these convictions:
>
> "*We believe* that the population problem must be recognized as a principal element in long-range national planning if governments are to achieve their economic goals and fulfill the aspirations of their people.
>
> "*We believe* that the majority of parents desire to have the knowledge and the means to plan their families; that the opportunity to decide the number and spacing of children is a basic human right.
>
> "*We believe* that lasting and meaningful peace will depend to a considerable measure upon how the challenge of population growth is met.
>
> "*We believe* the objective of family planning is the enrichment of human life, not its restriction; that family planning, by assuring greater opportunity to each person, frees man to attain his individual dignity and reach his full potential.
>
> "Recognizing that family planning is in the vital interest of both the nation and family, we, the undersigned, earnestly hope that leaders around the world will share our views and join with us in this great challenge for the well-being and happiness of people everywhere."

- In December, the General Assembly adopts by consensus a resolution on "Population growth and development" (2211, XXI) which emphasizes the necessity for accelerated action to implement the expanded programme recommended by the Population Commission and endorsed by ECOSOC. It provides that the United Nations and the Specialized Agencies "should assist, when requested, in further developing and strengthening national and regional facilities for training, research, information and advisory services in the field of population". The resolution recognizes "the sovereignty of nations in formulating and promoting their own population policies, with due regard to the principle that the size of the family should be the free choice of each individual family".

1967

- In May, the World Health Assembly adopts another resolution (WHA 20.41), requesting its Director-General "to continue to develop the activities of the World Health Organization in the field of health aspects of human reproduction" and "to assist on request in national research projects and in securing the training of university teachers and of professional staff".

- In June the International Labour Conference adopts a resolution calling upon the Director-General of the ILO "to undertake a comprehensive study on the influence and consequences of rapid population growth on opportunities for training and employment and on welfare of workers, with particular reference to developing countries, and to co-operate closely towards this aim with the United Nations and other competent international organizations . . .".

- In June also the Executive Board of UNICEF takes action in deciding that UNICEF can assist family planning as part of maternal and child health services, if so requested by a government, in accordance with a recommendation of a joint UNICEF/WHO Committee on Health Policy. The Executive Board further decides that the types of family planning projects which UNICEF could assist, subject in each case to the technical approval of WHO, will be (a) training in maternal and child health care, including family planning, for the health personnel, and (b) the expansion of the basic health services, including the maternal and child health services.

- In July, Secretary-General U Thant in his address to ECOSOC declares that "On the strength of a historic General Assembly resolution, the United Nations can now embark on a bolder and more effective programme of action in this field." He announces that he has decided to establish a trust fund for population activities "to which I hope governments and institutions will pledge voluntary contributions. This would help us to lay the ground for training centres as well as for pilot experiments which will assist the countries in establishing or expanding their own administration and programmes."

- In July-August, ECOSOC adopts a resolution (1279, XLIII, "Development of Activities in the Field of Population") which urges "all organizations within the United Nations system to make every effort, within their competence, with a view to developing and rendering more effective their programmes in the field of population, including training, research, information and advisory services . . . ."

- In September the first contribution to the new Trust Fund is made. The Government of Denmark pledges $100,000 on 11 September 1967.

- In November, the UNESCO Executive Board examines UNESCO's responsibilities in the field of population and endorses "the broad perspectives put forward by the Director-General for the next ten years in regard to UNESCO's action as part of the co-ordinated United Nations programme in the field of population" (77 EX/4.4.1).

- In November also the Conference of the Food and Agricultural Organization of the United Nations calls for a study of food and population problems. It recommends that "the Director-General increasingly involve the organization in the study of the food/population dilemma" and considers that home economics and agriculture extension programmes for women and youth and applied nutrition provide excellent channels to reach the family. The Conference recognizes the need to help families achieve, through appropriate policies and programmes, conditions that will increase well-being and will contribute to national development, and agrees that education and training activities in support of these national programmes, through better utilization of resources and improved nutrition, are within the competence of FAO. Accordingly, it recommends that on government request, FAO be prepared to provide assistance in the organization of educational programmes aimed at helping populations in their search for well-balanced family life.

- In October-November, the Population Commission draws up priorities of work for five-year and two-year programmes within the framework of its long-range 15-year programme, and recommends that greater emphasis should be put on "*action programmes*" at the regional and country levels, and on the establishment of programming machinery to assist governments in identifying population problems in preparing projects for technical co-operation on request.

- In December, Secretary-General U Thant issues another statement on Human Rights Day, on the occasion of being presented additional signatories to the Declaration on Population by World Leaders. He states: ". . . nowadays, population planning is seen not only as an integral part of national efforts for economic and social development but also as a way to human progress in modern society. We observe today rapidly changing attitudes towards the population problem, particularly in the developing countries where the rates of population increase are . . . so high. . . . The work of the United Nations itself in the population field has so far been relatively limited, given the importance of the problem. . . . Our aim is to expand our work in those countries where it is more needed and which request our help. . . ."

1968

- One of the first uses of the Trust Fund's resources comes in the spring to field a programming mission on population to a number of countries in Africa to make an assessment, at regional and country levels, of the present status and requirements for the development of training, research and operational activities in the population field and the steps needed to establish a regional infrastructure for the expansion of work in this field. The six-member mission visits twelve African countries and their recommendations provide the basis for an expansion of population activities at the headquarters of the Economic Commission for Africa and in individual countries of Africa.

[Serving as chairman of this mission was Halvor Gille, then Director of the Division of Social Affairs, United Nations Office at Geneva, who in 1970 was to transfer to the newly-named United Nations Fund for Population Activities and eventually become Deputy Executive Director of UNFPA.]

- In April, in Teheran, Iran, the International Conference on Human Rights, convened by the General Assembly and held during the International Year for Human Rights, meets to review the progress in the field of human rights in the twenty years since the adoption of the Universal Declaration of Human Rights and to formulate a programme for the future. The final act of the Conference - the so-called "Proclamation of Teheran" - states that "the protection of the family and of the child remains the concern of the international community. Parents have a basic human right to determine freely and responsibly the number and the spacing of their children. . . ." In a special resolution dealing with the "Human Rights Aspects of Family Planning" (Resolution XVIII, adopted by 56 votes to none, with 7 abstentions), the Conference declares that "couples have a basic human right to decide freely and responsibly on the number and spacing of their children and a right to adequate education and information in this respect" and urges "Member States and United Nations bodies and Specialized Agencies concerned to give close attention to the implications for the exercise of human rights of the present rapid rate of increase in world population".

[One of those attending the Conference as Chairman of the Philippine Delegation was Rafael M. Salas, who served as a Vice President of the Conference and who would the following year be named Director of the United Nations Fund for Population Activities.]

• In April also the Administrative Committee on Co-ordination attended by the heads of all organizations in the United Nations system, under the chairmanship of the Secretary-General, decides to establish as a subsidiary body an inter-agency Sub-Committee on Population.

• In May, the World Health Assembly reaffirms the considerations expressed in its earlier resolutions regarding WHO's role in population activities. Its resolution (WHA 21.43, Health Aspects of Population Dynamics, 23 May 1968) requests the Director-General "to continue to assist Member States upon their request in the development of their programmes with special reference to: (i) the integration of family planning within basic health services without prejudice to the preventive and curative activities which normally are the responsibility of those services; (ii) appropriate training programmes for health professionals at all levels".

• In May, with almost $1 million already contributed to the Trust Fund for Population Activities, Secretary-General U Thant appoints Richard Symonds of the Institute of Development Studies at the University of Sussex as Special Adviser to the Population Division to study the ways in which the Trust Fund for Population Activities can best be developed as a flexible arm of the United Nations programme in population. He is asked to conduct a study not only of United Nations population programmes financed from all sources, but of the relationship of these to the programmes of other agencies of the United Nations family.

• In May, ECOSOC is concerned with a resolution on "Family planning and the status of women" (1326, XLIV). Calling upon interested governments "to undertake national surveys or case studies on the status of women and family planning, taking into account such factors as the implication for the status of women of the effects of population growth on economic and social development, factors affecting fertility that relate directly to the status of women, the implications of family size for maternal and child welfare, the scope of existing family planning programmes in relation to the status of women, and current trends in population growth and family size and the protection of human rights, in particular the rights of women".

• In July, Secretary-General U Thant declares at the meeting of ECOSOC: "There is a call for United Nations leadership. Now that certain inhibitions have finally been lost, it is for us to establish the needed programming machinery in order to help governments in preparing projects, including the establishment of pilot-projects, in family planning. The financial requirements involved are not so considerable that they should be invoked against more widespread and effective efforts. This is a field where moderate resources, well-utilized, with the knowledge and skills available in the family of United Nations agencies, should produce important results. . . . I also know that some governments are willing to ear-mark additional resources for action projects. I hope that there is by now sufficient moral support so that we can face this challenge without too many financial constraints."

• In July, ECOSOC adopts a resolution on "Population and its relation to economic and social development" (1347, XLV) endorsing the recommendations of the Population Commission on the five-year and two-year programmes and priorities within the framework of the long-range work programme in the population fields. It also recommends that the United Nations Development Programme "give due consideration to applications submitted for financing projects designed to assist developing countries in dealing with population problems, primarily in the fields of economic and social development, including both national and regional projects".

• In September, Symonds submits his report to the Secretary-General on "The United Nations Trust Fund for Population Activities and the Role of the United Nations in Population Action Programmes" (ST/SOA/SER.R/10). After reviewing the activities of United Nations agencies in the population field, he concludes:

"The Trust Fund in its first year has made a useful contribution towards accelerating United Nations action programmes. Its scope, however, should be greatly broadened in the light of the new needs and population policies of governments and of the new mandates of the United Nations agencies. It is suggested that the Secretary-General should inform the organizations which are members of the ACC Sub-Committee on Population that the United Nations Trust Fund for Population Activities is available for use by them as well as by the United Nations, and that he intends to approach governments and private sources for considerably larger contributions in order to support an expanded programme in which the main but not exclusive emphasis will be on family planning. . . . Consideration should be given to the appointment of a Commissioner for Population Programmes who would attend meetings of ACC. The Commissioner would be responsible for raising resources and would preside over the machinery through which funds would be allocated to the agencies and by which their action programmes in the population field would be co-ordinated. His relationship with UNDP would be a matter for discussion between the Secretary-General and the Administrator."

• In September, the newly-named President of the World Bank, Robert S. McNamara, proposes to the Board of Governors "a programme of greatly increased activity by the World Bank Group", to inject new momentum into the global economic effort. He refers to the assistance given to developing countries during the sixties as "too little" and to the shadow cast over development efforts by the "mushrooming cloud of population explosion". He proposes three courses of action that the Bank will consider undertaking in the population field: "First, to let the developing nations know the extent to which rapid population growth slows down their potential development, and that, in consequence, the optimum employment of the world's scarce development funds requires attention to this problem. Second, to seek opportunities to finance facilities required by our member countries to carry out family planning programmes. Third, to join with others in programmes of research to determine the most effective methods of family planning and of national administration of population control programmes.''

[The response of the Board of Governors is positive and two months later the Bank decides to establish a Population Projects Department which is ultimately to carry out the operational work of the Bank in the population field.]

• In October, the first meeting of the Sub-Committee on Population of the Administrative Committee on Co-ordination is held.

• In November, the Governing Body of the International Labour Organisation adopts an enlarged mandate for action by the ILO in the population field.

• In November also, the General Conference of UNESCO approves three resolutions authorizing a special role in the population field for UNESCO (resolutions 1.241, 3.251, and 4.241) in the fields of education, social science, and communication.

• In December, the United States Government announces that it is contributing $1 million to the Trust Fund to finance projects in countries requesting aid for family planning programmes, in addition to its 1968 contribution of $735,000. In the same year, Sweden contributes $200,000, and the United Kingdom, $95,992.

1969

• In January-February, in response to a request of the Government of the United Arab Republic [Egypt], the United Nations fields a three-week, six-member mission, financed under the Trust Fund, to study the organization and administration of the family planning programme established by the Government in November 1965, to identify the needs for external assistance with particular reference to supplies, training, research, and education/motivational aspects, and to assist the Government in drawing up proposals for action projects that might be aided by the United Nations and its agencies.

• During the same two-month period, nine Population Programme Officers are trained at United Nations Headquarters. Upon completion of the course, they are assigned to countries in Africa, Asia, the Middle East and Latin America to assist governments in identifying population problems and in preparing projects in the population field. They are to work closely with Resident Representatives of the UNDP and with officers in the regional Economic Commissions and collaborate with regional and country representatives and experts of relevant United Nations agencies and with other organizations engaged in action programmes in population fields.

• In February, the Economic Commission for Africa, following the recommendations of the 1968 Programming Mission, adopts a Programme of Work and Priorities for 1969-70 which calls for an expanded regional programme in the population field, including enlargement of the population staff in the ECA secretariat and initiation of regional and country projects geared to the most immediate needs of countries in the region.

- In April, a United Nations Consultative Group of Experts convened by the Secretary-General recommends to the Population Commission that a third World Population Conference be held, that the year of such a conference be designated as "World Population Year", and that such a Year should focus world opinion on the humanistic and development aspects of the subject and on the efforts made by the United Nations system and its Member States.

- In April also, the Economic Commission for Asia and the Far East reviews the activities of the ECAFE secretariat in the field of population, and especially the work of the newly-created Population Division in the ECAFE secretariat.

- In May, agreement is reached between the United Nations and the United Nations Development Programme on the administration of the Trust Fund for Population Activities. In an exchange of letters between Secretary-General U Thant and Paul G. Hoffman, Administrator of the United Nations Development Programme, the Trust Fund becomes the "United Nations Fund for Population Activities", a memorandum on "Procedures for Providing and Utilizing the United Nations Fund for Population Activities" is agreed to, and the administration of the Fund is entrusted to UNDP.

- In May, a panel of experts established by the United Nations Association of the United States of America, under the chairmanship of John D. Rockefeller 3rd, in a report entitled, "World Population - A Challenge to the United Nations and its System of Agencies", recommends that a Population Commissioner be appointed within UNDP. The panel estimates that the demand upon the Fund will increase to an annual level of $100 million.

- In August, as a result of earlier discussions in the Philippines between Paul G. Hoffman and Rafael M. Salas, who was serving as Executive Secretary of the Philippines, Salas is appointed as Senior Consultant to the UNDP Administrator.

- In August also, in a letter sent to Member States of the United Nations by the Under-Secretary-General for Economic and Social Affairs, he notes: "It has become clear that the resources of the Fund should be increased substantially in order to enable it to be used to finance . . . new forms of activity in response to the needs of governments; and that the Fund, which has even in its initial stages attracted a number of requests for assistance from developing countries, should be the principal instrument for intensive action by the United Nations family." An attached aide-memoire notes that, "In addition to technical assistance to governments in the usual forms, e.g. advice, experts, study tours, fellowships and seminars, it is intended that the Fund should be available to provide other forms of assistance as appropriate. Among these may be: (a) payment of costs for field, pilot and demonstration projects; (b) payment of costs of training; (c) support for education, information and communication activities; (d) provision of transport, equipment and supplies; (e) support for research and development of statistics; (f) assistance in the local manufacture of supplies and equipment." It is recognized that "the needs of governments for international assistance vary widely in accordance with their situations. The Fund will be available for assistance to governments upon their request over the whole range of population activities. In some cases, for example, the emphasis will be on demographic problems, in some it will be on the formulation of population policies, and in others it will be on assistance in the planning and execution of programmes to implement population policies. Flexibility will, therefore, be maintained in the approach to the population problems of individual countries and in the management of the Fund."

- On 1 October, Paul G. Hoffman, Administrator of the United Nations Development Programme, names Rafael M. Salas to be Director of the re-constituted Fund.

[Note: Information about General Assembly and ECOSOC resolutions dealing specifically with the UNFPA is given in the section "Basic Principles Guiding the UNFPA" under the heading, "Guidelines for the UNFPA from its Governing Bodies".]

Chapter 1

BASIC PRINCIPLES GUIDING THE UNFPA

Defining "Population Activities"

- The words "population" or "population activities" [are] in the United Nations . . . broadly understood to include: population censuses, vital statistics, sample surveys on population, economic and social statistics related to population, related research projects, training facilities required, demographic aspects of development planning, family planning delivery systems, techniques of fertility regulation, planning and management of family planning programmes, support communications, population and family life education in schools and in out-of-school education, the World Population Year 1974, documentation centres and clearing houses on population matters, and inter-disciplinary population training. (29 January 1973)

- [An] illustration of the scope of the Fund's work may be furnished by a simple enumeration of the headings under which . . . projects [are planned, approved and implemented]:

  Basic population data, including population censuses, vital statistics, sample surveys, economic and social statistics, and supporting activities.

  Population dynamics, including research projects, training and research facilities, and population aspects of planning.

  Population policy, including assistance to countries in policy formulation, and implementation of policies.

  Family planning, including delivery systems, programme management, and fertility regulation techniques.

  Communication and education, including communication for motivation, in family planning population education in schools and in out-of-school programmes.

  Multisector activities, including World Population Year, documentation centres and clearing houses, inter-disciplinary training, and general programme support.

  Programme development. (4 May 1973)

- Programmes supported by the Fund can be classified in different ways. The geographical classification comprises various kinds of programmes, such as: country programmes, regional programmes, interregional programmes and global programmes. (21 May 1975)

• Within these categories [defined as "population activities"] a great deal of flexibility is required; an activity which has only marginal population content in one society may be vitally important in another. In each case, the particular conditions and concerns of the recipient country should be paramount. (21 November 1975)

[In late 1977, the United Nations Administrative Committee on Co-ordination adopted a "Standard Classification for Population Activities". The breakdown of population activities now is:

(1) basic data collection - census, surveys, registration systems, other systems; (2) population dynamics - analysis of demographic data, determinants of fertility, determinants of mortality, determinants of migration, determinants of other population trends, consequences of population trends, interaction of demographic and socio-economic variables, including modelling, demographic projections, other; (3) formulation and evaluation of population policies and programmes - formulation of policies, including legislation, evaluation of policies and programmes, integration of population factors in development plans and programmes, other; (4) implementation of policies - fertility, other than family planning, sterility, morbidity and mortality, internal migration, international migration, other; (5) family planning programmes - community-based delivery systems, other delivery systems, contraceptives, management and evaluation of programmes, other; (6) communication and education - communication for awareness of population issues, population education in schools, out-of-school education, other; (7) special programmes (n.e.c.) - status of women, children and youth, the aged, the economically active, the disadvantaged, other special groups; (8) multisector activities - inter-disciplinary, programme development. The specific kinds of activities under each of these broad categories are: general, training, research, support communication and dissemination of information, action programmes, and other.]

General Guidelines

• The role of the Fund will differ considerably from country to country, depending on each country's level of development and population patterns. Broadly, it can be envisaged in stages as:

(a) to assist governments in determining the size of populations and to assess population trends;

(b) to assist governments in understanding the consequences of population trends in relation to economic and social development;

(c) to assist governments in formulating population policies, taking into account all factors which affect fertility;

(d) to assist governments which adopt population policies in carrying out and evaluating measures to control fertility, including assistance in organization of family planning programmes and in training for an evaluation of such programmes;

(e) to assist governments in preparing requests for assistance in the form of projects.

It is not the UNFPA's intention that programmes financed by the Fund should compete with those financed from other sources.

The Fund [is] to be "action-oriented", that is, to be devoted to the most effective ways that can be found for the solution of population problems by those countries having such problems and requesting assistance of the Fund. (10 November 1969)

• We shall not solicit requests unless we have good reason to be confident of our ability to handle them financially and administratively. (18 November 1969)

• There are . . . instances where the UNFPA is a logical funder since useful capabilities to deliver a certain type of assistance clearly exist within the United Nations system, the activation of which in the population field is one of the Fund's responsibilities. In some instances, moreover, the Fund probably should try to fill gaps in the assistance furnished by other donor agencies. . . . It is also probably true that the UNFPA, as a donor agency, should enter certain national programmes primarily to extend the capabilities of the United Nations system so that this system may be more useful in the future. (16 October 1970)

• The United Nations Fund for Population Activities makes two fundamental assumptions in providing assistance - (1) the United Nations system does not prescribe any population policy to any country, and acts only when a country requests assistance, and (2) population programmes are not substitutes for economic development efforts, but are necessary complements to them.

The guidelines for the Fund's operations [are]:

(a) recognition of governments' sovereignty in determining their own policies, but responding to their requests for assistance;

(b) utilization, wherever possible, of the appropriate organizations in the United Nations system as executing agencies but, if necessary, also utilizing other channels for execution of the proposed intensified activities;

(c) aim at broadening, if necessary, requests received from governments or organizations in the United Nations system to include, as appropriate, one or several of the approaches outlined . . . as the policies of the UNFPA;

(d) utilization, to the fullest extent, of the Population Programme Officers* in the preparation of projects for UNFPA financial support;

*The Population Programme Officers of the United Nations Population Division were later replaced by UNFPA Field Co-ordinators.

(e) strengthening the implementation and follow-up activities of projects approved for UNFPA financing; and

(f) undertaking evaluations of the impact of the UNFPA's assistance to developing countries. (18 February 1971)

• While there is a considerable variation in the pattern by which UNFPA assistance is programmed, some basic elements must be considered in all cases.
Among these are:

(a) the assistance to be programmed must be in accordance with the priority needs identified by the government of the recipient country, sometimes jointly with a non-governmental organization, as necessary;

(b) the assistance is usually channelled through the co-ordinating authority established by the government;

(c) the effective co-operation and participation of the executing agencies of the United Nations system, and other non-governmental organizations, where relevant, must be sought at the earliest stages of programming;

(d) the effective co-ordination by the recipient government of all external assistance in the population field must be encouraged. (18 May 1972)

• We are neutral in so far as national population policies are concerned. The Fund does not prescribe any particular solution to population problems and acts only at the request of governments. Assistance is provided on all aspects of population to which governments attach importance.

This [policy] has enabled the Fund to support a wide range of projects in countries with very different political and economic structures and cultures. . . . Our concept of population problems covers much more than high fertility and rapid rates of population growth. We are concerned with low rates of population growth, high levels of infant mortality, international migration and urbanization [and] . . . we are fully prepared to respond to requests, if any, for support of activities concerning problems of underpopulation as related to economic and social development.

We are prepared to support population activities in developing countries which will advance economic and social development and improve the quality of life. In our activities, we take fully into account the great diversity of conditions and attitudes regarding population which prevail in various parts of the world. . . . (10 August 1972)

• Collaboration between the Fund and developing countries can only be successful if based on mutual respect and understanding. (1 November 1972)

• The Fund's approach to the global problem can be divided into three broad areas. In the first place, we promote government awareness of the social and economic implications of population problems. Secondly, we provide systematic and sustained assistance to developing countries seeking to define and solve these problems. Thirdly, the Fund helps organizations both inside and outside the United Nations system to become more effective and efficient in planning, programming and implementing projects supported by UNFPA.

Another important aim of UNFPA is the formulation of population policies in keeping with national development objectives and targets. (14 February 1973)

• The main objective of the Fund is, and must be, universal participation, as the only means of bringing the knowledge, skills, expertise, experience and financial resources of all nations to bear on a problem that *concerns* all nations.

Perhaps . . . this is a bold statement for any one person to make, and a difficult target for any United Nations agency to aim for. But [we] believe, and a great many governments seem to be of similar mind, that the policies being pursued by the United Nations Fund for Population Activities offer the best possibility, and perhaps the only possibility, of getting adequate international co-operation in the sensitive and complex area of population.

The Fund's operations resolve themselves into three fundamental principles - neutrality, flexibility, and innovation.

First, *neutrality*. UNFPA does not prescribe any particular approach or solution to population problems but provides assistance in those areas to which developing countries themselves attach importance. As a result, UNFPA assistance is not limited to one aspect of population problems but covers a broad spectrum, ranging from vital statistics to the development of improved methods of fertility control. Assistance is provided irrespective of the attitude of the recipient with regard to population growth.

This principle has made the Fund's assistance welcome in countries . . . which contest the neo-Malthusian approach to population questions, countries . . . with large Catholic populations, and in [countries] . . . where the government's objective is to increase fertility. It has also made it possible for countries with an equally wide range of political persuasions and economic systems to contribute to and participate in the Fund.

Secondly, *flexibility*. The Fund has always been extremely flexible in the types of assistance it provides. For example, it could, in certain strategic sectors, provide for local and construction costs. When contraceptive supplies and equipment are essential for a programme but locally unavailable, arrangements are made to meet such shortages.

Criteria for project appraisal are applied with close attention to national needs and conditions; and the implementation of projects is entrusted to the organizations both outside and inside the United Nations family which have the greatest competency in the particular area.

Above all, the Fund is flexible in the kinds of activities it undertakes. For example, it is willing, under certain circumstances, to support activities in which the area of direct population concern is only part of the overall project. This has arisen several times in connection with family planning when, in order to carry out this part of the programme, it has proved necessary to help support basic health services and facilities, and on other occasions, to give assistance to on-going projects in the field of manpower planning, workers' education, and out-of-school education projects, in order to obtain the framework for population programmes.

Thirdly, *innovation*. The Fund has attracted attention in the United Nations system because of its willingness to adopt new approaches whenever the need arises. This applies to headquarters as well as field operations. In a very short period of time, its headquarters secretariat has been reorganized in order to respond more efficiently to requests for assistance. Consultative arrangements have also been set up which give participating governments, United Nations agencies and non-governmental organizations a much greater say in programme formulation. Moreover, when specific problems arise, the Fund is not slow to use task forces of specialists to help solve them.

The Fund has also moved towards new relationships with recipient countries under which governments play an important part in the administration of external assistance. . . .

It is part of the complexity of population programmes that there is no operational blueprint. Time and time again, questions arise for which there are no precedents and no easy answers. (14 February 1973-B)

• The Fund, in accordance with its mandate, does not advocate any specific policies or prescribe any particular courses of action. Its entire programme closely reflects the stated needs and identified priorities of the countries themselves. (15 February 1973)

• The Fund [recently] . . . began to orient its activities increasingly towards responding directly to requests from governments for country level activities. The needs for assistance varied greatly from region to region, and indeed, from country to country, and it became apparent immediately that the UNFPA's approach would have to be flexible and multi-faceted. The pattern of activities which developed during 1970 and 1971 was thus shaped essentially by the wishes and needs of the developing countries themselves, as they saw them, rather than by any pre-ordained strategy. (8 March 1973)

• We must be sure that our projects and programmes really reflect the needs and wishes of countries. If they do not, it will not matter how good the design of the project may look on paper, the project is unlikely to be implemented effectively by the country in question and is virtually certain to do no lasting good once it has been terminated. (30 April 1973)

• Each commitment made is just that—an act of trust in the administrations concerned, a declaration that we are willing to rely on their judgement of conditions and needs in their own country and on their ability to carry through the complex and difficult work of implementation. Because of this fundamental demonstration of trust at the outset, we find, as the relationship proceeds, that we can make suggestions on policy as interested friends, not as creditors. We believe we can have a profound influence on the mechanism not only of the project or programme which we have financed, but on all areas of policy which touch on population and this means, in a developing country, on development policy itself.

To [some] the act of giving implies not gratitude or repayment but mutual respect and concern between giver and receiver. The relationship between the Fund and those with whom we work is of this kind, a true symbiosis in which giving is only the first stage.

We learn from our operations—and our mistakes—and we pass on our experience in turn. (25 August 1973)

• We take as our premises, firstly, that the Fund's work relates to the most delicate, the most intimate of all human activity, so that programmes must always be geared to the needs of the individual. Secondly, we and all who work in the field are relatively inexperienced in effective methods of approaching population problems, and must therefore be prepared to innovate. Thirdly, the environments in which we work, and the values with which we have to deal, are very different from the general run of Western experience. Fourthly, that the role of foreign assistance is marginal and must therefore be injected at the time, and in the area, where its effect will be to generate further activity. (18 October 1973)

• The United Nations Fund for Population Activities is a firm believer in the possibility of national development for the poorer countries of the world, and in its necessity for the whole of mankind. . . . (13 November 1973)

• We can only respond when we are asked, and a government must be sure when it asks us for help that it is aware of the real needs of its people. (2 April 1974)

• We have developed this philosophy of assistance partly through observing the experience of others, and partly through the necessities of the type of assistance we are offering. It is of the nature of population assistance that it operates on a personal level. It must reach and affect directly the behaviour of individual people—not like a loan for a factory or an airport, whose effects, good or bad, operate indirectly. (19 April 1974)

• The two major principles always followed by the Fund: that every nation has the sovereign right to determine its own population policy, and that each individual couple has the right to determine the size of its family. (27 January 1975)

• What . . . is the task of those of us who have been charged with the responsibility of working in the population field? The challenge, surely, is to continue and ever intensify our efforts to develop population awareness, to assist in identifying population problems, and to help as generously and effectively as possible in the solution of such problems. We must not lose heart because of the lengthy time perspective of population phenomena. (19 June 1975)

• Its neutrality, its responsiveness to national policies, and its flexibility in meeting changing needs have enabled UNFPA to become today the largest multilateral channel for international assistance in population. (23 June 1975)

• The World Population Conference in Bucharest did come up with a consensus: that population programmes be considered part of the development process—an approach that UNFPA has adopted ever since it started to deliver assistance to countries. (23 October 1975)

• Responsiveness has been the key to the rapid growth of the UNFPA. Its responsiveness to the needs of the developing world is the reason for its acceptability by countries and communities—donors as well as recipients—with very different political and cultural attitudes towards the population question, which . . . is one of the most sensitive issues in human relationships, though . . . it is not a controversial matter as far as the Fund and the governments with which it works in partnership are concerned.

The UNFPA has been evolving from its meagre beginnings into something more than a dispenser of funds for programmes executed by institutions within the United Nations family. The Fund has the responsibility for funding and co-ordinating projects in near-ly all the developing countries; it is an institution which governments, as well as non-governmental organizations, with special concerns and varying attitudes on population questions, have begun to regard as a trustworthy, neutral and sensitive instrument for international assistance on this subject. It is also a bank of ideas on population and an innovator of techniques designed to respond to needs by delivering assistance quickly. UNFPA has thus been evolving into a worldwide population programme.

Its manner of delivering assistance was designed to establish within the United Nations system a Fund that would be responsive both to the developed and developing coun-tries not just for the next few decades, but for as long as the United Nations considers the problem of people crucial. This time perspective we have always considered vital in the building of the institution. (20 February 1976)

- The Fund is concerned, as we always have been, with the totality of development, believing that only in this way can the purposes of population programmes be fulfilled. (2 June 1976)

- For some time now, the United Nations Fund for Population Activities has acted as "honest broker" between developed and developing countries in population questions, wherever possible assisting each group to discover the problems, needs and possibilities of the other and to move towards a consensus on this vital question. (12 January 1977)

- From the beginning, the Fund has assumed that population covers a far wider area than family planning, that population growth had to be seen within the context of each country's economic and social circumstances, and that programmes should reflect na-tional needs.

The principles . . . which have guided our work from the outset [are] that our task is to promote population activities, particularly in those countries whose need is the most urgent; to respect the sovereign right of each nation to formulate, promote and imple-ment its own population policies; to promote recipient countries' self-reliance; and to give special attention to the needs of disadvantaged population groups. That these principles have not only survived but have been strengthened by time is a tribute to the foresight of their progenitors. They have given, and continue to give us, a matrix on which the Fund and governments can co-operate harmoniously in making plans for the future. (2 June 1977)

- We serve developing countries; we do not ask them to serve us.

UNFPA believes, as the World Population Plan of Action states, that, "of all things in the world, people are the most precious". (5 July 1977)

• One of UNFPA's concerns is that population and development, as means and as ends [with respect to one another], are dovetailed with each other so that they work together for the common good. (26 March 1978)

Guidelines for the UNFPA from its Governing Bodies

• The main purposes of the United Nations Fund for Population Activities are:

(1) to extend systematic and sustained assistance to member countries desiring such assistance to assess and cope with their population problems;

(2) to assist governments in promoting an awareness of the social and economic implications of the population problem, and of possible solutions;

(3) to help to co-ordinate population programmes among various elements of the United Nations system; and

(4) to extend the capabilities of the relevant agencies of the United Nations system within the framework of their respective mandates and to provide them with the means for more efficient and effective assistance to member countries in planning, programming and implementing population projects.

The terms of reference of the Fund encompass assistance on all aspects of population which have an important bearing on economic and social development; and education, research and data gathering on any relevant factors may be supported. No population policy, and indeed no serious economic and social planning, can be formulated unless it is based on sound demographic and statistical foundations. Fund assistance will be provided in appropriate cases to help such foundations. In this initial stage of the Fund at least, however, primary emphasis will be placed on operational programmes and projects assisting to moderate fertility rates where such assistance is desired. (16 October 1970)

• The plan of action [regarding the work of the Fund and the other United Nations bodies in the population field], with the limited resources available for application and solution of the problems, should concentrate on moderating trends in fertility and population growth. It should cover within this area a considerable number of activities, including improvements in existing technology, the development of research facilities, and the training of personnel needed for policy making, research and action; and also the establishment of operational facilities for the preparation of effective logistics, communications and education. (4 November 1970)

• Our functions in UNFPA headquarters and in the field . . . are to appraise projects, to fund projects, to co-ordinate the formulation and execution of projects among agencies and of programmes executed by other agencies outside the United Nations system, to monitor projects and programmes funded by us, and to provide for their evaluation in suitable cases. (18 February 1971)

• The rapid expansion of the Fund has brought a number of changes in its wake affecting the policies, directions and structure of the Fund. The most significant development was the adoption of resolution 2815 (XXVI) by the General Assembly at its last session [1971]. The Assembly noted that the Fund has become a "viable entity in the United Nations system" and was "convinced that the Fund should play a leading role in the United Nations system in promoting population programmes - consistent with the decisions of the General Assembly and the Economic and Social Council . . . ." It "recognized the need for the executing agencies of the Fund to implement with dispatch, in close co-operation with the Fund, population programmes requested by developing countries in order that such programmes may have the desired impact". The operative paragraphs of the resolution read as follows:

[The General Assembly:]

"1.   *Invites* Governments which are in a position to do so and whose policies would allow it to make voluntary contributions to the United Nations Fund for Population Activities;

"2.   *Requests* the Secretary-General, in consultation with the Administrator of the United Nations Development Programme and the Executive Director of the United Nations Fund for Population Activities, to take the necessary steps to achieve the desired improvements in the administrative machinery of the Fund aimed at the efficient and expeditous delivery of population programmes, including measures to quicken the pace of recruiting the experts and personnel required to cope with the increasing volume of requests, as well as to consider the training of experts and personnel in the developing countries;

"3.   *Further requests* the Secretary-General to inform the Economic and Social Council at its fifty-third session and the General Assembly at its twenty-seventh session of the steps he has taken in the implementation of the present resolution and of any recommendations he may wish to make in this regard."

To give effect to this resolution, a Review Committee of the UNFPA Advisory Board was created under the chairmanship of Ernst Michanek, Secretary-General of the Swedish International Development Authority.* (18 May 1972)

• In reporting to the [UNDP] Governing Council and in appearing before it, we are conscious of all the provisions of General Assembly resolution 3019, including the provisions of operative paragraph 2, which states that the Governing Council of UNDP shall

---

*The Review Committee was appointed in March 1972 and made its report to the Secretary-General in October 1972. Indicating that "the Fund must have a clearly defined status and place within the United Nations system", the report made a series of 25 recommendations regarding the UNFPA, "by which it may more effectively discharge its responsibilities". In fact, the Fund had already taken measures itself to improve its administrative machinery and programming. See "Report to the Secretary-General of the United Nations from the Review Committee of the United Nations Fund for Population Activities", New York, October 1972, 50 pp.

be the governing body of UNFPA* "subject to conditions to be established by the Economic and Social Council", presumably to be enunciated at the April 1973 session of ECOSOC. (29 January 1973)

• After receiving the report [of the Review Committee of the UNFPA Advisory Board], the Secretary-General directed a note to the Twenty-seventh General Assembly regarding the affairs of the Fund. After debate, the General Assembly decided:

(1) to place the Fund under the authority of the General Assembly;

(2) "without prejudice to the overall responsibilities and policy functions of the Economic and Social Council", and "subject to conditions to be established by ECOSOC", to make the Governing Council of the United Nations Development Programme the governing body of the UNFPA;

(3) to invite the Governing Council to concern itself with the financial and administrative policies concerning the work programme, the fund-raising methods and the annual budget of the Fund; and

(4) to authorize the Governing Council in its Fifteenth Session, held this January, to apply to the UNFPA funding principles similar to those of the UNDP and to establish the necessary financial rules and regulations, subject to consideration by the Governing Council of a report prepared by the Executive Director of the UNFPA in consultation with the Administrator of the UNDP. (8 March 1973)

• In formulating its programmes of assistance the Fund has adhered to policy decisions and recommendations which have emanated from the General Assembly of the United Nations, the Economic and Social Council and governing bodies of other organizations of the United Nations system. Most notable are recognition of the sovereignty of governments with respect to the formulation and promotion of population policies; the right of parents to determine their family size and to obtain the necessary information and means required to do so; the voluntary participation of a country's population in action programmes; and respect for the wishes of governments with regard to the execution of programmes at the national level.

The Fund does not prescribe any particular policy or approach in dealing with population problems. It acts only on request, and with due respect for national and regional attitudes. It recognizes that population policies and programmes are not alternatives to, or substitutes for, economic and social development, and that population planning is not an end in itself. The Fund has seen its main responsibility as meeting the most urgent needs of developing countries for support in carrying out population activities which can contribute to economic and social development.

In some regards they [the recommendations of the Review Committee] are already be-

*General Assembly resolution 3019 (XXVII), 18 December 1972. In January-February 1973, at the 15th Session of the UNDP Governing Council, the UNFPA made its first report to it as the Fund's new governing body. Prior to this time, the Fund had as its governing body an Advisory Group appointed by the Secretary-General and made up of prominent individuals from a number of developing and developed countries. The Advisory Board met four times (twice in 1970, and in 1971 and 1972) to provide policy guidance to the UNFPA. With the naming of the UNDP Governing Council as the Fund's governing body, the Advisory Board was abolished.

ing executed by us, and in another, the matter of UNFPA's Advisory Board, they have been overtaken by the action of the General Assembly. (4 May 1973)

• General Assembly resolution 3019 . . . stipulated that the governing body of the Fund should carry out its functions "subject to conditions established by the Economic and Social Council". Accordingly, the Executive Director, in consultation with the Administrator of UNDP, submitted a written report to the 54th session of ECOSOC, in which he reviewed the development and policies of the Fund.

Taking note of the Executive Director's report, ECOSOC on 18 May passed a resolution (1763, LIV), the operative paragraphs of which

(i) established the aims and purposes of the Fund,

(ii) directed UNFPA "to invite countries to utilize the most appropriate implementing agents for their programmes, recognizing that the responsibility for implementing rests with the countries concerned", and

(iii) requested that the Governing Council of UNDP submit annually to ECOSOC a report on the activities of the UNFPA.

So that the Governing Council may understand and judge how UNFPA interprets these aims and purposes . . . it may be worthwhile to review them and for [us] to indicate, in connexion with each, the types of activities that the Fund contemplates undertaking.

Operative paragraph number one of the ECOSOC resolution gives these aims and purposes in four paragraphs, (a) through (d). . . .

(a) "To build up, on an international basis, with the assistance of the competent bodies of the United Nations system, the knowledge and the capacity to respond to national, regional, interregional and global needs in the population and family planning fields; to promote co-ordination in planning and programming, and to co-operate with all concerned". Basically we interpret this paragraph to urge the Fund, with the assistance of other elements of the United Nations system, to play a leading role among development assistance agencies in the efforts of the world as a whole to acquire the knowledge and capacity to cope with population problems. We visualize doing this in several ways.

First, we have been seeking to develop, in the UNFPA staff, capacity in the fields of project development, assessment, monitoring and evaluation. While we have no intention of duplicating the substantive capabilities of the United Nations or the agencies, we are aware that we cannot shirk our own decision-making responsibilities in the allocations process. Hence we have felt that we must build up a basic level of competence in the various fields to an extent which will permit us to seek and understand expert guidance when we need it.

Second, we are aware that the permanence of the effects of the programmes we are funding will depend to a major extent on our ability to build up institutional capacity on a regional and national basis permitting countries to understand and cope with their own population problems. Hence, we have to date spent more than one third of our resources on training. We have, moreover, devoted from between 15% to 20% of our resources to applied research in relevant fields.

Third, we have sought to co-ordinate our programmes with those of other donor agencies in the population field. On a country level, where we were qualified to do so, we have taken a leading role as co-ordinator among all external assistance agencies. On a headquarters level, UNFPA has had a consultative body called the Programme Consultative Committee, whose members were drawn from other agencies. . . . Since this Committee, although consultative, had certain aspects of a governing body, we suspended it after the General Assembly's appointment of the UNDP Governing Council as our governing body. Now that the affairs of the Fund have been considered by the fifteenth session of the Governing Council and by ECOSOC, and we have had some indications as to how these bodies visualize governing us, we believe that it would be reasonable and useful to reconstitute the Programme Consultative Committee as a technical advisory and programme co-ordination body, and have started exploratory steps in this direction. There were indications at the fifteenth session of the Governing Council that this was favoured by a number of the distinguished delegates. In addition to plenary sessions where general programme matters would be discussed, the Committee might have other sessions devoted to problems in specific functional fields, such as demographic data collection and analysis, family planning programmes, etc. As well as permitting us to benefit from the experience and advice of the unusually knowledgeable people who would be its members, the Committee would also serve as an international body in which programme co-ordination among the donor organizations represented could be effected.

(b) "To promote awareness, both in developed and in developing countries, of the social, economic and environmental implications of national and international population problems; of the human rights aspects of family planning; and of possible strategies to deal with them, in accordance with the plans and priorities of each country". The Fund has carried out its promotion of awareness in the light of its principle of respect for the sovereign right of all states to determine their own population policies. In this context, the Fund has conceived of its duties on several levels:

(i) on the level of a dialogue between the UNFPA and other entities of the United Nations system, on the one hand, and recipient governments on the other, to assist the latter better to visualize the effects of demographic factors in their economic and social development and the options open to them in dealing with these issues;

(ii) on the level of the public within states, the Fund supports communication or education projects only at the request, or with the knowledge and consent, of the governments concerned. The Fund's activities in connection with the World Population Year constitute a special effort to promote consciousness of, and interest in, population problems and activities. Again, however, the Fund's efforts to this end are limited to countries which wish to participate in the World Population Year and have so stated. The Fund's point of departure was, with the assistance of the Secretary-General, to urge governments to set up national commissions to serve as a focal point for official and unofficial groups within the country interested in population matters.

(c) "To extend systematic and sustained assistance to developing countries at their request in dealing with their population problems; such assistance to be afforded in forms and by means requested by the recipient countries and best suited to meet the individual country's needs." In the earliest phase of our administration of the Fund, it was only natural that a substantial proportion of the activities supported should have been of a promotional nature, hence many were initiated by the agencies. For the past several years, however, we have sought to give first priority to our response to requests for assistance with country population programmes. In this, moreover, we are seeking to assure ourselves that the projects and programmes developed really will reflect the country's wishes. . . . The Fund is appointing . . . UNFPA Co-ordinators in developing countries, to assist UNDP Resident Representatives. . . . We believe UNDP Resident Representatives, with the assistance of the UNFPA Co-ordinators, through their contacts with governments, will play a vital role in assuring that the programming developed with UNFPA resources does in fact reflect the real needs and wishes of the recipient countries.

(d) "To play a leading role in the United Nations system in promoting population programmes and to co-ordinate projects supported by the Fund." Since population problems, and hence their solutions, are multi-sectoral and multi-disciplinary, population programmes have often involved a number of United Nations agencies. It was thus only natural that the Fund should feel responsible for attempting to co-ordinate interrelating components of assistance furnished through a number of organizations in the United Nations system. For this purpose, we have held semi-annual meetings with the concerned agencies in the Inter-Agency Consultative Committee, to discuss programming, co-ordination and procedural matters. We are now taking further steps to increase the cohesiveness of the country, regional and global programmes we are funding. Several agencies, at our request, are now presenting all their regional, interregional and global projects to us in a single package so that, with them, we may make sure that they form a coherent whole.

As regards operative paragraph number two of the ECOSOC resolution, which directed UNFPA to "invite countries to utilize the most appropriate implementing agents for their programmes, recognizing that the primary responsibility for implementing rests with the countries concerned", the Fund has already taken some steps in this direction. (14 June 1973)

• UNFPA has been entrusted by the General Assembly with leadership within the United Nations system on population problems. But we are not in any sense a world population council. Our primary function is to assist [countries] in carrying out those activities to which they attach priority. (22 October 1973)

• In December 1972 the General Assembly terminated our status as a trust fund of the Secretary-General and made us a fund of the General Assembly. Subject to policy guidance by ECOSOC, the UNDP Governing Council was established as our governing body. The Fund thus achieved a clear legislative basis and was brought under the control of an appropriate inter-governmental body, both developments of which we had felt the need and which we had sought. At the January session of the Council and, more particularly, at its June session, we worked out with it the means by which it would govern us, and a general schedule for these activities.

We were authorized annual funding, under which only the anticipated expenses of the current year have to be held against current resources. It was agreed that we would present a four-year work plan together with a projection of anticipated resources and programme costs, to the Council annually at its June session. Under a "rolling plan" arrangement, it was agreed that these resource and programme cost estimates would be revised annually in the light of developments, as would be the "approval authority" which we requested of each June Council to cover the approvals which we anticipated having to make during the next 12 months.

The Council asked the Fund to bring to it for approval, at either its January or its June session, three categories of projects or programmes: comprehensive country agreements, projects of a total value of $1 million or more, and projects which because of their innovative character or policy implications were worthy of the Council's attention.

Authority to approve other projects, within the financial ceilings prescribed by the Council, was delegated to the Executive Director, "in consultation with the Administrator of UNDP".

In its May [1973] session, the Economic and Social Council passed a resolution (1763, LIV) with regard to the Fund which, largely on the basis of the Report of the Review Committee, reformulated UNFPA's aims and purposes. They differed from the previous statement on the subject primarily in two ways:

Increased scope was given to the Fund in its choice of implementing agents, whether inside or outside the United Nations system, and for more direct relations between the Fund and recipient countries. Indeed, in this latter regard, ECOSOC went beyond the language of the Report and stated that the Fund "should invite countries to utilize the most appropriate implementing agents for their programmes, recognizing that the primary responsibility for implementing rests with the countries concerned".

In accordance with this directive, UNFPA is experimenting carefully with various ways of using its own channels for passing resources directly to recipient governments. Even in such cases, however, the Fund envisages using another organization with substantive capabilities, normally the United Nations organization with a mandate in the field, to carry out whatever technical assistance component may be involved and to assist the Fund in monitoring substantive aspects of the project. If, of course, in accordance with the language of the ECOSOC resolution, the recipient country desires us to associate ourselves with an external organization other than the obvious choice from within the United Nations system, we shall, in consultation with the government, select one.

In addition, with regard to the Fund's promotion of "awareness" of the implications of population problems, the ECOSOC resolution specified "both in developed and in developing countries", whereas [the Fund's] previous formulation had only mentioned developing countries. (6 November 1973)

- We believe that henceforth the Fund and the Governing Council should address themselves seriously to the programming implications of the relationship between population and economic and social development. Although much literature has been devoted to the subject, a lot remains to be done to clarify specific aspects, as well as a whole range of practical steps that can be taken on both the national and international levels so that population programmes may truly serve as an integral part of broader economic and social programmes. We would hope that the World Population Conference in August of this year will clarify some of these issues in more concrete terms and that the next sessions of the Governing Council will consider the implications of this with regard to the work of the Fund. (30 January 1974)

- Last May's [1973] ECOSOC resolution . . . we believe, together with the Fund's newly recognized position in the United Nations system, offers us an adequate legal framework for making UNFPA assistance truly responsive to the needs and wishes of developing countries. It is now up to us to do this, and to arrange the efficient and timely delivery of the assistance programme. (27 February 1974)

- UNFPA is responding to the General Assembly's resolution 31/170 of 21 December 1976, which endorsed five important principles for the Fund's future allocation of resources.*

First, the principle that UNFPA should promote population activities proposed in international strategies. A number of international strategies have been adopted which are relevant to UNFPA, such as the International Development Strategy for the Second Development Decade, the Programme of Action on a New International Economic Order, the World Population Plan of Action, the World Plan of Action on Integration of Women in Development, and the World Plan of Action on Desertification. They are all giving us useful guidance.

The World Population Plan of Action adopted by consensus by 135 states attending the World Population Conference, which is of special importance to the work of UNFPA, emphasizes an integrated development approach to population. In this regard, UNFPA continues to collaborate in development programmes into which population activities can be integrated, particularly through our field staff and in collaboration with UNDP and other agencies and programmes. In such collaboration, UNFPA provides assistance for the population components in integrated programmes, while other development assistance bodies support the other components of integrated programmes as required.

The second general principle established by the General Assembly is "to meet the needs of developing countries which have the most urgent need for assistance in the area of population activities, in view of their population problems". While this principle does not deprive any country of assistance, because all countries are entitled to receive UNFPA support, it seeks the increasing application of our resources to support a group of forty priority countries. These countries have been selected on the basis of objective

*Earlier endorsed by the UNDP Governing Council at its Twenty-second Session in June 1976 and by ECOSOC in resolution 2025 (LXI) of 4 August 1976.

demographic and economic indicators endorsed by the Governing Council, which take into account rates of population growth, levels of fertility, infant mortality, population density on arable land, and per capita national income. Seventeen of the priority countries are located in Africa, fourteen in Asia and the Pacific, and the remainder are evenly distributed between the regions of Latin America and the Mediterranean and the Middle East. At present, around 45 per cent of our resources available for country programmes are committed to supporting activities in priority countries. We intend gradually to increase this share and hope to reach the goal established by the UNDP Governing Council of allocating two-thirds of our funding at the country level to the priority countries by 1980.

The three other important general principles in the resolution concern the respect of the sovereign right of each nation to determine its own population policies, the promotion of countries' self-reliance, and the importance of giving special attention to meeting the needs of disadvantaged population groups. These principles will mainly be applied by UNFPA through the formulation of basic needs programmes in the field of population. In order to determine basic population needs, we first identify the countries' population policies and programme objectives, then we assess the domestic resources available for furthering them, and finally we try to determine the assistance required from external sources. [We] should like to underline that these programmes are being prepared in full collaboration with the governments concerned and are being worked out *with* governments and not *for* governments.

In developing basic population needs programmes, UNFPA will give special attention to meeting the needs of disadvantaged population groups. The success of population and development policies depends very much on meeting the demands of these groups, which comprise a very large proportion of the population of many developing countries. (7 November 1977)

Flexibility

• We are conscious of . . . the need for the utmost flexibility in order to adapt our procedures to the very different situations prevailing in different countries. (10 November 1969)

• One of the reasons for the rapid expansion of UNFPA assistance is due to the flexibility of the Fund procedures for considering requests. This flexibility is possible because:

(a) Projects may be approved by the Executive Director of the Fund according to a flexible system of consultation.

(b) In addition to covering the financing of the usual technical co-operation aspects of a project, UNFPA is prepared to cover substantial local costs of specific projects. Such local costs may include salaries of locally employed personnel.

(c) Construction costs may be financed on a demonstration basis if they comprise a relatively small part of a programme.

I.P.A.—D

(d) The choice of executing agencies for Fund-supported projects is made in collaboration with the requesting country and in consultation with the appropriate body, if any, of the United Nations system.

(e) Innovative projects within the terms of reference of UNFPA are encouraged. (18 May 1972)

• The Fund is unusual among United Nations agencies in that it was set up to carry out specific tasks flexibly, as a Secretary-General's Trust Fund which until recently was without a formal governing body. This has made it easier for us to develop methods of work which permit a variety of different types of assistance and a faster response than is the case with some more formalized organizations within the system. (5 February 1973)

• The Fund will undoubtedly change as much in the coming years as it has in the past three. The built-in flexibility of our organization ensures our ability to adapt. (14 February 1973)

• Criteria for project appraisal are applied with close attention to national needs and conditions; and the implementation of projects is entrusted to the organizations both outside and inside the United Nations' family which have the greatest competency in the particular area.

Above all, the Fund is flexible in the kinds of activities it undertakes. For example, it is willing, under certain cirumstances, to support activities in which the area of direct population concern is only part of the overall project. This has arisen several times in connection with family planning when, in order to carry out this part of the programme, it has proved necessary to help support basic health services and facilities, and on other occasions, to give assistance to on-going projects in the fields of manpower planning, workers' education, and out-of-school education projects in order to obtain the framework for population programmes. (14 February 1973-B)

• The Fund . . . [recently] began to orient its activities increasingly towards responding directly to requests from governments for country-level activities. The needs for assistance varied greatly from region to region, and indeed, from country to country, and it became apparent immediately that the UNFPA's approach would have to be flexible and multi-faceted. The pattern of activities which developed during 1970 and 1971 was thus shaped essentially by the wishes and needs of the developing countries themselves, as they saw them, rather than by any pre-ordained strategy.

The operating policies of the UNFPA have retained their flexibility as our assistance has provided support not only for advisory services, seminars, fellowships, research, transportation, equipment and supplies but also for local cost items such as salaries, local cost of training, procurement of locally manufactured goods and construction of facilities.

The Fund applies its policies and criteria for project appraisal as flexibly as possible. We are, however, conscious of the fact that we should formalize these policies. The Fund is, therefore, compiling a handbook of policies and criteria for project appraisal, which will be useful not only for our own staff but also to countries. [We] want to stress that we recognize that one of the great advantages of the Fund is that it has the capacity to respond quickly and in a fashion which has been appropriate for meeting the requirements of requesting governments and organizations. It is hoped that, in the interest of the developing countries, this flexibility can be maintained in the future to the greatest extent possible. (8 March 1973)

• The Fund has been developing methods which may be applicable in other areas. They depend on flexibility of response to different needs; on a willingness to approach each new request for assistance without pre-conceived ideas or ready-made solutions; and on the ability to make resources available when and where they are needed with a minimum of delay. These three principles . . . make possible a relationship with governments stronger and deeper than is usual between donor and recipient. (25 August 1973)

• During this period of rapid development, the Fund has found that the utilization of a rolling plan system based upon a multi-year Work Plan has offered the greatest flexibility in meeting urgent population needs while at the same time ensuring the financial integrity of the Fund. (19 June 1975)

• An activity which has only marginal population content in one society may be vitally important in another. In each case, the particular conditions and concerns of the recipient country should be paramount. (21 November 1975)

• Over the years, one of the most important lessons we have learned has been the necessity to adapt to the changing needs of both recipient and donor. We have discarded what is not valid. We have streamlined and updated and modernized our operations to fit the needs of those countries which require assistance.

In being flexible, UNFPA has tried not to be bound by standard technical assistance models, but rather has attempted to meet the needs which countries feel most urgently, no matter what type of UNFPA assistance is required. (21 June 1977)

Neutrality

• United Nations agencies cannot prescribe any particular population policy for any country. The choice, formulation and adoption of a particular policy is left to each government. But once a policy is adopted and the assistance of the United Nations is requested, there is considerable latitude where the international assistance could vitally strengthen the national effort and minimize existing deficiencies in the implementation of programmes. (4 November 1970)

• UNFPA assistance is not limited to one aspect of population problems, but covers a broad spectrum, ranging from vital statistics to the development of improved methods of fertility control. Assistance is provided irrespective of the attitude of the recipient with regard to population growth.

This principle has made the Fund's assistance welcome in countries . . . which contest

the neo-Malthusian approach to population questions, countries . . . with large
Catholic populations, and in [countries] . . . where the government's objective is to increase fertility. It has also made it possible for countries with an equally wide range of
political persuasions and economic systems to contribute to and participate in the
Fund. (14 February 1973-B)

• [We] do not use *neutrality* as a synonym for *passivity*. It has always been the Fund's
policy to maintain a strict neutrality in regard to government decisions on the kind of
population programmes they wish to undertake. But it has been an equally firm Fund
policy to act as quickly as possible in giving assistance in advancing these programmes
once the decision has been taken. (23 March 1973)

• The terms under which the UNFPA was set up demand that it be neutral in its approach to population. This has the great advantage that the countries asking for our
assistance can do so confident that we will not attempt to impose any particular view
upon them or dictate any solution. We can and do support programmes aimed at increasing fertility as well as reducing it. But there is another side to this: We can only
respond where we are asked, and a government must be sure when it asks us for help
that it is aware of the real needs of its people. (2 April 1974)

• The United Nations Fund for Population Activities is an agency they [governments]
can trust because they themselves, along with the other Member States of the United
Nations, control its policies. Politically, they know, it will be neutral; even if they
wanted to increase population growth rather than decrease it, they could still ask for
and receive its help. (19 April 1974)

Innovation

• In the implementation of the programmes, it is essential that the Fund and the agencies
respond quickly and adequately to the country requests. Steps will be taken to employ
modern managerial techniques to minimize delays in implementation. (10 November
1969)

• The Fund has attracted attention in the United Nations system because of its willingness to adopt new approaches whenever the need arises. This applies to headquarters as well as field operations. In a very short period of time its headquarters
secretariat has been re-organized in order to respond more efficiently to requests for
assistance. Consultative arrangements have also been set up which give participating
governments, United Nations agencies and non-governmental organizations a much
greater say in programme formulation. Moreover, when specific problems arise the
Fund is not slow to use task forces of specialists to help solve them.

It is part of the complexity of population programmes that there is no operational
blueprint. Time and time again questions arise for which there are no precedents and
no easy answers. (14 February 1973-B)

• The Fund welcomed the responsibility . . . [for the World Population Year preparations because, *inter alia,* the Year] would hopefully stimulate a responsible interest in

population which could well result in the development of innovative approaches to population problems and open up new channels for interchanges and communication of population knowledge and experience. (23 March 1973)

• We and all who work in the field are relatively inexperienced in effective methods of approaching population problems, and must therefore be prepared to innovate. (18 October 1973)

• It is incumbent upon all of us who are involved in the administration or implementation of assistance programmes also to take a close look at what we are doing in order to see if we really are flexible enough to adjust to change, innovative enough to find new solutions, and responsive enough to put the real needs of countries, as defined by their governments, before any other consideration.

Population work, except for its demographic aspects, is largely a development of this decade. Thus it should be freely admitted that experience in population matters is relatively limited, and that for many years to come it will be necessary to try out a wide range of approaches by no means only representing the thinking of the industrialized regions. In fact, it is already apparent that some developing countries are well ahead in understanding population situations and in determining appropriate actions to deal with population pressures in whatever form they appear. (29 October 1973)

• The problems of governments in promoting development, and in the utilization of international assistance to development, are numerous. The establishment of effective management techniques may prove to be of vital importance, yet there may be many difficulties to be overcome. As one management expert said, "A mere transposition of techniques from developed to underdeveloped countries is bound to encounter many difficulties and can produce results which may be largely irrelevant".

Most of the modern management techniques available are best suited to short and medium-range tactical questions, whereas the problems of developing countries involve primarily strategic and long-range planning considerations. Again, the process of change in developing countries, although fast, is both uneven and erratic. The precise timing and nature of change is difficult to anticipate, and it is doubly difficult to coordinate changes in rational fashion.

Many decision-makers in developing countries are not sophisticated in the use of . . . models. This may lead, on the one hand, to impatience with . . . models, or to overblown expectations and consequent disappointment when they are put to use, and, on the other, to oversimplification, in the hope of making the model more readily comprehensible. However, it has been accurately pointed out that efforts to simplify operations research approaches and techniques with the intention of putting them within reach of personnel with little knowledge of operations research are not likely to produce models and results commensurate with the problems they attempt to solve.

Yet another difficulty relates to the uneven nature of funding capability in most developing countries. Most simply do not have the available funds to carry out the comprehensive studies which may be needed. This, too, requires systematic planning of a kind which is probably unfamiliar to most practitioners of management science in the developed world.

[Another] problem relates to programme design. Here the basic questions with which we are struggling are: Given a specific population policy direction, what types of programme structure are most effective, and how can the process of programme organization most effectively proceed at national, regional and local levels?

Much work is being done on this programme design question, but severe data constraints, especially, have hindered model development, thereby leaving decision-makers with few guidelines beyond experience. The need is still to define parameters, develop measures of effectiveness, identify controllable as against non-controllable variables, and examine the many relationships between inputs and programme objectives.

[Yet another] problem relates to specific programme implementation questions, particularly concerning family planning delivery systems. Given a delivery system and set of inputs, how can the efficiency of the programme processes be maximized? There are many discrete problems in this area where operations research seems particularly applicable. These include:

(1) Establishing targets for programme utilization,

(2) Establishing the most effective mix of service functions to meet the forecasted demand, and

(3) Designing clinic work flows and schedules.

Apart from the development of usable management information systems, the model-building challenge for us lies mostly in the areas of resource allocation and evaluation. With our limited resources we must meet the demands of over 90 countries for all kinds of projects. To allocate our resources on other than an arbitrary or ad hoc basis we need methods for defining the status of a country programme and establishing priorities, given the very political systems with which we interact. (13 November 1973)

• What we have done in the past, the services we have been able to offer, and the resources we have been able to provide are not going to be nearly enough to meet the challenges from governments who are being asked to think in terms of greater commitment to attacking the problems of poverty, environment and population and of coping not only with their own difficulties but of contributing to an international chain of assistance.

All this calls for dynamic leadership from the United Nations family in sponsoring innovative programmes, and in encouraging new ideas and approaches, even at the expense of traditional methods. (21 January 1974)

• Success, like failure, leads to further problems. The many . . . who have managed programmes share [a] conviction that a manager's work . . . is never done. . . . Quick and easy solutions in this field of development [population], as in other human endeavours, may not be available. What is called for . . . is a continuous intelligent effort, using the tools at hand and attempting to develop better ones, undiscouraged that the mammoth problems ahead can only slowly be reduced. (30 January 1974)

• As every mountain climber knows, after the upward climb there is always the other side of the hill. We are now at a point when serious thought must be given as to how the impetus built up by the [World Population] Year can be maintained; when we must ask ourselves what form continuing population programmes should take; and when we must prepare ourselves to take advantage of the doors that have been opened and the acceptance obtained for new and innovative approaches. (4 March 1974)

• We have responded to government criticisms of the costs, delays and eventual ineffectualness involved in the traditional system of supplying foreign expertise by increasingly turning towards reliance on local expertise and local programme managers and, where necessary, paid their salaries. The advantage of this innovation in dealing with such a culturally sensitive matter as population, not to mention the saving of time and expense, is self-evident. In line with this, we have provided funds for the purchase of local materials and equipment, wherever possible, and in a few cases, and in limited amounts, even for construction of facilities.

The reaction to these innovations and to their immediate impact on action programmes has been overwhelmingly supportive, and even laudatory, to judge by the statements made by countries at meetings of our Governing Council and of the Economic and Social Council. . . . (20 February 1976)

Chapter 2

BUCHAREST AND AFTER

World Population Conference 1974

[The 3rd World Population Conference was held at Bucharest, Romania from 19 to 30 August 1974. It was the first intergovernmental conference on population sponsored by the United Nations. It was attended by representatives of 136 States. Secretary-General Kurt Waldheim opened the Conference by indicating that it should be viewed not in isolation, but as one of an extended series of important international events which together could determine the course of the United Nations in the rest of the century. He particularly referred to the International Conference on Human Rights held at Teheran in 1968, the United Nations Conference on the Environment held in Stockholm in 1972, the special session of the General Assembly on raw materials and resources in April of 1974, the World Food Conference to be held in Rome in November 1974 and the Conference on Human Settlements to be held in Vancouver in 1976. Each of these events, he said, emphasized a particular aspect of the closely interconnected set of problems which confront the world. The global nature of these problems made complex demands on the United Nations system, he said, and impelled it to take the central position.]

• [We] hope that during World Population Year [1974] and the World Population Conference [at Bucharest in August 1974] the barriers of ideology will fall, and we shall all speak of the population problem as a common one, part of the whole problem of the future of man. (14 February 1973)

• The World Population Conference . . . will bring together government leaders and specialists, to exchange views on population issues and to consider a draft World Plan of Action being formulated by the Secretary-General. The achievement of a consensus on the different aspects of current population problems which could be embodied in an overall strategy would indeed be a major accomplishment. (14 February 1973-B)

• This exercise of heightening awareness in World Population Year is primarily designed to enable the nations of the world to formulate their own policies and to frame their plans for action, so that when they send their delegations to Bucharest in August 1974 to attend the World Population Conference . . . the discussions would be undertaken in an informed ambience which, hopefully, would make it possible for nations with vary-

24

ing viewpoints on population, viewpoints based on cultural and ideological differences of attitude and emphasis, to arrive at a workable consensus of opinion leading to a practicable World Plan of Action on population. (7 July 1973)

• The idea of population programmes as a legitimate area for national activity has spread . . . taking hold even in areas where there was traditionally strong ideological or cultural opposition. . . . We are now in a situation where we can begin to look for broad agreement between nations, at the World Population Conference next year, on the principles of a common World Population Plan of Action.

World Population Year in 1974 and the World Population Conference offer a new opportunity . . . to participate in an international discussion and action on every aspect of population, including this most vital one of international assistance. . . . Working together, governments and non-governmental organizations around the world have an opportunity to take the dialogue on population which has developed in the last few years, and mould it into a consensus acceptable alike to developed and developing, donor and recipient countries. (25 August 1973)

• The success of the [World Population] Year will depend almost completely on the extent to which demographers, economists, social scientists and communicators of all kinds, ranging from politicians and [educators] to journalists and broadcasters, give their attention to intensifying worldwide awareness of the population problem and of heightening interest in population matters, so that in 1974 there will be a large body of informed opinion contributing to, and supporting, the deliberations of the World Population Conference.

In such an atmosphere of informed awareness, there is every reason to believe that the delegations to the World Population Conference will arrive with well-formulated national policies and plans of action which will make it possible for them to air varying and often widely divergent political, cultural and ideological viewpoints. . . . (27 August 1973)

• It would be unrealistic to look forward to 1975 without anticipating that the Conference will lead to widened concepts of population, to re-thinking of national plans, to new approaches to population questions, and perhaps to radical transformations in the form and priorities of multilateral assistance.

For the first time, the basic issues of population will be considered by the world's principal governmental decision makers, within the context of the common needs for food, for education, for housing, for technology, for health services, for employment, as well as from the angle of specific national situations.

Each representative will have much to contribute to, and much to gain from, these discussions. And so will we. [We] confidently expect that those of us who are engaged in administering external assistance will receive better insights on ways of making this assistance more effective. But the implications of the Conference are infinitely more significant than the mere finding of solutions for current difficulties. (4 March 1974)

• The [World Population] Conference deserves more than cursory notice and preparation before the opening date, and will call for continuous attention and action long after it is over. . . . It is of primary importance to everyone. No one can afford to be disinterested, because it is the interest of everyone that is at stake. Population is you and me and our children and our friends and our colleagues and our acquaintances, our way of life and our hopes for the future. It is not something that only concerns the other fellow and his habits.

The basic fact that is confronting all of us at the present time—and which is the real theme underlying the Bucharest Conference—is that no matter what we do, the earth's population is going to double in 25 years. This, unless there is world catastrophe of mammoth size, is a mathematical certainty. The young men and women are already growing up and the children are already born that will make it so.

While the Conference cannot be expected to provide ready-made answers to population questions, it is an opportunity not to be missed as a forum for exchange of views, for examining national problems against an international setting, and for, hopefully, reaching a consensus on the need for worldwide attention to population matters, even if the problems, the policies and the programmes may differ from country to country. Accordingly, the success of this Conference . . . will depend on the contribution each delegation makes to it, and on the widened concepts of population that each delegation derives from it.

But [we are] not merely asking you to help make this Conference a landmark in population history, [we are] asking you to gear yourselves to give continuing and sustained support to the mounting United Nations effort to assist countries in dealing with their population problems, of which this Conference is only a single event. (6 March 1974)

• The Conference in August is not a culmination so much as a springboard from which population activities will take off. The debate which has already started will not be resolved in August, only encouraged, but, we hope, within the framework of mutual respect and understanding which the World Population Plan of Action will provide.

One of the key areas of debate [during the World Population Conference] will be the part which is to be played by population assistance. (16 May 1974)

• We are looking forward to the World Population Conference as a renewal of our commitment to the tasks that we have been assigned. (9 July 1974)

• Decisions [of the Conference] substantially validate the approach of the Fund to population assistance. In particular, UNFPA wholeheartedly welcomes the emphasis of the Bucharest Conference on population programmes as an integral part of overall economic and social development efforts, and agrees that many elements of the latter will themselves have important demographic effects.

It is an essential corollary to the Conference that governments should be in a position to prepare demographic goals, along with other goals in all elements of economic and social programmes. (7 October 1974)

• Only ten years ago population was a subject of such delicacy that the United Nations and its agencies felt unable to become involved in action programmes. The United Nations Fund for Population Activities was set up only five years ago in its present form. In that short space of time, countries have resolved their differences sufficiently to allow nearly all members of the United Nations to attend the Bucharest Conference and to agree on a World Population Plan of Action.

Even after Bucharest there are, of course, many differences remaining. But increasingly they appear to be differences of form rather than content. One nation may reject family planning as unnecessary in a well-ordered society, and at the same time include all known forms of contraception in universally available health services. Another may reject outright population control, yet at the same time carefully build up a sound demographic base for development planning, which will in all probability include indications of the desired level of population growth. (15 October 1974)

• Past experience has shown that interest in a particular area of the United Nations' concerns tends to die away soon after it peaks at a major conference, so that the valuable commitments made on such occasions are perhaps irretrievably lost. The awareness and understanding developed during World Population Year need to be nurtured and kept alive. (17 April 1975)

• The increasing awareness of population factors as variables in the development process, and the growing role of the Fund to assist developing countries in responding to their needs, have been particularly evident in the post-World Population Conference regional consultations that have been taking place since January. . . . These consultations, sponsored jointly by the UNFPA and the United Nations, in collaboration with the secretariats of the regional Commissions concerned, all voiced the hope for augmented funds to deal with population matters, as well as the urgent need for new and continued assistance for population activities. (14 July 1975)

• A few cynics condemned both the World Population Conference and the World Food Conference as failures because neither came up with ready-made solutions to the problems which they were set to confront. Such critics chose to look only at the superficial events of these conferences while ignoring their wide repercussions. . . . The [World Food] Conference provided an opportunity to raise the level of consciousness among the public, and to make the peoples of different countries aware of the problems of others—and of likely effects on themselves. This in itself would have provided a justification for the Conference.

The World Population Conference can show a similar educating effect on the public. Like the World Food Conference, it was the first occasion on which governments of nearly the whole world sat down together to discuss the subject. Many differences were visible in Bucharest, sometimes very bitterly expressed, but the result in the year since the Conference was held has been a consolidation of the consensus which was emerging before it. Population is now acknowledged by all governments to be a legitimate area of concern, whatever their views on population growth.

A vital part of the consensus reached at Bucharest was the idea that reduction of top-heavy population growth rates depends, in addition to family planning programmes, on the steady improvements in basic conditions of life for the poorer sections of the population - in most developing countries, the rural and agricultural majority. Even a small improvement in health, housing, education and other services can apparently have a significant effect on fertility rates. (26 September 1975)

• The World Population Conference . . . did come up with a consensus: that population programmes be considered part of the development process—an approach that UNFPA has adopted ever since it started to deliver assistance to countries. This is a positive acknowledgement by the world that population is an important problem to be acted on in accordance with each country's policy.

At Bucharest, the discussions were long and often acrimonious. Meetings between informal groups went on far into the night. . . . But the willingness to meet as often and as long as necessary is itself an indication that agreement is desired—and in fact a document emerged from the World Population Conference with the endorsement of the delegations present. This is no small achievement. Since then, further discussions have been going on at national and regional levels, which are producing the first indications of regional priorities.

The five regional Commissions of the United Nations, covering all the developing countries and Europe, have all met this year and have agreed on common approaches to population questions. There are wide variations in emphasis, as you would expect in such differing circumstances, but there are enough elements in common to make agreement on priorities a likelihood.

There was agreement at Bucharest that individual rights were all-important in the matter of fertility regulation. (23 October 1975)

• At Bucharest, it became clear that opposition to what was regarded as Western thinking on population was much deeper-rooted than had been thought. There was much suspicion of those who wished for decisive action to lower birth rates. On the other side, there were bitter accusations that the debate had been diverted from its real subject—population—into issues which were important in themselves but peripheral to the subject of the Conference. There was, in some cases, a mutual failure to see the point of view of the other side, so that a rather sterile debate seemed to be taking place between "development", on the one hand, and "population", on the other.

But even at the height of controversy, voices could be heard saying that there was no need for such polemics. The World Population Plan of Action acknowledges as much, at least on paper. In the year since the Conference, although scattered gunfire has been reported, there are some indications that the combatants are recognizing that they have several things in common. These include interest and concern in successful development programmes to meet the needs of growing populations, and involvement in population activities as a vital component of development strategy. (21 November 1975)

• In the United Nations, emphasis on the principle that population size and growth were a matter for national decision inhibited concerted international action on population matters for many years. The World Population Conference debated this principle for two weeks, during which ample evidence was provided that population remained a highly sensitive topic of debate. At the same time, sufficient agreement was reached to allow the impression that the subject had been dealt with adequately. . . .

At the same time, it is clear that most governments have accepted the view that in their own national circumstances there is a negative correlation between population growth and development, and that a long-term strategy of reducing the birth rate is not only prudent, but a necessary part of economic and social programmes. . . . Effectively, there is a consensus on population among developing nations.

We have now arrived at the curious position where there is an international consensus in a highly sensitive area of policy, but few internationally accepted quantitative goals. Although there has been a considerable shift in opinion even in the two years since the World Population Conference . . . the World Population Plan of Action remains the main evidence of world agreement on population—and that document is less than specific in several key areas. (12 January 1977)

• Over the eight years since the UNFPA was set up, the geographical and topical range of population activities has expanded enormously. This is particularly noticeable since the World Population Conference in 1974.

This is a response to [*inter alia*] acceptance of the role of international assistance in population activities. The watershed in this respect was the World Population Conference, during which it was internationally accepted that population and development efforts were essentially means to the same ends. This acceptance has made it considerably easier for governments to approach organizations such as UNFPA for assistance. (6 December 1977)

• The year 1974 was an important one for the population field. It marked the public coming-of-age of population discussion. Prior to the . . . World Population Conference . . . the dominant perception of population programmes was focused heavily on family planning. As with so many public perceptions, it was, unfortunately, misguided for many institutions and individuals, unlike the UNFPA, which from the inception of its operations acted upon a much broader view of population concerns.

The political forum of the Bucharest Conference . . . served to direct attention to, and interest in, a broader, less simplistic, more sophisticated view of the mutual interrelationships between population and development factors.

The conferees left Bucharest without agreement on a single definition of the population problem, but with greater awareness of the range of problems that exist, or are made more difficult, when "population growth, distribution and structure are out of balance with social, economic and environmental factors". They also brought home with them a greater awareness of the degree to which these factors have an impact upon population dynamics. The relation between population growth and economic growth, which was at the heart of the classical economic theory of Ricardo and others, and which had been to a large extent ignored in the fifties and sixties, was re-established, with deeper meaning. The neo-Malthusian position that population growth made rapid economic growth difficult was laid to rest on the basis of the historical evidence garnered during the preceding thirty years. Rather than looking at population in the aggregate, attention was directed to the components of the population. Population growth, assumed to have been independent of socio-economic development and change, was now seen as intimately and mutually related. Population, once viewed as exogenous by development planners, was now seen as endogenous. The maturation and sophistication of population thinking put an end to simplistic models of population change. (3 April 1978)

Developing a Sufficiency Society

• Development must be diffused socially and geographically throughout all levels and throughout all areas. A society of sufficiency for all, replacing the distortions of both excess and deprivation, must be our aim.

When we speak of a society of sufficiency for all, we are not just speaking of the developing countries. Sufficiency for all—in this sense of an absence of excess as well as an absence of deprivation—is a concept which is valid internationally as well as nationally.

We have already had one Development Decade. Now we are in the middle of the Second. Even though growth in terms of GNP has been at its highest ever in the developing world, most authorities agree that the economic gap between the developed and the developing countries has widened during this period. Is this fair? Is this just? Is this tolerable?

What makes the situation still worse is that the pursuit of increasing wealth has meant greater and greater production, consumption and waste, with consequently increasing damage to the ecological balance. Pollution does not respect national boundaries. Everyone—including the developing countries—is affected by the results of overloading the air and sea with waste products. Everyone - especially the developing countries - is affected by excess demand and the consequence of this demand on the supply of basic commodities which should by right be available at a fair and reasonable price to all.

Thus far, the concept of progress has been largely appreciated in economic terms, and the pursuit of wealth has set ever higher standards of affluence at which to aim. Is it possible now to limit our material demands? Can our priorities be changed so as to answer the needs of all?

For the sufficiency society of the future some values of both past and present may still be valid; but not values that spawn unbridled acquisitiveness. Rather, let us seek the values of co-operation and concern, of involvement in the lives of others, values which come from recognition that the lives and the fate of all are inextricably bound up with each other, that man is now interdependent between continents, as he once was within the confines of the village. Fortunately, these values still exist in many parts of the world and will, we believe, play a vital role in the future.

There are signs that the change in position and in attitudes has already begun. Growing national pride and self-confidence in many countries are bringing about a re-evaluation of national needs and wants which is both more in line with the realities of existing social structures and better adapted to the dictates of change. There is more willingness among national leaders to institute and accept change and to root out those aspects of the social and economic system which are obstacles to development.

Among industrialized countries there is a new willingness to participate in the evolution of new approaches. There is a growing acceptance that the values of growth and acquisition are not the most appropriate for our times, in a world whose resources and capacity to absorb the effects of human activity are limited. In the transition from scarcity to sufficiency, technologies and techniques are emerging, some new, some adapted, but in either case, appropriate to the needs and values of development.

This is the context in which the problems of population must be seen. The adoption of sensible and enlightened policies in this field is an essential step for all countries—whether developed or developing—on their road towards becoming "sufficiency societies". . . .

We need hardly add that the UNFPA can only discharge [its] historic task if those members of the international community who have supported us so generously in the past continue to support us even more generously in the future. If the concept of sharing in this "village world" means anything, if the concept of "sufficiency" means anything, then the goals and purposes of the World Population Plan of Action must surely be worthy of our utmost support—financial as well as moral.

[We] do not believe that it is possible to underestimate the challenge and the significance of this moment. To solve the population problems of countries will require more from us in a shorter time than ever before in the history of mankind. It will require a long-sustained effort without any guarantee that the final aim will be achieved. Yet without the effort, can there be any prospect for a just and peaceful world in the future? The ancient philosphers of Asia, in their wisdom, stressed the need for a balance and harmony between man and his world. Without a sane and orderly approach to the problems of population, there can be no balance and no harmony. (20 August 1974)

• Development assistance is only one element of international co-operation. In Bucharest, the Fund's presentation to the [World Population] Conference stressed the need to curb acquisitiveness and waste, to plan for the best use of the world's limited resources, to seek for ways in which excesses of consumption and deprivation may be ended. A world society, a society of sufficiency for all, is the best, and perhaps the only, hope for mankind. (15 October 1974)

• It is clear that we cannot have abundance for a few and privation for many—not for much longer. There is a level of poverty which human beings can perhaps tolerate, but there are too many millions now existing well below that line. Poverty and abject misery are different experiences, and 40 per cent of the world's people are condemned to misery. It is clear that our overheated consumption must level off so that our supplies of energy, raw materials and skills are put to less glamorous but more useful purpose. We have begun, only begun, to realize how interdependent our world is, however passionately we articulate our separate nationalisms and our cultural individuality. All the global concerns we are now involved with - hunger, the status of women, ethnic conflicts, the fair distribution of the resources of the land and the seas—are aspects of this interdependence, and indicate that the future must be guided by more egalitarian and equitable values if we are to survive.

That is why at Bucharest we made a plea for a Sufficiency Society. But sufficiency, given the limitation of means in a finite planet, is largely dependent on the number of people whose needs must be met. This realization is filtering through even to countries which once took the simplistic view that concern for population growth was a vicious plot to keep the poor poor. Whatever euphemism is employed to refer to the problem—maternal and child health, family welfare, or family health programmes—reducing fertility has been recognized as a priority for many developing countries. (27 September 1977)

World Population Plan of Action

• The idea of population action programmes as a legitimate area for national activity has spread . . . taking hold even in areas where there was traditionally strong ideological or cultural opposition. . . . We are now in a situation where we can begin to look for broad agreement between nations at the World Population Conference next year, on the principles of a common World Population Plan of Action. (25 August 1973)

• In an atmosphere of informed [global] awareness [which hopefully will be generated during World Population Year 1974], there is every reason to believe that the delegations to the World Population Conference will arrive with well-formulated national policies and plans of action which will make it possible for them to air varying and often widely divergent political, cultural and ideological viewpoints, and at the same time, in the end, arrive at a workable consensus leading to a practicable World Plan of Action on population. (27 August 1973)

• It would be unrealistic to look forward to 1975 without anticipating that the [World Population] Conference will lead to widened concepts of population, to re-thinking of national plans, to new approaches to population questions, and perhaps to radical transformations in the form and priorities of multilateral assistance.

The immediate effect will, of course, be an expansion of on-going activities. For example, it can be anticipated that the goals set by the [draft] World Population Plan of Action will push up the number of requests for assistance from countries setting quantitative growth targets, and from countries agreeing to take censuses between 1975 and 1985. It is also more than likely that migration problems and questions of urban explosion will feature more largely in future requests.

Other recommendations of the Plan of Action will undoubtedly give impetus to programmes in research and training; and the Fund in particular welcomes the proposal that an international training programme in population should be carried out concomitantly with national and regional programmes, a policy to which the Fund is already heavily committed.

As is stated in the World Population Plan of Action, a strategy has been formulated which makes population one of several factors which, taken together, constitute the multidisciplinary approach of the international community to the solution of world problems in the field of social and economic development.

This statement . . . changes everything. It is never going to be possible to view population activities in isolation again. Since population is the one element every other variable has in common, population may even turn out to be the binding force that makes the multidisciplinary approach . . . possible. (4 March 1974)

• The [draft] World Population Plan of Action which will be before the Conference is an initial step towards international thinking and planning in regard to the population variable. Two versions of this plan have been prepared; one, a summary version which will figure on the agenda of the Conference; the other, a detailed version which will be the background document.

In presenting this Plan to the Conference, it is pointed out that a number of strategies have already been formulated which, taken together, constitute the multidisciplinary approach of the international community to the solution of world problems. Examples of these are FAO's Indicative World Plan and the World Food Programme, ILO's World Development Programme, the World Plan of Action for the Application of Science and Technology to Development, and so on. But this is the first plan that deals explicitly with population, and while it must be viewed as part of the system of international strategies for economic and social development, it definitely brings a new dimension to the system as a whole.

The World Population Plan of Action concentrates on six main areas—population growth, morbidity and mortality, reproduction and family formation, population distribution and internal migration, international migration, and demographic structures—all of which, to a greater or lesser degree, and in an endless series of permutations, affect the very fabric of national life. (6 March 1974)

• There can be no blanket solution, and . . . even within countries, programmes must be adapted to take account of local needs. In considering the [draft] World Population Plan of Action . . . governments can take a lead in acknowledging local, national and regional differences, while insisting on the need for a global approach. (9 May 1974)

• We cannot think just three years ahead—from 1974 to 1977—even though the sums involved may seem large enough in all conscience. We have to think thirty years ahead—and more.

That is why the World Population Plan of Action could be a major milestone of the greatest importance. It could guide and reinforce the activities of the Fund, and at the same time, the Fund could play an important role in the realization of the Plan. The Plan will, of course, only take on its full meaning when it is translated into actual programmes at the international and national levels—programmes appropriate to the needs.

The draft Plan as it now stands is an affirmation of certain fundamental principles of action in the field of population. It emphasizes the different needs and priorities in the

I.P.A.—E

various parts of the world. In order to give the Plan substance, it will be necessary for countries and communities to design and put into effect their own national plans of action in accordance with their own special conditions, and with their own resources.

If the concept of sharing in this "village world" means anything, if the concept of "sufficiency" means anything, then the goals and purposes of the World Population Plan of Action must surely be worthy of our utmost support—financial as well as moral. (20 August 1974)

• There are three aspects of the Plan which [are] particularly important.

First, there is emphasis on the sovereign right of every nation to decide its policy for itself without external interference. This provision reflects the profound sensitivity of the whole population question, but it is also a positive indication, a recognition that each country's situation is different. There are still today a handful of nations whose policy it is to increase their numbers at least until the end of the century. In national terms there may be sound economic and social reasons for such a policy, even though the world situation may call for less rather than more growth overall. Other nations opt for an emphasis on quality rather than numbers; this, too, is their prerogative. It is not for the world community or international organizations to praise or condemn, but merely to ensure that the world facts are known and taken into consideration by governments when making policy.

The second point arises from the first: the sheer breadth of the Plan. Discussion in Bucharest ranged widely over an enormous variety of topics, and the Plan reflects this. Population is placed firmly in its perspective relative to other facets of social and economic development and the world structure. The depth and complexity of the interactions between population and many other variables—health, for example, nutrition, education, the status of women - is acknowledged. This too is a positive and hopeful sign for the future, because it marks the integration of this aspect of our social fabric with the whole. Simplistic, one-level approaches to population are clearly seen to be inadequate for our complex modern world; equally clear, on the other hand, is the necessity to include population considerations in discussions of other aspects of development.

The third point about the Plan . . . is its emphasis on the role of international agencies. In the context of the new world economic order called for by the last Special Session of the General Assembly, enormous shifts of financial and human resources will have to take place and many adjustments be made to the machinery of international trade and co-operation. International agencies have an especially important part to play in this process; as neutral brokers and at times also as innovators of new ideas and methods. They are, or should be, free from political bias and from cultural and economic prejudices to an extent which cannot, in the nature of things, be matched by governmental bodies. Considering population matters as part of the fabric of the new order, international organizations can make great contributions to international understanding and co-operation. (15 October 1974)

• One hundred and thirty-five [states] participating in that [World Population] Con-

ference adopted by consensus a World Population Plan of Action which constitutes today the most important policy document in the field of population. It represents the
formal recognition by the governments of the world of the legitimacy of, and the
necessity for, population policies as an integral part of overall socio-economic development. It recognizes the interaction between population and food, education, employment and the status of women in the development process. It addresses itself primarily
to governments but also contains important recommendations of relevance to international organizations and non-governmental bodies concerned.

The [World Population] Plan of Action has a bearing on food production in several
directions. The collection and analysis of demographic data, and research in such fields
as unemployment, starvation and poverty, are vital in planning future food production
policies. Knowledge of the location and concentration of peoples, their rates of natural
increase and migration, their economic and demographic status, are invaluable tools
for the planner and manager.

But above all, the World Population Plan of Action places emphasis on the production
of more food as a matter of utmost urgency, and recommends that governments give
high priority to improving methods of food production, the investigation and development of new sources of food, and more effective utilization of existing food sources.
These measures have to be taken with the view that the gaps in the standards of living in
many parts of the world be reduced and that the more rational utilization of natural
resources will avoid the deleterious effect of waste. (11 November 1974)

• [The] political consensus, involving 135 countries . . . reached on the adoption of a
World Population Plan of Action [is] a milestone . . . in the field of human development.

This same large consensus extended and strengthened one of the key conclusions of the
International Conference on Human Rights, held in Teheran in 1968, concerning
establishment of a new basic human right, expressed in the World Population Plan of
Action in this simple, crystal-clear language: "All couples and individuals have the
basic right to decide freely and responsibly the number and spacing of their children
and to have the information, education, and means to do so; the responsibility of
couples and individuals in the exercise of this right takes into account the needs of their
living and future children, and their responsibilities towards the community."

The same consensus underlined in the Plan that "Population and development are interrelated: population variables influence development variables and are also influenced by them; thus, the formulation of a World Population Plan of Action reflects
the international community's awareness of the importance of population trends for
socio-economic development, and the socio-economic nature of the recommendations
contained in this Plan of Action reflects its awareness of the crucial role that development plays in affecting population trends".

Some four months after the Bucharest Conference, the United Nations General
Assembly, in its resolution 3344 (XXIX) and resolution 3345 (XXIX), both adopted 17
December 1974, endorsed the Bucharest conclusions and in particular affirmed "that

the World Population Plan of Action is an instrument of the international community for the promotion of economic development, quality of life, human rights and fundamental freedoms within the broader context of the internationally adopted strategies for national and international progress''. (27 January 1975)

- The question before us is simple enough: How can we translate into action programmes the recommendations of the World Population Plan of Action? How can we make the Plan of Action operational at both the national and international levels?

The framers of this World Population Plan of Action were careful in the Plan they mapped out for us. While recognizing that population problems differ from country to country and that the main responsibility for national policies and programmes lies with national authorities, the framers of the Plan clearly suggest co-operative efforts at all levels. In fact, the Plan itself indicates that the primary aim "is to expand and deepen the capacities of countries to deal effectively with their national and subnational population problems and to promote an appropriate international response to their needs by increasing international activity in research, the exchange of information, and the provision of assistance on request".

In this interdependent world in which we live, it is clear that co-operation is the path that we all must travel—and travel together. This meeting, then, will help the nations of this area to decide the role that they want to play vis-a-vis the other nations of the world, the other regions, and in the world community itself. (24 March 1975)

- We are, of course, following up the recommendations of the General Assembly resolution,* but actually we had begun actions to implement the World Population Plan of Action almost as soon as the Fund's staff returned from Bucharest. . . . A few of these activities [are]:

Last September . . . a UNFPA Task Force [was appointed], consisting of staff members from all Fund divisions and sections, with the explicit task of examining, in detail, the World Population Plan of Action and its implications for the work of the Fund. The focus of this study was not on what the Fund has done, but rather on what the Fund could possibly do in light of the Recommendations for Action and for Implementation contained in the Plan of Action. The approach was to identify each group of recommendations, discuss generally UNFPA support to date in regard to the recommendations and point out examples of such support, and then, wherever possible, suggest the future role for the UNFPA in the areas under discussion. In other words, in light of the Plan, what *should* the Fund's programmes be?

The UNFPA, in conjunction with the United Nations Population Division and the regional Economic Commissions, initiated plans back in October to hold a series of regional consultations funded by UNFPA, to determine what the various countries around the world consider to be their priorities in the population field and which parts of the Plan are most relevant to them. . . .

Following these consultations . . . the UNFPA and the United Nations will jointly sponsor a meeting of experts from various countries, international agencies, and non-

'3344, 17 December 1974, *op. cit.*

governmental organizations, to solicit technical advice on how to make the World Population Plan of Action operational, and to translate the recommendations of the Plan into workable programmes.

In general, the Fund is prepared to use its experience of five years of programming, and its relationship with national governments everywhere, to perform its appropriate role in appraising, reviewing and giving substance to the recommendations of the World Population Plan of Action.

"Programme Co-ordination" is . . . the key. (17 April 1975)

• The [World Population] Plan [of Action] puts forward a series of useful guidelines for action and provides a logical and constructive framework within which governments could decide on their own population policies in the context of their strategy for development. (10 June 1975)

• The various international strategies such as the World Population Plan of Action, the International Development Strategy for the Second Development Decade, and the World Plan of Action focussing on integration of women and development, should provide guidance for the activities of the Fund. These strategies, particularly the first one, suggest that an integrated development approach to population be applied. This would mean that population activities would be funded increasingly in conjunction with activities in health, education, rural development, community development and other programmes of economic and social development. (21 November 1975)

• All population agencies, governmental as well as non-governmental . . . look to the Fund for giving substance, pace and direction to the World Population Plan of Action. . . . (20 February 1976)

• An international framework is necessary to support national efforts, and it is in this light that international instruments such as the World Population Plan of Action must be seen.

Both the World Population Conference and the World Population Plan of Action stressed the importance of making developing countries self-reliant as fully and rapidly as possible. (14 June 1976)

• The Bucharest Conference dealt with the question of population in its broadest development context. The final consensus was a political agreement, not a tactical blueprint; this was to be expected from the nature of the Conference, but it left unresolved the manner in which the objectives of the consensus were to be achieved. (8 August 1977)

• The [World Population] Conference established guidelines for future action which attested to the importance of population factors. The World Population Plan of Action . . . firmly established population as an important element in international strategies to promote development and to improve the quality of life, and set as an important goal the expansion and deepening of the capacity of countries to deal effectively with their national and subnational population problems. (3 April 1978)

The Role of the UNFPA in a Restructured United Nations Economic and Social Programme

• It is clear that the efforts . . . being made to restructure the United Nations apparatus concerned with economic development are intended to make the international community more responsive to human problems.

In determining the future structure dealing with development activities in the United Nations system . . . four factors should be considered:

(a) the subject matter

(b) the allocation of resources

(c) the delivery of project services

(d) the time frame of the activity

With respect to population activities, [we] believe that the experience of the UNFPA in these four areas is clearly relevant.

First, population, as a concern of the international community, has now reached a pivotal point in its evolution. . . .

Population, as a significant factor and a distinct variable in the complex of elements related to the problems of poverty, has taken a long time to manifest itself in public awareness, and is only now beginning to be given due recognition. Almost every developing country has demonstrated its awareness of the population factor by expressing a national population policy or by establishing a government council, agency or ministry to deal with population. This is not the time to risk reversing that trend by obscuring the distinctness of the population imperative.

Second, the allocation of resources for population activities is subject to significantly different considerations from those guiding other development efforts. The UNFPA's Governing Council and the Economic and Social Council have repeatedly stated that resources for population assistance should not be allocated according to a worldwide formula, as general development assistance is. Considering the sensitiveness of the population question and the varied nature of cultural and national approaches to it, population assistance policies must be responsive to the varying needs and requirements of different countries.

Third, the delivery of population programmes requires a constantly innovative and flexible approach. Our experience shows that the standard traditional methods of delivery have not been effective and that there is a danger that the imposition of a uniform method of delivery of development assistance would gravely affect the very high level of project implementation which the UNFPA has been able to achieve.

Fourth, the time frame of the increasing need for population assistance is finite. . . . [We] see the population programmes in which the international community as well as individual countries are now involved, as a self-liquidating process if they are to be of any value.

What is needed is effective action now . . . before the problem becomes impossibly big and complex to deal with in an orderly manner.

[We] have read the comments and recommendations of the Group of Experts on the Structure of the United Nations System with great interest and respect.

From the viewpoint of the Fund, the assumption they make that economic and social development and population are related is wholly acceptable. . . .

The Committee's recommendation that a Director-General be appointed to guide the overall economic and social programmes of the system recognizes the increased importance that needs to be given to the United Nations concern with the problems of poverty. . . .

[We] congratulate the experts on their perspicacity in placing emphasis, as they have done, on the need to simplify the system and make it more efficient through such well-known and time-tested means as drawing together related elements under a unified direction. [We are] sure they have considered . . . that there are inherent dangers in such a course of action, however well-intentioned and schematically unassailable it might appear to be. One danger is that related parts of the whole, which by their very purpose, their particular stage of evolution, and their essential distinctness in the nature of their work and their mode of operation, are clearly effective . . . may lose their essential character and usefulness in being too tightly or inappropriately integrated into a general system.

In the effort to avoid duplication of effort through an integration of related but different functions, effectiveness comes from establishing a clear definition of responsibilities and boundaries of functions, and not by integration for its own sake.

Consolidation of the resources now being made available for population assistance with other funds in the name of simplification . . . or of efficiency . . . may not be effective in this case. We fear that the momentum achieved by the Fund in raising contributions . . . may be irretrievably lost, and what is worse, an irreversible downward process may start. It is necessary to realize that it is not just a question of keeping distinct accounts, but one of maintaining a clear profile.

The UNFPA is such a special case and it should be regarded as such in your consideration of effective changes in the system. [We], therefore, suggest that it should be treated as a distinct programme, as its evolution warrants.

The rational, not to say natural, outcome of that process of evolution is that the Fund should become fully operational, in order to be as effective as it could be in the delivery of population assistance in a new international economic order.

To provide the necessary legislative and operational links with the system that will emerge from this exercise in restructuring, [we] suggest that we should go along with the links provided by the countries through the resolutions of the Economic and Social Council and our own governing body. The head of this population programme which [we] have in mind would accordingly report to the Economic and Social Council and the proposed Operations Board, in consultation with the principal officer responsible for the overall direction of assistance and development—presumably to be called the Director-General, and would also participate in any consultative or advisory institutions which may be established to co-ordinate the developmental activities of the United Nations and its Specialized Agencies.

We . . . realize that eventually the management of the Fund will pass to other responsible hands. Our view on reorganization was, therefore, always governed by this higher purpose—to keep the institution viable beyond our presence.

[We are] convinced that its [the Fund's] best value is to be obtained by maintaining a co-ordinated link to development as a distinct programme within the United Nations system. (20 February 1976)

New International Economic Order

• In the context of the new world economic order called for by the last Special Session [1974] of the General Assembly, enormous shifts of financial and human resources will have to take place, and many adjustments be made to the machinery of international trade and co-operation. International agencies have an especially important part to play in this process—as neutral brokers, and at times also as innovators of new ideas and methods. They are, or should be, free from political bias and from cultural and economic prejudices to an extent which cannot, in the nature of things, be matched by governmental bodies. Considering population matters as part of the fabric of the new order, international organizations can make great contributions to international understanding and co-operation.

Establishment of the new world economic order will require more from each one of us, from each organization, whether governmental, private or international, than ever before in the history of mankind. We can see now that we stand at a turning point. Over the past few years a whole way of approaching problems has become outmoded. In a world whose physical limits can now be observed and quantified, and in which interdependence is not just a phrase but a hard and sometimes unpleasant fact of life, narrow political and economic nationalism is rapidly becoming superfluous. Short-term solutions are seen to be no solutions at all, but postponements of a crisis which becomes more severe the more it is delayed. There is an immense fund of international goodwill, but goodwill on its own will not see us through. A complete restructuring of our systems of values, no less, is required if we are to meet the challenges which face mankind. The present shortages of food in many parts of the developing world are not a temporary or local difficulty, but indications of a global imbalance between need and supply. Pollution of the air, the earth and the sea is not a minor matter to be cleared up by a few emission controls, but a gigantic international problem which may threaten the delicate structure of global ecology and, with it, support for life itself.

Because of the long lead-time between any solution being worked out, put into action and taking effect, it is necessary to think in terms of the next thirty or fifty years. In population, for example, it takes two generations for a successful policy of population stabilization to take effect. At the United Nations Fund for Population Activities we freely acknowledge that we cannot affect today's problems—but insist that we must think for the next generation, and start planning and action now. (15 October 1974)

• Since then [the World Population Year and Conference], although population has received its measure of notice in world discussions, there has been little substantive discussion of the issue as part of the New International Economic Order debates. This has come as a surprise to some observers who have correctly pointed out that these discussions have been made necessary in part by population growth in the developing countries . . . as well as by disproportionate increases in consumption by the slower-growing populations of Europe, Japan, Australasia and North America.

The separation of population matters from the debate on the New International Economic Order results in precisely the opposite of that "integration of population and development" which was the expressed desire of nearly every nation attending the World Population Conference two years ago. The remaining areas of debate in population cannot be resolved within the context of the debate on the New International Economic Order; nevertheless, it is difficult to imagine a New International Economic Order such as the Third World countries seek, without some explicit recognition of the importance of population issues.

Moreover, it is possible to see that agreement may be achieved, because many of the staunchest supporters of the New International Economic Order are now also the most effective practitioners of a policy of limiting population growth.

There is a basis for discussion of the content and direction of population activities as part of the debates on the New International Economic Order. No one doubts that such an agreement would add to the progress already made in reshaping the international order, and might show the way for agreement in other areas. It is time that such an accord was reached. (12 January 1977)

• UNFPA has also taken due notice of the ECOSOC resolution (2051 (LXII)) last May [1977] on implementation of the recommendations of the World Population Plan of Action. We have followed the emphasis the Council has given in this resolution to the importance of population policies and activities in the establishment of a New International Economic Order and in determining the goals, objectives, policy measures and targets to be contained in the forthcoming new International Development Strategy. (7 November 1977)

• [The ECOSOC resolution, noted above, recommended that:] "When it considers the question of preparing a new international development strategy, the role of population and the importance of population policies and activities in their relationship to the establishment of a new international economic order should be given due weight, and should be duly integrated into the goals, objectives, policy measures and targets to be contained in any new strategy.". . .

The UNFPA stands ready, upon request, to assist the relevant organizations in the United Nations system that are charged with the preparation of the new International

Development Strategy for the Third Development Decade—and other relevant international strategies—in order to ensure that adequate recognition is given to population factors and activities in the formulation of such strategies and in the implementation of a new international economic order. (6 November 1978)

Technical Co-operation Among Developing Countries Programme

• Expert recruitment from a limited number of countries has . . . been a serious handicap to the effectiveness of external aid programmes. For many years the industrialized nations of the West had a virtual monopoly of modern technology and scientific advance. This is no longer the case. Regional and national reservoirs of expertise are being built up and it is the Fund's policy to encourage and assist the establishment of institutions and organizations to provide an increasing supply of experts needed for development and population programmes. (6 March 1974)

• On the important subject of technical co-operation among developing countries (TCDC), UNFPA has, from its inception, stressed support to programmes and projects which promoted national self-reliance, regional co-operation and collective self-reliance in the population fields. Indeed, much of UNFPA's assistance at the country and regional levels is aimed both at building up and improving the capacity of each country and each regional entity to administer such programmes themselves—and at using increasing amounts of TCDC-related inputs in accomplishing these important objectives.

The [World] Conference [on Technical Co-operation Among Developing Countries]* is of considerable interest to us, and we look forward to utilizing its insights and recommendations in our future activities. (21 June 1978)

[At the TCDC Conference, the Deputy Executive Director of the UNFPA, Halvor Gille, represented the Fund. In his statement to the Conference, he stated:

"From its inception, the Fund has concentrated on supporting programmes and projects which promote national self-reliance, regional co-operation and other forms of collective self-reliance in the population fields. All our endeavours are based upon respect for the sovereign right of each nation to formulate, promote and implement its own population policies according to its own conception of its population problems and needs. . . .

"[An] illustration of UNFPA's devotion to the concept and realization of TCDC is the extent to which we entrust to the developing countries themselves the execution of Fund-supported activities. This approach of so-called direct execution of technical co-operation activities including selection of expertise and procurement of equipment and supplies is functioning increasingly well. It has been found to be cost-efficient, to speed up implementation, and to promote development of responsibility, confidence and experience of institutions and individuals in developing countries. . . .

*Held in Buenos Aires, Argentina in September 1978.

"We give high priority to supporting human resources development through training programmes conducted in the developing world and transfer of the skills and technical know-how required for institution building at the national and regional levels, for strengthening the managerial, administrative and productive capabilities of the countries, and for exploring, through research and pilot projects, innovative approaches to deal with various aspects of population problems. . . .

"One of the cardinal principles for UNFPA, mandated by the General Assembly, is to give special attention to meeting the needs of disadvantaged population groups. We recognize that the main development objective of developing countries is to meet the human needs of their population, especially the needs of the poverty-stricken and underprivileged population groups. Population factors emerge as important—indeed central—elements in the formulation and implementation of needs-oriented development strategies and policies aiming at reducing poverty and economic and social inequalities between population groups. . . .

"We shall continue responding readily to individual and joint requests from governments and non-governmental bodies in various countries with the aim of promoting mutual self-reliance. We shall continue our efforts to enhance the capacities of developing countries to help themselves and each other by strengthening human resource development, institution-building and research capabilities.

"We shall also, in so far as possible and as appropriate, use our resources available for intercountry activities as instruments for promoting joint or collaborative population projects between developing countries. . . .

"Furthermore, we shall in areas within our competence continue to explore and apply new ideas and approaches for realization of the full potentialities of TCDC, such as, for example, establishment of production or distribution facilities for equipment and contraception supplies to meet the needs of several developing countries, strengthening of training and research facilities which may be of benefit to a number of countries and exploration of ways and means of dealing with problems of population distribution and migration within and between countries.

"Finally, we shall make every effort to mobilize our resources to play our role in helping to implement the Plan of Action which this Conference may adopt and which we note with appreciation in its draft gives recognition to the importance of population factors."]

- UNFPA actively participated in the recent successfully completed TCDC World Conference at Buenos Aires, which was highlighted by the adoption, by consensus, of a detailed Plan of Action for promoting and implementing technical co-operation among developing countries.

About two-thirds of the projects UNFPA assists at the country level support activities promoting national self-reliance—an indisputable foundation for TCDC. In addition, about half of the inter-regional, regional and sub-regional projects we support promote co-operation between technical personnel and institutions located in developing countries. (6 November 1978).

Chapter 3

CREATING AWARENESS OF POPULATION PROBLEMS

Promoting Awareness—UNFPA Role in

- The immediate step . . . is to promote an awareness of the [population] problem, particularly in countries which have not yet had to face up to the deprivations that excessive population brings in its wake. (26 August 1971)

- The Fund is in the process of making a number of arrangements to strengthen programmes at the country level. Among these are . . . a broad range of promotional activities aimed at heightening the awareness among high-level government officials of the effect of population trends on economic and social development efforts. . . .

To sustain current activities in the field of population and to develop more and better programmes, it is of utmost importance that the commitment of government leaders and those who are important in the development process be harnessed in support of the programme. The Fund requests the assistance of the [UNDP] Resident Representatives to develop further and deeper awareness among officials of the recipient countries, of the importance and relevance of population dynamics in their development efforts. (18 May 1972)

- The requests for assistance that the Fund has on hand far exceed available resources. This imbalance between demand for assistance and availability of resources, however, only proves the success of the Fund's efforts during World Population Year and the success of the World Population Conference in raising the "global consciousness" on population matters. (17 April 1975)

- The aims and purposes of the UNFPA, as laid down in ECOSOC resolution 1763 (LIV), cover the following: [*inter alia*] . . . to promote awareness, both in developed and developing countries, of the social, economic and environmental implications of national and international population problems; of the human rights aspects of family planning; and of possible strategies to deal with them, in accordance with the plans and priorities of each country. . . . (20 February 1976)

- From the nature of the requests for funds presented to us, we see a steadily increasing awareness of population issues in every region and a trend towards making family planning information and services available to every interested couple. The progression

44

continues, from gathering data, to forming population policy, to informing the people, to making available services. This process is further advanced and broader in application in some regions than in others, but is constantly accelerating in all geographic regions of the world. (7 November 1977)

World Population Year 1974—UNFPA Responsibility for

[In 1970, the General Assembly designated 1974 as World Population Year. Its action followed up that of the Economic and Social Council which had earlier the same year authorized the holding of a World Population Conference, which later was also set for 1974. In its designation of World Population Year, the Assembly indicated that "a way of focusing international attention on different aspects of the population problem would be for Member States and international organizations to devote the year 1974 especially to appropriate efforts and undertakings in the field of population in the context of their respective needs and areas of competence". In June 1972, ECOSOC assigned responsibility for preparations for World Population Year to the Executive Director of the UNFPA (resolution 1672, LII). In late 1972, Mr. Salas named Tarzie Vittachi of Sri Lanka, a journalist, as Executive Secretary of the World Population Year Secretariat.]

• This [responsibility for the formulation and promotion of an overall programme for the Year] includes encouraging governments, non-governmental bodies and individuals, as well as the organizations concerned in the United Nations system, to develop activities particularly related to the Year. This is a formidable task, but we are confident that our many contacts at the international and national levels will assist us in meeting this great challenge. The guiding principles and objectives of the Year are very much in accordance with those with which the Fund has operated since its inception, and have been the driving force behind our rapid growth. In a sense, for the Fund, every year is a world population year!

World Population Year will operate at three levels - the international, the national and the individual.

At the *international* level, the aim is to mobilize human and financial resources and to strengthen activities, so as to provide adequate and effective assistance as and when requested, in support of governmental and non-governmental forces to participate in promoting population activities within the context of the Year. Special attention will, therefore, be given to ways of increasing the volume and quality of international technical co-operation—bilateral, private, and multilateral—available to developing countries in dealing with population problems and policies. In this connection, it is hardly necessary . . . to stress that the World Population Conference, preceded by the preparatory symposia being organized by the United Nations, is an integral part of, and the main event around which, World Population Year activities will revolve.

At the *national* level, the objectives of the Year are to increase awareness and understanding of current and prospective population trends and their implications for economic growth and social progress; to further the application of population data to all pertinent aspects of developing planning, such as planning for better education, improved health facilities, housing, employment, and economic growth; to encourage discussion of alternative solutions to population problems; to provide research and training activities on population; and, where appropriate, to support the formulation and implementation of national policies and programmes relating to population. It is *not* our objective to persuade governments to adopt any particular population policies, but rather to encourage and assist them in taking the significance of population factors into account in planning for a better life for their citizens. The full participation of government agencies and non-governmental organizations in promoting the various activities of the Year at the national level will be enlisted in furthering this aim.

At the *individual* level, the aim is to increase awareness and understanding of population problems and their implications for the individual. This goal should be accomplished by promoting information and education activities using all appropriate channels. Furthermore, individuals, community organizations, and other local bodies should be encouraged to participate in population programmes, whether they be fact-finding in nature, or training or action programmes.

The availability of information and means to enable couples to decide freely and responsibly on the number and spacing of their children has been declared a basic human right. . . . A major objective of the Year should, therefore, be, in accordance with this resolution,* to encourage all governments, whatever their demographic objectives, to develop information and education on population and family life matters and to intensify family planning delivery systems.

The World Population Year is of concern to all. In this regard, it is important to recognize the involvement and key role which women and young people are playing as citizens, as well as that of mothers and future parents.

It may be objectionable, and even illogical, to consider women and young people as special population groups. Women and young people, after all, constitute at least half of the population of the world. However, the fact is that their participation and interest are often overlooked. We in the Fund, therefore, want to pay special attention to ways and means of ensuring their participation in the World Population Year activities, notably in national population programmes, as well as the World Population Conference itself. The Population Commission may assist us in making recommendations to governments and international organizations for the fullest possible representation and involvement of women and young people in various international undertakings for the Year.

As a first attempt in this direction, the Fund has supported the organization of a Working Party on Youth and Population convened by the United Nations Centre for Economic and Social Information (CESI). . . . Two important recommendations were made at this meeting of thoughtful, action-oriented young people. The first requests

*ECOSOC resolution 1672 (LII) of 2 June 1972, *op. cit.*

that the perspective which views population as one important variable within larger development concerns and problems be kept in mind at all times, especially when defining specific action programmes. The second suggests that a re-evaluation be made of national and international population programmes in terms of services, education and policy. A plea was made that young people's participation be encouraged in decision-making meetings and conferences.

The activities to be promoted within the framework of the World Population Year include promotion of the collection of basic population data, research, training and information activities.

As regards population statistics, the plans for the proposed World Fertility Survey have progressed considerably. With financial assistance from the Fund, the International Statistical Institute convened two expert meetings a few weeks ago to thoroughly consider the feasibility of organizing representative surveys on fertility patterns and the factors affecting them, on a world-wide basis. We have . . . received a request from the Institute to provide assistance for the detailed preparatory work to be carried out over the next two years, with the collaboration of the United Nations and the International Union for the Scientific Study of Population (IUSSP), for the effective launching of such fertility surveys in a large number of countries, as a part of the observance of the World Population Year. Furthermore, a number of governments have approached the Fund for assistance to organize population censuses and to develop vital statistics systems. . . . We in the Fund are particularly anxious to support these efforts, especially in countries which have so far never taken a population census, and to assist governments in establishing population census programmes as a permanent feature of government responsibilities.

In the field of population research, the Fund has already agreed to support a number of activities to be carried out by the United Nations, its Specialized Agencies concerned, the regional demographic centres and some national institutions. The establishment of the Committee for International Co-ordination of National Research in Demography (CICRED) offers an interesting and important new avenue for the promotion of vitally important research in population, to be carried out in different social and economic settings with the participation of local institutions in a large number of countries.

One of the main bottlenecks in promoting population activities in most developing countries is the lack of trained personnel. It is hoped that the World Population Year activities will include intensified efforts towards improving this situation. It may be appropriate here to refer to the recommendation made by this Commission at its Sixteenth Session, that a high-level programme of training should be initiated as soon as possible, and that the experience gained from such a programme would be useful in considering further the needs of an interdisciplinary training scheme in population matters. [We] wish to reaffirm the Fund's readiness to support such a programme if and when a request is submitted to us.

A number of publications are envisaged as a part of the activities for the Year. . . . In addition, some of the Specialized Agencies have plans for special publications, or special issues of their regular series of publications, giving special attention to relevant population aspects.

Most, although not all, organizations in the United Nations system concerned with population have now submitted their plans for the Year to the Fund and indicated the financial assistance needed to realize these plans. As a first step, infrastructure support has been approved. Requests for support from the Fund for various operational activities will soon be approved, such as, for example, the organization of seminars, the preparation of films and television spots, the organization of training programmes, and similar information and educational activities. After discussions with the various agencies, it has been agreed to co-ordinate many of these efforts by combining projects and developing joint distribution channels, for example, for the dissemination of publications, films and other materials. We are working towards an overall plan and timetable for information activities related to the Year.

[We] would welcome suggestions about the most appropriate theme to be adopted for the Year,* the ways and means of involving various key population groups such as community leaders, women and young people in the activities of the Year, and how to enlist fully the participation not only of organizations in the United Nations system, but also non-governmental organizations at the international, as well as national, levels. (10 August 1972)

• The essential purpose of World Population Year is to focus worldwide attention on population matters, in order to accelerate and intensify the entire range of population concerns and activities. . . . Our aim is for these activities to have a lasting impact, well beyond 1974. The Fund is also prepared to give the fullest possible assistance to countries engaged in population activities in connection with the World Population Year and to the World Population Conference, which will highlight the Year.

In a sense the Year is a consciousness-heightening event intended to raise worldwide awareness of population problems to a new platform, and not simply to subside when the next new year has been proclaimed. This is why information and the media are so important. Without them the Year as a focal point falls flat; with them, our efforts are enhanced, and popular understanding and support are enlisted for the benefit of all. (25 October 1972)

• We are already engaged in laying the foundations for what we hope will become a spectacular example of effective international co-operation. . . . Many programmes envisaged for the Year, such as the improvement of demographic data and services, expansion of maternal and child welfare facilities, and increased population training and educational programmes, will give new scope to on-going activities.

The Year will have failed if it does not result in activities of lasting and practical benefit to countries, particularly developing countries. (1 November 1972)

*The theme finally selected was "One World for All".

• [We] hope that during World Population Year and the World Population Conference the barriers of ideology will fall, and we shall all speak of the population problem as a common one, part of the whole problem of the future of man. (14 February 1973)

• The Fund welcomed this responsibility [for preparations for the World Population Year] for several reasons:

First, the activities of the Year would undoubtedly help to intensify and expand the organization's efforts—many of which were already directed towards the objectives that have been drawn up for the Year.

Secondly, the Year would provide the means of bringing members of the United Nations family, governments and bilateral agencies, as well as non-governmental organizations, into a more closely co-ordinated population effort that ever before.

Thirdly, the Year would provide an unprecedented opportunity of setting short-term targets for the achievement of population goals—which, as you are all aware, is difficult to do, given the long-term nature of population problems.

Fourthly, it would hopefully stimulate a responsible interest in population which could well result in the development of innovative approaches to population problems, and open up new channels for interchanges and communication of population knowledge and experience. . . .

In identifying and initiating the World Population Year projects, we kept in mind a number of basic principles which, in fact, differ very little from the Fund's normal policies and procedures.

The first of these was that World Population Year should not be regarded as an end in itself, but as the vital beginning of a sustained effort to achieve worldwide awareness of the need to find a rational balance between people and resources. Another was that a global undertaking of such complexity called for a flexible, dynamic and *neutral* approach which would be receptive to innovative ideas and capable of encompassing new dimensions. In this context [we] should like to emphasize that [we] do not use *neutrality* as a synonym for *passivity*. It has always been the Fund's policy to maintain a strict neutrality in regard to government decisions on the kind of population programmes they wish to undertake. But it has been an equally firm Fund policy to act as quickly as possible in giving assistance in advancing these programmes once the decision has been taken. . . .

The World Population Year projects divide into what might be called substantive programmes—such as demography and family planning—and communications and information type projects, with a heavy emphasis on the latter. This is inevitable. The primary stated purpose of the Year is to create awareness of population matters, and to this end we are endeavouring to mobilize all the assistance we can get in transmitting the message of the Year to people at all levels and in all walks of life.

The main thrust of the World Population Year programme is directed towards encouraging the maximum involvement of governments, both in promoting population activities in their own countries, and in participating to the fullest extent possible in international programmes and exchanges.

The Year calls for nothing less than universal commitment, and it is vitally important that industrialized nations should also take steps to set up national commissions and to make known their population programmes and policies. Only in this way will it bepossible to determine the contribution that these countries can make to the international sum of knowledge, and towards improving the dialogue and understanding between the rich and poor nations.

In the final issue, no matter how effective individual programmes may prove to be, the Year will not have accomplished its purpose unless it has brought about a new collaboration and pooling of resources between developing and more industrialized countries, in order to give substance, weight and direction to a long-term solution of the world's population problems. This can only be built up by a free flow of information, exchange of technical knowledge, and sympathetic understanding of the similarities and dissimilarities of each other's situations.

It is a communications job of *unprecedented* dimensions. But this is an era of unprecedented communications facilities and techniques. . . . Our major endeavour will be to try to convince communicators everywhere that the population question is a crucial global concern, requiring the commitment of their skills and resources as well as those of people directly and substantively involved in population work. After all, in this—probably more than any other aspect of human living—the problem of one is the problem of all. (23 March 1973)

• Miracles, as we all know, seldom make their appearance in the long-term haul of economic and social change. But [we are] astonished to see how many developments that bode well for the future have begun to emerge as by-products of the preparations for the Year. Some of these would, of course, have arrived with time, but undoubtedly, the sharp focus of attention on the Year and the [World Population] Conference has given momentum to a chain of events that might otherwise have occurred at a considerably slower pace.

Take, for example, the communications aspect of the Year. As one of the major objectives is to create a greater understanding and awareness of population matters, this has called for an intensification of population information at all levels. But to communicate, it is necessary not only to have the information to pass on, which we have, but also to have the means of doing so. . . . The contribution knowledgeable writers, broadcasters, publishers and public relations people can make in furthering understanding of population matters, in supporting government policies, and in placing population in the proper context within overall social and economic frameworks, is immeasurable. It would be sad indeed if we did not make every effort to expand and exploit the possibilities of this worldwide communications network long after the Year is over.

Of even greater significance are the national commissions being set up by governments as the co-ordinating centres for World Population Year activities. The majority of the countries receiving assistance from the UNFPA have already established such bodies. Many others have notified us that they are in the process of doing so. Even in the short time that such units have been in existence, they have led to closer relationships between people working at all levels, on a variety of on-going population activities, and have opened up new possibilities for effectively integrating programming in the future. It is notable that in almost every instance the governments have assigned high officials from ministries and planning authorities, as well as specialists directly concerned with population, to serve on the commissions. Though the immediate purpose is to activate World Population Year programmes, [we are] convinced that these organizations will prove so useful that they will well merit retention as co-ordinating centres for all national population liaison, planning and programming, and as the continuing links with the international movements and strategies in the future. Accordingly, the Fund stands ready to give the national commissions every support in carrying out their functions.

This trend towards the provision of permanent institutional underpinnings for action in the population field is . . . an early gain which can be fairly marked up to the World Population Year endeavours.

The time pressures of the Year and the Conference are also having an effect . . . a highly beneficial one—on the operational arrangements of many substantive projects in that, despite the long-term nature of most population undertakings, means are being sought of defining phased programmes which can be achieved within, and contribute to, the Year.

But even as we intensify our efforts to make 1974 memorable in the annals of population history, and as we scan every new development for breakthroughs which can be attributed to this endeavour, it must be remembered that the Year will be little more than a date on the calendar if it does not serve to advance, improve and strengthen the work that is already being done in the population field. (29 October 1973)

• Just as we at the UNFPA have always looked upon population as inseparable from other factors in social and economic development, so World Population Year is not an isolated phenomenon, but part of the United Nations Second Development Decade, and achievement of the aims of the Year part of our contribution to the overall purposes of the Decade. (30 November 1973)

• The activities of the Year and the major global World Population Conference will result in increasing the demand for more technical information on population, for more assistance in carrying out country programmes, for more reassurances and evidence that the problems of population are not just the problems of one but the problems of all. What we have done in the past, the services we have been able to offer, the resources we have been able to provide, are not going to be nearly enough to meet the challenges from governments who are being asked to think in terms of greater commitment to attacking the problems of poverty, environment and population, and of coping not only with their own difficulties, but of contributing to an international chain of assistance.

All this calls for dynamic leadership from the United Nations family in sponsoring in-novative programmes, and in encouraging new ideas and approaches, even at the ex-pense of traditional methods. It also calls for more money.

The real objective of World Population Year [is] . . . Action *Now*. (21 January 1974)

• Much credit for the intensification of World Population Year programmes is due to the United Nations and its Specialized Agencies, which have greatly expanded their information-type activities in order to reach their own particular audiences, and to add to the general availability of press and audio-visual material on population subjects. For example, at the present time . . . the United Nations has ready for distribution to television stations in both industrialized and developing countries, a series of tele-vision sequences covering population undertakings in Asia, Southeast Asia, Latin America, Africa and the Middle East, material that never existed before on population programmes.

Mention must also be made of the non-governmental organizations, both international and national, who have mobilized their members to take part in World Population Year activities and have launched numerous undertakings as a contribution to the Year. Their influence on general public opinion cannot be overestimated.

All these programmes are, however, directed towards having maximum impact over the twelve-month period designated for population emphasis.

A number of gains can already be chalked up to the Year. New contacts and working relationships have been established between the United Nations family and outside organizations and groups. It would be a pity if these were allowed to dissolve for lack of use. Governments have been drawn into an international community of concern on population which must be encouraged to increase rather than decrease. More and more people have been awakened to the population factor as it affects their daily life, and what it means in terms of personal responsibility to family and society. They have a right to expect the flow of information, which aroused their interest in the first place, to continue and to increase.

But awareness is one thing, action is another.

Definitely the most vital instruments for progress that have been developed in connec-tion with the Year are the national commissions, or similar authoritative bodies, which have been set up to give impetus to national population programmes. Over fifty governments have informed us that such units have been brought into operation. This number exceeds, if [we are] not mistaken, the overt governmental support that has been given to any previous special Year. It is already apparent that these units, func-tioning as a combined task force of governmental leaders and representatives of private organizations, are able to tackle the most sensitive population situations with an understanding and skill that cannot be written into any development plan; and they certainly should not be overlooked as a source of guidance and inspiration when it comes to determining the most effective ways of using external assistance. It is [our] sincere hope that governments will consider such bodies as an essential part of their organizational structures when the recommendations of the [World Population] Conference have to be turned into realities.

And it must not be forgotten that in the background, out of the limelight, the United Nations, through the UNFPA and the Specialized Agencies, has been able to keep going a steadily expanding programme of population assistance, which has proved to be extremely responsive to the new directions and needs arising from the World Population Year campaigns. In fact . . . without the backing of this substantive programme, the Year would have little meaning and even less possibility of lasting effect. (4 March 1974)

• Above all, we hope and believe that the Year will make a permanent contribution to the emerging consensus on population. Such a consensus is not based on a belief that all population problems are the same or that they are all susceptible to a single solution, but on the belief that population questions form a part of the fabric of social and economic development and as such must be accorded the importance they deserve. (21 May 1974)

• Six months of intensive activity are behind us.

We think that much has been accomplished thus far. Governments, United Nations agencies, citizen organizations, the communications media, and many individuals have focused their attention on world population matters, and we think it would be the rare individual indeed who has not in some way been touched by all the combined efforts throughout the world to increase understanding of population as it affects nations, communities, and individual families. (9 July 1974)

• The experience of World Population Year brought home to the Fund the need to maintain a continuing dialogue on population and its relationship with development, through governmental agencies directly concerned with the problem and through non-governmental organizations—particularly those concerned with economic development, the status of women and the role of youth—directed towards improving the understanding and the well-being of people everywhere.

Past experience has shown that interest in a particular area of the United Nations' concerns tends to die away soon after it peaks at a major conference, so that the valuable commitments made on such occasions are perhaps irretrievably lost. The awareness and understanding developed during World Population Year need to be nurtured and kept alive.

It is important to maintain the awareness of the economic and social implications of the population question generated in World Population Year, since, by its very nature, population will remain a pivotal issue in national planning for the foreseeable future. (17 April 1975)

• There is much greater awareness today, than there was two years ago, of the interrelationship between population and development issues and of the relevance and importance of the population factor in the development process. There is also evidence of increasing involvement of national governments in the population field, so much so that the demand for international assistance in population has fast outstripped available resources. (10 June 1975)

The Role of the Media

• There is no area in which more change is called for than that of attitudes and behaviour is regard to population.

[In what is] the most important area of all, measures are being taken [by the Fund] to try and improve communications techniques.

Communication, or rather the lack of it, is where the real problem lies. Not in carrying out successful population programmes once people know what it is all about, but in getting the necessary understanding in the first place.

When people are given the facts, when they are free to examine the cons as well as the pros, when they are able to develop their ideas and voice their opinions, then a general agreement soon emerges as to what would be for the common good . . . and after that, action follows fast.

To provide this free flow of information . . . is a major responsibility of the news media. Educators have an important part to play within specialized areas and among differing age groups. Researchers also have an important contribution to make in the form of findings and approaches. But when it comes to reaching all of the people, not just some of the people, the field is open to the professional who is capable of analysing developments, of taking an objective viewpoint, and of presenting the total picture in a way that the lay public can absorb. There *has* been considerable airing of population questions in the press but mainly of an uneven nature. . . . The time has come for the news media to adopt consistent editorial policies directed towards helping people to realize the influence population matters have on their own families, their own jobs and their own futures.

As a communications job, it is not an easy one. It raises more questions than there are answers. For example:

How do you get people to take daily heed and preventive action to avert a potential and not-too-well-defined crisis in thirty years' time?

How do you convince people that they must re-think the precepts that have been handed down from generation to generation as infallible ingredients of a secure society?

And finally, how do you get the public mind working on the broad concept that the well-being of the human race must transcend all cultural, ethical, racial and political differences? (15 February 1973)

• Although the UNFPA has no policy on the use of various family planning techniques, and will only assist projects provided that they are the subject of an official request by the government concerned, and provided that the individual right of couples to practise family planning techniques or not is preserved, UNFPA does feel that governments, as well as individual couples, should make their decisions in the full knowledge of all the alternatives and implications involved. This, again, necessitates communicating these alternatives to them.

At the individual's level, one further way of assuring this knowledge of the available options is through a programme of population education backed up by the latest audio-visual communications techniques.

Other kinds of basic demographic research, such as fertility surveys and medical studies related to fertility, are also being undertaken in many countries, including some developing countries which, for one reason or another, do not regard population increase as a "problem" or, in fact, wish to hasten the pace of their population growth. . . . For it must be emphasized that the awareness required is *informed* awareness on which rational individual and national population policies may be formulated and action programmes may be initiated.

It is no longer possible for the media in the developing world to stand aloof as amused observers of the passing parade, however entertaining or clever these observations might be. Professional detachment is one thing, lack of commitment to the improvement of human lives is quite another. It is no longer possible to ignore the social duty of serving as true educators, of communicating not only what you call "human stories"—stories, which . . . are too often limited to the trivia of social relationships—but also the truly human story of social change and social trends which have profound effects on the future of the people you try to reach. It is no longer sufficient . . . for communicators to react to events that have already taken place and neglect the task of reporting where the past, perhaps inevitably, is taking us all. Can communicators of today conscientiously wait until the deep social forces, that move inexorably underneath the daily public gaze, erupt suddenly into violence and crisis—even catastrophe—before they give their attention and column space and broadcasting time to such trends? Has the time not come for communicators everywhere, but more especially in the poor world, to begin to reassess their news values, to reconsider their judgements and to re-think their own personal responsibilities?

As you no doubt realize, this is a plea for commitment. [We] do not mean commitment to this or that particular point of view or policy on population, but to the importance of the communicator's role in studying, reporting and commenting on social problems. This is a plea for deploying some of your forces to specialization in reporting the development process in the developing world in which most of us live—specialization which would make it possible to report such matters as population trends in serious depth, and with continuous attention. . . . This is also a plea that you might consider refurbishing your techniques to make "soft" news of politics, crime, and colourful personalities. Population reporting . . . may not be about colourful persons, it is about people. (7 July 1973)

• It is of the first importance for the success of a population programme that people know what is being asked of them and why it is being asked, and that they accept and approve of the aims of the programme. It is as important, conversely, for the administrator to know the wishes of the people, what they think about his policies, and what they consider to be a viable policy, as it is for the people to know what the administration wants them to do. Communication cuts both ways.

In the international context, the problem is essentially the same, but magnified. How can developing countries communicate their urgency about the various problems of development to their industrialized neighbours in a way which will move them to make a real effort to assist? How can someone in London or New York be made to understand that the fate of the Indonesian slum-dweller is his concern? We must, somehow, create a climate of opinion in which indifference to the fate of others is impossible. This requires much more than demands for increases in the flow of international financial assistance. For aid to be effective, we need a far deeper understanding of the real needs of developing countries. The nature of this development process must be explored with compassion and sensitivity by those who know it at first hand, and the choices debated fully and in public.

The difficulty for newspapermen trying to write about all this is that there is so little in the way of hard news. There's nothing new about poverty, malnutrition, disease, ignorance and early death; they have been the lot of most men in most ages. For the United Nations, the problem of presenting the news is doubly difficult. Hard news stories involve conflict as an essential ingredient—but it is the United Nations' task precisely to avoid conflict, to remove its causes, or at least to damp it down.

Some attempts have been made—familiar phrases such as the "war on world poverty", "the crisis of change", "the population explosion" have in their time made good copy. But it is time that we went further than this and presented the news behind the news. This is where we need the co-operation of newspapermen, already skilled in the analysis of events, who are able to discern change, who can sense trends, who can report tomorrow's news today.

I understand and respect the principles of independence on which newspapermen base their attitudes because I have been in the newspaper business myself. I am familiar with the disenchantment among journalists with the performance of politicians, public servants and the whole machinery of bureaucracy—indeed I appreciate that part of the heritage of every journalist is the right to criticize the performance of public officials. The official spokesman is an ever-present standby on a slow day for news.

But administrations were not created solely so that they could make mistakes for an eager press to leap upon. They too have a job to do, and an informed, intelligent and thoughtful press can be of immeasurable benefit in helping to do it. I should like to quote you a view about the obligations of the journalist to his reader with which, as a consumer, I am totally in agreement.

"A journalist's required talent is the creation of interest. A good journalist takes a dull or specialized or esoteric situation and makes newspaper readers want to know about it. By doing so he both sells newspapers and interests people. It is a noble, dignified and useful calling."*

In dealing with problems, such as population, which involve the most deeply ingrained and intimate habits of human behaviour, and with the arcane sciences of statistics and demography, how can the public servant do his work unless the communicator is willing and able to serve as an interpreter, an advisor to people who are not specialized? Unless there is continuous and studious interpretation of problems such as the consequences of the growth of cities—to alert the administrator, the legislator, the law enforcement officer and the researcher—the hard news, when it breaks, will certainly be tragic. (2 April 1974)

• The need for communication is so vital, that without it there can be neither the public motivation to solve problems nor the active citizen participation needed to carry them through. (18 May 1974)

• Both governments and private organizations are coming to realize the value of communication, by which [we] do not mean propaganda, but responsible and reflective analysis of events, explaining the purposes of government to the people and responding in turn with the views, reactions, wishes and needs of the people themselves.

The question of press freedom is relevant here [in reporting to people and governments on development issues]. It is [our] view that it depends to a great degree on the quality of the performance of the press itself. Freedom is not a divine right of the media, but a social right belonging to the people, who delegate it to the press. Therefore the professionalization of journalism in terms of the skill and responsibility of its practitioners is of concern not only to the owners and workers in the media , but to the community as a whole. Where, as in many countries throughout the world, a large proportion of the population live in conditions which deny them even the most basic of rights . . . the function of the media takes on an added dimension of responsibility and sensitivity.

An informed, intelligent and sensitive press can provide services which even the most sophisticated of development policies cannot include. The reporter on the street and in the village can tell the true story of what population growth really means to the ordinary people. If the administrator is doing his job, he will listen. He knows as well as anyone that things do not always go according to plan, that people do not always behave as they are expected to, and that situations may develop which are beyond his experience and control. (20 May 1974)

Involving Parliamentarians in Population Issues

• Under the energetic leadership of [former Prime Minister] Mr. Nobusuke Kishi, the Japanese Parliamentary Federation on Population has become an extremely active organization and has engaged in a series of activities aimed at building up greater awareness and appreciation of population and development issues among parliamentarians. Its initiative in organizing this preparatory meeting [in Tokyo] for a World

*Written by journalist Nicholas Tomalin, who was killed in the Golan Heights in October 1973.

Conference of Parliamentarians on Population and Development, in co-operation with parliamentarians from several other countries, is to be warmly applauded, as it will enable legislators from both developed and developing countries to engage in a dialogue on population and development issues. UNFPA . . . is fully committed to this current initiative.

We . . . realize and appreciate the desire of national legislators to become aware of various facets of population and development issues. We consider the roles of the executive and legislative branches complementary; and we believe that population activities will benefit tremendously from the growing involvement of the legislators.

The decision of the United States House of Representatives in 1977 to set up a Select Committee on Population is but one example of the serious interest and concern being shown by legislators in the population issue.

The growing involvement of legislators in population and development issues is related to a world-wide trend generated by World Population Year and the World Population Conference in 1974. This trend can be discerned in several ways:

An increasing number of governments are becoming interested in population issues.

There is increasing understanding and acceptance of the complex interrelationship between fertility patterns and such areas as maternal and child health and nutrition, education, the status and role of women, and other vital development concerns.

As governments reformulate and refine their perceptions of population needs, on the basis of a better data and information base, the emphasis on various sectoral activities has begun to shift. The question of migration and dispersal of settlements, for instance, is emerging as a major sector of population activity and will require increasing international assistance.

[We] understand that this preparatory meeting will consider plans for a world meeting of legislators on population and development in 1979. . . . [We] would like to indicate UNFPA's willingness to help the preparations for such a meeting by (a) providing substantive documentation for the meeting (b) providing an opportunity to legislators to get acquainted with as many UNFPA-supported projects as possible and (c) supporting some of the financial costs of the World Conference, in conformity with our mandate to help promote "awareness-building" activities around the world.

[We] know that your decisions will have an enormous impact on the entire range of population activities—both governmental and non-governmental. . . . (28 March 1978)

• Following up on smaller informal meetings held in London and Bonn, parliamentarians from nine countries, namely Canada, Colombia, Federal Republic of Germany, India, Japan, Mexico, Sri Lanka, the United Kingdom and the United States met in Tokyo last March, at the invitation of the Japan Parliamentary Federation on Population, to begin preparations for an inter-parliamentary conference on population. This conference is now scheduled to be held in Sri Lanka in August 1979 and will be attended by parliamentarians interested in population and development from all geographic regions of the world. A Steering Committee of parliamentarians has been organized in co-operation with the Inter-Parliamentary Union and UNFPA.

As part of the Fund's ongoing work to fulfill its mandate "to promote awareness, both in developed and developing countries, of the social, economic and environmental implications of national and international population problems" as outlined in ECOSOC resolution 1763 (LIV), we will provide partial support to the preparatory activities for the conference and to the conference itself. [We] believe the increasing involvement of parliamentarians in issues of population and development will broaden and strengthen the efforts on population being undertaken by leaders in the executive branches of national governments. (21 June 1978)

Chapter 4

DATA COLLECTION

- No population policy, and, indeed, no serious economic and social plans, can be formulated unless . . . based on sound demographic and statistical foundations. (10 November 1969)

- No sound decision can be made on questions of population policy unless there is adequate demographic information. . . . The most urgent need is to assist countries which have as yet never taken a population census and countries whose experience and resources are very limited, especially in regard to planning and conducting census-taking and in processing the results.

  Although considerable progress has been made in recent years, most developing countries still lack a reliable vital registration system and they, therefore, lack important data required for economic and social planning. Intensified assistance is needed in building up and improving vital statistics, especially the establishment of demonstration projects and the provision of equipment. (4 November 1970)

- Basic demographic data required for economic and social development planning and the formulation of population policies are generally very scarce in most developing countries. Many developing countries have very little reliable information on the size and distribution of the population, levels of fertility and mortality, and rate of population growth. The dearth of data is particularly serious in Africa, south of the Sahara, where a number of countries have not yet taken a population census. Ten per cent or less of the births and deaths occurring in rural areas are recorded. (18 February 1971)

- Many countries have not engaged in population programmes so far for two main reasons. First, largely due to the lack of demographic information, they have not yet fully realized the close inter-relationship between population trends and economic and social development. Therefore, they do not recognize the significant influence that population factors have on advancing or hindering national progress. Secondly, they do not have the means nor the trained personnel to collect basic demographic data, to analyze it, and to utilize it as an essential tool for decision-making. (9 December 1971)

- Demographic activities are without doubt the most important of the population programmes being activated today. . . . In the first place they provide the only sure foundation on which to build any population action programme or, for that matter, social and economic development planning. And in the second place, demography is perhaps the only aspect of the complex, sensitive field of population which, in itself, is not controversial, in that it cuts across ideologies and does not offend cultural, ethical, traditional or political mores. Even governments which have not yet learned to use the sophisticated quantitative tools that demographic science is producing appreciate in a general sense the advantages of determining the size, composition and movements of their populations.

So it is hardly surprising that much of the credit for the increasing concern and attention being given to population belongs to the people of your calling [a gathering of demographers]. It is also not surprising that the involvement of the United Nations in population matters should have had its genesis in the United Nations Population Division, which over the years has obtained such eminence as a major source of demographic advice and guidance for all nations.

The consequences were, of course, that when, at the insistence of a number of member nations, the United Nations created the Fund for Population Activities, the Fund's original programme was heavily demographic in content. Even today, when the Fund's programme of assistance has expanded to encompass, in accordance with its mandate, every aspect of population, nearly a quarter of the total programme is still devoted to demographic undertakings.

We are not moving fast enough or consistently enough in helping governments to . . . use . . . demographic data in their policymaking operations—despite the fact that we are all well aware that the whole success or failure of population programmes of all kinds can depend to a major extent on the availability and informed use of demographic data.

This, in many countries, calls for assistance at three distinct levels. First, the setting up of infrastructure facilities for the collection of data, secondly, the training of personnel to handle and analyze the data and finally, the existence of government officials who understand and have the ability to take demographic conditions into account when formulating national and sub-national development plans. If population programmes per se are to be effective, we must take it as a priority commitment to see to it that every government is appraised of the basic needs.

We have no means of telling to what extent governments will use available data in their national planning processes and we are not even sure what kind of data should be developed to meet their needs.

Demography, like every other science, has developed its own language which is almost impossible for those not of the craft to understand.

The demographic communities, with a level of dialogue between nations already established, are in a better position than almost any other group to add still another dimension to their work and devise the means not only of communicating with their peers, but also of disseminating information in intelligible forms so that people to be touched by population problems—which really means everyone—should understand the implications of population as a factor in daily life. (27 August 1973)

• This type of programme [basic data collection] is the happy exception to most population work. Immediate results can be obtained. Practical programmes can be initiated to help provide the organizational structures for data collection, analysis and application. To help member countries through the preparatory phase and determine the most useful programmes for societies which can range from nomadic communities to urban dwellers in high-rise apartments, is the present demanding task being tackled by this Commission [Economic Commission for Africa]. The development of population policies related to economic and social planning still lies ahead. (21 January 1974)

• [We] wish to pledge the continuing support of the Fund for all activities aimed at improving the demographic base for population activities, according to the wishes and requests of the governments with which we are associated. In order to assist government ministries or agencies concerned with development planning, the Fund is prepared to assign teams of experts on a short-term basis whose task will be to analyze and assess the effects of demographic characteristics on development plans. (16 May 1974)

• In some cases, governments may be in a position to prepare demographic goals, along with other goals, in all elements of the economic and social programmes. Unfortunately, the theoretical basis for this is still weak. The Fund has been trying to promote better understanding of the interrelation between economic and social factors and demographic factors. As you know, we have strongly supported the collection of reliable census data. Our support of the World Fertility Survey is intended to assist in the procurement of more reliable [fertility] data and other economic and social data with which they may be correlated. And we have supported both macro and micro research projects also designed to clarify these relationships. We also stand ready to support, along with other donors, appropriate aspects of multipurpose . . . development projects if the demographic aspects of these can be designed in a promising way. (9 July 1974)

• Just as effective development depends on a reliable knowledge of natural and other resources, so does effective development planning depend upon reliable knowledge of the composition, growth and movement of population. (21 May 1975)

• Population activities can be seen as a vital part of the [development] framework, for it is on knowledge of the numbers and present condition of the people in a country that planning may be based. (23 October 1975)

• The collection and analysis of demographic statistics has been a valuable tool for making government decisions for over a hundred years; but recently the methods used have been considerably refined and extended even to the predominantly rural societies of the developing world. (30 March 1977)

• The knowledge has taken root [in developing nations] that censuses, surveys and analysis of the resulting data are the indispensable basis for planning population or any other kind of development programme. . . . We have been able to help many [countries] in the analysis of census data - an art in itself, but an essential link between the raw data and its use as a planning tool. (2 June 1977).

- Although a population census taken at regular intervals is a fundamental requirement for any modern government and is taken as a matter of course by citizens of developed countries, it must be recalled that many of the newly-independent countries of the world took their first census only recently. In most developing countries, the inadequacy or complete lack of basic data on the size, rate of growth, distribution and major characteristics of the population has been a serious handicap in economic and social planning. As a result, census-taking has received major UNFPA allocations, to help many countries take this first vital step towards planned management. A striking result of the African Census Programme, which is jointly sponsored by the United Nations and the UNFPA, is the fact that, of the 17 African countries which had never had a census, 10 had actually taken a census by the end of the 1970 census period. The UNFPA has given greater impetus to census-taking by the provision of direct financial support of the local personnel costs and equipment, and by the provision of external technical advisers. In addition, UNFPA has provided aid in the training of local personnel and in the strengthening of demographic training and research institutions, in order to help increase the technical capacity of developing countries in basic population data collection. (5 July 1977)

- All governments now fully realize that better knowledge of population trends and characteristics is a prerequisite both for action in the field of population and for the progressive integration of population factors with other aspects of development strategy and planning.

  The growing use of computer models . . . is a good indication of this sophistication. (8 August 1977)

- Data gathering, processing, analysis and research . . . necessitate the development of high-level units within governments to make the most effective use of what has been learned. Increasing attention is being paid by governments to the development of National Population Councils and/or Population Planning Units within National Offices, to assume responsibility for co-ordinating and facilitating these myriad activities, and for translating them into policies. (3 April 1978)

Chapter 5

DEVELOPING COUNTRIES

Responsibilities of

• In the long run, the Fund hopes that the developing countries themselves will fund substantially their respective population programmes and request assistance only when this is critically necessary and unavoidable. There are indications that the developing countries are now beginning to adopt this attitude. (4 November 1970)

• Collaboration between the Fund and developing countries can only be successful if based on mutual respect and understanding. . . . In the population field more than any other, it is in the developing countries themselves that the greatest experience and expertise are to be found. We must now go further, and encourage the governments of developing countries to take greater responsibility not only for the formulation of projects but also for their execution. (1 November 1972)

• Successful governments are organized so as to be able to deliver services effectively to the individual and to motivate people to take advantage of the services offered. This motivation is not limited to matters of fertility, but is part of a complete package including responsiveness to the expression of individual and local needs, which ties each individual into the larger society and gives purpose to individual action. This responsiveness and responsibility is notably lacking in many contemporary governments and population programmes, and general development efforts suffer as a result.

It is the responsibility of each government to devise responsive channels through which individual needs and desires can make themselves known.

[We] would suggest the following considerations as a continuing basis for this consensus [on the need to rationalize the world's population growth]: (1) The pressure of population on resources is increasingly making development efforts difficult in many parts of the world; (2) It is the responsibility of all governments to take stock of population growth and movements in their countries, and formulate appropriate policy; (3) Having determined their policy, governments have the responsibility to devise effective means of delivery of family planning and related services; (4) It is the responsibility of each government to devise responsive channels through which individual needs and desires can make themselves known; (5) Each government must recognize the need for international co-operation in research and in the transfer of skills and resources; (6) There must be a common acceptance that population is part of the wider issue of development and cannot be tackled on its own. (14 February 1973)

- Where there is a government actively committed to moving population programmes along, implementation rates are relatively high, even taking into consideration the usual unfortunate delays in implementation. (8 March 1973)

- It is one thing to recognize that each country must adopt its national population objectives; it is another and more difficult thing to pin the idea down, to formulate practical measures which will strengthen the capacity of the country to mobilize its resources behind this will and its realization.

A national population objective must not be just a "wish". It must be a clear and comprehensive statement of goals and policies arrived at by countries in accordance with their own particular needs and views. Target settings and policies should be arrived at, as much as possible, with the largest possible participation by the people who are to carry out these programmes, and taking into account all available information about relevant facts.

If this is done, there must be the necessary administrative infrastructure to carry them out. There are many countries today where the whole governmental and fiscal system was designed to answer the needs of another era—in some, the colonial era. Thus, developmental programmes which look very logical on paper are grafted onto these old systems; they fail to grow. The old systems do not move the men, the money and the necessary integrated action. There are vast wastages, great under-expenditures, gross delays. Very often these failures are blamed on other causes when, in fact, the fault lies in a system which was not designed to meet new needs—to move new materials to new places, to set up new organizations for new purposes, to administer better techniques, and to serve new kinds of recipients.

In addition to the acceptance of the need and the responsibility to solve the population problem in each country, there must also exist the skills and means to carry them out. This is the reason why the UNFPA, in its three years of operation, has devoted more than a third of its resources to training. Advisory services, equipment and supplies mean nothing when there is neither the skill nor the will to utilize them.

The most important component of the strategic effort to solve the population problem is adequate communication between the leaders and the led; between donors and recipients of assistance; between the governmental agencies and private organizations. The need for adequate information is so vital in the process that without it, there can neither be public motivation to solve this problem nor the citizen participation that is needed even to make a beginning. (6 May 1973)

- It is ultimately at the national level that population policies and actions are decided upon. (7 September 1973)

- [We] feel strongly that the key to solution of the problems of population and development lies first of all in obtaining the consent and commitment of individuals. This is true particularly of population, where everything depends on the decisions of the parents about family size. Thus the first aim of development must be to satisfy certain basic requirements which . . . have more to do with personal and social security than with any particular level of income. This will provide the basic motivation to accept long-term goals, such as optimal family size, which may then be backed up with the provision of services, advertising campaigns and other supporting activities.

This approach requires more sensitivity on the part of the administration to the feelings, beliefs and aspirations of the individual than more mechanistic programmes which rely solely on the operation of market forces, supply and demand curves and other such mystic formulae. It requires more than anything else that each member of the administration, whether in a ministry, local office, or village, is responsive to the needs of his community.

It is fundamental that each country work out the programme which suits its own circumstances and needs. (26 September 1973)

• As we have discovered in our work in the UNFPA, and as the administrators of the "Green Revolution" have found, the commitment of every single individual and family is required if development programmes are to succeed; this requires more than central direction backed up by occasional visits by "motivators" or extension workers, but calls for administrative involvement in the community at the most basic level. (18 October 1973)

• International organizations have an undoubted contribution to make in helping to formulate and stimulate support for global programmes, but it must be admitted that no outside body has the competence to identify and devise methods for the solution of problems at the national level. This capacity rests within the country itself. (29 October 1973)

• Our concern has been first to build up a working relationship with governments, to attempt to understand as completely as possible what their aims are and to fit our contribution into that framework. This sort of relationship with governments is particularly important, because as yet the connection between population and development is not well understood, and because it appears to be country-specific. The interaction varies according to the size of the country, its endowments of natural resources, the economic structure, income per head, levels of education and other factors. Both we and government policymakers need to understand better the economic and social implications of population policies and the implications for population of economic and social goals. (13 November 1973)

• Experience of a number of family planning programmes based on KAP [Knowledge, Attitudes and Practices] surveys have provided sufficient evidence that approaches imported from other parts of the world with different societies, cultures, and economies, simply do not work unless the national processes exist to adapt or discard methods unsuited to national conditions. (21 January 1974)

• "Governments do not have babies; people do". It is of the first importance for the success of a population programme that people know what is being asked of them and why it is being asked, and that they accept and approve of the aims of the programme. It is as important, conversely, for the administrator to know the wishes of the people, what they think about his policies, and what they consider to be a viable policy as it is for the people to know what the administration wants them to do. Communication cuts both ways. (2 April 1974)

• A real consensus is growing, based on the acceptance of what might be called the "third view" of population—that it is neither to be ignored as irrelevant nor treated as a more important factor, but accepted as a significant factor in the development process. (9 May 1974)

• Beyond the necessary resources and the will and determination to develop, a country must have skilled personnel to plan development programmes and carry them out.

Of equal importance is communication between governments and citizens. The need for communication is so vital, that without it there can be neither the public motivation to solve problems nor the active citizen participation needed to carry them through. (18 May 1974)

• Government must know what is happening in the streets and the villages if it is to function effectively, and supply the true needs and desires of the people for development. (20 May 1974)

• It is difficult to over-estimate the importance of the individual in matters of population. The figures which we read and the lines we see drawn on charts are the result of millions of individual decisions, to have or not to have children, to move from country to city, to seek work in another country. The most sophisticated policies will not succeed unless this is understood, and unless the policymakers allow for the complexity of the factors which affect personal decisions. (18 August 1974)

• In order to give the [World Population] Plan [of Action] substance, it will be necessary for countries and communities to design and put into effect their own national plans of action in accordance with their own special conditions, and with their own resources. We must never lose sight of the fact that the bulk of all development effort, and this includes the field of population, is undertaken by the developing countries themselves. (20 August 1974)

• All governments should consider realistically their long-term requirements for food and other basic necessities against the background of their natural resources and the availability of means—human, technological, institutional and financial—for utilizing them, and adopt, consistent with their needs and national goals, the appropriate population policies and programmes. (11 November 1974)

• Social structures and customs in rural areas are adapted to an age-old way of life. When development plans are being made, it follows that they should be sensitive to local conditions and adapted to them.

In many developing countries . . . populations are scattered, of different ethnic makeup or social habits, and correspondingly difficult to reach or to influence by centrally-directed programmes. Agricultural development, health or education pro-grammes must reach out to the village to be effective there. Once again, this implies thorough local knowledge among development personnel and a certain amount of local-level decision-making.

The interplay between different strands of the social web is so complex that it is fruitless to attempt to make changes in only one area. Family planning, for example, cannot effectively be introduced without the follow-up health services which are needed.

The picture which emerges from these generalizations is an integrated development process—integrated vertically through the different stages of production and horizon-tally across the various strands of the social pattern.

Translating political will into solid results requires a broad range of skills at all levels, but perhaps the crucial element is the managerial skill which allows the process of decision-making to proceed smoothly and to be given effect with the least delay.

This sort of skill often exists already in traditional social structures, which are often easier for the sensitive administrator to use than attempt to bypass or supplant. But where new departures are being taken, these structures may not be appropriate or exist at all. A new structure may be necessary. Formation of such structures and the training of people to manage them must be done with the utmost care, in order to fit them into already existing patterns, yet preserve their effectiveness.

There are enormous reservoirs of ability in Third World countries, which can be re-leased by, and may themselves become, effective management. Local entrepreneurs, for instance, have often proved that their knowledge of local people and conditions make them more effective implementors of local development schemes than city-based, theoretically-trained administrators. If credit is made available and effectively ad-ministered, both the entrepreneur and the community will benefit.

Development management is largely confined at the moment to centralized bureaucracies and their local offshoots. Effective management demands that the weight of expertise be located nearer to the development activity. Given the career pat-terns of most bureaucracies and the natural tendency in most countries towards the ur-ban centres, it may be necessary to reorganize or, where necessary, bypass the present government departments or agencies. This in itself is a decision which requires managerial skill in its execution. (26 September 1975)

• Development programmes of all kinds touch the life of the individual and change it for better or worse; and each development decision by the policymaker or administrator must have at least the tacit consent of the people whom the decision will affect, or run the risk of failure. The question of who makes the decisions, how they are made, and the reasons which lie behind them, therefore, are of paramount importance in bringing development successfully to the broad mass of the people.

Success can be expected in population programmes only when those who plan and ad-minister them are fully aware of the sensitivity of the issue and make full allowance for that.

Countries should regard their people as actors in development programmes rather than as mere passive recipients of development. The international parallel is that countries should regard themselves as the main motive force towards their own development, rather than relying on help from outside.

A great deal of good can come from international assistance, but in the end it is the countries, themselves, who must decide their own priorities and supply their own needs.

National and international population programmes have learned, sometimes with difficulty, that from United Nations headquarters to the village street, the consent and co-operation of the individual person, family or local group is needed before any real progress can be made. (23 October 1975)

• It is not for the Fund to set priorities for national programmes. This can only be done by the countries themselves.

Most . . . [population and general development] needs . . . can best be supplied by close attention to the behaviour and the requirements of local groups. (21 November 1975)

• Population programmes of whatever kind have been proved most effective when coupled with the concern and involvement of the community. (2 June 1976)

• In the planning and implementation of population, employment and social programmes, it is necessary to rely not merely on government alone but, insofar as possible, also on the active involvement and participation of all organized or unorganized segments of the community, such as trade unions, employers' associations, co-operatives, organizations of the rural poor, social security agencies, research institutes and other non-governmental groups.

[Both population and general development] programmes should be geared particularly to meet the needs of the poor population groups by reaching them through the most appropriate channels. Community-based distribution systems and frameworks should be utilized to accomplish this, rather than service points and institutional channels which will only reach the well-to-do in cities and towns. (14 June 1976)

• Governments, donors and agencies executing projects alike are most likely to achieve success in their programmes if they address themselves to the basic needs of those whom they serve, the people of the developing countries. In our experience, this approach can offer at least as good a ratio of costs to benefits in those things which can be quantified, and the indications are that it is a much more rewarding approach in the areas which cannot be quantified.

There must be a very strong element of participation in decision-making by those most directly affected. At the national level we have found that, while central direction can be very effective or even essential in starting or giving the necessary impetus to programmes, effective delivery cannot be sustained unless there is active participation by the community, right down to the smallest social units, the village or the street. Regardless of the political system, the important element is participation. If this is present, though the practical rewards may be few, the psychological satisfaction gained from being included in decision-making is a powerful motive to help in making programmes effective.

There are no fixed paths to a just global balance between population and economic resources. Each country, even each individual, will find the best path if allowed the means to do so, and this depends very much on the ability of administrators, governments and international organizations to listen, to determine what the needs really are, and to respond effectively.

[There is a] necessity, both at national and international levels, for the political will to effect change. Facts are useless without the energy and vision to turn them into policies and programmes for the future. In population we have seen this process of energization taking place in country after country during the last few years. (2 June 1977)

• The determination of what would constitute a basic needs population programme is not to be decided by the UNFPA but by the government concerned, helped by whatever technical assistance and experience the UNFPA and its executing agencies can provide.

The basic needs programme is intended as a set of guidelines for the entire donor community. UNFPA will, of course, provide as much assistance as is possible from its own resources to help implement such programmes. But, realistically, it cannot presume to be capable of fulfilling by any means all requirements for external assistance to meet basic needs of developing countries in population. The Fund will assist the governments concerned in each case to identify other external sources of possible funding for components of the programme it cannot undertake to support fully. Needless to say, it is entirely up to the government to decide on the sources of assistance it may want to utilize to assist in the implementation of a basic needs programme. (21 June 1977)

• The present decade has marked what can be described as a quantum leap in the recognition among developing countries of the importance of understanding, and of consciously trying to cope with, population issues. One cannot help but be encouraged by the changes which have taken place over the last few years. What is now lacking in the developing world is sufficient amounts of the technical, financial and administrative means required for the translation of policies and principles into concrete country-wide programmes. The limits are now far less those of awareness of the problems and the recognition of the urgency to take action, but far more those of the need for resources and for the broad managerial skills to implement and execute programmes. (21 June 1978)

Differences Between and Among Developing Countries on Population Matters

• Programmes and projects supported by the Fund differ considerably in countries at various levels of development and with varying population patterns.

In deciding on the kinds of assistance which the Fund should finance in one or another case, we are conscious that we must distinguish between various types of countries. In this regard, the kinds of things that the Fund should be willing to do for a country would differ considerably in the case of: (a) a country already expert in family planning, with adequate or even superior manpower, or (b) a country only now beginning to undertake a population programme in any serious way. Also relevant would be the question of whether a country was, in comparison with other developing countries, reasonably affluent or not. One relevant aspect of its financial situation to be considered would be to see whether or not it had acute foreign exchange problems. (16 October 1970)

• In giving assistance, the Fund divides countries into three types: (a) countries which have population policies and programmes . . . (b) countries which do not have population policies but are in the process of adopting one . . . and (c) those which do not have any population policies or programmes and may not have one for some time. . . .

We are prepared to consider calls for assistance from both the needy and the able. In the case of the needy, however, we shall want to be sure that programmes are designed realistically in view of the real capabilities of the country to carry them out. In the case of the able, on the other hand, if they are also relatively well off, we shall want their projects to serve a broader purpose in the solution of the world's population problems than that which might pertain only to their local situation. Here we may wish to support pilot or demonstration projects or training institutions of regional or worldwide significance. (18 February 1971)

• The needs for assistance vary to a considerable extent in different parts of the world. In some areas, assistance is required on a large scale for implementing effective population programmes, including family planning. In other areas, the major immediate need is the creation of awareness and understanding of population problems, their economic and social implications, and the formulation of policies and programmes. (3 November 1971)

• [In the early days of the Fund's operations] we discovered that under certain national circumstances well-tried approaches in family planning programmes do not always work.

And . . . we realized, such were the differences in national structures, customs, beliefs, religions and levels of progress, that the solutions to population problems must be developed within individual countries by the people themselves. As a result, the activities being supported by the Fund are as diverse as the national characteristics of the recipient countries. (15 February 1973)

• [In the World Population Plan of Action] there is emphasis on the sovereign right of every nation to decide its policy for itself without external interference. This provision reflects the profound sensitivity of the whole population question, but it is also a positive indication, a recognition that each country's situation is different. There are still today a handful of nations whose policy it is to increase their numbers at least until the end of the century. In national terms, there may be sound economic and social reasons for such a policy, even though the world situation may call for less rather than more growth overall. Other nations opt for an emphasis on quality rather than numbers; this too is their prerogative. It is not for the world community or international organizations to praise or condemn, but merely to ensure that the world facts are known and taken into consideration by governments when making policy. (15 October 1974)

- Looking at the overall [population assistance] scene, the number of important and striking changes that have taken place since 1969 is very impressive. In this short period, there are very few governments which have not become acutely aware of their own population situation and sought international aid in coping with it.

That population factors are now almost a universally accepted element of development policy in developing countries can be seen in the increasing emphasis given to population. A United Nations survey of 114 developing countries, taken during 1976, pointed up some interesting facts in this regard. . . .

> 83 of 114 developing countries have entrusted a central planning authority with the task of integrating population factors with development planning.

> 69 countries believe that the current rate of natural population increase imposes severe constraints on the attainment of population objectives.

> 63 per cent of the 114 developing countries surveyed are concerned with some aspect of their demographic situation - internal migration, morbidity and mortality, the current rate of population increase, international migration and so on.

> 54 developing countries consider that their rates of fertility are too high. Of these, 18 are in Asia, 18 in Africa, 16 in Latin America and 2 in the Middle East, and together they comprise 82 per cent of the population in the developing world.

> 82 governments themselves provide either direct or indirect support to fertility regulation measures, regardless of their own policies on natural increase and national fertility.

> Only 8 of the 114 developing countries surveyed deny access to the use of modern methods of fertility regulation.

> 95 countries consider that their population distribution is either substantially or extremely unacceptable.

> 79 countries view their levels of morbidity and mortality as a problem.

In addition, most governments have totally accepted the concept of population as a vital component of socio-economic development. The controversy that existed earlier, as to whether intervention to regulate population growth was permissible, is virtually over. Even governments which were previously opposed to intervention in population matters now have population programmes and are making strenuous efforts to ensure widespread availability of equipment and supplies to implement these programmes. (5 July 1977)

- Population issues are different in different countries and solutions to these need to be found in the context of the specific needs and requirements of each country. (28 March 1978)

Absorptive Capacity

- The rate at which the Fund is able to deliver assistance . . . depends almost completely on the absorptive capacity of the recipient countries and the speed with which the executing organizations can move on implementation. (3 November 1971)

- A number of factors determine the ability of a country and its government to absorb outside assistance—among them [are] its own awareness of its population situation, the political will of the country to do something about it, its level of knowledge and management skills in the population area, its institutional structure, and its cultural and social background and traditions.

Many UNFPA projects have increased the absorptive capacity of individual countries. Census projects have provided countries a data base not only for population planning, but for policy formulation and implementation in other areas, such as agriculture, industry, and transportation. Pilot family planning projects have led to expanded region-wide or nationwide activities. Education programmes for one sector of society have led to similar programmes for other sectors. Research projects have led to the build-up of institutional capacity and capability.

We believe that there is no problem of absorptive capacity. When [the problem of absorptive capacity] seems to exist, [very often] the real problem lies in the fact that the wrong inputs are made into the wrong project at the wrong time. . . . In being flexible, UNFPA has tried not to be bound by standard technical assistance models, but rather has attempted to meet the needs which countries feel most urgently, no matter what type of UNFPA assistance is required. (21 June 1977)

Developing Self-Reliance

- From its inception, the Fund has seen it as its main role to provide assistance to developing countries, upon request, to deal with their population problems, and in doing so to develop an institutional capacity in the recipient countries concerned, as well as in the United Nations system, to respond to the needs for assistance and to co-ordinate population programmes. (8 March 1973)

- The Fund realizes that any lasting contribution it may make will depend heavily on its success in helping countries themselves to deal with their own problems. Thus, the development of the skills needed for population activities in the developing countries has been a fundamental objective of UNFPA's programming. (4 May 1973)

- The Fund shares the belief of many development specialists that development assistance, if of the right type and given in the right way, can strengthen, rather than undermine, self-reliance. We are very much concerned in funding those areas and methods which represent the most effective contribution to national development programmes. . . . (13 November 1973)

- The Fund should aim at building up as quickly as possible the ability of recipient countries to meet their own needs. Therefore, we may limit the period of our assistance, particularly in developing countries falling outside the group of the least-developed. At the end of the period, activities should be handed over to an organization within the country concerned. This suggests that high priority should be given to supporting the following types of activity, in particular:

    (a) Human resource development, through training programmes and transfers of the skills and technical know-how required in various types of population programmes;

    (b) Institution-building at the national level, particularly in the fields of population data collection and analysis, policy formulation, and implementation of action programmes;

    (c) Operational research and pilot projects exploring innovative approaches to population problems, and diffusion of experience gained; and

    (d) Strengthening of management capability to enable the recipient countries to execute their programmes effectively themselves and obtain the maximum benefit from assistance. (21 November 1975)

• The term "sustained assistance" may, in so far as UNFPA is concerned, refer to assistance in a period of time required for a country to build up minimum programmes in the major areas of population. At the end of this time, the country may be expected to be self-reliant in the area concerned. (27 July 1976)

• Emphasis is . . . given to activities that will advance the development of human resources through a wide range of training programmes, and that will build up institutions at the national level. Emphasis is also being placed on strengthening the managerial, administrative and productive capabilities of recipient countries to enable them to execute population programmes effectively. . . .

While it is always difficult to gauge the impact of population work on a quantitative basis, there are encouraging signs that UNFPA and other external inputs into national population programmes have stimulated developing countries to greatly increase their own capacity to conduct their population programmes.

For example, one important indication of national interest is that many governments have readjusted their national budgets in order to make larger internal inputs to population programmes, in particular to family planning programmes. . . .

Another indication is the considerable speed-up in the implementation ratio of UNFPA funds by developing countries. In 1972, recipient countries were able to expend only 48.1 per cent of the UNFPA resources allocated to them. However, by 1976 the implementation ratio had increased to almost 86 per cent. This increased absorptive capacity demonstrates quite clearly that developing countries have been able to improve their infrastructure, as well as their administrative and managerial capability to formulate and implement their population policies. (5 July 1977)

• About two-thirds of the projects UNFPA assists at the country level support activities promoting national self-reliance. . . . (6 November 1978)

Involving Individuals in Decision-Making

• It is ultimately at the national level that population policies and actions are decided upon. If young people . . . wish to influence the formulation of population policies and the implementation of relevant programmes in this area, they must undertake an active and energetic role in contributing their viewpoints to the formulation of these policies and their energies to the implementation of them. (7 September 1973)

• Family planning programmes, in combination with their social services, should aim at responding, and where necessary readjusting to individual needs and desires. In the final analysis, it is only by paying attention to the individual that these programmes can be successful. (25 September 1973)

• The key to solution of the problems of population and development lies, first of all, in obtaining the consent and commitment of individuals. This is true particularly of population, where everything depends on the decisions of the parents about family size. Thus, the first aim of development must be to satisfy certain basic requirements which we might surmise . . . have more to do with personal and social security than with any particular level of income. This will provide the basic motivation to accept long-term goals, such as optimal family size, which may then be backed up with the provision of services, advertising campaigns and other supporting activities. (26 September 1973)

• The experience of World Population Year brought home to us the simple but essential truth that population is about people and it is therefore essential, in any action taken, to be sensitive to the cultural and ethical ambience of people.

To sustain this responsiveness, it is necessary to consult as many substantial viewpoints as exist, and to work with people and their institutions, official and unofficial, as close-ly as possible. (17 April 1975)

• Organic, integrated development requires, above all, the political will to succeed. The people involved at all levels must be energized, committed, convinced that the plans will work. Obtaining this commitment is not a matter of rhetoric or flamboyant leader-ship. It is much more a process of patient groundwork, during which decisions emerge from the various levels rather than being imposed from the top. People who have made their own decisions - even if they coincide with government policy - are that much more committed to making them work. (26 September 1975)

• [We] should like to see, alongside the New International Economic Order, a New Human Order, in which the individual man and woman, the family and the community are given their proper place as the resources for, and the reason for, development. (23 October 1975)

• Just as the New Economic Order will result in far-reaching changes in the structure of international relationships, there may be a case for a New Human Order, which will give expression to the aspirations of the individual and the human desire to live in peace, in health, and in happiness. Such a new order would provide the practical link between broad statements on the economic rights and duties of states and the specific safeguards of the Universal Declaration of Human Rights. It would make sense of human relationships just as the New International Economic Order should make sense of international economic relationships.

[We are] convinced that such a New Human Order is emerging. It can be seen in the practical expression in development programmes of respect for the dignity of the individual and of belief in individual capacity for self-reliance and self-determination.

Closer contact is needed between development workers and the people with whom they work, and much closer involvement of the individual in development schemes, as an agent of development as well as an "acceptor".

If it is desired to produce more food and achieve a satisfactory ratio of producers to consumers, the needs, desires and attitudes of the individual must be consulted. (21 November 1975)

- In the planning and implementation of population, employment and social programmes, it is necessary to rely not merely on government alone but, insofar as possible, also on the active involvement and participation of all organized or unorganized segments of the community, such as trade unions, employers' associations, co-operatives, organizations of the rural poor, social security agencies, research institutes and other non-governmental groups. (14 June 1976)

- There must be a very strong element of participation in decision-making by those most directly affected. At the national level we have found that, while central direction can be very effective or even essential in starting or giving the necessary impetus to programmes, effective delivery cannot be sustained unless there is active participation by the community, right down to the smallest social units, the village or the street. Regardless of the political system, the important element is participation. If this is present, though the practical rewards may be few, the psychological satisfaction gained from being included in decision-making is a powerful motive to help in making programmes effective. (2 June 1977)

Chapter 6

EDUCATION AND COMMUNICATION

• Education on population problems and their implications, as well as on the basic principles of human reproduction, should be an important component of family life education to be provided to all children and youth. (4 November 1970)

• Full use should be made of all channels for the dissemination of population materials, particularly in development programmes such as functional literacy, community development, workers' education, vocational training, home economics and rural development. Governmental bodies and voluntary organizations, including trade unions, youth organizations and mothers clubs, can also be enlisted in organizing educational activities.

Many programmes of out-of-school education also lend themselves to the incorporation of population components.

The development of the relevant curricula and teaching methods for the formal school system is an urgent priority.

In the final analysis, it is better understanding which is the key to action. Such understanding is unlikely to be achieved by means of saturation advertising and the repetition of exhortations to have fewer children. Rather, we need to pay much greater attention to education. Education on population problems and their implications, as well as the basic principles of human reproduction and family planning, are a key part of family life education to be provided to all children and youth. In this way, future generations of prospective parents would be prepared for their responsibilities. (1 November 1972)

• In population, more than any other area of development, communication is crucial. Whether the goal is a reduction in fertility, or a redistribution of population, or the basic task of gathering census statistics, the success or failure of population programmes, in the final issue, will probably hinge on the communication, education and information aspects of that programme. And it is not only a simple matter of efficient public relations. A lot of harm can be done if the quality of the information component—whether it is mass campaigns, face-to-face communication on birth control techniques, or general education to create an informed public opinion—is second-rate,

77

or if the message imparted is not in keeping with the audience receiving it. (14 February 1973-B)

- There is no area in which more change is called for than that of attitudes and behaviour in regard to population.

  [In what is] . . . the most important area of all, measures are being taken [by the Fund] to try and improve communications techniques.

  Communication, or rather the lack of it, is where the real problem lies. Not in carrying out successful population programmes once people know what it is all about, but in getting the necessary understanding in the first place.

  When people are given the facts, when they are free to examine the cons as well as the pros, when they are able to develop their ideas and voice their opinions, then a general agreement soon emerges as to what would be for the common good . . . and after that action follows fast.

  As a communications job it is not an easy one. It raises more questions than there are answers. For example:

    How do you get people to take daily heed and preventive action to avert a potential and not too well-defined crisis in thirty years' time?

    How do you convince people that they must re-think the precepts that have been handed down from generation to generation as infallible ingredients of a secure society?

    And, finally, how do you get the public mind working on the broad concept that the well-being of the human race must transcend all cultural, ethical, racial and political differences? (15 February 1973)

- The most important component of the strategic effort to solve the population problems is adequate communication between the leaders and the led; between donors and recipients of assistance; between the governmental agencies and private organizations. The need for adequate information is so vital in the process that without it, there can neither be public motivation to solve this problem nor the citizen participation that is needed even to make a beginning. (6 May 1973)

- There is . . . no area in which misinformation and misunderstandings flourish more easily [than population]. To present the facts as they are in regard to population, to assist countries to identify population problems and to find solutions for them, and to create a true awareness of the influence that population factors can have on every aspect of national life ranging from social and economic development to the day to day life of a single family, is the task [we] have been given by the United Nations.

  World-wide awareness of population implies an appreciation of the special situation in each country, and of the interrelationship between these situations at the community or national level, and of the world as a whole—the differences as well as the similarities in social needs and social attitudes between community and community and nation and nation; the correlation between population trends and economic potential; the consequences of unplanned population growth and their connection with urban slums, internal migration and the overburdening of social services; the structure of populations, and job opportunities, education policies, housing, medical services and other social amenities. All this means a massive programme of generating information—demographic information, economic research, and appreciation of traditional value systems, and developing an understanding of the political frames of reference in which population problems are viewed. It also means the need to disseminate this information as far as possible in intelligible forms, so that people whose lives are to be touched by the population problem should understand its implications, and that this information should not remain an esoteric science confined to demographers, economists, and other social scientists.

Furthermore, many activities assisted by the UNFPA by their very nature involve the need for planned communication campaigns at the project level, designed to elicit the public's active collaboration as opposed to indifference or even hostility. For, after all, a field-level project is merely an activity designed to assist a specified group of people to change their own way of life in a certain manner. . . .

Although the UNFPA has no policy on the use of various family planning techniques, and will only assist projects provided that they are the subject of an official request by the government concerned, and provided that the individual right of couples to practise-or-not family planning techniques is preserved, UNFPA does feel that governments, as well as individual couples, should make their decisions in the full knowledge of all the alternatives and implications involved, and this again necessitates communicating these alternatives to them.

At the individual's level, one further way of assuring this knowledge of the available options is through a programme of population education backed up by the latest audio-visual communications techniques.

Other kinds of basic demographic research, such as fertility surveys and medical studies related to fertility are also being undertaken in many countries, including some developing countries which, for one reason or another, do not regard population increase as a "problem" or, in fact, wish to hasten the pace of their population growth. . . . For it must be emphasized that the awareness required is *informed* awareness on which rational individual and national population policies may be formulated and action programmes may be initiated. . . . (7 July 1973)

• It is of the first importance for the success of a population programme that people know what is being asked of them and why it is being asked, and that they accept and approve of the aims of the programme. It is as important, conversely, for the administrator to know the wishes of the people, what they think about his policies, and what they consider to be a viable policy, as it is for the people to know what the administration wants them to do. Communication cuts both ways.

In the international context, the problem is essentially the same, but magnified. How can developing countries communicate their urgency about the various problems of development to their industrialized neighbours in such a way which will move them to make a real effort to assist? How can someone in London or New York be made to understand that the fate of the Indonesian slum-dweller is his concern? We must, somehow, create a climate of opinion in which indifference to the fate of others is impossible. This requires much more than demands for increases in the flow of international financial assistance. For aid to be effective, we need a far deeper understanding of the real needs of developing countries. The nature of this development process must be explored with compassion and sensitivity by those who know it at first hand and the choices debated fully and in public. (2 April 1974)

• Both governments and private organizations are coming to realize the value of communication, by which [we] do not mean propaganda, but responsible and reflective analysis of events, explaining the purposes of government to the people and responding in turn with the views, reactions, wishes and needs of the people themselves. . . . (20 May 1974)

• For the effective promotion of population programmes, you need above all a comprehensive and effective network of communication, information and education. Population programmes depend less on bricks and mortar than on the minds and hearts of men and women. A real and vital commitment is needed from everyone—this is the essential ingredient in the change of attitudes and change of values. . . . Communication is a two-way process. Individuals seldom become committed to programmes unless they first understand them. Governments and agencies cannot get them further committed and involved unless they adjust to what people ask and demand in return.

This is the reason why the Fund has consistently committed a considerable portion of its assistance to communication and education and has supported and initiated the creation of press and information institutions in the Third World. (20 August 1974)

• Integrated rural development programmes . . . may be used for education and information activities aimed at motivating people to adopt a rational attitude on population matters. (11 November 1974)

• UNFPA has supported population information and population education programmes which will promote the understanding of population dynamics and the socio-economic implications of population. This kind of assistance has been extended to a number of national population education programmes, either through the school system or out-of-school programmes.

A remarkable increase in the volume and nature of population education and information is accompanying this upsurge of interest [in population on the part of developing countries]. These programmes deal not only with reproduction and the basic techniques of family planning, but also with the economic and environmental impact of population growth. Population information is also being disseminated outside educational programmes, in churches, health centres and other community networks. (5 July 1977)

• Since its inception in 1969, the United Nations Fund for Population Activities has always maintained close relations with the academic community. From the universities all over the world, it has drawn necessary ideas and manpower to generate its own growth, and to respond to developing countries' needs to strengthen indigenous institutional capacities to cope with their self-defined population problems. But the Fund believes that the role of intellectuals does not end with their past contribution. As the Fund grows and enters its ninth year of operation, and countries become more self-reliant in integrating population concerns in their development strategies, the role of academia in mapping out the future of population studies in the enhancement of national development gains additional significance. It is obvious that in the Third World, universities have a different role to play than they do in the developed countries. They are encountering a host of intricate problems . . . for which they need to seek their own solutions with the help of a thorough understanding of the historical and national contexts which shape these problems. (4 April 1978)

Chapter 7

FAMILY PLANNING

General

- It is expected that the main volume of requests to the Fund will be for international assistance in controlling the expansion of population. (10 November 1969)

- It is the consensus in United Nations circles that the weakest link in the family planning programmes of developing countries is in devising activities aimed at overcoming obstacles and resistance to the practice of family planning. No doubt there are few clinical services offering assistance in family planning which could not be improved. However, there is hardly any report, survey or programme that does not call attention to the relevance of the socio-cultural factors in the implementation of family planning programmes or to the need for information and knowledge to circulate freely to motivate leaders, heads of families, or individuals, to accept family planning practices and reduce family size. (16 October 1970)

- General support will be provided [by the Fund] for the promotion of demonstration and pilot projects on family planning, for the purpose of trying various approaches, and to gain experience in the development of a comprehensive approach in the implementation of programmes. Pilot projects in vital statistics and for the improvement of other demographic statistics will also be supported. (4 November 1970)

- UNFPA and the United Nations system as a whole will take considerably more initiative, and will undertake projects, with the agreement of governments, which are intended to "improve the state of the art". This will include demonstration and pilot projects.

A few major demonstration projects making provision for family planning in connection with maternal and child health services are envisaged. For advice and services on family planning, the maternity-centred approach is one of the most effective means of reaching women. . . .

Supplies and equipment should be provided as required, on a large scale, as part of a comprehensive approach to family planning. The comprehensive approach should include provision of supplies, advisory services, training, equipment, and other requirements, rather than their provision as isolated inputs.

Clinical trials and pilot projects should be carried out on new techniques of contraception which may have demonstrated their effectiveness in research trials. The acceptability in developing countries and the impact of possible widespread use of potentially effective methods should [also] be studied through pilot projects. Their impact upon the administration, organization, ʈraining, incentives and the overall strategy of national family planning programmes should especially be studied. (18 February 1971)

- The family planning approach to the problem of high fertility was predicated on the results of KAP surveys (Knowledge, Attitude, Practice), which indicated considerable interest in and demand for contraception. However, popular response to the introduction of family planning advice and services has generally not been as enthusiastic as was expected. It is true that in most countries in the [Asian] region birth rates have declined, but in many cases the declines have been modest and it is not clear to what extent these declines have been brought about by national family planning programmes. Indeed, such evidence as does exist often suggests that these programmes have merely reinforced an already existing trend toward fertility decline. In most countries, too, initial success has been followed by some falling-off in the number of new acceptors. This, however, has not led most social scientists to question the surveys. Instead, they have usually accepted the validity of the findings and looked elsewhere for explanations—lack of an ideal contraceptive, the clinical orientation of programmes, insufficient motivation. All these are undoubtedly important. The question remains, however, why are couples in developing countries not taking full advantage of the services offered?

[We] do not think that present family planning programmes have failed—or that they should be discarded. On the contrary, such programmes should be improved and intensified. Indeed, support to family planning programmes through strengthening their critical components has been, and will continue to be, one of the first priorities for UNFPA. The sense of disenchantment and even frustration with current efforts may have arisen, in large part, because we have expected too much from family planning and underestimated the difficulties involved in "engineering" a decline in fertility.

Criticism of family planning programmes usually focuses on such factors as lack of commitment on the part of the government, poor design and planning, shortage of trained personnel, inadequate resources and so on. The poor quality of services may well be an equally important weakness, particularly since the programme is likely to be somewhat suspect anyway by virtue of being introduced from outside the community. The need to fill quotas and achieve targets may tend to lead to a deterioration in quality. It is a question of the means matching the objectives. Family planning is essential for reasons of individual and family health and well-being alone. But if the goal is a rapid reduction in fertility, we must accept the implications of such an undertaking and formulate appropriate programmes.

In formulating a new strategy for the problem of high fertility, we can . . . learn an important lesson from recent experience in the field of agricultural development. Until a few years ago there was a tendency to dismiss peasant society as lazy and ignorant and bound by superstition and tradition. Peasant farmers, in particular, were condemned for their unwillingness to innovate. There was hardly any question in the minds of the experts—generally foreigners or foreign-trained—that the peasant could have valid reasons to act as he did. The problem was defined simply as one of finding ways of modifying his behaviour along the lines deemed necessary or desirable by the development planners. This approach is now being increasingly challenged on the basis of studies which question automatic assumptions of peasant conservatism and which try to understand the functioning of subsistence farming through the eyes of the peasant himself. These studies have demonstrated that peasant farmers in developing countries have a deep practical understanding of their farming environment and its limitations and that, far from being unwilling to experiment, they are behaving in a perfectly rational fashion by adopting what we might call a minimal-risk strategy.

The analysis of reproductive behaviour in developing countries and prescriptions for fertility control strategy have often displayed the same kind of self-assurance and condescension. The high levels of fertility prevailing in most countries in the Asian region are the legacy of a long cultural tradition which has encouraged large-sized families. Indeed, it is only in recent history that high fertility has ceased to be essential for the survival of the species. And even now, in many areas death rates remain sufficiently high to preclude any thought of having fewer children. Nor can we ignore the fact that in rural areas a large family is still viewed as an economic asset. However, we have tended to assume that couples who want large families are behaving in an irrational fashion when, in fact, they merely do not share our values regarding family size.

We should seek to deepen our understanding of the factors influencing decisions about family size—as these are perceived by the population concerned. This involves in-depth, village-level research of the kind undertaken by anthropologists. Some studies of this kind have been carried out, but they have not received the attention they deserve. We should encourage case studies in different settings to be undertaken. . . .

Insufficient attention has also been paid to the effects of various social policy measures on fertility and to their potential use in support of family planning programmes and as a part of comprehensive population policy. . . .

The development of a comprehensive strategy taking into account all the factors affecting fertility may, however, still not be sufficient. It is common these days to refer to rapid population growth as the single most important obstacle to improved living standards in developing countries. It is not surprising that this point of view is challenged in many developing countries as simplistic and misleading. The real "obstacles" to development lie elsewhere, not merely in the rate of population growth, but in the compound effects of such factors as the neglect of agriculture, rigid social structures, imbalances in resource allocation as well as the unequal relations between rich and poor countries and the maldistribution of income. It would be illusory to imagine that a reduction in the rate of population growth will, of itself, raise living standards. . . .

The problem is . . . not so much that population action programmes will not "bite" until a certain threshold of modernization is reached. Changes in fertility behaviour are more likely to occur as an integral part of an overall process of social and economic change which is, generally speaking, not yet occurring on a sufficiently broad scale in most developing countries. . . .

Population specialists have rightly drawn attention to the consequences—political, economic, social, environmental—of rapid population growth, but they have done so mainly in order to demonstrate the need for deliberate efforts to moderate fertility. However, effective population control is a long-term undertaking and whatever success is achieved through current efforts to reduce fertility, the population of the developing regions will almost certainly double within the next twenty-five to thirty years. Population growth of this magnitude can seriously jeopardize hopes for any substantial improvements in living standards in the coming decades. . . . As population specialists we have a responsibility to draw attention to these problems. [And] as population specialists we have a role to play in their solution, not only through the formulation and implementation of population policies as such, but also as part of an integrated approach to economic and social development. . . . (1 November 1972)

• Some of the family planning programmes we have supported have demographic goals; others do not, and are conceived entirely as measures of individual and family welfare under the direction and supervision of the Ministries of Health. (29 January 1973)

• Population policies are too often confused with family planning.

Family planning should be regarded as a service within an overall population policy, taking into consideration such factors as demographic patterns, fertility levels, social and economic conditions, religious traditions and cultural heritage.

In family planning, the Fund will intensify its efforts to assist governments in providing information and facilities. Because general health services in many cases provide the best framework for family planning, UNFPA will provide assistance through governments as well as by means of non-governmental and private channels.

A high priority will be given to activities intended to strengthen education and communication about family planning. (14 February 1973)

• Place population policies within the context of an overall plan for economic and social development, which aims at eliminating starvation and malnutrition, at providing more jobs, better housing and more educational facilities, and at reducing inequalities in the distribution of national resources and personal income, and *then* we can look for specific reasons why family planning services are not being used to full advantage.

These are aspects to which the Fund is giving constant attention. (14 February 1973-B)

• It would appear that . . . significant change in . . . fertility pattern[s] . . . is related to three related factors—(1) increasing availability of family planning information and facilities to all sections of the community; (2) a high literacy rate, ensuring widespread dissemination and appreciation of population information; and (3) a rising standard of living, benefits of which are being shared by different sections of the community.

Some countries . . . do not necessarily desire a reduction in the fertility rate, but wish to provide access to their citizens to family planning information and services. Family planning in this context should be regarded as a social service, and not just as the means to limit births. [We] subscribe to the view that family planning programmes, in combination with their social services, should aim at responding, and where necessary readjusting, to individual needs and desires. In the final analysis, it is only by paying attention to the individual that these programmes can be truly effective. (25 September 1973)

• Over the last four years there has been a profound evolution in thinking, and the ground on which action programmes were built no longer seems quite as sound as it did several years ago. This is particularly evident in two key areas—fertility control and the relationship of population to development. In both fields, basic assumptions are being challenged and new approaches are being explored. There is a growing sense of the complexity of the relationships involved, of the importance of the context in which individual decisions about family size are made and of the need for a comprehensive approach . . . which goes beyond the traditional confines of demography and family planning.

One of the factors behind the upheaval is undoubtedly the lack of clear evidence that national family planning programmes are producing results quickly enough.

We may have expected too much too soon from family planning programmes as an instrument of social planning. At the same time, we cannot discount the possibility that, because priority was quite naturally given to involving governments and the world community in action programmes, the evidence and assumptions on which these programmes were to be based were not properly established.

Whatever the reason [for reassessment of family planning approaches] . . . it is to be welcomed. The consensus which seems to be emerging from the present state of flux represents . . . a more sophisticated approach and thus, one which is more likely to lead to success in the long run.

Where population and family planning activities are organized as a part of an already existing programme, for example, the integration of family planning services in MCH [maternal and child health programmes] or family life education within functional literacy, the results have been impressive. (22 October 1973)

• In motivating the individual, it has been learned that population cannot be the subject of "hard sell"; rather, it should be our purpose to promote awareness and understanding of the population question in such a way that the individuals can decide for themselves, on the basis of adequate knowledge and facilities, what they would like to do in regard to the size of their families and spacing of their children. (30 November 1973)

• We do not talk any more in terms of family planning as an answer to population growth, because we realize now that there is far more to population than family planning. In many parts of the world, particularly in Asia, it is indeed vital to slow down the rate of population growth, but [we] think that it is now realized that the number of children a family has depends on a very complex interaction, in which levels of education, the quality of housing, health and social security services play a part, and which is tied closely to the form which overall social and economic development is taking. (2 April 1974)

- It [is] important that we *not* look at family planning programmes as the complete panacea to the world's population problems. While family planning programmes and information will help couples to have the numbers of children they wish, other economic and social factors lie behind their ideas of desired family size. (9 July 1974)

- Family planning . . . cannot effectively be introduced without the follow-up health services which are needed.

  Our experience has led us to emphasize the introduction of family planning, mother and child care service, training, communication and other services as a complete package, part of an overall plan which will probably include census and demographic services. (26 September 1975)

- This [family planning] is the part of the field of population activities which for most people in the industrialized countries symbolizes—and is sometimes taken for—the whole field. There is no universal agreement that the present rate of world population growth is too high, and [we] do not expect that there will be. Nevertheless, of the 48 developing countries which perceive their national population growth rates as too high, 40 are acting to lower them. These countries contain some 80 per cent of the developing world's population and over half of that of the entire world. Further, though most of the nations of the world are satisfied with their growth rates or wish to raise them, only 15 out of 156 prevent access to contraceptive methods.

  In many countries, the activities which . . . would be described as "family planning" come under the heading of activities designed to promote health and social welfare, and contraceptive services are provided as part of a package of health and welfare services. This offers many advantages, not the least of which is that existing networks and personnel can be used to carry both motivation and means to the people who need them. It also avoids singling out fertility regulation and integrates contraceptive services with other population and development services.

  In these countries, it will often be claimed, even by government representatives, that they are opposed to family planning. By this it can be taken to mean that they are opposed to the concept of delivering family planning *in isolation,* without reference to other development services. Many of these governments have highly efficient means of motivating users and delivery of fertility regulation services. Some have succeeded in cutting their birth rates drastically—without, in some cases, ever admitting that this was their aim.

  At a personal level, . . . hostility [to modern means of contraception] can be aroused by insensitive approaches, and there are recent examples of useful and progressive programmes which have had to be scrapped because of crude or simply over-enthusiastic implementation.

  Both fertility and mortality rates may decline, whether or not family planning programmes are in operation . . . at a much lower level of income than was needed for the European demographic transition—provided certain conditions are met. These include access to housing, health services, education and employment. They may also include special attention to the position of women in society. Together they constitute the whole package of services which provide the essentials of a secure and hopeful existence.

Whatever the remaining constraints, there is no doubt that family planning, as well as other important sectors of population activities, is in a phase of rapid expansion worldwide. (30 March 1977)

• Eight years ago, family planning programmes undertaken for demographic reasons were normally vertical structures, though connected to health ministries. Today, family planning programmes, whether interventionist or not, are more likely to be integrated in the wider context of maternal and child health care, which is itself part of the total package of health services. Indeed, family planning is increasingly seen as a social welfare service. (2 June 1977)

• Project budgets already approved for future years confirm the trend in programme development of the past, that is, a growing demand for assistance in family planning and population growth limitation after data collection has improved and population policies have been established.

We have seen [in the eight years of the Fund's operations] a revolution in worldwide attitudes toward the subject of population in general and family planning in particular. The same [recent United Nations] survey [of 114 developing countries] shows that 54 developing countries now consider that their rates of fertility are too high. Of these, 18 are in Asia, 18 in Africa, 16 are in Latin America and two in the Middle East, and together they comprise 82 per cent of the population in the developing world. A total of 81 governments themselves provide either direct or indirect support to fertility regulation measures, regardless of their own policies on natural increase and national fertility. And in only eight of the 114 developing countries surveyed was access to the use of modern methods of fertility regulation limited in any way.

Family planning has [in the course of the Fund's eight years of operation] been removed from the polemics of "population versus development" which had constrained its adoption during the previous decade in many countries, and [from] its identification as basically a health and welfare and human rights-oriented measure, which could contribute to demographic change if that change were independently considered desirable.

Eight years ago, the health services infrastructures in many developing countries were poorly developed or practically non-existent. Countries wanting to institute family planning programmes had, of necessity, to establish vertical or parallel programmes, if they were to be initiated at all. UNFPA-funded family planning programmes provided the impetus for the initiation by the developing countries, not only of the development of their health services, but of the expansion of model family planning programmes as well.

As health services infrastructures have been built up, family planning programmes have been integrated with maternal and child health care programmes. The United Nations survey points up the fact that the governments of all of the 81 countries which have national family planning programmes consider these to be an essential means of achieving acceptable levels of maternal and child health and family welfare, and of satisfying the goals of human rights and the improved status of women. In this sense, the progrrammes are integral parts of health and social policies. Indeed, it is as a health policy that the most rapid and widespread diffusion of family planning programmes have been accepted by governments of developing countries of varied cultural and development characteristics. (21 June 1977)

• [An] important [recent] trend is that the population programmes, especially the family planning programmes, of many developing countries have been expanded to a remarkable extent, to provide services not only to urban population, but also to rural areas. One concrete measurement of this programme expansion is the mushrooming of family planning service delivery points. (5 July 1977)

• Although . . . the field of population is much broader than family planning, family planning is nonetheless essential to assist families in achieving the number and spacing of children that they desire. (3 April 1978)

• UNFPA is increasingly being called upon to support programmes on infant and maternal mortality with the direct objective of contributing to the regulation and reduction of fertility. . . . In other cases, such programmes are supported with the main objective of reducing infant mortality and maternal mortality and morbidity, while the influence upon fertility is only incidental and not a primary objective. . . . (21 June 1978)

Factors Affecting Fertility Trends

• It would appear that . . . significant change in . . . fertility pattern[s] . . . is related to three related factors—(1) increasing availability of family planning information and facilities to all sections of the community; (2) a high literacy rate, ensuring widespread dissemination and appreciation of population information; and (3) a rising standard of living, benefits of which are being shared by different sections of the community. . . .

Several . . . countries . . . which have achieved [a decline in their rate of population growth] during a period of five to ten years, also have a high literacy rate, sharing of benefits of progress by various sections of the community, and a well-organized system of providing information and facilities on family planning to their people.

This "island" approach, implemented through a task force set-up, which seems to have been so successful in these countries, can be equally applied to other countries of similar size. Even in the case of much larger countries, it may be possible to utilize this approach towards developing areas of successful experimentation and achievement which cound then be emulated by other areas and communities in the country. . . . This approach may also apply to those countries which do not necessarily desire a reduction in the fertility rate, but wish to provide access to their citizens to family planning information and services. Family planning in this context should be regarded as a social service, and not just as the means to limit births. [We] subscribe to the view that family planning programmes, in combination with their social services, should aim at responding, and where necessary readjusting, to individual needs and desires. In the final analysis, it is only by paying attention to the individual that these programmes can be truly effective. (25 September 1973)

• There is a direct relationship not simply between national prosperity and family size but between *relative* prosperity within a country and family size. . . .

This says more than simply that if incomes go up fertility goes down. Distribution of benefits is brought about in part typically by the provision of a whole package of health, welfare and education services. Personal security is thereby increased, the sense of injustice at the prosperity of others perhaps lessened, involvement and identification with group aims enhanced. Again, the very existence of efficiently-operating systems of this kind implies superior administration able to deliver not only these services but others, including family planning. . . . And most important, establishment of these services implies an involvement on the part of the administration in the day-to-day affairs of the community and the individual, which calls forth a response from the individual and helps ensure his commitment to the goals of his society. If one of these goals is a reduction in fertility, it is much more likely to be brought about through this process than by any amount of advertising or free distribution of contraceptives.

The key to solution of the problems of population and development lies first of all in obtaining the consent and commitment of individuals. This is true particularly of population, where everything depends on the decisions of the parents about family size. Thus, the first aim of development must be to satisfy certain basic requirements which we might surmise . . . have more to do with personal and social security than with any particular level of income. This will provide the basic motivation to accept long-term goals, such as optimal family size, which may then be backed up with provision of services, advertising campaigns and other supporting activities. (26 September 1973)

• [A recent study by the Overseas Development Council] shows that birth rates in developing countries do not usually decline in the absence of some improvement in well-being; in particular, assured food supply, improved health services and higher literacy. In countries where there is solid economic growth, family size drops if the resulting benefits are distributed throughout the community. Conversely, where increasing wealth is concentrated in a few hands, population growth continues to be very high. Now, this is not an apology for egalitarianism; such dispersal through the community of the benefits of growth implies highly efficient administrative systems which reach through all levels of the community. Such systems, designed to deliver services such as health and education, will not only be in a much better position to provide family planning services as needed, but the security provided by such a system itself conduces to smaller family size. (18 October 1973)

• There appear to be clear links between . . . high literacy rates and low completed family size in some developing countries, between low infant mortality and low fertility, and between the success of an administration in distributing the fruits of development and the willingness of parents to limit the number of their children. (13 November 1973)

• It has been clear for a long time that family planning campaigns on their own are largely ineffectual in producing a lower rate of population growth. However, experience in a dozen different countries has shown that population growth rates fall, even in the absence of organized campaigns, if certain conditions are met. These conditions generally include adequate housing for all, full employment, ready access to education and health services; in other words, precisely the conditions which would prevail in an area applying the small-scale theory of development. . . .*

We tend to assume that the established relationships between such factors as levels of education, urbanization, employment outside the home, domestic status and completed family size, are simple. In fact, they are not. Education alone probably has little or no effect on family size, but it is quite often found to be combined with outside employment and other factors which will, together, affect fertility. Employment among city women does not necessarily affect their child-bearing, although where relationships with the husband are on a basis of equality, and especially if the woman is educated, families tend to be smaller. Completed family size thus depends on a complex interaction of social and economic variables about which we need to know a great deal more than we do.

In such a delicate, complex and personal matter as determining family size, it is all the more important to ensure the commitment and participation of women, in whose hands the ultimate decision lies.

More women must be involved at all levels in decision-making. Rather than being merely passive tools of policy, they must become active participants in the decisions which will profoundly affect their lives. (25 February 1974)

• Nothing is more relevant to successful population programmes than successful development efforts. It has been shown quite clearly that population growth rates will drop, given the right economic and social conditions. It seems that people require more than anything else not prosperity, but a measure of security in housing, health, jobs, education and, above all, in food supply, before they will risk reducing the numbers of their children. (19 April 1974)

• A vital part of the consensus reached at [the World Population Conference at] Bucharest was the idea that reduction of top-heavy population growth rates depends, in addition to family planning programmes, on the steady improvements in basic conditions of life for the poorer sections of the population—in most developing countries, the rural and agricultural majority. Even a small improvement in health, housing, education and other services can apparently have a significant effect on fertility rates.

Organic, integrated development requires, above all, the political will to succeed. The people involved at all levels must be energized, committed, convinced that the plans will work. Obtaining this commitment is not a matter of rhetoric or flamboyant leadership. It is much more a process of patient groundwork, during which decisions emerge from the various levels rather than being imposed from the top. People who

See entry for this date in "Development Planning".

have made their own decisions—even if they coincide with government policy—are that much more committed to making them work. (26 September 1975)

• Closer contact is needed between development workers and the people with whom they work, and much closer involvement of the individual in development schemes, as an agent of development as well as an "acceptor". (21 November 1975)

• Economic constraints [to effective population policies] are a classic feature of the so-called "demographic transition". In the now-industrialized countries, the decline in fertility which took place in the second half of the nineteenth century was accompanied by a rise in the standard of living, and low fertility rates have usually been associated with economic prosperity. Recent research and experience have shown, however, that the standard of living need not be high before fertility decline sets in—provided certain conditions are met. The state of Kerala in India, for example, is poorer than the states which surround it, but its fertility and mortality rates are considerably lower. Other factors which make it different from its neighbours are that its income distribution is more even—thanks to effective land reform; levels of education and general literacy are higher; the level of political participation by the general public is higher; and health services are more efficient and widely used. (30 March 1977)

• There must be a very strong element of participation in decision-making by those most directly affected. At the national level we have found that, while central direction can be very effective or even essential in starting or giving the necessary impetus to programmes, effective delivery cannot be sustained unless there is active participation by the community, right down to the smallest social units, the village or the street. Regardless of the political system, the important element is participation. If this is present, though the practical rewards may be few, the psychological satisfaction gained from being included in decision-making is a powerful motive to help in making programmes effective. (2 June 1977)

• Along with increasing sophistication in population policy-making and practice is an increasing scepticism concerning the connection between high fertility and population growth rates on the one hand, and economic growth and poverty on the other. It used to be regarded as axiomatic that too rapid a rate of population growth would retard economic growth and, further, that rapid economic growth would accelerate the demographic transition. Today, much more variety in the interaction of population and economic growth is acknowledged. (8 August 1977)

• Population programmes are not against motherhood but for motherhood. The size of the family does not necessarily, in our time, indicate the extent of the love the parents have for their children. Often it is a sign of the fear they have, or have had, of children dying in infancy or at a very young age, from malnutrition and consequent susceptibility to disease. The relationship between the fall in infant mortality and the spread of voluntary acceptors of contraception in the state of Kerala in India is an excellent case in point. It is also interesting that the reduction of fertility has been achieved there without a proportionally impressive improvement in industrial development, which has been classically regarded as an essential key to lowering the rate of population growth. (27 September 1977)

- In Sri Lanka we have found that the drop in birth rates was connected with good health care and other social services, including family planning, high literacy, a tradition of relatively high age at marriage, and the full integration of women into the economic and social life of the community. These factors have been noted in other countries where birthrates have dropped. . . . They are desirable in themselves as ends of development, and also as means to the end of lowering the population growth rate—-just as a lower birthrate is both an end of development and a means towards it. (26 March 1978)

Socio-Cultural Factors Affecting Family Planning

- The high levels of fertility prevailing in most countries in the Asian region are the legacy of a long cultural tradition which has encouraged large-sized families. Indeed, it is only in recent history that high fertility has ceased to be essential for the survival of the species. And even now, in many areas death rates remain sufficiently high to preclude any thought of having fewer children. Nor can we ignore the fact that in rural areas a large family is still viewed as an economic asset. However, we have tended to assume that couples who want large families are behaving in an irrational fashion when, in fact, they merely do not share our values regarding desirable family size. (1 November 1972)

- The solution [to population problems] is not simply one of technical innovation, but of persuading individuals to accept change. On the land, it is possible to demonstrate the gains immediately available to the innovators. But it is not so easy to demonstrate the rewards of better health, longer life and more food for all, that could come with enlightened population policies. Results do not become evident for fifteen to twenty years.

Traditional values and attitudes resist change. In many developing countries, the belief persists that every new child brings its own fortune into the world. The extra child is not only an extra mouth to feed, but also an extra pair of hands to help increase the family's resources and to provide for parents in their old age. It is difficult to persuade families to risk their future for the promises of government planners. Pleas for a radical transformation of attitudes must be accompanied by action aimed at social and economic development. (14 February 1973)

- There is no area in which more change is called for than that of attitudes and behaviour in regard to population.

How do you convince people that they must re-think the precepts that have been handed down from generation to generation as infallible ingredients of a secure society? Should we re-phrase common sayings so that they go something like this:

"Increase and multiply" . . . yes, but carefully.

"Young people should be seen and not heard" . . . yes, but how long can a majority keep silent, particularly on issues which so vitally affect it?

"The hand that rocks the cradle rules the world". But have women a sufficient say in how many times the cradle should be filled? (15 February 1973)

• Society is on the move; more and more people are becoming city dwellers, and the village is changing in order to adapt to the needs of modern living. It is important for the healthy development of social and economic life that the implications of these changes are fully weighed. (16 May 1974)

• The experience of World Population Year brought home to us the simple but essential truth that population is about people, and it is therefore essential, in any action taken, to be sensitive to the cultural and ethical ambience of people.

To sustain this responsiveness it is necessary to consult as many substantial viewpoints as exist, and to work with people and their institutions, official and unofficial, as closely as possible. (17 April 1975)

• Social structures and customs in rural areas are adapted to an age-old way of life. When development plans are being made, it follows that they should be sensitive to local conditions and adapted to them. (26 September 1975)

• Family planning programmes in Asia . . . have gone as far as they can in many places through conventional means. Further acceptance is to be won as a result of changes in ways of looking at the world among a large class of the rural poor. For this to happen, important changes in approaches to development are needed. In particular, closer contact is needed between development workers and the people with whom they work, and much closer involvement of the individual in development schemes, as an agent of development as well as an "acceptor". (21 November 1975)

• Historically, governments' preoccupation has been with increasing populations—a growing population was a clear sign of prosperity, of freedom from hunger and disease, and was a source of strength against potential enemies. This perception of a strong positive correlation between population growth, economic development and security persisted in Europe and America until quite recently and still colours attitudes to population growth elsewhere. (12 January 1977)

• At a personal level, traditionalist distrust of modern means of contraception often ignores traditional reality—that women at all times, and in most societies, have known about and used, with or without knowledge, some form of contraception. Suspicion can and is being eroded by programmes which reconcile acceptance of contraception with the values of everyday life. On the other hand, hostility can be aroused by insensitive approaches, and there are recent examples of useful and progressive programmes which have had to be scrapped because of crude or simply over-enthusiastic implementation. (30 March 1977)

Contraceptives: Technology and Community-Based Distribution of

• The United Nations will attempt to strengthen applied and operational research in . . . human reproduction. . . . (4 November 1970)

- Clinical trials and pilot projects should be carried out on new techniques of contraception which may have demonstrated their effectiveness in research trials. The acceptability in developing countries and the impact of possible widespread use of potentially effective methods should be studied through pilot projects. Their impact upon the administration, organization, training, incentives and the overall strategy of national family planning programmes should especially be studied. (18 February 1971)

- This group [Expert Group Meeting on the Production and Distribution of Contraceptives in Developing Countries] should perhaps also consider the possibility of helping developing countries to . . . improve engineering and testing facilities. (22 November 1971)

- Attention is being given [by the Fund] to the promotion of research in human reproduction, especially to research which may lead to new methods suitable for use in developing countries. (15 February 1973)

- Family planning services in most developing countries have traditionally been provided through public health systems, especially in their early stages. This has been shown to be politically wise, especially where family planning has been a sensitive issue for political or religious reasons, and administratively logical because of the need for medical skill in prescribing pills or inserting IUDs. Nevertheless, this approach has confined family planning programmes largely to the towns, where clinics were already in place. Even where clinics have been established in rural areas, potential acceptors have been discouraged by the distances to be travelled and the waiting time on arrival. Shortages of doctors and nurses have also limited effectiveness.

Efforts are now being made to bring family planning services closer to clients by using local groups and people, by using networks already in place and integrated with the culture of their societies. In [many] countries, contraception is now routinely taken to the villages where most of the Third World's population lives, and into the increasingly crowded urban areas, by a variety of carriers—midwives, health visitors, housewives recruited for the purpose and, increasingly, through commercial outlets.

This new approach, often called the "community-based approach" or "community-based distribution of family planning services", emphasizes the increase in the capacity of a community to use its own resources for the welfare of its people, including family planning. Medical facilities and personnel serve to provide technical support; the programme develops the social and administrative structures of the community to deliver family planning information and services. Special emphasis is often placed on the participation of women, through their association with family as well as community decision-making, and on providing them with alternatives to childbearing as a source of self-identity and gratification. Through the community-based approach, efforts are also being made to strengthen a sense of community identification and to increase awareness of the consequences of population growth for the community as a whole as well as for the individual family. . . .

A key element of the contraceptive distribution centre scheme [in some developing countries] is the involvement of village leaders and the village community itself in family planning. Community leaders act as distribution points not only for contraceptives, as "village contraceptive depot holders", but also for the appropriate family planning information. They are also expected to make the community more sensitive to the needs of family planning acceptors by becoming attentive to difficulties associated with contraception and by providing adequate information. For this purpose, satisfied family planning acceptors, in their turn, are mobilized to help recruit and maintain new acceptors, through indigenous village institutions. (30 March 1977)

• The range of contraceptive methods available has widened considerably since the Fund came into existence. (2 June 1977)

[In a statement to the Economic and Social Council on 25 July 1978, the UNFPA's Deputy Executive Director, Halvor Gille, further outlined the Fund's policy regarding contraceptive technology. He stated:

"The Governing Council [has] indicated its views . . . with regard to research on contraceptive technology. During several previous sessions, the question about UNFPA support in this area, particularly the WHO Special Programme on Research, Development and Research Training in Human Reproduction, was discussed without any consensus being reached. Last month the Governing Council recognized in its decision the importance of contraceptive research as 'crucial to the attainment of the Fund's objectives' and in taking note of the UNFPA contributions made in 1977 and 1978 to this programme, the Executive Director was requested to provide for the Council's approval specific proposals for future UNFPA support of global programmes of an innovative character, including the WHO Special Programme."]

Assistance to Countries with Low Fertility

• The Fund is prepared to respond to requests for assistance in all aspects of population problems to which governments attach importance. Thus, while in many cases the problems are connected with rapid population growth resulting from high and sustained levels of fertility, in some, sterility and low fertility may be of concern, and the Fund is prepared to respond to requests for assistance in this regard. (3 November 1971)

• Our concept of population problems covers much more than high fertility and rapid rates of population growth. We are concerned with low rates of population growth, high levels of infant mortality, international migration and urbanization. (10 August 1972)

• The Fund never seeks to urge any particular population policy or programmes on any country. It is neutral with respect to policy. It has responded to requests to assist countries with problems of sub-fertility and sterility as well as those with problems with high fertility rates. (29 January 1973)

• Other kinds of basic demographic research [besides census taking] such as fertility surveys and medical studies related to fertility, are also being undertaken in many countries, including some developing countries which, for one reason or another, do not regard population increase as a "problem", or, in fact, wish to hasten the pace of their population growth. (7 July 1973)

- Many of the projects which we have supported since we started full-scale operations in 1969 have been directed towards lower fertility, but we have supported work in every aspect of population . . . [including] on occasion, studies of sub-fertility, where a country feels that its population growth is too slow to exploit development opportunities. (30 November 1973)

- Because we *are* neutral, we are assisting countries with underpopulation as well as countries that are concerned with overpopulation. (21 May 1975)

Chapter 8

FOLLOWING UP ON UNFPA-FUNDED PROGRAMMES

Implementation

• In the implementation of the programmes, it is essential that the Fund and the agencies respond quickly and adequately to the country requests. Steps will be taken to employ modern managerial techniques to minimize delays in implementation. (10 November 1969)

• The rate at which the Fund is able to deliver assistance . . . depends almost completely on the absorptive capacity* of the recipient countries and the speed with which the executing organizations can move on project implementation. The United Nations, the Specialized Agencies, and the Fund, as well as the requesting governments, must endeavour to improve the utilization of the allocations given by the Fund, in order to make a real impact on resolving population problems. (3 November 1971)

• With the adoption of a new UNDP reporting and monitoring system, the Resident Representatives can easily make available at the headquarters the necessary information on the state of implementation of all population projects. The Fund is also drawing up monitoring and evaluation procedures. With some modifications, these can be fitted into and adapted to the UNDP method of monitoring and evaluation.

The Fund also welcomes suggestions from the Resident Representatives on how to solve the ever-recurring problem of training, recruitment and placement of experts. The executing agencies of the Fund need an adequate system of information on the availability of trained manpower in all the fields of population. The Fund intends to devise a system, in collaboration with the executing agencies, whereby the process of recruitment and placement can be decentralized either on a regional or country level. In this regard, the Resident Representatives' knowledge of country requirements and availability of trained manpower in the recipient countries will be valuable. (18 May 1972)

• Where there is a government actively committed to moving population programmes along, implementation rates are relatively high, even taking into consideration the usual unfortunate delays in implementation.

The UNFPA is constantly involved in attempting to find new ways to hasten the implementation of projects. The new manual, *Instructions for Preparation of Project Re-*

See also "Absorptive Capacity" section.

quests . . . is most important in connection with the rapid and efficient processing of requests and with the computerization of project data. . . . If a request is prepared according to the instructions, it will contain all information necessary for prompt appraisal by UNFPA staff and, in addition, the project budget will be ready for computer financial controls. We have asked that . . . requests received from the governments [be checked by the UNDP Resident Representative] to ensure compliance with the instructions before forwarding the request to UNFPA Headquarters. . . .

Moreover, we hope that the use of the new forms for project requests will also diminish the length of time necessary to commence projects after approval by the UNFPA. The form is designed to focus the attention of officials preparing the request on a more realistic appraisal of the need for advisory services and equipment, and on a more realistic phasing of the entire project. There have been cases where equipment is requested long before it can possibly be utilized. While delays in delivery of equipment must be taken into consideration, so too must the almost universal problem of recruitment of experts. Consequently, in projects where an expert must first undertake an appraisal before the project can begin, the inevitable time lag should be taken into consideration when phasing the project. Better planning, more realistic assessments of capacities of agencies, both United Nations and national, can reduce the frustrations of .project delay. For example, are outside "experts" always needed in projects submitted to the UNFPA for funding? There have been cases where an expert is provided not for technical advice but for organizational and administrative skills. Surely government ministries or universities can sometimes meet this latter need, indeed, if not the need for technical advice as well. Attempts should be made to seek out nationals with the necessary skills to make a project work. [We] will expect UNFPA Co-ordinators to assess the need for experts in projects submitted to us for funding, bearing in mind both the cost and the delays inherent in agencies' supplying experts, and to advise us as to whether national staff can be substituted for international experts.

One continuing cause of delay in implementation of projects is found in the months of correspondence and reviews necessary to agree upon a plan of operation. This delay could possibly be resolved by pre-project funding of certain components which would prepare a project for full operations at a later date. (8 March 1973)

- We must be sure that our projects and programmes really reflect the needs and wishes of countries. If they do not, it will not matter how good the design of the project may look on paper, the project is unlikely to be implemented effectively by the country in question and is virtually certain to do no lasting good once it has been terminated. (30 April 1973)

- Implementing population programmes is not a unique activity—it is only the population problem in the larger sense that is unique. The funding and implementation of population projects exhibit the same challenges and are subject to the same managerial problems as projects directed towards other defined social and economic goals. (6 May 1973)

- We have been seeking to develop . . . UNFPA staff capacity in the fields of project development, assessment, monitoring and evaluation. While we have no intention of duplicating the substantive capabilities of the United Nations or the agencies, we are aware that we cannot shirk our own decision-making responsibilities in the allocations process. Hence we have felt that we must build up a basic level of competence in the various fields. . . . (14 June 1973)

• [Yet another] problem relates to specific programme inplementation questions, particularly concerning family planning delivery systems. Given a delivery system and set of inputs, how can the efficiency of the programme processes be maximized? There are many discrete problems in this area where operations research seems particularly applicable. These include:

   (1) Establishing targets for programme utilization,

   (2) Establishing the most effective mix of service functions to meet the forecasted demand, and

   (3) Designing clinic work flows and schedules. (13 November 1973)

• Perhaps the greatest hurdle external aid programmes have to surmount is the long time lags in delivering assistance. Consequently, the Fund's operational policies have been directed towards avoiding bottlenecks resulting from too-complicated procedures and towards being as responsive as possible to governments' wishes and needs—even to the point of abandoning established processes for the transmittal of technical co-operation from the central administering organization via an executing agency to the recipient government. In fact, governments being assisted by the Fund have already received considerable autonomy in respect to the supervision and implementation of Fund-assisted projects, and in some cases direct aid has been negotiated between the Fund and the government. (6 March 1974)

• [We] . . . believe . . . that with the increase of experience, countries and agencies—and we in UNFPA—are increasingly efficient in the operation of population projects. (27 January 1975)

• A . . . major development in our work is the welcome marked upturn in the rate of project implementation. . . . Implementation [is defined] as the ratio between budgets and expenditures. . . .

   While a full analysis of the reasons for the increase in our implementation ratio has not yet been made, it can be assumed that it was due primarily to the flexibility of the Fund in allocating resources under the rolling plan to projects which were ready for implementation, as well as the gathering momentum . . . of a number of projects which had long leadtimes. While inflation may have been an additional factor in raising expenditures, it was not a controlling one. (19 June 1975)

• The delivery of population programmes requires a constantly innovative and flexible approach. Our experience shows that the standard traditional methods of delivery have not been effective, and that there is a danger that the imposition of a uniform method of delivery of development assistance would gravely affect the very high level of project implementation which the UNFPA has been able to achieve. (20 February 1976)

- Another indication [of increasing national interest in population programmes] is the considerable speed-up in the implementation ratio of UNFPA funds by developing countries. In 1972, recipient countries were able to expend only 48.1 per cent of the UNFPA resources allocated to them. However, by 1976 the implementation ratio had increased to almost 86 per cent. This increased absorptive capacity demonstrates quite clearly that developing countries have been able to improve their infrastructure, as well as their administrative and managerial capability to formulate and implement their population policies. (5 July 1977)

- We have taken several steps to improve our performance:

  We have improved our internal programme planning mechanism to enable us to plan our activities over a full four-year period.

  We have improved our internal monitoring and implementation procedures.

  We have established a mechanism to review regularly with our executing organizations the status of implementation.

  We have strengthened our field staff, *inter alia,* by adding four new Co-ordinator posts in Africa to stimulate project development in a number of priority countries in that region, and national programming staff to assist several UNFPA Co-ordinators and UNDP Resident Representatives where no Co-ordinator is stationed.

With these steps, [we are] confident that a substantial increase in our programming and implementation capacity can be accomplished. (21 June 1978)

Monitoring

- In designing a project of any size we want to build in some kind of a mechanism whereby we can know what is going on in the project's execution so that we can judge whether the activity should be continued in a second phase and, if so, know what changes should be made. Where an expert component is to be included with a project, this, of course, provides us with a sensory mechanism which can help us in this regard. If, on the other hand, what we are providing to a project is primarily in the nature of resources, we may wish to call on and perhaps strengthen your [UNDP Resident Representatives] offices specifically to co-ordinate and monitor the project in question. (18 February 1971)

- We have been seeking to develop . . . UNFPA staff capacity in the fields of project development, assessment, monitoring and evaluation. While we have no intention of duplicating the substantive capabilities of the United Nations or the agencies, we are aware that we cannot shirk our own decision-making responsibilities in the allocations process. Hence we have felt that we must build up a basic level of competence in the various fields. . . . (14 June 1973)

- Implementation involves not only quantity but also quality. . . .

We have now [January 1976] instituted a new, systematic and detailed method of monitoring project implementation qualitatively as well as quantitatively. The new monitoring procedure will not only tell us more about the quantity of work in all UNFPA country projects, but will also improve the quality by providing a sort of early warning system whereby difficulties will come to light sooner than in the past, and, accordingly, with a greater likelihood of correction. The system we are instituting resembles somewhat the UNDP tri-partite review procedure, involving, for each project reviewed, the government concerned, the executing agency concerned, UNDP and ourselves. It will, in most cases, also produce an annual country review, showing the position on all UNFPA projects in each country. (19 January 1976)

- The [UNDP Governing] Council will recall that [we] described to you last June the monitoring process we were introducing in 1976, including annual country reviews and tripartite reviews. During 1976, the first year of operation, six annual country reviews were held. . . . We have carefully followed the operation of the system, while seeking comments of the various parties concerned, especially the UNFPA Co-ordinators and UNDP Resident Representatives and the agencies. During our most recent Inter-Agency Consultative Committee meeting the monitoring system was discussed with all United Nations agencies working with UNFPA.

We feel confident that the monitoring system, consisting of multi-party reviews, has greatly enhanced the quality of our ongoing activities while at the same time providing the basis for subsequent programme development. (28 January 1977)

Evaluation

- We have been seeking to develop . . . UNFPA staff capacity in the field . . . of . . . evaluation. (14 June 1973)

- Our methods of evaluation depend more on the experience of those who live in the country than on rigorous adherence to a model laid down by foreign experts, whose knowledge of conditions in the country concerned must in the nature of things be largely second-hand. (25 August 1973)

- Good programme evaluation is dependent, in the first instance, on good programme planning and project design. (13 November 1973)

- It is difficult to assess the effectiveness of most development programmes, and with population, so deeply embedded in the social fabric and so long-term in its effects, the task is even more difficult. (21 May 1974)

- Among many topics discussed [at a meeting of experts on evaluation] were questions of how to provide for eventual evaluation at the time of programming and how to obtain realistic evaluations despite the sensitivities involved.

UNFPA believes that evaluations should offer tools for decision-making, by determining the effectiveness of projects and programmes evaluated. This means that they should assess not only changes brought about by project inputs, but also the relevance of these changes to the long-range, as well as the immediate, objectives of the activity. (18 June 1974)

- In the broader area of evaluation, that is, evaluating the extent to which the Fund's programmes are contributing to the achievement of the goals of the Second Development Decade, there is no qualitative way of measuring the impact of projects that we have funded on a nation's population policy or its population goals or its total development efforts. Development is, after all, the sum total of many inputs and components of which population activity is only one.

While it may be relatively easy to forecast agricultural harvests, which take only a season to mature, but which also depend on a great number of variables such as rainfall, sunshine, availability of fertilizers, incidence of pests and so on, it is not that easy to forecast the future effects, for example, of a country's official population policy or its total efforts in the population field, which take at least a generation to take effect. We can measure, for example, the project effectiveness of information and education campaigns related to a family planning programme, and we can measure the number of family planning acceptors after the initiation of a comprehensive programme, but it is only in the long-range, over a period of years, that the impact of this particular kind of population programme will be felt. . . .

- But [we] have no doubt that all of the activities in the population field—by governments, by non-governmental organizations, as well as by the United Nations system—are having substantial effect and will continue to have effect even with the moderate funding that is currently available. (9 July 1974)

- Since they [evaluations] are conducted as objective and independent in-depth analyses and since evaluation reports are written with the same candour [as presented in a document to the Governing Council] . . . , they serve as valuable support for our programming activities. They provide important inputs in the appraisal of requests for new or continued assistance. They provide the basis for taking corrective measures, if any, in regard to ongoing activities. Furthermore, they guide future programming by pointing to the importance of clarifying, in advance, programme objectives and alternative means of meeting them. . . . We fully recognize that evaluation can be a sensitive subject and that no evaluation of country activities can, or shall, be undertaken without the consent and collaboration of the government or institutions concerned. (21 June 1978)

Cost-Benefit Analysis

- The [concept] of "cost-benefit analysis" . . . [is] related to the subject of priorities and [has its] rightful place in development planning, but . . . must also be further conceptualized and refined in order to make [it] applicable to our work.

Cost-benefit analysis is an approach frequently proposed to assess and evaluate the contributions made by population programmes to overall development. Although it has proven its value in many types of economic programmes, serious problems arise in the application of this type of analysis to the more complex population activities. It may be relatively easy and straightforward to measure and compare costs and benefits of a single-purpose project having clearly defined resource requirements, affecting a readily identifiable target population and having only minor spillover effects on the larger economy. But most UNFPA-supported programmes are not limited in scope, objectives, time-span of their benefits or in distribution of ultimate benefits.

Defining the benefits' function becomes very complex indeed when a population programme encompasses not only family planning programmes but also programmes related to basic population data collection, population dynamics, population policy formulation, information and communication, population education and multi-sector activities.

Much work remains to be done in sorting out the benefits due to one programme and the benefits due to . . . other programmes. Indeed, it is in the very nature of UNFPA projects that they are not only interrelated among themselves but also that they are intertwined and linked with other programmes of broad socio-economic development. Both inputs and outputs, benefits and costs, are part of larger flows.

This does not mean, however, that we should abandon our efforts to assess and evaluate vigorously the benefits of UNFPA-assisted population programmes. UNFPA may find it appropriate to use cost-effectiveness methods for the examination of the relative productivity of different programmes within a given category of population activity, such as family planning and population education. For example, it may be possible to use such analysis to examine alternative courses of assessing population growth rates with censuses, surveys, and sample vital registration schemes. Apart from this, we intend to continue and to expand our own staff efforts to conceptualize further our ideas, and in this regard we are currently investigating the general body of techniques called public expenditure analysis, of which cost-benefit analysis is only one. Unfortunately, the match between the needs of the UNFPA and the current state of the art of public expenditure analysis is not perfect, but we feel that such techniques, applied particularly at the country level, can help to play a major role in improving the management of international population assistance programmes. (21 June 1977)

Chapter 9

FUNDING POPULATION ASSISTANCE

Donors to the Fund

• In 1967 the Secretary-General of the United Nations established a Trust Fund for Population Activities (subsequently the United Nations Fund for Population Activities), to be financed by voluntary contributions from governments and other sources. . . .

Contributions will be accepted by the Secretary-General in freely usable currency. . . . It is hoped that the bulk of the resources of the Fund will be in this form. The Secretary-General would, however, be prepared to negotiate with interested donors the acceptance of non-convertible currencies to the extent that these could be utilized to finance specific projects consistent with the purposes of the Fund. He would also be prepared to consider the acceptance of contributions for uses designated by the donor, provided that any restrictions on the use of the contributions are not inconsistent with the purposes of the Fund. (10 November 1969)

• Some countries . . . consider the introduction of population programmes important for all economic and social progress. Some have even earmarked percentages of their total development aid for this purpose. The Norwegian legislature, for example, has provided that ten per cent of Norway's aid should be devoted to population assistance, both bilateral and multilateral. The Swedish executive has a policy of giving some nine per cent of its development assistance to the population field. If a country . . . were to tie even a modest percentage of its development assistance to population, this would make a substantial difference to the work that could be done and to the timely goals that could be reached. (26 August 1971)

• Additional contributors not only mean additional financing—some of this is in non-convertible currencies—but, almost more importantly, they mean governments giving tangible evidence of their concern about population matters and of the important role they feel the Fund should play in this regard. (3 November 1971)

• The Fund has grown rapidly . . . demonstrating in no uncertain terms the rise in governmental uneasiness in regard to population. (14 February 1973)

• The Fund has increased its resources very rapidly on the basis of international confidence in its effectiveness. (21 May 1974)

105

- Along with the growth of requests, it [the increase in pledges to the Fund] constitutes dramatic evidence of the increasing attention, and increasing recognition of responsibility of countries both in the developing and developed world, to come to grips with population matters. (27 January 1975)

- The Fund is now in its fifth year of programming operation, and during this time it has built up solid and substantial working relationships with donor governments and organizations as well as recipient governments and organizations. As trust and confidence in the Fund has grown, so have its resources. (17 April 1975)

- The [World Population] Plan [of Action] calls for considerable expansion of assistance in the population field; and this call was repeated by the last General Assembly, which urged "that assistance to developing countries should be increased in accordance with the goals of the Second United Nations Development Decade, and that international assistance in the population field should be expanded, particularly to the United Nations Fund for Population Activities, for the proper implementation of the World Population Plan of Action".* (10 June 1975)

- We have explored with a number of countries, individually and collectively, the possibility that they might be able to provide assistance for population projects beyond the amounts of financial assistance which they can make available to and through UNFPA. . . . [We are] pleased to report that progress, although slow, is steady . . . UNFPA is also acting as a clearinghouse for information on requests from non-governmental organizations, as well as a co-ordination centre for such activities, to ensure that donors do not provide overlapping or duplicating funds. (19 June 1975)

- The growing resources and the increasing number of requests for assistance that the Fund receives is evidence of the faith and trust that the developing countries and the donor countries have placed in us.

  We have endeavoured to broaden our fund-raising base by enlisting new donors. . . . (14 July 1975)

- This [the number of countries supporting the work of the Fund with their voluntary contributions] surely indicates some sort of a consensus; the work now going on is a practical demonstration of the reality of international agreement. (23 October 1975)

- It might be that donor governments should endeavour, of course, within the limitation of their constitutional processes of appropriations, to make pledges, or provisional pledges, to cover a period not of a single year, but of two or three years. The Fund will welcome a discussion with donors on possible procedures for doing this. (19 January 1976)

- Responsiveness is the reason for the readiness of developing countries . . . to contribute generously to the Fund's resources.

  A large number of developing countries . . . have made contributions to the Fund. This . . . is a measure of the almost universal response to the Fund's own responsiveness in managing the flow of United Nations assistance in the population field. (20 February 1976)

*Resolution 3344 (XXIX), 17 December 1974.

- [The Fund's] rapid growth eloquently indicates the increasing awareness of very many countries, on all continents, and in both developed and developing areas, of the important inter-relationship between population activities and economic and social development; an increasing perception that population is a significant, distinct, and independent variable in the efforts of the international community to cope with the problems of poverty; and a growing realization of the potential effects of population policies on the well-being and happiness of mankind. (3 November 1976)

- UNFPA would never have reached its present level of funding without the confidence of governments that their needs and wishes would dictate the type and pattern of our assistance. (2 June 1977)

- This . . . rapid and sustained growth bears witness . . . first, to the increasing awareness in almost all developing and developed countries on all continents of the important inter-relationships between population activities and economic and social development; and, second, to the increasing perception that population is a significant variable for the international community to take more fully into account in its various efforts to help nations cope more effectively with the crucial problems of poverty, in order to fulfill man's basic needs.

A very encouraging, concrete sign is the large and steadily growing number of developing countries that over the past three years have substantially increased the amounts of domestic financial and human resources being allocated to help meet the various types of population needs of their citizens and communities. UNFPA believes this growing trend within developing countries clearly indicates . . . that the population dialogue is no longer concerned, as it was in the past, with a question of intervention versus non-intervention, but rather with a question of priorities and strategies for population policies and programmes. (7 November 1977)

- The recent passing of the half-billion dollar mark in pledges is . . . significant for a voluntary fund of the United Nations because it is a clear indication of the increasingly enlightened attitude of both the United Nations and its members in addressing difficult population problems that confront Member States. (6 November 1978)

Resources Versus Demands for Assistance

- We intend . . . in administering the Fund, to keep overhead costs to a minimum. We shall not solicit requests unless we have good reason to be confident of our ability to handle them financially and administratively. (18 November 1969)

- The UNFPA at this stage controls only a fraction, perhaps a tenth, of the resources currently at the disposal of donor agencies to assist the developing countries with population programmes. (16 October 1970)

- The volume of requests has been growing rapidly. At present, we have a very large volume of project requests pending. . . . We shall, of course, process these requests carefully, but we do not expect to be able to fund them all by any means. (29 January 1973)

- Impressive as the growth in the Fund's capacity to assist has been, it still barely keeps up with requests for assistance. . . . (14 February 1973-B)

- Thanks to the generous assistance of . . . governments . . . resources available to the Fund have been rising and appear likely to continue rising. . . . While demand for these resources in 1973 outran the available supply, we have been able to make a reasonable "fit" through a more critical approach and better budgeting. It's painfully evident, however, that the overflow of demand . . . [soon] will be on a much more serious scale and will demand a far more stringent application of priorities. (6 November 1973)

- As the demand for resources outruns supply, in addition to having a well-thought-through programme budget, we need to elaborate further our criteria and procedures for project approvals. (14 January 1974)

- The problems of population are not just the problems of one, but the problems of all. What we have done in the past, the services we have been able to offer, and the resources we have been able to provide are not going to be nearly enough to meet the challenges from governments who are being asked to think in terms of greater commitment to attacking the problems of poverty, environment and population, and of coping not only with their own difficulties, but of contributing to an international chain of assistance.

  All this calls for dynamic leadership from the United Nations family in sponsoring innovative programmes, and in encouraging the new ideas and approaches, even at the expense of traditional methods. It also calls for more money. (21 January 1974)

- Up until last year we were fortunate enough to have the resources to meet our commitments. Now, demand has outstripped supply, and ways must be found of husbanding our resources through better management and clearer definition of priorities. . . .

  The Fund is in a good position to take on added responsibilities, *provided* it is realized that the estimates in UNFPA's four-year-plan do not attempt to leave margins for unforeseen demands arising from the [World Population] Year and the [World Population] Conference, and *provided* donor governments are prepared to equip the Fund to finance special programmes as they arise.

  It would be unrealistic to look forward to 1975 without anticipating that the Conference will lead to widened concepts of population, to re-thinking of national plans, to new approaches to population questions, and perhaps to radical transformations in the form and priorities of multilateral assistance.

  The immediate effect will, of course, be an expansion of on-going activities. For example, it can be anticipated that the goals set by the World Plan of Action will push up the numbers of requests for assistance from countries setting quantitative growth targets, and from countries agreeing to take censuses between 1975 and 1985. It is also more than likely that migration problems and questions of urban explosion will feature more largely in future requests.

  The stage is now set for greater involvement in international and global undertakings. The World Fertility Survey is one of the most ambitious projects ever undertaken and marks a major step forward in man's endeavour to know more about mankind. It is to be hoped that more projects of this type will be developed. There are many more identifiable areas, particularly in research, where the answers could come through a pooling of resources and experience.

In making this resumé of the types of requests that will probably arise within the next few months, [we are] not in any way discounting or attempting to second-guess the outcome of the very important discussions that will take place in August [at the World Population Conference].

For the first time, the basic issues of population will be considered by the world's principal governmental decision-makers, within the context of the common needs for food, for education, for housing, for technology, for health services, for employment, as well as from the angle of specific national situations. (4 March 1974)

• This increase [in the Fund's programme authority from 1974 to 1975] is, by a considerable margin, the largest now foreseen during 1975 by any arm of the United Nations. This is excellent as far as it goes; and, along with the growth of requests, it constitutes dramatic evidence of the increasing attention, and increasing recognition of responsibility of, countries both in the developing and developed world, to come to grips with population matters. (27 January 1975)

• Following Bucharest, far from there being a diminution in requests for assistance in the population field, there has been, in fact, a considerable increase in requests. Because of this increase, a great strain has been exerted on our existing resources and we believe that a quantum jump in assistance is essential, to enable us to meet the new challenge of a quantum jump in the readiness of needy nations to tackle their population problems themselves. (13 February 1975)

• What is welcome in this situation [of demands outstripping resources] is the evidence that countries throughout the world are becoming increasingly concerned with population matters. . . . But what is troublesome is to find ways to deal with the excess of demand over supply.

The indications are that recipient countries are committing more of their resources to population programmes, particularly in Asia. If this trend continues, multilateral assistance will be limited in the long run to indispensable but proportionately small inputs.

As urged by the [UNDP Governing] Council, [we] have worked diligently during these past months to discuss the Fund's purposes and needs with numerous governments, especially governments not heretofore involved, or not heavily involved, in our activities, including the oil-producing countries in the Middle East and Latin America. (19 June 1975)

• The growing resources and the increasing number of requests for assistance that the Fund receives is evidence of the faith and trust that the developing countries and the donor countries have placed in us. (14 July 1975)

• Requests for UNFPA collaboration . . . continue to outstrip our foreseen resources. Our inability in 1974 and 1975 to approve all aid-worthy requests has meant that governments have somewhat reduced the volume of requests. From the point of view of financial management, such a reduction in requests may indicate a reduction in problems, but it is not an encouraging development if one starts from the premise that every sound effort to deal with population deserves support. (19 January 1976)

• Yet [despite our increase in resources] all, in my opinion, is not quite as it should be with reference to UNFPA's financial capabilities. A large and growing number of countries, and the people constituting them, have been stirred by growing awareness of the implications of population factors. They have been awakened and informed by such efforts as the World Population Conference in Bucharest in 1974, by the activities of World Population Year, and myriad other research and education efforts. And governments, as a result, are asking us for more and more assistance—are presenting us with imaginative and excellent requests for collaboration and support in their population programmes, which we are unable to meet simply because we do not have the money. (3 November 1976)

• We are continuing to seek new sources of financing and to engage in special fund-raising initiatives. We also expect to see a significant expansion of assistance through multi-bilateral arrangements.

While we are most grateful for the increased pledges of support from all donors, we refuse to be complacent about our fund-raising efforts.

Our inability to take more positive action on many . . . worthwhile project requests is of real concern. Even for those countries not on the priority list, it is vitally important that the internal momentum and enthusiasm for population activities should not be slowed down, and that the UNFPA be able to provide assistance for new and innovative projects.

Both from the point of view of the donor and the point of view of the recipient, there is one basic question which faces us all: Do we, and will we, have the resources to meet the needs that are required to continue the momentum that has built up over the past eight years? We should all be aware that the level of resources transferred for population activities for the benefit of developing countries, taking worldwide inflationary trends and devaluation into account, has hardly increased since the World Population Year and the World Population Conference in 1974. [A recent paper* shows] that the magnitude of population assistance has not kept pace with overall development assistance and, in fact, assistance in the field of population, which in 1974 amounted to 2.3 per cent of total official development assistance, has since declined to 2 per cent or slightly less. Although a number of new donor governments to the population assistance field have come upon the scene and many of the early donor governments have substantially increased their contributions, these increases have not been large enough to maintain the overall growth rate of resources of earlier years, nor have they been able to keep up with inflation. (21 June 1977)

*Reprinted in Appendix D

Multi-Bi Funding

- Contributions will be accepted by the Secretary-General in freely usable currency for application by the Administrator of UNDP and the Director of the Fund to any, or all, of the purposes for which the Fund in intended. It is hoped that the bulk of the resources of the Fund will be in this form. The Secretary-General would, however, be prepared to negotiate with interested donors the acceptance of non-convertible currencies to the extent that these could be utilized to finance specific projects consistent with the purposes of the Fund. He would also be prepared to consider the acceptance of contributions for uses designated by the donor, provided that any restrictions on the use of the contributions are not inconsistent with the purposes of the Fund. (10 November 1969)

- The UNFPA can, together with donor governments, support Fund projects in other ways, including joint funding, consortium financing, funds-in-trust, and parallel financing. We are anxious to explore . . . all avenues of possible financing that could lead to closer collaboration. (21 May 1975)

- We have explored with a number of countries, individually and collectively, the possibility that they might be able to provide assistance for population projects beyond the amounts of financial assistance which they can make available to and through UNFPA . . . . [We] are pleased to report that progress, although slow, is steady . . . UNFPA is also acting as a clearinghouse for information on requests from non-governmental organizations, as well as a co-ordination centre for such activities, to ensure that donors do not provide overlapping or duplicating funds. (19 June 1975)

- Because the requests for assistance continually outstrip our resources—and in order to provide at least some modicum of encouragement to those developing countries whose projects we have had to defer or reduce in size—we are, in addition to trying to broaden our resources base, actively exploring alternative sources of financing, such as joint parallel multilateral-bilateral funding arrangements, the establishment of funds-in-trust and others. . . . We are going to prepare guidelines for funds-in-trust arrangements and adoption of the "noted projects" approach which UNICEF has applied so successfully within its field of responsibility.* (14 July 1975)

- Most, if not all, of the traditional donor countries have suggested to us that we actively explore—both with prospective recipients and possible donors—the possibility of using multi-bilateral finance to meet some of the costs of the projects being requested of us. We are, accordingly, making such preparations, in many cases with an encouraging outlook.

---

*For further information on multilateral/bilateral funding, see UNFPA pamphlet "UNFPA Multi/bi: A Concept for Funding Population Programmes and Projects in Developing Countries Around the World on a Joint Multilateral/Bilateral Basis". The pamphlet states that "The aim of UNFPA multi/bi is to bring together multilateral and bilateral donors to assist developing countries in their population programmes and projects. UNFPA multi-bi can be used to assist developing countries in formulating national programmes or specific projects, and enlisting the co-operation of donor agencies, to provide necessary resources for their implementation. Or UNFPA can simply act as a 'go-between' in bringing together donor governments and developing countries to provide support for population activities."

Two of the key provisions of [our] proposal [in multi-bilateral area] . . . are first, that a prospective recipient government must itself clearly approve a multi-bilateral approach to financing one or more of its projects, as a pre-condition to negotiations or any sort of agreement. Secondly, the multi-bilateral approach aims not to replace pledges made, or which could be made directly to UNFPA in the regular manner, but only to supplement and augment such pledges. The procedure, if adopted, will lead to a new category of projects, termed Designated Projects. And success in funding Designated Projects would, in turn, lead to an expansion in global resources for population work.

[We] also urge . . . that recipient governments consider the inherent usefulness, in many cases, of such a multi-bilateral approach. Countries with requests beyond what, at a given time, we can approve in the standard manner, will many times, [we] believe, welcome multi-bilateral finance.

And [we] suggest that countries with projects which UNFPA has already approved, and for which we have full financial cover, will be wise to give careful consideration to suggestions that some of their already-approved projects, or portions of them, be explored for multi-bilateral finance. UNFPA in such cases would never withdraw the project in question from our approved list unless and until multi-bilateral finance was secured.

What, a recipient government might ask, would be the gain in agreeing to the transfer of a project that has already been approved for regular UNFPA financing, to multi-bilateral financing? The answer is simple: What would be gained is more money for the totality of all requests. And this is consistent with another provision of [our] proposal, which is that, in assessing project requests, we apply the same criteria of aid-worthiness, of excellence, to all projects, whether they ultimately are supported from regular UNFPA finance or from multi-bilateral finance, or by a combination of both. . . . [This new approach] may well produce substantial additional resources. (19 January 1976)

• We are developing arrangements for the multi-bilateral funding of aid-worthy population projects. . . . We have developed procedural arrangements that we feel will be practical for such a programme. We are visiting governments, potential donors and potential recipients, for systematic discussions; and, of course, are working closely with the relevant agencies in the United Nations system. Our visits to countries are being undertaken to explain more fully the concept of multi-bilateral funding, to generally exchange information, to seek advice and co-operation, and to make clear that the Governing Council and we in the UNFPA Secretariat do not seek multi-bilateral assistance as a substitute for direct contributions to the Fund, but only as a means of obtaining resources not otherwise available to the programme. We are satisfied with the outcome to date of these conversations. We are encouraged that we will be able to obtain additional resources for important activities in developing countries.

There are . . . very reassuring indications that this programme of multi-bilateral collaboration will become an important tool whereby UNFPA will be able to increase the quantum of population assistance flowing to requesting countries, although it must be borne in mind that in multi-bilateral arrangements there often is a considerable time-lag between the preparation of a project and its actual funding. (3 November 1976)

• From a cautious beginning, [we] can now report a fair amount of progress with the operation of UNFPA/multi-bi.

Our experience thus far with multi-bilateral operations indicates only one change that [we] wish to recommend [to the Governing Council]. . . . [We] suggested last year that multilateral support should contemplate mainly large projects; experience today indicates that a number of both prospective recipients and prospective donors look

favourably upon multi-bilateral support also for smaller projects; and [we] recommend that you authorize the Fund to proceed accordingly. (28 January 1977)

• We . . . expect to see a significant expansion of assistance through multi-bilateral arrangements. Identifying and specifying projects for multi-bi funding takes time, but . . . a considerable number of donor and recipient countries have recently been consulted, and many have expressed a ready interest in participating in multi-bi arrangements. (21 June 1977)

• The bulk of the funds for population activities have come from rich industrialized countries for allocation to the developing world, following the traditional North-South pattern. But we were recently able to introduce an innovation by awakening an interest in the capital-rich countries of the Arab World - who themselves have no problem of overpopulation (quite the contrary, in some cases)—to pick up the tab for population programmes in poorer Arab countries who do. We have hopes that this example of horizontal aid—neighbourly assistance—will spread in other areas, such as Latin America, Africa and the Caribbean, where oil has changed the economic scene. (27 September 1977)

• Since I reported to the [Governing] Council last June, the response by both donor and recipient governments to the Fund's initiative in developing multi-bilateral funding arrangements has been most encouraging. This initiative is proving to be timely and of potential benefit to many of the developing countries. (21 June 1978)

Chapter 10

INTERNATIONAL ASSISTANCE, THE NATURE OF

General

• Nothing concerns aid administrators more today than the probability that the volume of development assistance, which showed an accelerated rate of increase in its early years, has now reached a plateau from which an ascent is difficult to foresee. This predicament is real, in spite of the multi-national commitment of donors and recipients to the strategies of the Second Development Decade, which set a desired rate of increase in the volume of assistance up to 1980.

The reasons for this are many and varied. The sharp changes taking place in the pattern of world trade have created difficulties in many countries, and not the least among the traditional donor nations. But the possibility that the flow of aid is levelling off is also known to arise from criticisms directed at the aid process itself. There is a crescendo of accusations that aid has not been effective—that is, that it does not appear to have produced the results which the donors hoped for. Measured in the available terms, the net per capita production is rising painfully slowly, and at times not rising at all, in many of the aided nations. Parallel with this criticism is another—namely, that the distribution channels of aid are cumbersome and wasteful, and also that the implementation of aided projects is faulty and dilatory.

On the side of the aid-receiving countries, too, there are rumbles of discontent. These include the nature of tied loans, allegations of the inflationary effects of some forms of aid, and the growing burden of repayment and loan-servicing.

In the early literature of development, writers . . . were speaking of a "will to develop". But as the study of development became more sophisticated and its disciplines more quantified, development administrators lost sight of the crucial role of this perspective. As a consequence, a great deal of external resources devoted to development were wasted in countries which had no purposeful desire to develop, and bred, as a consequence, widespread suspicion and distrust. (6 May 1973)

• Rapid growth of international assistance in the late fifties and early sixties was followed by a period towards the end of the first Development Decade where the flow of assistance levelled off, and even began to decline in real terms.

114

In the world of the nineteen-sixties . . . it seemed that very little in the way of results was being gained from the developed countries' inputs. With a few exceptions, the countries receiving aid appeared to be just as far away from the point of what was called economic "take-off" or "self-sustaining growth" as they ever were. Many reasons were put forward for this. It was said that trade arrangements were unfavourable to the poorer countries, that they had been going for the wrong type of development, that development schemes had been ill-conceived and badly administered, that development assistance was of the wrong type and was delivered in the wrong way.

An attitude which requires personal commitment on the part of both giver and receiver is needed today if we are to increase the flow of effective resources to the poorer nations and break through to true national development. The approach implies that the relationship is ongoing, that international assistance will be a feature of our lives for some time to come, and that there is nothing wrong with it. It is not "charity" or "enlightened self-interest", but an affirmation of belief in our fellow-men and their right to make a better life for themselves. (25 August 1973)

• If international assistance is involved [in a programme], the donor must understand the process and himself become committed to the ideas which lie behind it. This requires, on the part of the donor, an act of trust in the recipient, because each country will have, of necessity, a different way of approaching the problem, and there are few universal criteria which can be applied. Indeed, it is fundamental that each country work out the programme which suits its own circumstances and needs. After this is done, a programme of assistance can be worked out with the donor which will ensure that external funds are put to work where they will be most useful. It is true that the donor has rather less actual supervision and control over the way in which his funds are used than a donor who establishes his own criteria and demands that they be met, but there are bonuses which . . . far outweigh any disadvantages of this kind. By establishing from the outset a relationship of trust and mutual confidence, it is possible for the donor to take part in the decision-making process, to understand more fully the problems with which he is working, and to formulate lines towards their solution. He thus assures himself of the usefulness of the operation of which he is a part, makes a real contribution to its success and, in the process, safeguards his financial interest as far as is humanly possible. Faith, in this case at least, is not altogether blind.

Furthermore, the donor can see more clearly where injection of additional resources will have the greatest impact. External assistance has from the outset been a small fraction of total development resources, but it can have an effect out of proportion to its size. Like an extra pulley in a block and tackle, its effect in the right place is multiplied. (26 September 1973)

• The Fund shares the belief of many development specialists that development assistance, if of the right type and given in the right way, can strengthen, rather than undermine, self-reliance. We are very much concerned in finding those areas and methods which represent the most effective contribution to national development programmes, bearing in mind that external assistance is only a small fraction of the resources devoted in a given country to development efforts. (13 November 1973)

- To even the least critical eye, the international assistance programmes provided over the last quarter of a century, through multilateral, bilateral or private organizations, have fallen short of their goals. Much has been done but not enough. Poor countries are still poor. And over the years disappointment has been added to frustration.

The Fund has endeavoured to learn from the lessons of these programmes. Perhaps the greatest hurdle external aid programmes have to surmount is the long time lags in delivering assistance. Consequently, the Fund's operational policies have been directed towards avoiding bottlenecks resulting from too-complicated procedures and towards being as responsive as possible to governments' wishes and needs—even to the point of abandoning established processes for the transmittal of technical co-operation from the central administering organization via an executing agency to the recipient government. In fact, governments being assisted by the Fund have already received considerable autonomy in respect to the supervision and implementation of Fund-assisted projects, and in some cases direct aid has been negotiated between the Fund and the government.

Expert recruitment from a limited number of countries has also been a serious handicap to the effectiveness of external aid programmes. For many years, the industrialized nations of the West had a virtual monopoly of modern technology and scientific advance. This is no longer the case. Regional and national reservoirs of expertise are being built up, and it is the Fund's policy to encourage and assist the establishment of institutions and organizations to provide an increasing supply of experts needed for development and population programmes. (6 March 1974)

- In the [development] process, enormous amounts of money, some from the more developed countries, but most of it from the developing countries themselves, have been poured into scheme after scheme. Each of them, it was hoped, would break the vicious circle of poverty bred by poverty and breeding poverty in its turn; nevertheless, the basic problem remains. In the past, it was assumed that failure to achieve economic "take-off" or "self-sustaining growth", as it was called, was simply because not enough money had been invested. The developed countries were blamed for supplying only meagre amounts of assistance and the developing countries were told that they must have been using the money inefficiently. Both positions may have been correct, but it is by no means certain, even if vastly increased sums of money had been available, that permanent and sustained improvements would have been noted in the situation of the majority of the people in the developing countries. (19 April 1974)

- Chronic poverty, with a nation as with an individual, makes it difficult, if not impossible, to realize latent abilities. Many countries of the developing world are rich in natural resources, but lack the skills and finance needed to turn them for the benefit of their people. A heavy responsibility therefore lies on those countries which have the good fortune to be the possessors of present riches, to apply them for the benefit of their fellow-men.

In the past, the pattern of international assistance has been that the few industrialized countries provided help to a large number of developing countries. Whether they did this out of self-interest or charity is irrelevant; the fact is that they did, and are, doing it. But for the last few years assistance from traditional donors has been at a standstill, in real terms. At the same time a new force has come on the scene, in the form of nations rich in the one natural resource which is both easy to develop and is absolutely essential to the functioning of modern society.

Some of these are Arab countries. Still developing in terms of the application of their wealth, these nations nevertheless have the opportunity to be of real help to others which are experiencing difficulty in making full use of their own resources. As donors they are in a unique position, since they understand from their own experience some of the problems of development.

Not least among these problems is securing the efficient deployment of the most important resource of all, the people of the developing countries. The work of the United Nations Fund for Population Activities is crucial to this aspect of development. (18 May 1974)

• So far, international assistance has largely been one-way. . . . Maybe, the time has come for a transfer to be made in the opposite direction. What can the developing countries offer the rest of the world? One of the most important things . . . is a restored sense of values. In their desperate chase after the satisfactions which material wealth can provide . . . the people of the industrialized countries have lost sight of the goal which impelled them in the first place to seek wealth. There is a growing sense in the industrialized countries that something is missing from a life which includes many of the things that the earth can provide, but which has lost the deeper satisfaction which comes from a fundamentally sound relationship with the rest of creation. (20 May 1974)

• Much has already been done by way of investment and financial and technical assistance to developing countries. Combined with the efforts and resources of the developing countries themselves, significant advances have been made. But, with some exceptions, the expected results have not been achieved. One of the reasons for the relative lack of success of development efforts so far is that assistance and investment have been on the wrong social and cultural terms.

In the early days of the First Development Decade, massive industrialization, with its attendant patterns of education, health care, and infrastructural development, particularly in the cities, was considered the only viable form. In effect, this meant transplanting not only a technology, but a set of values which were often alien to the societies into which they came. In the most successful cases, this has led to a split between a small, highly developed industrial sector and a large, traditional agricultural sector; in the least successful, disused factories and rusting equipment are all that remain. Many thousands of young people have been educated to expect jobs which do not exist; expensive and elaborate health schemes serve only a small fraction of the people. Emphasis on urban growth has drawn millions into cities which are ill-equipped to cater to them.

At the same time, expansion in agriculture has not kept pace with growing demand for food. Our most pressing requirement now is for programmes adapted to the values and true needs of developing societies. This largely depends on the developing countries themselves, but the "will to develop" can be nourished by external assistance. There is a greater eagerness for change when it is perceived as the natural outgrowth of national history and culture. Help from outside should be sensitive to this, and its form and direction should take it into account. In this way, external investment and assistance can be made both acceptable and useful, so that the donor's choices as between high-cost and low-cost investment will be made easier, and the dilemma eased. Both the adaptation of programmes of assistance and their acceptability will be helped by the donor's attitude. A close working relationship with the recipient government and an atmosphere of mutual trust are essential.

As a United Nations body, with its neutrality guaranteed, the UNFPA has been able to establish such relationships with many governments, and this is why many donors have chosen UNFPA as a channel for their population assistance. For bilateral donors, it must be clear to the recipient that there is no conflict between policy and practice. This extends further than aid policies, into the whole realm of economic and social activity. It is, for example, of no use for a government to preach birth control in the interests of preserving the environment and limiting consumption of resources, while its own economy is dependent on the rapid growth of GNP with high rates of resource consumption and consequent environmental damage. Declarations of good faith must be backed by action. For some donors, who do not make a connection between their internal economic policies and their policies of external assistance, this will be a hard transition to make. But it is a necessary change, analogous to many which are being made in our increasingly interdependent times. (2 July 1974)

• If there is a need for caution [in population programmes] and for extreme sensitivity at a national level, for example, in dealings between official government agencies and individual families, this must be equally true of the dealings between external agencies and the government and people of any particular country.

External aid should be used at the point, and in the form, where the effect it produces will be of the greatest benefit to the recipient country. There is, therefore, inevitably a creative dialogue between donor and recipient. Sometimes, perhaps, we should call it "creative tension". (20 August 1974)

• Obviously such a structural re-organization in our thinking [embodying the concept of balanced, organic growth rather than exponential growth in one sector and stagnation in another] would lead to many changes in the relationship between the developed and the developing worlds. On the assumption that co-operation is more productive for all parties than conflict, international assistance would be regarded less as charity than as the due which is paid to secure greater rewards in the future. The content of assistance would also change. Instead of exporting technology wholesale, industrialized countries would invest in researching technologies appropriate to the needs of the non-industrialized. In the developing countries, thinking about the process of industrialization itself would change. Systems of education would change to prepare for a new world, rather than an imitation of the old one. Assistance would be accepted only so far as it made a genuine contribution to the goals set by the developing society for itself.

Application of assistance in this manner has many differences from the traditional aid package. First, there is nothing for the donor to see, to put his label on. Second, control of the expenditure by the donor is at best indirect; it is widely diffused in space and time, and passes through many different hands. Third, such assistance cannot be worked out by a donor and presented as a package. It depends very much on knowledge and understanding of local needs and conditions, on the sort of information only the local authorities themselves are liable to have. Therefore it cannot be tested by the conventional criteria of donors. A great deal must simply be taken on trust, or on the basis of mutual knowledge and respect between donor and recipient.

Those of you with experience in this field may have noticed similarities between this approach and that adopted in successful family planning programmes. This is no accident—in population work it has long been recognized that success depends on motivation, and that motivation depends on a complex of factors, and can be achieved successfully only by intimate knowledge of local conditions and the changes which are necessary.

In the United Nations Fund for Population Activities we have been working on such approaches for the past five years. (15 October 1974)

• The [World Population] Plan [of Action] calls for considerable expansion of assistance in the population field; and this call was repeated by the last General Assembly, which urged "that assistance to developing countries should be increased in accordance with the goals of the Second United Nations Development Decade, and that international assistance in the population field should be expanded, particularly to the United Nations Fund for Population Activities, for the proper implementation of the World Population Plan of Action". (10 June 1975)

• We [who are involved in development assistance] are now required to work in cooperation with many different sources of financial and technical help, in order to produce a regulated form of development. The new development will not permit of single-agency, isolated activities, except in isolated cases.

The same qualities of responsiveness and flexibility must be shown in aid agencies as in national bureaucracies, and in respect for the wishes and needs of governments as for those of local communities. (2 June 1976)

• It is not sufficient for donors merely to direct an increasing part of their resources to the poorest countries. The purposes and forms of assistance will have to be changed to provide for more support of local costs, recurrent expenditures, long-term commitments, and generally more flexibility in applying donor policies and principles. (14 June 1976)

• A major change . . . is taking place in the field of international assistance programmes. A number of recipient countries no longer require the assistance of international experts to carry out development programmes—there are an increasing number of national experts in these countries to direct and manage such programmes. What these countries do require, instead, is financial support to intensify the pace of their own development efforts. Looking ahead, [we] believe that in the population field we may be witnessing the reduction of the importance of international experts for country projects, with an increasingly large share of international assistance funds being transferred directly to recipient governments for the execution of development programmes. (28 June 1976)

• [International assistance is] an investment above all in peace, stability and the happiness of much of the human race. (30 March 1977)

• Governments, donors and agencies executing projects alike are most likely to achieve success in their programmes if they address themselves to the basic needs of those whom they serve, the people of the developing countries. In our experience, this approach can offer at least as good a ratio of costs to benefits in those things which can be quantified, and the indications are that it is a much more rewarding approach in the areas which cannot be quantified.

No blueprint for international assistance will ever be effective unless adapted with the fullest participation of each country affected. (2 June 1977)

• Demand [for international assistance] grows quickly after governments have adopted policies and built institutions to carry out their policies. And demand changes dramatically with political changes in recipient countries. (21 June 1977)

• The magnitude of the need for international assistance must be increased many times before population growth can begin to be brought into balance with the available resources. (27 September 1977)

• The growing felt needs of developing countries for population assistance are far from being met at even minimal levels. Although the resources of UNFPA have continued to increase, total resources made available by donor governments for population programmes have increased only modestly in recent years, and when viewed as a proportion or percentage of total official development assistance, have in real terms probably declined.

The donor community has yet to respond fully to the call of the World Population Plan of Action in paragraph 104 for "considerable expansion of international assistance in the population field". (7 November 1977)

External Assistance, the Marginality of

• International assistance, even when measured in its broadest terms, has never been more than a marginal addition to the total development resources of aid-receiving nations. In the field of population programmes, it is true that aid has often contributed a comparatively high proportion of the initial launching cost and implementation, but for its long-run effects we are being challenged by the examples of the two most populous states of Asia—China and India. China has today one of the most comprehensive family planning programmes, extensively delivered, with no international assistance. And in India, which has the longest experience in a government-initiated family planning programme, the foreign contribution to its total national outlay does not exceed the order of ten per cent.

What is more, we must recall that aid, *because* it is marginal, must be more than marginally effective. Economic theory teaches us that it is the marginal addition of resources which sets the standards of expansion—the costs, the benefits and the productivity. Thus it is not how much aid which is really in question—calculations of percentages of GNP, or amounts of aid per country or per capita, have this weakness. It is the marginal effectiveness of each added portion of aid which is important.

What do we conclude from this? One conclusion may be that we seek to assist only in those basic areas which will yield better returns in the long run within each country's accepted programmes. In the past, because of the promotional aspect of assistance, resources have been applied to a considerable extent to isolated and peripheral activities.

Viewed in this light, aid becomes not a "catalyst", as it has too often been described, but a "spur". The catalytic role for aid may indeed be relevant in times of short-term crisis, following war or famine or other autonomous events in the social and economic life of a nation. But in the long-term flow of assistance, the kind of endeavour which looks forward over the generations and not merely over the next harvest, the aid programme should not play such a catalytic role. That role can best be played by the national governments themselves, and by any international or regional mechanisms that these national governments may implement. The great marginal and effective role for aid in these circumstances is as a spur.

If international assistance is to act as a spur, by what mechanisms, by what means, should it operate? We may conceive of the main aim as the creation of clear national population objectives or goals towards which the country's human resources should be mobilized.

No doubt . . . in the years to come, there will be a continuing role for multilateral assistance in population. There are certain irreducible elements in these processes of exchange that only international organizations can perform adequately: the transmission of information; the lending of multinational experts; and the transmission of certain technological advances in the population field within the framework of internationally-agreed policies. But for aid-giving countries not too weary of the short-run lack of visibility of results in the field of population, the aid-receiving countries must, at the very start of the process, show that they have both the realistic and necessary population objectives and the will to carry their plans through.

It is with this view that we in the Fund will continue to assist countries, and deliberately apply a portion of the assistance to spurring the countries to undertake these programmes themselves, by continuing to train as much of each country's human resources as possible, and assisting in the building of their own institutions. (6 May 1973)

- External assistance has from the outset been a small fraction of total development resources, but it can have an effect out of proportion to its size. Like an extra pulley in a block and tackle, its effect in the right place is multiplied. (26 September 1973)

- There are undoubtedly considerable grounds for satisfaction at the rapid expansion of the United Nations system's involvement in population work, the support it is receiving, and the general acceptance of many of the approaches that have been advocated. But it would be unrealistic, and even ridiculous, to imagine that any external programme could substitute, in any way, for national action. (29 October 1973)

- The Fund shares the belief of many development specialists that development assistance, if of the right type and given in the right way, can strengthen, rather than undermine, self-reliance. We are very much concerned in finding those areas and methods which represent the most effective contribution to national development programmes, bearing in mind that external assistance is only a small fraction of the resources devoted in a given country to development efforts. (13 November 1973)

- It seems fairly clear . . . that an estimated total of around $300 million annually currently available for population assistance from international sources amounts to a small proportion of total estimated needs for external and internal resources for population activities. But we must remember also that, in financial terms, international assistance defrays only a small portion of the actual costs of the population activities undertaken in the developing world. For every dollar of international population assistance, many more dollars of resources must be provided locally. (21 June 1977)

- External assistance . . . is an essential element in raising national consciousness of population problems and enhancing national efforts to solve them. It provides the much-needed spark to overcome reluctance both by government and the community to commit the necessary financial, human and material resources required for worthwhile programmes. Furthermore, it gives the countries access to international expertise not available otherwise.

  While it is always difficult to gauge the impact of population work on a quantitative basis, there are encouraging signs that UNFPA and other external inputs into national population programmes have stimulated developing countries to greatly increase their own capacity to conduct their population programmes.

  For example, one important indication of national interest is that many governments have readjusted their national budgets in order to make larger internal inputs to population programmes, in particular to family planning programmes. (5 July 1977)

- No credible increase in assistance provided by the international community would begin to match the amounts now being spent by the governments of the developing countries themselves. (6 December 1977)

- Much more remains to be done in fulfilling the population objectives that developing countries have set for themselves; and while they continue to strengthen their own capacity for self-reliant development, they would require, for some time to come, international assistance in such crucial areas as training, research and innovative activities in family planning. (28 March 1978)

Chapter 11

INTERNATIONAL CO-OPERATION, THE NEED FOR . . .
IN POPULATION AND OTHER MATTERS

• The question can always be asked, why should a developed country contribute to this [population assistance] effort when it is saddled with its own social and economic problems? The answer has long been given by a distinguished citizen of this country [Canada], Lester B. Pearson, who in his Report to the Commission on International Development, said that the answer "is a moral one: that it is only right for those who have to share with those who have not. Concern with the needs of other and poorer nations is the expression of a new and fundamental aspect of modern age—the awareness that we live in a village world, that we belong to a world community. It is a recognition that concern with improvement of the human condition is no longer divisible."

Indeed, for mankind to solve its most serious problem—the growth of its numbers—a combined action and a common goal among the developed and developing nations of the world are needed over a long period of time. Little sacrifices are needed from the citizens of the developed world to preserve the peace in our generation. (4 November 1970)

• Population is not the concern of one nation or one region of the world. It is a global problem and must be solved by international action. The giver-and-receiver relationship has little place in this setting; we are all givers and all receivers. (5 February 1973)

• Today national economies have to be meshed into larger communities . . . in order to remain viable. The increasing number of problems we are compelled to handle at the international level is evidence of this need. To be successful, therefore, rationalization has to come at every level of society, from the village to the national level, and, finally, at the international level.

The UNFPA does not regard the [world population] problem as one for the developing countries alone. It is a global problem and can only be tackled by concerted international action.

The circumstances that compel the world towards a unified approach make ideology a luxury. In any case, ideological statements are not necessarily incompatible with apparently conflicting statements made in different terms. . . . If some countries have been more successful than others in slowing down the growth of their population, it is as much because of superior management as because of any inherent superiority of ideology.

If . . . ideological differences of approach are more apparent than real, it should be possible to look for an international consensus in matters of population.

It seems that we are already moving towards international agreement on the fundamental question of the necessity to rationalize the growth of the world's population. Even countries which a few years ago resolutely opposed any move in the United Nations to support population activities now give at least qualified endorsement to the work of the UNFPA.

Each government must recognize the need for international co-operation in research and in the transfer of skills and resources.

[We] hope that during World Population Year and the World Population Conference the barriers of ideology will fall and we shall all speak of the population problem as a common one, part of the whole problem of the future of man. (14 February 1973)

• Unfortunately, up till now the sum . . . of national and international action [in the population field] does not add up to much. This can be attributed to a number of reasons. First, in addition to cultural, ethical, religious and political considerations, there have been many other factors, such as: that the industrialized countries, cushioned by high productivity and know-how, have tended to see the population problem only in terms of developing countries. Secondly, that developing countries, particularly in Asia, while acutely aware of the problem of numbers versus resources, have lacked the means, except for a few, to carry out effective programmes.

Thirdly, that it has taken a long time for the idea to percolate that whatever policies one nation adopts in regard to population is not a matter for itself alone. And that what is called for is large-scale, inter-linked national and international programmes on a global scale. The opportunity to mount such a programme now exists through the United Nations.

The main objective of the Fund is, and must be, universal participation, as the only means of bringing the knowledge, skills, expertise, experience and financial resources of all nations to bear on a problem that concerns all nations.

Perhaps you feel that this is a bold statement for any one person to make, and a difficult target for any United Nations agency to aim for. But [we] believe, and a great many governments seem to be of similar mind, that the policies being pursued by the United Nations Fund for Population Activities offer the best possibility, and perhaps the only possibility, of getting adequate international co-operation in the sensitive and complex area of population. (14 February 1973-B)

• How do you get the public mind working on the broad concept that the well-being of the human race must transcend all cultural, ethical, racial and political differences? (15 February 1973)

• In the final measure, no matter how effective individual programmes may prove to be, the [World Population] Year will not have accomplished its purpose unless it has brought about a new collaboration and pooling of resources between developing and more industrialized countries, in order to give substance, weight, and direction to a long term solution to the world's population problems. This can only be built up by a free flow of information, exchange of technical knowledge, and sympathetic understanding of the similarities and dissimilarities of each others' situations.

After all, in this—probably more than any other aspect of human living—the problem of one is the problem of all. (23 March 1973)

• For aid-giving countries not too weary of the short-run lack of visibility of results in the field of population, the aid-receiving countries must, at the very start of the process, show that they have both the realistic and necessary population objectives, and the will to carry their plans through. (6 May 1973)

• The "One Boat" concept which emerged from the world conference on the environment*—the thought that all of humanity is in one boat—applies, at many points, to the population situation as well. (7 July 1973)

• It sometimes seems that there is a feeling of disillusion spreading among the developed nations, but . . . disillusion at this stage is mistaken. In the past we may have expected too much from too little too soon; it is not time now to give up the concept of international co-operation, but rather to change our understanding of it into something closer to the true meaning of the word. (26 September 1973)

• As is stated in the World Plan of Action, a strategy has been formulated which makes population one of several areas which, taken together, constitute the multidisciplinary approach of the international community to the solution of world problems in the field of social and economic development.

This statement . . . changes everything. It is never going to be possible to view population activities in isolation again. Since population is the one element every other variable has in common, population may even turn out to be the binding force that makes the multidisciplinary approach . . . possible. (4 March 1974)

• In looking ahead to the end of this century . . . we must envisage a situation in which a second world population of the same dimensions as the present one will have been added to the world's inhabitants.

Accept this fact and we have to accept the responsibility *now* for taking action to adapt, to conserve and to develop the resources which will be needed to sustain these increases in numbers in the 25-year spiral period.

If any example is needed to illustrate the urgency of doing so, the present energy crisis provides a timely warning. It also demonstrates that there are a rising number of problems in the world that are beyond the power of individual governments and countries to

*United Nations Conference on the Human Environment, held in Stockholm, Sweden in June 1972.

resolve—problems of such magnitude that they demand not only national action, but international co-operation on a worldwide scale. (6 March 1974)

• When we speak of a society of sufficiency for all we are not just speaking of the developing countries. Sufficiency for all—in the sense of an absence of excess as well as an absence of deprivation—is a concept which is valid internationally as well as nationally. (20 August 1974)

• For many years some far-sighted men such as the late Paul G. Hoffman, Administrator of the United Nations Development Programme . . . have warned about the dangers of ignoring the future. Often they have been dismissed as pessimists and their calls for co-operation rather than conflict between nations have been welcomed in theory but neglected in practice.

Hoffman spent the later part of his life trying to show that co-operation was not only viable but necessary in our modern world. To an extent he was successful; the United Nations Development Programme stands as his monument. But it is only very recently that it has been brought home to us that the world is an interlocking system, any part of which we ignore at our peril. Recent studies show in practice that co-operation is more likely to produce desired ends than conflict except in the very short term. . . . (15 October 1974)

• It is . . . possible for us . . . to think in terms which would have seemed impossibly romantic only a generation or two ago—of a world free from the three deadly enemies of humankind [war, disease and famine]. . . . It is now not only possible, but mandatory to think in these terms. [But] our position has been held, whether we like it or not, at the cost of some of our independence. There is not one nation, or any group of nations today, which can exist on its own resources. Whether for oil, or for industrial raw materials, or for manufactured products, interdependence has become the key to our economic survival. Conflict, hunger, disease in any part of the world affect us all. . . .

The implications of interdependence—not just a slogan now but a reality—are slowly being worked out by the international community. They are impelled by the knowledge that serious damage to one part of the world means almost certain disaster for the rest. This makes nonsense of the "triage" or "lifeboat" theories being put about by pessimists who have been seduced by their own rhetoric. Such people believe that our situation is so near to cataclysm that some poor countries must be sacrificed to assure the survival of the remainder. Their error is to believe that it is possible in practical terms to make this sort of choice. Instead, far from the rich world occupying a lifeboat and having the awkward choice of whom among the poor countries to haul aboard, we are all very much in the same boat. If the boat is overloaded or underpowered at one end, the whole crew is affected.

Expert after expert, book after book have told us in recent years that whatever the current problems of feeding the world and supplying its needs, the technical resources exist to do so. The speeches delivered at the recently concluded Special Session of the United Nations General Assembly showed that most governments also have confidence in humankind's technical ability to feed ourselves.

If this is accepted, then the only course open to any country is to co-operate with the rest to the fullest possible extent in order to ensure the safety and well-being of the whole of the world's present and future population.

Many of the structures of an interdependent world already exist and will hopefully be stronger in the future. In the last few years, new organizations for improved capital flow to developing countries, better trade arrangements, secure and adequate food supplies and international assistance to national population programmes have been set up on the framework of the United Nations system. Now it has been proposed that the system itself be overhauled in order to bring it more into line with the realities of the modern world.

One of the most difficult subjects of all [in rural agricultural development] is access to markets in other countries, especially the industrialized. Here only international co-operation can provide the necessary openings.

Every country has the obligation to its fellow-members of the international community to make its plans as effective as possible, because in our interdependent world, the success of all plans depends on the co-operation which must exist between nations to work together for the best interests of all. (26 September 1975)

• The experience of the last twenty years shows that consensus about, and success in, population programmes is only to be won on the basis of a shared acceptance of different national and personal attitudes.

Success in achieving consensus on the wider issues of international economics and development, as with population, will also consist in the exercise of restraint—a willingness to understand the different needs of other nations and accept them, even when in some cases they appear to run counter to self-interest.

The recognition . . . of economic interdependence with the rest of the world, and of the connections which must be made between different areas of national and international life . . . demands acceptance of other cultures and values. (28 September 1976)

• When the World Environment Conference convened in Stockholm in 1972, it proved to be only the first of a general international debate that has been going on ever since. We have discussed food, population, industrialization, women, trade, energy, employment, housing and the law of the sea at an unprecedented series of world meetings, with two special sessions of the General Assembly of the United Nations and a year-long round of discussions, the so-called "North-South Dialogue", in between. But whatever the venue, and whatever the subject, ostensibly being discussed, the underlying theme has been the same—the nature of the relationship between the industrialized countries and the developing. This is the Great Debate of the seventies, the outcome of which is likely to determine the shape of our world for generations to come. (12 January 1977)

• Both in national and international affairs, success in meeting the problems of the future seems to depend ultimately on the responsiveness of society to the real needs of its members, and its ability to adapt its structures accordingly. (2 June 1977)

- Given the historical sensitivity of the subject of population—evidence of which was amply provided [by the World Population Conference] at Bucharest—and given also that the World Population Plan of Action provided the basis for a large measure of agreement on many issues connected with population, it is interesting to note that the international conferences held since Bucharest, on Food, Women . . . and Human Settlements, all passed resolutions on population matters. It is even more significant that the Economic and Social Council of the United Nations passed at its spring meeting this year a resolution which recommended that the General Assembly give due weight to the role of population, and the importance of population activities, when preparing the new international development strategy.* (8 August 1977)

- [The ECOSOC resolution recommended that:] "When it considers the question of preparing a new international development strategy, the role of population and the importance of population policies and activities in their relationship to the establishment of a new international economic order should be given due weight, and should be duly integrated into the goals, objectives, policy measures and targets to be contained in any new strategy.". . .

The UNFPA stands ready, upon request, to assist the relevant organizations in the United Nations system that are charged with the preparation of the new International Development Strategy for the Third Development Decade—and other relevant international strategies—in order to ensure that adequate recognition is given to population factors and activities in the formulation of such strategies and in the implementation of a new international economic order. (6 November 1978)

*ECOSOC resolution 2051 of 5 May 1977.

Chapter 12

POPULATION AND DEVELOPMENT

Relationship Between Population and Development

• While some governments consider that high priority should be given to population activities, others have expressed the view that there are economic and social programmes
which are more important. The solution of population problems is no substitute for the
pressing and broader requirements of economic development. It is complementary,
and the mechanism of a separate Fund enables governments which wish to support or
receive assistance in the population field to do so without a diminution in the assistance
given in other fields through the United Nations Development Programme and the
regular budgets of the agencies.

Since population programmes relate to the total fabric of a society, projects and programmes will, in many cases, not break down neatly along the lines of academic
disciplines or organizational jurisdictions. (10 November 1969)

• In entrusting the administration of the UNFPA to the UNDP, [we] believe that the
Secretary-General hopes . . . to relate development assistance in the population field as
closely as possible to other types of development assistance. There are . . . many instances in which assistance with family planning services and information will be
understandable and acceptable only if they are set in the broader context of other types
of development assistance programmes. (16 October 1970)

• Developing countries equate development with modernization, better control of the environment and general welfare. Development is the universal goal of all countries,
regardless of the prevailing ideology or stage of political organization.

However, while development planning has been going on in the past two decades, it
was only recently that there has been a recognition of the importance of population
growth as a factor in planning. Development planners are now convinced that unless
the present population growth trend . . . in developing countries is reversed, development efforts will be thwarted and, in the end, lead to a progressive deterioration of incomes and levels of living. (4 November 1970)

• Development is a process in which each part is intimately interrelated to every other.
For one part to move forward, all other parts must be moving in the same direction. . . . (1 November 1972)

• It may well be that we . . . need to discard the notion of a population policy as a separate area of government action. Instead, population policy would be merged into existing structures so that, in each sector, consideration would be given to the demographic implications of alternative policy options. Population growth would be considered, not in terms of whether or not it is an obstacle to development, but as a function of manpower planning. Greater emphasis would be placed on adapting existing development strategies, to enhance the capacity of the society to absorb existing and anticipated births, while at the same time creating the economic and social conditions conducive to the transition to smaller families.

Since population is a factor affecting almost every aspect of social and economic development, many of the basic principles and lessons learned in early foreign aid programmes are relevant when it comes to population assistance. Similar problems arise in both areas in regard to delivery of equipment and supplies, in the recruitment of qualified experts, and in the achievement of an effective combination with national undertakings. But population programmes demand a sharper definition, a more flexible approach and a much greater degree of understanding and perception of specific situations. Population programmes must reach out to the individual—they are, after all, finally dependent on the individual for their success. (5 February 1973)

• It is difficult to persuade families to risk their future for the promises of government planners. Pleas for a radical transformation of attitudes must be accompanied by action aimed at social and economic development. It is a question of organizing our societies more intelligently so that population growth takes place commensurately with our ability to develop resources.

It is vital that we improve our knowledge and awareness of the interrelationship between population, food, health, employment, education and training and other aspects of economic and social development.

The pressure of population on resources is increasingly making development efforts difficult in many parts of the world.

There must be a common acceptance that population is part of the wider issue of development and cannot be tackled on its own.

If we can achieve an international consensus [on rationalizing the growth of the world's population], we shall have gone a long way towards a solution of the population problem. From here we can take the argument to the broader issue of development. The same criteria apply, and perhaps it will be possible eventually to arrive at a common attitude to development problems which will allow us truly to co-operate in their solution. (14 February 1973)

• Unlike many economic development projects which can show tangible results in a year or two, population projects often take a generation or more to take full effect.

The problems that arise from population trends are not acting in a vacuum and cannot be treated as if they were in a vacuum.

It would be illusory to imagine that a reduction in the rate of population growth will, of itself, raise living standards. Such a reduction will in many developing countries remove a serious obstacle to the attainment of economic and social goals, because where rates of development are low, a large proportion of any rise is swallowed up by the high rate of additions to the population. To remove or to moderate this obstacle may be very necessary; but it is equally necessary to prosecute positive policies of development of services, resources, output and distribution.

It is true that aid has often contributed a comparatively high proportion of the initial launching cost and implementation, but for its long-run effects we are being challenged by the examples of the two most populous states of Asia—China and India. China has today one of the most comprehensive family planning programmes, extensively delivered, with no internalional assistance. And in India, which has the longest experience in a government-initiated family planning programme, the foreign contribution to its total national outlay does not exceed the order of ten per cent.

If international assistance is to act as a spur [to national effort], by what mechanisms, by what means, should it operate? We may conceive of the main aim as creation of clear national population objectives or goals towards which the country's human resources should be mobilized.

The most important component of the strategic effort to solve the population problems is adequate communication between the leaders and the led; between donors and recipients of assistance; between the governmental agencies and private organizations.

[We] have no doubt that, in the years to come, there will be a continuing role for multilateral assistance in population. There are certain irreducible elements in these processes of exchange that only international organizations can perform adequately: the transmission of information; the lending of multinational experts; and the transmission of certain technological advances in the population field within the framework of internationally-agreed policies. But for aid-giving countries not too weary of the short-run lack of visibility of results in the field of population, the aid-receiving countries must, at the very start of the process, show that they have both the realistic and necessary population objectives and the will to carry their plans through. (6 May 1973)

- There are three crucial points which lie behind them [the criticisms of development schemes]. The first is that development, whether it is of the urban-industrial type favoured at the outset or the rural-based variety recently in vogue, takes a long time—longer, perhaps, than many of the early donors wished to admit. The second is that there must be a genuine will to development on the part of the government and people of the country concerned. This is a point often overlooked when aid is discussed. The most efficient-sounding scheme can be made to work only if the people concerned want it to work. The third necessity is a real will to assist on the part of the donor. This is not simply a matter of quantity. . . . International assistance supplies only a fraction of the total resources poured into the development effort. It is all the more important, therefore, to ensure that it is delivered at the point, and in the form, where its effect will be greatest.

People are the purpose of development, they are its raw material and the greatest resource that any government possesses. (25 August 1973)

- There are many people today who refer to rapid population growth as the single most important obstacle to improvement of living standards in developing countries. It is not surprising that this point of view is challenged in developing countries as being both simplistic and misleading. The obstacles to development lie, not merely in the rate of population growth, but in the compound effects of such factors as the neglect of agriculture, rigid social structures, and imbalances in resource allocation, as well as the unequal relationship between rich and poor countries and the maldistribution of income. Action on population matters, therefore, needs to be part of a concerted effort to tackle all of these problems simultaneously.

[We] do not believe that there is any longer any dispute that population is an important but dependent variable to be considered within larger development concerns. The question, however, remains what importance should be given to the population question, and what priority it should have in relation to other aspects of development. . . . If the relevance of population to development factors were to be properly understood and appreciated (and it does require further progress in collection of basic data, in provision of research and training facilities, and in establishment of informed policies), then . . . each country would be able to establish a population programme most relevant to its economic and social situation and to the desires of the community.

There are those who articulate the suspicion that assistance for population programmes is in some ways taking away resources which would otherwise be available for other development programmes. . . . This is not the case. In the United Nations system, the population assistance programme is linked to the overall development assistance programme while maintaining its separate identity; and the United Nations has never supported the view that population assistance should be promoted at the cost of other types of development assistance. A separate identity for the population assistance programme such as the one being run by UNFPA is, however, desirable because of the need to avoid another suspicion, i.e., that population planning may be made a prerequisite for development assistance. The suspicion is totally unfounded, as in the case of UNFPA we have provided assistance at the request of governments, without laying down any conditions as to what other activities ought to be undertaken in relation to the programme. . . . (7 September 1973)

- Our understanding of the effects of economic growth on population is improving, but we do not yet have a comparable knowledge of the effects of population growth on development. It is, for example, the case that the eras of greatest expansion of the economies of the present industrial powers took place during a time of rapid population growth, and that this very growth in the number of workers was a contributory factor to economic development. (26 September 1973)

- It seems that action to limit population growth *on its own* has little or no effect on birth rates, whereas combined with other measures of social and economic development, quite dramatic results have been noted. From this, some have concluded that there is no case for special action on population.

However, as . . . we are all now aware, there is no case for leaving to chance what can be brought about by design. As an eminent academic observed recently, "We are now observing some of the outer limits of the earth's 'carrying mass' in terms of food production." We cannot simply hope earnestly that population growth rates will come down with increasing prosperity, but must operate so as to ensure that they do come down, which means very close study of the conditions under which birth rates have been observed to drop, and unceasing efforts to bring about those conditions.

We take as our premises, firstly, that the Fund's work relates to the most delicate, the most intimate of all human activity, so that programmes must always be geared to the needs of the individual. Secondly, we and all who work in the field are relatively inexperienced in effective methods of approaching population problems, and must therefore be prepared to innovate. Thirdly, the environments in which we work and the values with which we have to deal are very different from the general run of Western experience. Fourthly, that the role of foreign assistance is marginal and must, therefore, be injected at the time, and in the area, where its effect will be to generate further activity. It has, therefore, been our purpose to provide opportunity for recipient countries themselves to generate programmes, and to establish within the Fund mechanisms for evaluating requests which will give the maximum flexibility of response.

This implies that the Fund will, where possible, provide direct assistance within the framework of the individual country's general programmes of development, although we do not exclude multi-country programmes where these appear most suitable from the standpoint of administrative efficiency. (18 October 1973)

• An important advantage of the present multi-agency approach is that it ensures that population concerns and activities are diffused throughout the different sectors of development assistance. Where population and family planning activities are organized as part of an already existing programme, for example, the integration of family planning services in MCH [maternal and child health programmes] or family life education within functional literacy, the results have been impressive. . . . We should seek to extend this concept to include other development programmes and, indeed, the development planning process itself. (22 October 1973)

• There are undoubtedly considerable grounds for satisfaction at the rapid expansion of the United Nations system's involvement in population work, the support it is receiving, and the general acceptance of many of the approaches that have been advocated. But it would be unrealistic, and even ridiculous, to imagine that any external programme could substitute, in any way, for national action. (29 October 1973)

• As yet the connection between population and development is not well understood, and . . . it appears to be country-specific. The interaction varies according to the size of the country, its endowments of natural resources, the economic structure, income per head, levels of education and other factors. Both we and government policymakers need to understand better the economic and social implications of population policies and the implications for population of economic and social goals.

At the strategic planning level we in the population field are struggling with two basic questions:

(1) What effect, if any, will a particular population planning policy have on population growth, per capita income, and other socio-economic variables in a given country or region?

(2) Given a set of socio-economic goals for a country or region, what types of population planning policies and programmes are likely to be "optimal", that is, most consistent with these goals? What are the trade-offs between expenditures for population planning and expenditures for education, agricultural development, industrial development, urban planning, or medical care?

Economists and econometricians have been working on these questions, although in most of the national planning models the impact of population changes on socio-economic variables has been included, but not the reverse relationship. (13 November 1973)

• As is stated in the World Population Plan of Action, a strategy has been formulated which makes population one of several factors which, taken together, constitute the multidisciplinary approach of the international community to the solution of world problems in the field of social and economic development.

This statement . . . changes everything. It is never going to be possible to view population activities in isolation again. Since population is the one element every other variable has in common, population may even turn out to be the binding force that makes the multidisciplinary approach . . . possible. (4 March 1974)

• We do not talk any more in terms of family planning as an answer to population growth, because we realize now that there is far more to population than family planning. In many parts of the world, particularly in Asia, it is indeed vital to slow down the rate of population growth, but . . . it is now realized that the number of children a family has depends on a very complex interaction, in which levels of education, the quality of housing, and health and social security services play a part, and which is tied closely to the form which overall social and economic development is taking. (2 April 1974)

• In the United Nations system we have been talking about development for nearly thirty years now; about four-fifths of United Nations activity, and by far the larger portion of its staff, are concerned in one way or another with development work. Not only the United Nations itself, but the United Nations Development Programme, the Food and Agriculture Organization in Rome, the World Health Organization and the International Labour Organisation in Geneva, and the United Nations Economic Commissions, together with thousands of staff in . . . Member States of the United Nations organization, are all working towards this one thing called "development".

This is paradoxical because nobody knows for certain what development is. Much work has been done, and more words written and spoken on the subject than would fill a . . . library, but no single authority has yet offered a definitive description of the development process. . . .

So far, attempts to bring about this development have been only spasmodically successful. . . . To make lasting improvements in the lives of the majority of the people of the developing world is very difficult.

We should not underestimate the achievements of the developing countries in this regard [economic development efforts]; all of them are supporting vastly increased and increasing populations, and in most countries the famines and epidemics which were regular features of life in the past have been eliminated. . . .

The UNFPA, along with most other development agencies, is well aware that there can be no successful programme of slowing down population growth without real and permanent increases in the standard of living of ordinary people. Really poor people do not care how many children they have, because they will still be poor; moreover, a large number of children will at least ensure that one or two survive to be a support to their parents in old age. More hands can always be used for the few weeks of planting, hoeing and harvesting the crop, even though they will be idle for the rest of the year.

So when the Fund talks with a government about population assistance, we do so in the knowledge that family planning is only a very small part of what we can do to help. We will discuss with the government its whole programme of development and try to ensure that our assistance, as small as it is in relation to the whole programme, is used at the points where it can be most effective. We know, for instance, that healthy families tend on the whole to be smaller families, so we may take part in a scheme to improve the health of mothers and children. Or the government may wish to know for its future planning how many people are drifting into the towns or the villages each year, and how fast the population in each area is growing. We can help here, too; in fact we are assisting twenty-one African countries at this moment to carry out full or partial censuses of their population. Or there may be a shortage of trained workers, nurses, health visitors, midwives or teachers, and the Fund will help to improve training services. Wherever it is possible, we try to fit our assistance into comprehensive plans for development, as we are doing in ten countries at the moment, offering a wide range of services over a period of several years.

We have developed this philosophy of assistance partly through observing the experience of others, and partly through the necessities of the type of assistance we are offering. It is of the nature of population assistance that it operates on a personal level. It must reach and affect directly the behaviour of individual people—not like a loan for a factory or an airport, whose effects, good or bad, operate indirectly. From this basis, it has become clearer that there may be a foundation here for a new philosophy of development which takes people rather than things as its starting point. For example, instead of building large prestige projects such as central hospitals or universities, it may make more sense for a government to establish a chain of local clinics and provincial colleges, where the services are geared to local needs. Even manufacturing can be decentralized in this way, reducing the pressure on urban services in the major cities, and contributing to widespread development which is not concentrated in a few centres.

There are obviously drawbacks and difficulties to this type of development. It requires, for instance, administrations which are highly efficient, whose members are able to work on their own, reacting to local conditions but with the common purpose in mind. It requires, above all, a considerable act of will on the part of both government and governed to make the effort successful. Everyone is involved, so everyone must be committed. (19 April 1974)

- If we do not yet have the solution to the puzzle of population and development, we can be reasonably sure that we now have [some] of the pieces. (9 May 1974)

- We have to learn to think in terms of quality rather than quantity. This approach provides a good touchstone for the success of development and population programmes: Are the available human resources being fully developed? Do the people benefit? Our aim should be the fullest expansion of the productivity and the creativity of each individual. (21 May 1974)

- We feel that we have been able to participate in the development of what might be called a "third view" of population. Until the last few years, opinion was polarized around the views that population was the only significant factor in development or that it was of no importance at all. Now . . . it is clear that nearly every government in the world, in both developing and developed countries, has a view on population, and it is clear that for most governments, whatever their view of their own situation, population is an important component in their development thinking and planning. (3 June 1974)

- The Fund has been trying to promote better understanding on the interrelation between economic and social factors and demographic factors.

This idea is certainly one that is stated in the draft of the World Population Plan of Action, for the central theme of the Plan is that the Plan must be considered "as an essential component of the system of international strategies which, when taken together, constitute the international community's over-all strategy for the promotion of economic development and quality of life". (9 July 1974)

- To put it simply, the classic development models—and the development trends themselves—have stressed urban as against rural growth, large-scale as against small, concentration against diffusion. But in fact, in order to meet our problems, it may be that quite the opposite emphasis is needed. The development of agriculture can meet the world's food shortages; rural development can relieve the immense burden on the cities; and, for the sake of dignity and self-respect, as well as to provide markets, both industry and agriculture must offer the individual the opportunity and the incentive to work, to earn, and to contribute to his society.

Development must be diffused socially and geographically throughout all levels and throughout all areas. A society of sufficiency for all, replacing the distortions of both excess and deprivation, must be our aim.

This is the context in which the problems of population must be seen. The adoption of sensible and enlightened policies in this field is an essential step for all countries—whether developed or developing—on their road towards becoming "sufficiency societies". . . . (20 August 1974)

• [We] fully appreciate the severity of other problems confronting most of the world: inflation, recession, unemployment, the energy crisis, environmental pollution. But [we] feel that development planners . . . should isolate population from these other problems because it underlines, and is vital and basic to, all of them. In our efforts to grapple with the present grave emergencies. . . . We should not permit work in the population area to flag or be abandoned. (27 January 1975)

• We must recognize that population assistance programmes have a specific purpose and responsibility, namely to support population activities rather than overall development programmes. The need is so tremendous that the Fund's . . . resources . . . could easily be lost without trace if they were spread too thinly. Although it is impossible to maintain a clear-cut distinction between what are and are not population activities, the time has come . . . to determine more clearly what "population activities" we should in principle support. So far as UNFPA is concerned, population activities may cover population aspects of development, including the characteristics, causes and effects of changes in fertility, mortality and morbidity as they affect developmental prospects and human well-being. The activities have conveniently been divided into collection of basic population data, population dynamics, population policy formulation and implementation, contraception and child spacing, and communication and education. Within these categories, a great deal of flexibility is required; an activity which has only marginal population content in one society may be vitally important in another. In each case, the particular conditions and concerns of the recipient country should be paramount. (21 November 1975)

• The time frame of the increasing need for population assistance is finite. . . . [We] see the population programmes in which the international community as well as individual countries are now engaged necessarily as a self-liquidating process if they are to be of any value.

What is needed is effective action *now*. We need to devise the institutions and programmes of action *now,* to deliver assistance as effectively as humanly possible, before the problem becomes impossibly big and complex to deal with in an orderly manner. (20 February 1976)

• Solutions to both population and development problems are long-term propositions. This fact should not be a deterrent. The development of a society is like that of any other organism, evolving gradually and as a whole.

Population growth and national development have implications which are of global concern. Yet both must remain firmly within the area of national decisions if policies are to be acceptable and effective, because the demographic and developmental state of each country is different and therefore its needs are different. (14 June 1976)

• [In the 1950's] there was an upsurge of academic interest in the relationship between population growth and economic and social development, culminating in the publication in 1958 of Coale and Hoover's seminal book "Population Growth and Economic Development in Low-Income Countries". . . . It is upon this and other work done at this time that the thesis [upon which many population programmes are based, was developed]: that rapid population growth can seriously hamper efforts toward social and economic development in poorer countries. (28 September 1976)

- The international community has a responsibility to assist both sides of programmes for reducing birth rates—directly through population assistance by supporting such bodies as the United Nations Fund for Population Activities, and indirectly through conventional aid and other methods of easing the transition from massive poverty and high rates of population growth to moderate levels of both income and fertility. (12 January 1977)

- So far in the history of population assistance, the "population" component has been seen as a rather small proportion of the total aid budget. . . . It is time now to look at the matter in a different way. [This is because] . . . first, . . . interest and investment in population activities are growing throughout the developing world, perhaps at a faster rate than other aspects of development programmes; second, . . . the implementation and effectiveness of population programmes are both increasing in efficiency, again perhaps faster than that of other development programmes; and third, . . . both trends are well-established and shows no signs of tailing off. This points to an ability to use resources which did not exist a few years ago, and is directly related to the growth of population as a discipline. Developing countries' programmes have grown very rapidly, and, with them, their ability to use additional resources. . . . Further, [the countries] . . . are developing the theoretical understanding of the conditions under which population programmes may be expected to succeed. (30 March 1977)

- A recent United Nations survey, which covered 114 developing countries, shows that eighty-three of these have entrusted a central planning authority with the task of integrating population factors with development planning. Sixty-nine countries believe that the current rate of natural population increase imposes severe constraints on the attainment of developmental objectives.

These findings are behind the emphasis being given to population in the concerned discussion of planners. They have led to an increased sense of urgency in the North-South dialogue on a New International Economic Order, and they have quickened the trend in countries most conscious of the pressure of growing numbers on resources, to increase the pace of their fertility limitation programmes even to the extent of adopting more stringent anti-natalist policies and programmes than would have been considered possible or desirable only a few years ago. In fact, many countries in which economic development is being hampered by population growth are already endeavouring to introduce social reforms, undertake new development strategies and draw up legislative measures which aim at influencing people to have smaller families.

We have seen developing countries with previously limited concern about their own population problems, turn about, and institute broad-based and extensive national family planning programmes. And we have seen developing countries with minor national inputs in their own national population programmes, and with heavy reliance on external assistance, completely reverse their expenditure ratios so that now national inputs are major and external assistance is minor.

It is a difficult task to estimate the future needs for international population assistance. Much depends on the criteria to be applied with regard to the types of population activities which are required, the extent to which support from external sources is needed, and the availability of local resources. It seems fairly clear, however, that an estimated total of around $300 million annually currently available for population assistance from international sources amounts to a small proportion of total estimated needs for external and internal resources for population activities. But we must remember also that, in financial terms, international assistance defrays only a small portion of the actual costs of the population activities undertaken in the developing world. For every dollar of international population assistance, many more dollars of resources must be provided locally.

It is erroneous to think that development assistance is a fixed amount. There are recent indications that development assistance will increase considerably in the coming years. It is only logical that a larger share of this increase should go to support population programmes, which are such an important prerequisite for the attainment of many social and economic goals. (21 June 1977)

• External assistance . . . is an essential element in raising national consciousness of population problems and enhancing national efforts to solve them. It provides the much-needed spark to overcome reluctance both by government and the community to commit the necessary financial, human and material resources required for worthwhile programmes. Furthermore, it gives the countries access to international expertise not available otherwise. (5 July 1977)

• Besides the inevitable differences of approach between countries in different situations, there are many gaps in our understanding of the interrelations between population and development. It is in this respect that the policymaker and the programme manager look to the scientist for guidance. Certain relationships must be noted, however, to make the guidance effective.

By stressing the links between population and development, and broader issues such as national sovereignty and human rights, the World Population Conference placed population questions in a new dimension and a new perspective. If traditional approaches are no longer sufficient and the population question must be seen in the broader context of development, several questions arise: How can population be integrated into development? What will be the respective role of demography, economics and other disciplines in this process?

This already difficult problem is further complicated by the evolution of thinking about development itself. . . . Development is no longer considered as purely or perhaps even predominantly an economic phenomenon, involving only increases in per capita income or in gross national product. The creation of investment capital and its allocation to sectors where it will secure the maximum rate of growth is no longer considered adequate as a description of development.

The concept of development, as it has now emerged in the last decade or so, affects all aspects of human existence which determine the quality of life. It encompasses a development strategy in all spheres of economic and social life: in industry and agriculture, in trade and finance, in employment and education, in health and housing, in science and technology.

From the beginning of the Second Development Decade, and the call of the International Development Strategy for increased opportunities for all, through a more equitable distribution of the benefits of development, to the more recent formulation of the "basic needs" approach, ideas are becoming more precise and their content clearer.

But at the same time, development thinking never moves along one track. A great variety of different approaches have been suggested and many are being tried in practice.

All these considerations boil down to the questions of, first, understanding the complex ways in which population variables interact, reciprocally, with socio-economic development variables, and secondly, of showing how action programmes can be mounted to integrate population activities with health care, education, rural development organization of agriculture, industrial development, and other economic and social programmes.

Here, then, is a great challenge to us. Specialists of different disciplines have tended to confine their research activities specifically to their own subjects. As a result, the much needed synthesis and interchange of ideas has not taken place. To be able to fill the enormous gaps in our knowledge about population and development, we have to reach out beyond the confines of our respective disciplines, and carry out common, inter-disciplinary research. (8 August 1977)

• Many governments . . . have moved towards comprehensively planned action in population, with the fullest possible co-operation between the different sectors, and with constant reference to the country's development goals. Certainly the question of population growth cannot be left to chance or the forces of natural selection. Nor can we rely on "development" alone to slow population growth to a reasonable level. There have been too many interventions in other directions for nature to be left to take its course. Conversely, we have learned that family planning programmes by themselves will not slow rapid rates of population growth, but that they are essential, given that other conditions are right, to speed the drop in birthrates. (26 March 1978)

• Population programmes are already creating an impact, and demographers now project a slowing down of population growth rates in many parts of the developing world. This should not, however, make us complacent. Much more remains to be done in fulfilling the population objectives that developing countries have set for themselves; and while they continue to strengthen their own capacity for self-reliant development, they would require, for some time to come, international assistance in such crucial areas as training, research and innovative activities in family planning. (28 March 1978)

• Through the years, UNFPA has been aware of the change in the population scenario and it is constantly exploring new areas of assistance in development. We are convinced that to stay ahead of new developments and to influence the course these might take, a new thinking—a new conceptualization of population activities in the framework of social and economic development—must be continuously generated. (4 April 1978)

• In assisting governments which show an increasing desire to make their population policies more comprehensive, UNFPA seeks to encourage in-depth exploration of the interaction between population factors and development. The emergence of population factors as vital elements in programmes designed to bring about economic and social changes at the national level should now also be fully reflected at the international level. (6 November 1978)

Development Planning

• The real "obstacles" to development lie . . . not merely in the rate of population growth, but in the compound effects of such factors as the neglect of agriculture, rigid social structures and imbalances in resources allocation, as well as the unequal relations between rich and poor countries and the maldistribution of income. It would be illusory to imagine that a reduction in the rate of population growth will, of itself, raise living standards.

There is a great need within the national planning body and the various sectoral planning agencies for experienced persons of sufficiently high levels not only to advise on the population policy implications of most aspects of the various types of planning, but also to participate in the national planning process itself, in all its phases. . . . As some of you may know, a proposal was made recently for the creation of high-level, interdisciplinary international training facilities. UNFPA is actively seeking to develop such facilities at the national, as well as the international, level. An important target audience is development planners whose time perspective does not encourage consideration of population as an endogenous variable.

Furthermore, research leading to the elaboration of systematic models of the development process should be intensified. One of the purposes of such research would be to explore what rate of population growth could be absorbed given alternative assumptions about capital-output ratios, patterns of resource allocation, access to foreign markets, availability of external assistance, changes in social structure and so on.

In the UNFPA we are very much interested in working with governments and nongovernmental institutions in developing a conceptual framework for a truly integrated approach to the problems of poverty, environment and population, and in assisting governments in dealing with population aspects of the formulation and implementation of comprehensive development strategies. Such assistance would include consideration of problems relating to migration and urbanization, and the development of population-related strategies in such fields as public health, nutrition, employment and urban and rural development. (1 November 1972)

• Too many development schemes have failed because they started in the office or the drawing board and not in the field. . . . (25 August 1973)

• Twenty years ago, when serious development programmes were beginning in the former colonial territories, there was little doubt that what was needed was capital investment in industry—urban development along the lines laid down in Europe and North America. During the 1960's, the First Development Decade, these policies paid off in many countries in terms of high annual rise in Gross National Product.

At the same time, however, it appeared that the increased national prosperity was not reaching a large proportion of the people of developing countries. There had been an optimistic theory that the benefits of growth would, as it was put, "trickle down" through the various strata of society, reaching even the very poor eventually. By the end of the First Development Decade, it was clear that this was not happening.

The emphasis on rapid industrialization has led to an emphasis on bigness in both industry and agriculture, in the belief that large units are necessarily more efficient than small ones.

We are now slowly groping towards a theory which will not only allow the majority of the people a share in growing wealth but which depends on them to produce it. The key to economic growth is savings and investment. It has now been shown, in countries with widely differing ideologies, that it is not only the prosperous who save. Relatively poor producers and workers will save too, if given the opportunity. But in order to do this they need to have access to health and education services; they need credit, the appropriate technology and advice on using it. In other words, the initial investment need not be in big operations, whether industrial or agricultural, but can be widely diffused over thousands of small undertakings.

Contrary to accepted wisdom in the sixties, this is not necessarily . . . an inefficient use of resources. (25 February 1974)

• [We] have been talking . . . of national development and national plans, because it is vital that each country find its own road. But no country will be able to do so without the advice and assistance of its fellow members in the United Nations. Everything [we] have said here, for example, is based on the shared experience of several nations in various stages of development. If these ideas have any value at all it will be because ideas, facts and theories were exchanged across national boundaries. (19 April 1974)

• Thinking about development in many parts of the world is currently undergoing drastic revisions. There is some agreement that industrialization on the Western model is not going to take place in many countries—and there is increasing doubt whether it would be the best form of development even if it were possible. Instead, current ideas start with what is already there, the people themselves and their knowledge, and their relationship to their environment. Development schemes reach out to the villages, restructuring local agriculture and industry in an organic way which is comprehensible to those who must operate the systems. Their support and commitment is obtained at the outset and adjustments are made in the course of experience, according to local needs and new information.

[Provision] of assistance in this manner has many differences from the traditional aid package. First, there is nothing for the donor to see, to put his label on. Second, control of the expenditure by the donor is at best indirect; it is widely diffused in space and time, and passes through many different hands. Third, such an assistance scheme cannot be worked out by a donor and presented as a package. It depends very much on knowledge and understanding of local needs and conditions, on the sort of information only the local authorities themselves are liable to have. Therefore, it cannot be tested by the conventional criteria of donors. A great deal must simply be taken on trust, or on the basis of mutual knowledge and respect between donor and recipient.

Those . . . with experience in the field may have noticed similarities between this approach and that adopted in successful family planning programmes. This is no accident—in population work it has long been recognized that success depends on motivation, and that motivation depends on a complex of factors, and can be achieved successfully only by intimate knowledge of local conditions and the changes which are necessary. (15 October 1974)

• Organic, integrated development requires, above all, the political will to succeed. The people involved at all levels must be energized, committed, convinced that the plans will work. Obtaining this commitment is not a matter of rhetoric or flamboyant leadership. It is much more a process of patient groundwork, during which decisions emerge from the various levels rather than being imposed from the top. People who have made their own decisions—even if they coincide with government policy—are that much more committed to making them work. (26 September 1975)

• For most people, development means very simple things—enough food, a job, somewhere to live, a future for their children—in other words, some sort of basic security in their lives. Achievement of a New International Economic Order will achieve nothing if these basic needs are not supplied, because "development" which does not touch the majority of the people is not development at all, and because it is on the ordinary people of the developing countries that development programmes depend for their success.

If it is desired to produce more food and achieve a satisfactory ratio of producers to consumers, the needs, desires and attitudes of the individual must be consulted.

By regarding the individual as a resource rather than [as] a liability, development programmes have been able to build houses, open schools, provide basic medical care and jobs.

Respect for the powers and the possibilities of the individual has another aspect. We have said the countries should regard their people as actors in development programmes rather than as mere passive recipients of development.

The individual man and woman, the family and the community are . . . the resources for, and the reason for, development. (23 October 1975)

• Development theory and practice is in general tending . . . towards greater involvement with the small, usually rural, group, family or village, towards the growth of self-reliance, and towards the acceptance of development as an integrated whole.

Closer contact is needed between development workers and the people with whom they work, and much closer involvement of the individual in development schemes, as an agent of development as well as an "acceptor". (21 November 1975)

- There is . . . a movement away from vast schemes towards more modest projects more firmly rooted in the society from which they spring, and in general a swing away from what has been called "giantism" to programmes manageable on a human scale. (2 June 1976)

- Population programmes and other development activities share many of the same features: To be effective both must reach the individual who makes the ultimate decision. This requires planning and execution of national policies that are sensitive to local wishes and needs in a flexible, responsive manner, by both the public and the private sectors.

Solutions to both population and development problems are long-term propositions. This fact should not be a deterrent. The development of a society is like that of any other organism, evolving gradually and as a whole.

Commitment to, and implementation of, development strategies for providing the basic needs to the population rest first of all with the national government.

The hard question of development is how to release the enormous resources of energy, of skill, of knowledge in the developing world for productive purposes. (14 June 1976)

- The experience of the last twenty years shows that consensus about, and success in, population programmes are only to be won on the basis of a shared acceptance of different national and personal attitudes.

Success in achieving consensus on the wider issues of international economics and development, as with population, will also consist in the exercise of restraint—a willingness to understand the different needs of other nations and accept them, even when in some cases they appear to run counter to self-interest.

The typical . . . approach to . . . development . . . has been that economic growth is of paramount importance, shading all other problems into insignificance. Without growth, the theory runs, no problems, whether population, employment, the environment or any other, can be solved. . . . This view . . . has been followed enthusiastically. . . . More recently the "growth at all costs" view has been challenged by the "limits to growth" view . . . which takes precisely the opposite viewpoint—that unless both population and economic growth are curbed, environmental and resource problems will run out of hand. A recent modified formulation . . . postulates a limitation of growth in the more highly developed countries of the world in order to allow faster growth in the less well-off. (28 September 1976)

- Conventional approaches to development have largely failed to produce these conditions [access to housing, health, education and employment—the whole package that constitutes a materially secure and hopeful existence] because they were not intended to. Now, however, there is a new spirit . . . perhaps best summed up by the phrase "meeting basic needs". This is the other face [in addition to its concern with external relations between nations] of the New International Economic Order—an internal restructuring and redistribution within developing countries, a direct attack on poverty and its causes. (12 January 1977)

• Both in national and international affairs, success in meeting the problems of the future seems to depend ultimately on the responsiveness of society to the real needs of its members, and its ability to adapt its structures accordingly.

The result of unprecedented population growth and the deficiencies of conventional development strategies both in slowing it down and turning it to productive purposes, has been to challenge conventional approaches.

Conventional thinking held, on the one hand, that increasing populations would become a resource for future growth, and, on the other, that the rate of population increase would be slowed by the application of modern techniques of contraception.

The assumption that both national and international economic and social systems were susceptible to rapid and exogenous change [has proven to be false]. But the international economic structure has not worked for the benefit of developing nations nor have national economies been geared to the needs of the poor. So, just as the present international economic system is now felt by many to be inadequate to achieve equity in global economic relationships, the validity of internal economic and social strategies is also being called into question. In both cases, the matter is seen as one for political decision.

On the international level, the perception takes the form of a series of discussions, of which the most important are probably those centering on the demand of the developing countries for a New International Economic Order. Nationally, a variety of alternatives to conventional development thinking have emerged. (2 June 1977)

• Development is no longer considered as purely or perhaps even predominantly an economic phenomenon, involving only increases in per capita income or in gross national product. The creation of investment capital and its allocation to sectors where it will secure the maximum rate of growth is no longer considered adequate as a description of development.

The concept of development as it has now emerged in the last decade or so, affects all aspects of human existence which determine the quality of life. It encompasses a development strategy in all spheres of economic and social life: in industry and agriculture, in trade and finance, in employment and education, in health and housing, in science and technology.

From the beginning of the Second Development Decade, and the call of the International Development Strategy for increased opportunities for all, through a more equitable distribution of the benefits of development, to the more recent formulation of the "basic needs" approach, ideas are becoming more precise and their content clearer.

But at the same time, development thinking never moves along one track. A great variety of different approaches have been suggested and many are being tried in practice. (8 August 1977)

• From the mid-forties until the latter part of the sixties, development economists were relatively optimistic concerning future possibilities for continued development in the Third World. They perceived development to be a gradual but continuous and cumulative process which could effectively rely on marginal adjustments in its spread among groups within nations, as well as across the boundaries between nations.

For nations to reach a take-off point, proper incentives needed to be created to perfect market mechanisms. Automatic equilibrating mechanisms would create order from conflict, and development would be assured.

The paradigm, although questioned, persists. For in development, as in other areas of human activity, it was, and still is, difficult for people to incorporate changes in concepts and practices once a commitment and investment has been made in them. As one economist recently observed: "It is difficult to admit that what once appeared axiomatic is, in fact, subject to limitations of time and space and must be doubted."

After twenty years of optimism, the seventies saw a healthy agnosticism concerning development thinking. Several economists have expressed doubts about the relevance of neo-classical and Keynesian economics to Third World development. The indirect approach to development, the so-called "trickle down" approach of the fifties and sixties, has been found wanting.

So, today we find ourselves without a clear paradigm for development. The earlier preoccupation with aggregate economic growth and industrialization is greatly diminished. In its place there is a greater concern for matters of absolute poverty, growing inequality and rising unemployment, as well as growth of the gross national product.

In the seventies, economists and other social scientists and planners have raised the appealing banner of the basic needs approach to development. But despite its appeal, there is less clarity as to what is entailed intellectually. And, partially as a result of this, there is also less clarity as to how to make the concept a reality.

Rather than succumb to the intellectual vice of over-simplicity that characterized at least some of the earlier thinking about development, the basic needs approach is now being defined as supplementing and complementing existing development strategies, rather than being an all-embracing strategy itself. Rather than focusing on industrial institutions solely, in the hope that they will provide the means for social and economic well-being for individuals, the focus is on the ends of health and education and the like, themselves.

The new strategy focuses on a concrete specification of human needs—such as water, sanitation, and education—rather than abstract concepts, such as the quality of life. It is also specific in terms of attempting to channel particular resources to particular groups. It focuses not only on the unemployed and the underemployed, but also on the poor, the devastated—the so-called unemployable.

While thinking about development exhibits uncertainty, the conceptualization of the population field shows increasing maturity and sophistication.

The year 1974 was an important one for the population field. It marked the public coming-of-age of population discussion. Prior to the United Nations World Population Conference held in Bucharest in that year, the dominant perception of population programmes was focused heavily on family planning. As with so many public perceptions, it was, unfortunately, misguided for many institutions and individuals, unlike the UNFPA, which from the inception of its operations acted upon a much broader view of population concerns.

The political forum of the Bucharest Conference—the first of its kind—served to direct attention to, and interest in, a broader, less simplistic, more sophisticated view of the mutual interrelationships between population and development factors. By consensus of the nations of the world, the Conference established guidelines for future action which attested to the importance of population factors. The World Population Plan of Action, adopted at Bucharest, firmly established population as an important element in international strategies to promote development . . . and set as an important goal the expansion and deepening of the capacity of countries to deal effectively with their national and subnational population problems.

The conferees left Bucharest without agreement on a single definition of the population problem, but with greater awareness of the range of problems that exist or are made more difficult when "population growth, distribution and structure are out of balance with social, economic and environmental factors". They also brought home with them a greater awareness of the degree to which these factors have an impact upon population dynamics. The relation between population growth and economic growth, which was at the heart of the classical economic theory of Ricardo and others, and which had been to a large extent ignored in the fifties and sixties, was re-established, with deeper meaning. The neo-Malthusian position that population growth made rapid economic growth difficult was laid to rest on the basis of the historical evidence garnered during the preceding thirty years. Rather than looking at population in the aggregate, attention was directed to the components of the population. Population growth, assumed to have been independent of socio-economic development and change, was now seen as intimately and mutually related. Population, once viewed as exogenous by development planners, was now seen as endogenous. The maturation and sophistication of population thinking put an end to simplistic models of population change. For as two specialists at the International Labour Organisation recently observed, "it is worth re-emphasizing that the view that population policies are unnecessary since economic development provides the answer to the population question is as faulty as the argument that population is the main (and even insuperable) obstacle to development".

Thus, having re-established the linkage, and the need for greater attention to . . . population and development . . . we find ourselves today standing at a new frontier. For, having identified the need to integrate population factors in development planning, there is still much territory to be explored to bring this idea to full fruition and implementation. (3 April 1978)

Chapter 13

POPULATION ASSISTANCE:
Global Role of UNFPA

Multilateral Population Assistance, Advantages of

- In some areas, for political reasons, the United Nations system has advantages over, or at least lacks the disabilities of, other donors. There are also instances where the UNFPA is a logical funder since useful capabilities to deliver a certain type of assistance clearly exist within the United Nations system, the activation of which in the population field is one of the Fund's responsibilities. In some instances, moreover, the Fund probably should try to fill gaps in the assistance furnished by other agencies. . . . At the same time, the flexibility in Fund procedures and, we hope, our bureaucratic courage, should permit us to fund some worthwhile activities which other funding agencies for one or another reason find hard to tackle. It is also probably true that the UNFPA, as a donor agency, should enter certain national programmes primarily to extend the capabilities of the United Nations system so that this system may be more useful in the future. (16 October 1970)

- Over its twenty-five years, the United Nations through its family of agencies and organizations has built up a form of multilateral technical co-operation which has succeeded in reducing, if not eliminating, the inevitable mistrusts and misunderstandings inherent in giving and receiving assistance. As a result, some extremely effective progress has been made in stimulating the economic growth and social advancement of developing countries.

  The Fund can draw on the expertise and resources of the whole world, and not just on the skills, however great, of any one nation. [It is not necessary to] enlarge on how this helps in minimizing the endless difficulties of language, religion, culture and other elements which can arise in project implementation. (26 August 1971)

- The international community is showing an increasing preference for the multilateral approach when dealing with population questions. This is to be compared to the attitude towards development assistance generally, where the emphasis has from the outset been on bilateral programmes. (5 February 1973)

- Since 1946 the United Nations system has built up within its Specialized Agencies and related organizations, reservoirs of technical, scientific, educational, industrial, financial and linguistic skills (to mention only a few) which cannot be equalled by any country however rich or powerful. These reservoirs belong to the nations of the world. They are unlikely to ignore such a heritage. (29 October 1973)

• The first step towards improving population programmes is to recognize the need for integrated approaches by countries and by region, and to open up effective channels for inter-communication. The second step is to recognize the indivisible relationship between population and development and therefore to place population programming within the larger setting of the formulation and implementation of comprehensive development strategies.

No organizations outside the United Nations system have the capacity to mount such programmes. No bodies within the system are in such a key position as the [regional] Economic Commissions to help place national programmes within regional formats and to link regional formats with global strategies. (21 January 1974)

• Current trends show a steadily increasing demand for the Fund's services. . . . This rapid expansion of demand on the Fund testifies to the viability of the multilateral approach in this most sensitive of all matters, and to the acceptability of the Fund's own procedures, developed as they have been in co-operation with the countries for whom we work. Out of this co-operation, a momentum has been generated, and an atmosphere has been created in which it is possible to think in terms of solutions to problems which at one time seemed insoluble. (20 August 1974)

United Nations Agencies, UNFPA's Relationship With

• The Secretary-General and the Administrator of UNDP have decided that programmes undertaken by the Specialized Agencies and by UNICEF may now be financed by the Fund, and that the scope of its activities will be expanded to include forms of assistance which have not normally been financed under United Nations technical assistance programmes.

The approach to the [Fund's overall] programme will be interdisciplinary, and will be made in close co-operation with the United Nations and the Specialized Agencies, in accordance with the mandates which they have received from their respective legislative bodies. (10 November 1969)

• During most of the post-war years, the United Nations Secretariat, and in particular its Population Division and Statistical Office, had played an important role in assisting countries to collect and interpret relevant demographic statistics concerning their own populations. Although most of the relevant United Nations agencies' governing boards had, in the last few years prior to the Secretary-General's action [which established the Fund in 1967], given these organizations wide mandates in the field of population, the Secretary-General felt that their ability to deliver effective development assistance in the population field would be greatly enhanced by having a source of extra-budgetary funds for these purposes.

The main purposes of the United Nations Fund for Population Activities are [*inter alia*] . . . to help co-ordinate population programmes among various elements of the

United Nations system; and . . . to extend the capabilities of the relevant agencies of the United Nations within the framework of their respective mandates, and to provide them with the means for more efficient and effective assistance to member countries in planning, programming and implementing population projects. (16 October 1970)

• The Fund would like to assist programmes and projects that in no way duplicate the activities of the agencies and the regional Commissions of the United Nations. . . .

Therefore, if a project for assistance presented to the Fund does not duplicate programmes being undertaken by the United Nations agencies and its regional Commissions, and intends to promote better and efficient delivery of services, the Fund would be willing to consider such a project for funding. . . . (22 October 1970)

• UNFPA . . . has made arrangements to fund projects through UNICEF. In particular, where UNFPA has undertaken to meet some local costs, we have taken advantage in certain cases of UNICEF's capabilities in handling supplies, equipment, and funds.

A second step in our attempt to gain co-ordination inside the United Nations system has been that . . . the agencies [should] consult with . . . [UNDP Resident Representatives'] offices . . . in the planning stage of projects of which they have knowledge, so that we may not be faced with narrow sectoral requests which should have other components or should otherwise be broadened in an interdisciplinary way. (18 February 1971)

• The United Nations, the Specialized Agencies, and the Fund, as well as the requesting governments, must endeavour to improve the utilization of the allocations given by the Fund, in order to make a real impact on resolving population problems. (3 November 1971)

• UNFPA programming is . . . separate from UNDP programming, and there has never been a hint from UNFPA or UNDP that UNFPA population programmes might be promoted at the expense of UNDP's economic and social assistance. Mutual exchange of information about programming both at the headquarters and field levels is, of course, necessary, but there are absolutely no obligatory connections between the two types of assistance. (29 January 1973)

• Though there has been a relatively short passage of time since population began to be recognized as the important element it is in national advancement, considerable progress has been made, and much of it undoubtedly due to the Economic Commissions. It goes without saying that many of the national programmes owe their genesis to the regional work carried out by the Commissions. Now an even more vital role is emerging for the Economic Commissions in relation to population—that of providing the regional framework within which national programmes can be co-ordinated, expanded and assisted in supplementing each other's efforts, and of establishing and maintaining the international links which can lead to the development of global agreements on population. (21 January 1974)

• Much credit for the intensification of World Population Year programmes is due to the United Nations and its Specialized Agencies, which have greatly expanded their information-type activities in order to reach their own particular audiences and to add to the general availability of press and audio-visual material on population subjects. (4 March 1974)

• With the continuing support of the governments on whom we rely both as donors and recipients of assistance, the Fund has become established as an integral part of the United Nations pattern of assistance. (16 May 1974)

• The Fund serves as the link between the policymaking bodies of the United Nations and the actual programme implementation within a single country. And that is, of course, what the Fund is all about. Under the umbrella of the policymaking bodies of the United Nations, the Fund serves as a link, bringing into being, not just a commitment of financial resources but, with a commitment of many man-hours of dedicated work by UNFPA and other United Nations agency staff members as well, a wide variety of population projects in countries around the world. (9 July 1974)

• The UNFPA—which . . . works in close relationship with the United Nations Development Programme and the United Nations Population Division—regards its activities not as an isolated operation, but as an important part of the total mechanism of international co-operation. (20 August 1974)

• From time to time we convene meetings . . . of our Inter-Agency Consultative Committee, made up of representatives of UNFPA executing agencies throughout the United Nations system, called together by us to review, inter alia, project implementation and implementation ratios. (27 January 1975)

• [We] should like to make a brief comment on the status of the UNFPA in the United Nations system, recognizing [ECOSOC's] present preoccupation with the proposals for improvements in its structure. It is a pleasure . . . to confirm our present good working relations with the United Nations Development Programme, under which our separate identity is recognized in accordance with General Assembly resolution 3019 (XXVII).* The present semi-autonomous status of the Fund is of vital importance in preserving our flexible policies and approaches to population problems, which enable us to respond effectively to meeting the needs of each developing country, taking into account its individual situation and policies. This present status contributes significantly to reinforcing the support we receive from both our donors and recipients. (14 July 1975)

• The Fund has benefited from the close co-operation with the world-wide network of the UNDP and its support services.

  We are . . . mindful of the important contribution made by the United Nations Population Division, the Specialized Agencies and other organizations, in the development, with the Fund's support, of national programmes. (20 February 1976)

• UNFPA continues to collaborate in development programmes into which population activities can be integrated, particularly through our field staff and in collaboration with UNDP and other agencies and programmes. In such collaboration, UNFPA provides assistance for the population components in integrated programmes, while other

*18 December 1972.

development assistance bodies support the other components of integrated programmes as required.

We have continued our support for inter-agency activities, especially those that the General Assembly has recently singled out as requiring high priority attention by the entire United Nations system. Thus, we will participate fully in the apppraisal of the World Population Plan of Action being undertaken by the United Nations next year. The International Year of the Child has our full support and we are already actively collaborating with UNICEF in making this effort a success. We welcome the special attention being given by UNDP to rural development programmes and will contribute, within our mandate, to furthering this effort. In the field of technical co-operation between developing countries, we have already made considerable progress through utilization of local human and material resources in the recipient countries and we will participate fully in the preparations for the World Conference on TCDC*. . . . We will contribute to the development of measures for the benefit of the Sudano-Sahelian region insofar as population data collection, migration and other population programmes are concerned, and we plan to actively involve UNFPA in the follow-up action programmes growing out of the recent World Conference on Desertification.** (7 November 1977)

Co-ordination, the Need for and the Fund's Role in

• A good flow of information among donors and between donors and recipients is . . . an absolute essential in the world's approach to its population problems if decay and waste are to be avoided; and it is very obvious that we can ill afford them. (18 November 1969)

• Development assistance in the population field, particularly where the problem is responding to countries who wish to reduce high rates of fertility, is inevitably an interdisciplinary matter and requires the closest co-ordination between agencies. It is [our] belief that on the ability of the United Nations system to bring about this kind of co-ordination, more than on any other single factor, its success in the population field will depend. Certainly it was one of the Secretary-General's major purposes in setting up the Fund and in entrusting its administration to UNDP, and is one of our donors' major purposes in making contributions to the Fund, to have it serve to increase co-ordination among the population programmes of the various United Nations agencies. We are very serious about trying to carry out this responsibility. We are, moreover, currently experimenting with methods of interrelating inputs by various United Nations agencies with a national programme in a coherent overall framework. (16 October 1970)

• The Fund would like to assist programmes and projects that in no way duplicate the activities of the agencies and the regional Commissions of the United Nations in this area.

*Held in September 1978 in Buenos Aires, Argentina.
**Held from 29 August - 9 September 1977 in Nairobi, Kenya.

Since the resources available to the Fund are limited, we are careful in allocating available [resources] only to activities that lead to co-ordinated effort rather than duplication. (22 October 1970)

• We have sought to promote co-ordination inside the United Nations family [in several ways]. . . . In the first instance, we have convened meetings every six months of an Inter-Agency Consultative Committee consisting of agency representatives, including the United Nations, ILO, FAO, UNESCO, WHO, World Bank, UNICEF and the World Food Programme. With these representatives, we have openly and frankly discussed our problems, our policies and programmes. We have received many suggestions from the agencies and these we have sought to take into account whenever possible.

A second step in our attempt to gain co-ordination inside the United Nations system has been that we have instructed the agencies that we wish them to consult with [UNDP Resident Representatives'] offices and the Population Programme Officers, when present and available, in the planning stage of projects of which they have knowledge, so that we may not be faced with narrow sectoral requests which should have other components or should otherwise be broadened in an interdisciplinary way. (18 February 1971).

• After nearly two years of operational activities in close association with the United Nations, UNDP and the Specialized Agencies and a number of bilateral and non-governmental organizations, [we are] convinced that the imperative need is for "co-ordination". The more we can bring together the technical competencies and resources of the various organizations, including the World Bank and UNICEF, and concentrate our resources in joint endeavours, particularly at the country level, the closer we will come to achieving a worldwide awareness among governments and peoples of the paramount importance of recognizing population problems and of taking the necessary measures to cope with them. (3 November 1971)

• Since population problems, and hence their solutions, are multi-sectoral and multi-disciplinary, population programmes have often involved a number of United Nations agencies. It was thus only natural that the Fund should feel responsible for attempting to co-ordinate interrelating components of assistance furnished through a number of organizations in the United Nations system. . . . We are now taking further steps to increase the cohesiveness of the country, regional and global programmes we are funding. Several agencies at our request are now presenting all their regional, inter-regional and global projects to us in a single package so that with them we may make sure they form a coherent whole.

We have sought to co-ordinate our programmes with those of other donor agencies in the population field. On a country level, where we were qualified to do so, we have taken a leading role as co-ordinator among all external assistance agencies. (14 June 1973)

• The . . . number of inter-governmental, interagency and other meetings of real importance to the Fund is very high. Beyond sessions of the General Assembly, ECOSOC, the Governing Council, and the Population Commission, those of many of the co-ordinating bodies chaired by the United Nations and many chaired by UNDP must be attended, as must, for example, the most important meetings on population held by OECD* and other international organizations outside the United Nations system. Attendance at meetings specifically devoted to population matters is not simply a representational matter; it permits co-ordination to be achieved and friction avoided in many important matters. (14 January 1974)

- At [its] fifty-fourth session in May 1973, ECOSOC defined the aims and purposes of UNFPA, and these have been the mainstream of our policies since that time. In line with the ECOSOC mandate in this and other resolutions by both ECOSOC and the General Assembly** to promote co-operation and co-ordination among all agencies in the United Nations system, we have intensified our efforts in this area. We have continued to find the Inter-Agency Consultative Committee a valuable co-ordination body by which agency suggestions and views on the manner of implementation and programming procedures of the UNFPA can be made.(9 July 1974)

- Our . . . role as co-ordinator of global population activities . . . no doubt goes back in part to the first General Assembly resolution concerning the United Nations Fund for Population Activities—2815 (XXVI) of December 1971—in which the General Assembly expressed its conviction "that the United Nations Fund for Population Activities should play a leading role in the United Nations system in promoting population programmes . . .", and also to the Economic and Social Council resolution of 1973—1763 (LIV)—which stated that the aims and purposes of UNFPA should be "to promote co-ordination in planning and programming". . . . (27 January 1975)

- It is necessary to consult as many substantial viewpoints as exist and to work with people and their institutions, official and unofficial, as closely as possible. (17 April 1975)

- UNFPA is . . . acting as a clearinghouse for information on requests [for multi-bilateral funds] from non-governmental organizations as well as a co-ordination centre for such activities to ensure that donors do not provide overlapping or duplicating funds. (19 June 1975)

[In a speech in December 1975 at a joint FAO-UNFPA meeting in Rome, the Fund's Deputy Executive Director, Halvor Gille, further outlined the contribution of the UNFPA in the co-ordination process. He stated:

"Regular consultations have been established with major bilateral organizations to explore the possibilities for joint funding or other forms of collaboration in specific country programmes. We may have the programme capacity and the projects—they may have the money. We may contribute with the population components—they may cover the requirements in the broader development areas such as rural development, health and community development. We may monitor progress in implementation and make our field staff available—they may participate in evaluation. In this way we can broaden our role in meeting the needs of the countries more effectively in spite of our shortage of resources."]

*Organisation for Economic Co-operation and Development.
**ECOSOC 1084 (XXXIX), ECOSOC 1763 (LIV), GA 2211 (XXI) and GA 3019 (XXVII).

• We have . . . initiated the review and assessment of regional, interregional and global activities supported by UNFPA in the past, with a view to developing an overall, integrated strategy for the future, as requested by the [UNDP Governing] Council. Our plans in this regard have been discussed with the United Nations and the Specialized Agencies concerned at the Inter-Agency Consultative Committee meeting, and we are planning to convene two meetings of this Committee in 1977, particularly to have further consultations on this matter. (28 January 1977)

Global Assistance, Changing Patterns in

New Trends in Population Programmes

• The Fund's initial programmes laid heavy emphasis on the importance of the work of the United Nations Population Division in research, training and advisory services in demography. (3 November 1971)

• We are [now—in mid-1976] moving through three phases of population assistance:

(1) Traditional technical assistance, that is, transfer of technical know-how, through the services of long-term experts and the build-up of the capacity of the organizations in the United Nations system;

(2) Financial support to assist governments and non-governmental bodies to expand their activities; and

(3) Phasing out of assistance or foreign experts as appropriate bodies at the country level are progressively taking over the full responsibilities for the programmes concerned.

Initially, of course, we concentrated on the first phase, but we are increasingly reducing our support in this area. A number of recipient countries no longer require the assistance of international experts to carry out population programmes—there are an increasing number of national experts in these countries to direct and manage such programmes. What these countries do require, instead, is financial support to intensify the pace of their own efforts. (27 July 1976)

• There is wider and deeper international agreement than ever before [on population issues] . . . [a] practical consensus whose elements [are]:

First, family planning. This is the part of the field of population activities which for most people in the industrialized countries symbolizes—and is sometimes taken for—the whole field. There is no universal agreement that the present rate of world population growth is too high, and [we] do not expect that there will be.

The right of access to the means of contraception is acknowledged almost universally today, though for millions of people, particularly in the rural areas of the developing world, the right remains without meaning because they have neither the means nor the information to avail themselves of it.

The second element of the emerging consensus is the general agreement that population factors cannot be considered in isolation, but only as part of the fabric of socio-economic development. . . . Eighty-three governments have now passed to their central planning bodies the responsibility for integrating population factors into development planning. . . . The important exceptions to this general agreement are the industrialized countries, in most of which the policy implications of population trends are matters for piecemeal consideration by different governmental departments, if indeed they are considered at all. A full consensus requires a recognition of responsibility in this area from developed and developing countries alike.

A further element of the consensus is acceptance of the wide range of activities which can be classified under the heading of "population". The collection and analysis of demographic statistics has been a valuable tool for making government decisions. . . .

Another aspect of population activities is the study and regulation of migratory patterns.

As a final example of the broad sweep of population activities today, we may take the concern with factors indirectly affecting the birth rate. Mortality, particularly infant mortality, is a concern for all developing countries, for its own sake as well as for its demographic effects. . . . Similarly, it has been shown that social factors have important effects on fertility—employment, education and the position of women, among them. (30 March 1977)

• In the early stages [of the Fund's operations], there was considerable difference in the kinds of programme assistance requested from the regions.

For instance, the Asian and Pacific countries opted heavily for family planning projects, while countries of Africa required assistance mainly for census and data collection and analysis. Countries of the Middle East asked for assistance and data collection and migration studies, while Latin American countries needed assistance to undertake studies related to population and socio-economic development.

By 1974, however, programme patterns in the geographic regions began to shift from basic population data collection activities to fertility limitation programmes. Since then, there has been an increase in the number of requests for funds for family planning linked with the maternal and child health services. (5 July 1977)

• Population policy is becoming more complex. The spectrum of concerns across the world is extremely wide. (8 August 1977)

• UNFPA-supported data collection activities are leading to a deeper understanding and a more thorough analysis of population problems, which, in turn, will bring about the formulation and adoption of appropriate population and related socio-economic policies in many countries. As a result, we can expect a further growth in demand for projects related to family planning, maternal and child health care, and other measures.

Along with the growing awareness of population as a key factor in promoting national prosperity, governments have also shown an increasing desire to make their population policies more comprehensive, and to directing their actions to many fronts rather than limiting themselves to considering only one or two demographic variables. Thus, they have shown definite interest in the geographical distribution of their population and in internal and international migration, in addition to the more "traditional" concerns with fertility and mortality.

In response to this trend, UNFPA has begun to support, or has under discussion, requests for assistance for studies in internal migration . . . and to pilot schemes on population redistribution and settlement of populations from congested or scattered areas. . . . In making support available, the Fund realizes that undertakings in these fields may often involve capital-intensive efforts. Yet the fact remains that nearly all the governments in the developing world have expressed dissatisfaction with the distribution of their population and a desire to adopt measures to resolve such problems, although the number of requests for assistance in this regard has so far been rather limited. It is our view that UNFPA has an obligation to respond to requests, albeit with great caution. [We] would like to assure the [Governing] Council that the Fund's policy has always been, and will continue to be, to support only activities in which the population participate voluntarily.

Another area of increasing government interest in UNFPA assistance is population activities in connection with rural development and community development. Requests are under consideration for support of research on the population implications of rural development and community development. . . .

The trend towards diversification of UNFPA does not mean that decreasing emphasis is being given to family planning as the main area of support. More and more countries are attaching high priority to family planning, in recognition of the fact that availability and provision of such services are important elements in promoting primary health care, in improving the status of women, and in securing basic human rights. But the measures required are being broadened and diversified. For example, UNFPA is increasingly being called upon to support programmes on infant and maternal mortality with the direct objective of contributing to the regulation and reduction of fertility. . . . In other cases, such programmes are supported with the main objective of reducing infant mortality and maternal mortality and morbidity, while the influence upon fertility is only incidental and not a primary objective. . . . (21 June 1978)

Regional Variations: Africa, Asia and the Pacific, Latin America, and the Middle East

• The high levels of fertility prevailing in most countries in the Asian region are the legacy of a long cultural tradition which has encouraged large-sized families. Indeed, it is only in recent history that high fertility has ceased to be essential for the survival of the species. And even now, in many areas death rates remain sufficiently high to preclude any thought of having fewer children. Nor can we ignore the fact that in rural areas a large family is still viewed as an economic asset. However, we have tended to assume that couples who want large families are behaving in an irrational fashion when, in fact, they merely do not share our values regarding desirable family size. (1 November 1972)

• Among all the regions of the world, Asia is the most sophisticated in its experience and policymaking in regard to family planning. Almost every Asian country has population programmes of one kind or another. The motivational stage has been passed long ago. The concept is understood. The principal concern is the delivery of general, medical, and technical information and the timely provision of equipment to support action programmes . . . and, of course, the training of qualified personnel at all levels to administer these programmes. . . . The Economic Commission for Asia and the Far East is already providing an endless source of advice and guidance in helping to overcome such organizational difficulties and in raising the standards of training in all aspects of population.

The Economic Commission for Africa, which is taking such a prominent part in the formulation and implementation of demographic-type projects, has quite a different set of circumstances in front of it. Few countries in Africa have the basic data on which to formulate sound economic policies. Twenty-one countries are engaged in their first census, others are carrying them out after a long space of time.

This type of programme is the happy exception to most population work. Immediate results can be obtained. Practical programmes can be initiated to help provide the organizational structures for data collection, analyses and application. To help member countries through the preparatory phase and determine the most useful programmes for societies which can range from nomadic communities to urban dwellers in high rise apartments, is the present demanding task. . . . The development of population policies related to economic and social planning still lies ahead.

The Latin American situation is infinitely more complex, involving a mix of ideological, cultural, political and religious elements not so pronounced in other parts of the world. It is greatly to the credit of the Economic Commission for Latin America and the Latin American Demographic Centre that they have made such a substantial contribution to the advancement of demographic work, thus paving the way for the dramatic changes in governmental attitudes we have witnessed in the last few years. . . .

The dimensions of the population task are further exemplified by the problems being encountered in the European countries, which the Economic Commission for Europe is studying with such care, and, to an extent, in the industrialized countries in general. Once again, population considerations take on another shape and form, as governments view the changes in society arising from internal migration, increases in urbanization, the need for urban renewal, fluctuations in resource supply, and ageing populations producing less and demanding more. (21 January 1974)

• We do not talk any more in terms of family planning as an answer to population growth, because we realize now that there is far more to population than family planning. In many parts of the world, particularly in Asia, it is indeed vital to slow down the rate of population growth, but [we] think that it is now realized that the number of children a family has depends on a very complex interaction, in which levels of education, the quality of housing, and health and social security services play a part, and which is tied closely to the form which overall social and economic development is taking. (2 April 1974)

• A real consensus is growing, based on the acceptance of what might be called the "third view" of population—that it is neither to be ignored as irrelevant nor treated as a more important factor, but accepted as a significant factor in the development process.

In the development of this consensus, Asian countries should naturally play a leading part. Much of the world's expertise was generated here, and many of the more successful programmes are operated here. Above all, only Asian countries have the sophisticated approach which is the result of many years of experience in confronting the peculiar problems of individual countries. Asian countries are well aware that there can be no blanket solution, and that even within countries, programmes must be adapted to take account of local needs. In considering the World Population Plan of Action, Asian governments can take a lead in acknowledging local, national and regional differences while insisting on the need for a global approach; because only they have the necessary depth of first-hand experience. (9 May 1974)

• A new force has come on the scene, in the form of nations rich in the one natural resource which is both easy to develop and is absolutely essential to the functioning of modern society.

Some of these are Arab countries. Still developing in terms of the application of their wealth, these nations nevertheless have the opportunity to be of real help to others which are experiencing difficulty in making full use of their own resources. As donors, they are in a unique position, since they understand from their own experience some of the problems of development. (18 May 1974)

• Some of the regional trends [as of 1975]:

In Latin America there has been an almost *seven fold* increase in the past two years in requests for projects in maternal and child health and family planning.

In North Africa, the bulk of UNFPA assistance is now requested for support of family planning programmes. . . . In Western Asia, requests for UNFPA assistance have trebled in the past two years, with the emphasis on the development of basic population data required for social and economic development planning, but with increasing interest in family health and planning. . . .

In Sub-Saharan Africa, strong interest continues in demographic data collection and analysis, and there is now also discernible a growing interest in family planning as part of their efforts to strengthen basic health services.

In Asia and the Pacific, over 95% of our project requests are for support to family health and planning programmes and related communication and education activities for fertility reduction. The amounts we are providing for Asia have doubled since 1973. And by the end of 1975, UNFPA will have a substantive multisectoral population programme in almost every country in Asia. Moreover, most programmes in Asia are now in a well-advanced stage of actual implementation.

Another important trend in requests—a global trend, although most manifest in Asia—is for assistance in meeting local costs and in providing equipment and supplies, as distinguished from the provision of expertise. Another trend is governments' requests of assistance to be directly implemented by them rather than by outside executing agencies. These trends, it is to be noted, are divergent from the traditional forms and modalities of technical assistance. (27 February 1975)

• Indications are that recipient countries are committing more of their resources to population programmes. . . . (19 June 1975)

• Family planning programmes in Asia . . . have gone as far as they can in many places through conventional means. Further acceptance is to be won as a result of changes in ways of looking at the world among a large class of the rural poor. For this to happen, important changes in approaches in development are needed. In particular, closer contact is needed between development workers and the people with whom they work, and much closer involvement of the individual in development schemes, as an agent of development as well as an "acceptor".

High priority areas of funding in the various regions [are]:

In Asia and the Pacific, our assistance may concentrate on institutionalizing and implementing the population policies established in these countries. In family planning, greater attention should be devoted to the planning and design of programmes, to innovative approaches, to training, and to management and evaluation aspects.

In Latin America, high priority should be given to supporting the collection and analysis of the data required for population programme planning. In the field of fertility regulation, support for the maternal and child health approach may continue to be of great importance, but other channels should be given increasing attention. Planning, managerial and training components of programmes also need support.

In West Asia, assistance in data collection through censuses, sample surveys, vital statistics and migration studies are important requirements, as well as the inclusion of fertility services in integrated health programmes.

Finally, in Africa, continued assistance will be required to improve the weak population data base, particularly through support to census-taking in countries which have never taken a census or taken only one. Support for training of various kinds is another high priority area, as well as assistance for delivery of fertility services in existing health services. (21 November 1975)

• Middle Eastern countries have also shown greater interest in family health and family planning, and the Fund has supported sizeable programmes in that region since 1975. . . . In this area, the UNFPA is assisting large projects related to family planning as well as other population activities such as demographic studies, censuses and strengthening of governments' planning and statistics institutions.

Most of the UNFPA funds allocated to projects in Sub-Saharan Africa, however, continue to support basic population data collection activities, though, over the last year, the number of family health and family planning projects in the region has increased substantially. This changing pattern of the UNFPA resource allocation seems to suggest that after their demographic capabilities have been strengthened, many of the developing countries feel ready to take greater action in the area of family planning. (5 July 1977)

• Population policy is becoming more complex. The spectrum of concerns across the world is extremely wide; migration is now a major concern, especially in Africa and Latin America; infant mortality is especially important in Africa, and fertility limitation in Asia. (8 August 1977)

• The bulk of the funds for population activities have come from rich industrialized countries for allocation to the developing world, following the traditional North-South pattern. But we were recently able to introduce an innovation by awakening an interest in the capital rich countries of the Arab World—who themselves have no problem of overpopulation (quite the contrary, in some cases)—to pick up the tab for population programmes in poorer Arab countries who do. We have hopes that this example of horizontal aid—neighbourly assistance—will spread in other areas such as Latin America, Africa and the Caribbean where oil has changed the economic scene. (27 September 1977)

Chapter 14

POPULATION CONCERNS, SPECIAL DIMENSIONS OF

An Overview

- [The] difference between population problems in developed and developing countries [is]:

    (1) The population problems of the developing world are very consequential for the welfare of their people: too rapid growth rates threaten their aspirations for improved living standards, education, health, nutrition, jobs, and "modernization" in general; and increasing concentration of population makes for different problems of employment, housing, education, acculturation, and assimilation.

    (2) The population problems of the developed world may be less recognized and less consequential in the short run, but are still highly important: distribution of population, the status of disadvantaged groups and environmental issues are distinctively important there. (4 November 1970)

- Population growth cannot be stopped, or even slowed down, at short notice or by sudden decision.

    There is good reason to believe that if we can bring together the experience and the skills and the will of all peoples, we can still materially improve our prospects for the future. [We] say "all peoples" because, owing to its effects on practically every aspect of human life, the population problem transcends differences of ideology and belief, and demands the attention and efforts of all mankind. (26 August 1971)

- [We] should . . . like to emphasize the . . . importance of universal participation in tackling population problems. The more countries that are involved, the more likely we are to find the solution. (9 December 1971)

- Though we have no time to spare, we still *have* time to take reasonably effective measures to deal with population problems, provided we are responsible enough to do so. (14 February 1973-B)

- The situation is critical, but not hopeless. . . . The point to realize is that our decisions today will count and that it is important to make the right ones.

162

How do you get people to take daily heed and preventive action to avert a potential and not too well-defined crisis in thirty years' time? (15 February 1973)

• Setting short-term targets for the achievement of population goals . . . is difficult to do, given the long-term nature of population problems. . . . (23 March 1973)

• Implementing population programmes is not a unique activity—it is only the population problem in the larger sense that is unique. (6 May 1973)

• There is no area in which more change is called for, and more re-thinking is necessary, than that of population. And there is also no area in which misinformation and misunderstanding flourish more easily.

Such problems as population and environmental pollution—matters which touch the very bases of human existence on this planet—do not yield simplistic solutions. They have to be assessed and approached with a profound appreciation of their complexity and with equally profound respect for the rights of people. On the question of population, these rights are even more jealously guarded against importunate meddling from outside because it concerns the most intimate of personal relationships. (7 July 1973)

• The nature of population assistance has been such as to open new lines of thought among development administrators. We touch here the most sensitive area of human activity, the act of love and the life mystique that surrounds it. In approaching it, great delicacy and care must be used, the greatest respect shown to the deepest feelings of the people concerned. Because it is such a personal matter, it must be dealt with on a personal level. Each couple must decide for itself what action to take about family planning; and this decision depends on many factors of which we know little. Even the most remote of administrators finds that a population programme cannot be dealt with in the same way as a bridge or a dam project. (25 August 1973)

• It seems that action to limit population growth *on its own* has little or no effect on birth rates, whereas combined with other measures of social and economic development quite dramatic results have been noted. From this, some have concluded that there is no case for special action on population.

However, as we are all now aware, there is no case for leaving to chance what can be brought about by design. (18 October 1973)

• The dimensions of the population task are further exemplified by the problems being encountered in the European countries . . . and to an extent in the industrialized countries in general. Once again, population considerations take on another shape and form as governments view the changes in society arising from internal migration, increases in urbanization, the need for urban renewal, fluctuations in resource supply, and ageing populations producing less and demanding more.

[We are] convinced that unless this pattern [of population needs region by region] is seen as a whole, there is very little hope that [the regional Economic Commissions'] efforts to improve the regional situation, that UNFPA's efforts to mobilize technical co-operation forces, and that government efforts to cope with national conditions will, in the end, prove to be little more than palliative measures which leave the root causes untouched. (21 January 1974)

- No one can afford to be disinterested, because it is the interest of everyone that is at stake. Population is you and me and our children and our friends and our colleagues and our acquaintances, our way of life and our hopes for the future. It is not something that only concerns the other fellow and his habits. (6 March 1974)

- The realization is spreading . . . that population problems are not confined to one area of the world. In the industrialized world their public faces are different, and they are called overcrowding, crime, environmental damage, transport crises and racial clashes. But they are problems of population none the less. Another aspect of this new understanding of population problems is that none can be solved without assistance and understanding. They are too vast and complex to be tackled alone. This is reflected in the rapid increase in international population assistance and in the move towards consensus in population matters. . . . Each country will follow its own path, but all will benefit from the experience of others. (2 April 1974)

- It is difficult to over-estimate the importance of the individual in matters of population. The figures which we read and the lines we see drawn on charts are the result of millions of individual decisions, to have or not to have children, to move from country to city, to seek work in another country. The most sophisticated policies will not succeed unless this is understood, and unless the policymakers allow for the complexity of the factors which affect personal decisions. (18 August 1974)

- Of all areas of development and social change, population is one of the most complex and perhaps the most sensitive. We have to understand clearly the complicated interrelationships of fertility, mortality, morbidity, migration, and the growth, distribution and structure of the population, and economic and social factors. We have to be sure that family planning and maternal and child health services are formulated and delivered consistently with these factors in mind. But above all these, population deals with the most delicate of human relationships—the act of love, the family and the mystique which surrounds it. In approaching these areas of human activity, the greatest care must be used, and the greatest respect shown to the feelings of those concerned. Whenever it is a personal matter, it must be dealt with on a personal level; projects in population cannot be approached in a mechanical way. We are dealing with individuals. That is something we must never forget.

[We] do not believe that it is possible to underestimate the challenge and the significance of this moment. To solve the population problems of countries will require more from us in a shorter time than ever before in the history of mankind. It will require a long-sustained effort, without any guarantee that the final aim will be achieved. Yet without the effort, can there be any prospect for a just and peaceful world in the future? The ancient philosophers of Asia, in their wisdom, stressed the need for a balance and harmony between man and his world. Without a sane and orderly approach to the problems of population, there can be no balance and no harmony. (20 August 1974)

- In population . . . it takes two generations for a successful policy of population stabilization to take effect. At the United Nations Fund for Population Activities, we freely acknowledge that we cannot affect today's problems—but insist that we must think for the next generation, and start planning and action now. (15 October 1974)

- By its very nature, population will remain a pivotal issue in national planning for the foreseeable future. (17 April 1975)

- Population will certainly be a perennial problem for man as long as he inhabits the earth.

  Population matters are exceedingly complex. Population action is not simply the distribution of contraceptives. We have learned that we must also help some countries to lower their infant mortality rates and take the first censuses in their history. We must help countries solve special problems, such as . . . migration and the need to increase skilled manpower. We must assist Ministries of Education and journalists and non-governmental organizations in Asia and Latin America and in the Middle East and Africa to understand population matters. (19 June 1975)

- There is an old saying that one man is a person, a thousand are a community, and a million are a statistic. Only a few years ago, population was a similar abstraction. The experts talked in millions, if not in billions; growth rates seemed the most important fact of life; and it seemed that you could not open a book on population without being confronted with rows of digits. Luckily for us, anxiety about population sizes and the growth rates considered in isolation has diminished in recent years and our fundamental concern for people has reasserted itself. In recent years, valuable connections have been made between population growth and the health, education, living standards and general well-being of individuals, and we have learned that growth rates are not to be affected by merely mechanical means. We have broadened our scope in population activities to consider the forces behind the growth and movement of population and to consider the effect of the individual's decisions upon his family, his community and his environment. (25 September 1975)

- Interest in population is not a concern with the figures on a chart or the curves on a graph alone, however important they may be, but essentially an involvement with the future of humanity itself. (21 November 1975)

- Population was for many years a subject of such delicacy to nations and to individuals that it was thought suitable for international discussion and action only at the level of collecting and analysing figures—a job which the Population Division of the United Nations has done superbly since 1947.

  We are aware now that all problems are interlocked—food, housing, health, population, but we also know that we must attack wherever we can find an opening. It is [our] submission that the development of population activities over the last ten years represents such an opening. (30 March 1977)

- To every generation before our own, an increasing population was a sign of national strength. To friends and enemies alike, it demonstrated prosperity and well-being, and the defeat, however temporary, of disease and famine.

The position today is almost entirely reversed. Nations with high population growth rates are coming to perceive them as a liability rather than an asset, and nearly two-thirds of the world's population live under governments which desire a lower rate of population growth. In the developing countries, where incomes are low and population growth rates high, the figure is four out of five. . . .

Despite enormous efforts and solid economic and social achievements, in most developing countries the needs of growing populations have not been met. Meanwhile, in the industrialized countries where population growth is low, living standards are generally high. In the midst of a world of apparent plenty, poverty remains the rule for the vast majority of people in the developing world.

Poverty, and everything that it implies—insufficient food, inadequate housing, ill health, poor education, little comfort and less hope—has complex connections with population growth. The persistence of high rates of growth and low incomes has brought shifts in thinking in many areas of economic and social life besides population—so much so that this period may well be seen by historians of the future as one not of temporary disturbance but of fundamental change in human institutions. . . .

[The] essential facts of population growth should be the most effective means of persuading us that we are in an era of epochal change, and a spur to our efforts to meet its challenge. For a start, we should redouble our efforts to achieve slower population growth sooner than the projections indicate, by all the means at our command.

The result of unprecedented population growth and the deficiencies of conventional development strategies both in slowing it down and turning it to productive purposes has been to challenge conventional approaches. . . .

In particular, the thinking which linked population growth and economic development in a linear way—more population growth would mean less growth in income per capita—was by the end of the sixties already giving way in many countries to a broader view which connected population with each of several other factors in development and which saw demographic growth as only one of many population issues.

Since the United Nations Fund for Population Activities started operations in 1969, this change in thinking has accelerated. Over the eight years of the Fund's existence, we have become and been made aware of the depth and complexity of population issues.

[For example:]

First, we have had evidence of the growing urgency with which population is viewed. When we began operations, we found only a few countries interested in obtaining population assistance. As global consciousness has risen, so have the number of requests. Today there are few developing countries which have *not* asked for our support; the ideological objections which seemed so important only a few years ago have been transcended. . . .

This growing urgency reflects a concern, not merely with population growth as such, but with the elements of population growth, distribution and structure, and with how they may be affected by programmes in all areas of population and development. . . .

Second has been the rapid acceptance of population as a vital component in the machinery of development. For example, early family planning programmes were designed for the well-being of women; later, their purpose was eventually to slow population growth according to the linear connection made between population and economic growth. . . . As such, they had only limited impact and acceptance in developing countries. From the beginning, the Fund had assumed that population covers a far wider area than family planning, that population growth had to be seen within the context of each country's economic and social circumstances, and that programmes should reflect national needs. . . .

Countries which only a few years ago took the attitude that intervention was not only unnecessary but probably harmful to development now have extensive programmes. Some are avowedly undertaken with the intention of lowering population growth rates as a precondition of development . . .; in others . . . population policies are aimed at reducing mortality and morbidity and increasing the life expectancy of the people. . . .

[The] third point has to do with population as part of the general approach to development. Thinking in developing countries is re-examining theories of economic growth *per se*. More attention is being given to meeting the needs of the population at large by the provision of services such as health, education and employment, both to improve their well-being and to realize their potential as producers.

It has been noted that the problem of balancing economic resources and population growth can be solved effectively in countries where the benefits of development most closely answer the basic needs of human beings. . . .

These [traditional methods of family planning, community health care, secure land tenure, concern for the status of women and their involvement in development, and a high level of participation among both men and women in the political and administrative process] are the essentials of a secure and dignified existence—the "basic needs" of human beings. It has frequently been observed that lower fertility goes along with lower infant mortality, higher literacy, and opportunities for women to be employed outside the home, among other factors. The "basic needs" strategy blends these elements into a coherent whole. . . .

[The] fourth point will serve to illustrate the third. Eight years ago, little attention was paid to the widespread availability of contraceptive methods. Yet we know that unless contraceptives are made available to people in urban and rural areas, family planning programmes are hardly likely to succeed. The trend is to bring family planning services closer to clients by using local groups and people, by using networks already in place and integrated with the culture of their societies. Already, in many countries, contraceptive services are now routinely taken to villages, where most of the Third World's population lives, and into the increasingly crowded urban areas, by a variety of carriers—midwives, health visitors, housewives recruited for the purpose, and, increasingly, through commercial outlets. . . .

As demand for and the volume of UNFPA assistance has increased, so has the proportion of resources for population programmes which comes from recipient countries themselves—and this is [the] fifth point. Developing countries with quite small national inputs only a few years ago are now operating greatly expanded programmes for which most of the funding is internal. External assistance, though it has increased in size, is now a small proportion of the total.

Sixth, the placing of family planning programmes within the government structure has reflected their changing position. Eight years ago, family planning programmes undertaken for demographic reasons were normally vertical structures, though connected to health ministries. Today, family planning programmes, whether interventionist or not, are more likely to be integrated in the wider context of maternal and child health care, which is itself part of the total package of health services. Indeed, family planning is increasingly seen as a social welfare service.

Seventh, we have experienced a remarkable increase in the volume and nature of population education and information. Eight years ago, if it existed at all, population education was likely to cover only reproduction and the basic techniques of family planning. Today, education and information is offered to children and adults, both inside and outside formal education, in churches, workplaces and health centres. It is likely to cover not only human sexuality and reproduction, but the economic and environmental impact of population growth. It may also cover home economics, hygiene, and nutrition. . . .

Eighth, the knowledge has taken root that censuses, surveys and analysis of the resulting data are the indispensable basis for planning population or any other kind of development programmes. When we started operations, many of the newly-independent countries . . . had never taken censuses. . . .

Finally, changing perception of the significance of population activities has drawn together the strands of policymaking and implementation in this area. Central government bodies in eighty-three developing countries now have the responsibility of integrating population factors with development planning.

It is possible to discern, in the changes which have already taken place, and in the fresh ideas and approaches which are emerging, attempts not only to cope with present problems but to anticipate and avoid those which might arise in the future. This exercise of the distinctively human quality of foresight will have its greatest effect in a generation's time; we may then see the full benefits of a slowly expanding population in which population services of all kinds are part of the general fabric of society. . . .

In our experience, in the principles which underlie our programmes and in the priorities which have been set for our activities, it may be seen that the Fund and the governments with which we work—whether as donors, as recipients or as members of our governing body—are acting consistently with a perception of the transition from one era to another.

Three conclusions may be drawn from what [has been said] so far. . . .

The first is that governments, donors and agencies executing projects alike are most likely to achieve success in their programmes if they address themselves to the basic needs of those whom they serve, the people of the developing countries. In our experience, this approach can offer at least as good a ratio of costs to benefits in those things which can be quantified, and the indications are that it is a much more rewarding approach in the areas which cannot be quantified.

A second conclusion, which follows from the first, is that there must be a very strong element of participation in decision-making by those most directly affected. At the national level, we have found that while central direction can be very effective or even essential in starting or giving the necessary impetus to programmes, effective delivery cannot be sustained unless there is active participation by the community, right down to the smallest social units, the village or the street. Regardless of the political system, the important element is participation. If this is present, though the practical rewards may be few, the psychological satisfaction gained from being included in decision-making is a powerful motive to help in making programmes effective.

At the international level, the same principle is to be found in respect for national needs. No blueprint for international assistance will ever be effective unless adapted with the fullest participation of each country affected. . . .

[The] third conclusion is the necessity, both at national and international levels, for the political will to effect change. Facts are useless without energy and vision to turn them into policies and programmes for the future. In population we have been seeing this process of energization taking place in country after country during the last few years. . . .

There are no fixed paths to a just global balance between population and economic resources. Each country, even each individual, will find the best path if allowed the means to do so, and this depends very much on the ability of administrators, governments and international organizations to listen, to determine what the needs really are, and to respond effectively.

A pattern thus emerges. Both in national and international affairs, success in meeting the problems of the future seems to depend ultimately on the responsiveness of society to the real needs of its members, and its ability to adapt its structures accordingly.

The quality of foresight which only humans possess carries a complementary responsibility; it must be used wisely. We have come to various recognitions in the last few years. These recognitions have shown us that we have many choices. We can see the possibility, for example, of a world in which humans and the humane values are given their full importance. But other, much less pleasant futures are possible—the developed countries retreating behind their economic and physical barriers; civil or international warfare for the control of essential resources; population growth limited not by choice but by starvation and disease. The world is changing. We are in the transition from one era to another. Attainment of a world fit to live in demands keener perception and deeper insights into these changes. (2 June 1977)

- The increase in numbers now demands a qualitative change in our search for solutions. The magnitude of the need for international assistance, the business the Fund is in, must be increased many times before population growth can begin to be brought into balance with the available resources. But that is not the only need. The way we respond to these magnitudes, our appreciation of the nature of the consequences of population growth where it is unsustainable—in other words, the values we use to understand the population problem need change. What is called for is a change in the quality of our understanding of the equitable use and distribution of the resources of the earth and the level of life at which people exist.

Population, therefore, is, in a very real sense, the problem of problems. (27 September 1977)

- Certainly the question of population growth cannot be left to chance or the forces of natural selection. (26 March 1978)

- While [current] thinking about development exhibits uncertainty, the conceptualization of the population field shows increasing maturity and sophistication.

In working with . . . countries, we are not simply extrapolating from the past, but looking toward a desirable future. We recognize that we cannot predict the future. We believe, however, that we can, by our actions now, help to mold the future. If we do not take the opportunities open to us and the nations of the developing world to create a desired and desirable demographic future, the road ahead will be more difficult. (3 April 1978)

- The present decade has marked what can be described as a quantum leap in the recognition among developing countries of the importance of understanding, and of consciously trying to cope with, population issues. One cannot help but be encouraged by the changes which have taken place over the last few years. What is now lacking in the developing world is sufficient amounts of the technical, financial and administrative means required for the translation of policies and principles into concrete country-wide programmes. The limits are now far less those of awareness of the problems and the recognition of the urgency to take action, but far more those of the need for resources and for the broad managerial skills to implement and execute programmes.

[We] should like to point out two major trends we have seen in the field of population since the World Population Conference was held four years ago: On the one hand, the growing desire to enlarge the magnitude and scope of action with respect to population issues; and, on the other hand, the increasing need to establish closer linkage between population activities and other economic and social development efforts. Thus, today, more than ever before, an awareness is prevailing that population problems are so intimately linked to all of the other large socio-economic problems that humanity must face, that none of them can usefully be considered and dealt with in isolation. (21 June 1978)

Population Projections

• The world population figure [is] moving inexorably upwards from its three and a half thousand million people recorded at the beginning of this decade, to at least six and a half thousand million projected for the year 2000.

The figures compel attention if you put them against the projections of the earth's capacity to keep on supplying the food, the water and the other necessary elements of life. (26 August 1971)

• It took all of recorded history until 1830 for the world to acquire its first one thousand million human beings. It took only one hundred years, between 1830 and 1930, for the second thousand million. Only thirty years, between 1930 and 1960, for the third. Today the world's population stands at around 3,700 million. If current trends of fertility persist, it could double by the year 2000. (14 February 1973)

• The world's population now stands at about 3,800 million. Of this number, perhaps one billion live in areas which could be described as developed, at levels well above subsistence. They have, for the most part, employment, housing, a fairly good level of nutrition and access to the basic social services. For the two and a half billion plus who live in the developing countries, none of this is true. With a few exceptions, the people of these countries live at a very low economic level, and a large proportion live in conditions which would be regarded . . . as intolerable.

Population growth rates in the majority of developing countries, [namely] the whole of Asia and Africa, and most of Latin America and the Caribbean, are very high - averaging about 2.8 per cent per year. At this rate the population of a country doubles in 25 years. This [high growth rate] is the result of a combination of factors, probably the chief of which is the introduction of pesticides and other public health measures since the Second World War, which have reduced the incidence of fatal disease. Despite this drop in death rates, birth rates have remained high, as in the past, so that in many developing countries the proportion of children under fifteen is approaching 45 per cent. The effect of this non-productive burden on countries whose resources are already strained, and the prospect that many will remain non-productive because of lack of opportunity to work, can be imagined. (13 November 1973)

• No matter what we do, the earth's population is going to double in 25 years. This, unless there is world catastrophe of mammoth size, is a mathematical certainty.

Thus, in looking ahead to the end of this century, not far off, we must envisage a situation in which a second world population of the same dimensions as the present one will have been added to the earth's inhabitants. These newcomers are not intruders. They don't come from Mars. They are us—some seven billion of us instead of three and a half billion, with the same needs, rights, demands and aspirations—and all dependent for food, water, energy, technical facilities, education, housing and jobs on the resources of this planet.

Accept this fact and we have to accept the responsibility *now* for taking action to adapt, to conserve and to develop the resources which will be needed to sustain these increases in numbers in the 25-year spiral period. We need also to be prepared to move forward determinedly with the studies, the research, the planning and the programmes directed towards the achievement of better national, international and, eventually, global management of life on this planet. Later will be too late. (6 March 1974)

• The process of doubling [of the world's population] is not something which will suddenly come upon us; it is happening now, relentlessly, like a snowball rolling down a hill, picking up mass and speed. And ironically, it is happening because advances in medicine and nutrition have allowed people to live longer lives. Even if world fertility were to fall immediately to near "replacement level"—an average family size of two children reaching maturity—world population would still increase by nearly two billion before it levelled off. Immediate "replacement level" is clearly an unrealistic hope, and even the most optimistic foresee a world population of about six billion by the year 2000. This does not mean that efforts now being made to reduce population growth are meaningless. On the contrary, any relaxation of such efforts would only intensify the pace of doubling after A.D. 2000. (18 May 1974)

• [By the early years of the next century] there will be many more old people to take care of, there will be many more inhabitants of cities which are already feeling the pressure of their present population, and there will be many more children. The number of dependents, people under 15 or over 65, is already high in all the countries of Asia. The prospect is that they will increase not only in numbers, but as a proportion of the total population. The ramifications of this growth, and their implications for development policy in the 21st century, must be thought of now. (20 May 1974)

• The people of thirty years hence are not a demographer's nightmare, but a fact. Experts may quibble about a few million either way, but to all intents and purposes we are dealing in 1975 with a world which will double in size within the probable lifetime of anyone . . . under thirty-five today. (23 October 1975)

• The demographic forecast is that before the United Nations is twice as old as it is now, there will be twice as many people as there are now who need to share the material resources of this planet as equitably as possible. (20 February 1976)

• The most recent projections of the United Nations show a downturn in the [global] growth rate—small but significant. The challenge before us now is to repeat and capitalize on this success—in agriculture, industrial development, employment, education, health and housing. (28 September 1976)

• Although the global rate has remained roughly steady at about 1.9 per cent per year, the United Nations recently revised downwards its estimates of the number of people at present on the planet and forecasts a slowing rate of growth in all areas in the world.

This does not allow room for complacency, however. A global rate of growth of 1.9 per cent means that the world's population will double in 37 years. In the developing world, where two-thirds of the world's people live, the "doubling time" is even shorter—about 25 years. The most likely outcome of the present trend is that the world's population will stabilize at about three times its present level, that is to say, at

12 billion, nearly a century from now—and that assumes a constantly falling rate of fertility. This, in turn, assumes constant efforts to produce the conditions which will bring this about. (30 March 1977)

• The most recent projections of United Nations demographers show world population growth continuing at its present rate—just under two per cent per annum—until about 1985, then beginning a slow downward trend. Growth in numbers will, of course, continue, but at a declining rate, and will eventually stabilize. Stabilization will take place at different times in different regions during the course of the next century. The best estimate is for a stable world population of about 12 billion in 2075. That is to say, we and our descendants must be prepared to create conditions permitting a healthy life for between 10 and 15 billion human beings who will probably inhabit the earth.

These projections take full account of the likely level of success in bringing down fertility rates by means of family planning programmes and economic and social development. They are not pessimistic, simply realistic, and what they say represents the most important single fact about the age in which we live. We know, as nearly as we can know anything, that world population will double again, and we can be fairly sure that growth will continue for nearly a hundred years.

The new era will be one of gradually slowing world population growth. But this growth, as we know, is badly skewed. An annual rate of well over two per cent in the developing countries is projected by the United Nations for the period 1975-80, while in the industrialized countries the rate will be considerably lower than one per cent. Growth in developing countries takes place on a base of 2.9 billion people, and will add more than three hundred and sixty million people in those five years - or more than the total population of Latin America.

We should redouble our efforts to achieve slower population growth sooner than the projections indicate, by all the means at our command. (2 June 1977)

• The realities of the imbalance between growing human numbers and accessible resources, some of them rapidly dwindling, remain, particularly in countries which are least able to sustain the increase in their numbers. It is well to bear in mind that, allowing for a wide margin of possible error, and despite an assumed further fall in fertility of as much as 33 per cent over the next two decades, the lowest forecast for the world's total population in the year 2000 is 5.8 billion (as against 4.2 billion today, and 3 billion in 1960, when the First Development Decade was launched).

The implications of this further huge increase for national policies in such important areas as employment, industrialization, migration, population distribution, housing, and the provision of health and education services will affect all areas of the world. However, with 85 to 90 per cent of the 1.5 to 2 billion estimated increase in the world's population before the year 2000 projected to occur in developing countries, it is obvious that these countries will bear the heavier burden as they face their many social and economic development challenges. For example, it is estimated that the combination of population growth and accelerating migration from the countryside will add nearly a billion additional people to the urban labour pool of developing countries by the end of the century. (6 November 1978)

Views on the Population Debate

• Population questions had been discussed in the United Nations since the early fifties, but for many years the sensitivity of some members prevented the Organization's programme involvement. The reservations of these members fell into two main groups -one view was that the solution of social and economic problems was the key to development and that separate consideration of population as an issue was at best an irrelevance, and at worst a deliberate diversion of attention from the real problem. The other view—primarily religious—was that it was impossible to intervene in population questions without contravening the teaching of the churches. Set against these was a group consisting mainly of Western countries, whose view was that without direct and positive action on population problems, progress in the developing countries would be slowed down or vitiated completely. This view may have stimulated a reaction in some quarters against what was seen as an attempt to substitute population control for development assistance. Meanwhile, some countries, notably in Asia, were pressing ahead with their own programmes of family planning and demographic studies, assisted by individuals and organizations outside the area.

A concrete example of an area where you could help us . . . is in the forging of a common and neutral language of population problems. In agriculture, for instance, there are common concepts whereby all agriculturists can share their progress and their problems. In population, we still have to find a vocabulary of this kind. Ideology still presents obstacles at times, and this breeds suspicion of motives. (5 February 1973)

• In . . . industrialized countries, as well as in developing nations, a debate is going on as to whether there is a place for a state population policy. The supporters of population policies argue that limited resources make it urgent to stabilize the birth rate. On the other hand, opponents of state-directed population programmes are extremely vocal about what they see as a threat to individual freedom.

The circumstances that compel the world towards a unified approach make ideology a luxury. In any case, ideological statements are not necessarily incompatible with apparently conflicting statements made in different terms. . . . If some countries have been more successful than others in slowing down the growth of their population, it is as much because of superior management as because of any inherent superiority of ideology. . . .

If . . . ideological differences of approach are more apparent than real, it should be possible to look for an international consensus in matters of population.

Even countries which a few years ago resolutely opposed any move in the United Nations to support population activities now give at least qualified endorsement to the work of the UNFPA. (14 February 1973)

• Unfortunately, up till now the sum total of national and international action [in the population field] does not add up to much. This can be attributed to a number of reasons. First, in addition to cultural, ethical, religious and political considerations, there have been many other factors, such as: that the industrialized countries, cushioned by high productivity and technical know-how, have tended to see the population problem only in terms of developing countries. Secondly, that developing countries, particularly in Asia, while acutely aware of the problem of numbers versus resources, have lacked the means, except for a few, to carry out effective programmes.

Thirdly, that it has taken a long time for the idea to percolate that whatever policies one nation adopts in regard to population is not a matter for itself alone. And that what is called for is large scale, inter-linked national and international programmes on a global scale. The opportunity to mount such a programme now exists through the United Nations. (14 February 1973-B)

- [When it was created in 1967] the Fund was envisaged as a fairly minor operation running at about $1 million a year. But it quickly became apparent that this was not a case where half a loaf was better than none. Either we had to mount a programme that would make a real impact on the population situation, or we might as well give up the whole business. (15 February 1973)

- We have noticed in the past decade a softening of opinion among the hardliners in the population debate. Ideologues are becoming less convinced that social and economic growth alone will answer all the problems of developing countries without recourse to special measures on population, and all important religious groups are now also fully prepared to recognize the necessity for action. The Fund operates in countries of all religious and political persuasions; for example, in a number of Catholic countries our programmes include provision for training social visitors who teach the rhythm method in the villages where they work. It is to be hoped that one of the main functions of World Population Year will be to bring still closer the different shades of opinion on the population question and make possible a genuine World Population Plan of Action which will have the positive backing of all members of the international community. (18 October 1973)

- In many developing countries the proportion of children under fifteen is approaching forty-five per cent. The effect of this non-productive burden on countries whose resources are already strained, and the prospect that many will remain non-productive because of lack of opportunity to work, can be imagined.

In these circumstances the surprise is not that residual ideological and religious objections to action in population have broken down, but that it has taken so long for this to happen. (13 November 1973)

- The United Nations is only as strong as its members wish it to be. [We] do not mean by this to attempt to excuse the failures of the United Nations, but it is only political backing which lends authority and effectiveness to its work. In . . . population, the United Nations was for many years prevented from taking any firm action by the sensitivity of various members on population questions. It was not until the mid-sixties that agreement was reached in the General Assembly to recognize population as an urgent issue. With agreement on this fundamental point, the way was opened for money and technical support to be poured into population activities.

With the lifting of the political floodgate, the whole question is opened for discussion, controversy and, hopefully, final agreement on ways towards a solution. Not only have more money, men and material been made available in the last few years, but there has been a growing sense of the urgency of the problem and of its true extent. We do not talk any more in terms of family planning as an answer to population growth, because we realize now that there is far more to population than family planning. In many parts of the world, particularly in Asia, it is indeed vital to slow down the rate of population growth, but [we] think that it is now realized that the number of children a family has depends on a very complex interaction in which levels of education, the quality of housing, health and social security services play a part, and which is tied closely to the form which overall social and economic development is taking.

One of the difficulties which have attended all attempts to gain agreement on action in respect to population is the mutually exclusive nature of the points of view expressed. During the last few years, there has been a retreat from entrenched ideological positions, but it is still possible to hear in certain countries of the developed world the opinion, or at least the implication, that the population question is essentially and exclusively a matter of overpopulation elsewhere. This breeds, in its turn, a conviction in the developing countries referred to, that concern about population is strictly an attempt to keep them in their place.

Our world now is having great and apparently increasing difficulty in feeding, clothing and housing itself. How shall we accommodate another world on top of this one?

Some suggest that there is only one possible end to the mounting problems of population, food, natural resources and the environment. They say that we have already run out of time, and that global catastrophe is inevitable in the foreseeable future. If they are right, we can all sit back and wait for the hardest "hard news" of all time to break upon our heads. If they are not right, and we sit back nevertheless, then our very inactivity may be the cause of our downfall.

The lemmings have one answer to this, apparently directed by the DNA molecule. Since we are rational beings, with the ability to look into our future and plan for it, we may choose life rather than suicide. But we shall need all our resources of tenacity, foresight and wisdom. We have the technology now which could feed, house and clothe the world if it were applied correctly. We have the ability to create a world in which all of us and our descendants can peacefully live. We have the capacity to become wise. We must find the means of turning this potential into fact. (2 April 1974)

- A real consensus is growing, based on the acceptance of what might be called the "third view" of population - that it is neither to be ignored as irrelevant nor treated as a more important factor, but accepted as a significant factor in the development process.

In the development of this consensus, Asian countries should naturally play a leading part. Much of the world's expertise was generated here, and many of the more successful programmes are operated here. Above all, only Asian countries have the sophisticated approach which is the result of many years' experience in confronting the peculiar problems of individual countries. Asian countries are well aware that there can be no blanket solution, and that even within countries, programmes must be adapted to take account of local needs. In considering the World Population Plan of Action, Asian governments can take a lead in acknowledging local, national and regional differences while insisting on the need for a global approach, because only they have the necessary depth of first-hand experience. (9 May 1974)

• There will be many differences in approach from country to country, and even within countries, according to differences in local situations. But differences can be fruitful. While all our efforts should contribute to [reaching] . . . a final consensus, an artificial consensus imposed where no real one exists can only be sterile. There will be much more debate in the future about optimum growth rates, the use of family planning, the place of family size in relation to development, migration, and many other topics. (16 May 1974)

• Even after [the World Population Conference held in August 1974 at] Bucharest, there are, of course, many differences remaining. But increasingly they appear to be differences of form rather than content. One nation may reject family planning as unnecessary in a well-ordered society, and at the same time include all known forms of contraception in universally available health services. Another may reject outright population control, yet at the same time carefully build up a sound demographic base for development planning, which will in all probability include indications of the desired level of population growth. (15 October 1974)

• The population question is non-ideological. It can affect societies whatever their politics. (27 January 1975)

• The population question now lies beyond ideology or sectarian controversy.

All member nations of the United Nations now recognize the significance of population as one of the important keys to the solution of world poverty, food shortages, social order and the future of energy supplies. The Bucharest Conference showed that their approach to the solution of population problems differs according to the local conditions and circumstances, but there is no doubt any longer that the population factor is central to the problems of economic development. This awareness has been growing in the past few years, it was heightened during World Population Year, and reached a peak at Bucharest, where political consensus, involving 135 countries, was reached on a population matters and, notably, on the adoption of a World Population Plan of Action: a milestone . . . in the field of human development. (13 February 1975)

• There is still some residual feeling [in the United Nations] that population is too hot to handle with safety.

[We] would like . . . to correct some misjudgements about the population scene today. [For one thing] national views are not irreconcilable [as demonstrated by the World Population Plan of Action consensus].

Differences often seem to boil down to a matter of rhetoric rather than reality. Some of those who were loudest in deploring international assistance for fertility regulation programmes [at the World Population Conference] have themselves efficient birth planning programmes. For this reason, the debate, in a sense, had more to do with the use of words like "family planning" than with the practices or the behaviour of people in different societies.

There are, of course, good reasons why differences in terminology are important. There are vast differences between cultures and ideologies. Marriage, the family, and children are the centre of concern in most societies and are accordingly very sensitive areas of discussion, especially with outsiders. But more and more in the international arena we appear to be talking the same language. (23 October 1975)

• Population has always been a controversial issue.

At Bucharest, it became clear that opposition to what was regarded as Western thinking on population was much deeper-rooted than had been thought. There was much suspicion of those who wished for decisive action to lower birth rates. On the other side, there were bitter accusations that the debate had been diverted from its real subject—population—into issues which were important in themselves but peripheral to the subject of the Conference. There was, in some cases, a mutual failure to see the point of view of the other side, so that a rather sterile debate seemed to be taking place between "development", on the one hand, and "population", on the other.

But even at the height of the controversy, voices could be heard saying that there was no need for such polemics. The World Population Plan of Action acknowledges as much, at least on paper. In the year since the Conference, although scattered gunfire has been reported, there are some indications that the combatants are recognizing that they have several things in common. These include interest and concern in successful development programmes to meet the needs of growing populations, and involvement in population activities as a vital component of development strategy.

There have also been some practical developments which give room for some optimism. In some countries where "family planning" is not a respectable phrase, programmes including the provision of contraceptive services are taking root and growing strongly. In others, a new interest in the mechanics and the implications of population growth and distribution is clearly discernible since the end of World Population Year. And in the past year, as if to demonstrate the worldwide upsurge in interest in population matters, demands on the United Nations Fund for Population Activities have increased beyond our means to meet them. . . .

One has a strange feeling about the whole controversy, that it is like the mythical beast which could only be seen from the corner of the eye. When looked at directly, it would vanish. That is not to say that it is harmless—but it does mean that we should be sure that we are looking at the issues as squarely as possible.

A priority for all who are interested in population matters [is] the development of an intellectual consensus in which discussion can go on with a minimum of rancour and a maximum of understanding. The foundation for this lies in the practical consensus which already exists. [A number of countries] have programmes which involve the distribution of contraceptives on request as part of a package of health services for mothers and children. There can surely be rational discussion between and among them (and the donor countries and agencies) as to the nature and purpose of their activities.

From this discussion, it would probably emerge that these . . . countries have different views about the function of their population situations, and different ideas about the function of population activities within their development framework. Indeed, it would make no sense if the priorities of . . . such different countries were the same—but different priorities do not necessarily mean disagreement, if the same overall purpose is acknowledged.

There is, therefore, a challenge before this [International Population] Conference. It is to pool our experience and our perceptions and arrive at a real consensus. The consensus must cover practical priorities, and must give a basis for a common language which will be free of the misunderstandings which have bedevilled us in the past. (21 November 1975)

• The main opposition to discussion of contraception [at the first World Population Conference, held in Rome in 1954] fell under three heads, which might broadly be described as religious, social and nationalist, though in the course of debate distinctions naturally became blurred. The oldest objection was on moral grounds. The Roman Catholic Church has set its face against artificial contraception and its attitude considerably influenced personal and political opinion in several European countries and in the United States. Among other groups the moral argument—that contraception was simply wrong—was combined with the position that it was wrong because it could be used as a means of controlling the natural increase of certain parts of the population—defined by race, religion or class—in their own interest or that of other groups. The nationalist argument was an extension of this; any interference in natural population growth was a threat to the state, which relied on a growing population for its strength compared with other nations.

Against these, the supporters of family planning deployed arguments both personal and social. . . . Though the campaign grew out of a concern for the health of the individual, it was soon naturally extended to arguments about the health of society. It was this approach, extended further to the international sphere, which was eventually to prevail, and is enshrined in the World Population Plan of Action adopted in 1974.

[In the 1950's] insensitivity on the part of family planning campaigners to the feelings and beliefs of their potential "acceptors" was reinforced by emergent nationalism. Some of the visionary nationalists—Mahatma Gandhi is an example—saw rejection of all innovation as a positive step towards the self-identification of ex-colonial peoples. The new breed of nationalists was also fiercely anti-colonialist, and while accepting Western technology as the means of progress, they were often deeply suspicious of the motives of their present or former masters and their allies. "Population control" was an obvious target for their suspicion. This was reinforced, if they happended to be Marxist, by the interpretation of Marx, Engels and Lenin as condemning interference with population growth as unnecessary and reactionary. For these people, burgeoning population should, and would, be provided for by social and economic advances.

[In the 1960's] some . . . apocalyptically-inclined commentators held that in order to achieve satisfactory growth rates, more or less compulsory means of fertility limitation would have to be used.

These predictions achieved worldwide notice at the time, but their effect on progress towards the achievement of a world consensus on population policy was at best mixed. In such a sensitive area, where, as we have seen, suspicions of developed countries still remained, the sometimes raucous and ill-judged publicity surrounding the predictions caused further confusion and doubt. At one point, indeed, the Swedish economist Gunnar Myrdal was moved to warn of the dangers of an "obsession" with population growth. A counter-movement to the pessimists quickly grew up, but most of its members seemed committed to economic growth along conventional lines as a solution to social problems including population, relying on the power of technology to solve the resources and environmental difficulties. A dangerous polarization, not only between advocates and opponents of family planning along the older lines, but between proposers and opposers of "population control", seemed possible.

Two reports during this period helped to bring matters into perspective. The first was the report of the Pearson Commission, "Partners in Development", which looked at the whole spectrum of aid and development, including population assistance. The second was the United Nations Association of the U.S.A. report by an extremely distinguished panel chaired by John D. Rockefeller 3rd. . . . While endorsing the view that expanding population posed a threat to environment and resources, the report recommended intensification of action through the channels already established rather than any extraordinary measures.

A firmly established action programme within the United Nations system . . . did not by any means represent an end to controversy over the place of population in development. Right up to and including the World Population Conference in August 1974 there was a debate, passionate at times, on the place of population in national development programmes.

The Fund has been able to work towards a climate of genuine consensus in population matters between governments with widely differing views and has worked with over a hundred countries on population projects of the widest possible variety.

Through the years of debate, several different strands of thinking on population have emerged. . . . The first regards the population/resources situation as a "crisis" which can be solved only by extraordinary means, perhaps by suspending for a time normal civil liberties, including freedom of choice in fertility. This view has gained some support but has no status in the United Nations, where the rights of national and individual self-determination have . . . long been an article of faith. It is doubtful, in fact, whether any progress at all would have been made in assistance to population programmes without such safeguards.

A second . . . holds that family planning services are essential to break the vicious circle of poverty. In this view, poverty and "over-population" are seen as symbiotic evils, and intervention in the direction of lower population growth is necessary to break their grip on each other.

A third view, which was dominant at the World Population Conference in Bucharest and at international meetings since, holds, first, that economic and social advancement in the poorer countries is the only way of dealing with the problems posed by population growth, and, secondly, that a reordering of the international economic system is needed to make this possible. No progress can be made, this view insists, until the economic balance is redressed in favour of the poorer countries. The extent to which this attitude has led to the rejection of even the appearance of acquiescence in the importance of fertility limitation can be seen by the insistence of many countries that they do not have "family planning" programmes. Governments whose development plans include the availability of contraceptive services, even some whose intentions are advowedly to lower the birth rate, will insist on this point.

Out of the discussions which have taken place before, during and since Bucharest, a possible compromise position seems to be emerging, in which population is given its due importance as an essential part of development planning, self-determination in fertility is acknowledged as a basic human right, and the unique situation of each country, including its right to decide on and implement its own population policy, is acknowledged. At the same time, the economic and social roots of population problems are recognized. . . . This consensus is a break-through, rather than a defeat, for family planning.

The roots of controversy in population run very deep; they touch not only the most sensitive aspects of our personal lives, but, by extension, the deepest feelings of national security and identity. To have reached this point of practical consensus, even though the language remains that of controversy, represents an immeasurable advance over the position twenty years ago. (28 September 1976)

• In the United Nations, emphasis on the principle that population size and rate of growth were a matter for national decision inhibited concerted international action on population for many years. The World Population Conference debated this principle for two weeks, during which ample evidence was provided that population remained a highly sensitive topic of debate. At the same time, sufficient agreement was reached to allow the impression that the subject had been dealt with adequately. . . .

At the same time, it is clear that most governments have accepted the view that in their own national circumstances there is a negative correlation between population growth and development, and that a long-term strategy of reducing the birthrate is not only prudent, but a necessary part of economic and social programmes. . . . Effectively, there is a consensus on population among developing nations.

We have now arrived at the curious position where there is an international consensus in a highly sensitive area of policy, but few internationally-accepted quantitative goals. Although there has been a considerable shift in opinion even in the two years since the World Population Conference at Bucharest, the World Population Plan of Action remains the main evidence of world agreement on population—and that document is less than specific in several key areas. (12 January 1977)

• There is wider and deeper international agreement than ever before [on population issues]. . . .

First, family planning. This is the part of the field of population activities which for most people in the industrialized countries symbolizes—and is sometimes taken for—the whole field. There is no universal agreement that the present rate of world population growth is too high, and [we] do not expect that there will be. Nevertheless, of the 48 developing countries which perceive their national population growth rates as too high, 40 are acting to lower them. These countries contain some eighty per cent of the developing world's population and over half of that of the entire world. Further, though most of the nations of the world are satisfied with their growth rates or wish to raise them, only 15 out of 156 prevent access to contraceptive methods.

The right of access to the means of contraception is acknowledged almost universally today, though for millions of people, particularly in the rural areas of the developing world, the right remains without meaning because they have neither the means nor the information to avail themselves of it.

The second element of the emerging consensus is the general agreement that population factors cannot be considered in isolation, but only as part of the fabric of socio-economic development. . . . Eighty-three governments have now passed to their central planning bodies the responsibility for integrating population factors into development planning. . . . The important exceptions to this general agreement are the industrialized countries, in most of which the policy implications of population trends are matters for piecemeal consideration by different governmental departments, if indeed they are considered at all. A full consensus requires a recognition of responsibility in this area from developed and developing countries alike.

A further element of the consensus is acceptance of the wide range of activities which can be classified under the heading of "population". The collection and analysis of demographic statistics has been a valuable tool for making government decisions. . . .

Another aspect of population activities is the study and regulation of migratory patterns.

As a final example of the broad sweep of population activities today, we may take the concern with factors indirectly affecting the birth rate. Mortality, particularly infant mortality, is a concern for all developing countries, for its own sake as well as for its demographic effects. . . . Similarly, it has been shown that social factors have important effects on fertility—employment, education and the position of women, among them.

Let us see how this consensus expresses itself in practice. In Asia, there is broad agreement among governments that rates of population growth are too high and that lowering them is a top priority in securing a balance between population and resources. . . .

Many of the techniques found to be successful—incentive and disincentive schemes, family life education, community-based distribution schemes, to give examples—are now being successfully used elsewhere. . . .

In Africa, there is no widespread agreement on the necessity for lower rates of population growth, although several governments in the region are working towards this end. There is, indeed, some distrust in African countries of the concept of "family planning'', but schemes integrating contraceptive services with other aspects of family life have met with some success. Collection and analysis of census data is a common concern . . . as is the level of mortality. UNFPA is also helping to discover the reasons for low fertility in a few countries with low rates of growth and small populations relative to their resources.

In the Western Asian region, there is naturally little concern with growth rates as such, except in the North African Arab countries, where policies of lowering rates of growth are vigorously pursued. There is, however, considerable and growing interest in mother and child health schemes to improve health and reduce mortality, in improving the quality of population data, in education on population matters, and in research.

In Central and South America, 21 of 27 countries actively support programmes to increase access to contraceptive techniques, reduce mortality and improve general health, while several are pursuing lower rates of population growth. . . . There are now several different models in operation which indicate not only how different rates of growth will affect policy decisions, but how policy decisions will affect population growth.

In [many] countries, it will often be claimed, even by government representatives, that they are opposed to family planning. By this it can be taken to mean that they are opposed to the concept of delivering family planning *in isolation*, without reference to other development services. Many of these governments have highly efficient means of motivating users and delivery of fertility regulation services. Some have succeeded in cutting their birth rates drastically - without in some cases, ever admitting that this was their aim.

Given that population matters are now widely accepted as an important part of development planning and policy, what are the remaining constraints to effective population policies?

Constraints may be divided into three kinds: social, economic and institutional. *Social* inhibitions to population activities use nationalist, racial or moral prejudice, against any sort of intervention, and sometimes are even extended to opposition to census-taking. Free access to family planning has been the chief victim here, and though nearly all governments are now not opposed, there remain ideological and moral barriers to certain, sometimes all, forms of contraception. There is still religious opposition to contraception, abortion and sterilization, on grounds of the sanctity of human life. Nevertheless, acceptable forms of fertility limitation are widely used in Roman Catholic countries, and many Islamic peoples find the teaching of the Koran quite compatible with the practice of contraception. In another direction, it was held by Marxist ideologues at one time that contraception and socialism did not mix, but many socialist countries . . . are now in the forefront of the movement to make the knowledge and means of contraception available as widely as possible as part of general programmes of social development.

At a personal level, traditionalist distrust of modern means of contraception often ignores traditional reality—that women at all times, and in most societies, have known about and used, with or without knowledge, some form of contraception. Suspicion can and is being eroded by programmes which reconcile acceptance of contraception with the values of everyday life. On the other hand, hositility can be aroused by insensitive approaches, and there are recent examples of useful and progressive programmes which have had to be scrapped because of crude, or simply over-enthusiastic, implementation.

Economic constraints are a classic feature of the so-called "demographic transition". In the now-industrialized countries, the decline in fertility which took place in the second half of the nineteenth century was accompanied by a rise in the standard of living, and low fertility rates have usually been associated with economic prosperity. Recent research and experience have shown, however, that the standard of living need not be high before fertility decline sets in—provided certain other conditions are met. The state of Kerala in India, for example, is poorer than the states which surround it, but its fertility and mortality rates are considerably lower. Other factors which make it different from its neighbours are that its income distribution is more even—thanks to effective land reform; the level of political participation by the general public is higher; and health services are more efficient and widely used.

The implication of this and other studies is that both fertility and mortality rates may decline, whether or not family planning programmes are in operation (as they are in Kerala), at a much lower level of income than was needed for the European demographic transition—provided certain conditions are met. These include access to housing, health services, education and employment. They may also include special attention to the position of women in society. Together they constitute the whole package of services which provide the essentials of a secure and hopeful existence. At the moment, and for the foreseeable future in many parts of the world, these conditions are not being fulfilled, and this . . . poses the greatest threat to attempts to bring down birth rates.

Institutional contraints are of many kinds and affect all areas of population programme formation and implementation, though to different degrees in different countries. Policy implementation is handicapped by lack of expertise, for example, in some African countries. On the other hand, in some Latin American countries effective programming at middle levels is hampered by lack of effective co-ordination higher up. Asian countries offer the best examples of highly sophisticated machinery for delivering contraceptive services. Nevertheless, no developing country even in Asia, with the possible exception of China, has devised a really effective means of delivering family planning to the people at large, especially the rural poor. This is also the main problem in providing the economic package of necessities . . . essential to the success of family planning programmes. (30 March 1977)

- When we began operations, we found only a few countries interested in obtaining population assistance. . . . Today there are few developing countries which have *not* asked for our support; the ideological objections which seemed so important only a few years ago have been transcended.

As the World Population Conference in 1974 showed, it is only when population is seen as something separate from other development activities that it is unacceptable [in the view of many governments]. (2 June 1977)

• During these [eight] years [of the Fund's operations], we have seen a recognizable consensus emerge on the need to relate population factors closely to other factors of development planning. It has been increasingly recognized that population is both an important activity on its own, and an essential component of development. As a result, governments of many developing countries are providing increasing allocations for population activities, activities which are being undertaken in close co-ordination with other development projects relating to health, nutrition, maternal and child welfare, education, status of women, and income redistribution.

The population dialogue is no longer concerned, as it was in the past, with the question of intervention versus non-intervention, but rather with the question of priorities and strategies for population policies and programmes.

Today, unlike 1969, most governments recognize population programmes as an important component of development policy. A recent United Nations survey, which covered all 114 developing countries, shows that 83 of these have entrusted a central planning authority with the task of integrating population factors with development planning. Sixty-nine countries believe that the current rate of natural population increase imposes severe constraints on the attainment of population objectives.

These findings are behind the emphasis being given to population in the concerned discussion of planners. They have led to an increased sense of urgency in the North-South dialogue on a New International Economic Order and they have quickened the trend, in countries most conscious of the pressure of growing numbers on resources, to increase the pace of their fertility limitation programmes even to the extent of adopting more stringent anti-natalist policies and programmes than would have been considered possible or desirable only a few years ago. In fact, many countries in which economic development is being hampered by population growth are already endeavouring to introduce social reforms, undertake new development strategies, and draw up legislative measures which aim at influencing people to have smaller families.

We have seen "consciousness" rise on a global scale regarding population matters. In 1969, very few policymakers and administrators addressed themselves to population problems or planned programmes to deal with them. Population growth was not thought of as a factor that could be consciously changed or directed. Today, there are few countries where the population factor has not entered the "consciousness" of policymakers and administrators. The recent study by the United Nations showed that of 114 developing countries surveyed, 63 per cent were concerned with some aspect of their demographic situation—internal migration, morbidity and mortality, the current rate of national population increase, or international migration.

We have seen a revolution in worldwide attitudes toward the subject of population in general and family planning in particular. The same survey shows that 54 developing countries now consider that their rates of fertility are too high. Of these, 18 are in Asia,

18 in Africa, 16 in Latin America and two in the Middle East, and together they comprise 82 per cent of the population in the developing world. A total of 82 governments themselves provide either direct or indirect support to fertility regulation measures, regardless of their own policies on natural increase and national fertility. And in only 8 of the 114 developing countries surveyed was access to the use of modern methods of fertility regulation limited in any way.

We have seen the acceptance of the population factor as a vital component in the development process and have, in fact, seen some developing countries indicate that solution of their population problems is a pre-condition to their development.

Family planning has been removed from the polemics of "population versus development" which had constrained its adoption during the previous decade in many countries, and [from] its identification as basically a health and welfare and human rights-oriented measure, which could contribute to demographic change if that change were independently considered desirable.

And governments have come to see the population factor in a broad sense, encompassing not just the population growth rate, but other objectives as well, such as programmes designed to reduce morbidity and mortality, the problems of internal and international migration, and the geographical distribution of populations within national territories. In fact, in the United Nations survey cited earlier, severe or serious levels of morbidity and mortality were viewed as a problem by 79 countries, and 95 countries considered that the population distribution was either substantially or extremely unacceptable. Some governments have indicated a strong interest in initiating studies to identify the effects of population distribution on cities and on rural areas.

Eight years ago few people discussed the subject of sterilization. If they did, it was primarily in a doctor's office on an individual basis. During these past eight years, many developing countries have instituted government-sponsored sterilization programmes, and millions of vasectomies and tubectomies have been performed. Though we have seen the consequences of over-enthusiasm in this area, the fact remains that voluntary sterilization is very much a part of the contemporary scene.

In 1969, little attention was paid to the question of the availability of contraceptives. Yet a common complaint has been, and continues to be, the inaccessibility of contraceptive supplies, particularly for people in rural areas . . . the trend now is to bring family planning services closer to clients by using local groups and people, by using networks already in place and integrated with the culture of their societies. . . .

We have seen developing countries with previously limited concern about their own population problems, turn about, and institute broad-based and extensive national family planning programmes. And we have seen developing countries with minor national inputs in their own national population programmes and with heavy reliance on external assistance, completely reverse their expenditure ratios so that now national inputs are major and external assistance is minor. For example, in Mexico the President's State of the Nation report in September 1973 is regarded as marking a major shift from non-intervention to a programme of responsible parenthood. From an expenditure base of very little in 1974, the contribution of the Government of Mexico to a national maternal/child health and family planning programme has increased to a committed amount close to $70 million, with external inputs of about $15 million.

Eight years ago, the health services infrastructures in many developing countries were poorly developed or practically non-existent. Countries wanting to institute family planning programmes had, of necessity, to establish vertical or parallel programmes, if they were to be initiated at all. UNFPA-funded family planning programmes provided the impetus for the initiation by the developing countries, not only of the development of their health services, but expansion of model family planning programmes as well.

As health services infrastructures have been built up, family planning programmes have been integrated with maternal and child health care programmes. The United Nations survey points up the fact that the governments of all the 81 countries which have national family planning programmes consider these to be an essential means of achieving acceptable levels of maternal and child health and family welfare, and of satisfying the goals of human rights and the improved status of women. In this sense, the programmes are integral parts of health and social policies. (21 June 1977)

• Most governments have totally accepted the concept of population as a vital component of socio-economic development. The controversy that existed earlier, as to whether intervention to regulate population growth was permissible, is virtually over. Even governments which were previously opposed to intervention in population matters now have population programmes and are making strenuous efforts to ensure widespread availability of equipment and supplies to implement these programmes. (5 July 1977)

• In the early 1970's two extreme views on the approach to population problems came into sharp focus. One school of thought insisted that rapid population growth was the cause of increasing poverty, and that the gains of whatever economic growth was being achieved by development efforts were being undermined by more people to feed and sustain. This school believed that population "control" was the only reasonable solution. The other school took the opposite view, that poverty was the cause of high population growth, and claimed that rapid development was the only way to reduce population growth. [That] in effect there was no population problem as such, only a problem of poverty caused by social injustice.

"Population" is not a problem for governments alone, for demographers alone, or for statisticians and economists alone. It is a problem of people. It involves not just numbers nor even just a workable balance between numbers and resources. It is not a question of quantity or quality but of both, because quantity, at some point, affects and determines quality. (27 September 1977)

Population Policies, Development of

• In the UNFPA, we have argued that every country should have a clear, well-defined and consistent policy with regard to population.

It may well be that we . . . need to discard the notion of population policy as a separate area of government action. Instead, population policy would be merged into existing structures so that, in each sector, consideration would be given to the demographic implications of alternative policy options. Population growth would be considered, not in terms of whether or not it is an obstacle to development, but as a function of manpower planning. Greater emphasis would be placed on adapting existing development strategies, to enhance the capacity of the society to absorb existing and anticipated births, while at the same time creating the economic and social conditions conducive to the transition to smaller families. (5 February 1973)

• In . . . industrialized countries, as well as in developing nations, a debate is going on as to whether there is a place for a state population policy. The supporters of population policies argue that limited resources make it urgent to stabilize the birth rate. On the other hand, opponents of state-directed population programmes are extremely vocal about what they see as a threat to individual freedom.

The main difficulty is that population policies are too often confused with family planning. Family planning should be regarded as a service within an overall population policy. . . .

It is the responsibility of all governments to take stock of population growth and movements in their countries, and formulate appropriate policy. (14 February 1973)

• There has been a mistaken tendency to use family planning programmes as a substitute for population policy.

Place population policies within the context of an overall plan for economic and social development, which aims at eliminating starvation and malnutrition, at providing more jobs, better housing and more educational facilities, and at reducing inequalities in the distribution of national resources and personal income, and *then* we can look for specific reasons why family planning services are not being used to full advantage.

These are aspects to which the Fund is giving constant attention. (14 February 1973-B)

• Responsiveness to individual needs, and close involvement at all stages of the decision-making process of those who are most intimately affected, are the elements of a successful population policy. The way in which assistance is given must include these elements. Therefore, the Fund has developed as close a relationship as possible with each government with which it is involved, in order to gain a full understanding of the nature and scope of its population policies, and has then tailored its programmes as closely as possible to those needs. (25 February 1974)

• [Although] nothing can be done about population growth rates in the immediate future, there is no case for ignoring their long-term importance and the possibility of change. It is the sovereign right of governments to decide upon the correct course of action; but some action must be taken. (16 May 1974)

• Every planning ministry is aware that its schemes will be useless unless they take into account [an] inexorable increase in population. (20 May 1974)

• The adoption of sensible and enlightened policies in this field [population] is an essential step for all countries—whether developed or developing. . . .

In order to give the [World Population] Plan [of Action] substance, it will be necessary for countries and communities to design and put into effect their own national plans of action in accordance with their own special conditions, and with their own resources. (20 August 1974)

• All governments should consider realistically their long-term requirements for food and other basic necessities against the background of their natural resources and the availability of means—human, technological, institutional and financial—for utilizing them, and adopt, consistent with their needs and national goals, the appropriate population policies and programmes. It should be recognized, however, that such policies and programmes take a relatively longer time to implement than most development programmes and their effects are often visible only after a generation or more of sustained effort. (11 November 1974)

• The formulation and implementation of population policies is the sovereign right of each nation. . . . (21 May 1975)

• The Fund's active but neutral approach to population . . . urges countries to adopt population policies and programmes, but leaves it to them to decide what the policies and programmes should be. (19 June 1975)

• There must be a guarantee that each country must be free to work out its own plans and put them into effect in its own way. (26 September 1975)

• Countries [are likely to] have different views of their population situations, and different ideas about the function of population activities within their development framework. Indeed, it would make no sense if the priorities of . . . [very] different countries were the same. (21 November 1975)

• To be effective both [population programmes and other development activities] must reach the individual who makes the ultimate decisions. This requires planning and execution of national policies that are sensitive to local wishes and needs in a flexible, responsive manner, by both the public and the private sectors.

Population growth and national development [activities both] have implications which are of global concern. Yet both must remain firmly within the area of national decision, if policies are to be acceptable and effective, because the demographic and developmental state of each country is different, and therefore its needs are different. . . . Formulae and practices deriving from other cultures may be useful if they are sensitively adapted, but will most certainly fail if they are imported and imposed wholesale. (14 June 1976)

• Population policy is a long-range strategic weapon. Its effects are felt not immediately, but a generation hence. But to be effective, it must be launched now . . . to have its maximum effect. . . . This would not in the least detract from the importance assigned to other aspects of development—food, employment, industrialization and the rest—but would add the missing element, the factor of people. (12 January 1977)

Chapter 15

POPULATION AND ITS UNIQUE RELATIONSHIP TO . . .

. . . Employment

• Many cities in developing countries are strained to the point of collapse by the numbers of people crowding into them in search of the work which they heard was to be found there; resources intended for development projects which would provide jobs must be diverted to supplying the basic needs of these new residents. (25 August 1973)

• Large families in the past have been a sign of prosperity, and large populations have in the past been thought of as enhancing a nation's strength. But we live in a time of great changes, and it may be that we have to revise our ideas about this, as about many other things. In the past, for example, the children of a poor man frequently died of disease or malnutrition. Now we have the means to keep those children alive, but in many cases we cannot provide the education and employment which would make them full members of society. This is one of the most acute problems now facing us. For people to have fewer children in itself will not improve conditions. Those for whom we must provide are here now, and there will be twice as many in 30 or 35 years' time.

A lot can be done by the adaptation of educational systems, and the adjustment of the economy to make the best use of available labour. Eventually, however, we have to learn to think in terms of quality rather than quantity. This approach provides a good touchstone for the success of development and population programmes: Are the available human resources being fully developed? Do the people benefit? Our aim should be the fullest expansion of the productivity and the creativity of each individual. (21 May 1974)

• Many thousands of young people have been educated to expect jobs which do not exist. . . . (2 July 1974)

• It is . . . readily apparent that population and employment are inextricably linked. They are both concerned with the welfare of the individual, the quality of life in society, and, by the same token, the development of the country.

Population programmes can reinforce the effect of other development activities, and can attain their objectives only in the presence of certain basic developmental re-

190

quirements. Among these . . . are the availability of employment, improved social conditions and better income distribution.

Population programmes are vitally linked to the success of efforts to achieve increased levels of employment, better income distribution and improved levels of living, because they are . . . concerned with the fulfillment of the basic needs of the individual as well as the community. For example, the ability to regulate fertility is important not only for maternal and child health reasons, but also because it enables women to become, or to continue to be, active participants in the labour force. Census and vital statistics data provide information on population growth structure and movements which permits planners and administrators to take action on employment, either to supply an existing demand or create new demand. Understanding of population trends and patterns in a given area and their interrelationships with employment can assist in the planning of effective employment policies.

[We are] convinced that closer linkage and harmonization should be brought about between population policies on the one hand, and employment, income equalization and social development policies on the other hand.

[The International Labour Organisation (ILO) and UNFPA] have worked creatively together on many projects within our respective mandates in support of national and international efforts.

A particularly important venture is research and action concerning population and employment which has been carried out as part of the World Employment Programme. For example, with the assistance of more than thirty research institutes and universities, much has been done towards explaining the relationship between population growth, distribution and movement, and employment and income change. Economic-demographic models in the BACHUE series have been developed to evaluate alternative development and population policies and generally to facilitate the incorporation of the population factor into national development planning. Further, the model provides the framework for studies of selected problem areas, for instance, the economics of fertility reduction, or the effects on migration of changes in employment or income distribution.

The ILO's unique tripartite constituency has been able, with financial contributions from UNFPA, to carry population education to the working people in many developing countries, and has greatly raised the general knowledge about this vital area. . . .

In the planning and implementation of population, employment and social programmes, it is necessary to rely not merely on government alone but, insofar as possible, also on the active involvement and participation of all organized or unorganized segments of the community, such as trade unions, employers' associations, cooperatives, organizations of the rural poor, social security agencies, research institutes and other non-governmental groups.

Research work including statistical surveys and development of economic-demographic models should be geared towards providing guidance for the formulation of strategies and policies to meet the needs of the disadvantaged groups by taking fully into account the interrelations between population factors and such elements as employment, migration, income distribution and social progress, particularly as related to poverty. (14 June 1976)

• If there are shortages of food, housing, energy, and jobs in today's world, with a population of four billion on the earth, such shortages can only worsen when the world's population grows to over six billion people twenty years from now. (5 July 1977)

• It is estimated that the combination of population growth and accelerating migration from the countryside will add nearly a billion additional people to the urban labour pool of developing countries by the end of the century. (6 November 1978)

. . . Food

• It is paradoxical that the breakthrough in population at the United Nations, when agreement was finally achieved to initiate action programmes as well as study and discussion of the matter, came at a time when scientific developments were about to create the most massive increase in agricultural productivity that the world has ever seen. For a while, it seemed that the Green Revolution, as it got underway at the end of the sixties, might make obsolete our worries about overburdening the earth with people. But even as the reports were coming in of enormous increases in crops of wheat and rice in Mexico, India, Pakistan, my own country—the Philippines, and others, warnings were being sounded of possible threats to the environment from the sort of technology needed for these increases.

Enormous efforts are being made in the developing countries to improve conditions. [But] the droughts, floods and other disasters of the past two years show something of what they are up against, and with what terrifying suddenness an apparently secure situation can turn into disaster.

Action to limit population growth is a long-term business, and can have no conceivable effect on the ratio of people to food supplies in the immediate future. More important, it seems that action to limit population growth *on its own* has little or no effect on birth rates, whereas combined with other measures of social and economic development, quite dramatic results have been noted. From this, some have concluded that there is no case for special action on population.

However, as . . . we are all now aware, there is no case for leaving to chance what can be brought about by design. As an eminent academic observed recently, "We are now observing some of the outer limits of the earth's 'carrying mass' in terms of food production."

[A recent] study [by the Overseas Development Council] concentrates on the population/food ratio. By showing that food production is limited very closely by the ecological cycle, it concludes that the main weapon against food shortage must be limitation of consumption. This is naturally directed more at the rich countries than the poor, but there is a clear warning that developing countries cannot pin their hopes on the Green Revolution, but must act so as to limit population growth. (18 October 1973)

• Food supply is a particularly urgent aspect of this [increasing rate of population] growth. As the Secretary-General of the United Nations has recently pointed out, the problem is not confined to any one area, but is world-wide. Whatever field of development work we are in, none of us can afford to ignore it. (16 May 1974)

• When the Green Revolution first began several years ago, many viewed it as a solution to the [hunger] problem. This is not the case. Only the stabilization of population will eventually solve the food problem. The Green Revolution is merely a means of buying time in which to put the brakes on population growth.

There were two ways in which family planning programmes were influenced by the Green Revolution. Some governments saw it as an excuse for relaxing efforts to slow population growth. Others derived hope from the Green Revolution. If largely illiterate farmers could respond to educational programmes and to incentives, changing traditional modes of behaviour and agriculture, then there was clearly reason to believe that the people could also change their attitudes towards desired family size, given the appropriate education and incentives to do so. Unfortunately, too many governments viewed the Green Revolution as a reason for reduced effort on the family planning front.

There is only one way to come out of our difficulties [regarding a decline in worldwide agricultural production], and that is to proceed with the utmost vigour on both the food and the population fronts simultaneously. The record shows that if the Green Revolution is to continue to spread and expand food production, it requires continuing high level management and an expanding supply of inputs, such as fertilizer and water, and of services, such as credit and technical advice. Governments in those countries which are lagging must awaken to the fact that the Green Revolution requires continued whole-hearted support and the highest level of management skills.

At the same time, there must be renewed and increased effort on the population and family planning front. These two efforts—on food and population—must be undertaken in parallel. They must complement each other and interact with each other.

We can only affirm that there is much more to learn about the relationship between population and food production. But there is hardly time to know everything before we undertake population programmes. . . . The lesson from food production is: learn by doing. (23 August 1974)

• Food and population problems have to be seen together.

The number of infants, young children and pregnant and lactating women have to be taken into account in determining food requirements. . . . Migratory movements do not only affect the demand, but also the processing, marketing and distribution of food. What Bangladesh and the countries of the Sahel region have experienced underlines dramatically the unavoidable necessity of relating food and population factors in comprehensive development policies and programmes.

The World Population Plan of Action places emphasis on the production of more food as a matter of utmost urgency and recommends that governments give high priority to improving methods of food production, the investigation and development of new sources of food, and more effective utilization of existing food sources. These measures have to be taken with the view that the gaps in the standards of living in many parts of the world be reduced, and that the more rational utilization of natural resources will avoid the deleterious effect of waste.

The collection and analysis of demographic data, and research in such fields as unemployment, starvation and poverty, are vital in planning future food production policies. Knowledge of the location and concentration of peoples, their rates of natural increase and migration, and their economic and demographic status, are invaluable tools for the planner and manager.

In considering the immediate steps to be taken in the solution of the food crisis, governments should not lose sight of the long-run effect of population growth, which will determine basically the nature, scope and intensity of future food problems. (11 November 1974)

• It [is] of great significance that the World Food Conference* adopted a resolution seeking the "Achievement of a desirable balance between population and food supply", endorsing the World Population Plan of Action, and noting [the world's] unprecedented population growth. . . . (27 January 1975)

• A few cynics condemned the World Population Conference and the World Food Conference as failures because neither came up with ready-made solutions to the problems which they were set to confront. Such critics chose to look only at the superficial events of these conferences while ignoring their wide repercussions. The World Food Conference started a chain of events which will culminate in the establishment of at least a minimum emergency reserve stock of major grains, and an International Agricultural Development Fund which should go far towards providing the finances for badly-needed agricultural and rural development. In addition, the Conference provided an opportunity to raise the level of consciousness among the public, and to make the people of different countries aware of the problems of others—and of likely effects on themselves. This in itself would have provided a justification for the Conference.

If this [the consensus reached at the World Population Conference] is linked to the consensus arrived at [by the World Food Conference] in Rome—that whatever the level of food aid, eventually the only answer to hunger is increased production in the developing countries themselves—a most important conclusion emerges: The answer to the two questions—"How to achieve a satisfactory rate of population growth?" and "How to eliminate hunger?" are the same in outline—concentrate development energies among the majority who live in the countryside.

*Held in November 1974 at Rome.

The implications are now being worked out in practice by countries with widely differing population and food needs. There are some important factors which are common to the needs of all, however.

Farmers are among the most conservative of groups, because their livelihood depends totally and directly on what they produce. They can only be persuaded to adopt new [farming] methods when they can be reasonably certain that they will work. As a corollary, many of the methods which look illogical or wasteful to an outsider are in fact the result of years or generations of experience. They are not lightly to be interfered with. This implies that agricultural development plans should be worked out *with* rather than *for* the farmer. Not surprisingly, the same sort of conservatism is found in approaches to family size, with the same implication.

Social structures and customs in rural areas are adapted to an age-old way of life. When development plans are being made, it follows that they should be sensitive to local conditions and adapted to them. As an example, it has been shown that small farms of three acres or less can be profitable in Asia, but clearly it would be of no use to offer such small farmers loans to buy full-size tractors.

The interplay of technology and social structure needs more understanding at all levels, but especially in its effects on agriculture. Many criticisms have been levelled at so-called "intermediate technology"—that it is "second best", that it tends to confirm the low status of the peasant rather than improve it, and so on. On the other hand, the dangers of the sudden introduction of the latest labour-saving, capital intensive technology have been clearly demonstrated.

Of equal importance is the integration of agricultural and other sectors. Lack of transport and adequate roads has left grain rotting in fields in many places in the past. Poor storage is still responsible for huge losses all over the developing world. Facilities for processing and manufacturing agricultural raw materials are often lacking—not always through lack of finance. And one of the most difficult subjects of all is access to markets in other countries, especially the industrialized. Here only international co-operation can provide the necessary openings.

The industrialized countries can, if they will, make vital contributions to effective development in the rural sector. In population activities over the last few years, there has been a marked shift in emphasis. From simply supplying products developed in the West and using Western promotion techniques, donor countries have moved towards an approach which is much more sensitive to the real needs of the recipients. Similarly, in agricultural development, the donors can contribute greatly in helping to develop appropriate technologies, for production, storage, transport and communications, marketing, and processing. . . .

Land reform must be accompanied by the provision of credit and other services to enable farmers to make use of what they have gained. (26 September 1975)

. . . Health and Nutrition

• The population problems of the developing world are very consequential for the welfare of their people: too rapid growth rates threaten their aspirations for improved living standards, education, health, nutrition, jobs and "modernization" in general. . . .

The United Nations will attempt to strengthen applied and operational research in . . . human reproduction and epidemiological studies. . . . (4 November 1970)

• A few major demonstration projects making provision for family planning in connection with maternal and child health services are envisaged. For advice and services on family planning, the maternity-centred approach is one of the most effective means of reaching women. . . . (18 February 1971)

• The immediate problem for the millions of people in developing countries is grinding poverty, inadequate housing and poor sanitation, unemployment or underemployment, malnutrition, disease and premature deaths—and little prospect of any substantial improvement in their lifetimes. Moreover, whatever success is achieved through current efforts to accelerate the demographic transition in developing countries, the population of the developing regions will almost certainly double within the next twenty-five to thirty years, and may double again by the year 2050. (10 August 1972)

• The high levels of fertility prevailing in most countries in the Asian region are the legacy of a long cultural tradition which has encouraged large-sized families. Indeed, it is only in recent history that high fertility has ceased to be essential for the survival of the species. And even now, in many areas death rates remain sufficiently high to preclude any thought of having fewer children. (1 November 1972)

• Rewards of better health, longer life and more food for all . . . could come with enlightened population policies. (14 February 1973)

• Place population policies within the context of an overall plan for economic and social development, which aims at eliminating starvation and malnutrition, at providing more jobs, better housing and more educational facilities, and at reducing inequalities in the distribution of national resources and personal income, and *then* we can look for specific reasons why family planning services are not being used to full advantage.

These are aspects to which the Fund is giving constant attention. (14 February 1973-B)

• [The forecast of recent] population projections . . . is not only a demographer's nightmare. It could be human tragedy. It is anybody's guess how many of the individuals making up that grand total will have any real expectations of adequate food, clothing, shelter, education, medical care, and job opportunities—in short, a life worth living. (15 February 1973)

• There is a direct relationship not simply between national prosperity and family size, but between *relative* prosperity within a country and family size. . . .

This says more than simply that if incomes go up fertility goes down. Distribution of benefits is brought about in part typically by the provision of a whole package of health, welfare and education services. . . . (26 September 1973)

- [A recent study by the Overseas Development Council] shows that birth rates in developing countries do not usually decline in the absence of some improvement in well-being; in particular, assured food supply, improved health services and higher literacy. (18 October 1973)

- Where population and family planning activities are organized as part of an already existing programme, for example, the integration of family planning services in MCH [maternal and child health programmes] . . . the results have been impressive. (22 October 1973)

- Existing difficulties in providing food, housing, education, medical attention and employment are going to compound themselves in accelerated ratio to population increases . . . unless rational solutions are sought and action taken, not when the swollen population figures are a reality, but *now*. (21 January 1974)

- We do not talk any more in terms of family planning as an answer to population growth, because we realize now that there is far more to population than family planning. . . . It is now realized that the number of children a family has depends on a very complex interaction, in which levels of education, the quality of housing, health and social security services play a part, and which is tied closely to the form overall social and economic development is taking. (2 April 1974)

- We know . . . that healthy families tend on the whole to be smaller families, so we may take part in a scheme to improve the health of mothers and children.

  It has been shown quite clearly that population growth rates will drop, given the right economic and social conditions. It seems that people require more than anything else not prosperity, but a measure of security, in housing, health, jobs, education and, above all, in food supply, before they will risk reducing the numbers of their children. (19 April 1974)

- Discussion in Bucharest ranged widely over an enormous variety of topics, and the [World Population] Plan [of Action] reflects this. . . . The depth and complexity of the interactions between population and many other variables—health, for example, nutrition, education, the status of women—is acknowledged. (15 October 1974)

- Some of the regional trends [as of 1975]:

  In Latin America there has been an almost *seven-fold* increase in the past two years, in requests for projects in maternal and child health and family planning. In Western Asia requests for UNFPA assistance have trebled in the past two years, with the emphasis on the development of basic population data . . . but with increasing interest in family health and planning. . . .

  In Sub-Saharan Africa, strong interest continues in demographic data collection and analysis, and there is now also discernible a growing interest in family planning as part of their efforts to strengthen basic health services.

In Asia and the Pacific, over 95% of our project requests are for support to family health and planning programmes and related communication and education activities for fertility reduction. (27 January 1975)

• Family planning . . . cannot effectively be introduced without the follow-up health services which are needed.

Our experience has led us to emphasize the introduction of family planning, mother and child care service, training, communication and other services as part of a complete package, part of an overall plan which will probably include census and demographic services. (26 September 1975)

• The various international strategies such as the World Population Plan of Action, the International Development Strategy for the Second Development Decade, and the World Plan of Action focusing on the integration of women and development, should provide guidance for the activities of the Fund. These strategies, particularly the first one, suggest that an integrated development approach to population be applied. This would mean that population activities would be funded increasingly in conjunction with activities in health, education, rural development, community development and other programmes of economic and social development. (21 November 1975)

• Most of the global problems that nations have recently addressed themselves to with increasing seriousness and intensity - world hunger, the need for a new international economic order, population growth, crime, environment, human settlements, the plight of Sub-Saharan Africa, unemployment, health, and vestigial colonialism, not to mention the need for an appropriate and equitable role for women in social and economic affairs—ultimately and essentially are bound up with the questions of poverty.

In dealing with poverty, one of the resources that humanity is running out of is time. The demographic forecast is that before the United Nations is twice as old as it is now, there will be twice as many people as there are now who need to share the material resources of this planet as equitably as possible. It is becoming evident, therefore, that the needs of food, shelter, health and education must be attended to now, before they become too heavy and complex to handle. (20 February 1976)

• High overall population growth, high fertility rates, high infant mortality and high population density—there is a close parallel between these characteristics in a nation and severe poverty among its people. (14 June 1976)

• In many countries, the activities which . . . would be described as "family planning" come under the heading of activities designed to promote health and social welfare, and contraceptive services are provided as part of a package of health and welfare services. This offers many advantages, not the least of which is that existing networks and personnel can be used to carry both motivation and means to the people who need them. It also avoids singling out fertility regulation and integrates contraceptive services with other population and development services.

As [an] . . . example of the broad sweep of population activities today, we may take the concern with factors indirectly affecting the birth rate. Mortality, particularly infant mortality, is a concern for all developing countries, for its own sake as well as for its demographic effects. . . . (30 March 1977)

• Poverty, and everything that it implies—insufficient food, inadequate housing, ill health, poor education, little comfort and less hope—has complex connections with population growth.

[When the Fund became operational] eight years ago, family planning structures undertaken for demographic reasons were normally vertical structures, though connected to health ministries. Today, family planning programmes, whether interventionist or not, are more likely to be integrated in the wider context of maternal and child health care. . . . Indeed, family planning is increasingly seen as a social welfare service. (2 June 1977)

• Eight years ago, the health services infrastructures in many developing countries were poorly developed or practically non-existent. Countries wanting to institute family planning programmes had, of necessity, to establish vertical or parallel programmes, if they were to be initiated at all. UNFPA-funded family planning programmes provided the impetus for the initiation by the developing countries, not only of the development of their health services, but of the expansion of model family planning programmes as well.

As health services infrastructures have been built up, family planning programmes have been integrated with maternal and child health care programmes. [A recent] United Nations survey points up the fact that the governments of all of the 81 countries which have national family planning programmes consider these to be an essential means of achieving acceptable levels of maternal and child health and family welfare, and of satisfying the goals of human rights and the improved status of women. In this sense, the programmes are integral parts of health and social policies. Indeed, it is as a health policy that the most rapid and widespread diffusion of family planning programmes has been accepted by governments of developing countries of varied cultural and developmental characteristics. (21 June 1977)

• Malnutrition, hunger, ill-health, untimely death, illiteracy, inequity, social injustice—problems with which we are embattled today—have provided the substance of our history, the cutting edge of our philosophy, the themes of our art, the authority of our religious teachings, and the force behind the eternal quest for the perfectibility of Man. But the old solutions, the familiar pace, and the habitual ways we have developed to turn our eyes away from the problem which always seemed to be caused by other people's foolishness or natural incompetence, will no longer do.

The size of the family does not necessarily, in our time, indicate the extent of the love the parents have for their children. Often it is a sign of the fear they have, or have had, of children dying in infancy or at a very young age, from malnutrition and consequent susceptibility to disease. The relationship between the fall in infant mortality and the spread in voluntary acceptors of contraception in the state of Kerala in India is an excellent case in point. (27 September 1977)

- There is increasing understanding and acceptance [by governments] of the complex interrelationship between fertility patterns and such areas as maternal and child health and nutrition, education, the status and role of women, and other vital development concerns. (28 March 1978)

- UNFPA is increasingly being called upon to support programmes on infant and maternal mortality with the direct objective of contributing to the regulation and reduction of fertility. . . . In other cases, such programmes are supported with the main objective of reducing infant mortality and maternal mortality and morbidity, while the influence upon fertility is only incidental and not a primary objective. . . . (21 June 1978)

- Another encouraging feature of the recent past has been the impressive gains made in the expectation of life at birth. In the last quarter century, life expectancy in the developing countries has increased on the average from 42 to 54 years, and in the developed world from about 65 to 71 years.

In the developing world, infant mortality continues to be the most important determinant of general levels of mortality. It is, therefore, encouraging to note that infant mortality rates, as well as overall death rates in developing countries, have fallen substantially during the recent past.

In the area of programme trends, there is a growing interest in turning to simpler community-based schemes, to give closer attention to the basic health needs of people. UNFPA, which has supported this strategy in maternal and child care, believes that such an approach for primary health care will prove effective in further reducing mortality and morbidity.

The implications of this . . . [projected] huge increase [of the world's population to 5.8 billion by the year 2000] for national policies in such important areas as employment, industrialization, migration, population distribution, housing and the provision of health and education services, will affect all areas of the world. (6 November 1978)

. . . Human Rights

- The availability of information and means to enable couples to decide freely and responsibly on the number and spacing of their children has been declared a basic human right. . . . The Economic and Social Council has, upon the recommendation of the Sixteenth Session of this [Population] Commission, adopted a resolution urging all member states "To ensure, in accordance with national population policies and needs, that information and education about family planning as well as the means to practise family planning effectively is made available to all individuals by the end of the Second United Nations Development Decade. . . .* A major objective of [World Population] Year should be, therefore, in accordance with this resolution, to encourage all governments, whatever their demographic objectives, to develop information and education on population and family life matters and to intensify family planning delivery systems. (10 August 1972)

*ECOSOC resolution 1672 (LII), 2 June 1972.

- Population is a question that basically concerns people. Decisions on overall plans and strategies need to be undertaken and implemented by governments. It is, however, the individuals whose lives are affected by these plans and strategies, and who need to be given adequate knowledge, information and facilities to enable them to make a meaningful choice in their own personal lives. The United Nations has recognized, through its resolution of 11 December 1969 (GA 2542 (XXIV)) that parents have the exclusive right to determine freely and responsibly the number and spacing of their children, and that provision of knowledge and means necessary to enable them to exercise that right should be made available to individuals. In a further resolution, of 15 December 1970*, the United Nations General Assembly has identified as a minimum target for the Second Development Decade, availability of the necessary information and advice to all persons who so desire it, to enable them to decide freely and responsibly on the number and spacing of their children, and to prepare them for responsible parenthood. (28 June 1973)

- We have recognized that the decision on family size is taken by individuals and [that] they should have access to the information and means to determine the size of their family and spacing of their children, in exercise of their basic human rights, as set forth in various United Nations declarations. (20 February 1976)

- Through the years of debate, several different strands of thinking on population have emerged. . . . The first regards the population/resources situation as a "crisis" which can be solved only by extraordinary means, perhaps by suspending for a time normal civil liberties, including freedom of choice in fertility. This view has gained some support but has no status in the United Nations, where the right of national and individual self-determination has . . . long been an article of faith. It is doubtful, in fact, whether any progress at all would have been made in assistance to population programmes without such safeguards. (28 September 1976)

- Coercive measures, as an extension of [national population] policies, have been widely discussed but not yet given legal sanction. Adoption of such measures, if they are sanctioned, will have to be regarded in the light of the Declaration of Human Rights and other international agreements endorsing the right of freedom of choice in fertility. The fact that they are even being considered attests to the severity of the pressures under which governments find themselves; but it is worth pointing out that sufficient emphasis on persuasive policies may well make coercive measures unnecessary. If it is sincerely desired to avoid coercion and all the complications which would ensue, support for persuasive policies should be intensified in developed and developing countries alike and in the United Nations, and every effort made to ensure that they succeed. (12 January 1977)

- In most countries, the great majority of couples do not yet have a real choice because contraceptive services are not available. . . . It has been estimated that fewer than one in five fertile couples in all developing countries practice contraception. This means that the realization of the principle of freedom of choice in family size is still far off.

*General Assembly resolution 2770 (XXV), 15 December 1970.

The right of access to the means of contraception is acknowledged almost universally today, though for millions of people, particularly in the rural areas of the developing world, the right remains without meaning because they have neither the means nor the information to avail themselves of it.

At the personal level, . . . hostility [to modern means of contraception] can be aroused by insensitive approaches, and there are recent examples of useful and progressive programmes which have had to be scrapped because of crude or simply over-enthusiastic implementation. (30 March 1977)

• Fully recognizing human rights, the Fund supports those activities in which participation is voluntary, especially in regard to fertility regulation. (5 July 1977)

. . . Law

• Reviews should be undertaken of laws and practices in developing countries related to population questions, to examine their effects, if any, upon population growth and distribution. Laws and practices concerning abortion, sterilization, sale of contraceptives, publicity about contraceptive techniques, age at marriage, tax rebates for married persons and their dependent children, family allowances, social security benefits to mothers and children and status of women are some of the many areas which should be investigated.* In many countries such laws and practices may have effects which are not in conformity with established population policies and goals. Research grants to local institutions, consultants, and advisers may be provided to arrange for such studies within a regional or global framework. (18 February 1971)

• Insufficient attention has been paid to the effects of various social policy measures on fertility, and to their potential use in support of family planning programmes and as a part of comprehensive population policy. Among such measures are tax and welfare benefits, including family allowances, maternity benefits, tax deductions for children, and housing provision for large families. It is desirable to scrutinize all relevant social legislation realistically from the point of view of its probable influence upon childbearing and population growth and, if necessary, to revise it to bring it into line with population policy goals. Special consideration should also be given to legislation raising the legal age at marriage. . . . (1 November 1972)

• Population law may be defined as "that body of the law which relates directly or indirectly to the population growth, distribution and those aspects of well-being affecting, as well as affected by, population size and distribution". . . . As such, population law is concerned not only with the problems posed by population size and distribution, but ultimately with human rights. Family planning, for example, should not be viewed as a goal in itself, but rather as a means to an end—opportunities for adequate food, health, clothing, shelter, education, work, recreation, old-age security, etc.—all of them basic human rights which family planning affects.

*See UNFPA publication, *Survey of Contraceptive Laws: Country Profiles, Checklists, and Summaries,* 143 pp., 1976. See also UNFPA publication, *The Symposium on Law and Population* (Proceedings, Background Papers and Recommendations), 309 pp., 1975, a report on a meeting held in Tunis from 21-24 June 1974, sponsored by the United Nations and UNFPA in co-operation with the Government of Tunisia, ILO, UNESCO, WHO, IPPF, and the International Advisory Committee on Population and Law.

But "right" and "duty" are two sides of the same coin. Acceptance of human rights necessarily entails a corresponding duty not only to refrain from activities which would impede the exercise of the right but, positively, to undertake the necessary measures for the realization and safeguarding of such a right. Furthermore, inherent in the concept of "right" is the discharge of it with "responsibility"—whether explicitly provided, as in the Teheran Proclamation on Human Rights, with respect to family planning as a basic human right, or implicit, as in the right to the freedom of speech, either in time of peace (e.g., libel, defamation, nuisance, obscenity) or during war or emergency (e.g., treason, sedition, censorship). Continuing the family planning right as an example, "responsible" parenthood must seek to balance the "individual" with the "collective" right. . . . The question of when exactly does the "individual" right give way to the "collective" is always difficult to answer—even in the case of freedom of speech, notwithstanding its centuries-old development and refinement. However, it is equally clear that inability to define with exactness the relationship between the individual and collective rights does not negate their existence. Problems such as these will remain to test the inventiveness and ingenuity of lawyers.

As far as the Fund is concerned, the degree of importance we attach to the Law and Population Project may be gleaned from the fact that it was the first project directly executed by the Fund. The project is conducted not merely as an academic study, but a dynamic project which will have long-felt effects on the behaviour of countries that respect the "rule of law". We would like to see the population factor formulated into policies and executed as operationally feasible programmes in all countries if possible, but never losing sight of the ultimate goal of human rights.

When the World Population Conference and Year are over, our tasks as lawyers are just beginning. For the World Population Plan of Action remains to be implemented, which means the removal of conflicting laws which frustrate such implementation and the adoption of new laws to further the objectives of the Plan. To us lawyers, every year is World Population Year. (21 June 1974)

• Incentives and disincentives of varying types and degrees of severity are increasingly being used to influence couples in the direction of smaller families. Many countries have examined legal provisions affecting family size and have acted to raise the minimum age at marriage, provide contraceptive services through workplaces and legalize sterilization, to take some random examples. (12 January 1977)

• Many countries in which economic development is being hampered by population growth are already endeavouring to introduce social reforms, undertake new development strategies, and draw up legislative measures which aim at influencing people to have smaller families. Moreover, old laws enacted at a time when the traditional social stance was pro-natalist are being rescinded or amended to meet modern social needs—legalized sterilization is an example. New laws are being introduced to remove barriers to making contraceptives available to the population at large. Efforts are also being made to lower fertility by raising the minimum age at marriage and by providing fiscal rewards to couples opting for smaller families. (21 June 1977)

. . . Peace and Stability

- The question can always be asked, why should a developed country contribute to this [population assistance] effort when it is saddled with its own social and economic problems? The answer has long been given by a distinguished citizen of this country [Canada], Lester B. Pearson, who in his Report to the Commission on International Development, said that the answer "is a moral one: that it is only right for those who have to share with those who have not. Concern with the needs of other and poorer nations is the expression of a new and fundamental aspect of the modern age—the awareness that we live in a village world, that we belong to a world community. It is a recognition that concern with improvement of the human condition is no longer divisible."

Indeed, for mankind to solve its most serious problem—the growth of its numbers—a combined action and a common goal among the developed and developing nations of the world are needed over a long period of time. Little sacrifices are needed from the citizens of the developed world to preserve the peace in our generation. (4 November 1970)

- Now, if we accept . . . and accept we must . . . that enormous burgeoning of populations cannot be confined by national or regional demarcations. And if we accept . . . and all mankind's history points to this . . . that the depressive economic and human miseries resulting from too many people and too little food and opportunity in one part of the world undoubtedly imperils the security and well-being of another . . . then surely we have already made a solid case for a worldwide population strategy. (26 August 1971)

- It is only very recently that it has been brought home to us that the world is an interlocking system, any part of which we ignore at our peril. Recent studies show in practice that co-operation is more likely to produce desired ends than conflict except in the very short term. . . . (15 October 1974)

- It is . . . possible for us to think in terms which would have seemed impossibly romantic only a generation or two ago—of a world free from the three deadly enemies of mankind [war, disease and famine]. [We must] go further than this. It is now not only possible, but mandatory to think in these terms. [But] our position has been held, whether we like it or not, at the cost of some of our independence. There is not one nation, or group of nations today, which can exist on its own resources. Whether for oil, or for industrial raw materials, or for manufactured products, interdependence has become the key to our economic survival. Conflict, hunger, disease in any part of the world affect us all.

The implications of interdependence—not just a slogan now, but a reality—are slowly being worked out by the international community. They are impelled by the knowledge that serious damage to one part of the world means almost certain disaster for the rest. This makes nonsense of the "triage" or "lifeboat" theories being put about by pessimists who have been seduced by their own rhetoric. Such people believe that our situation is so near to cataclysm that some poor countries must be sacrificed to assure the survival of the remainder. Their error is to believe that it is possible in practical terms to make this sort of choice. Instead, far from the rich world occupying a lifeboat and having the awkward choice of whom among the poor countries to haul aboard, we are all very much in the same boat. If the boat is overloaded or underpowered at one end, the whole crew is affected. (26 September 1975)

• [International assistance is] an investment above all in peace, stability and the happiness of much of the human race. (30 March 1977)

• We can see the possibility of a world in which humans and the humane values are given their full importance. But other, much less pleasant futures are possible—the developed countries retreating behind their economic and physical barriers; civil or international warfare for the control of essential resources; population growth limited not by choice but by starvation and disease. The world is changing. We are in the transition from one era to another. Attainment of a world fit to live in demands keener perception and deeper insights into these changes. (2 June 1977)

. . . Population Distribution

• Action programmes for which assistance may be provided are not limited to activities designed to affect fertility, but may, insofar as resources permit, also include programmes concerned with internal and international migratory movements. (3 November 1971)

• Our concept of population problems covers much more than high fertility and rapid rates of population growth. We are concerned also . . . with international migration and urbanization. (10 August 1972)

• [A] government may wish to know for its future planning how many people are drifting into the towns from the villages each year, and how fast the population in each area is growing. (19 April 1974)

• We are . . . supporting studies concerned with the implications of internal, regional and international migration.

The UNFPA has funded . . . special studies on internal migration . . . and expects to provide assistance for technical studies relating to settlement schemes, as well as studies on incentives to encourage the return of migrants from urban areas back to their rural settlements. These projects will have a vital impact on economic and social development. . . . (21 May 1975)

• In discussing action upon the creation and development of human settlements, governments should consider population policy as a basis upon which many decisions may be built. . . . (2 June 1976)

• Many developing countries have severe problems associated with the drift of country dwellers into the cities, others of different kinds of imbalance. Seventy-five developing, and twenty-five of the forty-two developed countries, have policies aimed at changing patterns of migration. (30 March 1977)

- An important population question in many countries is that of population redistribution and internal migration—in fact, most governments of developing countries consider such problems of major importance (in a United Nations survey, 95 out of 114 developing countries gave high priority to these problems). The mandate of UNFPA, as endorsed last year by the UNDP Governing Council, the Economic and Social Council, and the General Assembly, explicitly includes population redistribution, particularly in the context of population policy formulation and implementation, as one of UNFPA's areas of concern. This year we have received several preliminary expressions of interest from governments concerning assistance in this area. (7 November 1977)

- As governments reformulate and refine their perceptions of population needs, on the basis of a better data and information base, the emphasis on various sectoral activities has begun to shift. The question of migration and dispersal of settlements, for instance, is emerging as a major sector of population activity and will require increasing international assistance. (28 March 1978)

- In order to support and inform government policies and to assist planners in developing activities that are responsive to the needs of the people, as well as effective, the UNFPA is being asked [for example] to assist in research on transmigration. The goal is to learn more about the reasons why people migrate. Some of the questions for which answers are sought include: What elements of regional development have an important bearing on migration behavior? Is employment creation through regional development a sufficient incentive to migrate, given adequate flows? How do rural development policies influence net outmigration? What are the likely effects of labour and manpower policies, including wage policies, on migrants' decisions? Does the type of wage contract offered by the private sector encourage only short-term migration? The relationship between these population questions and [a] government's development policies is self-evident. (3 April 1978)

- Along with the growing awareness of population as a key factor in promoting national prosperity, governments have also shown an increasing desire to make their population policies more comprehensive and to direct their actions to many fronts rather than limiting themselves to consider only one or two demographic variables. Thus, they have shown definite interest in the geographical distribution of their population and in internal and international migration, in addition to the more "traditional" concerns with fertility and mortality.

In response to this trend, UNFPA has begun to support, or has under discussion, requests for assistance for studies on internal migration . . . and for pilot schemes on population redistribution and settlement of population from congested or scattered areas. . . . In making support available, the Fund realizes that undertakings in these fields may often involve capital-intensive efforts. Yet the fact remains that nearly all the governments in the developing world have expressed dissatisfaction with the distribution of their population, and a desire to adopt measures to resolve such problems. . . . It is our view that UNFPA has an obligation to respond to requests, albeit with great caution. . . . The Fund's policy always has been, and will continue to be, to support only activities in which the population participate voluntarily. (21 June 1978)

[The Deputy Executive Director of UNFPA, Halvor Gille, in a statement to the Governing Council in June 1978 further outlined UNFPA policy in this area: "Due to the growing understanding of the implications of population trends on development efforts and the increasing recognition of population factors as crucial in promoting economic and social development, governments are showing an increasing desire to make their population policies more comprehensive. This trend has recently manifested itself in a number of requests for population assistance in areas within the mandate of the Fund as determined by the Economic and Social Council but in which we previously had few requests. One of these 'new' areas requiring assistance from UNFPA is spatial distribution of the population and migratory movements. The increasing interest in support of population redistribution and migration programmes no doubt reflects the fact that this is an area of concern to a large number of developing countries. . . . It seems clear that UNFPA has a mandate to provide assistance in the area of population redistribution and migration. This would be in accordance with the main aim and purpose of the Fund, which is, as stated by ECOSOC, to extend systematic and sustained assistance to developing countries at their request in dealing with their population problems."*

At the ECOSOC meeting, the following month, Mr. Gille stated that "In view of the Fund's responsibility to respond to the needs of countries and governments in accordance with their own policies and priorities, assistance should be provided in the field of population distribution and related activities. It is recognized, however, that the Fund's resources are limited, and, therefore, it will not be possible to support action programmes aiming at population redistribution on a large scale as such activities could easily absorb a major part of available resources." He outlined the areas in which UNFPA assistance might be provided:

Assistance may be provided to improve the knowledge of migratory movements and causes for and attitudes towards migration and resettlement. Data collection activities may be supported not only in connection with population censuses but also current population statistics, sample surveys and other sources.

Support may be provided for studies on levels, trends and patterns of migratory movements, urbanization and distribution of the population as well as the determinants and consequences of such movements. Migration and population distribution factors should be analysed in relation to land use, location of industry, availability of social services, communication and transport facilities and other relevant economic and social factors.

The Fund may support activities which assist developing countries in developing plans and guidelines for programmes designed to deal with their population distribution problems.

Assistance may be provided to promote the training of personnel concerned with data collection, research, and policy formulation in the fields of population redistribution and migration.

*ECOSOC resolution 1763 (LIV), 18 May 1973.

Institutions in developing countries may be supported in fields of data collection, research and policy formulation concerning population redistribution and migration, particularly by strengthening existing facilities in statistical offices, planning units in various ministries, universities and research institutes.

The Fund may give support to small scale pilot projects and exploration of innovative approaches to deal with the problems concerned and with the aim of guiding the government and other authorities in formulating and implementing policies. UNFPA support in this area should be limited mainly to providing advisory services in such areas as urban planning, rural development, regional planning, demographic and health aspects and social welfare and community facilities for the benefit of migrant population.

In conclusion he noted that:

"UNFPA support for population distribution and migration activities should be provided primarily as a part of over-all development programmes in such fields as rural development, urban renewal, social or family welfare, community development, anti-poverty schemes, etc. The Fund should not provide financial support for the actual movements of families or individuals from one place to another either directly by funding transport costs or indirectly by providing vehicles for this purpose. Under no circumstance should UNFPA be involved directly or through multi-bi arrangements in projects in which the population concerned does not participate voluntarily."]

. . . Poverty

• Although an increasing number of countries have adopted policies aimed at achieving a reduction in the rate of population growth, such efforts should not be allowed to divert attention from the urgent problems that exist now as a result of past and present high rates of population growth. The immediate problem for the millions of people in developing countries is grinding poverty, inadequate housing and poor sanitation, unemployment or underemployment, malnutrition, disease and premature deaths—and little prospect of any substantial improvement in their lifetimes. Moreover, whatever success is achieved through current efforts to accelerate the demographic transition in developing countries, the population of the developing regions will almost certainly double within the next twenty-five years to thirty years, and may double again by the year 2050. Population growth of this magnitude has far-reaching implications for all aspects of development, and seriously jeopardizes hope for any substantial improvements in living standards in the coming decades.

The situation is such that consideration must be given to the need for alternative development strategies and to fundamental changes in the relations between rich and poor countries. It also indicates the need for much greater efforts by the international community to improve living standards in developing regions. (10 August 1972)

• In a very real sense, poverty breeds poverty; poorer families tend to have more children, who are dependent on the family for several years before they begin to make a contribution. In the family, as in the country as a whole, more dependents mean that there is less opportunity for savings, for investment and, therefore, for development. (25 August 1973)

• It is not at all clear that the present poverty of the majority of developing countries is caused by rapid growth of the population, nor that an improvement in economic conditions would necessarily follow a reduction in their population growth rates. Let us not delude ourselves that population control is an answer to the problem of poverty, but rather attempt to find out all we can about the relationship between population, poverty and development. (26 September 1973)

• Voluntary limitation of family size will not solve the problems of poverty, just as large families do not in themselves cause poverty, but can it be denied that many children would have had a better start in life if they had had fewer brothers and sisters with whom to share? (30 November 1973)

• Those from the countries of Europe, North America and Australasia must imagine a situation in which poverty is not the exception but the rule—and a poverty which can only feebly be described. It is not simply material poverty—although the national income per head of population in developing countries is only a fraction of that in the more developed—but a lack of most of the things which make life worth living, including, very often, hope.

The UNFPA, along with most other development agencies, is well aware that there can be no successful programme of slowing down population growth without real and permanent increases in the standard of living of ordinary people. Really poor people do not care how many children they have, because they will still be poor; moreover, a large number of children will at least ensure that one or two survive to be a support to their parents in old age. More hands can always be used for the few weeks of planting, hoeing, and harvesting the crop, even though they will be idle for the rest of the year. (19 April 1974)

• We should manage our everyday affairs with wisdom and foresight. Looking at the world today, can it be truly said that we have done this? . . . . Poverty is an ever-present condition of life for many people in today's world; perhaps it has always been so, but now the fruits of that poverty are being harvested. These are the crises of which we seem to hear every day, riots in one place, mass starvation in another, epidemic disease in a third. Can it truly be said that we are managing our affairs well when our worst problems are not faced squarely until they leap at us in the form of still another crisis?

Chronic poverty, with a nation as with an individual, makes it difficult, if not impossible, to realise latent abilities. (18 May 1974)

• Most of the global problems that nations have recently addressed themselves to with increasing seriousness and intensity—world hunger, the need for a new international economic order, population growth, crime, environment, human settlements, the plight of Sub-Saharan Africa, unemployment, health, and vestigial colonialism, not to mention the need for an appropriate and equitable role for women in social and economic affairs—ultimately and essentially are bound up with the question of poverty.

In dealing with poverty, one of the resources that humanity is running out of is time. The demographic forecast is that before the United Nations is twice as old as it is now, there will be twice as many people as there are now who need to share the material resources of this planet as equitably as possible. It is becoming evident, therefore, that the needs of food, shelter, health and education must be attended to now, before they become too heavy and complex to handle. (20 February 1976)

• It is readily apparent that poverty and population are inextricably linked. . . . They are both concerned with the welfare of the individual, the quality of life in society and, by the same token, the development of the country.

High overall population growth, high fertility rates, high infant mortality and high population density—there is a close parallel between these characteristics in a nation and severe poverty among its people. (14 June 1976)

• A serious attack on the problem of rapid population growth is clearly a priority with most governments of the developing world. . . . It is equally clear, however, that a con-certed attack on poverty must be made at the same time if population programmes are to have a chance of success. (12 January 1977)

• Poverty, and everything that it implies—insufficient food, inadequate housing, ill health, poor education, little comfort and less hope—has complex connections with population growth. (2 June 1977)

[In July 1977, at the meeting of ECOSOC, the Deputy Executive Director of the UNF-PA, Halvor Gille, further explained the UNFPA role in reaching the disadvantaged. He stated: "In developing . . . basic needs programmes there is one principle . . . which is especially important to keep in mind. That is, the urgency of meeting the needs of disadvantaged population groups. This principle is not merely justified as an act of altruism; the success of population and development policies depends very much on meeting the demands of these groups, which comprise a very large proportion of the population of most developing countries.

"By definition, disadvantaged, particularly poverty-stricken groups, are the most dif-ficult to reach, and are the most in need of population assistance. Often they remain in urban ghettos and slums or rural depressed areas, virtually untouched by economic growth and social development going around them. They are deprived in large measure of the basic human needs—health, nutrition, housing, education and employment. Mortality and fertility may remain high. Disease is common and life expectancy short. Among the poorest half of the population, fertility rates may be up to 50 per cent higher than the national average.

"Population activities can, of course, only meet some of the basic requirements of disadvantaged population groups for improving their lives and becoming part of the development process. Undoubtedly, when some of the basic development services have been provided, it will be easier to deliver family planning and other population pro-grammes. Nevertheless, access to the means of family planning and advice on how to use them is also a basic human right and need—a need of its own as well as related to other aspects of social progress. Moreover, many development activities such as basic health and nutrition services, including parasite control and encouragement of breast-feeding and basic education in schools as well as outside schools can be integrated with provisions for family planning supplies and services. Community-based distribution of family planning means through a very wide variety of channels is becoming the norm rather than the exception in an increasing number of developing countries. UNFPA will continue to support such integration of birth planning and other population programmes within the life of the community."]

• It is now widely agreed that assistance to developing countries who wish to reduce their rate of population growth, and assistance for developing their material and human resources, are not mutually exclusive efforts but essentially related, if poverty is to be minimized and contained, as smallpox and cholera have been, through concerted international action.

There is a level of poverty which human beings can perhaps tolerate but there are too many millions now existing well below that line. Poverty and abject misery are different experiences, and 40 per cent of the world's people are condemned to misery. (27 September 1977)

. . . Religion

• The Fund operates in countries of all religious and political persuasions. For example, in a number of Catholic countries our programmes include provision for training social visitors who teach the rhythm method in the villages where they work. (18 October 1973)

• We have, in UNFPA, given a great deal of attention to maintaining close relations with non-governmental groups, although we have never suggested any particular point of view on population that ought to be promoted by any private groups, including those related to the Church.

In the last year, UNFPA has given support to a number of Church-related activities in Africa, Asia and Latin America. . . . The regional and national attitudes which come through [in the conclusions and recommendations from these meetings and seminars] are clearly related to specific economic, social and cultural situations and needs of the the areas concerned. At the same time, we can find a number of common threads running through all of these statements. [There is] no better way of referring to these common points than restating what was said by the participants of the regional seminar organized by International Educational Development in Manila.

The statement suggests that we should support all efforts towards the solution of the population problem which lead to the fostering and preservation of human and moral values and to the true fulfillment of persons as individuals and as members of a community. In seeking vigorous and effective means to solve this problem, "it is the responsibility of the Church to assist men to form their consciences in the task of a truly human development".

Our purpose in 1974 [World Population Year] is nothing less than to raise the consciousness of the world on this one subject [that population is inseparable from other factors in social and economic development] and its implications for rich countries and poor alike . . . . Let us be more specific about what . . . members of the Church can do.

There is confusion and prejudice arising from ignorance of even the simplest facts of sexuality and reproduction. The Church's wise guidance and instruction is needed in this as in all aspects of family life. Beyond the family, on national and international issues, information and guidance is needed on the relationship of the rich world to the poor world, including issues such as the rate of consumption of natural resources, pollution and the environment, aid and trade, and population and development.

Secondly, Catholic aid agencies already do valuable work in grassroots development all over the world. Their work deserves the commitment of all Catholics. . . . In the United States and other developed countries, staff at headquarters and voluntary workers can render invaluable service in winning public support for the aims of the Year.

[A] third point leads on from the second: In its influence on decision-makers, the Church is without an equal. [We] would urge strongly that Church groups and individual lay and clerical members use their influence on governments and non-governmental organizations on behalf of the aims of World Population Year.

Finally a most important consideration . . . subsumes the rest. The question of poverty in the world and its eradication, the allied questions of development and population, are in the end questions of morality. We should not become so closely involved in consideration of the morality of specific means of family planning that we lose sight of the wider issue, which is no less than the physical, mental and moral well-being of two-thirds of mankind. . . World Population Year is concerned with the totality of the relationship between population and development. It is a concern . . . that all Catholics can share. (30 November 1973)

• The custodian of the quality of life in this [Western Asian region] and many other parts of the world is Islam. Population questions are, therefore, not irrelevant to the Islamic concern for social justice and human well-being. However, answers to these questions must come from within Islam and not from sources external to it. It is important for Moslem scholars to produce answers to population problems which are consistent with Islamic values and culturally meaningful for Moslems.* (21 May 1974)

• There is . . . religious opposition to contraception, abortion and sterilization on grounds of the sanctity of human life. Nevertheless, acceptable forms of fertility limitation are widely used in Roman Catholic countries, and many Islamic peoples find the teaching of the Koran quite compatible with the practice of contraception. (30 March 1977)

---

*For a fuller explanation of Islamic views concerning family planning and related issues, see International Planned Parenthood Federation, *Islam and Family Planning,* a two-volume English translation, issued in 1973, of the Arabic edition of the proceedings of the International Islamic Conference held in Rabat, Morocco in December 1973 under the sponsorship of the International Planned Parenthood Federation. The UNFPA provided a grant for the translation of the proceedings into English.

. . . **Resources**

- All mankind's history points to . . . [the fact] that the depressive economic and human miseries resulting from too many people and too little food and economic opportunity in one part of the world undoubtedly imperils the security and well-being of another. . . . (26 August 1971)

- The common underlying fear is that the earth resources will prove insufficient to support ever-increasing numbers of people.

  The pressure of population on resources is increasingly making development efforts difficult in many parts of the world. (14 February 1973)

- Population projections [that there will be seven to eight billion people by the year 2000] are so universally agreed upon, that for all practical purposes they must be accepted as facts. This is not only a demographer's nightmare. It could be human tragedy. It is anybody's guess how many of the individuals making up that grand total will have any real expectations of adequate food, clothing, shelter, education, medical care, and job opportunities—in short, a life worth living. (15 February 1973)

- Existing difficulties in providing food, housing, education, medical attention and employment are going to compound themselves in accelerated ratio to population increases . . . unless rational solutions are sought and action taken, not when the swollen population figures are a reality, but *now*. (21 January 1974)

- The basic fact that is confronting all of us at the present time . . . is that no matter what we do, the earth's population is going to double in 25 years. This, unless there is world catastrophe of mammoth size, is a mathematical certainty. The young men and women are already growing up and the children are already born that will make it so.

  Thus, in looking ahead to the end of this century, not far off, we must envisage a situation in which a second world population of the same dimensions as the present one will have been added to the world's inhabitants. These newcomers are not intruders. They don't come from Mars. They are us - some 7 billion of us instead of 3 and a half billion—and all dependent for food, water, energy, technical facilities, education, housing and jobs, on the resources of this planet.

  Accept this fact and we have to accept the responsibility *now* for taking action to adapt, to conserve and to develop the resources which will be needed to sustain these increases in numbers in the 25-year spiral period. We need also to be prepared to move forward determinedly with the studies, the research, the planning and the programmes directed towards the achievement of better national, international, and, eventually, global management of life on this planet. Later will be too late.

  If any example is needed to illustrate the urgency of doing so, the present energy crisis provides a timely warning. It also demonstrates that there are a rising number of problems in the world that are beyond the power of individual governments and countries to resolve - problems of such magnitude that they demand not only national action, but international co-operation on a worldwide scale. (6 March 1974)

• The realization is spreading . . . that population problems are not confined to one area of the world. In the industrialized world, their public faces are different and they are called overcrowding, crime, environmental damage, transport crises and racial crises. But they are problems of population none the less.

Our world now is having great and apparently increasing difficulty in feeding, clothing and housing itself. How shall we accommodate another world on top of this one? (2 April 1974)

• In a sense the developing countries are rich. They have enormous potential. They control well over half the world's supply of raw materials and contain two-thirds of the world's people. Despite the conditions in which many of them are forced to live, there are vast resources of energy and resourcefulness among the people of the developing countries which have not yet been tapped. The problem of development is to release these reserves, of natural resources, of human capability, and turn them to the service of the world. (19 April 1974)

• If doubling and redoubling of populations can be foreseen, there is no country, even the least populous, which does not need to take some positive steps now. Let us by all means protect the right of governments to opt for regional or total increases in their populations, but let us also recognize that our resources and our ability to exploit them usefully are finite. (9 May 1974)

• We must combine efforts to reduce population with plans for social and economic development. And somehow this must be done without polluting the earth and destroying its resources. (18 May 1974)

• There are massive disparities in the quantity and value of the resources available in different parts of the world, as well as within individual countries. Some years ago, development experts in their optimism looked forward to a future in which the resources of the world would supply a standard of living for the majority of people on a level equal to that of the richer countries. Better knowledge of the extent of our resources, and, perhaps more important, of the effects of their exploitation on our environment, has brought about a change in our thinking. Uncontrolled production and processing of raw materials, and certainly their consumption by a small minority of the world's people, cannot go on.

Eventually many of those people who now consume resources out of all proportion to their numbers will have to learn to limit their demands. We have to find ways to achieve this. . . .

What can the developing countries offer the rest of the world? One of the most important things . . . is a restored sense of values. In their desperate chase after the satisfactions which material wealth can provide, . . . the peoples of the industrialized countries have lost sight of the goal which impelled them in the first place to seek wealth. There is a growing sense in the industrialized countries that something is missing from a life which includes many of the things that the earth can provide, but which has lost the deeper satisfaction which comes from a fundamentally sound relationship with the rest of creation.

The great religions of Asia grew among people who were living under conditions of scarcity and in a limited, although unspoiled, environment. This kind of poverty, however, was rich in human values. For the sake of survival, each man had to recognize that his fate was bound up with the fate of every other member of the community. In such circumstances, sharing goes deeper than community of material things; there is an empathy, a deep sense of what is essential in the life of another, and a practical compassion for his fate. Despite, or perhaps because of its material poverty, Aisa continues to be wealthy in this dimension of human existence.

We live in a time where is considerable uncertainty about the future shape of the international community; but all our efforts to equalize disparities of wealth among nations, contain population growth and survive in a threatened biosphere will be meaningless if we cannot learn to overcome our acquisitiveness by developing a sense of limitation. A limitation of material desires, but an unlimited capacity to share human fulfillment, is imperative, especially as we move into an era when no nation or group will be able to command a massive share of the world's resources as if by right. (20 May 1974)

• The quality of the environment, living conditions, the state of agriculture and industry, and social change have a profound effect on family size. Nor is it sufficient to look only within national boundaries: in our time, the causes and effects of change are too complex and far-reaching to allow a narrow approach. While separate national viewpoints will be maintained, there is a growing recognition that our problems are to be solved only by international interchange and willingness to act together. . . . There can be no doubt that the world is passing through a time which will test to the full our willingness to work together for our mutual benefit. World food stocks are at their lowest level ever, while vast areas are being lost to cultivation through the combined effects of natural events and men's depredations; and it should be remembered that stocks are calculated on present rates of consumption—which are for many people already too low. To add to this, fisheries and forests are apparently suffering from overexploitation, while many of the other natural resources which we have taken for granted for so long may also be threatened. Our air, our water and the very earth itself suffer from the effects of industrial pollution. Meanwhile, the demands made upon the earth continue to grow with the ever-increasing numbers of mankind. Our dilemma presents itself in a stark form since, under present patterns of distribution of wealth and ability to mobilize resources, man's capacity to feed, clothe and house himself is limited. In the richer countries, the increasing demands of affluence put ever-increasing strains on supply, while at the same time fouling the environment and creating additional demands for energy to make it habitable. Costs are already high, and the creation of additional amenities, whether in the form of clean air or heavier crops, is correspondingly expensive. Meanwhile, in the developing countries, enormous resources of minerals, land and people go largely untapped because of a shortage of finance, skills and the indefinable quality which has been described as the "will to develop". Most people are poor in these countries, and many live close to the edge of starvation. The cost of development to supply their needs is not high, by the standards of the industrialized countries, either in cash or in environmental terms, and the margin between the resources available and those needed is quite narrow. The dilemma is that a choice must be made between high-cost development in the industrialized countries, which will increase already high standards of living, and low-cost development elsewhere, which will provide many with the necessities of life. The choice cannot be as simple as it looks, otherwise it would have been made long ago.

It is . . . of no use for a government to preach birth control in the interests of preserving the environment and limiting consumption of resources, while its own economy is dependent on the rapid growth of GNP with high rates of resource consumption and consequent environmental damage. Declarations of good faith must be backed by action. For some donors, who do not make a connection between their internal economic policies and their policies of external assistance, this will be a hard transition to make. But it is a necessary change, analogous to many which are being made in our increasingly interdependent times. (2 July 1974)

• Over the last several years . . . we have had to adjust our view of many elements of the world situation. We have learned that the world's abundance is finite; that the capacity of the biosphere to sustain life, including human life, is limited; and that quite extraordinary measures are needed if, in the struggle for survival, man is not to do irreparable harm both to himself and to the environment. Above all, we have come to recognize that population trends are vitally important factors in economic and social change, in the use or misuse of resources and in the conservation or destruction of the natural environment.

Development must be diffused socially and geographically throughout all levels and throughout all areas. A society of sufficiency for all, replacing the distortions of excess and deprivation, must be our aim.

When we speak of a society of sufficiency for all we are not just speaking of the developing countries. Sufficiency for all—in this sense of an absence of excess as well as an absence of deprivation—is a concept which is valid internationally as well as nationally.

Even though growth in terms of GNP has been at its highest ever in the developing world, most authorities agree that the economic gap between the developed and developing countries has widened during this period. Is this fair? Is this just? Is this tolerable?

What makes the situation still worse is that the pursuit of increasing wealth has meant greater and greater production, consumption and waste, with consequently increasing damage to the ecological balance. Pollution does not respect national boundaries. Everyone—including the developing countries—is affected by the results of overloading the air and sea with waste products. Everyone—especially the developing countries—is affected by excess demand and the consequences of this demand on the supply of basic commodities which should by right be available at a fair and reasonable price to all.

Thus far, the concept of progress has been largely appreciated in economic terms, and the pursuit of wealth has set ever higher standards of affluence at which to aim. Is it possible now to limit our material demands? Can our priorities be changed so as to answer the needs of all?

For the sufficiency society of the future, some values of both past and present may still be valid; but not values that spawn unbridled acquisitiveness. Rather, let us seek the values of co-operation and concern, of involvement in the lives of others, values which come from recognition that the lives and the fate of all are inextricably bound up with each other, that man is now interdependent between continents, as he once was within the confines of the village. Fortunately, these values still exist in many parts of the world, and will . . . play a vital role in the future.

If the concept of sharing in this "village world" means anything, if the concept of "sufficiency" means anything, then the goals and purposes of the World Population Plan of Action must surely be worthy of our utmost support—financial as well as moral. (20 August 1974)

• Pollution of the air, the earth and the sea is not a minor matter to be cleared up by a few emission controls but a gigantic international problem which may threaten the delicate structure of global ecology and, with it, support for life itself. (15 October 1974)

• Land settlement programmes provide, in many cases, excellent opportunities for achieving a better balance between population and natural resources. (11 November 1974)

• For many years now, their [the developed countries] consumption of resources has been rising far faster than population growth rates warranted. The time has come for the countries of the Northern Hemisphere to curb their prodigality, to look for ways in which they can conserve resources while still providing an adequate standard of life for their peoples, and to assist the peoples of the Third World in meeting their own needs. This is their internal responsibility, to be met by each country in its own way. (12 January 1977)

• There are no fixed paths to a just global balance between population and economic resources. Each country, even each individual, will find the best path if allowed the means to do so, and this depends very much on the ability of administrators, governments and international organizations to listen, to determine what the needs really are, and to respond effectively.

We can see the possibility . . . of a world in which humans and the humane values are given their full importance. But other, much less pleasant futures are possible—the developed countries retreating behind their economic and physical barriers; civil or international warfare for the control of essential resources. . . . (2 June 1977)

• One element in the equation of energy consumption to resources, and a vital element in the balance between food supplies and needs, that can be influenced by human intelligence, by humane and moral means, is the number of people depending on the limited food and energy supplies. (21 June 1977)

• The complex relationships between human beings and resources . . . are now determining the present and future quality of life on our small planet.

Throughout time, human beings have tried to cope with the consequences of the transitory nature of individual and social order. The fear of what tomorrow might bring is as old as life itself. The problems of change are, indeed, very familiar to all of us.

But the perception of change has itself undergone a change in our time. Consequently, the problems engendered are different. This difference is in magnitude, quality and pace. Malnutrition, hunger, ill-health, untimely death, illiteracy, inequity, social injustice—problems with which we are embattled today—have provided the substance of our history, the cutting edge to our philosophy, the themes of our art, the authority of our religious teachings, and the force behind the eternal quest for the perfectibility of Man. But the old solutions, the familiar pace, and the habitual ways we had developed to turn our eyes away from the problem which always seemed to be caused by other people's foolishness or natural incompetence, will no longer do. When we beat the drums just a few years ago about the "Population Explosion", the assumption many of us made was: "We have children, other people explode." When we spoke of Exploding Cities we, somehow, did not contribute to their explosiveness, only to their cultural or social ambience. When we spoke of millions of children going to bed hungry every night, they were always other people's children.

This sort of self-created remoteness was possible for a long time, even up to a few years ago. But the increase of numbers now demands a qualitative change in our search for solutions. The magnitude of the need for international assistance, the business the Fund is in, must be increased many times before population growth can begin to be brought into balance with the available resources. But that is not the only need. The way we respond to these magnitudes, our appreciation of the nature of the consequences of population growth where it is unsustainable—in other words, the values we use to understand the population problems—must change. What is called for is a change in the quality of our understanding of the equitable use and distribution of the resources of the earth and the level of life at which people exist.

Population, therefore, is, in a very real sense, the problem of problems.

It is now a question of how soon and how wisely we shall be able to use our technological, material and spiritual resources to reduce the impact of our past profligacy. It is clear that we cannot have abundance for a few and privation for many—not for much longer. . . . It is clear that our overheated consumption must level off so that our supplies of energy, raw materials and skills are put to less glamorous but more useful purpose. We have begun, only begun to realize how itnerdependent our world is, however passionately we articulate our separate nationalisms and our cultural individuality. All the global concerns we are now involved with—hunger, the status of women, ethnic conflicts, the fair distribution of the resources of the land and the seas—are aspects of this interdependence, and indicate that the future must be guided by more egalitarian and equitable values if we are to survive.

That is why at Bucharest [we] made a plea for a Sufficiency Society. But sufficiency, given the limitations of means in a finite planet, is largely dependent on the number of people whose needs must be met. This realization is filtering through even to countries which once took the simplistic view that concern for population growth was a vicious plot to keep the poor poor. Whatever euphemism is employed to refer to the problem—maternal and child health, family welfare, or family health programmes, reduc-ing fertility has been recognized as a priority for many developing countries.

Population growth is rightly regarded as a global problem, because the pressure on resources touches on the economic interdependence of the planet, not to mention the sense of neighbourly concern of all people. (27 September 1977)

. . . The Role of Women

• It is important to recognize the involvement and key role which women and young people are playing as citizens, as well as that of mothers and future parents. It may be ob-jectionable, and even illogical, to consider women and young people as special popula-tion groups. Women and young people, after all, constitute at least half of the popula-tion of the world. However, the fact is that their participation and interest are often overlooked. (10 August 1972)

• Special consideration should . . . be given to legislation raising the legal age at mar-riage, combined with measures such as education of girls, vocational training, increas-ed employment opportunities for women and general improvement of the status of women in the community. Such measures could have a significant impact on fertility patterns.

The necessity of involving women and youth cannot be overemphasized. In my opin-ion, the Year [World Population Year 1974] will have been well worthwhile alone if, as a result of intensified programmes, these two sectors will be more actively involved in population programmes at all levels. (1 November 1972)

• How do you convince people that they must re-think the precepts that have been hand-ed down from generation to generation as infallible ingredients of a secure society? Shouldn't we re-phrase such common sayings as "The hand that rocks the cradle rules the world", so that they take into account the right of women to have a say in how many times the cradle should be filled? (15 February 1973)

• [We are] particularly happy to see that increasing emphasis is being given to the par-ticipation of young women in population information programmes of this kind [World Assembly of Youth Seminar on Population and Development]. . . . Women need to contribute their viewpoints to the continuing discussion on population questions, as they have as much at stake as men, if not more, in whatever action is taken in this area. Very often, what is put forward as the popular opinion is the male point of view; and this situation can only be rectified if more women come forward to participate in the discussions, and ask for equal consideration of ideas and opinions.

Since [the Fund] took over the responsibility in the United Nations to prepare for World Population Year, [we] have consistently emphasized the special role of women and youth in promoting and achieving the objectives of the Year. (14 September 1973)

- Mounting interest in population as a factor in development, now reinforced by interest in small-scale or local development planning, has brought policymakers, however belatedly, to a realization of the true importance of women to the success of any scheme of development which has as its aim the direct involvement of the mass of the people in the development process.

  In many agricultural societies, women add to their activities as a wife, mother and cook, the care of the gardens in which many of the family staples are grown. Like so many of the things that women do, this is taken for granted. What is not perhaps fully realized is the significance of the contribution which such work makes to the family diet. Surely it makes sense to establish extension courses to help women to do this work better.

  Many women are prevented from realizing their full potential by the number and arduous nature of the tasks they have to do. Applied technology can make these tasks simpler and release their abilities for other work, for study, or simply for leisure to enjoy their families.

  The cumulative effect of apparently minor innovations such as these is far greater than it might appear. But perhaps more important are the effects on the way the woman thinks about herself. . . . Her life is no longer bound by the everyday tasks. She has the opportunity to widen her horizons and take a full part in the world around her. She has, perhaps for the first time, the freedom to choose.

  Employment among city women does not necessarily affect their childbearing, although where relationships with the husband are on a basis of equality, and especially if the woman is educated, families tend to be smaller.

  In such a delicate, complex and personal matter as determining family size, it is all the more important to ensure the commitment and participation of women, in whose hands the ultimate decision lies.

  More women must be involved at all levels in decision-making. Rather than being merely passive tools of policy, they must become active participants in the decisions which will profoundly affect their lives.

  In particular we hope that 1974 [World Population Year] will be a useful preparation for International Women's Year which comes in 1975, and that this year we shall gain a clearer appreciation of the true importance of women in the development of the full potential of all the world's people. (25 February 1974)

- The impact of employment of women in agriculture on fertility should be considered of prime importance. (11 November 1974)

- The General Assembly has designated 1975 as International Women's Year. We in UNFPA have a warm interest in this development, because of the tremendous importance, both real and potential, of women in all areas of development, and in particular in population matters. (27 January 1975)

- Women's aspirations and women's decisions are vital to any effective population policy. . . .

We have . . . enthusiastically supported the [programme for] . . . International Women's Year, which seeks to promote equality between men and women and to integrate women into economic development. (19 June 1975)

• For all of us who are concerned with international development, this [International Women's Year] Conference is particularly significant. The measures which are set out so clearly in the draft Plan of Action for International Women's Year will assist women's contributions to national development; but even more important, by broadening the opportunities available to women, such measures will allow them to enrich their own lives.

This is the very stuff of development, for, as one of the delegates to this Conference has already said elsewhere, development has a human face, not a harsh, pragmatic one. Equality does more than contribute to development; equality *is* development. . . .

For many people in developing countries, the restraints of traditional society are being broken down. Even the remotest village is aware nowadays of outside pressures to change. Some of the changes are life-enhancing, some are not; but given the freedom to adapt, change becomes a positive force. Many women, however, do not have this freedom. Their major role remains for the most part what it has always been—bearing and rearing children. Furthermore, there is considerable pressure, sometimes subtle, sometimes direct, to remain in this niche. For many women, the power of decision over this one basic function would represent a major step towards equality.

This power is not conferred by government decrees on equality, nor by the simple availability of the means of contraception. Even all these plus education and information programmes will not be enough without the economic and social context in which the freedom to choose becomes real. Those governments which have consciously attempted to bring down birth rates in their countries have found greatest success where a vigorous family planning service was combined with small but marked improvements in housing, employment, education, mother and child health care, and general health services—the fabric of a secure life. And there is a demonstrable connection between jobs outside the home, education for women, and smaller family size.

But freedom to choose is not only a matter of having fewer children. It is much more a question of setting women free to make the most appropriate contribution in their power to the society in which they live, whether it is having a family, or following a career, or simply escaping from poverty. A society which fails to free women from the reproductive treadmill takes enormous risks, not only in the wastage of human resources represented by unwilling motherhood, but in the inevitable decline in the quality of future populations—and this is to say nothing of the direct cost to society of pursuing an unpopular and unrealistic policy. In a world whose population must inevitably undergo massive increases during the next fifty years, these considerations are of the first importance.

The pursuit of a successful population policy and full equality for women both imply that women must be involved in formulating and carrying out policy. So far, even though population policy concerns women more intimately and directly than any other branch of development, and even though they are in the majority at the operational levels, women have not yet penetrated the administrative superstructure to any great extent. . . . If this is so marked in population, what must the situation be in other areas of development policy? This criticism applies universally—even those who boast of the numbers of women doctors and lawyers or senior civil servants in their own countries can only show a tiny minority of women in available posts.

The importance of women to successful population policies has never been far from the front of our minds at the United Nations Fund for Population Activities, and neither has the converse, that successful population policies have great importance for the successful achievement of equality for women. Naturally, a considerable part of our available funds are devoted to health care for mothers and children, and family planning. But we have also given support to work with a direct bearing on the status of women.

We plan to strengthen our support to programmes in these areas. We hope, at the same time, that the projects recommended by this Conference will focus, among other priority areas, on the family and population questions, and further, that close links will be maintained between UNFPA-supported programmes and those resulting from this Conference.

The extent to which we are involved, of course, depends on the determination of governments to put into effect the recommendations of the World Population Plan of Action and the Plan of Action for International Women's Year.

One of the most serious problems which still remains to be solved is the question of women as mothers as against women as workers, including the problems of involving women in government. But it is necessary for the future well-being of our world that they should be solved. One of the most important functions which this Conference could perform would be to bring this truth home to governments everywhere. . . .

Governments should acknowledge how important for women's *future* is the *freedom to choose*; governments should recognize by their policies the importance to national development of a female population which is able to achieve its aims, whether of motherhood, or a career, or both. (23 June 1975)

• The various international strategies, such as the World Population Plan of Action, the International Development Strategy for the Second Development Decade, and the World Plan of Action focusing on integration of women and development, should provide guidance for the activities of the Fund.

More attention should be given to women's participation in community development programmes, and to enlisting women in communication activities. (21 November 1975)

• The ability to regulate fertility is important not only for maternal and child health reasons, but also because it enables women to become, or to continue to be, active participants in the labour force.

Women, as homemakers, and as an actual and potential economic force, should also receive special attention. Little success can be expected for population activities without their active involvement. We, therefore, intend to give special attention to the participation of women in the management of population programmes, to the training of women, and to the development of services designed for them. (14 June 1976)

• [We have established] a Task Force on Women, Population and Development . . .[and] following up on the work of this Task Force . . . have issued guidelines for Programme Development, Project Formulation, Implementation, and Evaluation* to field staff and Resident Representatives, and to Specialized Agencies and others concerned with programming for population assistance, for implementation in the spirit of the recommendations of the World Population Conference and the International Women's Year Conference. (28 January 1977)

• [In the "community-based" contraceptives distribution approach] special attention is often placed on the participation of women . . . and on providing them with alternatives to childbearing as a source of self-identity and gratification. (30 March 1977)

• Women, in many countries, can be considered among the disadvantaged and vulnerable population groups, [to which the Fund accords high priority,] and UNFPA fully recognizes that in the population field, perhaps more than any other area of development, little success can be expected without the active involvement and full participation of women. (5 July 1977)

• The integration of population and development is a central theme in the World Population Plan of Action, and is repeated and reaffirmed in many other international declarations, in particular the Plan of Action for International Women's Year. (26 March 1978)

• As [we] have stressed in previous statements to this [Governing] Council and to other United Nations bodies—and more importantly, as the Fund has sought to demonstrate and foster in its programme, in its recruitment practices of professional staff, and in its Population Profile issue on *Women, Population and Development*—little can be accomplished in the population fields without the active involvement and full participation of women. Guidelines now being utilized by UNFPA headquarters and field staff . . . for programme development, project formulation, implementation, and evaluation call special attention to the need to take the vital links between the status and roles of women and population activities fully into account. UNFPA's recognition of the importance of women in formulating and executing its many-sided programme is also reflected in the fact that over one-third of the UNFPA's professional staff at headquarters and in the field are women. (21 June 1978)

⸰ The Fund has been, and remains, a pioneer within the United Nations system in supporting programmes directly aimed at increasing opportunities for the greater participation of women in population and development at all levels—as policymakers, programme planners and community workers. (6 November 1978)

*Contained in UNFPA Population Profile 7, *Women, Population and Development,* 1976, 47 pp.

. . . Rural Development

- [A government] may decide to go for rural-based development on a modest but widespread scale rather than large-scale urban development, which benefits a few but creates perhaps as many problems as it solves. It may find, in the process, that its population growth rates are dropping, and that it can plan without too much strain for its future growth and prosperity. (19 April 1974)

- In view of the fact that a large majority of people in the developing countries are living in rural areas, the role of rural development policies and programmes is of paramount importance. . . . This is indicated by the increasing emphasis governments are giving to integrated rural development programmes. Such programmes can be a major vehicle for bringing about social change and related changes in demographic behaviour. There is, indeed, a large scope for combining rural development and population programmes in all countries irrespective of their population policies and demographic goals.

In considering the problems of development, a proper emphasis should be given to the importance of rural development and its vital link with population policies and programmes. (11 November 1974)

[In a speech in December 1975 to a joint Food and Agriculture Organization and UNFPA meeting, the Deputy Executive Director of the Fund, Halvor Gille, indicated UNFPA thinking on the subject of rural development. He stated: "The fact that the rural masses in developing countries are generally very poor and under-privileged clearly suggests that population activities should be geared towards meeting their needs.

"Rural development and population programmes are closely interrelated. Our experience at UNFPA indicates that population programmes, in particular family planning and maternal and child health activities, are most effective when they are related to the totality of development efforts. Without adequate housing and health facilities, improvement in the status of women, and more equal distribution of income, it is difficult to be successful in carrying out action programmes on population.

"Many of the problems in rural development programmes are also to be found in population activities. All such programmes need to be adapted to the prevailing way of life and must be sensitive, geared towards the local conditions and adapted to them. This applies equally to programmes promoting farming and to those promoting family planning."]

- A new perception of cities and towns requires a complementary change in our view of rural areas. Rural people are neither hopelessly backward peasants, as some impatient developmentalists have seemed to imply, nor are they repositories of all that is valuable in our collective life, as some romantics have claimed. The land on which they live and work is the essence of human survival, and the environment in which they live is a precious heritage which once destroyed can never be replaced. The vitality of the rural areas, no less than of the city, is part of the balance which we must seek.

There is an increasing emphasis on rural development; a movement away from vast schemes towards more modest projects more firmly rooted in the society from which they spring, and in general a swing away from what has been called "giantism" to programmes manageable on a human scale. (2 June 1976)

• Villages [are] where most of the Third World's population lives. . . . (30 March 1977)

• We welcome the special attention being given by UNDP to rural development programmes and will contribute, within our mandate, to furthering this effort. (7 November 1977)

• Rural development is essential to create the preconditions for family planning, as well as to produce more food and cash crops. Family planning programmes must be brought into the villages as part of any scheme of rural development, and family planning education and publicity included in the general information made available by extension workers and other agents of the government. (26 March 1978)

• Another area of increasing government interest in UNFPA assistance is population activities in connexion with rural development and community development. (21 June 1978)

. . . Urbanization

• The problems of all cities are not all the same. There are vast differences between the situations of New York, Sao Paulo, Glasgow, and Shanghai, but there are also many problems shared in common, and there are many solutions successful in one city which can be successfully applied in others.

Perhaps even more important than this, the impact of change in one part of the world is not long in being felt in all others. The cities, as the nerve centres of modern civilization, are particularly sensitive to this effect, so that attempts to solve the pollution problems of Los Angeles are quickly felt by the motor manufacturers of Birmingham. If the supply of an essential industrial raw material is cut off by events in a developing country, workers in the cities of Europe and America are not long in feeling the pinch.

One known change which is going to take place before the end of the century is in the size of city populations. By 2001, perhaps as many as half of the people of the world will be living in cities—and this in a world which will be supporting twice the numbers of people that it did in 1970. (2 April 1974)

• Emphasis on urban growth has drawn millions into cities which are ill-equipped to cater for them. (2 July 1974)

• Human history up to this point has been one of movement. Gradually, though, the nature of movement has changed. The great migrations are past, and nomads and seasonal migrants are becoming fewer. In our own age, movement has been from poorer parts of the world to richer, and from country to city.

The great ebb and flow of populations across continents [in the past] has become a magnetic field polarized on the great cities.

Paradoxically, as man has become more mobile, his settlements have become more concentrated.

Examining the paradox, its true nature becomes clear. Improved transport and communications have reduced the need for personal contact in order to carry on the business of living and made feasible greater distances between people. So we see, at the same time that conurbations are bigger than ever before, a tendency to live and work away from the centre, and an enormously increased mobility between centres. . . . By the end of this century, man will be predominantly an urban animal, no longer dependent directly on the land for his living, nor yet on the great metropolis. We might call him Inter-urban Man.

Our literature, art and music, whole systems of culture and values derive from a basic connection with the land. . . . The culture and values of inter-urban man will have to cope with still-essential but indirect connection with the earth which gives him being, and with groups of people, sometimes in large numbers, with whom his connection is similarly indirect.

These problems are not new to industrial cities, but they show few signs of resolution—perhaps because the essential change in perception is not complete. There is a tendency still to think of the city-dweller as an aberration, even among city-dwellers themselves, and an unconscious refusal to learn to handle the reality of inter-urban life.

The facts must be faced; people will not return to the land in any significant numbers unless taken by force, and the tendency to congregate will in all probability continue. There are good reasons for this—cities and towns are vital sources of energy, ideas, technologies and artifacts. They offer a breadth and depth of experience which is not available anywhere else. They are the powerhouses of our civilization.

In the future, urban life will be the norm and . . . the life-force of a country or region is less likely to be a single great city, than a series of urban centres. (2 June 1976)

. . . Youth and the Aged

- It is important to recognize the involvement and key role which women and young people are playing as citizens, as well as that of mothers and future parents. It may be objectionable, and even illogical, to consider women and young people as special population groups. Women and young people, after all, constitute at least half of the population of the world. However, the fact is that their participation and interest are often overlooked. (10 August 1972)

- The necessity of involving women and youth cannot be overemphasized. In my opinion, the Year [World Population Year 1974] will have been well worthwhile alone if, as a result of intensified programmes, these two sectors will be more actively involved in population programmes at all levels. (1 November 1972)

- The programme [for World Population Year] would need to be launched at three levels. The *international* level to mobilize the resources both human and financial to expand the volume and the quality of international technical co-operation. The *national* level to stimulate country programmes, and the *individual* level in order to increase general understanding of population activities and to encourage the participation and support of the young men and women who, after all, will make the population decisions that count at all levels. [We] also felt, and still do, that in the next few months special attention should be given to ensuring that youth and women have a say in the programmes that so directly affect their lives and their futures. (23 March 1973)

• Since [the Fund] took over the responsibility to prepare for World Population Year, [we] have strongly emphasized the special role of women and youth in promoting and achieving the objectives of the Year. The reason is that young people have a number of very relevant and important ideas on population and development issues, and these should be brought up for an open and frank discussion. [We] also believe that young people, through both established and ad hoc groups, can help organize several major activities relating to the Year.

It is ultimately at the national level that population policies and actions are decided upon. If young people . . . wish to influence the formulation of population policies and the implementation of relevant programmes in this area, they must undertake an active and energetic role in contributing their viewpoints to the formulation of these policies and their energies to the implementation of them.

The continuing debate on the population question is useful, but its ultimate impact will be felt at the national level, and that is where young people and youth groups must use their abilities and energies. (7 September 1973)

• In the Caribbean countries, discussions among young people on population matters relate closely to concepts of family life. This, of course, involves consideration of such questions as marriage laws and practices, legal rights of spouses and children, laws relating to property and inheritance rights, and of traditional religious and social aspects of family life. [We] believe that ultimately each country will be able to find its own solution to these questions, on the basis of informed awareness of changes in social attitudes and habits. This process will certainly be facilitated by frank and open debate among young people themselves on these questions. (14 September 1973)

• Our World Population Year Secretariat . . . is paying particular attention to women's and youth organizations, in the belief that in their hands lies the key to the riddles of population and development. (18 October 1973)

• The dimensions of the population task are further exemplified by the problems being encountered in the European countries, . . . and, to an extent, in the industrialized countries in general. Once again, population considerations take on another shape and form, as governments view the changes in society arising from internal migration, increases in urbanization, the need for urban renewal, fluctuations in resource supply, and ageing populations producing less and demanding more. (21 January 1974)

• One of the things which has most encouraged me in recent months is that young people, in particular, seem to be especially conscious of this [the need for both developed and developing countries to adopt population policies on their road towards becoming "sufficiency societies"]. World Population Year has demonstrated the vigour and enthusiasm with which young people are facing their new world. . . . (20 August 1974)

- The portion of the population under 15 years of age in many developing countries today is approximately 40 per cent. During the 1980s, many of these . . . will become young adults. How they will behave with respect to fertility will markedly affect the prospects and progress that can be made towards reaching socio-economic goals in many countries.

Another population-related concern that the United Nations recently began to focus more attention on is the growing problem of ageing of the population, caused by the decline of fertility coupled with the prolongation of life expectancy in both developed and developing countries. The number of people over 60 years of age is already well over 300 million. By the year 2000, it is estimated the figure will exceed 580 million, and that 60 per cent of that total—or some 348 million people—will be residing in developing countries.

In response to a General Assembly resolution of last December,* which directly invites UNFPA, within its mandate, "to provide financial assistance to developing countries, upon request, in improving the conditions of the ageing", the Fund has recently begun to assist work in this field. (6 November 1978)

---

*General Assembly resolution 32/131 of 16 December 1977.

Chapter 16

PROGRAMMING POPULATION ASSISTANCE

Appraising Proposed Population Projects

• In looking at a potential request, we try to assure ourselves that it is addressed to a real problem.

Second, we . . . assure ourselves that the government or non-governmental organization requesting the project has given evidence of its will to do something about the problem. This, in most instances, is evidenced by willingness to put up at least some counterpart contribution to the project. Without this, there can be no assurance that the project will enjoy the priority which it needs from the government (or the non-governmental organization) in order to have a reasonable chance of success.

Third, we must ask ourselves: Are the means suggested in the project request feasible? Will they be efficient? Do they promise to be efficient relative to costs?

Fourth, we must ask ourselves whether the proposed UNFPA input is justified within the terms of reference of the Fund. . . .

A fifth criterion is, of course, that the United Nations system directly or indirectly have capabilities for executing the project.

In looking at the question of UNFPA funding for the project, moreover, we must answer the question: Why should this assistance be extended by the United Nations system rather than by some other donor or donor agency? (18 February 1971)

• The Fund applies its policies and criteria for project appraisal as flexibly as possible. We are, however, conscious of the fact that we should formalize these policies. The Fund is, therefore, compiling a handbook of policies and criteria for project appraisal which will be useful not only for our own staff but also to countries. . . . We recognize that one of the great advantages of the Fund is that it has the capacity to respond quickly and in a fashion which has been appropriate for meeting the requirements of requesting governments and organizations. It is hoped that, in the interest of the developing countries, this flexibility can be maintained in the future to the greatest extent possible.

The new manual, *Instructions for Preparation of Project Requests* . . . is most important in connection with the rapid and efficient processing of requests and with the computerization of project data. . . . If a request is prepared according to the instructions, it will contain all information necessary for prompt appraisal by UNFPA staff and, in addition, the project budget will be ready for computer financial controls. We have asked that . . . requests received from the governments [be checked] to ensure compliance with the instructions before forwarding the request to UNFPA Headquarters. . . .

Moreover, we hope that the use of the new forms for project requests will also diminish the length of time necessary to commence projects after approval by the UNFPA. The form is designed to focus the attention of officials preparing the request on a more realistic appraisal of the need for advisory services and equipment, and on a more realistic phasing of the entire project (8 March 1973)

• The substantive or technical aspect of programming is, of course, always of importance. There are two other aspects . . . of particular importance to all in the next year and a half in building the record we need.

The first is the administrative and financial aspects of programming. We need projects to be spelled out in well-thought-through work plans understood by all the parties who must co-operate to implement the project. We need project budgets with realistic costing and realistic phasing. If we have exaggerated costing or unrealistically optimistic phasing, we shall be tying up on behalf of one project some of our limited resources which should be applied to other projects which would result in useful activity.

Second, we must be sure that our projects and programmes really reflect the needs and wishes of countries. If they do not, it will not matter how good the design of the project may look on paper, the project is unlikely to be implemented effectively by the country in question and is virtually certain to do no lasting good once it has been terminated. (30 April 1973)

• A government coming to us with a request for assistance knows that it will be examined on the viability of the project. . . . There is no pressure to somehow make a project "pay", or to organize other branches of policy so that a loan can be paid off, with interest, over a given period. . . . This is not to say that we give money away without inquiring where it is going; but our methods of evaluation depend more on the experience of those who live in the country than on rigorous adherence to a model laid down by foreign experts whose knowledge of conditions in the country must in the nature of things be largely second-hand. We have our Co-ordinators. . . . We can draw on the wide knowledge and experience of the Resident Representatives of the United Nations Development Programme in each country, and call in other agencies in the United Nations system for their assessment. (25 August 1973)

• No attempt is made to establish the Fund's own "model" for each country into which requests must fit. Rather, with the advice and assistance of our . . . country Co-ordinators and of the Resident Representative of the United Nations Development Programme in each country, governments are encouraged to develop their own models. A process of consultation thus develops which draws the Fund into the decision-making process. Governments identify and choose their own sources of technical assistance, going outside the United Nations system if desired.

Conventional analysis of a request may show that it has certain weaknesses. It may be in the interests of the Fund and of the relationship with the government concerned not to insist at this point on changes being made in the project, for two reasons; firstly, conventional analysis may not be sufficiently sensitive on local conditions, and secondly, a demonstration of trust in a government at the outset of a relationship may pay dividends in terms of access to decision-making processes at a later stage. (18 October 1973)

• Our criteria in [appraising] requests for assistance have been very much those of the country making the request. If a government makes a request to us, the project has usually been discussed with the United Nations Development Programme representative in that country, and possibly also with one of the . . . Co-ordinators which the Fund employs in key centres. It is then [appraised] in New York by our Programme Division, on the basis not of the Fund's opinions as to what policy in that country *should* be, but on the basis of what that policy *is* and the aims which have been laid down by the government. Our concern has been first to build up a working relationship with governments, to attempt to understand as completely as possible what their aims are and to fit our contribution into that framework. In the process we have developed rather more than a business relationship with many governments, and can make a real contribution, on the basis of first-hand knowledge, to their development planning.

This sort of relationship with governments is particularly important, because as yet the connection between population and development is not well understood, and because it appears to be country-specific. The interaction varies according to the size of the country, its endowment of natural resources, the economic structure, income per head, levels of education and other factors. Both we and government policymakers need to understand better the economic and social implications for population of economic and social goals. (13 November 1973)

• Expert recruitment from a limited number of countries has . . . been a serious handicap to the effectiveness of external aid programmes. For many years the industrialized nations of the West had a virtual monopoly of modern technology and scientific advance. This is no longer the case. Regional and national reservoirs of expertise are being built up, and it is the Fund's policy to encourage and assist the establishment of institutions and organizations to provide an increasing supply of experts needed for development and population programmes. (6 March 1974)

• Our major concern has been to improve the effectiveness of our programming. In doing so we have built up a close and cordial relationship with many governments. . . . At the same time, a considerable body of expertise has been built up in the formulation and implementation of programme assistance. (9 May 1974)

• In order to identify the developing countries with the most urgent need for population assistance, the Fund is proposing the use of a set of criteria which includes high overall population growth, high fertility rates, high infant mortality and high population density. (14 June 1976)

• The Governing Council [in June 1976] requested that the UNFPA should, in making future allocation of resources, apply the following general principles which we suggested and which fall within our mandate: (a) promote population activities proposed in international strategies; (b) meet the needs of developing countries which have the most urgent requirements for population assistance; (c) respect the sovereignty of recipient countries on matters of population policies; (d) build up the recipient countries' self-reliance; and (e) support activities of special benefit to disadvantaged population groups.

The Governing Council also approved in principle the criteria for establishing priorities. All developing countries should, irrespective of their size, be entitled to assistance if required, but high priority should be given to countries which are especially in need of population assistance taking into account their present demographic situation, the major population problems and the progress made in dealing with them. We will prepare, as requested by the Governing Council, certain minimum or basic population programmes at the country level, taking into account the diversity of country situations as regards population problems and policies, and approaches to dealing with them. (27 July 1976)

Delivery of Programmes

• In the implementation of the programmes, it is essential that the Fund and the agencies respond quickly and adequately to the country requests. Steps will be taken to employ modern managerial techniques to minimize delays in implementation. (10 November 1969)

• In view of the country programme orientation of the UNFPA and our bias towards promoting action-oriented projects, the Fund is more inclined to assist programmes and projects that will improve the delivery of services in the countries requesting assistance. (22 October 1970)

• In looking at a potential request . . . we must ask ourselves: Are the means suggested in the project request feasible? Will they be efficient? Do they promise to be efficient relative to costs? (18 February 1971)

• The rate at which the Fund is able to deliver assistance . . . depends almost completely on the absorptive capacity* of the recipient countries and the speed with which the executing organizations can move on project implementation. The United Nations, the Specialized Agencies, and the Fund, as well as the requesting governments, must endeavour to improve the utilization of the allocations given by the Fund, in order to make a real impact on resolving population problems. (3 November 1971)

• There have been cases where equipment is requested long before it can possibly be utilized. While delays in delivery of equipment must be taken into consideration, so too must the almost universal problem of recruitment of experts. Consequently, in projects

*See "Absorptive Capacity" section.

where an expert must first undertake an appraisal before the project can begin, the inevitable time lag should be taken into consideration when phasing the project. Better planning and more realistic assessments of the capacities of agencies, both United Nations and national, can reduce the frustrations of project delay. For example, are outside "experts" always needed in projects submitted to the UNFPA for funding? There have been cases where an expert is provided not for technical advice but for organizational and administrative skills. Surely government ministries or universities can sometimes meet this latter need, indeed, if not the need for technical advice as well. Attempts should be made to seek out nationals with the necessary skills to make a project work. [We] will expect UNFPA Co-ordinators to assess the need for experts in projects submitted to us for funding, bearing in mind both the cost and the delays inherent in agencies' supplying experts, and to advise us as to whether national staff can be substituted for international experts.

One continuing cause of delay in implementation of projects is found in months of correspondence and reviews necessary to agree upon a plan of operation. This delay could possibly be resolved by pre-project funding of certain components which would prepare a project for full operations at a later date. (8 March 1973)

• In addition to the acceptance of the need and the responsibility to solve the population problem in each country, there must also exist the skills and the means to carry them out. This is the reason why the UNFPA, in its three years of operation, has devoted more than a third of its resources to training. Advisory services, equipment and supplies mean nothing when there is neither the skill nor the will to utilize them.

The Fund will continue to assist countries, and deliberately apply a portion of the assistance to spurring the countries to undertake these programmes themselves, by continuing to train as much of each country's human resources as possible, and assisting in the building of their own institutions. (6 May 1973)

• The United Nations agencies are still our main source of technical expertise. At the same time, we are building up a capable, knowledgeable field staff to whom considerable autonomy will be allowed. Headquarters will thus become the support unit of the organization, with its main role as general policy guidance and co-ordination. We have always put a high value on speed, aiming for the minimum delay between receipt of programme requests and implementation of the project. This decentralization should further accelerate our programming. (18 October 1973)

• [Another] problem [in promoting development] relates to specific programme implementation questions, particularly concerning family planning delivery systems. Given a delivery system and set of inputs, how can the efficiency of the programme processes be maximized? There are many discrete problems in this area where operations research seems particularly applicable. These include:

(1) Establishing targets for programme utilization,

(2) Establishing the most effective mix of service functions to meet the forecasted demand, and

(3) Designing clinic work flows and schedules. (13 November 1973)

- Perhaps the greatest hurdle external aid programmes have to surmount is the long time lags in delivering assistance. Consequently, the Fund's operational policies have been directed towards avoiding bottlenecks resulting from too-complicated procedures, and towards being as responsive as possible to governments' wishes and needs—even to the point of abandoning established processes for the transmittal of technical co-operation from the central administering organization via an executing agency to the recipient government. In fact, governments being assisted by the Fund have already received considerable autonomy with respect to the supervision and implementation of Fund-assisted projects, and in some cases direct aid has been negotiated between the Fund and the government. (6 March 1974)

- We shall . . . do our best to continue to keep the costs of delivering the programme down. The experimentation that we have been doing, in accordance with the directives of ECOSOC in its May 1973 resolution, in passing some resources directly to countries through UNDP/UNFPA channels, while using the agencies in technical assistance and monitoring roles, represents one line of development which we believe may help keep down the costs of delivering our programme. . . . (13 June 1974)

- Our experience has shown that countries deliver programmes better if . . . there are adequate cadres of trained personnel to execute them. The success of projects depends to a large extent on the leadership and the quality of training that workers have before undertaking these projects. But there is still a large gap in our knowledge of specific country training requirements and the training programmes that are necessary to meet the goals set in each country. A better understanding and insight on this problem is needed. The Fund regards this as one of the priorities over the coming years. (20 August 1974)

- All of these [directly-funded] projects are administered through the offices of the UNDP Resident Representatives in monitoring and evaluating projects of this type. Where required, UNFPA also provides funds for local programme and administrative field staff in the Resident Representative's office, to furnish the necessary programme support services. (19 June 1975)

- UNFPA [has recognized the need] to introduce new managerial methods and techniques in delivering assistance. We have moved progressively in the past few years, providing direct funding to government agencies or government-approved agencies.

We have responded to government criticisms of the costs, delays and eventual ineffectualness involved in the traditional system of supplying foreign expertise, by increasingly turning towards reliance on local expertise and local programme managers and, where necessary, paid their salaries. The advantage of this innovation in dealing with such a culturally sensitive matter as population, not to mention the saving of time and expense, is self-evident. In line with this, we have provided funds for the purchase of local materials and equipment, wherever possible, and in a few cases, and in limited amounts, even for construction of facilities.

The reaction to these innovations and to their immediate impact on action programmes has been overwhelmingly supportive, and even laudatory, to judge by the statements made by countries at meetings of our Governing Council and of the Economic and Social Council. . . .

The delivery of population programmes requires a constantly innovative and flexible approach. Our experience shows that the traditional methods of delivery have not been effective and that there is a danger that the imposition of a uniform method of delivery of development assistance would gravely affect the very high level of project implementation which the UNFPA has been able to achieve. (20 February 1976)

- We have taken several steps to improve our performance:

  We have improved our internal programme planning mechanism to enable us to plan our activities over a full four-year period.

  We have improved our internal monitoring and implementation procedures.

  We have established a mechanism to review regularly with our executing organizations the status of implementation.

  We have strengthened our field staff, *inter alia,* by adding . . . new Co-ordinator posts in Africa to stimulate project development in a number of priority countries in that region, and national programming staff to assist several UNFPA co-ordinators and UNDP Resident Representatives where no Co-ordinator is stationed.

With these steps, [we are] confident that a substantial increase in our programming and implementation capacity can be accomplished. (21 June 1978)

Direct Funding

- It is expected that ultimately responsibility for the execution of projects will lie more directly with the recipient governments, using the services of United Nations or other organizations for any essential technical assistance. Indeed, the movement away from small projects to more comprehensive country programmes—a trend that is gradually gaining momentum—foreshadows this development. (4 May 1973)

- In accordance with this directive [from ECOSOC] UNFPA is experimenting carefully with various ways of using its own channels for passing resources directly to recipient governments. Even in such cases, however, the Fund envisages using another organization with substantive capabilities, normally the United Nations organization with a mandate in the field, to carry out whatever technical assistance component may be involved and to assist the Fund in monitoring the substantive aspects of the project. If, of course, . . . the recipient country desires us to associate ourselves with an external organization other than . . . from within the United Nations system, we shall, in consultation with the government, select one. (6 November 1973)

- We shall . . . do our best to continue to keep the costs of delivering the programme down. The experimentation that we have been doing, in accordance with the directives of ECOSOC in its May 1973 resolution, in passing some resources directly to countries through UNDP/UNFPA channels, while using the agencies in technical assistance and monitoring roles, represents one line of development which we believe may help keep down the costs of delivering our programme. . . . (13 June 1974)

- [In] the year that has passed since I last had the privilege of addressing the Second Committee [of the General Assembly], . . . the principle that recipient countries should themselves administer Fund-supported projects whenever possible, has been extended in practice. (7 October 1974)

- [With regard to] direct funding, . . . UNFPA has continued the practice authorized by the Economic and Social Council of arranging for the execution of projects by recipient countries themselves. In 1974, approximately $7 million of project budgets were executed in this fashion. (19 June 1975)

- In agreement with UNDP, we are taking over from UNDP the headquarters' financial management of directly-funded projects, in which governments themselves execute UNFPA-assisted projects. This is a large area of our activity, amounting in 1975 to about $15 million annually. . . . (28 June 1976)

- We initiated this innovative approach a few years ago, but we did it cautiously in the beginning in view of the many practical difficulties involved. (27 July 1976)

- Population growth is rightly regarded as a global problem because the pressure on resources touches on the economic interdependence of the planet, not to mention the sense of neighbourly concern of all people. But it is important to realize that people live within the territorial boundaries of nations and as long as the world is made up of sovereign nationalities, all population policies and programmes are the direct responsibility of national governments and national institutions. This is why the Fund has increasingly moved towards providing direct assistance to national governments and non-governmental organizations in the population field rather than working exclusively through international or regional agencies. (27 September 1977)

- In the important . . . area of direct execution by recipient governments of UNFPA support for population activities, a new high level was reached in 1977 when a total of $22.4 million, or some 27.4 per cent of overall programme support, was allocated directly to governments for their own direct implementation of some 175 population projects.

  Direct [funding] of UNFPA-supported population projects . . . provides excellent opportunities for dialogues and interaction between the recipient governments and the Fund. (21 June 1978)

- This approach of so-called direct execution of technical co-operation projects, including utilization of national personnel and procurement of equipment and supplies, is functioning increasingly well. It has been found to be cost-efficient, to speed up implementation, and to promote further development of responsibility, confidence and experience of institutions and individuals in developing countries. It also takes into account the considerable level of expertise in population matters already acquired by a growing number of developing countries. (6 November 1978)

Executing Agencies

[In UNFPA terminology, an "executing agency" is an international organization which executes projects sponsored by the UNFPA, that is, an international organization that is responsible for seeing that the project is carried out. Such organizations include United Nations agencies, regional commissions, and non-governmental organizations. Not all projects are implemented with the aid of executing agencies. In cases where the government directly executes projects, the government executing agency is called the "Implementing Agency". In the early years of UNFPA operations, most Fund projects were executed by various United Nations organizations. The range of executing agencies was expanded to include a variety of non-governmental organizations. In recent years, however, the trend of UNFPA programming has been "direct execution" of UNFPA-funded projects by governments themselves.]

- The UNFPA is not an operating agency. It normally chooses executing agencies for a project from among . . . the United Nations agencies. The Fund, however, may choose as the executor of a project an agency outside the United Nations system if it seems advisable for it to do so. (16 October 1970)

- The Fund is collaborating with the World Bank [in a major population effort being launched in Indonesia]. Also, for the first time, a non-governmental organization—the Population Council—will join the United Nations agencies, in this case WHO and UNICEF, in executing certain components. It is also hoped that the United Nations will participate on the demographic side. . . . Everything has now been satisfactorily arranged for what [we] hope will turn out to be a . . . successful undertaking as a result of using the many specialized skills of the participants to best advantage. (21 March 1972)

- One of the reasons for the rapid expansion of UNFPA assistance is due to the flexibility of the Fund procedures for considering requests. This flexibility is possible because [*inter alia*] . . . the choice of executing agencies for Fund-supported projects is made in collaboration with the requesting country and in consultation with the appropriate body . . . of the United Nations system. (18 May 1972)

- The implementation of [Fund-financed] projects is entrusted to the organizations both outside and inside the United Nations family which have the greatest competency in the particular area. (14 February 1973-B)

- Most of the projects financed by UNFPA are being implemented with the assistance of organizations of the United Nations system, within their respective fields of competence, namely the United Nations itself (including its regional Economic Commissions), United Nations Development Programme (UNDP), United Nations Children's Fund (UNICEF), United Nations Industrial Development Organization (UNIDO), International Labour Organisation (ILO), Food and Agriculture Organization of the United Nations (FAO), United Nations Educational, Scientific and Cultural Organization (UNESCO), and World Health Organization (WHO). Collaborative arrangements have been made with the International Development Association (IDA), an affiliate of the World Bank, and with the World Food Programme. We have held two meetings a year with these agencies, in a collective body called the Inter-Agency Consultative

Committee, to discuss the Fund's programmes, operational policies and procedures, and to facilitate the co-ordination of Fund-supported projects carried out by these organizations.

In this way, the Fund has been able to take full advantage of the experience, contacts and expertise of these organizations, and of the opportunities for associating or incorporating UNFPA contributions to on-going development programmes and projects. A few projects are being executed through international non-governmental organizations. It is expected that ultimately responsibility for the execution of projects will lie more directly with the recipient governments, using the services of United Nations or other organizations for any essential technical assistance. Indeed, the movement away from small projects to more comprehensive country programmes—a trend that is gradually gaining momentum - foreshadows this development. (4 May 1973)

• As regards operative paragraph number two of the ECOSOC resolution (1763 (LIV))—which directed UNFPA "to invite countries to utilize the most appropriate implementing agents for their programmes, recognizing that the responsibility for implementing rests with the countries themselves"—the Fund has already taken some steps in this direction. (14 June 1973)

• There have been many modifications and new directions in the Fund's programme since its beginning. None are more significant than the process which is being carried out at the present time in accordance with the directive contained in [this] ECOSOC resolution. . . . (29 October 1973)

• In its [ECOSOC's] . . . resolution with regard to the Fund . . . increased scope was given to the Fund in its choice of implementing agents, whether inside or outside the United Nations system, and for more direct relations between the Fund and recipient countries. (6 November 1973)

• The great bulk of UNFPA-financed projects—country projects, regional projects, interregional projects, and global projects—are executed by agencies of the United Nations system—the United Nations, ILO, FAO, UNESCO, WHO, UNIDO, and UNICEF—and we are most pleased with the working relationships that have developed between us and all these partners in our UNFPA work. (19 June 1975)

• UNFPA's limited support to non-governmental organizations is being increasingly directed towards national programmes which form part of overall strategies formulated by the respective national governments. (7 November 1977)

Foreign Experts, Recruitment of

• The Fund . . . welcomes suggestions . . . on how to solve the ever-recurring problem of training, recruitment and placement of experts. The executing agencies of the Fund need an adequate system of information on the availability of trained manpower in all the fields of population. (18 May 1972)

• While delays in delivery of equipment must be taken into consideration [in planning a project], so too must the almost universal problem of recruitment of experts. Consequently, in projects where an expert must first undertake an appraisal before a project can begin, the inevitable time lag should be taken into consideration when phasing the project. Better planning and more realistic assessments of capacities of agencies, both United Nations and national, can reduce the frustrations of project delay. For example, are outside "experts" always needed in projects submitted to the UNFPA for funding? There have been cases where an expert is provided not for technical advice but for organizational and administrative skills. Surely government ministries or universities can sometimes meet this latter need, indeed, if not the need for technical advice as well. Attempts should be made to seek out nationals with the necessary skills to make a project work. (8 March 1973)

• Expert recruitment from a limited number of countries has . . . been a serious handicap to the effectiveness of external aid programmes. For many years, the industrialized nations of the West had a virtual monopoly of modern technology and scientific advance. This is no longer the case. Regional and national reservoirs of expertise are being built up, and it is the Fund's policy to encourage and assist the establishment of institutions and organizations to provide an increasing supply of experts needed for development and population programmes. (6 March 1974)

• We have responded to government criticisms of the costs, delays and eventual ineffectualness involved in the traditional system of supplying foreign expertise by increasingly turning toward reliance on local expertise and local programme managers. . . . The advantage of this innovation in dealing with such a culturally sensitive matter as population, not to mention the saving of time and expense, is self-evident. (20 February 1976)

• There are clear signs that many of the major changes in population assistance provided by the Fund are setting the pattern for similar trends in other areas of development assistance. We are moving through three phases of population assistance:

(1) Traditional technical assistance, that is, transfer of technical know-how, through the services of long-term experts and the build-up of the capacity of the organizations in the United Nations system;

(2) Financial support to assist governments and non-governmental bodies to expand their activities; and,

(3) Phasing out of assistance or foreign experts as appropriate bodies at the country level are progressively taking over the full responsibilities for the programmes concerned.

Initially, of course, we concentrated on the first phase, but we are increasingly reducing our support in this area. A number of recipient countries no longer require the assistance of international experts to carry out population programmes—there are an increasing number of national experts in these countries to direct and manage such programmes. What these countries do require, instead, is financial support to intensify the pace of their own efforts. Long-term foreign experts are normally provided only where expertise is not available locally. Where such advisers are provided, their responsibility is clearly confined to technical tasks in the planning and execution of activities.

Whenever possible and needed, short-term advisers are provided on a regional or sub-regional basis to cover several disciplines or to service several countries, rather than providing resident advisers. We also want to stress the importance of training local personnel, to enable them to make the need for foreign advisory services superfluous. . . . Actually, we finance approximately twice as many man-months of local personnel as international experts. (27 July 1976)

Budgeting

[In the early days of the UNFPA, budgeting practices involved full funding of all of UNFPA's commitments against current resources, that is, holding all funds committed to projects in abeyance until used up. This continued until 1973, when UNFPA asked its new governing body, the UNDP Governing Council, to adopt separate financial rules and regulations for the UNFPA, putting the UNFPA on an annualized funding basis, that is, permitting the UNFPA to programme unutilized resources.]

• Full funding is an inefficient basis for the operations of a well-established funding organization. It faces the organization with two alternatives, both of which are undesirable: (1) to limit commitments to one year, a basis too short for effective planning by recipient governments, or (2) to immobilize the assets granted by donor governments for an unnecessarily long period by making multi-year commitments. (29 January 1973)

• We were authorized* annualized funding, under which only the anticipated expenses of the current year have to be held against current resources. It was agreed that we would present a four-year work plan, together with a projection of anticipated resources and programme costs, to the Council annually at its June session. Under a "rolling plan" arrangement, it was agreed that these resources and programme cost estimates would be revised annually in the light of developments, as would be the "approval authority" which we requested of each June Council to cover the approvals which we anticipated having to make during the next 12 months. (6 November 1973)

• The [Fund's 1974-1977] Work Plan will . . . incorporate changes in demand and the further elaboration of UNFPA funding principles. These financial planning exercises have been important steps towards the establishment of explicit and coherent programming practices. (12 November 1973)

• Under the rolling plan concept, UNFPA requests the UNDP Governing Council to authorize the total approval authority shown in the first year of the Work Plan submitted . . . and portions of the approval authority shown in the Work Plan for the second and third years, in order to permit multi-year programming.

During this period of rapid development, the Fund has found that the utilization of a rolling plan system based upon a multi-year Work Plan has offered the greatest flexibility in meeting urgent population needs while at the same time ensuring the financial

*By the UNDP Governing Council at its 15th Session, January 1973.

integrity of the Fund. (19 June 1975)

• Our UNFPA financial system features a four-year rolling plan, financial control focused tightly on project allocations rather than on cash expenditures, and the use of estimated actual costs, rather than standard costs, for experts. In addition, we have established and maintain . . . a fully-funded operational reserve. (19 January 1976)

• Through the years, the Fund has remained financially viable by maintaining an un-programmed reserve of $20 million, and by authorizing expenditure only on the basis of firm commitments for financial contributions. (20 February 1976)

• We are prudently managing the funds [the UNDP Governing Council] have entrusted to us. . . . We have not overprogrammed. We have continued to use actual costs of experts, not standard costs; we have always been able, and are now able, to meet all of our obligations; and our operational reserves are intact. (28 June 1976)

Infrastructure* Support

• We have extended a limited amount of support to the [United Nations] agencies to help them with additional staffing, at least over the first few years of expanded programmes in the population field. (18 February 1971)

• The capacity of the United Nations and the Specialized Agencies concerned to meet requests has . . . been greatly strengthened by the infrastructure support provided by the Fund.

The Fund is supporting a very wide range of projects which, contrary to the belief of some, is far from being entirely devoted to family planning activities. For example, the Fund's initial programmes laid heavy emphasis on the importance of the work of the United Nations Population Division in research, training and advisory services in demography. (3 November 1971)

• The Fund is in the process of making a number of arrangements to strengthen programmes at the country level. Among these are . . . the strengthening of agency regional offices by granting UNFPA support for the establishment of posts for population specialists and the strengthening of population units at the regional Economic Commissions and the Specialized Agencies, thereby strengthening the planning assistance available to governments in the population sector. . . . (18 May 1972)

• Where required, UNFPA . . . provides funds for local programme and administrative field staff in the Resident Representative's office, to furnish the necessary programme support services. (19 June 1975)

• We have held fruitful discussions [regarding infrastructure support] with these [United Nations] organizations within the framework of the Inter-Agency Consultative Committee. An agreement has been reached with them about a clearer definition of in-

---

*In UNFPA terminology, the word "infrastructure" is defined as financial support for personnel in other United Nations organizations who are responsible for administering and co-ordinating population activities at the headquarters, regional, and in some cases, country level.

frastructure support, since a number of posts which in the past were considered as infrastructure really were for specific project activities. Insofar as real infrastructure posts are concerned, we are in consultation with the organizations concerned, with a view to a gradual reduction of our support to infrastructure. Considerable progress has already been made by several organizations towards absorbing some infrastructure costs provided by UNFPA in the past. . . . (28 January 1977)

• We have reached agreement with the United Nations organizations that are members of UNFPA's Inter-Agency Consultative Committee on a common definition of infrastructure posts that is applicable to all of them. It was agreed that infrastructure be defined as posts of an administrative, financial or co-ordinating nature at agency headquarters. It was further agreed that all other posts should be considered as project posts and included in the project budgets and terminated when the project activities cease.

The proposals from other organizations call for reconciliation and adjustment in the various financial and budgetary organs of the United Nations system. [We] urge the governments concerned to be consistent in their views on these matters, both in these bodies and the Governing Council. (21 June 1977)

Local Costs, Funding of

• The Fund may be used to finance technical assistance and . . . sector-type projects through provision of expert services, equipment, fellowships abroad, including those at [United Nations] Regional [Demographic Training and Research] Centres, and organization of training courses and seminars. . . . In view of the importance, urgency and special nature of the population problem, however, consideration may be given to use of the Fund to provide other types of assistance, including the payment of local costs and counterpart services. Among these may be:

Local Costs for Field Research Projects. There is, in most countries, and even in different regions of large countries, a need for applied research into such questions as motivation towards family planning and attitudes towards use of various methods of contraception. Some countries, particularly in Asia, have had considerable experience in running family planning programmes. Provided financial assistance were available, governments could identify institutions which could then carry out such research with little outside expert assistance. In principle, the Fund may be used for such research, with due provision for the results to be made available through the agencies of the United Nations system to other countries and for visits to the projects by representatives of the United Nations agencies.

Local Costs for Training. While the Fund is likely to be used to finance training abroad, and particularly at Regional Centres, it may also be used in appropriate circumstances to finance training at the national level along the same sort of lines as in UNICEF-financed programmes.

Local Costs for Other Operational Activities. The question has arisen, in countries which have serious budgetary problems, of contributions towards local costs of operational programmes. Though the implications would need careful examination in each case, the possibility of such contributions is not excluded.

Transport and Equipment. Transport and equipment for family planning programmes will be included in the support provided by the Fund.

Manufacture of Equipment and Supplies. The question has arisen in some countries as to whether assistance in the manufacture of equipment and supplies may be possible. The possibilities of the Fund providing capital assistance for this purpose will depend on a considerable expansion of its resources.

Research. Among the types of research which may be usefully conducted in one or another developing country might be research into the economic and social consequences of demographic trends, the social and economic factors leading to current fertility trends, and the appropriateness and effectiveness in the area of one or another type of family planning programme or contraceptive.

All the above activities would only be contemplated in the context of projects, and not as general budgetary support. (10 November 1969)

• We are finding that the question of what types of local costs to bear and when to bear them is one of the most thorny problems we have to face. Although we have no hard and fixed rule about local costs, as, for example, does the UNDP in its Technical Assistance or Special Fund projects, we do regard the willingness of governments to bear part of the local expenses of a project as an indispensable indication of their seriousness concerning the project, without which the project's chances of success would be dubious indeed. (16 October 1970)

• In some appropriate cases UNFPA can support local costs of projects and even, in some instances, capital costs, although we are rather anxious, wherever possible, to avoid construction costs and hope to be able to leave these to the population programmes of the World Bank or to other donors. (18 February 1971)

• One of the reasons for the rapid expansion of UNFPA assistance is due to the flexibility of the Fund procedures for considering requests. This flexibility is possible because . . . in addition to covering the financing of the usual technical co-operation aspects of a project, UNFPA is prepared to cover substantial local costs of specific projects. Such local costs may include salaries of locally employed personnel. Construction costs may be financed on a demonstration basis if they comprise a relatively small part of a programme. (18 May 1972)

• The Fund has always been extremely flexible in the types of assistance it provides. For example, it could, in certain strategic sectors, provide for local and construction costs. When contraceptive supplies and equipment are essential for a programme but locally unavailable, arrangements are made to meet such shortages. (14 February 1973-B)

• We have provided funds for the purchase of local materials and equipment, wherever possible. . . . (20 February 1976)

• Population programmes normally require more funds for local costs than other traditional technical assistance, and UNFPA has been in the forefront of the movement away from traditional provision of experts and equipment, towards funding of local costs. We remain convinced that this is vital to promotion of population activities where governments have not yet been able to commit all the budgetary support necessary. (21 June 1977)

Multi-Country Activities, UNFPA Support of

[Initially, most of UNFPA's resources were allocated to what are called "regional, inter-regional and global" population activities. The purpose was to build up the organizational capacity of regional, inter-regional and global institutions so that they in turn could assist developing countries in meeting their population needs by, for example, providing training to nationals in demography, etc. As the developing countries began to build up their own capacities to implement population projects, the UNFPA began increasingly to provide more funds to the developing countries themselves. And the proportion of UNFPA resources allocated to regional, inter-regional and global population activities began to decline, although there remained many multi-country projects which deserved financing. The question was: What should be the mix of country funding to multi-country funding? The search for the answer to this question resulted in a study directed by the UNFPA's Deputy Executive Director, Halvor Gille, which was presented to the UNFPA's governing body, the UNDP Governing Council, in June 1978. The study is included as Appendix F in this volume.]

• It has . . . been our purpose to provide opportunity for recipient countries themselves to generate programmes, and to establish, within the Fund, mechanisms for evaluating requests which will give the maximum flexibility of response.

This implies that the Fund will, where possible, provide direct assistance within the framework of the individual country's general programmes of development, although we do not exclude multi-country programmes where these appear most suitable from the standpoint of administrative efficiency. (18 October 1973)

• Consistent with the views strongly expressed by many of you [Governing Council] at your 19th Session in January, we are continuing in 1975 our programming trend of 1973 and 1974, whereby requests for country projects are given higher priority than requests for regional, inter-regional and global activities. In 1974, UNFPA allocations were maintained to permit regional, inter-regional and global activities at a similar level as in preceding years (though receiving a decreasing proportion of our increasing resources), but in 1975 it has been necessary to reduce substantially the level of support as compared with 1974. It is our present plan to maintain future regional, inter-regional and global activities at least at the 1975 level.

Many such multi-country projects are in our view highly important to the overall UNFPA objectives assigned to us by the General Assembly and the Economic and Social Council. Many tasks of awareness-building, training and research are significant and vital in the full perspective of UNFPA's responsibilities, and yet often cannot be carried out in the form of country projects, as, for example, the United Nations demographic centres now operating in six countries and serving all developing regions, population aspects of the ILO World Employment Programme, FAO research and case studies on the effects of different rates of population growth on agricultural development, UNESCO regional programmes in the development of population education, WHO research concerning sterilization and abortions, and the UNICEF revolving fund stockpile of contraceptives. (19 June 1975)

• In all cases, multi-country activities carried out at the regional and inter-regional levels are constantly being revised to further relate them to the varying needs of developing countries. We expect this effort to result in the streamlining of current inter-country operations in the United Nations system, and in a multidisciplinary approach. (3 November 1976)

• We have . . . initiated review and assessment of regional, inter-regional and global activities supported by UNFPA in the past, with [a] view to developing an overall, integrated strategy for the future. (28 January 1977)

• Regarding UNFPA-funded inter-country activities, a review of past and present UNFPA-supported projects in this area has been completed. It is clear that, while the amount of funding has remained nearly the same since 1974, the proportion of UNFPA programme resources allocated to inter-country activities as a whole has declined steadily. . . . (21 June 1977)

• In order to arrive at a strategy which is viable, and on the basis of which new inter-country operations will be designed, UNFPA is conducting an analysis of regional needs, and has also looked at the main substantive fields in population activities and their future directions. In the process, UNFPA is involving the concerned Specialized Agencies of the United Nations. . . . (20 January 1978)

• This study ["Support of Inter-country Activities"] is the outcome of the Fund's intensive efforts over the past year, which included the preparation of a comprehensive summary of past UNFPA support to inter-country activities. . . . In preparing the recommendations in the documents, UNFPA has reviewed the major areas requiring support at the inter-country level, taking into account the main findings of evaluations undertaken by UNFPA of relevant programmes, and benefiting from extensive consultations held with UNFPA's executing organizations in the United Nations system and interested non-governmental organizations.

With regard to the report, the ^Governing] Council's attention is drawn particularly to the rationale for UNFPA support of inter-country activities and the suggested priority areas of future support. In each of the main programme areas within the Fund's mandate, the types of activities that require support are identified, keeping in mind the principles and criteria for selecting such inter-country activities. . . . In view of the fact that the perceived needs extend beyond the resources UNFPA can be expected to have available for this purpose, recommendations of the priority areas and programmes which the Fund may support in the foreseeable future have been outlined for the Council's consideration.

It is in recognition of the close relationship between UNFPA-supported country and inter-country programmes and the desirability that it should continue, that [we] propose in the document before the members that a percentage level within a certain range of the Fund's programme resources be established [to replace the ceiling of an absolute amount] established by the Council in 1975. [We are] convinced that the approval of a range of 25-30 per cent would be essential to meet critical gaps in the major sectors at the inter-country level, while at the same time ensuring that the important needs of country programmes for technical support will be met.

It should be noted that almost one-half of UNFPA's resources currently allocated at the inter-country level is providing direct technical support to country programmes, which is a continuing need. Furthermore, commitments have been made to support, for some time to come, the regional and inter-regional demographic centres. And block allocations for international fellowships on population, as well as other vitally important training programmes, undoubtedly have to be provided for. This means that the scope for support of other recommended activities is quite limited indeed. Imposition of a more restrictive ceiling than the one [we] have recommended to the Council could in the long run be detrimental to meeting the overall objectives set for UNFPA at the inter-country as well as the country levels.

In this document, it is proposed that the Council should, in the future, review and approve, on a rotating basis, major inter-country programmes for UNFPA support. It is also indicated that arrangements will continue to be made for intensified and regular consultations with organizations and experts, before approval of inter-country programmes are made. Maintaining such procedures should ensure members of the Council that the allocations for inter-country activities will be of the greatest relevance to meeting the needs of the developing countries, and be addressed to the most urgent areas of gaps in knowledge. (21 June 1978)

Non-Governmental Organizations, UNFPA's Relations with

• A number of bilateral agencies have been giving substantial assistance in several countries, as have private organizations such as the Population Council, the International Planned Parenthood Federation, and the Pathfinder Fund. It is not the UNFPA's intention that programmes financed by the Fund should compete with those financed from other sources. However, consultations with representatives of other agencies should help to indicate where in each country the most useful activities can be undertaken by the Fund. (10 November 1969)

• The United Nations system and the IPPF [International Planned Parenthood Federation] . . . should be mutually supportive. . . . In some instances, the UNFPA intends to fund projects through the IPPF. This, [we] think, will be particularly true in areas . . . where the governments wish family planning activities to take place but sometimes do not wish to have official policies or programmes supporting such activities. In such cases, the work of the IPPF may be, and in many instances has been, an indispensable bridge on the road to official government policies and programmes of the sort which the United Nations system can support through its own agencies. (16 October 1970)

• The Fund is capable of responding to requests from non-governmental organizations in developing countries, provided that . . . the government in question will not object to UNFPA's funding the activity. With regard to NGO's [non-governmental organizations], we have it in mind not to open the doors to all comers . . . but, whenever possible, to entertain requests from non-governmental organizations such as the International Planned Parenthood Federation, or, for example, the International Alliance of Women and the International Council of Women, which can judge the coherence and capabilities of the local NGO and which, if need be, could serve as a channel for our assistance, even as "executing agency". (18 February 1971)

• As we all know, there are many extensive bilateral programmes of aid, and well-planned and executed assistance in population matters being provided by other international and private organizations. Foremost among these is, of course, the IPPF. The co-operation and counsel of this organization is much valued by the Fund. So it is only reasonable to ask what particular contribution this comparatively new Fund can make that could not be achieved by increasing support to these other efforts.

[We are] not suggesting the Fund as an alternative to these other programmes. The need is so great that all forms of assistance, however mobilized, are needed if even a dent is to be made in overcoming the major problem. (26 August 1971)

• Non-governmental organizations . . . are of key importance when it comes to reaching the community level, and [we] hope that those already involved with population programmes will stimulate the active participation of various groups such as professional and scientific associations, trade unions, farmers, and community centres. (1 November 1972)

• UNFPA has, since its inception, worked closely with a number of major non-governmental organizations. This has enabled UNFPA to benefit from their knowledge and experience, and to utilize their particular capabilities in implementing several UNFPA-supported projects.

Other organizations and groups, national and international , in developing as well as developed countries, are performing useful functions in the population field, mainly in training, research and communications, with support from UNFPA. These NGO activities, in order to be most effective, have to relate closely to the overall population and development policies and programmes of the countries concerned, and therefore in each case UNFPA ascertains that the government concerned has no objection to the proposed programme.

UNFPA's involvement with non-governmental organizations has thus grown steadily over the last three years. It was, therefore, considered necessary and useful to initiate a process of regular consultation with them, as a group. This meeting in London [Non-Governmental Organizations Consultation] provides the first such occasion. It is our hope that this meeting will provide the opportunity for the representatives of a number of major NGOs to inform us about their current programmes and future plans in the population field. We in UNFPA also invite them to give us suggestions and comments on how the relationship between UNFPA and NGOs can be strengthened further in the future. It is my hope that we shall have a full and free exchange of information and ideas at this meeting—and my colleagues and I from UNFPA look forward to participating in these discussions.

Though UNFPA has given increasing support to NGOs, the question is still raised as to why UNFPA should be providing support to, and working with, NGOs. The answer is . . . rather simple. UNFPA has been given a leading and important role in the United Nations system in the promotion of population programmes, and has identified a number of areas of activity as being of particular importance in this context. As in several of these areas NGOs have particular competence, UNFPA will utilize their services to fulfill the established objectives. It goes without saying that NGO efforts in the population field, must complement those of governments. The primary responsibility for setting goals and objectives in the population field, in relation to other aspects of development and for implementing operational programmes, rests with the governments, and NGO efforts must fit into the broad framework worked out by the governments for the activities in this area. I know, at the same time, from contacts with a variety of governments, that they keenly appreciate the services rendered by non-governmental and private groups in their countries in promoting awareness and understanding of population problems. Governments also appreciate that they are undertaking innovative and pioneering efforts in the field of family planning—and they would be happy to utilize the particular capabilities of NGOs in some of these areas in the future. There is, thus, a continuing role for NGOs in the population field.

The emphasis, in the final analysis, is . . . on individuals, on people. Non-governmental organizations are run by people, and are, therefore, attuned and responsive to their needs and requirements. It is clear to me that NGOs have, thus, a major and important role to play in bringing proper awareness and understanding of the population question to people, and in helping them to decide how they wish to exercise their individual rights and enrich their personal lives.

As the activities and roles of national governments have widened, it might be thought—and indeed it once *was* thought—that the role of private and voluntary agencies would correspondingly diminish. With the establishment of full-scale national health services, for instance, it was at one time expected that health insurance schemes would disappear. This has not, in fact, happened at all. The need for the unique person-to-person relationships that are the special virtue of the voluntary organizations has not diminished, but grown. Even at the level of financing alone, the needs of the social services are great, and the available resources of national governments are not infinite. The voluntary organizations thus play an enormous role in supplementing governmental efforts.

In the area of research, studies and surveys, organizations like IUSSP [International Union for the Scientific Study of Population] and CICRED [Committee for International Coordination of National Research in Demography] are performing highly significant functions. Population education, particularly non-formal population education, is the concern of a wide variety of international NGOs, such as the International Council of Women, the International Alliance of Women, the World Assembly of Youth, ISMUN [International Student Movement for the United Nations], etc. In the field of communications, youth groups and women's groups continue to play an increasingly important and effective role.

Apart from these sectoral activities, there are multi-disciplinary activities which are being supported by NGOs, or in which NGOs can provide a meaningful contribution. World Population Year 1974 should, in this sense, be regarded as a multidisciplinary activity, and [we are] hopeful that WPY will really provide an incentive to extend and intensify many of the sectoral activities while, at the same time, strengthening the overall purpose—to bring the urgency and the relevance of population and development questions to the attention of people everywhere in the world.

UNFPA has supported, through specific grants, a variety of NGO activities, ranging from seminars and conferences to implementation of country level programmes. We shall continue to provide support in the future to such activities which meet the UNFPA criteria for support and fit into the guidelines of our Work Plan. It is, however, obvious to us that we can be only one of the channels for providing support for such activities. As NGO activities expand in this area, it is our hope that they will be able to obtain from a variety of national and international agencies the basic support required for the programmes in the population field they wish to undertake. Whenever through partial subsidy or assistance we can encourage or help initiate such activities, we shall be willing to do so. The major responsibility, however, for finding support for these programmes, on a long-term basis, must rest with the organizations concerned. UNFPA funds are designed to act as a spur to action in the future. (28 June 1973)

• Non-governmental organizations occupy a key position in the relationship between government and people. (25 August 1973)

• In some countries, family planning associations continue to be responsible for running family planning services, and have achieved results comparable to any government programme. Generally, however, national programmes can best be operated by the public health authorities. This does not necessarily diminish the role of voluntary agencies. In the course of visits to many countries in the last few years, [we] have been repeatedly struck by the quality and vitality of the work. . . . Governmental action and voluntary effort must go hand in hand. The challenge now facing you [IPPF] . . . is to identify and concentrate on developing those areas in which you have a comparative advantage. It is not for [us] to tell you what to do. And, obviously, the contribution will vary from situation to situation. But, with your permission, [we believe there are] three areas in which . . . the IPPF and its member associations can make a vital contribution.

The first such area is that of innovation. Voluntary agencies do not operate under the same constraints as governmental programmes. Consequently, they have a vital role to play in the development of new approaches, particularly with regard to the delivery of family planning services and to communication programmes. This would include such things as model clinics, distribution of oral contraceptives without prescription, pilot projects for particular groups, and so on.

A second area in which voluntary agencies can make a special contribution is by acting as a link between government programmes and the population at large. This is not just a question of mobilizing popular support for action programmes or complementing government efforts. It must also include acting as a channel for the expression of popular attitudes and values with regard to population and family planning. . . .

The third area in which [there is] a continuing role for voluntary agencies, both nationally and internationally, is that of a proselytizing group. Although many governments have accepted some responsibility for family planning, we are still far from universal acceptance of family planning as a basic human right. In other fields, such as sex education and abortion law, there is an even greater need to promote public debate and press for legislative reform.

It is not your role of "friend, critic, educator and guide" which is in question, but rather how best to fulfill it in the years to come. (22 October 1973)

• We have, in UNFPA, given a great deal of attention to maintaining close relations with non-governmental groups, although we have never suggested any particular point of view on population that ought to be promoted by any private groups. . . . (30 November 1973)

• It is difficult to over-estimate the importance of the individual in matters of population.

It is through the personal involvement and commitment of individuals that non-governmental organizations were established, and they are kept in being by the continuing enthusiasm of their individual members. They are, therefore, of enormous importance in shaping and carrying out policy, not only in population, but in every kind of activity. Governments can only be as good as their lines of communication to their people; non-governmental organizations are in a position to inform governments of the wishes and needs of those whom they represent. As communicators and creators of a common will out of millions of personal attitudes and opinions, they are unequalled.

Non-governmental organizations, therefore, take on even more importance when they are seen in the context of economic and social development. Changing views of the development process have given more and more significance to the individual as an active participator rather than a passive tool of policy.

For their part in helping to shape these views, tribute should be paid to the pioneering work of the private groups and individuals who have been instrumental in establishing, for example, rights within the family, which now have the sanction of the whole international community. Governments and international agencies have good reason to value the voice and the activity of the non-governmental organizations, and should be prepared to listen at all times, even when the voices are critical.

UNFPA has always held that the individual is the key to successful development efforts, and has committed a consistently high proportion of its resources to non-governmental organizations in every field of activity, from demographic research to women's rights. They have responded by throwing their whole-hearted support behind our work. In particular, World Population Year has seen a tremendous increase in non-governmental activity and owes its success to the enthusiasm and dedication of you who are attending this [Population] Tribune and to many thousands of people in every country of the world.

At UNFPA we have relied since our foundation on the support of non-governmental organizations for the success of our work. In turn, we have committed our moral and material support to them. [We] look forward to continuing our association in the future, and hope that . . . it may be improved still further. (18 August 1974)

• The task before us . . . is to find resources to meet increasing demands in the population field; and to continue to strengthen the population component in development planning. It is a task primarily undertaken by governments. But [we] can see a major role also for non-governmental organizations and private groups in this area. There are still significant gaps in the understanding and appreciation of the importance of the population question within the development process, and NGOs are admirably suited for the task of educating and informing people of these issues. There is also a need for innovative programming in the population field which would point out new ways of dealing with the complexities of the population problem. NGOs, which have in the past shown a great deal of initiative, courage and conviction in undertaking such programmes, should continue to perform this function.

We in UNFPA have always recognized the importance of NGOs and have backed up this recognition with substantial support to NGO activities. . . . Most of this support has gone toward national activities in family planning, research studies and surveys, and information, education and communication projects. As national population activities increase, the pressure on us to provide greater support to governmental plans also increases. A major part of our resources has to go to national governments, as we believe in the efficacy of national programmes undertaken by the governments themselves. But we also believe that NGOs will continue to have an important role, and remain prepared to provide them support for programmes which fit into national action programmes on population.

We will continue to support a selected number of NGO activities which are relevant to national population activities, through financial grants.

We will continue to look [to] NGOs for support in the task that is ahead of us—further national action needed for dealing with and rationalizing population trends while seeking the economic threshold which would make the lives of millions worth living, and therefore worth self-regulating. (10 June 1975)

• The interest and momentum of the work of non-governmental organizations, which look to the Fund for leadership and support, needs to be nurtured and sustained. The large number of non-governmental organizations with which we collaborate include, for example, the International Planned Parenthood Federation and its large membership of national planned parenthood organizations, and the International Statistical Institute, which is the executing agency for the World Fertility Survey. (19 June 1975)

• Many governments . . . have moved towards comprehensively planned action in population, with the fullest possible co-operation between the different sectors, and with constant reference to the country's development goals. But this co-operation will not be adequately meaningful unless . . . there is rapport between governmental and non-governmental organizations. (26 March 1978)

Population Needs, Assessment of

• It is our intention to undertake a study, region by region, of the types of basic population programmes required to meet the needs of countries at various stages of development, and identify the types of programmes the countries need to deal with their major population problems in accordance with their own policies. In doing this we would try to take into account factors such as the availability of resources in the countries themselves, the priorities indicated by the regional consultations held after the Bucharest [World Population] Conference, and the availability of other resources of foreign aid. (21 November 1975)

• Governments, donors and agencies executing projects alike are most likely to achieve success in their programmes if they address themselves to the basic needs of those whom they serve, the people of the developing countries. In our experience, this approach can offer at least as good a ratio of costs to benefits in those things which can be quantified, and the indications are that it is a much more rewarding approach in the areas which cannot be quantified. (2 June 1977)

• The three other important general principles endorsed in the [General Assembly] resolution* concern the respect of the sovereign right of each nation to determine its own population policies, the promotion of countries' self-reliance, and the importance of giving special attention to the needs of disadvantaged population groups. These principles will mainly be applied by UNFPA through the formulation of basic needs programmes in the fields of population. In order to determine basic population needs, we first identify the countries' population policies and programme objectives, then we assess the domestic resources available for furthering them, and finally, we try to determine the assistance required from external sources. [We] should like to underline that these programmes are being prepared in full collaboration with the governments concerned and are being worked out *with* governments and not *for* governments. (7 November 1977)

• During 1978 we expect the [Fund's] programme to enter into new frontiers. First of all, some programmes and projects will be based on basic needs assessments. Secondly, and increasingly, the population distribution concerns of a number of developing countries will be translated into action programmes, either with the purpose being to relieve over-urbanized centres or to cluster a dispersed population into viable centres. Thirdly, requests for activities concerned with infant mortality, employment, and education of women and teenagers are increasing. (20 January 1978)

*31/170 of 21 December 1976, which outlined five principles for the future allocation of UNFPA resources, the first two being "To promote population activities proposed in international strategies . . . " and "To meet the needs of developing countries which have the most urgent need for assistance. . . ."

- In the appraisal of programmes, and in view of the limited resources at the Fund's disposal, we have to assess the country's needs more carefully. Only in this way can the long-term goal of complete self-reliance be attained. Therefore, we have developed a method of establishing needs by means of a thorough study, not only of a country's population situation, but of the economic and social context in which population activities will be carried out.

These studies will tell us more about the special needs of the different countries. Because we recognize that each country is an individual case, we are not intending to impose a pattern on the studies. In the more advanced countries, the information on needs assessment will come mainly from the government itself, with external advice and analysis as needed. In others with less sophisticated policy and planning mechanisms, much of the work will be done by outside consultants, in association with the government.

The studies will have certain features in common. All of them will discuss the current economic and social situation, and prospects for the future. All will look at the general development plans and activities of the government, and the specific development problems of each country. They will then go on to analyze the population situation, and planning and programming in this area. Particular attention will be paid to the way in which population programmes and activities are linked with other areas of development. Finally, the studies will identify gaps in the structure of population policy and programming and will make recommendations for filling them. Following the study, missions will visit the country to prepare specific requests for assistance. (26 March 1978)

- In the seventies, economists and other social scientists and planners have raised the appealing banner of the basic needs approach to development. But despite its appeal, there is less clarity to what is entailed intellectually. And, partially as a result of this, there is also less clarity as to how to make the concept a reality.

Rather than succumb to the intellectual vice of over-simplicity that characterized at least some of the earlier thinking about development, the basic needs approach is now being defined as supplementing and complementing existing development strategies, rather than being an all-embracing strategy itself. Rather than focusing on industrial institutions solely, in the hope that they will provide the means for social and economic well-being for individuals, the focus is on ends of health and education and the like, themselves.

The new strategy focuses on a concrete specification of human needs—such as water, sanitation, and education—rather than abstract concepts, such as the quality of life. It is also specific in terms of attempting to channel particular resources to particular groups. It focuses not only on the unemployed and underemployed, but also on the poor, the devastated—the so-called unemployable. (3 April 1978)

- The needs assessment exercise will, in the long run, speed up the programming cycle. Towards this end, we have taken steps to standardize the format and speed up the procedures for developing basic population programmes, although we fully recognize that there are limits to what can be done in this regard, realizing that each recipient country, to a large extent, is unique in its problems, objectives, policies and programmes. (21 June 1978)

Priorities, Determining . . . in the Allocation of UNFPA Resources

[In 1974, it became increasingly apparent to the UNFPA that demands for international population assistance were far outstripping the Fund's resources. Much of the rise in demand was due to the success of the World Population Year and World Population Conference in 1974. A major question facing the UNFPA was: In view of the limited resources available, how should the Fund's resources be allocated, particularly in view of the principles outlined in the World Population Plan of Action? The development of a major UNFPA programme of priorities in the future allocation of UNFPA resources was the responsibility of the Fund's Deputy Executive Director, Halvor Gille.* The general principles on which the Fund's priority programme is based were approved by the Economic and Social Council (resolution 2025, LXI, 4 August 1976) and by the General Assembly (resolution 31/170, 21 December 1976).]

• A more long-term strategy for activities during the Second Development Decade has . . . been drafted by the Fund. This strategy reflects the priority needs of the developing countries, but at the same time, it recognizes the important regional and national differences which exist. It is very much action-oriented, but at the same time, it is also geared towards supporting relevant research activities, in particular in the fields of applied research, and assisting in the widest possible dissemination and application of research findings in developing countries. Training is another important area, with the aim of building up, as soon as possible, the human resources needed in the developing countries to deal effectively with population matters. Also, the development of demonstration and pilot projects is given a prominent place in the strategy, with the objective of improving the "state of the art" rather than achieving early spectacular results. (3 November 1971)

The very success of the initial promotional stage of the Fund has meant that demand for resources is beginning to outrun supply in a dramatic way. Thus, we need to apply priorities in the allocation of resources. . . . We need, moreover, a better method of judging the quality of individual project requests so that, if not all, at least the best may be funded. (30 April 1973)

• The increasing demand upon the resources of the Fund has created a new situation which brings the question of priorities for funding into the forefront. The World Population Plan of Action, adopted by consensus by 135 nations at the World Population Conference last year, has opened up much wider areas of population activities for international action. With the current re-thinking of the structure of the United Nations, the time may have come to re-examine the Fund's mandate, its criteria for approval of requests, and its priorities for allocation of resources among various types of

*See UNFPA Publication, "Priorities in Future Allocation of UNFPA Resources", reprinted as Appendix E in this volume.

population programmes and among various requesting governments and organizations. (14 July 1975)

• The resources [compared to requests] gap produces a . . . basic problem. When funds can no longer meet *all* requests, it becomes necessary to choose *between* requests, i.e., to establish operating priorities. The establishment of priorities is inherently difficult. . . . The World Population Plan of Action . . . broadened and enlarged the objectives of programming. But to produce a synthesis of global priorities for assistance is difficult. (24 October 1975)

• In determining priorities for use of UNFPA's resources, the following main principles may be established:
(1) The various international strategies such as the World Population Plan of Action, the International Development Strategy for the Second Development Decade, and the World Plan of Action focussing on integration of women and development should provide guidance for the activities of the Fund. These strategies, particularly the first one, suggest that an integrated development approach to population be applied. This would mean that population activities would be funded increasingly in conjunction with activities in health, education, rural development, community development and other programmes of economic and social development. . . .

We may state it as a fundamental condition of the Fund's assistance that population projects must be shown to be an integral part of development programmes. However, we must recognize that population assistance programmes have a specific purpose and responsibility, namely to support population activities rather than overall development programmes. The need is so tremendous that the Fund's own resources . . . could easily be lost without trace if they were spread too thinly. Although it is impossible to maintain a clear-cut distinction between what are and are not population activities, the time has come . . . to determine more clearly what "population activities" we should in principle support. So far as UNFPA is concerned, population activities may cover population aspects of development, including the characteristics, causes and effects of changes in fertility, mortality and morbidity as they affect developmental prospects and human well-being. The activities have conveniently been divided into collection of basic population data, population dynamics, population policy formulation and implementation, contraception and child spacing, and communication and education. Within these categories, a great deal of flexibility is required; an activity which has only marginal population content in one society may be vitally important in another. In each case, the particular conditions and concerns of the recipient country should be paramount.

(2) It will be increasingly necessary to concentrate our resources in supporting the most urgent requirements in those developing countries which have the greatest need in the population fields. This suggests that the least-developed countries, of which there are now 29—the majority in Africa—should be given preference in the allocation of the Fund's resources. In the present year, 14 per cent of our resources were allocated to these countries. We are considering the possibility of widening the concept of "least developed countries" to take into account some of the demographic components. We

may come up with a list of countries to be given preferential consideration, based upon appropriate criteria for levels of fertility and mortality, as well as on per capita gross domestic product and balance of payments positions.

(3) The Fund should aim at building up as quickly as possible the ability of recipient countries to meet their own needs. Therefore, we may limit the period of our assistance, particularly in developing countries falling outside the group of the least-developed. At the end of the period, activities should be handed over to an organization within the country concerned. This suggests that high priority should be given to supporting the following types of activity, in particular:

(a) human resource development, through training programmes and transfers of the skills and technical know-how required in various types of population pro-grames;

(b) institution-building at the national level, particularly in the fields of population data collection and analysis, policy formulation, and implementation of action programmes;

(c) operational research and pilot projects exploring innovative approaches to population problems and diffusion of experience gained; and

(d) strengthening of management capability to enable the recipient countries to ex-ecute their programmes effectively themselves and obtain the maximum benefit from assistance.

(4) Finally, in accordance with the spirit of Bucharest, special attention should be given to meeting the needs of disadvantaged groups such as the poorest among rural populations, under-privileged sectors in urban areas, and women in low-income families. High priority should be given to action programmes designed to ensure population participation and [to] explore all avenues for promoting community-based activities and involvement of all organized groups. This would mean that more atten-tion should be given to women's participation in community development programmes and to enlisting women in communication activities.

Any good planning for the future has to deal with alternatives. In the Fund, we are ten-tatively considering three alternative levels of resource development over the next five years:

A low-funding level which will merely maintain the present level in real dollar value, providing only for anticipated inflationary cost increases.

A medium-level funding which would enable us to provide assistance to developing countries within the concept of population activities . . . but applying strict priorities on the types of assistance we could give.

Finally, a high-funding level which would allow the Fund to support programmes within the immediate area of population activities but, at the same time, allow us to be more flexible in supporting some activities falling on the fringe.

It is our intention to undertake a study, region by region, of the types of basic popula-tion programmes required to meet the needs of countries at various stages of develop-ment, and to identify the types of programmes the countries need to deal with their major population problems in accordance with their own policies. In doing this, we would try to take into account factors such as the availability of resources in the countries themselves, the priorities indicated by the regional consultations held after the Bucharest [World Population] Conference and the availability of other resources of foreign aid.

Let me give a few illustrations of high priority areas of funding in the various regions:

In Asia and the Pacific, our assistance may concentrate on institutionalizing and implementing the population policies established in these countries. In family planning, greater attention should be devoted to the planning and design of programmes, to innovative approaches, to training, and to management and evaluation aspects.

In Latin America, high priority should be given to supporting the collection and analysis of the data required for population programme planning. In the field of fertility regulation, support for the maternal and child health approach may continue to be of great importance, but other channels should be given increasing attention. Planning, managerial and training components of programmes also need support.

In West Asia, assistance in data collection through censuses, sample surveys, vital statistics and migration studies are important requirements, as well as the inclusion of fertility services in integrated health programmes.

Finally, in Africa, continued assistance will be required to improve the weak population data base, particularly through support to census-taking in countries which have never taken a census or taken only one. Support for training of various kinds is another high priority area, as well as assistance for delivery of fertility services in existing health services.

It is not for the Fund to set priorities for national programmes. This can only be done by the countries themselves. (21 November 1975)

• The allocation of resources for population activities is subject to significantly different considerations from those guiding other development efforts. The UNFPA's Governing Council and the Economic and Social Council have repeatedly stated that resources for population assistance should not be allocated according to a worldwide formula, as general development assistance is. Considering the sensitiveness of the population question and the varied nature of cultural and national approaches to it, population assistance policies must be responsive to the varying needs and requirements of different countries. (20 February 1976)

• [In addition to building countries' self-reliance and giving priority to countries with the most urgent needs] we also propose to give special attention to population activities for the benefit, and with the participation, of the poorest among the rural poor, the underprivileged in urban areas, poor migrants and poor families in densely populated areas. Women, as homemakers, and as an actual and potential economic force, should also receive special attention. (14 June 1976)

I.P.A.—T

- In preparing this report [to the Governing Council on the question of criteria and priorities for the future allocation of our resources] we have . . . consulted informally with a number of governments and organizations as well as individuals. In its preparation, we have kept in mind the World Population Plan of Action and the role which UNFPA should play in its implementation.

The document outlines various basic principles which the Fund may adhere to in the future . . . in the allocation of its resources. It also recommends certain criteria to be applied in making priorities. . . . The arrangements [we] propose may be briefly summarized as follows:

The chief portion of the Fund's resources would be devoted to respond to requests made by governments. In order to achieve the most efficient use of the Fund's resources, a core programme of population activities has been outlined which is in accordance with the Fund's mandate. Within this core programme, it is suggested that we identify the basic population problems and policies and determine the minimum [or basic population] programmes—at the country as well as inter-country levels—required for the implementation of such programmes. Actually, the Fund has already initiated work on these lines based upon country reviews, with the assistance of an experienced consultant; and with the approval of the Governing Council, we intend continuing the exercise with the full collaboration of the governments and organizations concerned.

In meeting countries' needs for assistance to establish basic population programmes, it is proposed that high priority should be given to requests from countries which are especially in need of population assistance in view of their demographic situation and other relevant considerations. It should be understood that countries not included in the high priority group would still be eligible for assistance, but at more modest levels and for support of more selected activities.

Turning from country projects, a further portion of UNFPA resources would be reserved for support of activities at the regional, inter-regional and global levels, to be determined in due course after a thorough review of past activities and the preparation of an overall integrated strategy for future activities to be supported by the Fund.

The approach . . . briefly outlined would enable us to concentrate the Fund's resources in areas of the greatest need and where our support would be most significant in order to further the formulation and implementation of population policies of governments, to build up self-reliance in developing countries, to meet the requirements of disadvantaged groups, and to assist in the implementation of relevant international strategies, particularly the World Population Plan of Action. (28 June 1976)

- The Governing Council [at its 22nd Session in June] requested that the UNFPA should, in making future allocation of resources, apply the following general principles which we suggested and which fall within our mandate:

  (a) Promote population activities proposed in international strategies;

  (b) Meet the needs of developing countries with the most urgent requirements for population assistance;

(c) Respect the sovereignty of recipient countries on matters of population policies;

(d) Build up the recipient countries' self-reliance; and

(e) Support activities of special benefit to disadvantaged population groups.

The Governing Council endorsed the proposed core programme of UNFPA assistance, the main areas of which are: basic population data collection and analysis; population policy formulation and programme implementation, including family planning and population redistribution; population education and training; and applied research; as well as communication activities in support of these programmes.

The Governing Council also approved in principle the criteria for establishing priorities. All developing countries should, irrespective of their size, be entitled to assistance if required, but high priority should be given to countries which are especially in need of population assistance taking into account their present demographic situation, the major population problems and the progress made in dealing with them. We will prepare, as requested by the Governing Council, certain minimum or basic population programmes at the country level, taking into account the diversity of country situations as regards population problems and policies, and approaches to dealing with them. Minimum programmes will be outlined for the various sectors of population activities, keeping in mind that they are interrelated and have to be viewed in their totality. The assistance required to enable countries to implement these programmes in stages should be determined. (27 July 1976)

• Another means [in addition to fund-raising and multi-bilateral arrangements] whereby we are attempting to deal with the gap between UNFPA resources and the requests of governments for assistance from those resources, has been our effort to establish priorities.

Briefly, we conceptualized and identified the areas of population activities falling within the mandate of UNFPA. Further, we outlined criteria for the selection of certain developing countries for high priority consideration, particularly taking into account their population problems, but still maintaining the principle that all countries are entitled to receive support from the Fund. We also outlined proposals for preparing minimum [or basic population] programmes of support to recipient countries, and for the development of a strategy for our support of inter-country activities. The Governing Council approved all these suggestions.

Subsequently, the Economic and Social Council also considered the question of priorities, and adopted a resolution (2025 (LXI), 4 August 1976) endorsing five general principles for UNFPA, which emphasize that the Fund should aim particularly at meeting the needs of countries with the most urgent requirements for population assistance, building up the countries' self-reliance, and supporting activities of special benefit to disadvantaged groups. (3 November 1976)

• The designation of a group of priority countries does not preclude other developing countries from receiving UNFPA assistance, since all countries are entitled in principle to receive such aid; and indeed, according to [our] proposal, at least one-third of all our resources for country activities will be allocated to non-priority countries. Moreover, the Fund intends to stand firmly behind all commitments earlier made. . . . Thus, the application of the high priority countries concept will be a gradual process, and it will be done with some flexibility, bearing in mind that some donors may wish to make ear-marked contributions to the Fund to assist selected countries or specific activities of special interest to them. . . .

We have proceeded to develop the concept of minimum population programmes at the country level, with the aim of identifying the areas and amounts of assistance required. (28 January 1977)

• In order to meet the problem of limited resources, the Fund has established a "core programme" of activities especially relevant to population, and has named a group of countries eligible for priority treatment. Even so, many perfectly eligible projects have had to be turned down for shortage of resources. The Fund has a responsibility to meet not only demands within the "core programme", but to reach out to other agencies in the development field in order to set up programmes bearing less directly on population but most important for the full integration of population within development. We are already trying to do this by funding population components within development projects and seeking bilateral assistance to supplement UNFPA resources, but the only long-term solution is an increase in the resources made available to the Fund by the major donors. (30 March 1977)

• The priorities which our governing body has set for the Fund recognize that our resources will inevitably be limited, and that we must not attempt more than is practicable in fulfilling our mandate. Thus, a core programme of population activities has been delineated to be our prime concern; [and] "high priority" countries have been named on the basis of their need for assistance. In addition, basic population programmes are being developed for each of the major areas of the core programme, by identifying the most essential steps countries would have to take in census-taking, data analysis, delivery of family planning services, communication support services, training, population policy and population education. . . . (2 June 1977)

• The application of the revised indicators* has yielded a group of 40 priority countries. The largest number of priority countries is in the African region, which is expected to receive the highest percentage increase in assistance in the coming years.

At the end of February 1977, UNFPA had comprehensive agreements with, or large-scale projects in, 10 of the 40 priority countries. Of the 10, 5 are in the Asia and Pacific region, 2 in Africa, 2 in the Mediterranean and Middle East, and 1 in Latin America. At present, around 45 per cent of total resources available for country programmes are being committed to supporting projects in priority countries. We have . . . continuing

---

*These revised indicators, approved by the Governing Council at its 23rd Session in January 1977, consist of the criterion of a per capita national income below $400 per annum and two or more of the following demographic criteria: (i) annual rate of population growth of 2.75 per cent or higher; (ii) fertility, in terms of gross reproduction rate, of 2.75 per cent or higher; (iii) infant mortality of 176 or more infant deaths per 1,000 live births; and (iv) agricultural population density on arable land of 2.2 or more persons per hectare. By applying these, the UNFPA has designated a group of 40 priority countries for population assistance (PCPA's) out of a total of 128 developing countries.

commitments to many non-priority countries up to 1980, but we are gradually moving towards the goal of allocating up to two-thirds of resources for programmes in priority countries. Furthermore, we intend to give special attention to countries which may not be on the present priority list but which are borderline cases.

UNFPA has begun its efforts to assist countries in identifying the minimum or basic needs of their population programmes. In that this exercise will help to enable UNFPA and other donors to channel population assistance to areas of greatest need, it will serve as one of the means to maximize the impact of increasingly scarce resources. Moreover, it will constitute an important tool to promote better co-ordination among donors of population assistance. . . .

It may be appropriate . . . to clarify the concept of these programmes. First, it is not the Fund's intention to render, through this exercise, the mere "minimum" of assistance to countries. Rather, the aim . . . is to identify the basic needs in the fields of population, and the assistance required to make the recipient countries self-reliant. Secondly, . . . the determination of what would constitute a basic needs population programme is not to be decided by the UNFPA but by the government concerned, helped by whatever technical assistance and experience the UNFPA and its executing agencies can provide.

Thirdly, the basic needs programme is intended as a set of guidelines for the entire donor community. UNFPA will, of course, provide as much assistance as is possible from its own resources to help implement such programmes. But, realistically, it cannot presume to be capable of fulfilling by any means all requirements for external assistance to meet the basic needs of developing countries in population. The Fund will assist the governments concerned in each case to identify other external sources of possible funding for components of the programme it cannot undertake to support fully. Needless to say, it is entirely up to the government to decide on the sources of assistance it may want to utilize to assist in the implementation of a basic needs programme.

The UNFPA will, of course, continue to allocate its resources in accordance with the general principles which have been endorsed by the Economic and Social Council and the General Assembly. These, inter alia, enjoin the UNFPA to give primary attention to the needs of developing countries which have the most urgent requirements for population assistance. They also require that the UNFPA should support programmes that will help to build up the self-reliance of developing countries; and perhaps the most onerous charge of all, that the UNFPA should assist activities which would bring special benefits to disadvantaged population groups. . . . The large majority of the population in developing countries comes under this latter category. (21 June 1977)

• The main thrust of UNFPA programming has always been, and will continue to be, at the country level. But because its resources are limited, priority is given to urgent and critical requirements for population assistance in the poorer developing countries.

A major share of the Fund's resources available for activities at the country level is being provided to these priority countries, in order to assist them in meeting the targets of their basic population programme objectives. At present, around 45 per cent of total UNFPA resources available for country programmes are being committed to supporting projects in priority countries. We are gradually moving towards our stated goal of allocating up to two-thirds of the Fund's resources for programmes in priority countries. Developing countries which are not designated as priority countries will by no means be excluded from receiving assistance from UNFPA. But the assistance will be more limited, and allocations more selective, for these countries.

A . . . principle of the Fund is to accord high priority to support population activities for the benefit, and with the participation, of such disadvantaged population groups as poverty-stricken elements of rural populations, under-privileged sectors in urban areas, migratory groups, and low-income families in densely populated sub-national areas. The problem of "exploding cities" is of major importance in many developing countries and will become even more so in the future. Women, also, in many countries can be considered among the disadvantaged and vulnerable population groups and UNF-PA fully recognizes that in the population field, perhaps more than in any other area of development, little success can be expected without the active involvement and full participation of women. (5 July 1977)

- In developing basic population needs programmes, UNFPA will give special attention to meeting the needs of disadvantaged population groups. The success of population and development policies depends very much on meeting the demands of these groups, which comprise a very large proportion of the population of many developing countries. (7 November 1977)

- As a further means of placing our resources where they will be most effective in promoting self-reliance and decreasing dependence on aid, we are in the process of formulating programmes of basic needs in population. We first identify a country's policies and programme objectives, then assess the domestic resources available and finally, determine the minimum requirements for establishing self-reliance. [We] should emphasize that these programmes are being prepared in full collaboration with the governments concerned. They are being worked out *with* governments, not *for* governments. (6 December 1977)

- Many of these countries [on the priority list] have only a limited capacity to plan a programme and implement population activities. Often, improvements in basic population data and training of key personnel are needed before a major population programme can be expected to evolve. In other countries, reformulation and review of on-going activities have been necessary in order to make more effective use of increased resources available from the Fund. (21 June 1978)

Country Programming

- We are . . . currently experimenting with methods of interrelating inputs by various United Nations agencies with a national programme, in a coherent overall framework. (16 October 1970)

- It would be well to consider two important points with regard to the foreseeable assistance from the United Nations Fund for Population Activities.

(1) The first is that the Fund would like to assist programmes and projects that in no way duplicate the activities of the agencies and the regional Commissions of the United Nations in this area. Since the resources available to the Fund are limited, we are careful in allocating available amounts only to activities that lead to co-ordinated effort rather than duplication.

(2) In view of the country programme orientation of the UNFPA and our bias towards promoting action-oriented projects, the Fund is more inclined to assist programmes and projects that will improve the delivery of services in the countries requesting assistance.

Therefore, if a project for assistance presented to the Fund does not duplicate programmes being undertaken by the United Nations agencies and its regional Commissions, and intends to promote better and efficient delivery of services, the Fund would be willing to consider such a project for funding. . . . (22 October 1970)

• In deciding on the kinds of assistance which the Fund should finance in one or another case, we are conscious that we must distinguish between various types of countries:

(1) Countries which have formulated a national population policy and adopted a government-sponsored programme of family planning;

(2) Countries without a population policy as yet, but which may be expected to evolve one during the decade; and

(3) Countries which may not adopt a national population policy but which will need to study the implications of population trends and take demographic factors into account in development planning.

Also relevant would be the question of whether the country is, in comparison with the other developing countries, reasonably affluent or not, or whether or not it suffers from an acute foreign exchange problem. (4 November 1970)

• [We] would like to mention the role which the Fund could and should play in country programming exercises. As population is one of the most important aspects of social and economic development, the country programming exercise should take account of the needs and possible assistance in the area of population planning. This can be done either through a national population programme or by adding population components to other UNDP-financed development assistance projects. The finances will not be taken from the country target, instead they are additional to the funds committed by UNDP. There are, moreover, also cases where programmes supported with World Food Programme resources, especially programmes in community development and maternal and child health, could be related to population programmes.

It is anticipated that the expanded activities will, in many cases, be executed through one or several of the organizations in the United Nations system, as appropriate, but the UNFPA may also arrange for execution through appropriate non-governmental organizations, or provide assistance directly to local institutions in developing countries, or take a direct initiative. . . . (18 February 1971)

- In regard to country programming . . . the Fund and the United Nations recently reach-ed an agreement on . . . [field] services, and the Fund has decided to appoint Senior Advisers, to be attached to the [UNDP] Resident Representatives' Staff, to perform the dual function of advising and assisting the Resident Representatives on population matters, and also of supervising the implementation of fund-financed activities.

This is of particular importance since there is an increasing tendency for governments to request assistance in carrying out large-scale multi-disciplinary projects encompass-ing many different aspects of population activities on a countrywide basis. As these major projects will inevitably involve the competencies and co-operation of several organizations in the United Nations system at one and the same time, the Senior Ad-visers will serve as project co-ordinators. (3 November 1971)

- We . . . anticipate a growth in the number and the importance of . . . [country] agreements will result from our participation in the overall country programming exer-cises being scheduled by the UNDP.

Since the inception of the Fund, it has been one of its guiding principles that assistance provided by UNFPA will be closely co-ordinated with other types of assistance and with overall development planning. With the introduction of country programming by UNDP, it has become even more important to ensure that population assistance is fully integrated in overall development assistance. The Fund is actively exploring ways of en-suring its full participation in country programming.

Resources supplied by the Fund are intended to supplement, and not supplant, the sup-port being given to population activities from the regular budgets and other funding sources within the United Nations system. In accordance with this principle, UNFPA assistance will therefore continue to be additional to the indicative planning figures which provide the order of magnitude within which financial assistance from UNDP proper can be programmed in advance.

In general, one can say that the concept of country programming is fully applicable to the programming of UNFPA assistance, although the institutional means for effecting it may be a little different. (21 March 1972)

- The main expenses anticipated by the Fund are those connected with large-scale com-prehensive country programmes.

Even before the adoption of the country programming approach which placed the Resident Representatives at the focal point for co-ordination at the country level of all United Nations inputs, the Resident Representative had a vital role to play in the im-plementation of Fund-supported population activities. The adoption of the country programming approach for UNDP assistance offers new opportunities for even closer collaboration in programming. . . .

An overall programming effort of this order of magnitude will require considerable ef-fort on the part of both the Resident Representative and the UNFPA. Accordingly, the Fund is in the process of making a number of arrangements to strengthen programmes at the country level. Among these are: (a) The appointment of UNFPA Senior Advisers to Resident Representatives, to assist Resident Representatives in their larger role of programming funds for projects in the population sector; (b) A broad range of promotional activities aimed at heightening the awareness among high-level government officials of the effect of population trends on economic and social development efforts; and short-term advisory services to national planning offices or other bodies with a responsibility for the formulation of national population policies, to help in identifying areas where UNFPA assistance could be made available; (c) The strengthening of agency regional offices by granting UNFPA support for the establishment of posts for population specialists, and the strengthening of population units at the regional Economic Commissions and the Specialized Agencies, thereby strengthening the planning assistance available to governments in the population sector; and (d) The strengthening of the Programme Division at UNFPA Headquarters with a small number of subject specialists and experts on a consultancy basis who will have easy access to up-to-date information on relevant developments in the population field.

It is hoped that, with these measures, a foundation will have been laid for the effective decentralization of the programming of UNFPA assistance to the country level. As the experience with the first round of UNDP country programming exercises has shown, there may be wide variations in the way such an exercise is conducted. The UNFPA, therefore, does not specify any hard and fast rules on how to carry out the programming of UNFPA assistance at the country level, but wants to encourage suggestions from the UNDP and the Resident Representatives on how this decentralization could be effected. (18 May 1972)

• In October 1970 the Fund entered into an agreement with the Government of Pakistan for a comprehensive programme of assistance to the national family planning programme. This initiative set the pattern for what has become a key feature of the Fund's operations—the development of major country projects through which a comprehensive range of inputs can be provided to national action programmes over a period of years and involving several international agencies. Since then, the Fund has concluded similar agreements with [a number of other governments]. . . . Projects under these agreements have covered all aspects of family planning programmes, including planning and management, evaluation and research, as well as support communication and education. We feel that these projects are perhaps the most important contribution which the Fund has made to the development of multilateral assistance in the population field. (8 March 1973)

• It is expected that ultimately responsibility for the execution of projects will lie more directly with the recipient governments, using the services of United Nations or other organizations for any essential technical assistance. Indeed, the movement away from small projects to more comprehensive country programmes—a trend that is gradually gaining momentum—foreshadows this development. (4 May 1973)

• The funding and implementation of population projects exhibit the same challenges and are subject to the same managerial problems as projects directed towards other defined social and economic goals. (6 May 1973)

- [In discussing five-year population assistance agreements] we are aware that this is a long period and that the sums of money in several cases are large. At the same time, we believe that it would be helpful for the recipients to have a five-year perspective on the activities being programmed. Thus, the [Governing] Council may wish to authorize the Fund to enter into agreements described, with the five-year totals specified as planning figures, and simultaneously to authorize UNFPA to allocate appropriate funds for the first two years of the agreements. This would mean that after two years the Fund would report back to the Council on the status of the programmes. (18 June 1974)

- "Country agreements" are meant to help states in their nationwide population efforts, not just in specific projects. (21 May 1975)

- Our experience has led us to emphasize the introduction of family planning, mother and child care service, training, communication and other services as a complete package, part of an overall plan which will probably include census and demographic services. (26 September 1975)

- Developing countries with quite small national inputs only a few years ago are now operating greatly expanded programmes for which most of the funding is internal. (2 June 1977)

- The main thrust of UNFPA programming has always been, and will continue to be, at the country level. But because its resources are limited, priority is given to urgent and critical requirements for population assistance in the poorer developing countries.

In the first three years of UNFPA's operations, nearly fifty per cent of available resources was allocated for intercountry activities, mostly executed by various organizations within the United Nations system. The objective was to build up the organizational capacity of interregional and regional institutions so that they could meet the population needs of the countries within the region. By 1975, intercountry activities had declined and direct country requests for assistance had increased. Today, 69 per cent of UNFPA's available resources are being allocated directly to country programmes. (5 July 1977)

- Another issue with which UNFPA and its Governing Council are grappling is the distribution of UNFPA's resources between country programmes and intercountry activities—that is, regional, interregional and global activities. The proportion of our programme resources allocated to intercountry activities has declined steadily. (7 November 1977)

- As a further measure to increase our effectiveness, we are refining our internal planning process so that we can identify the demand for country programme funds with more certainty. We are establishing a pipeline of country project requests which will enable us to identify the demand for country programme funds more specifically. (6 December 1977)

- In the appraisal of programmes, and in view of the limited resources at the Fund's disposal, we have to assess the country's needs most carefully. Only in this way can the long-term goal of complete self-reliance be attained. Therefore, we have developed a method of establishing needs by means of a thorough study, not only of a country's population situation, but of the economic and social context in which population activities will be carried out.

These studies will tell us more about the special needs of the different countries. Because we recognize that each country is an individual case, we are not intending to impose a pattern on the studies. In the more advanced countries, the information on needs assessment will come mainly from the government itself, with external advice and analysis as needed. In others with less sophisticated policy and planning mechanisms, much of the work will be done by outside consultants, in association with the government.

The studies will have certain features in common. All of them will discuss the current economic and social situation, and prospects for the future. All will look at the general development plans and activities of the government, and the specific development problems of each country. They will then go on to analyze the population situation, and planning and programming in this area. Particular attention will be paid to the way in which population programmes and activities are linked with other areas of development. Finally, the studies will identify gaps in the structure of population policy and programming and will make recommendations for filling them. Following the study, missions will visit the country to prepare specific requests for assistance. (26 March 1978)

Research

• There is, in most countries, and even in different regions of large countries, a need for applied research into such questions as motivation towards family planning and attitudes towards use of various methods of contraception. . . . Provided financial assistance were available, governments could identify institutions which could then carry out such research with little outside expert assistance. In principle, the Fund may be used for such research, with due provision for the results to be made available, through the agencies of the United Nations system, to other countries, and for visits to the projects by representatives of the United Nations agencies.

Among the types of research which may be usefully conducted in one or another developing country might be research into the economic and social consequences of demographic trends, the social and economic factors leading to current fertility trends, and the appropriateness and effectiveness in the area of one or another type of family planning programme or contraceptive. (10 November 1969)

• The United Nations will attempt to strengthen applied and operational research in:

(1) Demographic studies, as in the inter-relationships between population trends and economic and social factors;

(2) Human reproduction and epidemiological studies;

(3) Operational research, such as the study of the organization and administration of family planning programmes under different governmental systems; and

(4) Environmental and social policy, such as the study of the ecological consequences of the application of science and technology. (4 November 1970)

- Social science research should be promoted, particularly by providing grants to existing
institutions in developing countries. Such activities should be geared towards
strengthening the operational activities of ongoing programmes, including their planning, organization and evaluation. Furthermore, data on attitudes towards family size
should be collected, as well as data on motivations for changing family norms and
means of communicating information on family planning. (18 February 1971)

- We should seek to deepen our understanding of the factors influencing decisions about
family size—as these are perceived by the population concerned. This involves in-
depth, village-level research of the kind undertaken by anthropologists. . . . We should
encourage case studies in different settings to be undertaken.

Research leading to the elaboration of systematic models of the development process
should be intensified. One of the purposes of such research would be to explore what
rate of population growth could be absorbed given alternative assumptions about
capital-output ratios, patterns of resource allocation, access to foreign markets,
availability of external assistance, changes in social structure, and so on. (1 November
1972)

- The interrelationship between population and national development is often talked
about. But there are many relationships that are not clear. For example, what is the impact of population density on national development?

In fact, apparently very little is known about the whole subject of the impact of
population density. There are, of course, obvious ways of solving density problems in
the physical sense, through immigration, emigration and other forms of re-distribution
of population. But is it certain that the dispersion of concentrations of people will in
the long run advance the development process and alleviate anything more than temporary pressures on space and social services?

Obviously, more and more of these areas where present knowledge is inadequate are
going to emerge. Equally obviously, the Fund must be prepared to take urgent action
to acquire that knowledge, and to support the research and evaluation programmes
which can produce it. (14 February 1973-B)

- [In the early days of the Fund's operations] we learned that there were total areas like,
for example, the impact of population density on national advancement—on which
there were many theories and few answers. And the best we can do is to try and encourage more research and more pilot projects to find out what really is going on. Attention is being given [by the Fund] to the promotion of research in human reproduction, especially to research which may lead to new methods suitable for use in developing countries. (15 February 1973)

- The Fund attaches [the] utmost importance . . . [to] demographic research. . . . Studies
. . . on fertility and fertility planning, urbanization and population distribution,
economic aspects of population, educational aspects of population, and on the

development of analysis where basic population data are defective, are all invaluable contributions towards filling the gaps in our present knowledge. (27 August 1973)

• Among all the regions of the world, Asia is the most sophisticated in its experience and policymaking in regard to family planning. . . .

It is essential, however, that the background and experience being gained in these countries should not be confined within national frontiers or regional boundaries. (21 January 1974)

• Besides the inevitable differences of approach between countries in different situations, there are many gaps in our understanding of the interrelations between population and development. It is in this respect that the policymaker and the programme manager look to the scientist for guidance.

Here . . . is a great challenge to us. Specialists of different disciplines have tended to confine their research activities specifically to their own subjects. As a result, the much needed synthesis and interchange of ideas have not taken place. To be able to fill the enormous gaps in our knowledge about population and development, we have to reach out beyond the confines of our respective disciplines, and carry out common, interdisciplinary research. (8 August 1977)

[In August 1977, in a statement to the Directors of Demographic Research Centres, in Mexico City, the Fund's Deputy Executive Director, Halvor Gille, further outlined the Fund's policy regarding research. He stated:

"The increasing demand from developing countries for UNFPA assistance to operational activities has tended to limit the resources available for research. However, at the same time, it is recognized by the Fund that the overall scarcity of resources makes it more important than ever, in the interest of cost effectiveness, to explore, through research, various alternatives and approaches in order to develop appropriate solutions to meeting the needs of the countries. The resolution adopted by the World Population Conference, suggesting that UNFPA devote a certain percentage of its resources to research, has not been implemented, particularly in view of the fact that it is difficult to determine and maintain borderlines between research and other activities. Instead, the role of the Fund in supporting research activities is now being determined systematically at the intercountry as well as country levels.

"A major part of the global, interregional and regional activities supported by the Fund is for demographic research. A thorough review of past activities has been completed and a strategy for future activities is under preparation. In preparing this strategy, it is intended to give special attention to the needs of developing countries and the desirability of making them self-reliant in research and other fields, to promote population research of special importance for planners and policy makers and to develop common methodologies to deal with population issues of common concern to several countries. In this connection, our Governing Council has requested us to bear in mind global research programmes of an innovative nature.

"At the country level basic needs population programmes are being prepared in collaboration with the governments concerned with the objective of promoting the countries' self-reliance in the formulation and implementation of population policies. High priority will, in this connection, be given to supporting institution-building at the national level, particularly in the fields of population data collection and demographic research.''']

• While action cannot await the findings of research, there is a great need to learn more about the dynamics of population change so that countries are in a better position to plan programmes and policies accordingly. (3 April 1978)

Training

• While the Fund is likely to be used to finance training abroad, and particularly at [United Nations] Regional [Demographic Training and Research] Centres, it may also be used, in appropriate circumstances, to finance training at the national level. (10 November 1969)

• A basic prerequisite for the effective planning and execution of large-scale population programmes is a realistic and comprehensive review of manpower requirements and the assessment of needs for training of various types of personnel. Several of the organizations in the United Nations system can make essential contributions to such manpower planning and development by assisting in estimating the needs at country and international levels. The major efforts in training of national personnel for population programmes will naturally rest with the governments and organizations in the developing countries themselves. However, the international organizations can assist training institutions by providing advice, and developing pertinent curricula, and by exchanging the international experience gained. (4 November 1970)

• The training of nationals . . . is a primary concern of the Fund. Workshops and regional seminars for exchange of information among senior census personnel, and training centres for middle-level personnel, are being organized; fellowships for training nationals abroad are also provided. Other projects receiving support include staff strengthening [at regional demographic training centres]. . . .

The Fund is also helping to improve training and research facilities in demographic fields at universities and similar institutions. . . . Fellowships for postgraduate work in demography abroad are being provided in connexion with these activities. (18 May 1972)

• The main activity in the next four-year period will be to improve the collection and analysis of population data. The establishment of registration systems and the training of personnel will be an important extension of this work. (14 February 1973)

• An increase in the supply of trained manpower has been especially important for the success of the comprehensive country projects which the Fund is assisting. As a result, over a third of UNFPA's allocations has been for training, which includes fellowships, special courses and seminars for leadership groups, support to training institutions, the preparation of teaching materials, and research on training. (4 May 1973)

- In addition to the acceptance of the need and the responsibility to solve the population problem in each country, there must also exist the skills and the means to carry them out. This is the reason why the UNFPA, in its three years of operation, has devoted more than a third of its resources to training.

  The Fund will continue to assist countries, and deliberately apply a portion of the assistance to spurring the countries to undertake these programmes themselves, by continuing to train as much of each country's human resources as possible, and assisting in the building of their own institutions. (6 May 1973)

- Qualified people are hard to find. Even when they have the necessary training, language barriers often hamper their performance. Means must be devised of providing training and research facilities at different levels in all countries and of introducing regular procedures for constant exchanges of experience, technology and expertise. (27 August 1973)

- Since the fifties, training in the field of population has been engaging the attention of the United Nations, international agencies, academic institutions and some governments. Several factors have been responsible for attracting attention to training needs: the problems caused by the accelerated growth of population, the momentum generated by independence of a large number of countries of the developing world and their need for studies on economic and social prospects and trends, and the decision made by most countries to participate in the 1960 world-wide population census programme advocated, promoted and supported by the United Nations. Shortage of trained persons has always been a handicap in countries which are making a determined effort towards economic and social development. In spite of the efforts made by the United Nations and other agencies, however, progress has been slow.

In recent years, many of the developing countries have introduced population policies intended to reduce rapid population growth in as short a period as possible. These and related developments, such as the need for improved population statistics in a planned economy and rapidly growing interest of many countries in family planning programmes, have greatly increased the demand for trained personnel. Moreover, the activities of governments in the field of population and family planning are now assisted by increased activities of international agencies such as the United Nations, UNFPA, WHO, ILO, UNESCO and UNICEF, all of whom are now also looking for trained persons in the field of population. In addition, private organizations such as the Population Council, IPPF, and other private foundations concerned with population issues are now stimulating the demand for trained persons.

Population problems and programmes now require persons with multi-disciplinary skills who can formulate, implement and evaluate the programmes relating to population control, public health, education, city planning, employment and unemployment, and so on. Faced with this changing and growing demand, more recently several national and international conferences have been generated to discuss the need and type of training prgrammes. One point of general agreement is that in view of the increasing demand for population studies in a planned economy and the complexities involved in the population problems, there is an urgent need, requiring top priority, for interdisciplinary training programmes. In this respect, there is considerable scope for co-operation among the international and private agencies who have committed themselves in the field of population. (17 October 1973)

• So far, one of the difficulties in the developing countries has been to provide the trained and committed manpower to operate the kind of efficient administration which is needed. A great number of educational and training opportunities have been made available by donor countries, but these have suffered from the inevitable drawback that they related more to conditions in the donor country than in the trainee's homeland. When the need is for a system sensitive to conditions which may be far different from those found in Western countries, this is not always adequate. (18 October 1973)

• [In a particular country] there may be a shortage of trained workers, nurses, health visitors, midwives or teachers, and the Fund will help to improve training services. (19 April 1974)

• Our experience has shown that countries deliver programmes better if . . . there are adequate cadres of trained personnel to execute them. The success of projects depends, to a large extent, on the leadership and the quality of training that workers have before undertaking these projects. But there is still a large gap in our knowledge of specific country training requirements and the training programmes that are necessary to meet the goals set in each country. A better understanding and insight into this problem is needed. The Fund regards this as one of the priorities over the coming years. (20 August 1974)

• Translating political will into solid results requires a broad range of skills at all levels, but perhaps the crucial element is the managerial skill which allows the process of decision-making to proceed smoothly and to be given effect with the least delay.

This sort of skill often exists already in traditional social structures, which are often easier for the sensitive administrator to use than attempt to bypass or supplant. But where new departures are being taken, these structures may not be appropriate or exist at all. . . . A new structure may be necessary. Formation of such structures, and the training of people to manage them, must be done with the utmost care, in order to fit them into already existing patterns, yet preserve their effectiveness. (26 September 1975)

• We . . . want to stress the importance of training local personnel, to enable them to make the need for foreign advisory services superfluous. (27 July 1976)

• The success of all these programmes [data collection, policy formulation, family planning, and communication and education] requires well-trained personnel at the national and sub-national level. And the UNFPA has invested considerable sums in assisting the developing world to become self-reliant in their population activities. At regional and then at national levels, training programmes for nurse/midwives, educational planners, development specialists—the list could be extended beyond the time available to us today—have been undertaken, pointing to the day some time in the future when the developing nations will need only financial support to meet their population needs and to achieve their demographic transition. (3 April 1978)

UNFPA Co-ordinators, Their Role in the Field

• The authorized representatives of the UNFPA in the field are the UNDP Resident Representatives. (16 October 1970)

• In regard to country programming, the Fund has no field services of its own as yet. [We are], therefore, glad to report that the Fund and the United Nations recently reached an agreement on such services, and the Fund has decided to appoint Senior Advisers, to be attached to the Resident Representatives' Staff, to perform the dual function of advising and assisting the Resident Representatives on population matters and also of supervising the implementation of Fund-financed activities.

As these major projects [country programmes] will inevitably involve the competencies and co-operation of several organizations in the United Nations system at one and the same time, the Senior Advisers will serve as project co-ordinators. (3 November 1971)

• We are . . . taking steps to strengthen UNFPA's representation in the field. . . . Senior Advisors to Resident Representatives are being posted in countries where we have million dollar programmes or anticipate having projects of this magnitude. . . . It is our hope that further reorganization of field staff of the United Nations and the Fund will lead to the Fund's being represented in other countries by regional UNFPA Co-ordinators. (21 March 1972)

• At the end of last year, in consultation with the Administrator of the UNDP, a decision was taken to expand the Fund's field staff. The Resident Representatives in countries where the Fund is supporting or anticipating large-scale multidisciplinary programmes have been advised of the probable appointment, with their concurrence, of UNFPA Senior Advisers.

Agreement has also been reached by the Fund and the United Nations Population Division that Population Programme Officers will be phased out as soon as a UNFPA Senior Advisor is appointed to a country. The Senior Advisor will have the dual function of advising and assisting the Resident Representative on population matters, and supervising the implementation and execution of the large multidisciplinary projects.

The Administrator of the UNDP has also been requested to authorize the establishment of . . . additional posts for UNFPA regional Co-ordinators, to be assigned to certain field offices to look after countries with smaller population programmes.

Even before the adoption of the country programming approach which placed the Resident Representatives at the focal point for co-ordination at the country level of all United Nations inputs, the Resident Representative had a vital role to play in the implementation of Fund-supported population activities. The adoption of the country programming approach for UNDP assistance offers new opportunities for even closer collaboration in programming. . . .

I.P.A.—L

An overall programming effort of this order of magnitude will require considerable effort on the part of both the Resident Representative and the UNFPA. Accordingly, the Fund is in the process of making a number of arrangements to strengthen programmes at the country level. Among these are . . . the appointment of UNFPA Senior Advisors to Resident Representatives, to assist Resident Representatives in their larger role of programming funds for projects in the population sector. . . .

It is hoped that with these measures a foundation will have been laid for the effective decentralization of the programming of UNFPA assistance to the country level. As the experience with the first round of UNDP country programming exercises has shown, there may be wide variations in the way such an exercise is conducted. The UNFPA, therefore, does not specify any hard and fast rules on how to carry out the programming of UNFPA assistance at the country level, but wants to encourage suggestions from the UNDP and the Resident Representatives on how this decentralization could be effected.

In addition to programming exercises to be initiated in connection with the development of UNFPA government agreements, the Fund hopes to involve Resident Representatives in a broad range of other measures which will serve the needs for forward planning of the UNFPA work programme in the light of the priorities for assistance and the resources expected to be available to the UNFPA.

At a later stage, the UNFPA may propose that Resident Representatives might hold, from time to time, informal meetings with government representatives, country and field representatives of Specialized Agencies, and of donor organizations from outside the United Nations system, for the purpose of joint forward planning of population programmes. It is expected that the . . . Fund headquarters would assume the responsibility of periodically reviewing the advance information that might be generated in such planning meetings, in the light of UNFPA policies and priorities.

The Fund would like to encourage the Resident Representatives to give due attention to the population components of UNDP country programmes. The revised sector classification, developed by UNDP on the basis of a proprosal by the Consultative Committee on Administrative Questions, gives due recognition to population as one of the sectors to which development efforts are to be addressed. In the future, most of the expansion of assistance to country population programmes will be financed out of UNFPA resources.

The Fund requests the assistance of the Resident Representatives to develop further and deepen awareness among officials of the recipient countries of the importance and relevance of population dynamics in their development efforts. (18 May 1972)

• We believe UNDP Resident Representatives, with the assistance of the UNFPA Coordinators, through their contacts with government, will play a vital role in assuring that the programming developed with UNFPA resources does in fact reflect the real needs and wishes of the recipient countries. (14 June 1973)

• We have . . . been extending our scope in the last year or so, by putting a Fund Coordinator in each of the areas where we are most active. He or she supports the local

United Nations Development Programme Resident Representative and assures the all-important personal contact between governments and ourselves. (26 September 1973)

- The United Nations agencies are still our main source of technical expertise. At the same time, we are building up a capable, knowledgeable field staff to whom considerable autonomy will be allowed. Headquarters will thus become the support unit of the organization, with its main role as general policy guidance and co-ordination. We have always put a high value on speed, aiming for the minimum delay between receipt of programme requests and implementation of the project. This decentralization should further accelerate our programming. (18 October 1973)

- By placing the Co-ordinators on the staff of the Resident Representatives, the effort to incorporate population programmes into general economic and social development plans and programmes should be greatly facilitated. (12 November 1973)

- We continue to believe . . . that the present arrangement [of funding Co-ordinators from project funds] results in lower programme development costs and allows greater flexibility of action. It offers . . . definite advantages during at least the early period of our reinforcement of the Resident Representatives' offices. There are several reasons for this:

  (1) As project personnel, the Co-ordinators do not create a permanently enlarged administrative staff. Their posts as advisers are established specifically for the countries in which they serve and may be terminated upon conclusion of the programme within the country. Under the administrative budget, on the other hand, UNFPA would assume certain responsibilities for continuation of employment beyond the requirements in a particular country. Recruitment procedures also fall under simpler and more flexible rules.

  (2) The Co-ordinators are furnishing essentially project development and co-ordination services, not administrative services. The costs of their services are, therefore, more properly a charge against programme development rather than administration.

  (3) UNFPA is not establishing a network of field offices. It is, rather, providing senior assistance for population programming and co-ordination of implementation to the Resident Representative at his request. When there is no longer a need for a population advisor, the post will be abolished. (13 June 1974)

- The Resident Representatives, assisted by now in most cases by UNFPA Co-ordinators, are markedly increasing their knowledge of our programme and performing increasingly important services on our behalf. We hope, moreover, since they are the field representatives of the UNDP and the UNFPA, as well as some other United Nations assistance programmes, they can play an increasingly valuable role in harmonizing UNFPA projects and programmes with those of UNDP and other United Nations agencies. (18 June 1974)

- All of these [directly-funded] projects are administered through the offices of the UNDP Resident Representatives. The UNFPA field Co-ordinators assist the Resident Representatives in monitoring and evaluating projects of this type. Where required,

UNFPA also provides funds for local programme and administrative field staff in the Resident Representatives' office, to furnish the necessary programme support services. (19 June 1975)

Appendix A

List of Statements from which Quotations Are Taken

*10 November 1969
"The Formative Years: The Beginnings of the United Nations Fund for Population Activities". Statement to the 15th Session of the United Nations Population Commission, Geneva, Switzerland.

18 November 1969
Statement to the Development Centre of the Organisation for Economic Co-operation and Development (OECD), Paris, France.

*16 and *22 October 1970
"Designing Population Assistance Programmes". Statements to the Conference of the Western Pacific Region of the International Planned Parenthood Federation (IPPF), Tokyo, Japan, and the Southeast Asian Ministerial Conference on Family and Population Planning, Kuala Lumpur, Malaysia, printed together under the above title.

4 November 1970
Lecture at "World Week", Windsor, Canada.

*18 February 1971
"Establishing Criteria for United Nations Population Activities". Statement to the Global Meeting of Resident Representatives of the United Nations Development Programme (UNDP), New Delhi, India.

26 August 1971
Statement at a Dinner for German Parliamentarians, Königshof Hotel, Bonn, Federal Republic of Germany.

*3 November 1971
"The Task Ahead". Statement to the 16th Session of the United Nations Population Commission, Geneva, Switzerland.

22 November 1971
Expert Group Meeting on the Production and Distribution of Contraceptives in Developing Countries, New York.

9 December 1971
Statement to the African Population Conference, Accra, Ghana.

21 March 1972
Statement to the 4th Session of the UNFPA Advisory Board, New York.

*Printed statement. Copies available.

*18 May 1972

"Strengthening the UNFPA". Statement to the Regional Meeting of UNDP Resident Representatives for Africa, Addis Ababa, Ethiopia.

10 August 1972

"World Population Year, 1974". Statement to the 1st Special Session of the United Nations Population Commission, New York.

25 October 1972

Statement to the Multimedia Meeting on World Population Year and World Development Information Day, New York.

*1 November 1972

"Asia: An Area Assessment". Statement to the Second Asian Population Conference, Tokyo, Japan.

*29 January 1973

"Scope and Direction: First Report to the Governing Council". Statement to the 15th Session of the UNDP Governing Council, United Nations, New York.

*5 February 1973

"Increasing the Effectiveness of Population Programmes". Statement to the One Asia Assembly, New Delhi, India.

*14 February 1973

"Population Consensus—The Need for a Common Idiom". Statement to the Royal Institute of International Affairs, Chatham House, London, England.

14 February 1973-B

Statement to the Parliamentary Group Meeting, London, England.

15 February 1973

Statement at the Foreign Press Association Luncheon, London, England.

8 March 1973

Statement to the Annual Meeting of UNDP Resident Representatives of the Asian Region, Bangkok, Thailand.

23 March 1973

Statement to the 2nd Special Session of the United Nations Population Commission, United Nations, New York.

30 April 1973

Statement to the 8th Session of the UNFPA Inter-Agency Consultative Committee (IACC), New York.

4 May 1973

Statement to the Economic Committee of the 54th Session of the United Nations Economic and Social Council (ECOSOC), United Nations, New York.

6 May 1973

"International Population Assistance - A Spur to National Effort". Statement at the Institute of Man and Science, Rensselaerville, New York, U.S.A.

14 June 1973

Excerpts from a statement to the 16th Session of the UNDP Governing Council, Geneva, Switzerland.

28 June 1973

Statement to Non-Governmental Organizations (NGO) Consultation, London, England.

7 July 1973

"The Need for Commitment". Statement to the Latin American Development Journalists Association (ALACODE), Santa Marta, Colombia.

*25 August 1973

"Population Assistance and National Development: The Search for Commitment". Statement to the Conference of the Australian Council for Overseas Aid, Canberra, Australia.

27 August 1973

Statement to the 1973 General Conference of the International Union for the Scientific Study of Population (IUSSP), Liège, Belgium.

7 September 1973

Statement to the Seminar of Communicators, San José, Costa Rica.

14 September 1973

Statement to the World Assembly of Youth (WAY) Seminar on Population and Development, St. Augustine, Trinidad.

25 September 1973

Statement to the Seminar sponsored by the Population Reference Bureau, Boca Raton, Florida, U.S.A.

26 September 1973

Statement to the Overseas Development Council, Washington, D.C ., U.S.A.

17 October 1973

Statement to the Committee on Inter-Disciplinary Training in Population, New York.

18 October 1973

Statement to the Development Assistance Committee of the High Level Meeting of the Organisation for Economic Co-operation and Development (OECD), Paris, France.

*22 October 1973

"Government Programmes and Voluntary Action: Partnership in Planned Parenthood". Statement to the "IPPF 21" (21st Anniversary) Conference, London, England.

29 October 1973

Statement to the 17th Session of the United Nations Population Commission, Geneva, Switzerland.

6 November 1973

Statement to a meeting of members of the recently disbanded UNFPA Programme Consultative Committee (PCC), New York.

12 November 1973

Statement to the Second Committee of the 28th United Nations General Assembly, United Nations, New York.

13 November 1973

Statement to the Operations Research Society of America, San Diego, California, U.S.A.

*30 November 1973

"Catholics and World Population Year - A Question of Morality". Statement to the Centre of Concern Seminar, New York.

14 January 1974

Statement to the 17th Session of the Budgetary and Finance Committee of the UNDP Governing Council, United Nations, New York.

21 January 1974

Statement to the Meeting of Executive Secretaries of the United Nations regional Economic Commissions, United Nations, New York.

30 January 1974

Statement to the 17th Session of the UNDP Governing Council, United Nations, New York.

*25 February 1974

"Women and World Population Year: Decision-making for Development". Statement to the Women's Forum on Population and Development, New York.

27 February 1974

Statement to the 10th Session of the UNFPA Inter-Agency Consultative Committee (IACC), New York.

4 March 1974

Statement to the 3rd Special Session of the United Nations Population Commission, United Nations, New York.

6 March 1974

Statement at the "1974 Dialogue", Bogotá, Colombia.

2 April 1974

Statement to the Sunday Times Exploding Cities Conference, Oxford, England.

19 April 1974

"Population, Development and the United Nations". Statement to the United Nations Orientation Meeting, New York.

9 May 1974

Statement to the United Nations Economic Commission for Asia and the Far East (ECAFE) Regional Consultation Preparatory to the World Population Conference, Bangkok, Thailand.

*16 May 1974

"The 'Third View' - Population in the African Context". Statement to the Regional Consultation on the World Population Plan of Action, Addis Ababa, Ethiopia.

18 May 1974

Statement at the Arab Regional Centre for Development Journalism, Cairo, Egypt.

*20 May 1974

"Population and the Media: an Added Dimension". Statement at the Editors' Round Table, Bangkok, Thailand.

21 May 1974

Statement to the Regional Consultation on the World Population Plan of Action, Damascus, Syria.

3 June 1974

Statement to the Inaugural Meeting of the United Nations Economic Commission for Western Asia (ECWA), Beirut, Lebanon.

13 June 1974

Statement to the Budgetary and Finance Committee of the 18th Session of the UNDP Governing Council, Manila, Philippines.

18 June 1974

Statement to a Plenary Meeting of the 18th Session of the UNDP Governing Council, Manila, Philippines.

21 June 1974

Statement to the Symposium on Law and Population, Tunis, Tunisia.

2 July 1974

Statement to the Japan Population Conference, Tokyo, Japan.

9 July 1974

Statement to the 56th Session of the United Nations Economic and Social Council (ECOSOC), Geneva, Switzerland.

18 August 1974

Statement at the Population Tribune, World Population Conference, Bucharest, Romania.

*20 August 1974

"Population Assistance and the UNFPA - Responding to the Countries' own Assessments of their Needs". Statement at the World Population Conference, Bucharest, Romania.

23 August 1974

"The Green Revolution in the Philippines". Statement at the Population Forum, World Population Conference, Bucharest, Romania.

7 October 1974

Statement to the Second Committee of the 29th United Nations General Assembly, New York.

15 October 1974

"Population, Development and the Future". Statement at Georgetown University, Washington, D.C., U.S.A.

*11 November 1974

"Food: The Population Factor". Statement to the World Food Conference, Rome, Italy.

*27 January 1975

"A Time for Consolidation". Statement to the 19th Session of the UNDP Governing Council, United Nations, New York.

13 February 1975

Statement at a Press Conference at United Nations Headquarters, New York.

24 March 1975

Statement at the Economic Commission for Western Asia (ECWA) Post-World Population Conference Regional Consultation, Doha, Qatar.

17 April 1975

Statement on Agenda Item 11, "Population Questions", to the Economic Committee of the 58th Session of the United Nations Economic and Social Council (ECOSOC), United Nations, New York.

*21 May 1975

"Population and Development in the Arab World". Statement at the League of Arab States Ministerial Conference on Population Activities, Cairo, Egypt.

10 June 1975

Statement to the International Council of Voluntary Agencies (ICVA) Working Group, Geneva, Switzerland.

*19 June 1975

"Progress and Performance: The Need for Sustained Effort". Statement to the 20th Session of the UNDP Governing Council, Geneva, Switzerland.

*23 June 1975

"Women and Population - The Freedom to Choose". Statement to the International Women's Year Conference, Mexico City, Mexico.

14 July 1975
Statement to the 59th Session of United Nations Economic and Social Council (ECOSOC), Geneva, Switzerland.

25 September 1975
Congratulatory Address to the Second Japan Population Conference, Tokyo, Japan.

*26 September 1975
"Idealism as Practical Politics: The Future for Rural Development". Statement at the Second Japan Population Conference, Tokyo, Japan.

*23 October 1975
"Development is People". Statement at World Development Information Day, United Nations, New York.

*24 October 1975
"Assessments: The Operational Scene". Statement to the Second Committee of the 30th United Nations General Assembly, United Nations, New York.

*21 November 1975
"Population Assistance Since Bucharest - Developing a Consensus on Priorities for Population Resources". Statement at the International Population Conference, Washington, D.C., U.S.A.

*19 January 1976
"New Directions: the UNFPA in 1976". Statement at the 21st Session of the UNDP Governing Council, United Nations, New York.

*20 February 1976
"Responsiveness and Innovation: The Role of the UNFPA in a Restructured United Nations Economic and Social Programme". Statement to the Ad Hoc Committee on the Restructuring of the Economic and Social Sectors of the United Nations System, United Nations, New York.

*2 June 1976
"Interurban Man: The Dynamics of Population in Urban and Rural Life". Statement at the United Nations Conference on Human Settlements, Vancouver, Canada.

*14 June 1976
"Population and Employment". Statement at the Tripartite World Conference on Employment, Income Distribution, Social Progress and the International Division of Labour, Geneva, Switzerland.

*28 June 1976
"The UNFPA in Mid-1976". Statement to the 22nd Session of the UNDP Governing Council, Geneva, Switzerland.

*27 July 1976

"Priorities and Trends". Statement to the 61st Session of ECOSOC, Geneva, Switzerland.

*28 September 1976

"World Population and the United States - The Development of an Idea". Statement at The United States in the World International Conference, Washington, D.C., U.S.A.

*12 November 1976

"Operational Activities for Development". Statement to the Second Committee of the 31st United Nations General Assembly, New York.

*12 January 1977

"Population and the New International Economic Order". Statement at the University of Michigan, Ann Arbor, Michigan, U.S.A.

*28 January 1977

"UNFPA Progress Report, January 1977". Statement to the 23rd Session of the UNDP Governing Council, United Nations, New York.

*30 March 1977

"Population Trends and Implications". Statement at the Conference on Population Trends and Implications, sponsored by the Conference Board, Dallas, Texas, U.S.A.

*2 June 1977

"The Implications of Change". The 1977 David Owen Memorial Lecture, at the David Owen Centre for Population Growth Studies, University College, Cardiff, United Kingdom.

*21 June 1977

"The UNFPA - An Overview: Present and Past". Statement to the 24th Session of the UNDP Governing Council, Geneva, Switzerland.

5 July 1977

"Programmes and Policies of the United Nations Fund for Population Activities". Statement at the Population Institute, East-West Center, University of Hawaii, Honolulu, Hawaii, U.S.A.

8 August 1977

Statement at the International Union for the Scientific Study of Population (IUSSP) Conference, Mexico City, Mexico.

27 September 1977

"People's Problems". Statement to a meeting of press representatives, sponsored by the Epoch B Foundation, Mohonk, New York, U.S.A.

7 November 1977

"Operational Activities for Development". Statement to the Second Committee of the 32nd United Nations General Assembly, United Nations, New York.

6 December 1977

Statement to the International Working Group of Parliamentarians on Population and Development, London, England.

20 January 1978

Statement to the final meeting of the 18-20 January 1978 Meeting of the UNDP Governing Council, United Nations, New York.

*26 March 1978

"New Dimensions in Family Planning Development". Keynote Address to the Opening Session of the Silver Jubilee Celebrations of the Family Planning Association of Sri Lanka, Colombo, Sri Lanka.

28 March 1978

Statement to the International Working Group of Parliamentarians on Population and Development, Tokyo, Japan.

*3 April 1978

"The Need for Paradigms". Statement at the Japan Economic Research Centre, Tokyo, Japan.

4 April 1978

Statement at Commencement Exercises, Yonsei University, Seoul, Republic of Korea.

*21 June 1978

"The UNFPA: Progress Report 1978". Statement to the 25th Session of the UNDP Governing Council, Geneva, Switzerland.

*6 November 1978

"UNFPA Operations - Report to the General Assembly". Statement to the Second Committee of the 33rd United Nations General Assembly, United Nations, New York.

Appendix B

Selected Statements of the UNFPA Executive Director

[Because of their content, a few of the statements of Rafael M. Salas, Executive Director of the UNFPA, are reprinted here in their entirety.]

THE FORMATIVE YEARS
The Beginnings of the United Nations Fund for Population Activities

Statement to Fifteenth Session of the Population Commission, United Nations, Geneva, 10 November 1969

I am happy to have the opportunity to appear before this distinguished body, the Population Commission. I have only been officially connected with the United Nations for a very short time. Five weeks ago, Paul Hoffman, Administrator of the United Nations Development Programme, whom I am representing here, nominated me for the post of Director of the United Nations Fund for Population Activities.

It was only in May of this year that the Secretary-General asked Mr. Hoffman to assume responsibility for administering the Fund. Since my appointment, I have been engaged in an intensive round of consultations with the specialized agencies and other major entities in the United Nations family whose mandates give them a special interest in population activities.

This is a formative period for the Fund and we are engaged in formulating definite proposals regarding the Fund's principles and procedures. Some things which we shall propose have already emerged fairly clearly. A few matters of procedure remain to be fully discussed and worked out in detail. I will thus report to you those things regardingthe Fund which can be said now with confidence, and as regarding the others, promise you that we shall have formulated definite proposals covering them shortly.

Creation of the Fund

As you know, in 1967, the Secretary-General of the United Nations established a Trust Fund for Population Activities*, to be financed by voluntary contributions from governments and other sources in order to enable the level of programmes of the

*The title has subsequently been changed to the United Nations Fund for Population Activities.

United Nations agencies to be increased, as approved by the Population Commission. The Fund has been used to finance, among other activities, programming missions to ascertain the needs of governments in the field of population and family planning and to finance family planning evaluation missions; some of these have been conducted by the United Nations itself and some in collaboration with the specialized agencies. It has also been used to expand the activities of the Economic Commission for Asia and the Far East, the Economic Commissions for Africa, and the United Nations Economic and Social Office in Beirut in the population field as well as of the United Nations Regional Demographic Centres and to enable ten Population Programme Officers to be trained and sent into the field.

Expansion of the Fund

The Secretary-General and the Administrator of UNDP have decided that programmes undertaken by the specialized agencies and by UNICEF may now be financed from the Fund and that the scope of its activities will be expanded to include forms of assistance which have not normally been financed under United Nations technical assistance programmes.

Interested governments will be assisted in preparing project requests by the Population Programme Officers as well as by the representatives of other specialized agencies as appropriate. Requests to the Fund, when formulated, will be submitted to the headquarters of the United Nations Development Programme through the offices of the Resident Representatives, who, in turn, will send copies for information to the agencies concerned.

Scope of the Programme

It is the underlying premise of the UNFPA programme that assistance from the Fund shall be given only to countries which request such assistance.

The role of the United Nations and specialized agencies will differ considerably from country to country, depending on each country's level of development and population patterns. Broadly, it can be envisaged in stages as:

(a) to assist governments in determining the size of populations and to assess population trends;

(b) to assist governments in understanding the consequences of population trends in relation to economic and social development;

(c) to assist governments in formulating population policies, taking into account all factors which affect fertility;

(d) to assist governments which adopt population policies in carrying out and evaluating measures to control fertility, including assistance in organization of family planning programmes and in training for an evaluation of such programmes;

(e) to assist governments in preparing requests for assistance in the form of projects.

The approach to the programme will be interdisciplinary and will be made in close co-operation with the United Nations and the specialized agencies in accordance with the mandates which they have received from their respective legislative bodies.

Demography and Family Planning

In future years, it is expected that the main volume of requests to the Fund will be for international assistance in controlling the exansion of population. Nevertheless, no population policy, and indeed no serious economic and social plans, can be formulated unless they are based on sound demographic and statistical foundations. For this reason, the Fund is available to finance activities over the entire population field. This is a point which may not be sufficiently understood by governments.

Conventional Types of Technical Assistance

The Fund may be used to finance technical assistance and Special Fund sector-type projects through provision of expert services, equipment, fellowships abroad, including those at Regional Centres, and organization of training courses and seminars. While the activities of the Fund will be reported to the Governing Council for information, projects and programmes financed by the Fund will not be submitted to it for approval. They will, moreover, in no way be competitive with project requests for technical assistance or Special Fund sector financing.

Related Assistance

In view of the importance, urgency and special nature of the population problem, however, consideration may be given to use of the Fund to provide other types of assistance, including the payment of local costs and counterpart services. Among these may be:

Local Costs for Field Research Projects. There is, in most countries, and even in different regions of large countries, a need for applied research into such questions as motivation towards family planning and attitudes towards use of various methods of contraception. Some countries, particularly in Asia, have had considerable experience in running family planning programmes. Provided financial assistance were available, governments could identify institutions which could then carry out such research with little outside expert assistance. In principle, the Fund may be used for such research with due provision for the results to be made available through the agencies of the United Nations system to other countries and for visits to the projects by representatives of the United Nations agencies.

Local Costs for Training. While the Fund is likely to be used to finance training abroad and particularly at Regional Centres, it may also be used in appropriate circumstances to finance training at the national level along the same sort of lines as in UNICEF-financed programmes.

Local Costs for Other Operational Activities. The question has arisen in countries which have serious budgetary problems of contributions towards local costs of operational programmes. Though the implications would need careful examination in each case, the possibility of such contributions is not excluded.

Transport and Equipment. Transport and equipment for family planning programmes will be included in the support provided by the Fund.

Manufacture of Equipment and Supplies. The question has arisen in some countries as to whether assistance in the manufacture of equipment and supplies may be possible. The possibilities of the Fund providing capital assistance for this purpose will depend on a considerable expansion of its resources.

Research. Among the types of research which may be usefully conducted in one or another developing country might be research into economic and social consequences of demographic trends, the social and economic factors leading to current fertility trends, and the appropriateness and effectiveness in the area of one or another type of family planning programme or contraceptive.

All of the above activities would only be contemplated in the context of projects, and not as general budgetary support.

The Need for Flexibility

The involvement of United Nations agencies in population programmes, and in particular family planning programmes, on any considerable scale is new. We are conscious of the urgency of the problem in many countries and of the need for the utmost flexibility in order to adapt our procedures to the very different situations prevailing in different countries.

In the implementation of the programmes, it is essential that the Fund and the agencies respond quickly and adequately to the country requests. Steps will be taken to employ modern managerial techniques to minimize delays in implementation.

Relationships with Other Programmes

Although the United Nations has long-established demographic programmes, the United Nations agencies have not until recently been very active in the family planning field. A number of bilateral agencies have been giving substantial assistance in several countries as have private organizations such as the Population Council, the International Planned Parenthood Federation, and the Pathfinder Fund. It is not the UNFPA's intention that programmes financed by the Fund should compete with those financed from other sources. However, consultations with representatives of other agencies should help to indicate where in each country the most useful activities can be undertaken by the Fund.

The Need for a Population Fund

I am happy to have been asked to serve as Director of the United Nations Fund for Population Activities, since I believe both in the extreme seriousness of the population problem in the world and in the vital role which the United Nations and its family of agencies can play in its solution. The UNFPA can, I believe, play a crucial role in this. While some governments consider that high priority should be given to population activities, others have expressed the view that there are economic and social programmes which are more important. The solution of population problems is no substitute for the pressing and broader requirements of economic development. It is complementary and the mechanisms of a separatte Fund enables governments which wish to support or receive assistance in the population field to do so without a diminution in the assistance given in other fields through the United Nations Development Programme and the regular budgets of the agencies.

Resources of the Fund

Some $4.9 million has been contributed to the Fund to date of which as of now about $2.9 million have been obligated. There are valid requests now in process on which the balance of $2 million will be allocated. Donor countries to date have included the United States, Sweden, Norway, Denmark, the United Kingdom, Finland, the Netherlands, Trinidad and Tobago, and Pakistan. I would like to stress the fact that the Fund will endeavour in the next and following years to increase the contributions and number of contributors from the developed as well as the developing countries.

Contributions will be accepted by the Secretary-General in freely usable currency for application by the Administrator of UNDP and the Director of the Fund to any, or all, of the purposes for which the Fund is intended. It is hoped that the bulk of the resources of the Fund will be in this form. The Secretary-General would, however, be prepared to negotiate with interested donors the acceptance of non-convertible currencies to the extent that these could be utilized to finance specific projects consistent with the purposes of the Fund. He would also be prepared to consider the acceptance of contributions for uses designated by the donor, provided that any restrictions on the use of the contributions are not inconsistent with the purposes of the Fund.

Action Orientation

The Secretary-General and Mr. Hoffman intend the Fund to be "action-oriented", that is, to be devoted to the most effective ways that can be found for the solution of population problems by those countries having such problems and requesting assistance of the Fund. Both in the aggregate and in many instances in detail, this represents a staggering task. Its direct relevance to human welfare, however, makes it a fitting task for the United Nations family to face squarely. Since population problems relate to the total fabric of a society, projects and programmes will, in many cases, not break down neatly along the lines of academic disciplines or organizational jurisdictions. An imaginative approach and the closest possible co-operation and co-ordination on population programmes and projects will thus be required among the various elements of the United Nations system.

ASIA:
An Area Assessment

Statement to the Second Asian Population Conference,
Tokyo, Japan, 1 November 1972

It is a great pleasure and honour for me to address this Second Regional Population Conference in Asia. The first Conference held in 1963 was of great significance, both for the United Nations system, and for the development of population programmes all over the Asian region. The decision to hold the first Conference was characteristically bold. It came at a time when the international community was deeply divided on population questions. During the 1950's and early 1960's the majority of member states of the United Nations were reluctant to face up to the implications of rapid population growth. It was the Asian countries which kept population issues alive in international forums and which began an international laboratory for the formulation and implementation of strategies to deal with population problems. The deliberations of the first Asian Population Conference, and the recommendations adopted unanimously, led directly to the historic decision of the United Nations Economic and Social Council in 1964 to authorize the United Nations to give technical assistance to action programmes on population and the General assembly resolution of 17 December 1966 which resulted in the creation of the United Nations Fund for Population Activities in 1967. We in the Fund are very conscious of the debt which the entire United Nations system in this regard owes to the member states of the Asian region.

At the time of the first Asian Population Conference there were only three countries—India, Republic of Korea and Pakistan—which had adopted policies aimed at bringing about a reduction in fertility and had organized national family planning programmes. Since then, one country after the other has adopted similar policies, with the result that there are very few countries remaining in the region where family planning is not a part of overall economic and social development planning. If it is recalled that India, the first country to embark on a national family planning programme did so only in 1951, the recognition which Asian Governments have given to the problem of rapid population growth, is indeed, phenomenal.

Approaches to Family Planning

The family planning approach to the problem of high fertility was predicated on the results of KAP surveys (Knowledge, Attitude, Practice), which indicated considerable interest in and demand for contraception. However, popular response to the introduction of family planning advice and services has generally not been as enthusiastic as was

291

expected. It is true that in most countries in the region birth rates have declined, but in many cases the declines have been modest and it is not clear to what extent these declines have been brought about by national family planning programmes. Indeed, such evidence as does exist often suggests that these programmes have merely reinforced an already existing trend toward fertility decline. In most countries, too, initial success has been followed by some falling-off in the number of new acceptors. This, however, has not led most social scientists to question the surveys. Instead, they have usually accepted the validity of the findings and looked elsewhere for explanations—lack of an ideal contraceptive, the clinical orientation of programmes, insufficient motivation. All these are undoubtedly important. The question remains, however, why are couples in developing countries not taking full advantage of the services offered?

Please do not misunderstand me. I do not think that present family planning programmes have failed—or that they should be discarded. On the contrary, such programmes should be improved and intensified. Indeed, support to family planning programmes through strengthening their critical components has been and will continue to be one of the first priorities for UNFPA. The sense of disenchantment and even frustration with current efforts may have arisen, in large part, because we have expected too much from family planning and underestimated the difficulties involved in "engineering" a decline in fertility.

Criticism of family planning programmes usually focusses on such factors as lack of commitment on the part of the government, poor design and planning, shortage of trained personnel, inadequate resources and so on. The poor quality of services may well be an equally important weakness, particularly since the programme is likely to be somewhat suspect anyway by virtue of being introduced from outside the community. The need to fill quotas and achieve targets may tend to lead to a deterioration in quality. It is a question of means matching the objectives. Family planning is essential for reasons of individual and family health and well-being alone. But if the goal is a rapid reduction in fertility, we must accept the implications of such an undertaking and formulate appropriate programmes.

In formulating a new strategy for the problem of high fertility we can, I think, learn an important lesson from recent experience in the field of agricultural development. Until a few years ago there was a tendency to dismiss peasant society as lazy and ignorant and bound by superstition and tradition. Peasant farmers, in particular, were condemned for their unwillingness to innovate. There was hardly any question in the minds of the experts—generally foreigners or foreign-trained—that the peasant could have valid reasons to act as he did. The problem was defined simply as one of finding ways of modifying his behaviour along the lines deemed necessary or desirable by the development planners.

This approach is now being increasingly challenged on the basis of studies which question automatic assumptions of peasant conservatism and which try to understand the functioning of subsistence farming through the eyes of the peasant himself. These studies have demonstrated that peasant farmers in developing countries have a deep practical understanding of their farming environment and its limitations and that, far from being unwilling to experiment, they are behaving in a perfectly rational fashion by adopting what we might call a minimal-risk strategy.

The analysis of reproductive behaviour in developing countries and prescriptions for fertility control strategy have often displayed the same kind of self-assurance and condescension. The high levels of fertility prevailing in most countries in the Asian region are the legacy of a long cultural tradition which has encouraged large-sized families. Indeed, it is only in recent history that high fertility has ceased to be essential for the survival of the species. And even now, in many areas death rates remain sufficiently high to preclude any thought of having fewer children. Nor can we ignore the fact that in rural areas a large family is still viewed as an economic asset. However, we have tended to assume that couples who want large families are behaving in an irrational fashion when, in fact, they merely do not share our values regarding desirable family size.

Village-Level Research

As a first step, then, we should seek to deepen our understanding of the factors influencing decisions about family size—as these are perceived by the population concerned. This involves in-depth, village-level research of the kind undertaken by anthropologists. Some studies of this kind have been carried out, but they have not received the attention they deserve. We should encourage case studies in different settings to be undertaken.

Findings of such research will make it easier to help couples in developing countries to understand their predicament, for, in the final analysis, it is better understanding which is the key to action. Such understanding is unlikely to be achieved by means of saturation advertising and the repetition of exhortations to have fewer children. Rather, we need to pay much greater attention to education. Education on population problems and their implications, as well as the basic principles of human reproduction and family planning, are a key part of family life education to be provided to all children and youth. In this way future generations of prospective parents would be prepared for their responsibilities. The development of the relevant curricula and teaching methods for the formal school system is an urgent priority. Many programmes of out-of-school education also lend themselves to the incorporation of population components. Full use should be made of all channels for the dissemination of population materials, particularly in development programmes such as functional literacy, community development, workers' education, vocational training, home economics and rural development. Governmental bodies and voluntary organizations including trade unions, youth organizations and mothers clubs can also be enlisted in organizing educational activities.

Insufficient attention has also been paid to the effects of various social policy measures on fertility and to their potential use in support of family planning programmes and as a part of comprehensive population policy. Among such measures are tax and welfare benefits, including family allowances, maternity benefits, tax deductions for children and housing provision for large families. It is desirable to scrutinize all relevant social legislation realistically from the point of view of its probable influence upon childbearing and population growth and, if necessary, to revise it to bring it into line with population policy goals. Special consideration should also be given to legislation raising the legal age of marriage, combined with measures such as education of girls, vocational training, increased employment opportunities for women and general improvement of the status of women in the community. Such measures could have a significant impact on fertility patterns.

The development of a comprehensive strategy taking into account all the factors affecting fertility may, however, still not be sufficient. It is common these days to refer to rapid population growth as the single most important obstacle to improved living standards in developing countries. It is not surprising that this point of view is challenged in many developing countries as simplistic and misleading. The real "obstacles" to development lie elsewhere, not merely in the rate of population growth, but in the compound effects of such factors as the neglect of agriculture, rigid social structures, imbalances in resource allocation as well as the unequal relations between rich and poor countries and the maldistribution of income. It would be illusory to imagine that a reduction in the rate of population growth will, of itself, raise living standards.

Development and Population

Development is a process in which each part is intimately interrelated to every other. For one part to move forward, all other parts must be moving in the same direction. The immediate problem for the millions of people in our countries is grinding poverty, malnutrition, ill health, poor sanitation, little or unsatisfying work—and little prospect of any substantial change in their lifetimes. The problem is thus not so much that population action programmes will not "bite" until a certain threshold of modernization is reached. Changes in fertility behaviour are more likely to occur as an integral part of an overall process of social and economic change which is, generally speaking, not yet occurring on a sufficiently broad scale in most developing countries.

If what I have said is true, where does this leave the population specialist?

Population specialists have rightly drawn attention to the consequences—political, economic, social, environmental—of rapid population growth, but they have done so mainly in order to demonstrate the need for deliberate efforts to moderate fertility. However, effective population control is a long term undertaking and whatever success is achieved through current efforts to reduce fertility, the population of the developing regions will almost certainly double within the next twenty-five to thirty years. Population growth of this magnitude can seriously jeopardize hopes for any substantial improvements in living standards in the coming decades. The situation is such that urgent consideration must now be given to the need for alternative development strategies on the one hand and fundamental changes in the relations between rich and poor countries on the other. As population specialists we have a responsibility to draw attention to these problems. I think, also, that as population specialists we have a role to play in their solution, not only through the formulation and implementation of population policies as such, but also as part of an integrated approach to economic and social development.

Training of Personnel

Until now the involvement of population specialists in the formulation anb implementation of strategies for economic and social development has been largely limited to the collection and analysis of population data including preparation of projections. There is a great need within the national planning body and the various sectoral planning agencies for experienced persons of sufficiently high levels not only to advise on the population policy implications of most aspects of the various types of planning, but also to participate in the national planning process itself, in all its phases. Such persons will probably have to be crossbred. As some of you may know, a proposal was made recently for the creation of high-level, interdisciplinary international training facilities. UNFPA is actively seeking to develop such facilities at the national as well as the international level. An important target audience is development planners whose time perspective does not encourage consideration of population as an endogenous variable.

Furthermore, research leading to the elaboration of systemic models of the development process should be intensified. One of the purposes of such research would be to explore what rate of population growth could be absorbed given alternative assumptions about capital-output ratios, patterns of resource allocation, access to foreign markets, availability of external assistance, changes in social structure and so on.

In UNFPA we are very much interested in working with governments and nongovernmental institutions in developing a conceptual framework for a truly integrated approach to the problems of poverty, environment and population, and in assisting governments in dealing with population aspects of formulation and implementation of comprehensive development strategies. Such assistance would include consideration of problems relating to migration and urbanization and the development of population related strategies in such fields as public health, nutrition, employment and urban and rural development. In this connection, our close links with UNDP and the steps we are taking to associate UNFPA more closely in country programming will be of great importance.

Collaboration between the Fund and developing countries can only be successful if based on mutual respect and understanding. As you know, UNFPA does not prescribe any particular approach or policy in dealing with population problems. We seek to be as flexible as possible in appraising projects submitted to us realising that, in the population field more than any other, it is in the developing countries themselves that the greatest experience and expertise are to be found. I think we must now go further and encourage the governments of developing countries to take greater responsibility not only for the formulation of projects but also for their execution.

World Population Year—1974

Many of these ideas will, we hope, be developed further during World Population Year. As you know, the General Assembly has designated 1974 as World Population Year. The preparations for this important undertaking have been entrusted to me by the Economic and Social Council and we are already engaged in laying the foundations for what we hope will become a spectacular example of effective international cooperation. In one sense, every year is population year for UNFPA. Many programmes envisaged for the Year, such as the improvement of demographic data and services, expansion of maternal and child welfare facilities and increased population training and educational programmes, will give new impetus and scope to on-going activities. At the same time, the Year provides us with an opportunity to develop imaginative and innovative activities, using new technologies and skills which, we hope, will open up new areas for support by UNFPA in the future.

The Year will have failed if it does not result in activities of lasting and practical benefit to countries, particularly developing countries. To this end the Fund has already begun to bring into play the network of communication and interrelationships between the United Nations, its regional economic commissions, governments and other bodies. However, the success of programmes promoted in conjunction with the Year will depend to a major extent on the full participation of organizations and individuals in the countries themselves. Non-governmental organizations, for example, are of key importance when it comes to reaching the community level, and I hope that those already involved with population programmes will stimulate the active participation of various groups such as professional and scientific associations, trade unions, farmers and community centres.

In this connection the necessity of involving women and youth cannot be overemphasized. In my opinion, the Year will have been well worthwhile alone if, as a result of intensified programmes, these two sectors of the population will be more actively involved in population programmes at all levels. The countries of Asia, in particular, have a notable contribution to make in this regard and the Fund is only too ready to support activities that will lead in this direction.

The highlight of the World Population Year will, of course, be the World Population Conference. It is fortunate for the United Nations to have such a distinguished person as Don Antonio Carrillo Flores in charge of this Conference. Like the first Asian Population Conference, the World Population Conference in 1974 will be composed of government representatives and will make recommendations for action by the United Nations and by governments. This in itself is a measure of the historic importance of the first Asian Population Conference. Despite the considerable achievements which have been made in recent years in our understanding of population problems and in finding effective but human solutions, we still have much to learn. I believe that this Second Asian Population Conference, coming as it does less than two years before the World Population Conference, can also be of great significance. You will be considering many of the problems to which I have alluded and I am certain that at the end of the Conference you will have found workable solutions to them. I wish you every success in your work.

SCOPE AND DIRECTION
First Report to the Governing Council

Statement at the Fifteenth Session of the UNDP Governing Council,
United Nations, New York, 29 January 1973.

The United Nations Fund for Population Activities has reported to the UNDP Governing Council on several occasions since the time in 1969 when the Administrator assumed responsibility for the administration of the Fund. Our reports on those occasions, however, were for information only, since during that period UNFPA was a Trust Fund of the Secretary-General. This is the first time, in accordance with General Assembly Resolution 3019 (XXVII) of 18 December 1972, we are reporting to you as our governing body. We welcome this development, indeed we sought it, since we need your help and guidance.

Before I come to the specific points raised in my written report in connexion with which the Council might consider acting at this time, however, I would like to make a few general remarks about the Fund by way of introduction.

While many of the distinguished delegates know a great deal about the Fund, there are a few basic points about the Fund's operation that need to be emphasized.

First, UNFPA programming is entirely separate from UNDP programming and there has never been a hint from UNFPA or UNDP that UNFPA population programmes might be promoted at the expense of UNDP's economic and social assistance. Mutual exchange of information about programming both at the headquarters and field levels is, of course, necessary, but there are absolutely no obligatory connexions between the two types of assistance.

Second, the Fund never seeks to urge any particular population policy or programmes on any country. It is neutral with respect to policy. It has responded to requests to assist countries with problems of sub-fertility and sterility as well as those with problems of high fertility rates.

Third, the words "population" or "population activities" in the United Nations are broadly understood to include: population censuses, vital statistics, sample surveys on population, economic and social statistics related to population, related research projects, training facilities required, demographic aspects of development planning, family planning delivery systems, techniques of fertility regulation, planning and management of family planning programmes, support communications, population and family life education in schools and in out-of-school education, the World Population Year 1974, documentation centers and clearing houses on population matters, and inter-disciplinary population training.

Forty-four per cent of the Fund's resources have been allocated to these various programmes other than family planning and support communications. A substantial proportion—some 28 per cent—has been devoted to wholly demographic projects—census and vital registration programmes often in countries which have no family planning programmes. The Fund is, for example, preparing to respond favourably to requests for assistance with censuses from twenty African countries, seventeen of which have never had a population census and three of which have not taken censuses in many years. It is preparing, moreover, to expand its assistance in demographic data gathering and interpretation to other areas, such as Latin America in response to interest shown by countries there. That adequate demographic data is essential for meaningful economic and social development planning is a fact that needs no elaboration.

In response to requests from many countries, by no means confined to Asia, we have responded to requests for assistance with family planning programmes and support communications and have devoted some 56 per cent of resources to the purpose. Some of the family planning programmes we have supported have demographic goals; others do not and are conceived entirely as measures of individual and family welfare under the direction and supervision of the Ministries of Health.

Fourth, support for and interest in the Fund has been rapidly growing since 1969. We have received contributions from 60 countries, and have responded favourably to project requests from 72 countries. We have more than 500 projects under way at present.

Fifth, the volume of requests has been growing rapidly. At present, we have a very large volume of project requests pending. The annual cost of 1973 project requests which we have already received or about which we have advance information, for the first year of their operation if funded, would come to some $72 million. We shall, of course, process these requests carefully but we do not expect to be able to fund them all by any means.

In reporting to the Governing Council and in appearing before it, we are conscious of all the provisions of General Assembly Resolution 3019, including the provisions of operative paragraph 2 which states that the Governing Council of UNDP shall be the governing body of UNFPA "subject to conditions to be established by the Economic and Social Council", presumably to be enunciated at the April 1973 session of ECOSOC. It is with this in mind, in view of the very specific authorization which the General Assembly in paragraph 4 of its Resolution gives to the 15th Session of the Governing Council, and in light of urgent problems facing the Fund in connexion with the subject matter of paragraph 4, that we restricted the scope of the Fund's written report to you to certain financial questions.

In paragraph 4 of Resolution 3019 the General Assembly authorized "the Governing Council at its 15th Session to apply to the United Nations Fund for Population Activities funding principles similar to those of theUnited Nations Development Programme and to establish the necessary financial rules and regulations, subject to consideration by the Governing Council of a report, prepared by the Executive Director of the United Nations Fund for Population Activities in consultation with the Administrator of the United Nations Development Programme, and of the full implications thereof."

In this connexion, we have prepared our report to the Governing Council. It suggests that the Council might wish to take five actions concerning our financial affairs:

(1) to authorize the Executive Director, in consultation with the Administrator of UNDP, to work out financial regulations and rules for the Fund and to submit these to the 16th session of the Governing Council in June;

(2) to authorize the Executive Director, in consultation with the Administrator, to continue to conduct the financial operations of the Fund under the appropriate financial regulations and rules of UNDP, taking into account the separate identity and character of the Fund;

(3) to authorize the Executive Director to work out, in consultation with the Administrator, funding principles of UNFPA similar to those of UNDP, taking into account the separate identity of UNFPA and its funding arrangements; to set aside an operational reserve of approximately 7.5 per cent of the total programme costs for the period 1973-1976; and to programme on the basis of a four-year resource projection assuming new resources as follows:

1973	$42.0 million
1974	$54.0 million
1975	$64.0 million
1976	$74.5 million

(4) to authorize the Executive Director to present a revised version of the programme projections in UNFPA's Work Plan, a document on which the programme cost projections in our report are based, to the 16th Session of the Governing Council together with a revised statement following any further adjustments in the estimates of annual programme costs for the period 1973-1976;

(5) to authorize the Executive Director to examine various possibilities for regularizing the Fund's pledging process, which in the past has been irregular and unpredictable with pledges often being made very late in the year to which the pledges refer.

All of these subjects are important but the most important of them from the Fund's point of view is the question of the Governing Council's authorization of the Fund now to adopt principles of annualized funding. The General Assembly has specifically authorized the 15th Governing Council to grant this.

When he assumed responsibility for UNFPA in 1969, the Administrator of UNDP continued to operate the Fund as a Secretary-General's Trust Fund. This involved fully funding all of UNFPA's commitments against current resources.

As is not unusual with new programmes, a lag between allocations and expenditures opened up. Partly to meet the needs of countries for financial assurances extending over a number of years to permit rational planning and programming, future commitments of the Fund became heavier than had been foreseen. This factor, coupled with a volume of pledges less than the Fund had hoped to receive, caused the Fund late in 1972 to defer temporarily approval of new activities.

However, despite the very modest programming balance which the Fund now has under the rules of full funding, a substantial amount of resources could be liberated for programming and for our operational reserve were the Fund to be permitted authorization to adopt the principles of annualized funding. Cumulative pledges and other income as at 31 December 1972 were approximately $79 million and all cumulative commitments of the Fund totalled at that date approximately the same amount. Thus, under the rules of full funding we had a zero programming balance. On the other hand, using the accounting system authorized under an annualized funding system, from these cumulative resources of $79 million, programme costs and programme support costs of only some $33 million would have to be subtracted leaving a figure of some $46 million which could be considered as un-utilized resources as at 31 December. This would yield the $20 million we calculate we would need as an operational reserve as well as some $26 million which would be released for programming.

Full funding, as the Council recognized some years ago with regard to UNDP, is an inefficient basis for the operations of a well-established funding organization. It faces the organization with two alternatives, both of which are undesirable: (1) to limit commitments to one year, a basis too short for effective planning by recipient governments, or (2) to immobilize the assets granted by donor governments for an unnecessarily long period by making multi-year committments. In considering our request for authorization for annualized funding the Council should bear these long-term considerations in mind as well as our shorter-term needs for specific sums of money now tied up by full funding rules.

These are, of course, matters for the Council, as the Fund's sovereign governing body, to decide.

INTERNATIONAL POPULATION ASSISTANCE:
A Spur to National Effort

Remarks at the Institute of Man and Science, Rensselaerville, New York, 6 May 1973

After three years of intensive work in multilateral assistance through the UNFPA, one begins to gain a firmer insight on the process of delivering population assistance and its inevitable links to other types of development assistance. With this insight, however, comes the apprehension that what has happened to development assistance in the last two decades could happen—and in a much shorter time—to assistance in population.

Nothing concerns aid-administrators more today than the probability that the volume of development assistance which showed an accelerated rate of increase in its early years has now reached a plateau from which an ascent is difficult to foresee. This predicament is real, in spite of the multi-national commitment of donors and recipients to the strategies of the Second Development Decade which set a desired rate of increase in the volume of assistance up to 1980.

The reasons for this are many and varied. The sharp changes taking place in the pattern of world trade have created difficulties in many countries, and not the least among the traditional donor nations. But the possibility that the flow of aid is levelling off is also known to arise from criticisms directed at the aid process itself. There is a crescendo of accusation that aid has not been effective—that is, that it does not appear to have the results which the donors hoped for. Measured in the available terms, the net per capita production is rising painfully slowly, and at times not rising at all, in many of the aided nations. Parallel with this criticism is another—namely, that the distribution channels of aid are cumbersome and wasteful, and also that the implementation of aided projects is faulty and dilatory.

On the side of the aid-receiving countries, too, there are rumbles of discontent. These include the nature of tied loans, allegations of the inflationary effects of some forms of aid, and of the growing burden of repayment and loan-servicing.

Thus, the present state of development assistance in general is not a very encouraging one. This does not hold true for population assistance as yet. The volume of resources available here has so far been adequate to meet the demands of countries in need and in their capacity to absorb the assistance. The prospects for increases in the volume are good as we approach 1974. But a few years after the World Population Conference, which would be about seven or eight years after the initial large-scale investment in multilateral-assisted population programmes, donor countries might begin to ask the same questions that they are now seeking answers for in the development field. Where are the "results?" What are the "benefits?"

301

Time of Re-thinking

The prospect of having to answer these questions points to a time of re-thinking for aid-donors, aid-receivers and aid-administrators. More so, because, unlike many economic development projects which can show tangible results in a year or two, population projects often take a generation or more to take full effect. Implementing population programmes is not a unique activity—it is only the population problem in the larger sense that is unique. The funding and implementation of population projects exhibit the same challenges and are subject to the same managerial problems as projects directed towards other defined social and economic goals.

This is because the problems that arise from population trends are not acting in a vacuum and cannot be treated if they were in a vacuum. It is sometimes claimed that rapid population growth is the single most important obstacle to improved living standards in many countries of the world; but such an opinion is not strictly tenable. There are many obstacles to development—the neglect of agriculture, the lack of adequate infrastructure to develop markets, rigid social structures, inequality of opportunity and income, and the maldistribution of resources.

It would be illusory to imagine that a reduction in the rate of population growth will, of itself, raise living standards. Such a reduction will in many developing countries remove a serious obstacle to the attainment of economic and social goals, because where rates of development are low, a large proportion of any rise is swallowed up by the high rate of additions to the population. To remove or to moderate this obstacle may be very necessary; but it is equally necessary to prosecute positive policies of development of services, resources, output and distribution.

International assistance, even when measured in its broadest terms, has never been more than a marginal addition to the total development resources of aid-receiving nations. In the field of population programmes, it is true that aid has often contributed a comparatively high proportion of the initial launching cost and implementation, but for its long-run effects, we are being challenged by the examples of the two most populous states of Asia—China and India. China has today one of the most comprehensive family planning programmes, extensively delivered, with no international assistance. And in India, which has the longest experience in a government initiated family planning programme, the foreign contribution to its total national outlay does not exceed the order of ten per cent.

What is more, we must recall that aid *because* it is marginal, must be more than marginally effective. Economic theory teaches us that it is the marginal addition of resources which sets the standards of expansion—the costs, the benefits and the productivity. Thus it is not how much aid which is really in question—calculations of percentages of GNP, or amounts of aid per country or per capita, have this weakness. It is the marginal effectiveness of each added portion of aid which is important.

Aid as a Spur

What do we conclude from this? One conclusion may be that we seek to assist only in those basic areas which will yield better returns in the long run within each country's accepted programmes. In the past, because of the promotional aspect of assistance, resources have been applied to a considerable extent to isolated and peripheral activities.

Viewed in this light, aid becomes not a "catalyst," as it has too often been described, but a "spur." The catalytic role for aid may indeed be relevant in times of short-term crisis, following war or famine or other autonomous events in the social and economic life of a nation. But in the long term flow of assistance, the kind of endeavour which looks forward over the generations and not merely over the next harvest, the aid programme should not play such a catalytic role. That role can best be played by the national governments themselves, and by any international or regional mechanisms that these national governments may implement. The great marginal and effective role for aid in these circumstances is as a spur.

If international assistance is to act as a spur, through what mechanisms, by what means, should it operate? We may conceive of the main aim as the creation of clear national population objectives or goals toward which the country's human resources should be mobilized. In the early literature of development, writers like Arthur Lewis were speaking of a "will to develop." But as the study of development became more sophisticated and its disciplines more quantified, development administrators lost sight of the crucial role of this perspective. As a consequence, a great deal of external resources devoted to development were wasted in countries which had no purposeful desire to develop, and bred, as a consequence, widespread suspicion and mistrust.

National Objectives

But it is one thing to recognize that each country must adopt its national population objectives; it is another and more difficult [thing] to pin the idea down, to formulate practical measures which will strengthen the capacity of the country to mobilize its resources behind this will and its realization. Let us attempt an exposition of a few of its aspects:

One: A national population objective must not be just a "wish." It must be a clear and comprehensive statement of goals and policies arrived at by countries in accordance with their own particular needs and views. Target settings and policies should be arrived at, as much as possible, with the largest possible participation by the people who are to carry out these programmes, and taking into account all available information about relevant facts.

Two: If this is done, there must be the necessary administrative infrastructure to carry them out. There are many countries today where the whole governmental and fiscal system was designed to answer the needs of another era—in some, the colonial era. Thus development programmes which look very logical on paper, are grafted onto these old systems; they fail to grow. The old systems do not move the men, the money and the necessary integrated action. There are vast wastages, great under-expenditures, gross delays. Very often these failures are blamed on other causes when, in fact, the fault lies in a system which was not designed to meet new needs—to move new materials to new places, to set up new organizations for new purposes, to administer better techniques, and to serve new kinds of recipients.

Three: In addition to the acceptance of the need and the responsibility to solve the population problem in each country, there must also exist the skills and the means to carry them out. This is the reason why the UNFPA, in its three years of operation, has devoted more than a third of its resources to training. Advisory services, equipment and supplies mean nothing when there is neither the skill nor the will to utilize them.

Four: The most important component of the strategic effort to solve the population problems is adequate communication between the leaders and the led; between the governmental agencies and private organizations. The need of adequate information is so vital in the process that without it, there can neither be public motivation to solve this problem nor the citizen participation that is needed even to make a beginning.

I have no doubt that, in the years to come, there will be a continuing role for multilateral assistance in population. There are certain irreducible elements in these processes of exchange that only international organisations can perform adequately: the transmission of information; the lending of multi-national experts; the transmission of certain technological advances in the population field within the framework of internationally agreed policies. But for aid-giving countries not too weary of the short-run lack of visibility of results in the field of population, the aid-receiving countries must, at the very start of the process, show that they have both the realistic and necessary population objectives and the will to carry their plans through.

It is with this view that we in the Fund will continue to assist countries, and deliberately apply a portion of the assistance to spurring the countries to undertake these programmes themselves, by continuing to train as much of each country's human resources as possible, and assisting in the building of their own institutions.

POPULATION AND THE MEDIA
An Added Dimension

Statement to Editors' Round Table, Bangkok, Thiland, 20 May 1974.

One day many years ago in the newsroom of the Times of London, a few sub-editors were discussing the most boring headlines they could think of. The eventual winner was "Small earthquake in Chile; not many killed." Until quite a short time ago, a close second might have been "Experts give another warning on Asian population growth." Last month, however, a sister paper of the London Times held a conference on "The Exploding Cities." Many journalists and experts attended—some of whom are here today—and the resulting newspaper, radio and TV coverage in both developed and developing countries on this crucial aspect of population is still coming in.

But it has taken newspapermen outside Asia a long time to get to the point where they not only take population issues seriously but are prepared to bring them out into the open and discuss them with the attention that their importance merits. The Asian press has given a most valuable lead in this respect, as we saw at last month's conference.

In the last two months there have been three regional consultations of governments in Latin America, Asia and Africa to discuss the World Population Conference and Plan of Action. Each region has its own contribution to make, but it was clear from the discussions that Asian governments have a measure of sophistication and expertise which other countries have not yet attained.

In part at least, this extra dimension can be ascribed to the close attention which the Asian press and broadcast media have paid to population questions in the past. It is frequently clear, after it has been adopted, that this or that policy was logical and necessary, but it is a tribute to the responsiveness of Asian journalists to the dictates of social change that nearly every country in Asia now has an official population policy. The Asian press was the first to recognize the need for specialist reporting of population questions and the integral nature of population and development. Perhaps I may cite the consistent policy in this regard of the Press Foundation of Asia, and the success of its DEPTHnews service. Both the PFA and the National Press Institute of Asia have maintained a consistent programme of training journalists to seek out the significance for development of stories in the news, and to write up stories which would not otherwise have seen the light of day. Several hundred newspapermen have been trained by these organizations to look for what might be called the news behind the news and to report it in a critical and responsible way.

This experience is now being sought in other Third World countries where the problems are similar and an awakening is only now taking place. The success of the PFA experiment has encouraged newspapermen in Latin America to take a similar initiative in establishing ALACODE, the Latin American Development Writers Association, set up last year. I have just come from Cairo, where a meeting of newspapermen from Arab countries agreed to set up an organization of the same kind in the Middle East. The value which is placed by the international community on this work is reflected by UNFPA's funding of the programmes which I have mentioned to the extent of more than $1 million.

But support from UNFPA and other international organizations can only be seed or start-up finance. For the continuing success of these organizations, support from within the community is required. Both governments and private organizations are coming to realize the value of communication, by which I do not mean propaganda, but responsible and reflective analysis of events, explaining the purposes of government to the people and responding in turn with the views, reactions, wishes and needs of the people themselves. As I know from my experience as an administrator in Asia, government must know what is happening in the streets and the villages if it is to function effectively, and supply the true needs and desires of the people for development. Such two-way communication cannot exist without a well-informed and expert corps of pressmen. The "Asian" recently published an essay on the training of journalists which contains one of the most effective short descriptions of the journalist's work that I have seen. Some of you will no doubt already have heard it, but it bears repetition. The writer says. "A journalist's required talent is the creation of interest. A good journalist takes a dull or specialist or esoteric situation and makes newspaper readers want to know about it. By doing so he both sells newspapers and educates people. It is a noble, dignified and useful calling."

The question of press freedom is relevant here. It is my view that it depends to a great degree on the quality of the performance of the Press itself. Freedom is not a divine right of the media, but a social right belonging to the people, who delegate it to the press. Therefore the professionalization of journalism in terms of the skill and responsibility of its practitioners is of concern not only to the owners and workers in the media, but to the community as a whole. Where, as in many countries throughout the world, a large proportion of the population live in conditions which deny them even the most basic of rights, the right to eat, the right to work, the right to live in peace, the function of the media takes on an added dimension of responsibility and sensitivity.

One important aspect of this in many Asian countries is the phenomenon of a rapid growth in the numbers of people demanding satisfaction of their basic rights. Population throughout the world is growing at an average rate of about two per cent. In Asia, growth is even faster, about 2.3 or 2.4 per cent. Nearly every Asian country now has a policy aimed at reducing the speed of this growth; but this by itself is not enough. If all such policies achieved their aims tomorrow, it would take some seventy years for population growth to attain stability. The children already born would see to that. There have been some considerable successes in Asian population programmes, but every planning ministry is aware that its schemes will be useless unless they take into account this inexorable increase in population.

Nor are we talking simply about another Asia on top of this one by the early years of next century. There will be many more old people to take care of; there will be many more inhabitants of cities which are already feeling the pressure of their present population; and there will be many more children. The number of dependents, people under 15 or over 65, is already high in all the countries of Asia. The prospect is that they will increase not only in numbers but as a proportion of the total population. The ramifications of this growth, and their implications for development policy in the 21st century must be thought of now. Once more, an informed, intelligent and sensitive press can provide services which even the most sophisticated of development policies cannot include. The reporter on the street and in the village can tell the true story of what population growth really means to the ordinary people. If the administrator is doing his job, he will listen. He knows as well as anyone that things do not always go according to plan, that people do not always behave as they are expected to, and that situations may develop which are beyond his experience and control. The Press can act as his eyes and ears; and where necessary, as his conscience.

Population growth then, is only one aspect of the Asian future. Alongside population growth are the problems of mobilization of the resources to provide for increased numbers of people. This, we know, is not confined to one country or one region. There are massive disparities in the quantity and value of the resources available in different parts of the world, as well as within individual countries. Some years ago development experts in their optimism looked forward to a future in which the resources of the world would supply a standard of living for the majority of people on a level equal to that of the richer countries. Better knowledge of the extent of our resources, and, perhaps more important, of the effects of their exploitation on our environment, has brought about a change in our thinking. Uncontrolled production and processing of raw materials, and certainly their consumption by a small minority of the world's people, cannot go on.

In the future, the peoples of Asia will demand as their right a bigger share of the world's wealth. Much expansion can still take place, but eventually many of those people who now consume resources out of all proportion to their numbers will have to learn to limit their demands. We have to find ways to achieve this and I can see that perhaps Asian communicators will have a part to play in the process. So far, international assistance has been largely one-way, in the form of transfers of technology, skills and financial resources from the industrialized to the developing countries. I think maybe the time has come for a transfer to be made in the opposite direction.

What can the developing countries offer the rest of the world? One of the most important things I believe is a restored sense of values. In their desperate chase after the satisfactions which material wealth can provide, I feel that the peoples of the industrialized countries have lost sight of the goal which impelled them in the first place to seek wealth. There is a growing sense in the industrialized countries that something is missing from a life which includes many of the things that the earth can provide, but which has lost the deeper satisfaction which comes from a fundamentally sound relationship with the rest of creation.

The great religions of Asia grew among peoples who were living under conditions of scarcity and in a limited although unspoiled environment. This kind of poverty, however, was rich in human values. For the sake of survival each man had to recognize that his fate was bound up with the fate of every other member of the community. In such circumstances sharing goes deeper than community of material things; there is an empathy, a deep sense of what is essential in the life of another, and a practical compassion for his fate. Despite, or perhaps because of its material poverty, Asia continues to be wealthy in this dimension of human existence.

We live in a time when there is considerable uncertainty about the future shape of the international community; but all our efforts to equalize disparities of wealth among nations, contain population growth and survive in a threatened biosphere will be meaningless if we cannot learn to overcome our acquisitiveness by developing a sense of limitation. A limitation of material desires, but an unlimited capacity to share human fulfillment is imperative, especially as we move into an era when no nation or group will be able to command a massive share of the world's resources as if by right.

I should like to throw out a challenge to the writers and broadcasters of Asia; no less a task than to transmit to the privileged an awareness of their responsibility to the rest of the world, and the consciousness that by fulfilling the needs of others they will be restoring their own humanity and thus fulfilling themselves.

POPULATION ASSISTANCE AND THE UNFPA
Responding to the Countries' own Assessments of their needs

Statement to World Population Conference, Bucharest, Romania, 20 August 1974.

This is an historic occasion. It is the first time the governments and people of the world have come together to discuss and to debate, in solemn assembly, the problems of population.

Now that this World Conference is at last taking place, it seems almost extraordinary that it should have been delayed so long. Over the last several years, often under the pressure of circumstances, we have had to adjust our view of many elements of the world situation. We have learned that the world's abundance is finite; that the capacity of the biosphere to sustain life, including human life, is limited; and that quite extraordinary measures are needed if, in the struggle for survival, man is not to do irreparable harm both to himself and to the environment. Above all, we have come to recognize that population trends are vitally important factors in economic and social change, in the use or misuse of resources and in the conservation or destruction of the natural environment.

This recognition has been given a new and sharper edge by the current unprecedented and sustained population growth experienced in major parts of the world. The fact that most of this growth is taking place in those countries least able in their present situation to support it, has lent force to the feeling that this is a legitimate area of international concern.

But we are not here to rest upon our laurels. We are not here to indulge in self-congratulation. It is one thing to recognize the problem. It is quite another thing to know what should be done about it and to plan and implement the steps to be taken, both on a national and an international level.

For the last five years, the United Nations Fund for Population Activities has served the needs of countries in the field of population. On the basis of its experience, we would like to offer some thoughts on the relationship of population to economic and social development, and to give some indication of the possible future direction, as we see it, of both national and international action.

A View On Development

I know nobody here wants to listen to a lecture on economic theory and particularly not during the first speech of the morning. To put it briefly, though, I think we can all agree that the classic development models were based on an interpretation of the process which took place in the developed countries. The emphasis was on capital-intensive industrialization, advanced technology, large-scale productive units and urban growth. It was believed that savings and investment would be increased by concentrating development in key areas. After the initial period, it was expected that the benefits would trickle down through the rest of the economy. In particular it was hoped that the agricultural sector would respond to increasing demand by modernizing itself.

The results, however, have not followed the expected pattern. Without sufficient inputs of capital and skills, changes in the rural sector have proceeded only slowly. Even the coming of the Green Revolution to the countryside has carried with it largely unforeseen problems such as income distribution, and agricultural production has not risen enough to avoid shortages. Nor did the urban sector respond quite in the way intended. Instead of being dispersed evenly throughout the economy, the benefits of development have remained concentrated in small areas.

Today, in cities all over the developing world, flourishing modern areas exist side by side with old centres, decaying slums and the shanty towns thrown up by those who have flocked in from the countryside.

To put it simply, the classic development models—and the development trends themselves—have stressed urban as against rural growth, large-scale as against small, concentration against diffusion. But in fact, in order to meet our problems, it may be that quite the opposite emphasis is needed. The development of agriculture can meet the world's food shortages; rural development can relieve the immense burden on the cities; and, for the sake of dignity and self-respect, as well as to provide markets, both industry and agriculture must offer the individual the opportunity and the incentive to work, to earn and to contribute to his society.

The implication of all this is that development must be diffused socially and geographically throughout all levels and throughout all areas. A society of sufficiency for all, replacing the distortions of both excess and deprivation, must be our aim.

When we speak of a society of sufficiency for all we are not just speaking of the developing countries. Sufficiency for all—in this sense of an absence of excess as well as an absence of deprivation—is a concept which is valid internationally as well as nationally.

We have already had one Development Decade. Now we are in the middle of the Second. Even though growth in terms of GNP has been at its highest ever in the developing world, most authorities agree that the economic gap between the developed and the developing countries has widened during this period. Is this fair? Is this just? Is this tolerable?

What makes the situation still worse is that the pursuit of increasing wealth has meant greater and greater production, consumption and waste, with consequently increasing damage to the ecological balance. Pollution does not respect national boundaries. Everyone—including the developing countries—is affected by the results of overloading the air and sea with waste products. Everyone—especially the developing countries—is affected by excess demand and the consequence of this demand on the supply of basic commodities which should by right be available at a fair and reasonable price to all.

Thus far, the concept of progress has been largely appreciated in economic terms and the pursuit of wealth has set ever higher standards of affluence at which to aim. Is it possible now to limit our material demands? Can our priorities be changed so as to answer the needs of all?

Sufficiency Society and Human Values

For the sufficiency society of the future some values of both past and present may still be valid; but not values that spawn unbridled acquisitiveness. Rather, let us seek the values of co-operation and concern, of involvement in the lives of others, values which come from recognition that the lives and the fate of all are inextricably bound up with each other, that man is now interdependent between continents, as he once was within the confines of the village. Fortunately these values still exist in many parts of our world and will, I believe, play a vital role in the future.

These are signs that the change in positions and in attitudes has already begun. Growing national pride and self-confidence in many countries are bringing about a re-evaluation of national needs and wants which is both more in line with the realities of existing social structures and better adapted to the dictates of change. There is more willingness among national leaders to institute and accept change and to root out those aspects of the social and economic system which are obstacles to development.

Among industrialized countries there is a new willingness to participate in the evolution of new approaches. There is a growing acceptance that the values of growth and acquisition are not the most appropriate for our times, in a world whose resources and capacity to absorb the effects of human activity are limited. In the transition from scarcity to sufficiency, technologies and techniques are emerging, some new, some adapted, but in either case appropriate to the needs and values of development.

Population An Integral Part of the Sufficiency Society

This is the context in which the problems of population must be seen. The adoption of sensible and enlightened policies in this field is an essential step for all countries—whether developed or developing—on their road towards becoming "sufficiency societies" in the sense that I have used that term. One of the things which has most encouraged me in recent months is that young people in particular seem to be specially conscious of this. World Population Year has demonstrated the vigour and enthusiasm with which young people are facing their new world, and the Youth Population Conference which has just ended here has produced ideas and suggestions which are worthy of the most serious attention.

Certainly, the experience of many governments represented here—and of UNFPA itself—has shown us that, of all areas of development and social change, population is one of the most complex and perhaps the most sensitive. We have to understand clearly the complicated interrelationships of fertility, mortality, morbidity, migration and the growth, distribution and structure of the population and economic and social factors. We have to be sure that family planning and maternal child health services are formulated and delivered consistently with these factors in mind. But above all these, population deals with the most delicate of human relationships—the act of love, the family and the mystique which surrounds it. In approaching these areas of human activity, the greatest care must be used and the greatest respect shown to the feelings of those concerned. Whenever it is a personal matter, it must be dealt with on a personal level; projects in population cannot be approached in a mechanical way. We are dealing with individuals. That is something we must never forget.

Population Assistance and the UNFPA

If there is a need for caution and for extreme sensitivity at a national level, for example, in dealings between official government agencies and individual families, this must be equally true of the dealings between external agencies and the government and people of any particular country. The cardinal principle which has governed UNFPA's activities over the last five years is that the Fund should respond to countries' own assessments of their needs and priorities.

Of course, external aid should be used at the point and in the form where the effect it produces will be of the greatest benefit to the recipient country. There is, therefore, inevitably a creative dialogue between donor and recipient. Sometimes, perhaps, we should call it "creative tension". But I think it is fair to say that so far the Fund's programmes have been agreed to in an atmosphere of full confidence and mutual trust.

Perhaps I could give two or three examples of the way in which the Fund operates.

Many countries have now undertaken extensive family-planning and maternal child health programmes and the Fund actively assists in the furtherance and expansion of these services when needed by the countries. At the same time, our experience indicates that to be even more effective, these programmes must be related to the totality of the development effort. Family size is affected not only by income level but a complex of social and economic factors as well. The existence of adequate housing, education and health services, improvement in the status of women and the redistribution of income may be of crucial importance.

Population programmes must therefore be closely co-ordinated with—indeed they must form an integral part of—the total development effort. And this should be true of external aid as well. Certainly, the UNFPA—which as you know works in close relationship with the United Nations Development Programme and the Population Division of the United Nations—regards its activities not as an isolated operation but as an important part of the total mechanism of international cooperation.

Again, for the effective promotion of population programmes, you need above all a comprehensive and effective network of communication, information and education. Population programmes depend less on bricks and mortar than on the minds and hearts of men and women. A real and vital commitment is needed from everyone—this is the essential ingredient in the change of attitudes and change of values about which I spoke earlier. Communication is a two-way process. Individuals seldom become committed to programmes unless they first understand them. Governments and agencies cannot get them further committed and involved unless they adjust to what people ask and demand in return. This is the reason why the Fund has consistently committed a

considerable portion of its assistance to communication and education and has supported and initiated the creation of press and information institutions in the Third
World.

Yet again, we have found that the managerial requirements of population is another
vital area. Our experience has shown that countries deliver programmes better if,
besides a consensus on the validity of these programmes, there are adequate cadres of
trained personnel to execute them. The success of projects depends to a large extent on
the leadership and the quality of training that workers have before undertaking these
projects. But there is still a large gap in our knowledge of specific country training requirements and the training programmes that are necessary to meet the goals set in each
country. A better understanding and insight on this problem is needed. The Fund
regards this as one of the priorities over the coming years.

Growth of the Fund

I have given—I hope—some small insights into the operations of the Fund and its
underlying philosophy. But what, you may ask, does it all add up to? What is the
totality of the effort, as opposed to these individual glimpses?

Perhaps the word "explosion" is overworked, particularly at population meetings.
But we can truly say in all modesty, that these last five years have indeed seen an explosion within UNFPA, both in terms of activities and resources.

So far, the Fund has supported population activities in some 90 developing countries
and areas or almost all of the developing world. We have financed, or helped to finance
more than nine hundred projects covering such diversified fields as census taking, improvement of vital statistics registration, maternal and child health programmes, family planning services, communication and education, studies on law and population,
and training of personnel and institution building in many different areas. The largest
programme, amounting to US$ 40 million over five years, has very recently been for-
mulated and agreed upon with the Government of India. That our approach is also acceptable to donors is clear from the fact that they have increased in number from five
to sixty-seven—most of them developing countries—in a brief span of five years and
have made available in support of the Fund's activities nearly US$ 175 million over this
same period.

If you consider that the Fund in 1969 had less than three million U.S. dollars, you
will I am sure agree that I am justified in speaking of the "Population Fund
explosion".

I would not, however, like to give the impression that our coffers are bursting. Indeed the very reverse is the case. Current trends show a steadily increasing demand for
the Fund's services—at present we estimate that about US$ 500 million will be needed
for the period 1974-77 to respond to the most urgent requirements of the developing
countries for the Fund's support. This rapid expansion of demand on the Fund testifies
to the viability of the multilateral approach in this most sensitive of all matters, and to
the acceptability of the Fund's own procedures, developed as they have been in co-
operation with the countries for whom we work. Out of this co-operation, a

momentum has been generated, and an atmosphere has been created in which it is possible to think in terms of solutions to problems which at one time seemed insoluble. The question we put to you today is this: Will that momentum and that atmosphere be maintained?

The World Population Plan of Action

This brings me to the World Population Plan of Action. We cannot think just three years ahead—from 1974 to 1977—even though the sums involved may seem large enough in all conscience. We have to think thirty years ahead—and more.

That is why the World Plan of Action which will I hope be adopted by this Conference could be a milestone of the greatest importance. It could guide and reinforce the activities of the Fund and at the same time the Fund could play an important role in the realization of the Plan. The Plan will, of course, only take on its full meaning when it is translated into actual programmes at the international and national levels—programmes appropriate to the needs.

The draft Plan as it now stands is an affirmation of certain fundamental principles of action in the field of population. It emphasizes the different needs and priorities in the various parts of the world. In order to give the Plan substance, it will be necessary for countries and communities to design and put into effect their own national plans of action in accordance with their own special conditions, and with their own resources. We must never lose sight of the fact that the bulk of all development effort, and this includes the field of population, is undertaken by the developing countries themselves. The UNFPA, with the co-operation of the United Nations system and other inter-governmental and non-governmental bodies is ready to offer every possible assistance to enable countries to solve these problems themselves in the long run.

We need hardly add that the UNFPA can only discharge this historic task if those members of the international community who have supported us so generously in the past continue to support us even more generously in the future. If the concept of sharing in this "village world" means anything, if the concept of "sufficiency" means anything, then the goals and purposes of the World Population Plan of Action must surely be worthy of our utmost support—financial as well as moral.

I do not believe that it is possible to underestimate the challenge and the significance of this moment. To solve the population problems of countries will require more from us in a shorter time than ever before in the history of mankind. It will require a long-sustained effort without any guarantee that the final aim will be achieved. Yet without the effort, can there be any prospect for a just and peaceful world in the future? The ancient philosophers of Asia in their wisdom, stressed the need for a balance and harmony between man and his world. Without a sane and orderly approach to the problems of population, there can be no balance and no harmony.

A TRIBUTE TO GENERAL WILLIAM H. DRAPER, JR.

Statement at Memorial Service for General William H. Draper, Jr., Church Center for the United Nations, New York, 18 February 1975

I am honoured to be here to pay my respects to a friend—a very close friend and a special friend of the United Nations Fund for Population Activities.

In a sense, those of us gathered here to honour General Draper honour ourselves as well, for as a poet once said, we are a part of all that we have met, and General Draper is a part of all of us. Certainly his is a legacy we all share.

Several years ago at a conference in Japan, General Draper said, "I do not speak for my own government, nor for the United Nations Fund for Population Activities, nor the International Planned Parenthood Federation, although I work closely with all of them. I speak only for myself." But because his presence loomed large on every horizon, because he was the epitome of the concerned citizen in a sometimes apathetic world, he spoke not just for himself but for all organizations he felt responsible for. He was a kind of *amicus curiae*—a friend of the court—but in this case, his court was the world and he was a friend of the world. He spoke for all of us who have worked for years in the field of population. And, what we in this field have achieved—or will achieve—will be, I believe, a testament to the man and a monument to his memory.

We ask ourselves today, What kind of man was General Draper? How does one sum up a long lifetime of activity in a few sentences?

If I had to put my finger on one quality above all, I would cite his energy. He drove himself tirelessly, searching for solutions to the many problems that confront us. He always demanded more of himself than others. He traveled everywhere—China, India, to the countries of Africa and Latin America—anywhere at all, to look for allies, colleagues, ideas, good will, funds, and, above all, to learn how people in differing circumstances and traditions felt and thought and acted. He had an enthusiasm and an eagerness for the causes for which he worked that was unmatched among his colleagues. He was magnanimous in his praise, but critical when he felt criticism was necessary. He never claimed credit for his victories, but shared them with all of us—which, to me, was the mark of a true leader.

One of my last memories of General Draper took place on an evening before the World Population Conference. Some of his friends got together to help him celebrate his eightieth birthday. And it seemed right that it should take place in Bucharest on the eve of an event which he had worked so hard to bring about. For many, an eightieth birthday might seem to be an occasion for looking back. But for General Draper it was another new beginning. Not very many knew that he was an avid amateur magician and

315

he spent the evening entertaining us with his tricks. But the real magic of that performance was not in the tricks, but in the vision of his dialogue which he spoke with the vigor of a young man on his first job—of how he foresaw the countries solving their population problems not with millions but with billions of dollars he would help produce.

Indeed, he was the senior statesman of population. But he was also ageless. He made one completely forget his age as he himself forgot it. Too often we tend to believe that the youth of the world have a monopoly on idealism as well as the enthusiasm with which to pursue it. If that is true, then General Draper was perpetually young. Age was simply a state of mind that he refused to acknowledge. He had too many things to do and too many miles to travel.

In the days and years ahead, when the work we share becomes more and more complex and urgent, as we know it will, we shall miss General Draper's reliable presence. But we shall always remember with gratitude the years he was with us.

POPULATION ASSISTANCE SINCE BUCHAREST
Developing a Consensus on Priorities for Population Resources

Statement at the International Population Conference, Washington, D.C., 21 November 1975.

Last September, just over one year after the World Population Conference ended, the United Nations began a special meeting of the General Assembly in New York. Its purpose was to continue to debate and reach some conclusions on the distribution of the world's resources. During the debate, nearly all the major issues of our time were subjects of discussion—food, agriculture, industry, technology, international assistance, trade and financial arrangements. Yet there was one topic conspicuously absent from the agenda—population.

This struck some observers as odd, given the fact that the growth of the world's numbers was one of the major forces creating the pressure which brought the world's governments together in New York, given, too, the fact that growth in humanity's numbers will be a major force determining the future shape of the world. The absence of population from the agenda is significant, and it may be worthwhile to look at some possible explanations. We shall not achieve any neat solutions, but we may be able to gather some pointers towards possible courses of action in the future.

Population has always been a controversial issue. Was it still considered too controversial for such a delicately-balanced occasion as the September meeting? Or, on the other hand, was it felt that one year after Bucharest there was nothing left to talk about, that agreement in population matters was so complete that it was no longer a matter for discussion?

Of course, neither explanation is true. But there are elements of truth in each. First, the controversy. At Bucharest, it became clear that opposition to what was regarded as Western thinking on population was much deeper-rooted than had been thought. There was much suspicion of those who wished for decisive action to lower birth rates. On the other side, there were bitter accusations that the debate had been diverted from its real subject—population—into issues which were important in themselves but peripheral to the subject of the Conference. There was, in some cases, a mutual failure to see the point of view of the other side, so that a rather sterile debate seemed to be taking place between "development," on the one hand, and "population," on the other.

But even at the height of the controversy, voices could be heard saying that there was no need for such polemics. The World Population Plan of Action acknowledges as much, as least on paper. In the year since the Conference, although scattered gunfire

317

has been reported, that are some indications that the combatants are recognizing that they have several things in common. These include interest and concern in successful development programmes to meet the needs of growing populations, and involvement in population activities as a vital component of development strategy.

There have also been some practical developments which give room for some optimism. In some countries where "family planning" is not a respectable phrase, programmes including the provision of contraceptive services are taking root and growing strongly. In others, a new interest in the mechanics and the implications of population growth and distribution is clearly discernible since the end of World Population Year. And in the past year, as if to demonstrate the worldwide upsurge in interest in population matters, demands on the United Nations Fund for Population Activities have increased beyond our means to meet them, even with an increased budget.

One has a strange feeling about the whole controversy, that it is like the mythical beast which could only be seen from the corner of the eye. When looked at directly, it would vanish. That is not to say that it is harmless—but it does mean that we should be sure that we are looking at the issues as squarely as possible.

I see as a priority for all who are interested in population matters, the development of an intellectual consensus in which discussion can go on with a minimum of rancour and a maximum of understanding. The foundation for this lies in the practical consensus which already exists. India, Kenya and Cuba, to take these examples, all have programmes which involve the distribution of contraceptives on request as part of a package of health services for mothers and children. There can surely be rational discussion between and among them (and the donor countries and agencies) as to the nature and purpose of their activities.

From this discussion, it would probably emerge that these three countries have different views of their population situations, and different ideas about the function of population activities within their development framework. Indeed, it would make no sense if the priorities of three such different countries were the same—but different priorities do not necessarily mean disagreement if the same overall purpose is acknowledged.

There is, therefore, a challenge before this Conference. It is to pool our experience and our perceptions and arrive at a real consensus. The consensus must cover practical proirities and must give a basis for a common language, which will be free of the misunderstandings which have bedevilled us in the past.

Since I have posted the challenge, it is fitting that I should be the first to make my contribution to developing this consensus.

International assistance in population has grown enormously in recent years, and an attempt should now be made to see in a clearer light what its objectives should be. I know that most multilateral and bilateral bodies in this field are also struggling with the issue. I would like to share with you here the position as UNFPA perceives it—and invite your suggestions and comments.

In determining priorities for use of UNFPA's resources, the following main principles may be established.

(1) The various international strategies such as the World Population Plan of Action, the International Development Strategy for the Second Development Decade, and

the World Plan of Action focussing on integration of women and development should provide guidance for the activities of the Fund. These strategies, particularly the first one, suggest that an integrated development approach to population be applied. This would mean that population activities would be funded increasingly in conjunction with activities in health, education, rural development, community development and other programmes of economic and social development. One of the greatest challenges for us is to determine how population activities can be promoted effectively as an integral part of such development programmes and how population problems can be dealt with through socio-economic transformation.

We may state it as a fundamental condition of the Fund's assistance that population projects must be shown to be an integral part of development programmes. However, we must recognize that population assistance programmes have a specific purpose and responsibility, namely to support population activities rather than overall development programmes. The need is so tremendous that the Fund's own resources, which are still well below $100 million a year, and even the total of international population assistance, which is approximately $300 million annually, could easily be lost without trace if they were spread too thinly. Although it is impossible to maintain a clear-cut distinction between what are and are not population activities, the time has come, I believe, to determine more clearly what "population activities" we should in principle support. So far as UNFPA is concerned, population activities may cover population aspects of development including the characteristics, causes and effects of changes in fertility, mortality and morbidity as they affect developmental prospects and human well-being. The activities have conveniently been divided into collection of basic population data, population dynamics, population policy formulation and implementation, contraception and child spacing, and communication and education. Within these categories, a great deal of flexibility is required; an activity which has only marginal population content in one society may be vitally important in another. In each case, the particular conditions and concerns of the recipient country should be paramount. I should like your reaction to this concept of "population activities" as described.

(2) It will be increasingly necessary to concentrate our resources in supporting the most urgent requirements in those developing countries which have the greatest need in the population fields. This suggests that least-developed countries of which there are now 29—the majority in Africa—should be given preference in the allocation of the Fund's resources. In the present year, 14 per cent of our resources were allocated to these countries. We are considering the possibility of widening the concept of "least-developed countries" to take into account some of the demographic components. We may come up with a list of countries to be given preferential consideration, based upon appropriate criteria for levels of fertility and mortality as well as on per capita gross domestic product and balance of payments positions.

(3) The Fund should aim at building up as quickly as possible the ability of recipient countries to meet their own needs. Therefore, we may limit the period of our assistance, particularly in developing countries falling outside the group of the least-developed. At the end of the period, activities should be handed over to an organization within the country concerned. This suggests that high priority should be given to

supporting the following types of activity, in particular:

(a) human resource development through training programmes and transfers of the skills and technical know-how required in various types of population programmes;

(b) institution-building at the national level, particularly in the fields of population data collection and analysis, policy formulation and implementation of action programmes;

(c) operational research and pilot projects exploring innovative approaches to population problems and diffusion of experience gained; and

(d) strengthening of management capability to enable the recipient countries to execute their programmes effectively themselves and obtain the maximum benefit from assistance.

(4) Finally, in accordance with the spirit of Bucharest, special attention should be given to meeting the needs of disadvantaged groups such as the poorest among rural populations, underprivileged sectors in urban areas, and women in low income families. High priority should be given to action programmes designed to ensure population participation and explore all avenues for promoting community-based activities and involvement of all organized groups. This would mean that more attention should be given to women's participation in community development programmes and to enlisting women in communication activities.

Any good planning for the future has to deal with alternatives. In the Fund, we are tentatively considering three alternative levels of resource development over the next five years:

A low-funding level which will merely maintain the present programme level in real dollar value providing only for anticipated inflationary cost increases.

A medium-level funding which would enable us to provide assistance to developing countries within the concept of population activities outlined above but applying strict priorities on the types of assistance we could give.

Finally, a high-funding level which would allow the Fund to support programmes within the immediate area of population activities but, at the same time, allow us to be more flexible in supporting some activities falling on the fringe.

It is our intention to undertake a study, region by region, of the types of basic population programmes required to meet the needs of countries at various stages of development and to identify the types of programmes the countries need to deal with their major population problems in accordance with their own policies. In doing this we would try to take into account factors such as the availability of resources in the countries themselves, the priorities indicated by the regional consultations held after the Bucharest Conference and the availability of other sources of foreign aid.

Let me give a few illustrations of high priority areas of funding in the various regions:

In Asia and the Pacific, our assistance may concentrate on institutionalizing and implementing the population policies established in these countries. In family planning, greater attention should be devoted to the planning and design of programmes, to innovative approaches, to training, and to management and evaluation aspects.

In Latin America, high priority should be given to supporting the collection and analysis of the data required for population programme planning. In the field of fertility regulation, support for the maternal and child health approach may still continue to be of great importance, but other channels should be given increasing attention. Planning, managerial and training components of programmes also need support.

In West Asia, assistance in data collection through censuses, sample surveys, vital statistics and migration studies are important requirements as well as the inclusion of fertility services in integrated health programmes.

Finally, in Africa, continued assistance will be required to improve the weak population data base, particularly through support to census-taking in countries which have never taken a census or taken only one. Support for training of various kinds is another high priority area as well as assistance for delivery of fertility services in existing health services.

It is not for the Fund to set priorities for national programmes. This can only be done by the countries themselves. The priorities which I have mentioned have been developed as a result of our experience and contacts in developing countries and reflect as closely as possible a marriage of their needs and our ability to supply them.

From this brief survey of priorities, it can be seen that most of the needs expressed can best be supplied by close attention to the behaviour and the requirements of local groups. Family planning programmes in Asia, for example, have gone as far as they can in many places through conventional means. Further acceptance is to be won as a result of changes in ways of looking at the world among a large class of the rural poor. For this to happen, important changes in approaches to development are needed. In particular, closer contact is needed between development workers and the people with whom they work, and much closer involvement of the individual in development schemes, as an agent of development as well as an "acceptor."

Interestingly enough, development theory and practice is in general tending this way, towards greater involvement with the small, usually rural, group, family or village, towards the growth of self-reliance and towards the acceptance of development as an integrated whole.

Perhaps these changes in population and development thinking point to the conclusion that something is needed besides the New International Economic Order which was discussed so much this year. Just as the New International Economic Order will result in far-reaching changes in the structure of international relationships there may be a case for a New Human Order, which will give expression to the aspirations of the individual and the human desire to live in peace, in health and in happiness. Such a new order would provide the practical link between broad statements on the economic rights and duties of states and the specific safeguards of the Universal Declaration of Human Rights. It would make sense of human relationships just as the New Economic Order should make sense of international economic relationships.

I am convinced that such a New Human Order is emerging. It can be seen in the practical expression in development programmes of respect for the dignity of the individual and of belief in individual capacity for self-reliance and self-determination. It can be seen in the increasing recognition in practice of interdependence between citizens of developed and developing countries. It will be instrumental in putting an end to one-way development and in assisting the growth of an interchange between countries and continents, which will make possible a solution to the problems both of underdevelopment and over-development. It starts with the adoption of the sort of consensus about which I have talked.

I should like to propose as a further challenge to members of this Conference that they begin the consideration of the content of this New Human Order. For, interest in population is not a concern with the figures on a chart or the curves of a graph alone, however important they may be, but essentially an involvement with the future of humanity itself.

RESPONSIVENESS AND INNOVATION:
The Role of the UNFPA in a Restructured United Nations Economic and Social Programme

Statement to the Ad Hoc Committee on the Restructuring of the Economic and Social Sectors of the United Nations System, New York, 20 February 1976

I am very happy to have been given the opportunity to present my views to this Committee. Designing a new and effective structure to undertake the economic and social functions of the United Nations system is one of the most challenging tasks that has ever been given to any United Nations Committee. The complexities involved are indeed formidable, but your recommendations will be of the utmost importance because the impulse behind your efforts is the increasing concern with the need to fashion the instruments which would enable the United Nations system to be more efficient and responsive in dealing with the basic human problem of all—the problem of poverty.

Most of the global problems that nations have recently addressed themselves to with increasing seriousness and intensity—world hunger, the need for a new economic order, population growth, crime, environment, human settlements, the plight of Sub-Sahara Africa, unemployment, health, vestigial colonialism, not to mention the need for an appropriate and equitable role for women in social and economic affairs—ultimately and essentially are bound up with the question of poverty. I would like to make a few observations based on my experience in dealing with poverty in an Asian country, particularly the managerial problem arising from the first impact of the Green Revolution, as well as from my six years of experience at the United Nations Fund for Population Activities (UNFPA).

Every honourable delegate in this hall is aware that in dealing with poverty one of the resources that humanity is running out of is time. The demographic forecast is that before the United Nations is twice as old as it is now, there will be twice as many people as there are now who need to share the material resources of this planet as equitably as possible. It is becoming evident, therefore, that the needs of food, shelter, health and education must be attended to now before they become too heavy and complex to handle. We need to give a new dynamism to the common assault on poverty in countries that are threatened by intolerable need, along with a longer term strategy of reordering priorities in the use and distribution of depleting resources and of developing new resources.

At the Fund, which I have the honour of managing, we have always seen the question of population as a problem of people and it is my experience that whatever our shortcomings, people everywhere look to the United Nations as a symbol of hope in a threatening world. This faith should not go unrequited.

It is clear that the efforts now being made to restructure the United Nations apparatus concerned with economic development are intended to make the international community more responsive to human problems.

Responsiveness has been the key to the rapid growth of the UNFPA. Its responsiveness to the needs of the developing world is the reason for its acceptability by countries and communities—donors as well as recipients—with very different political and cultural attitudes towards the population question which, as we all know, is one of the most sensitive issues in human relationships, though, let me add, it is not a controversial matter as far as the Fund and the governments with which it works in partnership are concerned. Responsiveness is the reason for the readiness of developing countries, also, to contribute generously to the Fund's resources.

The experience of the Fund in substantiating this responsiveness in programmes of action may, therefore, be relevant and useful to this Committee.

International concern with the question of population was initiated in the United Nations system which in the early 50's responded to the need for assistance on population activities such as census taking, data analysis, and training and research on the relationships between population trends and social and economic factors.

However, for many years most international assistance for population was supplied by voluntary humanitarian organisations including the International Planned Parenthood Federation. The United Nations response to this need was on a very modest scale during those years but the needs of countries for multilateral assistance led to the Secretary-General to establish a Trust Fund in 1967 to strengthen the capacity of the United Nations to support demographic activities. The Trust Fund began with one contribution of one hundred thousand dollars which, with two more contributions, grew in a year to a million dollars. As demands for assistance grew, the Secretary-General transferred the Fund to the care of the Administrator of the United Nations Development Programme (UNDP) where it was lodged until such time as the General Assembly resolved to place it under its own authority. In 1969 when I had the privilege of being appointed Executive Director of the Fund, its available resources stood at two and a half million dollars. In six years the cumulative resources of the Fund increased to 250 million dollars—a hundred-fold growth.

The credit for this impressive growth must surely go to our major donors and to the developing countries themselves who have evinced great enthusiasm and interest in population activities. While the bulk of our contributions came from several major donors, I am glad to say that a large number of developing countries—at least sixty at present—have made contributions to the Fund. This, I think, is a measure of the almost universal response to the Fund's own responsiveness in managing the flow of United Nations assistance in the population field.

A brief account of certain institutional and other developments regarding the Fund is appropriate here. In 1971, the General Assembly recognized that the UNFPA had become a viable entity in the United Nations system and called upon the Fund to play a leading role in promoting population programmes (General Assembly resoulution 2815 (XXVI). In 1972, UNFPA was made a Fund of the General Assembly and the Governing Council of the UNDP was designated as the Governing Council of UNFPA, subject to the policies and conditions to be established by the Economic and Social Council. In fulfilling these functions, the Governing Council was asked to take into account the separate identity of the Fund (General Assembly resolution 3019 (XXVII).

The Fund's character has changed considerably from the time it was established as a Trust Fund. The aims and purposes of the UNFPA, as laid down in ECOSOC resolution 1763 (LIV), cover the following:

(a) to build up, on an international basis, with the assistance of the competent bodies of the United Nations system, the knowledge and the capacity to respond to national, regional, inter-regional and global needs in the population and family planning fields; to promote co-ordination in planning and programming; and to co-operate with all concerned;

(b) to promote awareness, both in developed and developing countries, of the social, economic and environmental implications of national and international population problems; of the human rights aspects of family planning; and of possible strategies to deal with them, in accordance with the plans and priorities of each country;

(c) to extend systematic and sustained assistance to developing countries at their request in dealing with their population problems, such assistance to be afforded in forms and by means requested by the recipient countries and best suited to meet the individual country's needs;

(d) to play a leading role in the United Nations system in promoting population programmes, and co-ordinate projects supported by the Fund.

Overall, the Fund is now supporting nearly 1400 projects, large and small, in more than 100 developing countries. To give you a few representative examples of the wide range of these activities I may point to the following projects:

Data Collection: In Africa and the Middle East over 20 census programmes, most of them being the first censuses taken;

Family Health: Programmes for family planning in India, Bangladesh and Tunisia and for maternal and child health purposes in Cuba and Mali;

Population Policy: Services to Planning Councils in El Salvador and Guatemala;

Research and Training: In addition to national programmes, UNFPA supports regional and interregional centres established in Accra, Bombay, Bucharest, Cairo, Santiago and Yaounde.

In addition to individual projects, the Fund supports large-scale multisectoral programmes in 20 countries in the developing world.

You will have gathered from what I have said so far that the UNFPA has been evolving from its meagre beginnings into something more than a dispenser of funds for programmes executed by institutions within the United Nations family. The Fund has the responsibility for funding and co-ordinating projects in nearly all the developing countries; it is an institution which governments as well as non-governmental organisations with special concerns and varying attitudes on population questions have begun to regard as a trustworthy, neutral and sensitive instrument for international assistance on this subject. It is also a bank of ideas on population and an innovator of techniques designed to respond to needs by delivering assistance quickly. UNFPA has thus been evolving into a worldwide population programme.

This development has been helped further by the activities undertaken in the context of the World Population Year, which was co-ordinated by UNFPA, and the World Population Conference in Bucharest, which was supported by UNFPA through financial contributions in the amount of $1.9 million, and through involvement in all the preparatory activities.

All population agencies, governmental as well as non-governmental, now recognise the leadership role given to the UNFPA by the General Assembly and the Economic and Social Council* and look to the Fund for giving substance, pace and direction to the World Population Plan of Action adopted by consensus by 135 states at the World Population Conference of 1974.

I would like to place on record that in carrying out this role I have always enjoyed an excellent working relationship with the Administrator of the UNDP and the Fund has benefited from the close co-operation with the worldwide network of the UNDP and its support services. I am also mindful of the important contribution made by the United Nations Population Division, the Specialised Agencies and other organisations in the development, with the Fund's support, of national programmes.

What are the principles and techniques which have made it possible for an institution within the United Nations system to attract this degree of support and trust from such a wide variety of governments and people in dealing with population growth, which involve the most sensitive and intimate of all human relationships? All UNFPA programmes have been governed by three cardinal principles:

We have recognised the sovereign right of nations to formulate and promote their own population policies and programmes.

We have recognised that the decision on family size is taken by individuals and they should have access to the information and means to determine the size of their family and spacing of their children, in exercise of their basic human rights, as set forth in various United Nations declarations.

We have recognised that the most important contribution of assistance is the development of self-reliance in the communities.

These are the considerations which led the UNFPA to introduce new managerial methods and techniques in delivering assistance. We have moved progressively in the past few years towards providing direct funding to government agencies or government-approved agencies.

We have responded to government criticisms of the costs, delays and eventual ineffectualness involved in the traditional system of supplying foreign expertise by increasingly turning towards reliance on local expertise and local programme managers and, where necessary, paid their salaries. The advantage of this innovation in dealing with such a culturally sensitive matter as population, not to mention the saving of time and expense, is self-evident. In line with this, we have provided funds for the purchase of local materials and equipment, wherever possible, and in a few cases, and in limited amounts, even for construction of facilities.

The reaction to these innovations and to their immediate impact on action programmes has been overwhelmingly supportive, and even laudatory to judge by the statements made by countries at meetings of our Governing Council and of the

*General Assembly resolution 2815 (XXIV) of 14 December 1971 and ECOSOC resolution 1763 (LIV) of 18 May 1973.

Economic and Social Council to which the Executive Director of the UNFPA now reports regularly.

It is worth noting here that the Fund's rapid evolution toward a worldwide population programme and the innovative techniques of delivering assistance amounting to 80 million dollars for 1975 have been achieved by a small staff of 50 professionals at headquarters and some 20 in the field. The UNFPA's administrative costs are thus very low but its record of delivery of programme assistance is high. Through the years, the Fund has remained financially viable by maintaining an unprogrammed reserve of $20 million, and by authorizing expenditure only on the basis of firm commitments for financial contributions.

From the tenor of the comments made by country delegations to our governing bodies on this record we believe that countries feel that the managerial techniques which have made it possible should be encouraged to gather increased momentum in that direction and that it would be damaging to hamper or deflect that process.

I would like to now to summarize the information I have given to you and to relate it to the reorganisation of the economic and social development efforts of the United Nations with which you are concerned in giving effect to the proposals for a new international economic order.

In determining the future structure dealing with development activities in the United Nations system it seems to me that four factors should be considered:

(a) the subject matter;
(b) the allocation of resources;
(c) the delivery of project services;
(d) the time frame of the activity.

With respect to population activities, I believe that the experience of the UNFPA in these four areas is clearly relevant.

First, population, as a concern of the international community, has now reached a pivotal point in its evolution, particularly with regard to the formulation of national policies and the implementation of national programmes.

Population as a significant factor and a distinct variable in the complex of elements related to the problems of poverty has taken a long time to manifest itself in public awareness and is only now beginning to be given due recognition. Almost every developing country has demonstrated its awareness of the population factor by expressing a national population policy or by establishing a government council, agency or ministry to deal with population. This is not the time to risk reversing that trend by obscuring the distinctness of the population imperative.

Second, the allocation of resources for population activities is subject to significantly different considerations from those guiding other development efforts. The UNFPA's Governing Council and the Economic and Social Council have repeatedly stated that resources for population assistance should not be allocated according to a worldwide formula as general development assistance is. Considering the sensitiveness of the population question and the varied nature of cultural and national approaches to it, population assistance policies must be responsive to the varying needs and requirements of different countries.

Third, the delivery of population programmes requires a constantly innovative and flexible approach. Our experience shows that the standard traditional methods of delivery have not been effective and that there is a danger that the imposition of a uniform method of delivery of development assistance would gravely affect the very high level of project implementation which the UNFPA has been able to achieve.

Fourth, the time frame of the increasing need for population assistance is finite. It is not a matter of numbers but a question of balance between population and accessible resources. I see the population programme in which the international community as well as individual countries are now engaged necessarily as a self-liquidating process if it is to be of any value.

What is needed is effective action NOW. We need to devise the institutions and programmes of action NOW, to deliver assistance as effectively as humanly possible, before the problem becomes impossibly big and complex to deal with in an orderly manner.

I have read the comments and recommendations of the Group of Experts on the Structure of the United Nations System with great interest and respect.

From the viewpoint of the Fund the assumption they make that economic development and population are related is wholly acceptable as it has always been a basic consideration in our activities. This assumption has been endorsed by consensus at the United Nations World Population Conference and is a guiding principle in the World Population Plan of Action.

The Committee's recommendation that a Director-General be appointed to guide the overall economic and social programmes of the system recognises the increased importance that needs to be given to the United Nations concern with the problems of poverty which I referred to in my opening remarks.

I congratulate the experts on their perspicacity in placing emphasis as they have done on the need to simplify the system and make it more efficient through such well-known and time-tested means as drawing together related elements under a unified direction. I am sure they have considered, as I have, that there are inherent dangers in such a course of action, however well-intentioned and schematically unassailable it might appear to be. One danger is that related parts of the whole which by their very purpose, their particular stage of evolution, and their essential distinctness in the nature of their work and their mode of operation, are clearly effective and so assessed by the countries whose needs they seek to serve, may lose their essential character and usefulness in being too tightly or inappropriately integrated into a general system.

In the effort to avoid duplication of effort through an integration of related but different functions, effectiveness comes from establishing a clear definition of responsibilities and boundaries of functions and not by integration for its own sake.

The rate of acceleration of the growth of contributions and the number of contributors to the UNFPA especially at a time of economic restraint when other fund-raising efforts have been experiencing difficulty is a clear indication that countries view population assistance as a distinct and urgent concern. Consolidation of the resources now being made available for population assistance with other funds in the name of simplification—which, in itself, may be a good thing—or of efficiency—which is, in itself, a good thing—may not be effective in this case. I fear that the momentum achieved by the Fund in raising contributions not only in the developed countries but also in the developing countries for this separate activity of evident concern to them, may be irretrievably lost, and what is worse, an irreversible downward process may start. It is necessary to realize that it is not just a question of keeping distinct accounts but one of maintaining a clear profile.

With respect, I suggest for the reasons I have stated here today, that the UNFPA is such a special case and that it should be regarded as such in your consideration of effective changes in the system. I, therefore, suggest that it should be treated as a distinct programme, as its evolution warrants.

The rational, not to say natural, outcome of that process of evolution is that the Fund should become fully operational in order to be as effective as it could be in the delivery of population assistance in a new international economic order.

To provide the necessary legislative and operational links with the system that will emerge from this exercise in restructuring I suggest that we should go along with the links provided by the countries through the resolutions of the Economic and Social Council and our own governing body. The head of this population programme which I have in mind would accordingly report to the Economic and Social Council and the proposed Operations Board, in consultation with the principal officer responsible for the overall direction of assistance and development —presumably to be called the Director-General, and would also participate in any consultative or advisory institutions which may be established to co-ordinate the developmental activities of the United Nations and its specialised agencies.

This suggestion, in my view, will ensure that the growing concern with population matters is not relegated to a position in the new scheme which might imperil its evolution and retard the dynamic drive it has shown in its rapid growth.

I have been detailed in my description of the growth of the Fund, and specific in my recommendations about what I consider to be its appropriate place in a reorganised United Nations system.

Six years have passed since, I, with my colleagues, undertook the management of the UNFPA. Its manner of delivering assistance was designed to establish within the United Nations system a Fund that would be responsive both to the developed and developing countries not just for the next few decades but for as long as the United Nations considers the problem of people crucial. This time perspective we have always considered vital in the building of the institution. And we equally realize that eventually the management of the Fund will pass to other responsible hands. Our view on reorganization was, therefore, always governed by this higher purpose—to keep the institution viable beyond our presence.

I wish to assure the Distinguished Members of the Committee that the recommendations I have made for the future of the UNFPA have been made without regard to my own future. Whatever that might be, whoever is given the resposibility for managing the UNFPA, I am convinced that its best value is to be obtained by maintaining a co-ordinated link to development as a distinct programme within the United Nations system.

INTERURBAN MAN:
The Dynamics of Population in Urban and Rural Life

Statement at the United Nations Conference on Human Settlements, Vancouver, Canada, 2 June 1976

This conference continues the great international debate on aspects of the human condition which began with the Stockholm Conference on the Environment in 1972. But it is unique in its organization and structure; and in its proclaimed intention of being action-oriented. I am honoured to be invited to make a contribution to the Conference on behalf of the UNFPA.

From the great migrations of whole peoples across Asia and Europe to the massive influx of immigrants to this continent, human history up to this point has been one of movement.

Gradually, though, the nature of movement has changed. The great migrations are past and nomads and seasonal migrants are becoming fewer. In our own age movement has been from poorer parts of the world to richer and from country to city.

The great ebb and flow of populations across continents has become a magnetic field polarised on the great cities. Paradoxically, as man has become more mobile, his settlements have become more concentrated.

Examining the paradox, its true nature becomes clear. Improved transport and communications have reduced the need for personal contact in order to carry on the business of living and made feasible greater distances between people. So we see, at the same time that conurbations are bigger than ever before, a tendency to live and work away from the centre, and an enormously increased mobility between centres. But the inexorable movement from rural to urban goes on, so that by the end of this century, man will be predominantly an urban animal, no longer dependent directly on the land for his living, nor yet on the great metropolis. We might call him Interurban Man.

All this implies in the course of a few generations a phase shift in human perception of the world. Our literature, art and music, whole systems of culture and values derive from a basic connection with the land which provides our food and shelter. The culture and values of inter-urban man will have to cope with still essential but indirect connection with the earth which gives him being, and with groups of people, sometimes in large numbers, with whom his connection is similarly indirect.

These problems are not new to industrial cities, but they show few signs of resolution—perhaps because the essential change in perception is not yet complete. There is a tendency still to think of the city-dwellers as an aberration, even among city-dwellers themselves, and an unconscious refusal to learn to handle the reality of inter-urban life. The facts must be faced; people will not return to the land in any significant numbers unless taken by force, and the tendency to congregate will in all probability continue. There are good reasons for this—cities and towns are vital sources of energy, ideas,

330

technologies and artifacts. They offer a breadth and depth of experience which is not available anywhere else. They are the powerhouses of our civilization.

A new perception of cities and towns requires a complementary change in our view of rural areas. Rural people are neither hopelessly backward peasants as some impatient developmentalists have seemed to imply, nor are they repositories of all that is valuable in our collective life, as some romantics have claimed. The land on which they live and work is the essence of human survival, and the environment in which they live is a precious heritage which once destroyed can never be replaced. The vitality of the rural areas no less than of the city is part of the balance which we must seek.

The shift in perception which is now taking place and of which this conference is a sign, implies first, that in future urban life will be the norm and, second, that the life-force of a country or region is less likely to be a single great city than a series of urban centres. The shift is marked by a change in approach to the problems of urbanization and industrialization. There is an increasing emphasis on rural development; a movement away from vast schemes towards more modest projects more firmly rooted in the society from which they spring, and in general a swing away from what has been called "giantism" to programmes manageable on a human scale.

In the area with which the Population Fund is concerned, this is certainly the case. Population programmes of whatever kind have been proved most effective when coupled with the concern and involvement of the community. Our experience has been duplicated in agricultural development, in health care—and in human settlements.

Management of this kind of development requires a special expertise; it requires the creation of an administration which is flexible and sensitive enough to respond to local and individual needs while executing the purposes of a broader plan. It requires above all the willingness, from the political leadership to the lowest administrative level, to go through the long, slow and sometimes painful processes of gaining and implementing consent.

Given that this is the way in which the theory and practice of development is moving, how does international assistance to the process fit in? The same qualities of responsiveness and flexibility must be shown in aid agencies as in national bureaucracies, in respect for the wishes and needs of governments as for those of local communities. This is the way in which we have attempted to work in the UN Population Fund; with, it seems, a certain amount of success, if the demands now being made on us are a criterion.

Given the number and nature of the agencies both multilateral and bilateral now offering assistance in development, specific demands are placed upon them by the changing concepts of development. We are now required to work in co-operation with many different sources of financial and technical help, in order to produce a regulated form of development. The new development will not permit of single-agency, isolated activities except in isolated cases.

UNFPA is already active in many aspects of human settlements and is extending its means of co-operation with local and international development agencies. So many aspects of development touch upon population considerations that it has been a major concern of the Fund to establish priorities for the use of our limited resources. We have therefore determined a core programme including the principal aspects of population activities and are suggesting for discussion means by which these activities can be combined productively with other areas of development work.

Thus the Fund supports collection and analysis of basic data on population growth and movement and programmes developed on the basis of this data designed to affect fertility, mortality and mobility. But these areas are so vast that we must further refine our priorities so that in a community-based health scheme, for example, the Fund may support that part directly concerned with fertility; or in an urban renewal project the establishment of services for registration of vital statistics.

Establishing priorities does not mean limiting scope. The Fund is concerned as we always have been with the totality of development, believing that only in this way can the purposes of population programmes be fulfilled. I should like to recommend that in discussing action upon the creation and development of human settlements, governments should consider population policy as a basis upon which many decisions may be built; and that they bear in mind that development decisions are taken in the end not by governments or international institutions, but by millions of individual men and women. They are both the reason for which development decisions are taken and the resources by which they are made reality.

POPULATION AND THE NEW INTERNATIONAL ECONOMIC ORDER

Statement at the University of Michigan, Ann Arbor, Michigan, 12 January 1977

When the World Environment Conference convened in Stockholm in 1972, it proved to be only the first round of a general international debate that has been going on ever since. We have discussed food, population, industrialization, women, trade, energy, employment, housing and the Law of the Sea at an unprecedented series of world meetings, with two Special Sessions of the General Assembly of the United Nations and a year-long round of discussions, the so-called "North-South Dialogue", in between. But, whatever the venue and whatever the subject ostensibly being discussed, the underlying theme has been the same—the nature of the relationship between the industrialized countries and the developing. This is the Great Debate of the seventies, the outcome of which is likely to determine the shape of our world for generations to come.

The publicity surrounding the population issue in the late sixties and early seventies culuminated in the World Population Year and Conference in 1974. Since then, although population has received its measure of notice in world discussions, there has been little substantive discussion of the issue as part of the New International Economic Order debates. This has come as a surprise to some observers, who have correctly pointed out that these discussions have been made necessary in part by population growth in the developing countries—virtually all of Africa, Asia and Latin America—as well as by disproportionate increases in consumption by the slower-growing populations of Europe, Japan, Australasia and North America.

To those of us who have been embroiled in the debate during the seventies however, the absence of population from the debates of the New International Economic Order was not such a shock. The size and rate of growth of a nation's people have always been highly sensitive matters. Historically, governments' preoccupation has been with increasing populations—a growing population was a clear sign of prosperity, of freedom from hunger and disease, and was a source of strength against potential enemies. This perception of a strong positive correlation between population growth, economic development and security persisted in Europe and America until quite recently and still colours attitudes to population growth elsewhere. In the United Nations, emphasis on the principle that population size and rate of growth were a matter for national decision inhibited concerted international action on population matters for many years. The World Population Conference debated this principle for two weeks, during which ample evidence was provided that population remained a highly sensitive topic of debate. At the time, sufficient agreement was reached to allow the impression that the subject had been dealt with adequately. It is hardly surprising, therefore, that

333

the subject should not appear on the agenda in the recent discussions.

At the same time, it is clear that most governments have accepted the view that in their own national circumstances there is a negative correlation between population growth and development and that a long-term strategy of reducing the birthrate is not only prudent but a necessary part of economic and social programmes. There are still a few countries the human resources of which are insufficient to exploit their natural potential, but these are a tiny proportion of the world's population. Effectively there is a consensus on population among developing nations.

We have now arrived at the curious position where there is an international consensus in a highly sensitive area of policy, but few internationally-accepted quantitative goals. Although there has been a considerable shift in opinion even in the two years since the World Population Conference at Bucharest, the World Population Plan of Action remains the main evidence of world agreement on population—and that document is less than specific in several key areas.

The separation of population matters from the debate on the New International Economic Order results in precisely the opposite of that "integration of population and development" which was the expressed desire of nearly every nation attending the World Population Conference two years ago. The remaining areas of debate in population cannot all be resolved within the context of the debate on the New International Economic Order; nevertheless, it is difficult to imagine a New International Economic Order such as the third world countries seek without some explicit recognition of the importance of population issues.

Moreover, it is possible to see that agreement may be achieved, because many of the staunchest supporters of the New International Economic Order are now also the most effective practitioners of a policy of limiting population growth. Let me give some examples of what I mean by this. First, in several countries, with governments of widely differing political persuasions, great progress has been made towards building into health, nutrition, education and other development programmes, the capability of giving advice and delivering the means of limiting fertility. The era of contraception delivered only by doctors in hospitals or clinics is passing; in most countries contraception is now routinely taken to the villages where most of the third world's population lives, and into the increasingly crowded urban areas, by a variety of carriers—midwives, health visitors, housewives recruited for the purpose, and increasingly through commercial outlets. Usually their functions are not limited to, or even consist principally of, delivering family planning.

Second, at the planning level, building different population growth curves into planning models has become increasingly sophisticated and there are now several different models in operation which indicate not only how different rates of growth will affect policy decisions in other areas, but also how policy decisions will affect population growth. Although problems remain in giving practical effect to this theoretical understanding, this is an effective acknowledgement of the dual importance of population in development.

Thirdly, we at the United Nations Fund for Population Activities are finding that we have little expertise to add to what is already known about the successful delivery of population programmes; in fact our colleagues in government are increasingly instructing us on what sort of assistance is most effective in what circumstances. Increasingly, also, they are requesting our assistance in programmes bearing on the integration of population and development, one of the main points of agreement at the World Population Conference.

Finally, under steadily increasing pressure of population on resources, many countries are contemplating or have implemented stronger measures, both direct and indirect, to slow population growth. Incentives and disincentives of varying types and degrees of severity are increasingly being used to influence couples in the direction of smaller families. Many countries have examined legal provisions affecting family size and have acted to raise the minimum age at marriage, provide contraceptive services through workplaces and legalize sterilization, to take some random examples. The new emphasis on sterilization is worth looking at more closely, because it underscores the extent of the change that has taken place in recent years.

Sterilization has been of minor importance until recently. Those accepting it, whether men or women, tended to be aging, with a complete family of several children. It was seen perhaps as an interference, permanent and irreversible, with the essence of manhood or womanhood. Despite the difficulty of reversibility which remains for most people in developing countries, acceptance has increased considerably in recent years. Where it has been promoted by family planning campaigns, it has in general met with little opposition. In particular, the number of vasectomies has increased so rapidly that a reservoir of untapped demand must be assumed. Techniques are improving all the time, improving speed and safety and with less inconvenience to the life of the individual.

The effect of increasing emphasis among developing countries on population programmes can be seen in increasing demand for the services of the United Nations Fund for Population Activities. We have responded to this changing pattern by sharpening definitions of our own areas of competence. We have determined that the United Nations Fund for Population Activities should continue using its resources to support population activities rather than becoming involved in assisting overall development, the needs of any one area of which could easily absorb the Fund's total resources and more. In this context, the UNFPA has conceptualized a programme of "core" activities. The main areas of this "core programme" are: basic population data collection and analysis, formation and implementation of population policy, including family planning and population redistribution, population education and training, and applied research and communication activities. At the same time, in order to adhere to the integrated approach recommended by the World Population Plan of Action, the Fund encourages support by other development assistance agencies for the development activities vital to the success of population programmes. We also encourage other organizations to include population components in their development assistance, and in some instances joint funding may be arranged between the United Nations Fund for Population Activities and other development aid organizations.

Another general principle guiding the allocation of our resources is to assist countries with particularly urgent population problems. The lack of population data in many developing countries is a problem here, but estimates on population growth, fertility, infant mortality and population density on arable land are generally available.

They indicate the main population problems and, to some extent, the level of development and welfare. Various threshold levels for these demographic indicators have been explored using the most recent information available. Furthermore, in order to concentrate the Fund's scarce resources where they are likely to contribute most, consideration has also been given to the country's population and its economic condition as indicated by national income per capita.

On this basis, we are helping to arrive in population at a concentration of effort which might perhaps serve as a pointer for similar definition in other areas of development.

These measures and others like them are based on a realistic appraisal of the opportunities for genuine development in most third world countries within the constraints of available resources. The cost of the two most vital elements—food and energy—is continually rising, and though most developing countries are not yet approaching the limit of the theoretical "carrying capacity" of their territories, very few are in a position to make the investments necessary to exploit them.

The difficult problem now facing third world governments is how to convey these perceptions to the people who will make the ultimate decisions on population—those billions of ordinary men and women who are not involved in the debate about the greater issues of world economics or the availability of resources, but in whom lies the only responsibility for balanced, just development.

One group of means of conveying these perceptions, direct and indirect encouragement of family planning, has already been discussed and is in operation is most countries. Coercive measures, as an extension of these policies, have been widely discussed but not yet given legal sanction. Adoption of such measures, if they are sanctioned, will have to be regarded in the light of the Declaration of Human Rights and other international agreements endorsing the right of freedom of choice in fertility. The fact that they are even being considered attests to the severity of the pressures under which governments find themselves; but it is worth pointing out that sufficient emphasis on persuasive policies may well make coercive measures unnecessary. If it is sincerely desired to avoid coercion and all the complications which would ensue, support for persuasive policies should be intensified in developed and developing countries alike and in the United Nations, and every effort made to ensure that they succeed.

The second approach is less direct. It has been shown that fertility decline may set in, whether or not family planning programmes are in operation, at a much lower level of income than was needed for the European "demographic transition" of the nineteenth century—provided certain conditions are met. These include access to housing, health, education and employment—the whole package that constitutes a materially secure and hopeful existence. At the moment and for the foreseeable future in many parts of the world, these conditions are not fulfilled, and this to my mind poses the greatest threat to attempts to bring down birth rates.

Conventional approaches to development have largely failed to produce these conditions, because they were not intended to. Now, however, there is a new spirit abroad, perhaps best summed up by the phrase "meeting basic needs". This is the other face of the New International Economic Order—an internal restructuring and redistribution within developing countries, a direct attack on poverty and its causes. With it, attempts to lower population growth rates will have an excellent chance of success. Without it, programmes of contraception may well be regarded by the mass of the third world's poor as at best irrelevant to their needs, and at worst a crude attempt to eliminate the problem by eliminating the people.

The international community has a responsibility to assist both sides of programmes for reducing birth rates—directly through population assistance by supporting such bodies as the United Nations Fund for Population Activities and indirectly through conventional aid and other methods of easing the transition from massive poverty and high rates of population growth to moderate levels of both income and fertility.

Recent attempts to model the future of the world economic system underscore the necessity for this holistic approach. The second report to the Club of Rome and the Leontief study for the United Nations show that both internal and international restructuring of political and economic systems will be necessary if a real impact is to be made on the problems of poverty and population. The Tinbergen report, *Reshaping the International Order,* puts it in this way:

"New perceptions of population growth have shown us that there can be no single solution to balancing birth and dealth rates. High birth rates clearly have a cause and effect relationship with poverty, illiteracy and under-development. To curb high growth rates calls for a concerted attack on poverty, unemployment, illiteracy, hunger, malnutrition and disease; and for the provision of essential social services as well as population limitation measures".

To sum up—a serious attack on the problem of rapid population growth is clearly a priority with most governments of the developing world. Many have instituted or are considering strong measures towards this end. It is equally clear, however, that a concerted attack on poverty must be made at the same time if population programmes are to have a chance of success. This will require action from both developed and developing countries. Within the third world, the international responsibilities of countries demand that population growth be lowered, but to do that they must prove themselves responsive to the needs of their peoples. For the developed countries, international responsiveness implies assistance both direct and indirect for the assault on poverty and population growth rates. This carries its own imperative for the internal policies of the developed; for many years now their consumption of resources has been rising far faster than population growth rates warranted. The time has come for the countries of the northern hemisphere to curb their prodigality, to look for ways in which they can conserve resources while still providing an adequate standard of life for their peoples and to assist the peoples of the third world in meeting their own needs. This is their internal responsibility, to be met by each country in its own way.

Population policy is a long-range strategic weapon. Its effects are felt not immediately but a generation hence. But to be effective it must be launched now; and to have its maximum effect on the basis of international discussion and agreement on problems and policies. This would not in the least detract from the importance assigned to other aspects of development, food, employment, industrialization and the rest, but would add the missing element, the factor of people.

For some time now, the United Nations Fund for Population Activities has acted as "honest broker" between developed and developing countries in population questions,

I.P.A.—Z

wherever possible assisting each group to discover the problems, needs and possibilities of the other and to move towards a consensus on this vital question. The importance of the task in which we have been engaged is shown by the steep increases in the Fund's resources and in requests for these resources in recent years. The developments which I have outlined show that there is a basis for discussion of the content and direction of population activities as part of the debates on the New International Economic Order. No one doubts that such an agreement would add to the progress already made in reshaping the international order, and might show the way for agreement in other areas. It is time that such an accord was reached.

Let me ask a question of the distinguished members of this audience. I hope I have shown how wide an area of agreement on population there is in practice. The question is "What can the academic community do to secure recognition of this agreement in discussions on the New International Economic Order?"

THE IMPLICATIONS OF CHANGE

Statement for the 1977 David Owen Memorial Lecture at the David Owen Centre for Population Growth Studies, University College, Cardiff, United Kingdom, 2 June 1977.

To every generation before our own, an increasing population was a sign of national strength. To friends and enemies alike, it demonstrated prosperity and well-being, and the defeat, however temporary, of disease and famine.

The position today is almost entirely reversed. Nations with high population growth rates are coming to perceive them as a liability rather than an asset, and nearly two-thirds of the world's population live under governments which desire a lower rate of population growth. In the developing countries, where incomes are low and population growth rates high, the figure is four out of five.

The reasons for this radical alteration in our view of the world are too complex for detailed examination in the course of a brief lecture. The central fact may be said to be that despite enormous efforts and solid economic and social achievements, in most developing countries the needs of growing populations have not been met. Meanwhile, in the industrialized countries where population growth is low, living standards are generally high. In the midst of a world of apparent plenty, poverty remains the rule for the vast majority of people in the developing world.

Poverty, and everything that it implies—insufficient food, inadequate housing, ill health, poor education, little comfort and less hope—has complex connections with population growth. The persistence of high rates of growth and low incomes has brought shifts in thinking in many areas of economic and social life besides population—so much so that this period may well be seen by historians of the future as one not of temporary disturbance but of fundamental change in human institutions.

My aim in this lecture will be to describe briefly the elements of this change as they affect population and to indicate courses of action which may enable us to make the transition successfully.

First, the facts of population growth. We are all, I take it, familiar with the history of world population growth—how it took until the middle of the nineteenth century to reach one billion, how population had doubled by 1930 and has now doubled again.

The most recent projections of United Nations demographers show world population growth continuing at its present rate—just under two per cent per annum—until about 1985, then beginning a slow downward trend. Growth in numbers will, of course, continue, but at a declining rate and will eventually stabilize. Stabilization will take place at different times in different regions during the course of the next century. The best estimate is for a stable world population of about 12 billion in 2075. That is to say, we and our descendants must be prepared to create conditions permitting a healthy life for between 10 and 15 billion human beings who will probably inhabit the earth.

These projections take full account of the likely level of success in bringing down fertility rates by means of family planning programmes and economic and social development. They are not pessimistic, simply realistic, and what they say represents the most important single fact about the age in which we live. We know, as nearly as we can know anything, that world population will double again and we can be fairly sure that growth will continue for nearly a hundred years.

The new era will be one of gradually slowing world population growth. But this growth, as we know, is badly skewed. An annual rate of well over two per cent in the developing countries is projected by the United Nations for the period 1975-80, while in the industrialized countries the rate will be considerably lower than one per cent. Growth in developing countries takes place on a base of 2.9 billion people and will add more than three hundred and sixty million people in those five years—or more than the total population of Latin America.

These essential facts of population growth should be the most effective means of persuading us that we are in an era of epochal change, and a spur to our efforts to meet its challenge. For a start, we should redouble our efforts to achieve slower population growth sooner than the projections indicate, by all the means at our command.

The result of unprecedented population growth and the deficiencies of conventional development strategies both in slowing it down and turning it to productive purposes has been to challenge conventional approaches.

Conventional thinking held, on the one hand, that increasing populations would become a resource for future growth, and, on the other, that the rate of population increase would be slowed by the application of modern techniques of contraception.

Implicit in this thinking was the assumption that both national and international economic and social systems were susceptible to rapid and exogenous change. But the international economic structure has not worked for the benefit of developing nations nor have national economies been geared to the needs of the poor. So, just as the present international economic system is now felt by many to be inadequate to achieve equity in global economic relationships, the validity of internal economic and social strategies is also being called into question. In both cases, the matter is seen as one for political decision.

On the international level, the perception takes the form of a series of discussions, of which the most important are probably those centring on the demand of the developing countries for a new international economic order. Nationally, a variety of alternatives to conventional development thinking have emerged.

In particular, the thinking which linked population growth and economic development in a linear way—more population growth would mean less growth in income per capita—was by the end of the sixties already giving way in many countries to a broader view which connected population with each of several other factors in development and which saw demographic growth as only one of many population issues.

Since the United Nations Fund for Population Activities started operations in 1969, this change in thinking has accelerated. Over the eight years of the Fund's existence, we have become and been made aware of the depth and complexity of population issues.

Let me give a few examples of what I mean.

First, we have had evidence of the growing urgency with which population is viewed. When be began operations, we found only a few countries interested in obtaining population assistance. As global consciousness has risen, so have the number of requests. Today there are few developing countries which have *not* asked for our support; the ideological objections which seemed so important only a few years ago have been transcended.

This trend has become more marked during the eight years of the Fund's existence; the urgent sense of purpose which has become visible in population programmes is one of the more remarkable phenomena of our times. Eighty-two per cent of the developing world's population is now covered by government population programmes. In response to a recent United Nations survey, which covered 114 developing countries, ninety-five governments expressed concern over extremely or substantially unacceptable spatial distribution of their population. Severe or serious levels of morbidity and mortality were viewed as a problem by 79 governments. Sixty-nine countries believe that the current rate of natural population increase imposes severe constraints on the attainment of development objectives.

This growing urgency reflects a concern, not merely with population growth as such, but with the elements of population growth, distribution and structure, and with how they may be affected by programmes in all areas of population and development. At the United Nations Fund for Population Activities, for example, we have now committed just over half of our available resources to family planning. The remainder of our work has been in the collection and analysis of basic population data, the dynamics of population growth, the formation of policy, in research, and in communication and education.

Second has been the rapid acceptance of population as a vital component in the machinery of development. For example, early family planning programmes were designed for the well-being of women; later, their purpose was eventually to slow population growth according to the linear connection made between population and economic growth which I mentioned earlier. As such, they had only limited impact and acceptance in developing countries. From the beginning, the Fund has assumed that population covers a far wider area than family planning, that population growth had to be seen within the context of each country's economic and social circumstances, and that programmes should reflect national needs. On this basis, we have seen the upsurge in requests which I have mentioned. As the World Population Conference in 1974 showed, it is only when population is seen as something separate from other development activities that it is unacceptable.

Countries which only a few years ago took the attitude that intervention was not only unnecessary but probably harmful to development now have extensive programmes. Some are avowedly undertaken with the intention of lowering population growth rates as a precondition of development, as in Mexico; in others, for instance several African countries, population policies are aimed at reducing mortality and morbidity and increasing the life expectancy of the people.

My third point has to do with population as part of the general approach to development. Thinking in developing countries is re-examining theories of economic growth *per se.* More attention is being given to meeting the needs of the population at large by the provision of services such as health, education and employment, both to improve their well-being and to realize their potential as producers.

It has been noted that the problem of balancing economic resources and population growth can be solved effectively in countries where the benefits of development most closely answer the basic needs of human beings.

In the State of Kerala in India, for example, population growth has slowed without the traditional accompaniments of rising income and urbanization. Although Kerala is poor, even compared with neighbouring Indian States, its birth and death rates are both much lower than the Indian average; infant mortality is half the national rate and life expectancy is fifteen years higher. Development programmes have promoted—in addition to the traditional methods of family planning—community health care, secure land tenure, concern for the status of women and their involvement in development, and a high level of participation among both men and women in the political and administrative process.

These are the essentials of a secure and dignified existence—the "basic needs" of human beings. It has frequently been observed that lower fertility goes along with lower infant mortality, higher literacy, and opportunities for women to be employed outside the home, among other factors. The "basic needs" strategy blends these elements into a coherent whole.

My fourth point will serve to illustrate the third. Eight years ago, little attention was paid to the widespread availability of contraceptive methods. Yet we know that unless contraceptives are made available to people in urban and rural areas, family planning programmes are hardly likely to succeed. The trend is to bring family planning services closer to clients by using local groups and people, by using networks already in place and integrated with the culture of their societies. Already, in many countries, contraceptive services are now routinely taken to the villages, where most of the third world's population lives; and into the increasingly crowded urban areas, by a variety of carriers—midwives, health visitors, housewives recruited for the purpose, and, increasingly, through commercial outlets. Indonesia is one of the many developing countries which has adopted the community-based approach on a large scale. In Java and Bali, some 27,000 village pill and condom depots have been established. Women needing supplies come to the distribution centre—frequently a private home—or attend meetings of the mothers' clubs *(Apsari)* which have been set up or have grown out of existing clubs.

Also, the range of contraceptive methods available has widened considerably since the Fund came into existence. Eight years ago, for example, few people discussed sterilization on a large scale as a serious option; since then several million voluntary vasectomies and tubectomies have been performed. Though we have seen the consequences of over-enthusiasm in this area, the fact remains that voluntary sterilization is very much a part of the contemporary scene. Medical termination of pregnancy is also becoming more widely available.

As demand for and the volume of UNFPA assistance has increased, so has the proportion of resources for population programmes which comes from recipient countries themselves—and this is my fifth point. Developing countries with quite small national inputs only a few years ago are now operating greatly expanded programmes for which most of the funding is internal. External assistance, though it has increased in size, is now a small proportion of the total. A good example of this process is Tunisia where a national programme has been in operation since 1966 and under the direction of a semi-autonomous Government agency since 1973. For the period of 1974 to 1978 the national family planning programme has a budget of $18,000,000 of which half is direct counterpart to family planning-related activities for which UNFPA has provided $4,000,000. However, the Government's total appropriation for family programmes during the period 1979 to 1981 is expected to be $35,000,000 of which UNFPA will again be providing $4,000,000.

Sixth, the placing of family planning programmes within the government structure has reflected their changing position. Eight years ago, family planning programmes undertaken for demographic reasons were normally vertical structures, though connected to health ministries. Today, family planning programmes, whether interventionist or not, are more likely to be integrated in the wider context of maternal and child health care, which is itself part of the total package of health services. Indeed, family planning is increasingly seen as a social welfare service.

Seventh, we have experienced a remarkable increase in the volume and nature of population education and information. Eight years ago, if it existed at all, population education was likely to cover only reproduction and the basic techniques of family planning. Today education and information is offered to children and adults, both inside and outside formal education, in churches, workplaces and health centres. It is likely to cover not only human sexuality and reproduction, but the economic and environmental impact of population growth. It may also cover home economics, hygiene, and nutrition. Kenya's Planning for Better Family Living Programme includes all these elements in an integrated approach to population and development at the level of the village.

Eighth, the knowledge has taken root that censuses, surveys and analysis of the resulting data are the indispensable basis for planning population or any other kind of development programme. When we started operations, many of the newly-independent countries, particularly in Africa, had never taken censuses. When a catastrophe such as the Sahel drought occurred, for example, governments were quite unprepared for the number of refugees arriving in their capitals. Today fourteen African countries have completed their first censuses, and we have been able to help many others in the analysis of census data—an art in itself, but an essential link between the raw data and its use as a planning tool.

Finally, changing perception of the significance of population activities has drawn together the strands of policymaking and implementation in this area. Central government bodies in eighty-three developing countries now have the responsibility of integrating population factors with development planning.

It is possible to discern, in the changes which have already taken place, and in the fresh ideas and approaches which are emerging, attempts not only to cope with present problems but to anticipate and avoid those which might arise in the future. This exercise of the distinctively human quality of foresight will have its greatest effect in a generation's time; we may then see the full benefits of a slowly expanding population in which population services of all kinds are part of the general fabic of society.

A similar sense of vision has moved the governments which form UNFPA's ruling bodies to set out the principles and priorities under which we operate.

The principles are basically those which have guided our work from the outset—that our task is to promote population activities, particularly in those countries whose need is the most urgent; to respect the sovereign right of each nation to formulate, promote and implement its own population policies; to promote recipient countries self-reliance; and to give special attention to the needs of disadvantaged population groups. That these principles have not only survived but have been strengthened by time is a tribute to the foresight of their progenitors. They have given and continue to give us a matrix on which the Fund and governments can co-operate harmoniously in making plans for the future.

Similarly, the priorities which our governing body has set for the Fund recognize that our resources will inevitably be limited and that we must not attempt more than is practicable in fulfilling our mandate. Thus, a core programme of population activities has been delineated to be our prime concern; but since available resources would still not cover all activities within the core programme, further priorities have been set. Forty "high priority" countries have been named on the basis of their need for assistance. In addition, basic population programmes are being developed for each of the major areas of the core programme, by identifying the most essential steps countries would have to take in census-taking, data analysis, delivery of family planning services, communication support services, training, population policy and population education. Negotiations on minimum programmes are now in progress with several governments in the high priority group. I should like to make it clear that countries outside the high priority group are also entitled to our assistance on request, and a third of our resources has been set aside for this purpose.

In our experience, in the principles which underlie our programmes and in the priorities which have been set for our activities, it may be seen that the Fund and the governments with which we work—whether as donors, as recipients or as members of our governing body—are acting consistently with a perception of the transition from one era to another.

Three conclusions may be drawn from what I have said so far. They are certainly applicable to our experience in the population field and many well have relevance for other areas of development.

The first is that governments, donors and agencies executing projects alike are most likely to achieve success in their programmes if they address themselves to the basic needs of those whom they serve, the people of the developing countries. In our experience this approach can offer at least as good a ratio of costs to benefits in those things which can be quantified, and the indications are that it is a much more rewarding approach in the areas which cannot be quantified.

A second conclusion, which follows from the first, is that there must be a very strong element of participation in decision-making by those most directly affected. At the national level, we have found that while central direction can be very effective or even essential in starting or giving the necessary impetus to programmes, effective delivery cannot be sustained unless there is active participation by the community, right down to the smallest social units, the village or the street. Regardless of the political system, the important element is participation. If this is present, though the practical rewards may be few, the psychological satisfaction gained from being included in decision-making is a powerful motive to help in making programmes effective.

At the international level, the same principle is to be found in respect for national needs. No blueprint for international assistance will ever be effective unless adapted with the fullest participation of each country affected. UNFPA would never have reached its present level of funding without the confidence of governments that their needs and wishes would dictate the type and pattern of our assistance.

My third conclusion is the necessity, both at national and international levels, for the political will to effect change. Facts are useless without energy and vision to turn them into policies and programmes for the future. In population we have been seeing this process of energization taking place in country after country during the last few years.

Having said this, we must question our own certitudes. There are no fixed paths to a just global balance between population and economic resources. Each country, even each individual, will find the best path if allowed the means to do so, and this depends very much on the ability of administrators, governments and international organizations to listen, to determine what the needs really are, and to respond effectively.

A pattern thus emerges. Both in national and international affairs, success in meeting the problems of the future seems to depend ultimately on the responsiveness of society to the real needs of its members, and its ability to adapt its structures accordingly.

The quality of foresight which only humans possess carries a complementary responsibility; it must be used wisely. We have come to various recognitions in the last few years. These recognitions have shown us that we have many choices. We can see the possibility, for example, of a world in which humans and the humane values are given their full importance. But other, much less pleasant futures are possible—the developed countries retreating behind their economic and physical barriers; civil or international warfare for the control of essential resources; population growth limited not by choice but by starvation and disease. The world is changing. We are in the transition from one era to another. Attainment of a world fit to live in demands keener perception and deeper insights into these changes.

THE UNFPA: Progress Report 1978

Statement at the Twenty-fifth Session of the UNDP Governing Council,
United Nations, Geneva, 21 June 1978

In my statement today I would like, particularly, to review briefly the progress made in the activities of the UNFPA during the past twelve months; inform the Governing Council about the successful fund-raising efforts which have resulted in all major donor Governments substantially increasing their contributions to the Fund in 1978; outline the steps taken and the progress made in the implementation of priorities established by the Council in the allocation of the Fund's resources; report on the process of assessing basic needs in the fields of population which we have initiated; and outline to the Council new programming challenges and needs for population assistance in such areas as population distribution and migration, rural development, desertification, infant mortality, youth, women and the aged.

Progress Made in the Past Year

The Council has before it a full report of the activities of UNFPA in 1977 and the projected activities for the period 1978-1982. Let me mention a few highlights and update some of the data.

By the end of 1977, UNFPA had allocated $81.4 million for population projects for the year, bringing the cumulative total for the Fund's total programme operations to $339 million. Our implementation rate for 1977 was 82 per cent.

Of the 1977 programme budgets, 48 per cent were approved in response to requests from Governments for projects directly related to family planning. This is an increase over the percentage level of 1976 which was at 44.5 per cent. The closely-related category of communication and education activities received 13 per cent of the programme approved. Projects in basic population data, including support for national population censuses, required 15 per cent of total programme resources. The UNFPA-supported data collection activities are leading to a deeper understanding and a more thorough analysis of population problems which, in turn, will bring about the formulation and adoption of appropriate population and related socio-economic policies in many countries. As a result, we can expect a further growth in demand for projects related to family planning, maternal and child health care, and other measures.

In 1977, there was a fifteen per cent increase in the Fund's resources as compared with 1976, but programme allocations and expenditures remained at about the same level.

There were several reasons for this temporary levelling off of allocations and expenditures, namely, the arrangements required to undertake comprehensive assessment of national needs in the fields of population; the increasing concentration of the Fund's resources in the priority countries, and various political and socio-economic events which delayed and reduced UNFPA-supported activities in a number of countries.

The year 1977 was the first year in which the Fund initiated detailed appraisals of national population programme needs. As the Council will recall from last year's debate, these basic needs assessments are designed to enable developing countries, especially the forty priority countries, to foresee and deal more effectively with their major population problems in a comprehensive manner. Soon after adoption by the Council of this new approach to programming, it became clear that basic needs assessment exercises would require considerable time for preparation and execution and would thereby delay, to some extent, the approval and actual starting dates of new technically sound programme activities in a number of countries.

During our first year of experience with appraisals of basic needs on population, we have learned that it takes from nine to fourteen months from the time a mission is fielded until resulting projects are formulated and, subsequently, approved by UNFPA.

In the interim period, UNFPA often makes available some preliminary financing as authorized in the case of prospective major programmes by the Council in order that projects can be started without too much delay. While this rather long lead time in some cases has temporarily caused some delays in programming, the needs assessment exercise will, in the long run, speed up the programming cycle. Towards this end, we have taken steps to standardize the format and speed up the procedures for developing basic population programmes, although we fully recognize that there are limits for what can be done in this regard, realizing that each recipient country, to a large extent, is unique in its problems, objectives, policies and programmes.

In full co-operation with the Governments concerned, appraisals of the basic needs in the fields of population were undertaken last year in the following eight countries: Afghanistan, Bangladesh, Democratic Yemen, Honduras, Liberia, Mali, Senegal and Viet Nam. Copies of these appraisal reports are available for distribution to interested Council members. Other reports will be finalized soon and mailed to members of the Council. New large-scale country programmes that evolved from this work and in the case of Afghanistan and Viet Nam are being submitted to the present session of the Governing Council for its consideration and approval.

During the first five months of this year, appraisal reports have been completed for four countries, namely, Haiti, Malaysia, Mauritania and Paraguay and missions have been undertaken or are scheduled to be sent to El Salvador, Gambia, Kenya, the Philippines, Sri Lanka, Sudan, and Thailand.

Another factor, which has made our overall programming efforts more difficult and time-consuming, is the implementation of the decision of the Council to allocate an increasing proportion of resources available for country programmes to the forty priority countries for UNFPA assistance and to give special attention to the fourteen non-priority countries which are borderline cases. Many of these countries have only a limited capacity to plan a programme and implement population activities. Often, improvements in basic population data and training of key personnel are needed before a major population programme can be expected to evolve. In other countries, reformulation and review of ongoing activities have been necessary in order to make more effective use of increased resources available from the Fund. However, in spite of such problems, the proportion of our total country programme allocations to priority countries increased in 1977 to 46 per cent from 39 per cent in 1976. In 1978 we expect that slightly over half our total allocations to countries will be channelled to priority countries.

Finally, during 1977 we encountered more than the usual number of disruptions in the flow of allocations and expenditures because of major political or socio-economic events in recipient countries such as abrupt changes in governments, large-scale civil disturbances, strikes and important population policy changes. It was unavoidable that such developments would affect our programming and implementation performance.

The Council can rest assured that the temporary slowing down of the increase in UNFPA's allocations and expenditures that occurred in 1977 will not continue in 1978. We have taken several steps to improve our performance:

- We have improved our internal programme planning mechanism to enable us to plan our activities over a full four-year period.
- We have improved our internal monitoring and implementation procedures.
- We have established a mechanism to review regularly with our executing organizations the status of implementation.
- We have strengthened our field staff *inter alia* by adding four new Co-ordinator posts in Africa to stimulate project development in a number of priority countries in that region and national programming staff to assist several UNFPA Co-ordinators and UNDP Resident Representatives where no Co-ordinator is stationed.

With these steps, I am confident that a substantial increase in our programming and implementation capacity can be accomplished. The level of our allocations for 1978 already equals $105 million—the level of approval authority endorsed by the Governing Council at its Twenty-fourth session last June. We have additional project requests which will be ready for approval shortly, thereby enabling us to increase our 1978 programming level to at least $115 million. With the concurrence of the Council, it is my intention to approve projects for allocation, in 1978, up to an additional amount of $10 million by utilizing unallocated resources and, in this way, reducing the available carry-over from last year by nearly one-half.

UNFPA's 1978 Fund-raising

On the status of UNFPA's fund-raising activities, I am gratified to be able to inform the Council that we will reach our initial fund-raising target for 1978 of $105 million. We already have firm pledges and knowledge of other pledges awaiting only parlimentary approval that total approximately this amount. All of the Fund's nine major donor Governments have increased their pledges for 1978, led by the Federal Republic of Germany with an increase of approximately 70 per cent, and followed by Japan and

Norway with increases each of approximately 50 per cent. Other large real and percentage increases were received from the United Kingdom (30 per cent) and the Netherlands (25 per cent).

1979 Approval Authority

We have proposed that the UNFPA approval authority for 1979 be $120 million, subject to the availability of funds. Pledges so far foreseen for next year bring such an approval authority level well within reach. We expect to receive aid-worthy project requests in excess of $120 million for implementation during 1979. Thus, should UNFPA once again be able to fulfill its fund-raising target, unallocated or reprogrammable resources in hand from the previous year would permit us to programme prudently beyond the $120 million level for 1979, subject to the approval of the Council.

1979 Administrative Budget Estimates

The 1979 UNFPA budget estimates for administrative and programme support services are contained in a document before the members. In accordance with the request of the Governing Council and the recommendation of the ACABQ, the 1979 budget presentation includes, for the first time, information on workload indicators in support of staffing proposals. On a net basis, the 1979 administrative budget estimates amount to $5.4 million. This represent 4.5 per cent of the proposed level of approval authority for 1979; if the estimated costs of UNFPA's field co-ordinators are added, this percentage will be 6.7. These percentages have remained at about the same level as in the past four years.

Field Co-ordinators' Budgets

As previously, the Field Co-ordinators' budgets are not included in the appropriation estimates for the 1979 administrative budget. In response to the request of the Council made at its twenty-fourth session, a document is before the Council, reporting on the feasibility of including the costs of the Co-ordinators in the administrative and programme support budget. The members will note that I recommend, on the grounds of flexibility and other management considerations, that the Governing Council once again reiterate its approval of continuation of the present practice of funding the UNFPA Co-ordinator posts from programme funds at the country level.

Support of Intercountry Activities

As a further stage of the process of establishing priorities in allocation of UNFPA resources, I am pleased to submit for the Council's consideration recommendations concerning support of regional, interregional and global population activities in a document, entitled "Support of Intercountry Activities". This study is the outcome of the Fund's intensive efforts over the past year which included the preparation of a comprehensive summary of past UNFPA support to intercountry activities which was circulated, by mail, to members of the Council last September. In preparing the recommendations in the documents, UNFPA has reviewed the major areas requiring support at the intercountry level, taking into account the main findings of evaluation undertaken by UNFPA or relevant programmes, and benefiting from extensive consultations held with UNFPA's executing organizations in the United Nations system and interested non-governmental organizations.

With regard to the report, the Council's attention is drawn particularly to the rationale for UNFPA support of intercountry activities and the suggested priority areas of future support. In each of the main programme areas within the Fund's mandate, the types of activities that require support are identified, keeping in mind the principles and criteria for selecting such intercountry activities which the Governing Council took note of at its twenty-fourth session last June. In view of the fact that the perceived needs extend beyond the resources UNFPA can be expected to have available for this purpose, recommendations of the priority areas and programmes which the Fund may support in the foreseeable future have been outlined for the Council's consideration.

It is in recognition of the close relationship between UNFPA-supported country and intercountry programmes and the desirability that it should continue that I propose in the document before the members that a percentage level within a certain range of the Fund's programme resources be established to replace the ceiling in an absolute amount established by the Council in 1975. I am convinced that the approval of a range of 25-30 per cent would be essential to meet critical gaps in the major sectors at the intercountry level, while at the same time ensuring that the important needs of country programmes for technical support will be met.

It should be noted that almost one-half of UNFPA's resources currently allocated at the intercountry level is providing direct technical support to country programmes which is a continuing need. Furthermore, commitments have been made to support, for some time to come, the regional and interregional demographic centres. And bloc allocations for international fellowships on population as well as other vitally important training programmes undoubtedly have to be provided for. This means that the scope for support of other recommended activities particularly in the field of research and exploration of new and innovative approaches is quite limited indeed. Imposition of a more restrictive ceiling than the one I have recommended to the Council could in the long run be detrimental to meeting the overall objectives set for UNFPA at the intercountry as well as the country levels.

In this document, it is proposed that the Council should, in the future, review and approve on a rotating basis major intercountry programmes for UNFPA support. It is also indicated that arrangements will continue to be made for intensified and regular consultations with organizations and experts before approvals of intercountry programmes are made. Maintaining such procedures should ensure members of the Council that the allocations for intercountry activities will be of the greatest relevance to meeting the needs of the developing countries and be addressed to the most urgent areas of gaps in knowledge.

Infrastructure Support

Since June 1977, when the Council took note of my report on infrastructure support for population posts in the organizations in the United Nations system, the dialogue between UNFPA and its executing organizations on the subject has continued. There has been a net reduction of 24 professional posts among the infrastructure posts supported by the Fund, of which nine were absorbed into the regular budgets of the organizations concerned.

Projects Submitted for Approval

At the present session, proposals for new large-scale UNFPA programme support in Afghanistan, the Republic of Korea, Tunisia and Viet Nam are being submitted for the Council's approval. With regard to the Viet Nam programme, the project component on "Population activities in the New Economic Zones" will be revised to deal with family planning and population education activities estimated at an approximate amount of $3.4 million. At the same time, the Programme Reserve will be increased from $1.4 million to $4.8 million maintaining the total programme level of $17 million. After the Governing Council session, the Executive Director will, together with the Government of Viet Nam, programme the Reserve. The views expressed by the members of the Governing Council on UNFPA support to population redistribution activities will be taken into account by the Executive Director when programming in this area. In accordance with previous Council decisions, we are also submitting for approval the concluding portions of the ongoing programmes in Haiti, Jordan, Nigeria and the Syrian Arab Republic, as well as of the programme at the United Nations-Romanian Demographic Centre. With regard to the last mentioned programme we are going to initiate discussions soon with the Romanian government about future support after the expiration of the present project next year.

Technical Co-operation Among Developing Countries

On the important subject of technical co-operation among developing countries (TCDC), as the Council is aware, UNFPA has from its inception stressed support to programmes and projects which promoted national self-reliance, regional co-operation and collective self-reliance in the population fields. Indeed, much of UNFPA's assistance at the country and regional levels is aimed both at building up and improving the capacity of each country and each regional entity to administer such programmes themselves—and at using increasing amounts of TCDC-related inputs in accomplishing these important objectives.

We are participating fully in the preparatory meetings for the World Conference on Technical Co-operation Among Developing Countries and plan to be represented at the Conference itself. The Conference is of considerable interest to us and we look forward to utilizing its insights and recommendations in our future activities. A special publication, highlighting the Fund's experience in TCDC, is being prepared and will be issued prior to the Conference.

Direct Government Execution of UNFPA Projects

In the important related area of direct execution by recipient Governments of UNF-PA support for populations activities, a new high level was reached in 1977 when a total of $22.4 million, or some 27.5 per cent of overall programme support was allocated directly to Governments for their own direct implementation of some 175 population projects.

Direct implementation of UNFPA-supported population projects has functioned increasingly well in that it has been found to be cost-efficient, to speed up implementation and to promote development of experience and confidence of individuals and institutions in developing countries. Furthermore, it provides excellent opportunities for dialogues and interaction between the recipient Governments and the Fund.

This approach of increasingly entrusting Governments and institutions with the responsibility for executing technical co-operation activities which was pioneered by UNFPA in 1973 has since received full recognition in the United Nations system for development assistance in general and has been endorsed by the General Assembly in its resolution 3405 (XXX), adopted 28 November 1975.

Evaluation

At previous sessions, I have reported regularly on the outcome of evaluations and on follow-up action taken based thereon. At the present session, the Council has before it, as requested, a comprehensive document presenting for the first time a detailed description of the purpose and methodology of UNFPA-conducted evaluations as well as an analytical summary of the experience gained in five years of work in this area.

During this period, we have conducted twenty evaluations, most of them dealing with major UNFPA-supported regional, interregional or global projects.

Since they are conducted as objective and independent in-depth analyses and since evaluation reports are written with the same candour as the document before the Council, they serve as valuable support for our programming activities. They provide important inputs in the appraisal of requests for new or continued assistance. They provide the basis for taking corrective measures, if any, in regard to ongoing activities. Furthermore, they guide future programming by pointing to the importance of clarifying, in advance, programme objectives and alternative means of meeting them.

Due note has been taken of the suggestion made in the Council to undertake more evaluations of population activities supported at the country level. This will be reflected in the selection of programmes and projects to be evaluated in the coming years. We fully recognize that evaluation can be a sensitive subject and that no evaluation of country activities can, or shall, be undertaken without the consent and collaboration of the Government or institutions concerned.

Multi-Bilateral Arrangements

Since I reported to the Council last June, the response by both donor and recipient Governments to the Fund's initiative in developing multi-bilateral funding arrangements has been most encouraging. This initiative is proving to be timely and of potential benefit to many of the developing countries.

Through our multi-bilateral arrangements, we have to date received firm offers or commitments from donor Governments totalling more than $7 million. The Government of Norway has entered into an agreement with UNFPA under which a trust fund has been created mainly to support needs assessments and population programmes in priority countries. The agreement was approved in response to a note verbale circulated to Council members on 22 November 1977, and it is now being implemented. The Norwegian Government has already pledged some $2.4 million to this trust fund.

In June 1976, the Council approved UNFPA support to the Government of Mexico for a sex education programme in 1976-1979, financed by the Government of Sweden through funds-in-trust arrangements. I wish to inform the Council that recently agreement has been reached between the three parties concerned, to review the project somewhat, insofar as the research and action components are concerned, without changing the project's overall scope and content and, at the same time, to extend its duration for an additional two-year period (1980-1981) at the same level of overall support at around $2 million.

Public Information Activities

In addition to our regular periodical publications, *UNFPA Newsletter* and *POPULI*, we have continued the successful series entitled, "Population Profiles". The monographs in this series deal with the population situation in selected countries or regions, as well as with various population topics. They have achieved a wide and interested readership because of their success in making a complex subject interesting and readable. During the last twelve months, the following monographs have been issued: (1) *Asia: Home of Half the World;* (2) *Women, Population and Development;* (3) *Thailand;* (4) *Barbados;* (5) *The English-speaking Caribbean;* (6) *Population Education.* Monographs scheduled for publication in 1978 include Sri Lanka; Papua New Guinea; Indonesia; the Philippines; and the Arab Republic of Egypt. A new series of UNFPA publications entitled *Reports* and *Documentation* began in 1978 with *Priorities in Future Allocation of UNFPA Resources.*

The new fourth edition of the *Inventory of Population Projects in Developing Countries Around the World* for 1976/1977 was published last month. This unique publication has proven to be most useful to agencies and individuals throughout the world since it fills an important information need. Two copies of the new edition have been distributed to each of the Permanent Missions of the United Nations in New York.

The Role of Women in UNFPA's Activities

As I have stressed in previous statements to this Council and to other United Nations bodies—and more importantly, as the Fund has sought to demonstrate and foster in its programme, in its recruitment practices of professional staff and in its Population Profile issue on *Women, Population and Development*—little can be accomplished in the population fields without the active involvement and full participation of women. Guidelines now being utilized by UNFPA headquarters and field staff of UNFPA for programme development, project formulation, implementation, and evaluation call special attention to the need to take the vital links between the status and roles of women and population activities fully into account. UNFPA's recognition of the importance of women in formulating and executing its many-sided programme is also reflected in the fact that over one-third of the UNFPA's professional staff at headquarters and in the field are women.

Inter-Parliamentary Conference on Population

I would like to take this opportunity to inform the Council of some encouraging, concrete examples of the rapidly growing interest of parliamentarians around the world in population activities and the linkages between population and development. Following up on smaller informal meetings held in London and Bonn, parliamentarians from nine countries, namely Canada, Colombia, the Federal Republic of Germany, India, Japan, Mexico, Sri Lanka, the United Kingdom and the United States met in Tokyo last March at the invitation of the Japan Parliamentary Federation on Population to begin preparations for an inter-parliamentary conference on population. This conference is now scheduled to be held in Sri Lanka in August 1979 and will be attended by parliamentarians interested in population and development from all geographic regions of the world. A Steering Committee of parliamentarians has been organized in co-operation with the Inter-Parliamentary Union and UNFPA.

As part of the Fund's ongoing work to fulfill its mandate "to promote awareness, both in developed and in developing countries, of the social, economic and environmental implications of national and international population problems" as outlined in ECOSOC resolution 1763 (LIV), we will provide partial support to the preparatory activities for the conference and to the conference itself. I believe the increasing involvement of parliamentarians in issues on population and development will broaden and strengthen the efforts on population being undertaken by leaders in the executive branches of national governments.

Programme Trends

Members of the Council will note that in the printed version of the Fund's Annual Report for 1977, a preface is included entitled, "Perspectives", in which some of the notable changes that have occurred in population in recent years are summarized, especially as regards population growth, fertility, mortality and morbidity, migration and urbanization, population composition and population policies.

The present decade has marked what can be described as a quantum leap in the recognition among developing countries of the importance of understanding and of consciously trying to cope with population issues. One cannot help but be encouraged by the changes which have taken place over the last few years. What is now lacking in the developing world is sufficient amounts of the technical, financial and administrative means required for the translation of policies and principles into concrete country-wide programmes. The limits are now far less those of awareness of the problems and the recognition of the urgency to take action but far more those of the need for resources and for the broad managerial skills to implement and execute programmes.

As understanding of the implication of population factors on development efforts becomes more widespread, considerable progress has been achieved in developing countries on all continents in recognizing population policies and action programmes as part and parcel of each country's development strategy. This recognition has not only resulted in increased demand on the Fund's resources but has also served as a catalyst in efforts to seek new modalities of assistance. The general acceptance of an integrated approach to population and development has brought with it opportunities to include population components in programmes related to primary health care, human settlements, environmental concerns, desertification, youth, the aged, etc. The basic needs programming exercises being undertaken at the country level lend themselves most aptly to capitalizing on these opportunities.

Along with the growing awareness of population as a key factor in promoting national prosperity, Governments have also shown an increasing desire to make their population policies more comprehensive and to directing their actions to many fronts rather than limiting themselves to consider only one or two demographic variables. Thus, they have shown definite interest in the geographical distribution of their population and in internal and international migration in addition to the more "traditional" concerns with fertility and mortality.

In response to this trend, UNFPA has begun to support, or has under discussion, requests for assistance for studies on internal migration such as in Indonesia and to pilot schemes on population redistribution and settlement of population from congested or scattered areas such as in Burundi, Democratic Yemen, Peru and Viet Nam. In making support available, the Fund realizes that undertakings in these field may often involve capital intensive efforts. Yet the fact remains that nearly all the Governments in the developing world have expressed dissatisfaction with the distribution of their population and a desire to adopt measures to resolve such problems, although the number of requests for assistance in this regard has so far been rather limited. It is our view that UNFPA has an obligation to respond to requests, albeit with great caution. I would like to assure the Council that the Fund's policy always has been and will continue to be to support only activities in which the population participate voluntarily.

Another area of increasing Government interest in UNFPA assistance is population activities in connexion with rural development and community development. Requests are under consideration for support or research on the population implications of rural development and community development submitted by Jordan and the ASEAN group of countries. A major project on population policy in the context of rural and community development is already being funded in Egypt.

The trend towards diversification of UNFPA does not mean that decreasing emphasis is being given to family planning as the main area of support. More and more countries are attaching high priority to family planning in recognition of the fact that availability and provision of such services are important elements in promoting primary health care, in improving the status of women and in securing basic human rights. But the measures required are being broadened and diversified. For example, UNFPA is increasingly being called upon to support programmes on infant and maternal mortality with the direct objective of contributing to the regulation and reduction of fertility in Colombia and Sri Lanka. In other cases, such programmes are supported with the main objective of reducing infant mortality and maternal mortality and morbidity, while the influence upon fertility is only incidental and not a primary objective, such as in Afghanistan, Central African Empire, Jordan, Mali, Peru and Sudan.

In concluding, I should like to point out two major trends we have seen in the field of population since the World Population Conference was held four years ago: On the one hand, the growing desire to enlarge the magnitude and scope of action with respect to population issues; and, on the other hand, the increasing need to establish closer linkage between population activities and other economic and social development efforts. Thus, today, more than ever before, an awareness is prevailing that population problems are so intimately linked to all of the other large socio-economic problems that humanity must face, that none of them can usefully be considered and dealt with in isolation.

It is essential that the Fund continue to respond adequately to this challenge under the guidance of the Governing Council .

Appendix C

[In June 1978, the Executive Director of the UNFPA issued his first "State of World Population" report. These reports, which will be issued annually, comment on population trends, the present and the future. The reports for 1978 and 1979 are reprinted here in their entirety.]

State of World Population Report: 1978

As the UNFPA approaches its tenth anniversary notable changes are occurring in the "population climate" in which its work is done. We have traversed what may be seen in retrospect as a period of recognition of the nature and significance of the population question as a whole, and are entering a period which might appropriately be described as one of responsive action.

In the four years following the World Population Conference at Bucharest the activities of the Fund have become nearly universal, almost all the member countries of the United Nations participating either as donors or recipients of assistance, or both. This is a clear indication of the extent of the recognition of the importance of population as a cardinal concern of the international community. The next steps are to consolidate the gains made, maintain the momentum, respond to the heightened awareness of need and to the demographic trends that are now being discerned and to assess their implications, and their interrelationships with policy and programmes of action.

Population Growth

The realities of the imbalance of growing human numbers and accessible resources, some of them rapidly dwindling, remain awesome and are likely to become more unmanageable with the increase in the size of population, particularly since the bulk of this increase will occur in countries which are least able to sustain the increase in their numbers. It would be well to bear in mind that allowing for a wide margin of possible error, and despite an assumed fall in fertility of as much as 30 per cent in the next two decades, the lowest forecast for world population in the Year 2000 is 5.8 billion [1] (as against 4 billion in 1975). The most conservative estimates which, again, make adequate allowance for error, but do not assume the intrusion of catastrophe as a means of solving human problems, suggest in the next 22 years, a world of a very different order of magnitudes from that with which we are familiar.

In 1950 only 4 countries (China, India, the United States and the USSR) had populations exceeding 100 million. In 1975 this number had grown to 7 (including Indonesia, Japan and Brazil). In 1950, 5 countries (Brazil, Japan, Indonesia, the United Kingdom of Great Britain and Northern Ireland and the Federal Republic of Germany) had populations exceeding 50 million. By 1975 this number had increased to 15. [2]

By the Year 2000 the indications are that:

- 2 countries (China and India) will have populations exceeding 1 billion
- 11 countries (including Pakistan, Bangladesh and Mexico) will exceed 100 million
- 27 countries will have populations exceeding 50 million. [3]

This 'giantism' should not be regarded as a spectre but as a probable reality which needs to be confronted boldly so that the increased demands on the planet's resources that will be made in the not so distant future will be taken into account in making government policy and planning programmes for the development and deployment of those resources.

In this period of consolidation of efforts to respond to the changing needs in the population field some other considerations of intense current concern relate to trends in mortality, health, migration, the role of women and to problems common to both the developed and developing worlds such as the growth of cities, the consequences of increased longevity and, at the other end, demographic and social implications of the increase in the number of young adults in most countries.

Fertility

There are clear signs of a decline in fertility. While changes from the early to the late 1960's were so modest as to be considered inconclusive, the drop since the late 1960's has been marked. Most impressive is that the drop has occurred where registration is either complete or at least reliable; it has occurred in the smaller, predominantly island countries containing roughly 12 per cent of the developing world and it has been reported in large mainland countries containing 30 per cent or more of the developing world. Overall since the 60's birth rates have fallen by approximately 15 per cent in some 3 to 4 dozen countries representing from at least 40 per cent to possibly two-thirds of the developing world. [4]

It is an impressive alteration of pace but it is essential for any serious purpose to modulate any sense of satisfaction or achievement which it might engender by giving due weight to certain caveats. First, the pattern of decline noted has been very uneven: certain countries, especially islands or small nations with dense populations relative to their size have achieved a marked decline in their fertility. Second, and this is perhaps the most important of the caveats, the signs of levelling off or fall in fertility rates, however encouraging they might be, should not obscure the reality that it is occurring at a very high level of actual numbers of people whose lives must not only be sustained in terms of basic needs but also improved considerably if they are to be made worth living.

In the past decade we have experienced the beginning of the third wave of fertility transitions in the world. The first took place in Western Europe and North

America in the nineteenth century, the second in Eastern Europe and Japan after World War II when fertility rates turned sharply downwards.

Has human fertility behaviour reached such an epoch-making point of change? Will world fertility continue to fall? Will the fall decelerate and plateau at a lower level? Will fertility rise once more and continue along the familiar historical lines? These are some of the issues at the centre of the debate now going on among the demographers and no answers may appear until the dust has settled. Even the reasons for the current decline in fertility rates in various countries—whether it has been caused by the effectiveness of family planning programmes, by increased literacy, by the improved status of women, by a rise in the average age at marriage, by international migration—or a combination of these factors—are not agreed. Such questions do not yield themselves to a catch-all explanation. In some countries, many of these reasons apply, in others only some, but, at best, these are only partial explanations of highly individualised and localised conditions.

Nevertheless it needs to be said that the decline in many countries is sufficiently marked to demand serious scholarly assessment in order to reveal its true correlations with other factors such as rates of mortality—particularly infant mortality—health, literacy, education and value change, industrialisation, migration, urbanisation, employment, distribution of economic opportunities and the gains of economic growth, the change in the social condition of women and the effective management and delivery of family planning. The lessons of that experience need to be urgently garnered and assimilated to encourage other countries to adapt them to their own situations.

Unfortunately the task is made more difficult because the data base on which scholars are expected to work is deplorably inadequate and offers only precarious footholds for the serious analyst. No more than 200 million among the 3 billion people living in the less developed world are covered by proven and reliable data on fertility. [5] This is surely a fragile basis for making any but the most tentative conclusions about fertility trends and then, only with appropriately apologetic qualifications. The findings of the World Fertility Survey funded by the UNFPA and USAID have recently begun to appear in quantity but more work needs to be done to strengthen their value as tools for analysing trends.

Fortunately, the signs of declining fertility in the less developed world are borne out by the fact that many of the countries where this trend has become noticeable do have reliable data. Admittedly these countries are relatively small (one of the possible reasons for the reliability of their statistics) but the downward trend is sufficiently impressive in nearly all of them to remove any doubt that fertility has fallen sharply.

What about the big countries in the developing world? Can nothing meaningful be said about them despite the lack of proven data? Judging from indirect evidence as well as some statistical information from Chinese sources, many analysts are inclined to believe that birth rates have dropped to near 25 per 1000. [6] The drop in the last decade alone is estimated at around 20 per cent. [7] If true, this indicates that a major transformation of fertility patterns has occurred in the most populated nation in the world.

In India, estimates based on sample registration data, indications from population programme sources, and the low rate of increase found in the intercensal period in the sixties, suggest that a 10 per cent fall in fertility may have occurred over the past decade.

Indonesia too is reported by a recent sample survey to have achieved a 10-15 per cent drop in fertility within a decade. [8]

In Sub-Saharan Africa there is no evidence of a fall in fertility rates. On the contrary, the possibility is that it has risen as a result of better health facilities becoming available.

In Latin America recent indications suggest that in Chile, Colombia, Costa Rica, Dominican Republic, Guyana and Mexico the traditional trend towards rising fertility has been reversed and, what is more, a sharp downtrend may have been set in Mexico. [9] It is possible that the Government's policy change in favour of lowering fertility and the programmes which followed have played an active role in this transformation.

Welcome as these signs are, it would be unwise to conclude that the population problems of individual nations or of the world as a whole are at an end or anywhere near it.

The benefits of a demographic transition in the developing world can be said to have been achieved in substantial measure only when most of its people have the means and opportunities to make life-choices of consequence to themselves and their children.

Mortality and Morbidity

A remarkable feature of the period was the unprecedented rise in life expectancy. In the developing world average life expectancy increased from 42 to 54 years and in the developed world from about 65 to 71 by the mid 1970s. [10] Here too the statistical picture would be illusory if what it suggests is not qualified by recognition of the diversity of mortality and longevity figures between and within regions. For instance, according to recent estimates [11] the expectation of life at birth varied between 38 and 73, a wide spectrum by any measurement. Latin America has an average life expectancy of 62 years, Asia 56 and Africa around 45. It is clear that there is considerable work ahead to lower the level of premature mortality in the developing world. That a gap of 26 years in life expectancy between Africa and the developed world should exist despite the technology and knowledge that could be harnessed for this purpose is a tragic comment on our ability to give substance to the rhetoric of global interdependency.

In the developing world infant mortality continues to be the most important determinant of general levels of mortality. Ten years ago the rate of infant mortality in the developing world as a whole was estimated to be 180, with a high of over 200 per 1000 live births in the poorest countries, as against 57 in the developed world. [12] There are encouraging indications of a steep fall in infant mortality in certain areas of the Third World, a trend which is reflected in a decline in overall mortality. It has been suggested that the fall in infant mortality along with improvements in the provision of health and education facilities, in the status of women and more equitable income distribution in some developing nations has been directly responsible for the relative success of family planning programmes and a consequent sharp drop in fertility rates in those areas.

One of the platitudes of social science has been that a fall in fertility has taken place in every nation that has achieved economic progress. The experience of Sri Lanka and the State of Kerala in South India seems to belie this because the decline in fertility there has been achieved without a commensurate growth of the economy. The improvement of social welfare—the provision of health and educational facilities for all disadvantaged families and the betterment of social and economic opportunities for the female population—have evidently taken the place of economic success as a factor in bringing fertility rates down. The implication is that these welfare measures have been powerful determinants in the lowering of infant mortality and a decline in fertility. This has been interpreted by some social scientists, particularly in India, as being due to parents no longer feeling impelled to have as many children as they could have to replace those who were dying in infancy before the social welfare programmes were instituted. It is an interesting hypothesis but many scholars are inclined to doubt the validity of this replacement theory on the ground that there is insufficient evidence to educe a general theory of a correlation between a decline in infant mortality and a decline in fertility. They prefer to think that income distribution has been the determining factor in decreasing fertility. Possibly the experience mentioned above should be regarded as special cases arising from circumstances peculiar to them. Nevertheless it is worth asking whether it would be feasible or useful to adopt some or all of those special circumstances in other areas where fertility has shown little or no signs of changing.

Certain disturbing features which are bound to have a serious effect on mortality have recently appeared. Prominent among these is the resurgence of malaria, a disease which was believed to have been vanquished 30 years ago. Malaria has once again become a major health problem in many developing countries in Asia and Africa, widespread enough to suggest that a new "epidemic" is rampant. In 1966 in India there were 40,000 cases reported. In 1972 this number rose to 1,430,000 and in 1967 to 6 million. [13] Pakistan, Bangladesh, Sri Lanka, Indonesia and the Philippines have been severely affected. On the continent of Africa alone 50 million clinical cases and a million deaths from malaria were recorded in 1975. Some 13 per cent of all hospital patients in tropical Africa are malaria victims. The reasons for the return of malaria appear to be that there is more mosquito breeding and new strains of mosquitos resistant to DDT as well as malaria parasites resistant to existing remedies have emerged. But what is of concern here is that the most vulnerable populations are those already suffering from malnutrition, particularly young children. The extent of the danger may be measured by the fact that nearly 400 million children are known to be malnourished. What impact a serious increase of infant mortality might have on the decline in fertility rates is still to be seen but it will not take long to know whether or not there is a direct and strong causal link between fertility and infant mortality.

In contrast with these disturbing developments there is a hopeful sign of growing interest in setting up simplified schemes to provide primary health care, designed to give communities responsibility in managing their own health programmes. A major improvement in coverage and better attention to basic health concerns may result. The effectiveness of this interesting departure in distinction to the more structured national health systems deserves studious attention in the coming years.

The Food Factor

An important connected factor which has a direct bearing on mortality as well as the level of health in the developing world is the supply of food. The gloomy prognostications of the decade of recognition received a great deal of reinforcement by the famines in Sub-Saharan Africa and Ethiopia, and the food shortage in 1974 caused by prolonged drought in the Indian sub-continent. The sense of urgency which pervaded the United Nations Food Conference was an indication that the ancient population-food equation, despite proof that agricultural technology has increased food supplies far beyond what could have been foreseen by Thomas Robert Malthus, remains a constraint at the back of many minds. These fears were soon eased when the rains came to the Sahel and to the sub-continent, and India produced a succession of record harvests which yielded unprecedently large reserves. The Biblical injunction about the need to conserve the gains of the fat years to avoid deprivation in the lean is being followed more devoutly and methodically than it has been for a long time. Agricultural economists continue to issue warnings that it would be unwise to suppose that the lean years will not come again bringing redoubled human suffering, that reserves of croplands are becoming exhausted, and that the cost of bringing marginal lands under the plough is becoming impractically high. It would indeed be unwise to discard these warnings out of hand as being ideologically tainted because they distract attention from questions of unbridled consumerism, extravagance and the crucial need for more rational and equitable distribution of food and the means to produce more. None of these considerations need be taken as being mutually exclusive.

It is a sobering thought that there is no technology now being evolved in the research institutes that promises the possibility of a quantum increase in food production in the order of magnitude offered 15 years ago by the Green Revolution. A possible breakthrough might be made in increasing photosynthetic efficiency and by breeding new varieties of cereal that can fix nitrogen in the soil thus solving the mounting problem of fertilizer costs. [14] Such innovations are still not advanced far enough to encourage the belief that science will once again intervene to rescue society from the consequences of its own improvidence.

Migration and Urbanisation

At current rates of growth cities in every region are expected to grow in the next two decades to magnitudes totally unfamiliar to town planners. Projections [15] for a few cities will illustrate this trend:

Tokyo-Yokohama with nearly 15 million in 1970 may have 26 million in the year 2000

Greater Cairo with 5.6 million in 1970 may have 16.3 million in the year 2000

Lagos with 1.4 million in 1970 may have 9.4 million by the year 2000

Mexico with 8.5 million in 1970 may have 31.6 million by the year 2000.

There is a widespread recognition of the urgent need for national policies and programmes, not only to manage the problems of crowded cities and reverse the flow not by facile recourse to compulsion but by developing "growth poles" which would attract settlers to areas depopulated through migration and to previously underpopulated regions by planned provision of schools, health facilities, housing, roads, transportation, water for irrigation, industrial use and domestic consumption and, above all, job opportunities for the young. Despite the extent of the importance accorded to policies concerning rural development by governments of many developing countries for two or three decades, very little has been achieved. The principal reason for this is the cost of establishing the "growth poles" as counter-attractions which could provide credible substitutes for the hopes of finding employment and social amenities that have drawn people to metropolitan centres at a gradually accelerating pace for many centuries.

In dealing with resettlement projects it is necessary for international aid agencies to anticipate a larger number of requests for grants than for loans. A case in point is the request to the UNFPA from the Socialist Republic of Vietnam for assistance in resettling the rural areas which were depopulated in order to lessen the burden of the bulging cities in which people had sought refuge during the long years of war and give large numbers of people the opportunity of finding a fuller life than they now have by hanging on to the edge of survival in a seething city.

Another is Sri Lanka which has sought assistance to resettle farming families in rural areas being opened up to agriculture and nascent agro-industry as a result of the Mahaveli Development Project.

In contradistinction, industrialised countries also experiencing the problems of over-urbanisation may be able to finance the reversing of the flow to the cities with support from the rural commercial and banking infrastructures which already exist in the less populated areas and are strong enough to invest in the development of new growth centres. The most noteworthy recent instance of this possibility is perhaps the renewed greening of the "sun-belt" in the southern areas of the United States now enjoying a regeneration of economic activity and an in-migration of people from crowded cities of the North.

An interesting and possibly pragmatic solution being proposed by some social scientists is to stimulate the planned development of half-way towns located between the big cities and the villages by inducing industry to locate their activities away from densely populated areas through fiscal concessions such as graduated tax benefits and by providing improved transport services. It is not a new idea and it needs the infusion of lessons learned by Indonesia, Brazil and other developing nations in their two-decade long efforts at diffusing density but it has prima facie merits to warrant serious study.

International migration has historically been a response to centrifugal political and social pressures within countries. In the post war years too migration has been caused by such pressures but, increasingly, the motives behind these movements have been economic necessity and the prospect of firm material security or professional advancement. Inadequate economic growth rates to sustain rapidly increasing numbers in many developing countries combined with what has been called the revolution in rising expectations have been strong enough to uproot many millions from their native soil and propel them to seek jobs, social amenities and a future for their children abroad. The magnitude of this movement and its increased momentum in the past two decades has caused the host countries in the developed world, even those which in more expansive times considered it a matter of national pride to be hospitable to strangers, to reinforce their immigration barriers.

International migration, intra-regional as well as inter-regional involves many levels of abilities ranging from unskilled labour to high professionalism and has generated new problems of cultural assimilation as well as criticisms of a Brain Drain. One solution to the first set of problems being suggested is to bolt the door tight against immigrants, an idea that appears to be a reaction to the high level of unemployment in the host countries of the developed world as well.

As for the migration of technical and professional skills it is being increasingly recognised by administrators in developing countries that its basic cause is that education and training designed to serve the needs of an industrial society which many non-industrial countries continue to provide will almost inevitably lead to such skills flowing out to wherever they can find useful and profitable employment. Changes in education policy are therefore necessary to make the content of education more relevant to national needs. Increased attention to the need for preventive health education as distinct from the familiar medical schooling is beginning to be paid in certain countries who have been inspired by the example of the paramedical services available to the rural communities in China.

A shift in the centre of gravity of health education and health services in the developing world from curative to preventive medicine will, apart from being cheaper, have a considerable effect on morbidity and mortality in the rural communities in which the vast majority of people live.

The Young and the Old

Reference has been made above to some of the common population problems of the developed and developing worlds and to some of the interlinked issues such as international migration. There are two other major shared concerns:

The first relates to the increase of the proportion and size of the youth cohort relative to the total population. The implications of this feature on national policies on fertility trends, employment, industrialisation, education and housing touch all areas of the world but, again, the developing world bears its heaviest impact because of the numbers involved in relation to the resources needed to respond to the change.

The number of young adults increased from 488 million in 1955 to 740 million in 1975 and is expected to grow to 879 million in 1985. The surge is higher in the developing world where their number is expected to increase from 548 million to 688 million in 1985.[16]

The portion of the population under 15 years of age has drawn considerable attention in recent years. These young people are dependents and in some countries constitute over 40 per cent of the population. Thus they can become a severe drain on economic and social development resources. Over the next 10 years these people will become young adults. The enormous number of children under 15 will soon be entering their child-bearing years. How this cohort behaves with respect to fertility will markedly affect the progress towards the socio-economic goals in many countries. At present about 20 per cent of populations are in the 15-25 age group in all regions of the world.[17]

This age group has special needs with respect to social services. Foremost are their needs in the educational field, particularly vocational education as increasing numbers finish what formal schooling is available. The difficulty of providing further education and/or employment for school leavers is enhanced as the numbers are increased. Also this age group has recreational, housing and transportation needs, often requiring provision of special services. Clearly if youth are a rapidly increasing proportion of the population, provision of appropriate social services becomes even more difficult than at present.

These young adults will also need adequate family planning services. The question of adolescent fertility is already a cause of concern to many developing countries, and will become a much more urgent and serious problem as the percentage of young people below 25 rises in the population. Serious studies of this question are needed in the specific social and cultural contexts of different regions and different countries so that the governments concerned may devise suitable programmes to provide information, counselling and services to young people in need.

There is indeed a potential for massive increases in fertility, as a result of increasing numbers of youth in developing country populations. How governments approach this issue and provide for increasing proportions of youth, is a question which should receive greater attention over the next decade.

The other shared concern is the problem of ageing caused by the decline of fertility rates and the prolongation of life expectancy resulting in marked changes in the age structure of populations in both areas. The ageing of the world's population and recent projections for the two ensuing decades point to the need for national policies and institutional responses to a problem which was not anticipated until the early seventies. It is important to realize that while the proportion of the total population over 60 years of age may be small—representing only 8.4 per cent of the world population in 1970 and forecast to be 9.3 per cent in the year 2000—the aggregate number of people over 60 years of age is sizeable.[18] In 1970 it stood at 304 million but this figure is expected to be 581 million at the end of the next two decades—almost double. The impact of these numbers will fall most heavily on the less developed countries. It may be anticipated that the less developed world will have 377 million people over 60 years—65 per cent of the world's total.

Another significant feature of the trend is that the ageing of population is associated with an increase in the number of females who outlive the male population. These proportions are likely to increase in the next two decades while the aggregate for each also rises.

Recent surveys of changes in the concept of the family too need to be taken into account when formulating social policies. In both the developed and developing worlds the traditional dependency relationship between the old and the younger members of the family is also changing. In the developed world the notion of the family is changing with the increase in longevity from a two and three generation to a four generation relationship. In the less developed world where social security systems such as old age pensions and annuities are lacking, similar changes are taking place which make an increasingly heavier impact on traditional family dependency relationships.

It is necessary, therefore, to set about studying these changes in specific detail at the national, urban and village levels in order to shift from the traditional stereotypes about families and ageing to what is current and relevant for the immediate future so that appropriate economic, fiscal and social welfare policies, institutions, training facilities and programmes may be designed to deal effectively with the problem caused by increased longevity and the alteration of the age structure of populations. Some of these stereotypes such as the practice of forcibly retiring people at the chronological age of 60 or 65 are being seriously challenged in the West. The practice came about, as it was said, "to make room for the younger generation" and became a matter of absolute doctrine in the past few decades, thus setting up one age group against another in a struggle for survival resolved by making the winners pay the cost of the dependency of the losers.

There is also a growing need to re-examine many of the old assumptions and attitudes related to ageing because with the change in population size, location, density and structure, many of the ideas and values that have become the basis of such social legislation, are also undergoing radical changes.

Policy Changes

The most significant principle emerging from this brief overview of the state of world population in 1978 is that changes taking place in demographic processes should be recognised as powerful determinants of relevance in the formulation of social and economic policy and plans in every major area of national concern. Most governments have shown increasing awareness of the need to integrate the population factor in national development efforts during the seventies, particularly since the World Population Conference. It is therefore a matter for regret to note that practice is lagging too far behind precept in many developing countries where progress in incorporating the population element in development planning is deplorably slow. In some countries this is due to a lack of an integrated philosophy and methodology of national development; in some by a lack of know-how, in some by the lack of population data, in some by the inadequacy of commitment and direction from the top, and in others, by a continuing reluctance to take a public position on a problem which may have culturally sensitive implications. This reluctance is reflected in the absence of an essential subject such as population in major international discussions on a new order in international economic affairs.

However, it is encouraging to report that more and more countries have begun to realize that no development effort can any longer afford to ignore the question of population, whether a particular country is concerned with reducing or increasing its rate of growth of its numbers. It's interrelationship with policies on education, food and agriculture, industrialization, urbanisation, employment, health facilities, the improvement of the status of women and other disadvantaged sectors and with numerous other areas of development is being acknowledged as a pivotal consideration for all societies irrespective of their differences in political creed or economic standing.

A significant increase has also taken place in the number of countries that consider their fertility levels "too high". The number rose from 42 in 1974 to 54 in 1976. Of these, 18 are in Asia, 18 in Africa, 16 in Latin America and 2 in the Middle East. Together they comprise 82 per cent of the population in the developing world. Fifty-three developing countries, with 17 per cent of the population of the developing world (25 in Africa, 10 in the Arab World, 9 in Latin America and 9 in Asia) consider their trends satisfactory. There are seven developing countries with one per cent of the population of the developing world which want to raise the level of national fertility.[19]

It is noteworthy that only 8 of the 144 developing countries surveyed by the United Nations restrict in any way access to the use of modern methods of fertility regulation. Actually, 29 of the developing countries which indicated no desire to change national fertility rates provide direct support to fertility regulation activities. In total, 82 developing countries provide either direct or indirect support to fertility regulation efforts, their policies on fertility notwithstanding.[20]

If population growth rates were to follow the trends desired by the governments as indicated in the United Nations enquiry, world population would be 280 million less than the 6.25 billion which is the United Nations medium projection for the year 2000.[21] It may be more useful therefore to assist governments to realize their aspirations than to try to change them.

Allocation of Resources

The trend is also reflected in the increasing number of developing countries that seek assistance from the Fund, in the variety of the types of programmes for which assistance is sought and in the widespread willingness of recipient nations to enlarge the proportion of national resources allocated for population programmes relative to multilateral, multibilateral and bilateral foreign contributions. By way of illustrating this last trend it is worth noting that government contributions to family planning programmes alone have increased notably in the past few years. To name a few cases without prejudice to others:

Nepal increased its allocation for family planning programmes from $185,000 in 1971 to $1,138,000 in 1975. Costa Rica, which was spending $40,000 on maternal/child health and family planning programmes in 1971 allocated $643,000 in 1975. Mexico, which began spending government funds on population programmes in 1974, following the adoption of an official population policy, increased its allocations from around $7 million in 1974 to more than $70 million in 1978. (The 1978 figure, if adjusted for the devaluation of the Mexican peso in 1976 will show 60 per cent more expenditure in local currency in 1978.)

Some Future Perspectives

The UNFPA's policy of direct funding and assisting countries to develop their own expertise, has paid dividends by saving costs and time. Also, its responsiveness to population needs and priorities as perceived by individual countries has enabled the Fund to achieve near universal acceptance.

The next phase, of consolidating these trends by assisting governments to integrate population in their basic needs programmes and to respond to economic and social change foreseen as a result of changes in the demographic processes noted above, suggests that international population assistance would have to grow to a new order of magnitude if it is to match adequately the effort that developing countries will have to make to meet the challenges of the last two decades of this millennium. The slowing down of the rate of population growth, as previously noted, gives us an opportunity to make crucial choices for the future.

International efforts made during the decades of recognition now need to be consolidated. The emergence of population as a vital element in programmes designed to bring about social and economic change at the country level should now be also reflected in a comprehensive effort at the international level in order to achieve maximum impact. Work in population now involves a large number of individuals and groups both in the public and private sectors who are engaged at various levels of policy making, planning and implementing a wide range of programmes. While there is universal recognition that population is a key determinant of content, pace and direction of the general development process, there is also a widespread acknowledgement of the need for population programmes to keep a clear profile to prevent diffusion of their effectiveness in the more generalised aspects of development with which their purpose is related. Thus, some of the most far reaching choices for the international community concern the design and implementation of a clear and coherent worldwide effort to give substance to the recommendations of the World Population Plan of Action and to assist countries to give effect to the policies they have since formulated. The sincerity and wisdom brought to bear on making those choices would greatly determine the quality of life that will be bequeathed to children already born and to those who will be born in the next ten years.

References

1. **United Nations,** *Selected World Demographic Indicators by Countries, 1950-2000,* **New York, 1975**
2. *Ibid.*
3. *Ibid.*
4. **United Nations,** *Levels and Trends of Fertility Throughout the World, 1950-1970,* **New York, 1977**
5. **George Stolnitz, United Nations Population Division, New York, in written statement to the U.S. House of Representatives Select Committee on Population, Washington D.C., 9th February 1978**
6. **United Nations,** *Levels and Trends of Fertility (Op.Cit)*
7. **United Nations,** *Selected World Demographic Indicators (Op.Cit)*
8. **United Nations,** *Population and Vital Statistics Report,* **(Statistical Series 'A' Vol. xxv-xxx, New York, 1973-1978 respectively);** **W. Parker Mauldin,** *Fertility Trends, 1950-1975,* **in the Population Council, New York, Studies in Family Planning, September 1976; Geoffrey McNicoll and Si Gde Made Mamas,** *The Demographic Situation in Indonesia,* **Central Bureau of Statistics, Jakarta 1973**

9. For Mexico *Vide* Stolnitz *(Op.Cit)*
10. United Nations, *Selected World Demographic Indicators (Op.Cit.)*
11. Ibid
12. United Nations, *Demographic Year Book, 1972-1976,* New York, 1973-1977 respectively
13. United Nations Environment Programme, Executive Director's Report to the Governing Council, 1978
14. Lester R. Brown, *The Twenty-ninth Day,* Worldwatch Institute, Washington D.C., 1978
15. United Nations, *Trends and Prospects in the Population of Urban Agglomerations, 1950-2000, as Assessed in 1973-1975,* New York, 1975
16. United Nations, *Population by Sex and Age for Regions and Countries, 1950-2000, as Assessed in 1973: Medium variant,* New York, 1976
17. Ibid
18. Ibid
19. United Nations, *Concise Report of Monitoring of Population Policies,* New York, 1976
20. *Ibid*
21. United Nations, *Selected World Demographic Indicators (Op.Cit)*

State of World Population Report: 1979

The decline in world fertility referred to in this Report last year with appropriate caution is now confirmed. Both in the developed world and in many areas of the developing world where the largest numbers of the planet's population live, the trend towards smaller families has become evident and there is no reason to expect a reversal in the foreseeable future, if we were to ignore minor temporary fluctuations.

Caution is needed, however, in drawing conclusions from a reading of these trends. It would be a grave error of judgement to make the tempting leap from pessimism to optimism, and suppose that the "population problem" has been solved. The rate of decline in fertility projected over the two remaining decades of this millennium will not prevent the world's population from increasing by nearly two billion who must inhabit a world whose economic balance is already distorted by worsening poverty for most and affluence for a few. At the end of the current decade alone three quarters of a billion people will be added to the 1970 count, nearly all of them in the poorest countries.

Apart from this, the very fact of a fertility transition has brought in its train some unfamiliar but very real population problems which need recognition and attention now if they are to be prevented from developing into a crisis in the next decade or two. The most serious population problem of the more developed parts of the world is the tendency for family size to drop below replacement levels. In the Federal Republic of Germany, for instance, the average family has already dropped below two children, a

I.P.A.—BB

trend which is appearing in other Western countries also. Another problem which is only now being recognised as a major concern, is aging and its impact on employment and the fiscal and social policies of the developed world. There are others, which will be mentioned further on in this report.

As for the developing world, the Fund's primary concern, the decline in fertility combined with the fall in mortality - which began earlier - has set off a phase of structural change within populations which is likely to place intolerably heavy burdens on the working population by greatly increasing the overall dependency on an already overburdened group. This and other aspects of the impact of trends in fertility and mortality patterns are set out in more detail below.

What has taken place, therefore, is not an elimination or even a substantial reduction of the "population problem" but rather a transformation of its character and magnitude which calls not for complacency and relaxation of effort but for new perceptions and a renewed willingness to design policies and programmes to deal with the consequences of change.

The 1980s will no doubt witness sweeping changes in world population patterns and also determine the character of a New International Economic Order in which demographic factors will need to be recognised as being central. This period will also mark the second decade of UNFPA operations. It seems unthinkable that the Fund would ever have been called into existence at all, had it not been for the momentous demographic trends of the 1950s and 1960s when the consequences of unbridled population growth in the poorest countries rose to the surface of public awareness. One can also point to a significant converse interrelation. The national policy efforts which the Fund has helped to encourage and sustain, have become substantial factors affecting change in the nature and pace of the trends themselves.

The 1980s will unfold vast new needs and opportunties for effective demographic policies. Major population movements are momentous factors in the lives of nations but what is especially challenging now is the fact that we are living in a period of revolutionary shifts in world and regional demographic processes. In each of the world's geographic regions, as in almost every large or small country, societies are entering new demographic realms, characterised by breakaway tendencies or turning points which will soon take them far from where they were only short decades ago.

It follows that continuous attention to today's and tomorrow's demographic dynamics is essential, if population policies are to measure up to national needs. Otherwise, having succeeded in securing recognition of population policy as a priority in national agendas for development in all dimensions - political, social and economic - we risk losing the momentum gained and the success it promised in the years ahead.

It also follows, as will be clear from the review of population trends and issues set out below, that this is no time for complacency on any population policy front - national, regional or international. Indeed, the main lesson of the Fund's experience is that action called for by population policy has hardly begun. By the end of the current decade global numbers will have risen by some 738 million people, with nearly 90 percent of the increase occurring in the less developed regions. It is worth noting here that the total population in the developing world is about as much as the world's entire population of 3 billion in 1960.

Apart from the structural change taking place within national populations, the following issues will continue to be important in the foreseeable future:

Preventable mortality and morbidity is still far too high in many areas of the globe. Traditional fertility aspirations formed when death rates were much higher than they are now, continue very typically to be well beyond the social goals and individual means of hundreds of millions, even billions, of human beings. Infertility continues to be an entrenched global affliction, while undesired teenage pregnancy bids rapidly to become one. The tendency towards poorly balanced internal spatial distribution of population is perceived by governments on all continents to be a substantial deterrent to national development. In recent years, international migration, often of an unfamiliar kind - for example the labour migration to the Gulf States - is acquiring considerably heightened importance on the agenda of cross-country political issues requiring new approaches and solutions.

Related to all of these is an over-arching new policy need. This is to achieve new types and degrees of integration between population policies and development goals in its many facets: individual human rights, role of family, status of women, environmental quality, food supply, employment and per capita income, among others.

Although the very dynamics of current demographic trends add greatly to the difficulties of forecasting, six underlying realities will surely determine the direction, shape and substance of population fact and policy in the decade ahead. They are:

(1) the fertility transformations which are apparently gathering force in most of the less developed, low-income regions of the world;

(2) the new face of mortality-development interrelations in these regions;

(3) the impetus of the trends to bare-replacement or below-replacement fertility in the developed regions;

(4) the close of a 100 to 200-year era of mortality decline patterns in the developed or higher-income countries;

(5) accelerating urbanisation everywhere, and

(6) the appearance of demographic programming and policy goals as essential elements in socio-economic developing planning.

Singly and in combination, these realities rank with the foremost determinants of social developments of our times. Each marks a clear watershed between the first and second halves of this century and all have momentous human implications for as far ahead as we can see. A brief review of each of these tendencies is in order, therefore, before turning to some main policy challenges and issues.

Some Watersheds in World Population Dynamics: A Brief Review

Policy Implications of Fertility Decline

It now seems evident beyond question that a gradual process of fertility decline is spreading over much of the less developed regions. Since June last year much new and impressive evidence has emerged to confirm this conclusion. It was noted then that some 40 per cent and possibly more of the Third. World populations lived in areas where fertility has shown remarkable downturns within a short recent period, roughly within the last decade or so. Of the three to four dozen nations so described - in Northern Africa, Latin America and East Asia in particular - about half were small or island areas and half, large or mainland areas. Today, according to recent estimates made available by United Nations analysts, it appears likely that the percentage of Third World populations experiencing rapid declines can be expanded perceptibly, with Brazil the outstanding addition in terms of size. India, because of serious setbacks to its family planning programme, cannot yet be confidently assessed for either degree or sustainability of previously estimated declining trends. If, however, India is included with appropriate caution as an area of significant downtrends, no less than two of the three billions in Third World countries can be said to have been reducing their fertility substantially. Even with India excluded, it is no longer unreasonable to conclude that the Third World's breakaway from its very long-standing fertility patterns differs significantly from earlier fertility transitions which were experienced in developed countries. Not only does it involve far greater numbers of people and national areas, but it is occurring under an array of much more diverse regional and cultural circumstances.

Reduced marital fertility and delayed age of marriage have been the main contributing factors. Although the relative importance of these causes have obvious major implications for analysis and policy, they seem to be best seen as being complementary rather than as alternatives. Rising age of marriage, for example, is itself an indication that the cultural, social and psychological factors affecting child-bearing after marriage are undergoing significant change. And conversely, reduced fertility expectations within marriage can be a cogent factor influencing the age at marriage - a point too seldom considered in assessing the direct and indirect effects of family planning and sex education programmes. Moreover, "third forces" also may well be at play which would lead to postponed marriage and reduced child-bearing, simultaneously, acting as an interrelated pair. Confidence in further reductions in mortality, for example, seems to be such a force, indeed a major one, by raising the anticipated lifetimes of both parents and children.

None of this, obviously, provides any ground for relaxation of efforts in family planning programme areas. The evidence of fertility declines in the less developed regions suggests only that their burdens from previously high rate of reproduction have just begun to be reduced. Almost everywhere, they are far from being adequately reduced or eliminated.

Growth of numbers in the Third World regions overall, as in many of its parts, is not far today from where it was 20 years ago. Although the pace may have slackened over the last decade, it is still over 2 per cent in aggregate and higher still in numerous sub-regions. That this is excessive is the clear perception, not only of the great majority of analysts working in the area of demographic development interrelations, but also the perceptions of national governments in countries inhabited by some 82 per cent of the Third World's population.

Effect of Changes in Mortality Patterns

With respect to mortality as well, events of recent decades pose fresh challenges for the future. It now seems assured that a revolutionary change has taken place in the inter-relations which link levels of income, consumption and education in less developed nations with their attainable levels of life expectancy, infant mortality and overall (crude) death rates. Levels of life expectancy of under 45 or 50 years, infant mortality rates of 200 or higher, and crude death rates exceeding 20 per thousand were the prevalent orders of magnitude in all less developed regions until recently. Today, expectation of life at birth in most of the Third World has advanced far beyond its mid-century average of some 40-plus years. Similar major-scale trends could be shown for infant mortality and general death rates.

The challenge to effective policy—in public health, medical and health education is clear. Precisely because today's technical potentials for enhanced death and disease control have become so much more independent of the constraints of social and economic underdevelopment, they open fresh opportunities for achieving major gains throughout the less and least advantaged parts of Africa, Asia and Latin America.

Given internal political stability, and even moderate increases of international assistance to areas of especially high mortality such as in sub-Saharan Africa, South Asia and the Middle East it is reasonable to expect that 5-year gains or more in life expectancy at birth can be achieved within a decade. Recent setbacks in malaria control programmes give reason for some pause in making this statement, but do not deny its essential and apparently well established accuracy.

The force of mortality change as a social catalyst acting along almost all developmental dimensions of significance is of primal importance. It is hard to believe, for example, that major declines in mortality, once deeply embedded in social and individual expectations, would fail to have large impacts on family formation attitudes and behaviour.

Effect of Falling Fertility in Developed World

Turning to the developed regions—essentially Europe, including the USSR, North America, Australia, New Zealand and Japan—current fertility for their combined populations is barely, if at all, at replacement level. As a result of sharp declines over most of these areas in the past 10 to 20 years, many individual nations are manifesting fertility levels which are lower than ever recorded, or below replacement, or combinations of the two; United Nations projections which have just been issued suggest that bare replacement is a prominent possibility for the rest of this century. These trends appear to be essentially independent of fluctuations in economic activity, being as likely to continue in periods of prosperity as during recessions or even depressions. Rather, current low fertility in industrialised societies has been linked to such transformed parts of the social fabric as the declining importance of the family; the changing role of women; new sexual premises and norms; and the rapid rise of non-family households.

How nations will, or should, respond to the new prospects—indeed in some cases to the already existing fact—of near zero or even negative natural increase is sure to occupy governments increasingly over the decade ahead and beyond. Involved in addition to numbers of births and people are the manifold social and economic consequences that arise when the relative size of a population's younger-age members declines rapidly: rising average age of the population and increasing proportions of the aged; the need to shift resources from familiar forms of young-age dependency such as assistance for child health and education, to welfare systems for the aged; major impacts on residential and labour-force mobility; probable needs for changes in political attitudes towards immigration and much more.

The seemingly entrenched tendencies in nearly all industrial nations to a rapid aging of the population because of falling fertility will be further reinforced by the very different mortality prospects they face compared to the past. Contrary to a popular misconception, past mortality downtrends in these nations throughout the modern era have tended to reduce the average age of their populations, not raise it. For, although chances of surviving to the upper ages of life have increased greatly, the proportion of survivors in the younger age groups has consistently risen even more.

Mortality of Developed World: End of an Era

The post-1950 decades have come close to ending mortality patterns which have endured for the better part of the past 100 to 200 years. The rise of life expectancy at birth during that period, from some 40 years to 70 or 75 years was due mainly to the conquest or near elimination of infectious disease and substantial reduction of premature mortality. Today, the leeway for further progress in each of these directions has become so sharply limited in all parts of the more developed regions that any further effects on longevity would be small in the future.

A World of Exploding Cities

The fifth basic demographic reality concerns the pace of urbanisation everywhere. Latest United Nations estimates suggest that world urban population has doubled since mid-century and may well double again before the century is over. These are phenomenally rapid trends by any historic standards we know about, and are bound to have radical-to-revolutionary implications for national economic and social structures.

In the more developed regions, about half of their total population lived in urban areas as of 1950, two-thirds do so today and three-quarters are expected to do so by the year 2000. These increases in ratios have been caused in part by the broadest declines in rural numbers ever known to have taken place in the past 300 to 400 years.

In the less developed regions, despite rapidly rising numbers in rural areas, the urban proportion has risen from about 1-to-6 in 1950 to almost 1-to-3 today; it could become almost 1-to-2 within the next 3 decades. Urban population in Africa tripled during 1950-1975 and is expected to triple again during 1975-2000, while the corresponding multipliers for Asia and Latin America range between 2 and 3.

Although the expected urban proportion in the population of the more developed regions by the year 2000 will be almost twice as high as the fraction estimated for the less developed regions, (about 80 per cent in the developed regions compared to roughly 40 per cent in the less developed), the size of urban populations will run much the other way. The United Nations' estimates suggest that, in terms of size, the urban population in the less developed areas will be about twice that in the developed.

These facts go far to explain why national governments, when asked to indicate their main population policy concerns, speak of unsatisfactory spatial distribution more often than all other demographic trends as an obstacle to their development goals. This is not surprising, given the immediacy of such concerns as population distribution and redistribution for industrial location policies, development investment allocations, schools, hospitals and housing needs.

Population Policy "Takes Off"

The sixth and last general point concerns the new place of population policies as viewed by governments. The battle for acceptance of the need for such policies has been largely won. Such need is no longer a matter for debate in international fora, much unlike the situation only a decade ago—surely one of the most striking instances of a major policy reorientation on record since the appearance of national development planning on a widespread scale.

An inquiry conducted by the United Nations during the past year suggests that about 80 per cent of the Third World population live in countries whose governments favour "direct intervention" to reduce their rates of natural increase. Access to modern methods of fertility regulation is directly or indirectly supported, or at least not limited, by the governments of practically the entire Third World's population a perceptibly higher percentage, incidentally, than is found among the more developed regions. To put it another way, over half the governments of the Third World report the use of fertility policy approaches intended to foster their development goals.

Policy measures for redistributing population are the most frequently used demographic policy approaches of all in the less developed regions, being applied by no less than nearly 95 per cent of their governments. Almost the same number of governments report the use of non-demographic measures which have been adopted or are intended to affect demographic trends indirectly.

In the more developed areas, the extent of population policy interest, as reported to the United Nations, is substantially smaller. It is, however, by no means minor. Governments of some 40 per cent of the population of these areas perceive a need to raise natural increase, and half of all developed-area governments favour direct intervention to achieve this end. About half, too, of such governments report the use of demographic or non-demographic measures, or both, for demographic policy purposes.

Modern population policy as an arm of development policy is still too new to permit identification of trends or degrees of success. The results now becoming available through the World Fertility Survey, an internationally coordinated programme of studies being conducted in 40 to 50 less developed countries and in 15 to 20 more developed ones, is beginning to provide important new light on the payoff possibilities to be expected from recent family planning programmes. Other population policy areas as well should soon become increasingly amenable to trend analysis and evaluation, assuming as we may that such policies continue to become increasingly time-tested, comprehensive and development-oriented.

In short, the last 10 to 15 years have witnessed a remarkably rich and promising "take off" phase in the international evolution of population policy-making. Widespread political acceptance of the need for such policies, and their initial translation into operating programmes, have been hallmarks of the period. Both as a body of social goals and as a process of social action, population policy will loom increasingly large throughout the rest of this century and for as far ahead as one can see.

Some Policy Looks Ahead: Needs, Issues, Possibilities

1980s — Decade of New Integrations

If the past decade can be regarded as marking a "take off" phase of demographic policy-making, the next decade might be described as one involving a "drive to maturity".

Briefly, we are dealing with a global establishment which has soared phenomenally from nearly zero-level beginnings only 10 to 15 years ago to already imposing levels today.

With these developments must come growing accountability. Population policy is fast transcending the point where it can be regarded as a fiscal sideshow. Rather, much enhanced sophistication will be necessary in future in selecting among policy alternatives, in assessing their benefits and cost effectiveness, and in allowing for demographic-development reciprocities. Not least among the coming decade's major needs for improved demographic policy-making will be the rapid evolution of evaluative tools for analysing all of these questions. Such tools might well, in time, come to constitute entire new areas of research in the social sciences and in the literature on administration.

Events of the past decade, and realistic expectations for the future, make it appear certain that demographic policies in the decade ahead will feature an ever-widening array of "New Integrations" with development policy. The integrations envisaged will complement, yet go far beyond, government concerns with death and disease control—important though these will continue to be. They will also far transcend focus on family planning, though this will continue to be a primary concern.

One of the "New Integrations" to be expected in the 1980s is that which proceeds from development planning, and from socio-economic programming more generally, to population planning and/or programming. In a number of countries planning boards have been set up to integrate population variables in economic development programmes.

The extension of educational and employment opportunities for women, especially when combined with growing liberalisation of life styles, can have significant impact on age at marriage and fertility. Yet we have few examples, if any, of alert population-planning adaptations designed to take account and advantage of such basic shifts in social contexts. Sex education as an adjunct to general education planning and policies has still to prove itself. National investment policies, whether of a social overhead nature or aimed at selective industrial expansion, can have major impacts on the location or relocation of labour force and population, but such impacts are seldom fully enough anticipated by either the development or population planner. Transportation and international trade policies are often primary catalysts of development. Rarely, however, are their potentials for population change adequately allowed for—not only with respect to internal migration, city-size distributions and the like, but also as they concern probable fertility impacts or required restructurings of public health and family planning programmes.

The list of potentially important examples is nearly endless, but the principle is essentially the same: Population planning needs to become a more effective arm of overall development planning, not only as an active change agent in its own right, but also as a resource closely attuned to other realms of policy for actively affecting development.

To these probable major areas of new substantive integrations should be added a variety of evolving or relatively novel integrations of a procedural administrative nature—another general concern of this review. In particular, two such items might be mentioned.

One is that country-to-country (or region-to-region) technical assistance by Third World areas among themselves needs to be increased as experience and expertise in demographic-development policy-making accumulate in these areas. The UNFPA already has a small but valuable body of experience in such horizontal assistance on which such an increase may be founded.

A second is that international agencies in the population assistance field will have to concern themselves increasingly not only with fertility and mortality but also with spatial distribution, if its activities are to become more closely consonant with practical development needs in aid-receiving areas. As an adjunct to such activities, as we have found, institution-building and expanded support of national research capabilities for meeting own policy needs could prove to be especially valuable.

Relative newness of population policy directions is not, of course, equivalent to relative priorities. Undoubtedly over the next decade, and almost surely for many decades to come, major policy attention by national and international agencies will continue to focus on family size and birth planning, in short on fertility.

Concluding Comment

The changing population picture over the past three decades may be usefully viewed in three thematic frames: The Fifties was the decade in which the "population problem" was perceived and studied by demographers primarily as questions of morbidity and mortality. The reason for this was that since there had been a rough and ready balance over centuries between birth rates and death rates, population increase had been relatively slow. But soon after World War II when the programmes to eradicate infectious disease were successfully launched, the demographic balance changed drastically. This concern was reflected in the demographic literature of the period.

The rapid increase in population growth that became apparent in the decades of the Sixties demanded and brought about a shift of emphasis to the fertility factor in population growth.

In the Seventies the awareness of the need to regard population as an important and integral factor in the entire process of development increased and was given universal political recognition.

The decade that lies ahead, taking into account the trends in fertility, mortality and other demographic factors, and their impact on development, demands the substantiation of that recognition. The Eighties, therefore, will be the decade in which population would be integrally embodied in development policies and programmes. It makes it essential, therefore to include population issues as one of the central concerns of the International Development Strategy.

Appendix D

Recent Trends in International Population Assistance*

by

Halvor Gille, Deputy Executive Director, United Nations Fund for Population Activities

Introduction

The history of international population assistance is brief, but spectacular. As recently as ten to fifteen years ago, there was little consensus among governments as to the need for assistance to the Third World except in the fields of demography and statistics. [1] On the contrary, the forces opposing assistance to such activities as family planning and population policy on religious, cultural, or political grounds were still generally dominant. Within many developed countries the promotion of family planning was still, to a large extent, seen as the exclusive concern of voluntary endeavours, supported by private philanthropy. Today, technical co-operation and financial assistance for a wide spectrum of population activities in developing countries are fully recognized as the legitimate concern of, and high priority for, governments and the international community.

In the early 1950s, the United Nations began to assist developing countries with census-taking, training in demography and the preparation of studies of the relationships between population trends and social and economic factors as well as with some action oriented research activities. In 1952, two non-governmental agencies concerned with assistance to population were established—the International Planned Parenthood Federation (IPPF) and the Population Council. The Ford and Rockefeller Foundations also began to assist population-related activities. Together these four non-governmental agencies were the main sources of assistance for population and related activities until the late 1960s when governmental resources became available on a large scale.

*Prepared as of September 1978. The views expressed are those of the author and do not necessarily reflect the policies or directions of the United Nations or any of its Member States.
[1] A clear-cut, and generally agreed upon definition of the term "population activities" is not available, but it is clear that it covers much more than demography or delivery of family planning services but not the entire scope of the World Population Plan of Action. Population activities covered by international assistance have been broadly classified by the United Nations organizations concerned into the following major subject areas: (1) basic population data; (2) population dynamics; (3) population policy formulation, implementation and evaluation; (4) family planning; (5) bio-medical research; and (6) communication and education. It includes a wide spectrum of data collection, training, research, information and operational activities in population.

The first government to give assistance for family planning to a developing country was Sweden in 1958. This was in support of an experimental programme in Sri Lanka, and was followed by similar assistance to the government of Pakistan in 1961. The United Kingdom initiated its bilateral population assistance programme on a modest scale in 1964. The U.S. government began to include population activities in its development assistance in 1965. In the early 1970s a number of governments followed the lead provided by Sweden, the United Kingdom and the United States. These included Canada, Denmark, the Federal Republic of Germany, Japan, the Netherlands and Norway.

The barriers which, to a large extent, had handicapped the United Nations system in responding directly to the needs of developing countries for assistance in the fields of population, particularly in family planning, began to lift around the mid 1960s. A consensus was reached in the General Assembly in 1966 concerning the provision of population assistance, from governments upon request, in the areas of training, research, information, and advisory services. In response, the following year, the Secretary-General established a Trust Fund for Population Activities—later renamed the United Nations Fund for Population Activities (UNFPA)—which rapidly grew into a major source of international population assistance, both in terms of financial resources as well as programme development. In the meantime, a number of United Nations Specialized Agencies and UNICEF broadened their mandates to include those aspects of population and family planning falling within their areas of competence. In 1968, the World Bank [2] began to take into consideration the need of developing countries for assistance to family planning programmes and related activities and made its first loan in this area to Jamaica in 1970.

One of the most important events in the history of international population assistance occurred in 1974 when the World Population Conference was held in Bucharest. A World Population Plan of Action was adopted at the conference by consensus of 135 states *inter alia* calling upon developed countries as well as other countries to increase their assistance to developing countries: "In view of the magnitude of the problems and the consequent national requirements for funds . . . considerable expansion of international assistance in the population field is required for the proper implementation of this Plan of Action." [3]

To what extent has this call been heard? Have the main features of international population assistance changed since the Bucharest Conference? What is the outlook for the future role of such assistance?

Current Levels of Population Assistance

Total international assistance for population activities amounted to only about $2

---

[2] The International Bank for Reconstruction and Development (IBRD) and the International Development Association (IDA).
[3] "World Population Plan of Action," in *United Nations Report of the United Nations World Population Conference, 1974,* New York, 1975, paragraph 104.

million in 1960 and $18 million in 1965, but it increased rapidly to $125 million in 1970 and to nearly $350 million by 1977 or an estimated net amount, excluding double counting, of $345 million (see Table I in the Annex). [4]

This dramatic increase in population assistance is a clear indication of the growing commitment of governments and international organizations concerned to collaborate in, and contribute to, tackling the urgent population problems of the developing world. It is important to note, however, that the rapid growth in resources made available for international assistance has not been maintained in recent years. A peak was reached in 1974 when the annual growth in resources for population assistance reached an all time high level of some $50 million. The timing of this peak could be interpreted as a response to the spirit of the World Population Year and Conference, but is more likely a result of the devaluation of the U.S. dollar which automatically increased the U.S. dollar equivalent of the amounts pledged by many donors in their own currency.

In the following years the average rate of growth in resources fell well below the level reached earlier in the 1970s. The percentage annual increase was only 8-12 per cent in the years 1975-1977, as compared with 20 per cent on the average in the years 1970-1974. In view of the substantial inflationary trends worldwide and the devaluation of the U.S. dollar, the growth in international population assistance has, to a great extent if not entirely, been offset by the decline in purchasing power. Measured in constant U.S. dollars (consumer price index), the average annual increase since 1974 has been around 3 per cent. Therefore, the level of resources transferred for population activities for the benefit of the developing countries has only increased very modestly since the World Population Year and Conference (Fig. 1).

The magnitude of population assistance has barely kept pace with overall development assistance since the World Population Conference (Annex, Table II). In 1974, assistance in the field of population amounted to 2.3 per cent of total development assistance; it declined to 2.1 per cent in 1975 but increased to 2.3 per cent in 1976 and in 1977 mainly due to stagnation in the overall level of official development assistance.

The main factor in the slowing down of the trend in resources for international population assistance was that the largest donor, the United States, did not continue to make substantial increases in its population assistance as it did in the late 1960s and early 1970s, but actually reduced its annual contributions from year to year in the period 1972 through 1975. An upward trend, however, appears to have begun in 1976 and an annual increase of around 12 per cent took place in 1977 and 1978. Although a number of other donor governments of developed countries at the same time showed a growing recognition of the importance of population assistance by increasing substantially their contributions, these increases were not large enough to maintain the overall growth rate of resources available for population assistance.

The dominating position of the United States in the donor community has recently been considerably reduced. Before 1974, three-quarters or more of all government

---

[4] Differences in definition of population activities and difficulties in identifying population components in multi-purpose or integrated development programmes make it necessary to exercise some caution in interpretation of international statistics on population assistance.

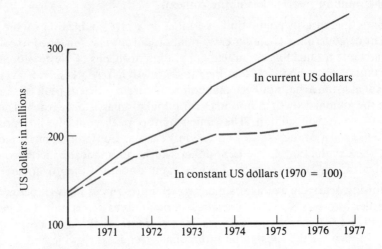

Fig. 1. *Total International Population Assistance* (excluding double counting) *1971-1977*

resources for population assistance and well over half of all funds came from the United States Government. In 1977, total contributions from all other governments was about equal to that of the United States and the latter provided about 40 per cent of the total of population assistance funds (Annex, Table II).

Sources of Population Assistance

Although over eighty governments have, at one time or another, contributed to international population assistance, the major share comes from less than a dozen countries. The largest contributor, the United States, spent around $146 million on population assistance in 1977 or 2.8 per cent of its total development assistance. Around one-fifth of this amount was channeled through private and voluntary international organizations based in the United States; nearly one-quarter went to UNFPA and IPPF; about one-fifth was grants to universities and other governmental and non-governmental institutions in the United States for research and training related to population issues of developing countries, and the remainder, over one-third provided direct bilateral support to population and family planning projects in developing countries.

Sweden and Norway are the two largest donor governments after the United States. In 1977, the total Swedish financial contribution reached a level of around $37 million amounting to around 4 per cent of its total development assistance. Norway, which has sharply increased its population assistance since 1974 by more than tripling it, contributed about $36 million in 1977 which represented nearly 13 per cent of the total Norwegian development assistance programme—the highest proportion of any donor country.[5]Denmark and Finland also gave comparatively high priority to population assistance with contributions in 1977 of $6 million and $2 million respectively, or around 3 per cent of their total assistance programme. Other major contributors were Japan, with over $15 million, Canada, the Federal Republic of Germany and the Netherlands with around $9 million and the United Kingdom with around $7 million—but in all these countries, population assistance constituted merely around 1 per cent of total official development assistance. A significant recent development has been the interest shown by a number of Arab governments, particularly of oil-exporting countries in contributing to international population assistance; in 1976, these governments, which had not previously given support in this area made contributions amounting to around $10 million.

A number of donors provide bilateral population assistance amounting to about 28 per cent of total governmental population assistance (1975), but only in three countries is the population component of the total bilateral governmental assistance programme of major significance, namely in Norway, Sweden and the United States where it constituted around 4 to 5 per cent of the total.

Around 62 per cent of total population assistance provided by governments is channelled through multilateral organizations—about 35 per cent to inter-governmental bodies and 27 per cent to international non-governmental organizations. (About 11 per cent of governments' population assistance is spent in institutions in the donor countries themselves.) A number of governments utilize multilateral channels for most of their support of population activities: Belgium, Canada, Denmark, the Federal Republic of Germany, Japan, New Zealand and Norway. The Netherlands has phased out all bilateral population programmes and concentrates its resources entirely on multilateral aid.

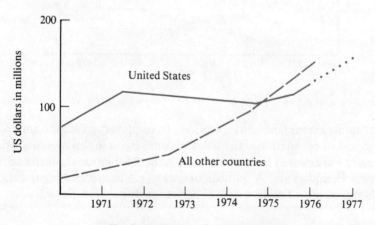

Fig. 2. *Government Donors, 1971-1977*

---

[5] The Norwegian law on development assistance stipulates that 10 per cent of all assistance should be for the fields of population.

Multilateral population programmes have grown markedly. Until the mid-1960s, the role of the organizations within the United Nations system was restricted, not merely by limited mandates in the population fields and lack of funds, but also by the fact that few governments had yet formulated national population policies or foreign aid policies on population. Around 4 per cent of total government development assistance provided to multilateral programmes is for population activities. Most of the resources available for population activities undertaken by the United Nations and its Specialized Agencies (excluding UNFPA whose resources are entirely from voluntary government contributions) are provided by governments as voluntary extra-budgetary contributions and only about one-sixth is provided by assessed contributions to their regular budgets from member states.

Before the World Population Conference, UNFPA had already emerged as the largest multilateral source of population assistance. Since 1974 the Fund has continued to grow rapidly, at twice the rate of increase in population assistance in general.[6] Today, it is the largest source of direct assistance for population activities in developing countries (Fig 3).[7]

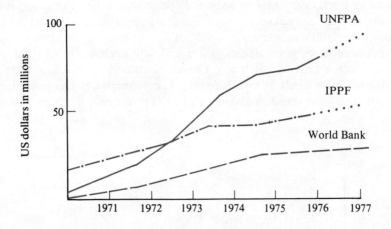

Fig. 3. *Major Multilateral Donors, 1971-1977*

A number of non-governmental organizations have played an important pioneering role in the support of population activities. The four largest in this regard are the International Planned Parenthood Federation (IPPF), the Population Council and the Ford and Rockefeller Foundations. A number of other smaller private organizations also contribute. Some of them function exclusively in the population fields; others support

[6] From 1975 to 1976, the nine major Government donors to UNFPA, IPPF and UNDP increased their contributions to UNFPA by 19 per cent and to each of the two other organizations by 6 per cent.
[7] In 1976, the level of direct UNFPA expenditures in developing countries amounted to $51 million; the United States spent bilaterally $38 million during the same period (in both cases including share of administrative costs).

population activities within a broad range of purposes and programmes. All these organizations provide a channel for private financial contributions, though many also draw, to some extent, on governmental or multilateral funds, and some rely on the contributions of volunteers and part-time workers.

Involvement in assistance has also spread to professional organizations in the population field, such as the International Union for the Scientific Study of Population, the International Confederation of Midwives and the International Association of Schools for Social Work. Other organizations are primarily concerned with assisting special target groups mainly through education, information, and advisory services on population questions of concern to their affiliates and members.

Mass organizations, such as trade unions, co-operatives, youth and women's organizations, and other key institutional forces with international responsibilities are also beginning to support the development of population policies and programmes, although the primary focus of their activities may not be on population issues.

Furthermore, a number of universities and other educational institutions, mostly American but also some European ones, conduct training programmes specifically oriented towards the needs of developing countries, as well as support or carry out research activities relevant to selected population issues in developing countries.

Types and Areas of Assistance

Almost all donors make their contributions to population assistance in grants, but a few governments (Canada, Denmark, Finland, the Federal Republic of Germany, and the United States) also make loans available. Inter-governmental and non-governmental organizations all provide grants except the World Bank, which only gives loans or credit. All donors make contributions in cash, but some also provide grants in kind, mainly equipment and contraceptive supplies (Australia, Denmark, Finland, the Federal Republic of Germany, Japan, Sweden, and the United States).

In 1975, about 48 per cent of the total resources available for population assistance supported family planning programmes. However, a substantial part of the resources devoted to "multisector activities" which amounted to around 20 per cent of all resources and, to some extent, some of the activities in the fields of communication and education, supported family planning activities directly or indirectly. Thus, the share of total resources supporting family planning was undoubtedly well over 50 per cent. Around 15 per cent of total resources was devoted to statistical and demographic activities and a smaller share, just under 10 per cent, to biomedical research including contraceptive development.

From a geographical point of view, the largest share of support, over 40 per cent, was devoted to interregional and global activities, many of them carried out in developed countries. As for the remainder, the largest share went to the region of Asia and the Pacific, namely around 30 per cent, followed by Africa with 14 per cent, Latin America 10 per cent and the Mediterranean and the Middle East 5 per cent.

I.P.A.— CC

A comparison between the assistance provided in 1975 by the three largest donors illustrates notable differences in programmatic emphasis. The United States spent over 75 per cent of its resources in supporting family planning programmes, while the comparable figure for Sweden was about 50 per cent and for the UNFPA slighly less. On the other hand, about 19 per cent of UNFPA resources supported basic data collection, the comparable figure for the United States was only around 9 per cent and for Sweden, negligible. Both the United States and the UNFPA devoted around 10 per cent of their population assistance to the field of population dynamics. Biomedical research, including contraceptive development, received over 40 per cent of Sweden's population assistance, about 5 per cent of the United States' population assistance and only less than 1 per cent of UNFPA resources. From a geographical point of view, the United States spent around 67 per cent of its resources on interregional and global projects, while for Sweden the share was just under 50 per cent and for the UNFPA almost 24 per cent. As for assistance to activities at the country level, all three donors spent the largest shares in Asia and the Pacific; this is particularly true of Sweden and the United States, while UNFPA had a more even distribution among regions.

The Need for, and Impact of, International Population Assistance

It is a difficult, if not an impossible task, to estimate the future needs for international population assistance. Much depends upon the criteria to be applied with regard to the types of population activities which are required, the extent to which support from external sources is needed, the availability of local resources and the absorptive capacity of the developing countries.

The UNFPA has attempted to make estimates of the costs of developing comprehensive population programmes to meet various targets or goals such as: to provide information and services on family planning for the entire population in the developing countries; to conduct a complete population census in all countries at least every ten years; to establish vital statistics registration systems with a coverage of at least 90 per cent; to provide population education in and out of schools; to train personnel required for population programmes; and to support research required for planning and implementing effective population programmes, including operational research and development of improved contraceptive techniques.

An approximate total annual cost for all relevant population activities is estimated at $1.50 per capita or $2900 million (1976 prices) for the developing world as a whole. The provision of family planning and maternal and child health services according to established minimum requirements accounts for over half of this or an estimate of $0.84 per capita.

Although no accurate estimates can be made of the need for population programmes and the estimates provided here may not take fully into account certain concomitant needs in the economic and social fields, it seems fairly clear that the estimated total of around $300 million available for population assistance from international sources amounts to a small proportion, probably only around 10 per cent of total estimated needs for external and internal resources for population activities.

In financial terms, international assistance defrays only a small portion of the actual costs of the population activities undertaken in the developing world. While it is recognized that such assistance cannot be, and should never be, more than a marginal addition to the development efforts of recipient countries, there is no question, however, that the role and significance of international population assistance go far beyond the often comparatively modest financial inputs. It constitutes, in many cases, an essential element in promoting national efforts and enlisting local resources. In many instances, the activities supported would probably not have taken place at all without the interest and contributions of donor governments and agencies. Very often, international assistance provides the important spark needed to overcome reluctance at the local level to expend the necessary financial, human, and material resources for worthwhile activities. Sometimes the will and the necessary local sources may be there, but crucial inputs of equipment and supplies cannot be obtained due to foreign exchange difficulties unless international assistance is made available. The African Census Programme is a case in point, under which a number of developing countries are involved for the first time in taking a population census.

At the same time, the role of international assistance should not be exaggerated to imply that without it major results cannot be accomplished in tackling population problems in the developing world. The People's Republic of China is an excellent example, where the effective delivery of family planning services at all levels, measures dealing with internal population distribution problems, and contraceptive research have been undertaken successfully without any assistance from abroad. Still, the majority of developing countries need and want international assistance to expedite the process of dealing with their population problems.

One of the most significant accomplishments of population assistance is probably the contribution it has made to promoting awareness worldwide and in individual countries of population problems and issues, their implications and the need for policies and programmes to deal with them. It is not possible, in general, to demonstrate definite effects upon population trends, and in any case, results cannot be expected in the short span of a few years. Support provided for the training of personnel, for research and evaluation, for institution building, and for related education and communication activities often has important multiplier effects and long-term benefits which are difficult to measure in quantitative terms.

Priorities in Future Programmes

More and more attention is being devoted to setting priorities in assistance to population programmes for two main reasons. On the one hand, increasing awareness of the impact of population factors on development and the adoption of population policies by more and more governments have led to rapid growth in the demand from developing countries for such assistance. On the other hand, developments at the World Population Conference have led many donors to review and reassess their development co-operation policies, with particular regard to population.

Reviews have been undertaken or are in progress in Canada, Sweden, the United Kingdom, the United States, UNFPA, the World Bank and IPPF, often resulting in new strategies or policies for population assistance. Various concepts of setting priorities for allocation of resources have emerged or have been refined. Most donors apply more than one criteria for setting priorities. UNFPA has developed a system for setting priorities based on economic and demographic data reflecting needs.

The following resume of criteria for priority setting is not intended to give complete coverage for all donors but reflects mainly new strategies for population assistance resulting from recent reviews, revision, or reaffirmation of policies.

Priority Countries

Some donors intend to concentrate their resources in, or give special attention to, the needs of certain countries.

In the case of several bilateral programmes, the political situation of the recipient countries or special geographical, historical, cultural, or trade considerations play an important role (Australia, Canada, Denmark, Japan, New Zealand, Sweden, the United States).

Some donors are particularly interested in assisting the poorest of the developing countries based upon criteria on estimated per capita income (UNFPA, Canada, the United Kingdom) or the extent to which they are seriously affected by balance-of-payments problems (New Zealand, the United Kingdom).

Sometimes demographic criteria are taken into account in identifying countries with the most urgent need for population programmes (Canada considering birth rate, death rate, infant mortality, current and future potential population growth; the United States concentrating on countries with large populations contributing most to world population growth and where prospects for reducing fertility are best; UNFPA using rate of population growth, fertility, infant mortality, and agricultural population density; and the World Bank taking into account population size, growth rate, population density, government's policy commitment to reduce fertility, and prospective demographic impact).

Priority Objectives

Most donors are giving increasing attention to support for population activities as an integral part of development such as rural development, family health, social welfare, participation of women in development, etc. (Finland, Federal Republic of Germany, Japan, Norway, Sweden, the United Kingdom, the United States, UNFPA, ILO, FAO, WHO, the World Bank, Ford Foundation, and the Population Council). Some support population components in such programs (UNFPA, the Population Council).

Several donors are giving priority attention to promoting activities at the local level through community or family based programmes (the United States, UNICEF, the

World Bank, IPPF). Priority is given by some donors to assisting population activities for the benefit of poverty-stricken and other disadvantaged population groups (UNF-PA, ILO).

Attempts are being made to determine recipient countries' basic needs in population and related fields (the United States, UNFPA, UNICEF, ILO, WHO).

Priority Areas of Assistance

Most donors of population assistance will continue giving high priority to support for family planning activities designed to attain fertility reduction, health, social welfare, or other socio-economic development objectives. Contraceptive supplies are provided by a number of donors (Japan, Sweden, the United States, UNFPA, IPPF). Only certain donors provide financial or technical assistance for abortion and sterilization programmes (Sweden, the United States (sterilization only), UNFPA, the World Bank, WHO, IPPF, and a few other non-governmental organizations). Injectables are available only from a few donors (the United Kingdom, UNFPA, WHO, the Population Council).

Most donors are giving high priority to the training of local personnel for population programmes. Many are also giving special attention to research such as in human reproduction and contraceptive development (Canada, Sweden, WHO, Ford Foundation, the Population Council, Rockefeller Foundation); to operational research (the United States, UNFPA, the World Bank); and to demographic and social science research (United Nations, UNFPA, the World Bank, Ford Foundation, the Population Council).

Prospects for the Future

It is, of course, difficult to make a long-term prediction of the future resource situation for international population assistance. Very much depends upon the prospects for overall development assistance. Several donors have reached, or will soon reach, the overall goal for development assistance in the Second Development Decade of 1 per cent of the gross national product and their population assistance may not increase substantially beyond the equivalent of increases in its national income.

On a short-term basis, however, prospects seem quite good for a substantial increase in resources; the United States has increased its population assistance from $119 million in 1976 to $146 million in 1977 and is likely to contribute around $160 million or higher in 1978, which is an average annual increase of nearly 20 per cent. Japan may increase its assistance in 1977 by a similar percentage and UNFPA's programme expenditure in 1977 was around 17 per cent higher than that in 1976. If contributions from other governments than the United States should continue to increase at the same level as in the past three years, total population assistance may reach about $400 million by 1978.

It seems too early to assess the impact of the World Population Conference and the

World Population Plan of Action upon population assistance. Several major donors have reviewed and revised their policies mainly to broaden the approach to deal with population issues. Many donors seem still to stress fertility control as the major objective of their population assistance, although the World Population Plan of Action gives considerable emphasis to other areas as well. Problems of urbanization and spatial distribution, according to a United Nations inquiry, are those population problems which most governments are concerned with, but very limited population assistance is provided in these areas. There has not been any discernible increase in the attention given to biomedical research, including contraceptive development despite the stress on it in the Plan of Action.

Donor governments and organizations have become more concerned with the views, needs and policies of recipient countries. However, a considerable part of international population assistance is still supporting research, training and other activities located in the donor countries themselves. Further attention should be given to building up the technological infrastructure in developing countries in some cases on a sub-regional or regional basis. More use should be made of the local expertise and production facilities in the recipient countries rather than sending advisers, equipment, and supplies from the industrialized world. The main emphasis should be on building up self-reliance of developing countries.

At the moment, international population assistance finds itself in a dilemmatic situation with forces pulling in opposite directions.

With the greater availability of data and trained personnel and the establishment of population policies by more and more governments, absorptive capacity for population assistance in recipient countries has substantially increased. This increase is generating a rapidly growing demand not only for population assistance itself, but also for a greater say regarding the sources and uses of such assistance. Yet, the donor community, having become more conscious of the need for better co-ordination to maximize the effectiveness of its inputs as a result of resource constraints, is involved in setting priorities to regulate the direction, areas, and modes of assistance.

It is as important to resolve this situation, perhaps on an *ad hoc* basis, as it is to seek financial means to minimize the widening gap between the demand for, and supply of, international population assistance. Apart from striving to ensure a continuous growth in the resources available for population assistance, the donor community should focus greater attention on channelling such assistance to help developing countries meet their basic needs for promoting self-reliance in the formulation as well as the implementation of population policies. It is, however, not only a matter of stepping up technical co-operation and providing financial assistance to these countries. More concerted action should also be promoted towards developing a global strategy to assist developing countries in dealing with their major population problems, rather than merely effecting a transfer of funds between donors and recipients.

Annex

Table I. *Trends in Development and Population Assistance. 1961-1977*

	Total official development assistance[1] (in millions of US$)	Population assistance[2]	Population assistance as percentage of total assistance (in per cent)
1977	14,759	345	2.3
1976	13,666	320	2.3
1975	13,588	286	2.1
1974	11,302	257	2.3
1973	9,400	182	2.0
1972	8,700	171	2.0
1971	7,700	155	2.0
1970	6,800	125	1.8
1969	6,600	86	1.3
1968	6,300	58	0.9
1967	6,600	30	0.5
1966	6,000	34	0.6
1965	5,900	18	0.3
1964	6,000	16	0.3
1963	5,800	11	0.2
1962	5,400	5	0.1
1961	5,200	6	0.1

Notes: [1] Excluding export credits, private investment, and other commercial transfers.
[2] Net totals excluding double-counting due to transfers between donors. Grants by voluntary organizations are not included for the years 1961-1969. In 1970 these grants amounted to $0.9 million.

Sources: Organization for Economic Co-operation and Development, governments and annual reports of development assistance agencies and organizations.

Table II. *Population Assistance by Major Donors, 1971-1977*[1]

Governments	1971	1972	1973 (in thousands of US$)	1974	1975	1976	1977
Australia	—	357	579	639	1,587	967	1,065
Belgium	147	18	75	837	476	934	900
Canada	2,496	2,997	4,159	5,498	7,183	8,989	9,116
Denmark	1,918	2,289	2,035	4,784	3,548	4,978	6,200
Finland	507	892	1,033	2,587	2,026	1,578	1,852
Germany Federal Republic of	1,657	2,435	4,392	5,770	13,400	8,739	8,611
Japan	2,090	2,196	2,812	5,293	7,971	12,920	15,400
Netherlands	1,106	2,232	3,718	5,785	6,695	8,954	9,649
New Zealand	—	77	40	580	880	607	573
Norway	3,870	5,539	8,600	10,800	18,500	27,400	36,363
Sweden	7,446	12,739	17,123	21,468	26,169	28,743	31,417

Table II (cont.)

Switzerland	168	191	189	190	200	242	500
United Kingdom	2,311	3,257	3,861	3,032	6,450	6,983	7,168
United States	109,567	121,133	115,106	110,146	106,036	119,027	145,367
Others	1,283	1,592	1,747	2,325	3,580	11,356	12,000
Sub-total	$134,566	$157,944	$165,469	$179,734	$204,701	$242,417	$286,181
Inter-Governmental Organizations							
United Nations	6,995	5,952	8,459	20,786	24,234	28,009	27,952
UNICEF	2,382	2,371	3,711	5,753	6,725	6,611	6,700
UNFPA	8,937	19,840	34,684	57,000	71,213	75,781	78,000
ILO	165	989	2,259	3,827	4,901	6,483	6,775
FAO	607	574	1,370	1,539	2,238	—	—
UNESCO	38	28	2,554	4,130	5,337	4,042	5,034
WHO	2,823	6,374	15,991	18,932	22,979	29,324	34,679
World Bank[2]	1,600	5,700	11,200	18,600	24,900	27,000	28,200
Others	5,200	6,577	1,789	6,225	6,300	6,300	6,500
Sub-total	$28,747	$48,405	$82,017	$139,219	$168,827	$183,550	$195,200
Non-Governmental Organizations							
Ford Foundation	15,221	14,647	12,353	13,774	10,700	10,800	8,900
IPPF	19,294	24,935	33,798	42,910	42,584	45,554	51,198
Population Council	14,084	17,360	16,128	15,582	12,076	11,000	11,338
Rockefeller Foundation	2,864	6,608	6,370	9,007	8,516	8,500	6,178
Others	3,877	4,400	7,400	6,400	6,400	6,400	7,900
Sub-total	$55,340	$67,950	$76,049	$87,673	$80,276	$83,000	$85,514
Total	$218,653	$274,299	$323,535	$406,626	$453,804	$508,967	$566,895
Total excluding double counting[3]							
(a) in current US$	$161,519	$183,785	$208,651	256,812	$285,663	$320,011	$345,268
(b) in constant US$ (1970 = 100)	$154,860	$170,645	$182,387	$202,214	$206,106	$218,280	$221,179

Notes:

[1] Actual expenditures except that some of the 1977 figures are estimates based upon allocations. All figures refer to calendar year.

[2] Annual estimates for the World Bank based upon its commitments according to loan or credit agreements and the planned duration of project execution.

[3] Arrived at by deducting the following from the total.

     Governments' contributions to UNFPA;

     USAID contributions to IPPF, Pathfinder Fund and the Population Council;

     UNFPA contributions to organizations in the United Nations system;

     Contributions from one foundation to another.

Sources: See Table I. In addition, United Nations document E/5673, "Report of the Administrative Committee on Co-ordination on Expenditure of the United Nations system in relation to programmes," and U.S. Consumer Price Index, United Nations, *Statistical Yearbook and Monthly Bulletin of Statistics.*

Table III. Government Assistance for Population Activities as Percentage of Total Official Development Assistance in Major Donor Countries 1973 -

Country	1973	1974	1975	1976	1977
	(in per cent)				
Australia	0.2	0.1	0.3	0.3	0.2
Belgium	-	0.3	0.1	0.3	0.2
Canada	1.2	0.8	0.8	1.0	0.9
Denmark	3.1	2.8	1.7	2.3	2.4
Finland	1.1	6.8	4.2	3.1	3.8
Germany, Federal Republic of	0.4	0.4	0.8	0.6	0.6
Japan	1.3	0.5	0.7	1.2	1.1
Netherlands	1.8	1.3	1.1	1.2	1.1
New Zealand	-	1.5	1.3	1.1	1.1
Norway	8.0	8.2	10.1	12.6	12.3
Sweden	4.4	5.3	4.6	4.7	4.0
Switzerland	0.3	0.3	0.2	0.2	0.4
United Kingdom	1.7	0.4	0.7	0.8	0.8
United States	3.8	3.2	2.6	2.7	3.5

Sources: See Table I.

Appendix E

UNFPA Priorities in Future Allocation of Resources

[As demands upon the resources of UNFPA increased so did the evidence that the Fund would have to set up a priority system regarding the future allocation of the Fund's resources. As a result, a UNFPA task force, headed by the Fund's Deputy Executive Director, Halvor Gille, worked out a priority system for the allocation of the Fund's resources. Because of this major development in the UNFPA programme, the paper setting forth the rationale and the specifics of the Fund's priority system is reprinted here. As indicated in the Introduction to the paper, the UNFPA general principles and criteria for establishing priorities have been endorsed by the UNDP Governing Council, ECOSOC, and the General Assembly.]

I. Introduction

The United Nations Fund for Population Activities has grown rapidly since its operations began in late 1969. The cumulative programme level for the period 1969-1972 was 50 million dollars. By 1977, the Fund's programme had doubled and is now operating at an annual programme level of 100 million dollars. The remarkable growth in resources available to UNFPA, however, has been more than matched by an equally rapid rise in demand for UNFPA assistance, particularly as a result of the World Population Year and the World Population Conference 1974.

The worldwide information and communication programme undertaken in World Population Year heightened awareness among Governments as well as individuals of the many facets of population, while the broad concept of population activities adopted at the World Population Conference made it possible for a large number of Governments to accept the need for intensifying or initiating population projects within the context of economic and social development planning. Moreover, the World Population Plan of Action [WPPA] adopted by consensus among 135 states at the Conference established clear links between population factors and improvement of the quality of life; it also identified broad areas of activity for Governments, non-governmental organizations and organizations in the United Nations system.

Within the framework of the Plan's many guidelines and recommendations, UNFPA has reassessed its mandate according to the new perceptions of population and to changes in the international population assistance scene, in particular the increasing need for assistance. It was felt that despite the Fund's neutrality on population policies and objectives, certain general principles should be evolved to serve as guidelines in the future allocation of resources and give overall direction to its assistance. With the broadening of the concept of population activities, it was also necessary to define a core programme of UNFPA assistance to provide a means of day-to-date interpretation of its mandate.

The UNFPA has developed two complementary mechanisms for setting priorities in the future allocation of its resources to countries. One of these refers to the *types of activity* to be given priority because of their importance to the promotion of national self-reliance. These activities are defined by minimum requirements or basic needs in the various population sectors. The other is the designation of a group of developing countries as *priority countries* for UNFPA population assistance by applying a set of demographic indicators for which data are generally available and which are considered indicative of a country's population problems. In this exercise also the economic conditions of countries have been taken into consideration by including per capita income as an additional qualifying factor.

Apart from activities at the country level, UNFPA supports intercountry activities. Before 1974 some 60 per cent of UNFPA resources supported intercountry activities and the remainder activities at the country level. by 1976 these proportions have been reversed to 30 per cent and 70 per cent respectively. With this change in emphasis in the UNFPA assistance programme, division of resources in the future has become an important consideration. A review of past UNFPA support to intercountry activities has been undertaken on the basis of which UNFPA will determine its priorities between country and intercountry activities and within the latter.

The following policy statements were presented by the Executive Director to the Governing Council, which discussed and endorsed them in three successive sessions, namely in June 1976 and in January and June 1977. Moreover, the general principles and criteria for establishing priorities received the endorsement of the sixty-first session of the United Nations Economic and Social Council [1] and the thirty-first session of the United Nations General Assembly in August and December 1976 respectively. [2]

II. Aims and Purposes of UNFPA

In May 1973, the Economic and Social Council established the main aims and purposes of UNFPA. These aims and purposes, under which the Fund is still operating, are as follows:

(a) "To build up, on an international basis, with the assistance of the competent bodies of the United Nations system, the knowledge and the capacity to respond to national, regional, interregional and global needs in the population and family planning fields; to promote co-ordination in planning and programming, and to co-operate with all concerned". [3]

[1] Economic and Social Council resolution 2025 (LXI).
[2] General Assembly resolution 31/170.
[3] Resolution 1763 (LIV), operative paragraph 1.

UNFPA and other organizations and governments have already built up considerable knowledge and capacity to respond to needs in the population and family planning fields at both national and international levels, and this continues to be an important objective for UNFPA. In the early years of the Fund, most of its resources were devoted to furthering understanding and knowledge of population matters and strengthening, on an international basis, the capacity of the United Nations Organizations to meet needs for population assistance at the regional, inter-regional and global levels. Recently, however, increasing demand from developing countries for direct assistance to national activities has reduced the share of UNFPA resources available for intercountry activities, particularly those provided through organizations in the United Nations system. As the largest direct—and in some areas the only major—source of international population assistance, UNFPA will continue to support activities on an international basis, but the emphasis in future will be on back-stopping country-level activities and on exploring innovative approaches to population issues.

(b) "To promote awareness, both in developed and in developing countries, of the social, economic and environmental implications of national and international population problems; of the human rights aspects of family planning; and of possible strategies to deal with them, in accordance with the plans and priorities of each country".[4]

As a result of the accomplishments of the World Population Year and Conference and of other activities promoted by UNFPA, other international organizations, Governments and non-governmental bodies, considerable progress has been made in the promotion of awareness of the implications of national and international population problems. Some 40 developing countries with a total of about 80 per cent of the developing world's population have as part of their overall economic and social development programmes national policies to reduce the rate of population growth. In addition, 71 developing countries have established policies in favour of disseminating information on, and distributing the means of, family planning as a basic human right and for the improvement of health, status of women, and family life. All organizations concerned in the United Nations system and many other organizations—intergovernmental and non-governmental—have established population programmes of their own within their mandates and responsibilities.

Considerable effort, particularly in developing countries is still required to promote awareness of the many aspects of population problems. Awareness is often limited to Government officials and educated groups while large segments of the population in many countries, even in those with established national population policies, still do not recognize the importance of population problems and their significance to the promotion of human well-being, the quality of life and basic human rights. This, together with limited recognition of the need for action programmes to cope with population problems, often constitutes a major handicap to delivery. Greater stress will be laid on reaching important population groups such as women, youth, local community leaders, as well as religious, political and other organized groups. Non-governmental

[4] Ibid

organizations can play an important role in this regard and UNFPA's collaboration with such bodies will continue.

(c) "To extend systematic and sustained assistance to developing countries at their request in dealing with their population problems; such assistance to be afforded in forms and by means requested by the recipient countries and best suited to meet the individual country's needs". [5]

This remains the principal objective of UNFPA and will continue to absorb the greater share of the Fund's human and financial resources. The growing demand for population assistance among developing countries, however, may make it necessary to introduce certain limitations in the stated objective. Unless the Fund's resources expand very substantially and beyond current expectations, it will not be possible to continue providing "systematic and sustained" UNFPA support to all developing countries. Assistance may in many cases have to be limited in time, and will gradually be phased out to release resources for new activities in the same country or elsewhere.

Furthermore, the concept of "population problems" as stated by the Economic and Social Council in 1973 must be clarified and its scope defined so far as UNFPA population assistance is concerned. It has always been the policy of UNFPA to respond, to the best of its ability, to the needs and priorities for population assistance as determined by the developing countries themselves. Thus, the Fund has responded not only to requests for assistance for taking population factors into account in development planning, for the collection and analysis of basic population data, and, for disseminating information on and the means of fertility regulation; support has also been extended to help solve problems of migration, distribution and structure of population and, in a few cases, insufficient rates of population growth. The broadening concept of population activities and the need to view population problems within the wider context of economic and social development, as urged by the World Population Conference and the World Population Plan of Action, make it desirable to determine more clearly the areas of principal concern to UNFPA and to which the Fund's limited resources should be devoted.

(d) "To play a leading role in the United Nations system in promoting population programmes and to co-ordinate projects supported by the Fund".[6]

Significant progress has been made by the Fund in this regard but there is considerable need for further co-ordination. The Fund has recently been encouraged by several other funding organizations and Governments with bilateral aid programmes to play a more vigorous role in co-ordinating international population assistance; the increasing difficulty felt within the international assistance community of meeting the demand with available resources makes such co-ordination more important than ever.

The Fund will redouble its efforts to

    (i) develop joint or co-ordinated funding arrangements with other aid organizations;

[5] Ibid
[6] Ibid

   (ii) search for strategies to solve population problems effectively in various settings; and

   (iii) identify approaches to integrating population components with social and economic development programmes.

Such an expansion of the Fund's co-ordinating function will not greatly affect the allocation of resources since it can be made without substantial additional resources. This expansion is not intended to interfere in any way with the right and responsibility of recipient countries to determine the types of programmes and sources of funding they prefer.

III. General Principles for Future Allocation of Resources

In making future allocation of resources, UNFPA will insofar as possible apply the following general principles:

   (a) to promote population activities proposed in international strategies;

   (b) to meet the needs of developing countries which have the most urgent requirements for population assistance;

   (c) to respect the sovereignty of recipient countries on matters of population policies;

   (d) to build up the recipient countries' self-reliance; and,

   (e) to support activities of special benefit to disadvantaged population groups.

Each of these principles is discussed briefly below.

(a) A number of international strategies have been adopted which provide the framework for international co-operation and which recognize population and related matters as an integral part of socio-economic development. Such strategies include the International Development Strategy for the Second Development Decade, the United Nations World Plan of Action on a New International Economic Order, the World Population Plan of Action, the World Plan of Action on Integration of Women in Development and the Draft Plan of Action to Combat Desertification. It is within the mandate of UNFPA to support the population elements of these instruments and to base its policy guidelines and the overall framework of its work programme on them.

The World Population Plan of Action (WPPA), of special importance to the work of UNFPA, emphasises an integrated development approach to population. This Plan suggests that population activities be increasingly supported as elements of activities in health, education, rural development, community development and other programmes to promote economic and social development. The greatest challenges posed by the WPPA are to determine how population and related activities can be promoted effectively as an integral part of such development programmes and how some population problems can be solved through socio-economic transformation.

The UNFPA is actively seeking ways to identify development programmes into which population activities can be integrated, particularly through increased use of its field staff and in collaboration with UNDP country programming exercises. The Fund will give increasing attention to responding to the WPPA and to the needs of developing countries in this regard by collaborating with other organizations within the United Nations system as well as with bilateral aid programmes and interested non-governmental bodies. In such collaborative efforts, UNFPA will be prepared to fund the population components while other development assistance bodies may support the non-population components of integrated programmes as required. At the same time, the Fund will encourage development assistance bodies to support development programmes which are needed for the promotion and effective implementation of population prorgrammes and to include population components, whenever possible, in their development assistance.

(b) Recognizing that the UNFPA's main thrust will continue to be at the country level, various approaches to distributing resources among countries were considered. In June 1975, the advantages and disadvantages of UNFPA's adopting an indicative planning figure (IPF) system similar to the one applied by United Nations Development Programme were considered by the Governing Council and it was decided that the adoption of the IPF system in the field of population was not an appropriate or practical measure.

Nonetheless, it was considered necessary to concentrate the Fund's limited resources on the urgent requirements of those developing countries with the greatest need for population assistance and to promote programmes which have a measurable impact in countries with urgent needs rather than spreading the Fund's resources thinly among some 130 developing countries. As outlined in Section IV(b) below, various alternatives by which certain countries may be assigned priority in the allocation of the Fund's resources without introducing the inflexibility of an IPF system were considered. The most appropriate solution has been found to be the adoption of some population-related grouping of developing countries as priority countries for UNFPA assistance, based mainly upon a set of criteria reflecting in general terms the major problems with which the Fund has been set up to deal.

(c) From its inception, the UNFPA has fully appreciated the sovereign right of each nation to formulate, promote and implement its own population policies as recognized and reconfirmed by the General Assembly.[7] It is for each Government to determine its population programme and approaches to meeting established policy goals. In allocating its resources, the UNFPA respects national priorities for population activities, but this does not obviate the problem of priorities of UNFPA or oblige it to play a completely passive role. In view of their past experience in dealing with population programmes, the Fund and its various executing organizations are prepared and willing, upon request, to advise Governments on setting priorities in accordance with their established population objectives and on the adoption of the most effective approaches. Furthermore, the increasing demands made upon its scarce resources suggest the need as well as the opportunity for the Fund to make choices regarding the nature

[7] General Assembly resolution 2211 (XXI) and 3344 (XXIX) adopted 17 December 1966 and 17 December 1974 respectively.

and size of the support to be provided. This may reflect but not necessarily be identical with national priorities in every case.

While maintaining its neutrality on matters of population objectives and policies, UNFPA provides assistance in accordance with certain basic policies and principles adopted internationally. One of these is that UNFPA supports activities designed for the voluntary participation of the population at large, especially with regard to family planning. This policy is in accordance with General Assembly resolution 2211 (XXI) which recognized "the sovereignty of nations in formulating and promoting their own population policies, with due regard to the principle that the size of the family should be the free choice of each individual family".[8]

Other guidelines may be applied in determining the Fund's own priorities, such as the principle of giving preference to activities designed to strengthen the recipient countries' self-reliance in population matters and to those which benefit disadvantaged population groups.

(d) The World Population Conference and the WPPA stressed the importance of making developing countries self-reliant as fully and rapidly as possible. Furthermore, the General Assembly has decided that the promotion of self-reliance in developing countries should be a basic purpose of technical co-operation[9] and serve as a guideline for future UNDP operations. Therefore, UNFPA support will aim particularly at building up the capacity and ability of recipient countries to respond to their own population needs. To achieve this end assistance should, as far as possible, be phased and limited to a definite period of time, especially where recipient countries have already developed basic population programmes. During the period of assistance the activity should gradually be taken over by the Government or non-governmental organization concerned. In order to avoid UNFPA assistance displacing funds which would or could be committed by recipient Governments or organizations,—the Fund's support should increasingly be devoted to programmes for which the recipient Governments and organizations are committed to making their own contributions and to taking over full financial responsibility gradually.

In accordance with the principle of promoting self-reliance, high priority will be given to supporting the following activities (not listed in order of priority):

(i) Human resource development through training programmes and transfer of skills and technical know-how required in population programmes;

(ii) Institution building at the national level, particularly in the fields of population data collection and analysis, policy formulation and implementation of action programmes;

(iii) Strengthening of managerial, administrative and productive capabilities of recipient countries to enable them to execute population programmes effectively, including ensuring eventual provision of equipment and supplies locally

[8] This principle was confirmed by the Declaration on Social Progress and Development adopted by the General Assembly (Resolution 2542 (XXIV)) which declared "that parents have the exclusive right to determine freely the number and spacing of their children".
[9] General Assembly resolution 3405 (XXX) of 28 November 1975.

whenever possible and to deliver services at the local level to the population at large; and

(iv) Operational research and pilot projects exploring innovative approaches to dealing with various aspects of population problems that may improve or encourage future action.

(e) In accordance with the WPPA, special attention will also be given to meeting the needs of disadvantaged population groups. This is a monumental task in view of the fact that the large majority of the population in most developing countries may be classified as belonging to such groups. This would clearly be in line with the importance given by the General Assembly to reaching the poorest and most vulnerable population sections in meeting the needs of developing countries for development assistance.[10]

The Economic and Social Council has endorsed the recommendation of the Administrative Committee on Co-ordination that alleviation of poverty, particularly in connexion with rural development, should become a major criterion influencing the design of activities and the allocation of resources of organizations in the United Nations system with the primary objective of improving the quality of life through the involvement of the rural poor in the development process.[11]

Towards this end, UNFPA will give high priority to supporting population activities for the benefit and with the participation of groups such as the poorest among rural populations, under-privileged people in urban areas, disadvantaged migratory groups and low-income families in densely populated localities. The problem of "exploding cities" is of great and growing importance in many developing countries, resulting, in many cases, in pockets of extreme poverty in inner cities. Existing organizational and institutional frameworks for reaching these sectors of the population will be fully utilized and supported. Action programmes aiming at widespread popular participation will explore all avenues for promoting community-based activities, involving particularly the underprivileged and other population groups often not greatly affected by or benefiting from development efforts.

Among disadvantaged and vulnerable groups, special attention will be given to women as an active and effective force in development in accordance with the recommendations of the World Conference of the International Women's Year. In the population field, perhaps more than in any other area of development, little can be accomplished without the active involvement and full participation of women, many of whom belong to the poorest of the poor in developing countries. They are vitally concerned as individuals, as actual or potential mothers, as homemakers and as an economically active force.

UNFPA has developed a set of guidelines for emphasizing, in its day to day operations, the inextricable link between the status and roles of women and population activities. These guidelines, which deal with programme development, project formulation, implementation and evaluation, are not meant to be used in the development of special

[10] General Assembly resolution *op. cit.*
[11] Economic and Social Council Resolution 175 (LXI) of 5 August 1976.

"women's projects" but rather as directions applicable to all programmes and projects within UNFPA's mandate. They outline how issues relating to the involvement of women in development may be taken into account in population policies, research in population, data collection and analysis, information, education and service programmes.

IV. Core Programme of UNFPA Assistance

In its broadest sense, "population activities" may be defined as comprising all programmes related to the determinants and consequences of population trends including economic, social, demographic, biological, geographical, environmental and political aspects. The limited financial and human resources available for international population assistance suggest that they be devoted primarily to supporting "the population aspects of development, defined as the causes, conditions and consequences of changes in fertility, mortality and morbidity as they affect developmental prospects and the human welfare resulting therefrom".[12]

The primary concern of UNFPA is to support activities aimed at bringing about a fuller understanding of the population aspects of development and at influencing population factors through the formulation and implementation of policies concerning the size, growth, structure and distribution of population, to improve levels of living and quality of life.

Within this broad scope of activities a core programme of assistance has emerged for which the Fund is now a major international source of funding. The main areas of this UNFPA core programme are the following (not listed in order of priority): basic population data collection and analysis, population policy formulation and implementation including family planning and population redistribution, population education and training, and applied research. It includes communication activities in support of these programmes.

The main emphasis in the core programme is on activities directly related to and required for population policy formulation and implementation. Such activities include:

- taking censuses of population;
- registration of vital events;
- population surveys;
- research particularly on matters relevant to decision making and action programmes;
- training of personnel;
- strengthening population policy units in Governments;
- meetings and seminars on the inter-relationships of population and socio-economic development;
- delivery of family planning services, including integration of family planning services with health and other social programmes;

[12] UNFPA/UN Interregional Consultative Group of Experts on the World Population Plan of Action, "Final Report", (UNFPA/WPPA/20/Rev. 1), p. 17.

- measures to deal with sterility and subfecundity;
- migration policy measures;
- introduction of population education into the curricula of schools and out-of-school education for various organized groups;
- activities designed to disseminate population information to target groups and the public at large.

On the other hand, programmes with the primary objective of, for example, reducing mortality, improving general health conditions, strengthening basic statistical services to improve general data collection, undertaking clinical trials of new contraceptives and providing general and professional education for health personnel, statisticians, teachers, administrators and rural extension workers should, generally speaking, to be considered as falling outside the UNFPA core programme.

The Fund's present and prospective limited resources indicate that primary concern will have to be directed to supporting activities falling within the core programme. Other population activities are not necessarily considered of secondary importance for development but it does not appear to be feasible for the UNFPA to devote a substantial part of its limited resources to activities which fall outside the main objectives of the Fund and for which other sources of funding may be available.

It is neither desirable nor possible, however, to establish clear-cut borderlines for UNFPA-supportable activities. Some flexibility will be maintained to allow the Fund to support activities in areas outside the core programme—but they will be limited mainly to types of activities which are related to the formulation and implementation of activities within the core programme, for example, expansion and strengthening of maternal and child health delivery systems; adaptation of regional, rural and community development programmes to include population elements and measures to deal with spatial distribution of population, including urbanization.

The core programme and, to a limited extent, activities in related areas, indicate the types of population activities for which UNFPA support should be available in the future. The fact is, however, that the scarcity of foreseen resources will most likely make it impossible for the Fund to respond favourably to many of the requests for assistance even within these limits, thus making it necessary to be selective and to establish further priorities. In doing so the need for population assistance as well as the capacity and ability of developing countries to absorb it will be taken into account.

In order to set such priorities the following considerations will be taken into account: types of programmes needed at the national level, population problems of recipient countries, and the role of intercountry activities. The types of programmes will be considered with reference to countries' basic needs at the various stages in the evolution, formulation and implementation of national population policies. National population problems will be taken into account in designating high priority countries for UNFPA assistance. The role of intercountry activities within UNFPA's programme will be reassessed through a review of past UNFPA support to such activities in order to draw up an integrated strategy for such support in the future.

(a) Basic Needs at Various Stages in the Evolution of National Population Policies and Programmes

There are marked differences throughout the developing world in approaches to population matters, in the degree of concern for population questions and in the level of sophistication of the measures taken to deal with population issues. This is not merely because population probelms are different in the various parts of the world but also because attitudes are the outcome of a complex mix of circumstances in a continuous process ending in full "population consciousness". Various steps in the evolution of national population policies and programmes can be identified.

One or several of the following steps in the development of policies may require assistance at the country level:

   (i) promotion of awareness and understanding of population factors as related to economic and social development;

  (ii) determination of the size, growth, structure and distribution of the population;

 (iii) assessment of population trends in relation to economic and social development and appreciation of the causes and consequences of their inter-relationships;

 (iv) formulation of population policies based on the country's perception of population trends and their socio-economic aspects.

In implmenting population policies, programmes may be required for spacing births, reducing fertility, sterility or subfecundity, raising age at marriage, influencing internal migration, redistributing population, or other types of activities.

The World Population Plan of Action provides general guidance on what is needed in various population sectors for the developing countries to become self-reliant in the development of population policies relating to population size, growth, distribution and structure. It is, of course, up to each Government to decide what its policies, population objectives, targets and means of implementation are to be, but the recommendations made in the Plan of Action are meant to guide Governments and international organizations.

The UNFPA will develop guidelines for providing countries with assistance in implementing programmes to meet basic needs in the fields of population, taking into account the priorities indicated by the countries themselves and their own resources as well as sources of external assistance.

Basic needs programmes will be drawn up for all interested developing countries, with a view to identifying (mainly within the UNFPA core programme) the most essential steps to be taken in, for example, census taking, vital statistics, data analysis, delivery of family planning services, communication support services, training and population education. Special attention will be given in this process to the five general principles stated in section III above, particularly building up recipient countries' self-reliance through strengthening the human resource base, institution building and developing other capabilities to meet their needs. This task will be carried out with the participation of experts from the relevant disciplines and in consultation with the Government(s) concerned.

Since this exercise would also be of use to other major organizations and Governments concerned with population assistance, the study may not be limited to the UNFPA core programme in order to be of maximum usefulness. Furthermore, it may not be limited to needs in the governmental sector, but could also take into account the role and contribution of nongovernmental bodies, particularly in promoting activities at the grassroots level.

In each case, the basic needs for population assistance will be identified within the context of the country's population goals, policies and existing capacities. After discerning the population objectives of a country, and its existing policy and capacity to carry it out, a programme will be drawn up of the most essential steps to set the country on the road to self-reliance in the formulation and implementation of population policies. This programme will include components that may be supported by the UNFPA, other multilateral organizations or bilateral donors. It is, of course, up to the government to decide which donor will provide what parts of the assistance required.

In developing basic needs programmes, UNFPA is beginning with studies of interested priority countries (see below) and will eventually study all interested developing countries requesting assistance from the Fund. It is not the Fund's intention to prepare blueprints for population programmes for individual developing countries—only they can do that themselves—but to prepare the framework for international population assistance within a balanced and integrated programme, taking into account differences in population objectives, policies and approaches.

Within such a framework the role of various international, intergovernmental and nongovernmental organizations and bilateral programmes as well as joint or collaborative efforts between them can be clarified and an improved division of labour developed. Such a co-ordinated approach should be of considerable benefit to recipient developing countries and will strengthen the impact of population assistance, making it more attractive to donors to continue and increase their support. The UNFPA should lead and help to co-ordinate this approach. Efforts will also be made to promote population components in related economic and social development activities, particularly through UNDP country programming.

In allocating its resources to countries, the Fund will give priority to assisting (in co-operation with other funding agencies) the establishment of basic population activities. However, the Fund will not be able to respond to all requests for assistance to such activities; further priorities must therefore be established to determine the extent to which countries should be assisted and which countries should receive assistance first.

(b) Priorities Between Countries

Allocation of UNFPA resources to countries has in the past been based largely upon the size of government requests, the types of programmes for which assistance was sought, and what internal and other external resources were available. In 1976, countries in Asia and the Pacific received the largest share of the Fund's programme resources, just over 30 per cent; Africa received around 13 per cent, Latin America around 25 per cent, and Europe, the Mediterranean and Middle East 13 per cent, while the remainder supported interregional and global activities. Over the years the share of UNFPA programme resources allotted to Asian and Pacific countries has remained fairly constant, while moderate to sharp increases have taken place in Europe, the Mediterranean and the Middle East, Africa and Latin America. Allocations to the two last regions have increased two to threefold. 1977 allocations, however, show increases in the percentage of resources for countries in Asia and the Pacific (from 30 to 34 per cent), Europe, the Mediterranean and the Middle East (from 13 to 16 per cent respectively), and Africa (from 13 to 15 per cent) and a decrease for Latin American countries (from 25 to 18 per cent).

The large share allotted to countries in Asia and the Pacific may be explained by the fact that particularly in the earlier years of the Fund's existence they were, and in general terms still are, more "population conscious" and have more comprehensive action programmes than elsewhere. Population size and density of this region are also much higher than elsewhere so that more support for population activities is needed, although not necessarily in proportion to the difference.

An analysis of the Fund's 1976 allocations shows that countries in Asia and the Pacific actually received assistance at the lowest per capita level of all the regions (two US cents), Latin America had the highest per capita level (six US cents), while Africa and Europe, the Mediterranean and the Middle East were at an intermediate level (three US cents each).[13] In relation to national income, UNFPA input was largest in the African region followed by Asia and the Pacific, Latin America and Europe, the Mediterranean and the Middle East.[14]

In order to respond to the most urgent and critical needs of developing countries and to maintain the programme approach applied in the past in accordance with the general principles mentioned earlier, various approaches to setting priorities in the allocation of resources among countries have been considered.

The use of indicative figures for the allocation of resources among the major developing regions rather than for individual countries was considered, but it was found difficult to fix criteria that would take into account the specific role of the Fund. Such indicative figures would have to be established by the governing bodies of the Fund as political decisions.

The Fund explored various other possibilities for identifying a group of developing

[13] Figures are for country as well as regional activities. For country activities alone: Asia and the Pacific one US cent, Latin America four US cents, Africa three US cents and Europe, the Mediterranean and the Middle East three US cents. Support provided in 1977 at the country level indicates no change in Latin America, and slight increases in all other regions viz. in Asia and the Pacific to two US cents, in Africa to four US cents and in Europe, the Mediterranean and the Middle East also to four US cents;
[14] The 1975 UNFPA contributions amounted to $179 per one million dollars national income (1971) in Africa, $145 in Asia and the Pacific, $78 in Latin America and $62 in Europe, the Mediterranean and the Middle East.

countries to be given special attention in the future allocation of resources, with the provision that assistance to other countries will continue on a more selective basis.

In the execution of the United Nations Development Programme[15] special attention is given to countries recognized as least developed countries.[16] This group includes 17 countries in Africa, eight in Asia and the Pacific, one in Latin America and three in Europe, the Mediterranean and the Middle East: total estimated population of 244 million or about 12 per cent of all developing countries.[17] This concept is not considered the most appropriate for assigning high priority for UNFPA assistance; it is based primarily on economic considerations,[18] most of the countries included are comparatively small (only six of them have a total population exceeding 10 million each) and many of them have population problems which are not considered more severe than those of countries not included in the group. The least developed countries urgently need assistance for their development programmes in general but may not necessarily be in urgent need of population assistance in particular.

Another group of developing countries has been designated by the General Assembly as most seriously affected countries.[19] These are developing countries suffering from serious balance-of-payments problems,[20] and benefitting from a Special Programme of Emergency Measures adopted by the Assembly. Most but not all of the least developed countries (24 of 29) as well as some eighteen additional developing countries are included. Of these 25 are located in Africa, nine in Asia and the Pacific, four in Europe the Mediterranean and the Middle East and four in Latin America with an estimated 41 per cent of the population of all developing countries. Since the concept of most seriously affected countries is based largely on the existence of serious balance-of-payments problems, it is also considered unsuitable for use as a criterion for priority treatment in the allocation of population assistance. In the allocation of UNFPA resources some consideration may be given to the existence of serious foreign exchange problems, but this should only be one among several indicators of needs and it is to some extent already taken into account in a general way in the Fund's assessment of requests.

It became clear that a special system of selection of high priority countries for population assistance would have to be designed in order to take fully into account the general principle that the Fund is supposed to assist particularly countries with urgent population problems. To select high priority countries, a few demographic indicators are applied. The lack of population data in many developing countries restricts the choice of demographic indicators but estimates on population growth, fertility, infant mortality and population density on arable land are generally available. They are, in general

[15] General Assembly Resolution 3405 (XXX) of 28 November 1975.
[16] General Assembly Resolution 2768 (XXVI) of 18 November 1971 and Economic and Social Council Resolution 1976 (LIX) of 30 July 1975.
[17] Included in UNDP's second programming cycle 1977-1981.
[18] The criteria applied includes per capita gross domestic products ($125 or less or $150 in some border line cases), share of manufacturing in the gross domestic product (10 per cent or less) and percentage of literates in the adult population (20 per cent or less).
[19] General Assembly Resolution 3202 (A/RES/3202/S-VI) of 1 May 1974.
[20] Following the upsurge in the prices of essential imports without corresponding increases in export earnings.

terms, indicative of major population problems and, to some extent, of the levels of development and welfare. Various threshold levels for these demographic indicators were explored using the most recent information available. Furthermore, in order to concentrate the Fund's scarce resources in areas where they are likely to contribute most towards solving the population problems of the developing world and where assistance is most needed, consideration is also given in a general way to the economic situation of countries as indicated by the level of per capita national income.[21]

By applying the criteria of a per capita national income below $400 per annum and two or more of the following demographic criteria:

(i) annual rate of population growth of 2.75 per cent or higher;

(ii) fertility in terms of gross reproduction rate of 2.75 per cent or higher;

(iii) infant mortality of 176 infant deaths or more per 1,000 live births; and

(iv) agricultural population density on arable land of 2.2 persons or more per hectare,

the UNFPA has designated a group of 40 developing countries as priority countries for population assistance (PCPA's) out of a total of 128 developing countries.[22]

All 40 countries but one meet the criterion of fertility. In all cases the added determining demographic indicator is population growth; in seven cases infant mortality and in seven cases agricultural population density. In 14 cases, in addition to fertility, two demographic indicators prevail, population growth and density in nine cases, and population growth and infant mortality in the remainder. In the one case where fertility is below the threshold level, the criteria of infant mortality and density are met.

Of the group 17 are in Africa, 14 in Asia and the Pacific, five in Europe, the Mediterranean and the Middle East and four in Latin America (see Annex). In 1977, these countries had a total population estimated at 1.2 billion, or 53 per cent of that of all developing countries and territories,[23] and received about 45 per cent of the Fund's total resources provided at the country level. Nineteen out of 29 of the least developed countries as determined by the General Assembly and the Economic and Social Council[24] are also PCPA countries.

A ceiling of two-thirds of total programme resources available to UNFPA for population activities at the country level has been established for assistance to priority coun-

---

[21] Application of social indicators were also explored but abandoned in view of lack of data and the fact that several of the demographic indicators are already strongly correlated with social factors. Material provided by the ILO on estimated ranking of a large number of countries in terms of poverty seems to indicate that all the countries selected using the criteria proposed above half of more of their population falling below an arbitrarily set poverty line; less than one third of the developing countries which do not meet the criteria are in this position.

[22] Countries and territories for which the UNDP Governing Council has established indicative planning figures for 1977-1981.

[23] See Footnote 22.

[24] General Assembly resolution 2768 (XXVI) of 18 November 1971 and Economic and Social Council resolution 1976 (LIX) of 30 July 1975.

tries as a group; the level of assistance of each of these countries is to be determined largely by its basic needs in population. The ceiling is tentative until more experience is gained in determining the need and capacity of high priority countries for carrying out basic needs population programmes.

It is the Fund's intention to review and revise the PCPA group periodically. As the demographic situation in recipient countries changes, some countries will leave the group while new data may result in the addition of new countries. The present group was identified on the basis of data available in 1976 from United Nations and Food and Agriculture Organization sources.[25]

UNFPA intends to maintain some flexibility in applying the concept of priority countries. Concentration of the Fund's resources on high priority countries can be implemented only gradually because commitments have already been made for most of the resources for 1978 and, to a lesser extent, for the following years. Only as commitments expire and additional resources become available will it be possible to implement the newly established priorities effectively. Furthermore, the preparation of basic needs programmes in collaboration with the Governments and the United Nations Organizations concerned will take time. Wherever UNFPA has helped countries to build up population programmes, assistance should not be reduced or terminated suddenly; but the aim should clearly be for the countries themselves eventually to take over full responsibility for the activities concerned.

It is fully recognized that since comparable official statistics are not available for all countries, the designation of countries is sometimes less than definitive. A number of countries, although strictly not within the adopted demographic and economic criteria based upon the data available in 1976, were fairly close to the threshold levels used. Thirteen of the 88 countries outside the priority list of 40 would qualify if a two per cent variance from the threshold levels were allowed. These include eight countries in Africa, two in Asia and the Pacific, two in Latin America and one in Europe, the Mediterranean and the Middle East region. In the allocation of resources among non-priority countries, it is intended to give special attention to borderline cases (for lists of such countries see Annex).

It is recognized that the amount of assistance desired and needed by each developing country depends on the nature of its population problems, the degree of knowledge and recognition of its population issues, the approaches to dealing with such problems, the policies which may have been adopted and the level of sophistication of the measures planned or already taken. These factors vary considerably between regions and countries. Many countries, particularly in Asia and the Pacific, and to a growing extent also in Latin America, are advanced in the evolution of policies and programmes and, have a higher capacity to absorb population assistance. Others, particularly in

[25] United Nations, Department of Economic and Social Affairs, Statistical Office, *Statistical Yearbook* 1974 (ST/ESA/STAT/SER.S/2). New York, 1975, table 188; *Selected World Demographic Indicators* by Countries, 1950-2000 (ESA/P/WP.55), prepared by Population Division, Department of Economic and Social Affairs of the United Nations Secretariat, New York, 1975; Food and Agriculture Organization of the United Nations, Production Yearbook, 1974, Vol. 28-1, Rome, 1975, tables 1 and 5.

Africa, where two-fifths of all the priority countries are located, are at an early stage in policy and programme evolution, concentrating to a large extent on data collection, population dynamics and training activities, and therefore often have a fairly limited need for population assistance. By determining countries' basic population needs, it is intended to respond to varying local conditions and allow for flexibility in developing UNFPA assistance. Until these programmes have been established, it is difficult to specify, either for priority countries or for borderline cases the types of population activities and the amount of assistance UNFPA will provide.

It should be pointed out that resources within the two-thirds ceiling not required for support of basic needs population programmes in high priority countries will be available for assistance in other developing countries. Support for population activities in the latter countries will have to be on a selective basis and will focus more on specific and urgent needs. Although, in principle, all developing countries and territories are entitled to support from UNFPA, those with a comparatively high per capita income may receive it on a funds-in-trust or reimburseable basis.

Allowance will be made for the possibility that one or several donors may wish to assist through UNFPA selected countries of special interest to them in their own region or to support activities which may be related to but not within UNFPA core areas of population assistance. Furthermore, multibilateral funding, funds-in-trust arrangements and other means of supplementing regular UNFPA resources will contribute to flexibility.

(c) Priority regarding intercountry activities

Many intercountry activities receiving UNFPA support, such as exchange of information and experience on population policies and action programmes, experimentation with new approaches, utilization of talent and research facilities in various countries and high level training abroad are essential to the self-reliance of individual developing countries. Furthermore, in view of their widespread ramifications, population problems and policies often have to be seen and dealt with on a broader than purely national scale.

The objectives of UNFPA support to intercountry activities are as follows.

  (i) to create awareness of population issues;
  (ii) to develop an international capacity for supporting activities at the country level;
  (iii) to promote development of innovative concepts and approaches; and
  (iv) to provide technical backstopping for activities at the country level.

In the early years of UNFPA, most of its resources were devoted to supporting intercountry activities through the various United Nations Organizations, but gradually more and more attention has been given to providing direct assistance to developing countries. The proportion of UNFPA programme resources allocated to intercountry activities has declined from some 60 per cent before 1974 to just under 30 per cent in 1977. This trend has been caused partly by a sharp increase in demand from countries for the Fund's resources and the high priority given to meeting these needs, and partly by an attempt to concentrate on activities most essential to meeting the objectives of intercountry activities stated above for which other sources of funding are not available. In order to determine its priorities for supporting intercountry activities, the UNFPA has completed a review of its past support to such activities. This review examined the trends and emphases of UNFPA-supported intercountry activities over the years from geographical and substantive points of view. The main findings of this review, together with the findings of several major evaluations of UNFPA-supported intercountry projects, will contribute to the development of an integrated strategy for future support at the intercountry level.

In preparing a strategy for future UNFPA support of regional, interregional and global activities, the five general principles for future allocation of the Fund's resources outlined in Section III above will be applied. As in the case of activities at the country level, UNFPA support will be directed primarily to the core areas of UNFPA assistance indicated above.

Programmes should aim at providing essential technical backstopping for national activities, so that developing countries can be assisted towards self-reliance. To this end, international capacity to deal with shared population problems should be strengthened and programmes which would encourage collaboration between disciplines and exchanges of experiences between countries should be promoted.

Support to research has always been important in UNFPA's assistance to intercountry activities and will continue to play a significant role in the future. It is the Fund's intention to concentrate its future support on research which will provide early operational results, in particular innovative approaches to population issues of concern to several countries and to effective implementation of country programmes. With a view to an integrated approach to development, research required to enable planners and policy-makers to take population factors into account in promoting economic and social development will also receive special attention.

In developing the Fund's strategy for future support to intercountry activities, the capacity and experience of the international organizations concerned will be taken fully into account and utilized for the maximum benefit of developing countries. In accordance with the instruction of the Governing Council in June 1977, the downward trend of the proportion of UNFPA support at the intercountry level will continue. Resources will be concentrated on a relatively small number of large programmes of an interdisciplinary nature, emphasizing those which have the greatest multiplier effect at the country level.

V. Summary and Conclusions

Until recently the UNFPA was able to accommodate most requests received from the Governments of developing countries. However, the recent sharp increase in the demand for assistance—to a large extent due to the Fund's success in accomplishing its main objectives—is making it increasingly necessary and indeed essential for the Fund to become more selective in granting assistance and in determining the criteria for establishing priorities.

The general principles for establishing priorities in future allocation of UNFPA resources will be: to implement relevant international strategies, to support population activities in developing countries with the greatest needs for population assistance, to give special attention to disadvantaged population groups and to promote recipient countries' self-reliance.

The Fund's resources will be devoted mainly to supporting a core programme of population activities directly related to development, particularly activities required for or connected with population policy formation and implementation. However, it is clear that the Fund's resources will not be sufficient to support all technically sound requests falling within the core programme. It is desirable, then, to concentrate on supporting activities in countries which are especially in need of population assistance, taking into account *inter alia* their demographic situation, their major population problems and the progress made in dealing with them.

Certain basic needs population programmes will be developed at the country level taking into account the diversity of countries' population problems and policies, and approaches to them. Basic population needs programmes will be outlined for interested developing countries in which the assistance required to enable countries to implement these programmes in stages will be clearly set out. This exercise will concentrate on the core areas of UNFPA support, but may go beyond so that its findings may be of use to other donors. This major task will be undertaken in collaboration with the Governments and Organizations concerned.

Up to two-thirds of the Fund's total resources available for country programmes will be devoted to meeting basic population needs in priority countries. The remaining third will go towards meeting basic needs in other developing countries, particularly those identified as deserving special attention in the future allocation of UNFPA resources to countries. However, activities in countries with a high per capita income may be supported on a funds-in-trust or on a reimburseable basis.

As regards intercountry or regional, interregional and global programmes the emphasis in future will be on promoting and reinforcing country programmes, on developing innovative approaches applicable in developing countries and on facilitating implementation of the WPPA. An overall integrated strategy for future UNFPA support to intercountry activities is being prepared. The aim will be to concentrate UNFPA support on a smaller number of major programmes dealing with the most urgent problems and with the greatest multiplier effect upon activities in developing countries.

In applying priorities overall flexibility will be maintained. In many cases, UNFPA support has helped countries to gain momentum in building up population programmes and assistance will not be reduced or terminated abruptly. Allowance will also be made through earmarking arrangements for the special interest of some donors in a particular region, country, or area, which may or may not fall within the UNFPA core areas of assistance.

It has to be recognized that the priorities outlined above cannot be fully applied immediately. The Fund has already made certain commitments into the next three years. Only when these commitments expire will it be possible to implement effectively the priorities indicated. Furthermore, the establishment of priorities is a long term, continuing process and should be subject to periodical review and revision.

UNFPA support to country programmes is often relatively small compared with other sources of population assistance and inputs from local Governmental and non-governmental organizations which are usually very substantial. Yet UNFPA assistance is of great significance, particularly in generating new programmes and new approaches which have to be proved successful in order to attract regular Governmental or other funds. The visibility of UNFPA assistance makes it especially important that it be provided effectively to areas with the greatest need.

Annex

Priority countries for population assistance

Afghanistan
Bangladesh
Burundi
Democratic Kampuchea
Democratic Yemen
Ecuador
El Salvador
Ethiopia
Gambia
Ghana
Guinea
Honduras
India
Jordan
Kenya
Lao People's Democratic Republic
Liberia
Madagascar
Maldives
Mali

Mauritania
Morocco
Nepal
Niger
Pakistan
Paraguay
Philippines
Rwanda
Samoa
Senegal
Socialist Republic of Viet Nam
Solomon Islands
Somalia
Sudan
Thailand
Tonga
Uganda
United Republic of Tanzania
Upper Volta
Yemen

Other countries to be given special attention*

Benin
Central African Empire
Gilbert Islands and Tuvalu
Guatemala
Indonesia
Malawi
Namibia

Nigeria
Peru
Swaziland
Syrian Arab Republic
Togo
United Republic of Cameroon

*Countries which would qualify as priority countries for population assistance if a 2 per cent variance from the threshold levels were allowed.

Appendix F

UNFPA Support of Intercountry Activities

[Another aspect of the Fund's newly-adopted priority system (see Appendix E) is that of the UNFPA's funding of intercountry activities. It was clearly indicated in the work involved in the development of the priority system that as more and more funds were allocated to countries, less funds would be available for regional, interregional and global activities. With this in mind, the Fund's Deputy Executive Director, Halvor Gille, at the request of the Fund's Executive Director and its governing body, sought to develop a strategy for the future funding of intercountry activities. Because the Fund's strategy in this area is intimately related to its priority system, the paper describing the Fund's intercountry strategy is reprinted here, as presented by the UNFPA to the UNDP Governing Council in June 1978.]

Introduction

1. The Governing Council at its twenty-second and twenty-third sessions held in June 1976 and January 1977 respectively, as part of the process of establishing priorities in the allocation of UNFPA resources, identified the core areas of population activities for UNFPA assistance, designated certain priority countries and established a concept of basic population needs programmes.[1] As a further step in the development of a priority system, the Council requested the Executive Director to develop a strategy for future support to intercountry activities. At its twenty-fourth session in June 1977, the Council took note of certain principles and criteria proposed by the Executive Director to be applied in the exercise[2] and requested the Executive Director, in preparing an integrated strategy, to bear in mind "the needs identified in the formulation of basic

[1] *Official Records of the Economic and Social Council, Sixty-first Session, Supplement No. 2A,* para, 594 (d); and *Sixty-third Session, Supplement No. 3,* para. 371 (c). See also Chapter I of the UNFPA report on 1977 activities and future programmes (DP/308).

[2] DP/263, paras. 19 and 20.
Paragraph 19 indicated: "It is recommended that in preparing a strategy for future UNFPA support of regional, interregional and global population activities:

"(a) The five general principles for future allocation of UNFPA resources adopted by the Economic and Social Council and General Assembly should be applied;

"(b) The population activities to be supported at the intercountry level should fall mainly within the core areas of UNFPA assistance as outlined in DP/186;

"(c) The capacity and experience of the appropriate international organizations concerned should be taken fully into account and utilized for the maximum benefit of developing countries; and

"(d) The resources available should be concentrated mainly in supporting a relatively small number of major intercountry programmes, exploring fully the possibilities for interdisciplinary activities".

415

population programmes, and to include in this strategy consideration of the role of UNFPA in research."[3]

2. At the request of the Council,[4] UNFPA circulated to Governing Council members, in September 1977, a summary of UNFPA-supported intercountry activities. In preparing the present document UNFPA has taken into account that review as well as the findings of evaluation of some such activities. Consultations held with the Fund's executing organizations at meetings of the UNFPA Inter-Agency Consultative Committee (IACC) and with interested non-governmental organizations under the auspices of the International Council of Voluntary Agencies have also been taken into consideration as far as possible.

I. Types of intercountry activities

3. The term intercountry activities is used here to include activities undertaken at the regional, interregional and global levels. Regional activities are those which involve or relate to countries in any one of the four UNFPA geographical regions. Interregional activities are those which involve or relate to countries located in two or more, but not all regions. Global activities involve or relate to a number of, if not all, developing countries in all regions.

4. The dividing lines between regional, interregional and global activities are not always clear and, sometimes, somewhat arbitrary. For example, a project may be classified as

---

Footnote [2] continued.

Paragraph 20 indicated: "Furthermore, it is recommended that in selecting intercountry programmes for future UNFPA support, the following criteria be applied:

"(a) The programmes should provide essential technical backstopping for population activities at the country level, so that developing countries can be assisted in meeting their basic needs in order to become self-reliant;

"(b) Support should go to activities which can be carried out most effectively and economically at the intercountry level and which have the greatest multiplier effect at the country level;

"(c) Innovative ideas and approaches to dealing with population issues and to promoting effective implementation of country programmes should be explored, particularly through research and pilot and demonstration projects;

"(d) Comparative studies on population trends and issues in regions and subregions should be encouraged;

"(e) Research activities should aim at developing common methodologies to deal with population issues of common concern to several countries and at providing early operational results;

"(f) Research required to enable planners and policy-makers to take population factors into account in promoting social and economic development should be supported;

"(g) Programmes which would encourage the collaboration of several disciplines and lead to an exchange of experience between countries through international efforts should be promoted;

"(h) Dissemination of population information and data should be promoted both within and among regions;

"(i) Training activities at the intercountry level should be limited to specific technical fields for which institutions, teachers and teaching materials are not available at the national level;

"(j) Regional capacity to deal with population problems common to a number of countries within each region should be strengthened; and

"(k) Activities should be supported only if other resources are not available at the national or international levels".

[3] *Official Records of the Economic and Social Council, Sixty-third Session, Supplement No. 3A*, para. 496 A 3 (c)

[4] *Ibid.*, para. 496 A 3 (b)

interregional instead of regional because of the geographical location of the countries involved, while it may actually be regional in nature. Thus, the Cairo Demographic Centre, which is essentially a regional institution, is considered an interregional project because the countries it serves are located in the region of Europe, the Mediterranean and the Middle East as well as in the African region. The distinction between inter-country and country activities may also be insignificant at times. For example, a number of fellowships are provided in various fields within the framework of country programmes, but others are provided to countries as a part of a global block allocation of fellowships, or are provided at the regional level for attendance at regional training institutes. Many intercountry activities may actually be a part of, or essential for, country programmes.

5. The types of activities supported by UNFPA at the intercountry level comprise research; training; advisory services; meetings and workshops for the creation of awareness or exchange of views and experience; and the preparation and dissemination of instructional materials and research designs. UNFPA support to the infrastructure[5] of some of the executing organizations in the United Nations system is limited to posts of an administrative or managerial nature and therefore is not included among inter-country activities discussed in the present report mainly from a programme point of view.

6. The majority of UNFPA-supported intercountry programmes are carried out by organizations in the United Nations system, mainly the United Nations proper, in-cluding its regional economic commissions, the International Labour Organisation (ILO), the Food and Agriculture Organization (FAO), the United Nations Educa-tional, Scientific and Cultural Organization (UNESCO), the World Health Organiza-tion (WHO), and United Nations Children's Fund (UNICEF). Around 85 per cent of UNFPA support at the intercountry level was made available through organizations in the United Nations system in 1977. Population activities of several regional in-tergovernmental bodies outside the United Nations system are supported, such as the Intergovernmental Co-ordination Committee based in Malaysia, the Association of South-East Asian Nations based in Indonesia and the Union douanière et économique de l'Afrique Centrale based in the Central African Empire. Intercountry activities are also carrried out with the Fund's support by such international non-governmental organizations as the International Statistical Institute, the Population Council, the In-ternational Alliance of Women, the Committee for International Co-operation on Na-tional Research in Demography and the International Union for the Scientific Study of Population.

II. Magnitude and trends

7. In the early years of UNFPA nearly 60 per cent of the Fund's programme resources were devoted to activities at the intercountry level (Table 1). Much of this support was designed to strengthen the capacity of organizations in United Nations system to enable

---

[5] Infrastructure support expenditures amounted to $3.3 million in 1975, $3.4 million in 1976 and an estimated $4.3 million in 1977.

them to carry out population activities, in accordance with their own mandates, mainly in the areas of training and research for the benefit of the developing countries.

Table 1. *Country and intercountry expenditures and estimated allocations, by years*
(in percentages)

	1969-1973	1974	1975	1976	1977	1978	1979-1982
Country	42.3	53.5	60.5	69.7	69.0	68.9	70.00
Intercountry							
Regional	21.3	19.1	16.9	14.8	15.0	14.1	14.0
Interregional	28.6	15.7	9.7	7.6	7.0	17.0	16.0
Global	7.8	11.7	12.9	7.9	9.0		
Subtotal	57.7	46.5	39.5	30.3	31.0	31.1	30.00
Grand Total	100.0	100.0	100.0	100.0	100.0	100.0	100.0

Note: 1969/73 to 1976 data based on actual expenditures according to Management Information Systems reports.

1977 data are provisional expenditures as of end of December 1977, according to Management Information Systems reports.

1978 to 1982 data are based on estimated allocations made in the work plan submitted in the report on 1977 UNFPA Activities and the Future Programme (DP/308).

Infrastructure, overhead and administrative costs are excluded.

8. In recent years, an increasingly larger proportion of the Fund's resources has been allocated to respond to the growing number and magnitude of requests from Governments of developing countries for population assistance at the national or subnational levels. In 1977 support of intercountry activities had declined to about 32 per cent of allocations of total programme resources. The bulk of the decrease had taken place at the interregional and global levels: from 36 per cent of the total programme resources before 1973 it steadily decreased to 18 per cent in 1977. Activities at the regional level, on the other hand, had experienced a much smaller decrease: from some 20 per cent until 1973 to 15 per cent in 1977.

9. The distribution of UNFPA support to regional projects in 1977 was as follows: Latin America and the Caribbean, 32 per cent; Asia and the Pacific, 31 per cent; Sub-Saharan Africa, 25 per cent; and Europe, the Mediterranean and the Middle East, 12 per cent. In absolute terms, resources allocated to regional activities in Latin America and the Caribbean have almost tripled over the period 1973-1977, while in Europe, the Mediterranean and the Middle East they have increased approximately two and one-half times over the same period; funds for regional activities in Sub-Saharan Africa increased by around 130 per cent and in Asia and the Pacific by some 70 per cent.

10. UNFPA has supported intercountry activities in all of its major programme sectors, namely in basic data collection; population dynamics; population policy; family planning; communication and education; and multisector activities. Chart 1 illustrates the proportionate share of UNFPA support to the various sectors at the intercountry level. Up to the end of 1977, the largest share of intercountry support went to research and training in population dynamics especially through the interregional and regional

demographic centres. Next in importance was support to activities in communication and education, family planning and programme development, in descending order. Around 14 per cent of intercountry support went to multisector activities, mostly projects initiated in conjunction with the World Population Year. Basic data collection and population policy received the smallest share (12% of intercountry support). The distribution of UNFPA support between intercountry and country activities varies considerably from sector to sector. Table 2 shows the distribution by major population sectors in 1977. Intercountry support was of primary importance for activities in population dynamics and population policy; over 70 per cent and 60 per cent respectively of UNFPA inputs to these sectors were at the intercountry level. Over 50 per cent of support to communication and education were provided through intercountry activities. In basic data collection and family planning, intercountry support was of lesser importance, only around 27 per cent and 10 per cent respectively of total support to these sectors.

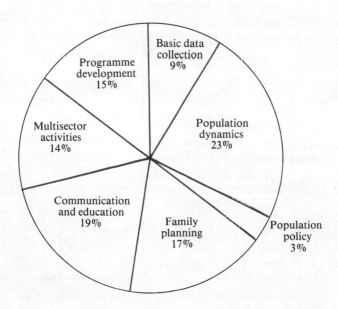

Chart 1. UNFPA support to intercountry activities by major sectors[6] 1969/72-1977

[6] The subsectors included in each of these sectors are as follows: Basic data collection - population censuses; vital statistics and civil registration; sample surveys; economic and social statistics; and supporting activities. Population dynamics - research projects; training and research facilities; and population aspects of planning. Population policies - policy formulation and implementation of policies. Family planning - delivery systems; programme management; and fertility regulation techniques. Communication and education - communication for family planning; population education in schools; and out-of-school programmes. Multisector activities - World Population Year; documentation centres, clearinghouses; and interdisciplinary training. Programme development - field staff and infrastructure.

Table 2. Distribution of intercountry and country support in the major population sectors in 1977 (in percentages)

	Basic data collection	Population dynamics	Population policy	Family Planning	Communication and education
Country	72.7	27.3	37.0	89.9	41.8
Intercountry					
Regional	9.1	39.6	31.4	3.6	35.3
Interregional	2.5	20.6	4.7	2.3	15.0
Global	15.7	12.5	26.9	4.2	7.9
Subtotal	27.3	72.7	63.0	10.1	58.2
Grand Total	100.0	100.0	100.0	100.0	100.0

Note: Estimated expenditures as of 31 December 1977.

11. The magnitude and distribution of regional activities by major substantive sectors in each region is illustrated in Chart 2.

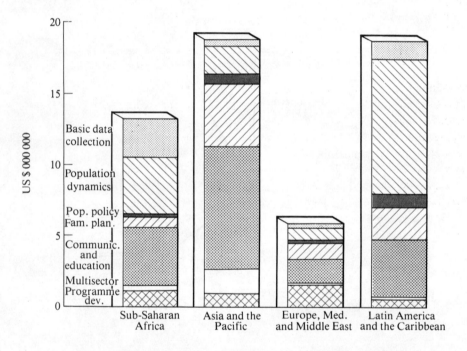

Chart 2. UNFPA support to intercountry activities by regions and major sectors 1969/72-1977

12. As seen in this chart, the areas of emphasis vary considerably from region to region. In Sub-Saharan Africa, basic data collection, population dynamics and communication and education are of almost equal importance. In Europe, the Mediterranean and the Middle East, communication and education and programme development activities are the main areas of support. In Asia and the Pacific, communication and education activities are of predominant importance, while in Latin America and the Caribbean the largest share of regional resources went to projects in population dynamics.

13. Some 44 per cent of UNFPA support to intercountry projects in 1977 was allocated for technical backstopping, principally through advisory teams, for country activities.

About 26 per cent in 1977 was allocated for support of research activities, around 15 per cent for training and the remainder for support communication activities.

14. At its twentieth session in June 1975, the Governing Council, at the recommendation of the Executive Director, decided that UNFPA support to intercountry activities should, for the time being, be "stabilized at the 1975 level, making some allowance for increased costs and subject to availability of resources."[7] The 1975 allocations to intercountry activities amounted to $33.2 million. This level of support has actually not been maintained; total allocations at the intercountry level in 1976 were only around $25.5 million and in 1977, $27.6 million.[8] This is due principally to two reasons: first, in accordance with the instruction of the Council to concentrate assistance on country activities, UNFPA has devoted most of its attention to programming at the country level. Second, the imposition of a ceiling at a specific point in time has tended to hamper programming of new activities and the development of initiatives. UNFPA's preccupation with reviewing its past support of intercountry activity and with developing a strategy for the future has also led to caution in allocating resources for intercountry programmes.

III. Rationale for UNFPA support

15. While fully recognizing that it is desirable and necessary to continue increasing emphasis on country programmes, the Executive Director believes that intercountry activities are, and should remain, an integral and substantial part of UNFPA's assistance programme. It was largely as a result of the Fund's initial, proportionately large, investments in the latter that the current demand for population assistance at the country level has come about. The early UNFPA supported intercountry activities not only strengthened the international capacity for population programmes but were also instrumental in promoting "population consciousness" among developing countries and in shaping the modalities of support to population activities at the country level. It is true that the thrust of UNFPA's assistance is now directed more towards operational than promotional activities but that does not mean that intercountry programmes are no longer necessary.

16. Increased awareness of population problems and the more widespead desire to undertake population programmes have been matched by a concomitant growth in technical capacity in developing countries in only a few cases. Technical cooperation continues to be necessary not only in the formulation phase of programmes, but also for their implementation and evaluation. To provide advisory services and training at the intercountry level is often a much more economical way of technical assistance than

[7] DP/118, paragraph 16(d) and *Official Records, Economic and Social Council, Fifty-ninth Session, Supplement No. 2A,* para. 494(d).
[8] Actual expenditures amounted to $28.5 million in 1975 and $23.4 million in 1976 or 42.4 per cent and 33.7 per cent respectively of total project expenditures in these years. Expenditures for 1977 are estimated at around 90 per cent of allocations. This is representative of the increasingly high implementation ratio of UNFPA intercountry support; historically it has been consistently higher than that of support at the country level.

to give such support on a country by country basis. Increasingly, developing countries have indicated their preference for short-term advisory services provided through regional or global arrangements rather than for international expertise through resident advisers and consultants.

17. Some specialized programmes cannot be promoted in individual developing countries, particularly in smaller ones, because cost-effectiveness is low. Joint ventures or other forms of intercountry collaboration are often the only way some countries can participate in, and benefit from, population assistance. Furthermore, intercountry technical co-operation makes available to developing countries the combined expertise of the international population community. Training and research programmes at the country level can be encouraged, strengthened and given a wider perspective if they are developed within a broader international framework and can provide exchange of experience, common methodology and technical backstopping.

18. There are certain population problems that are transnational in nature and have to be dealt with at the intercountry level, such as international migration or the problems of the drought-stricken Sahel region. Their solutions have to be sought from an intercountry perspective, and are assured only if there is full multi-country collaboration.

19. New dimensions of population problems need to be systematically explored and new solutions assiduously sought. In many instances, intercountry programmes provide the ideal setting for devising new and innovative concepts, methodologies and approaches not only because they are more economical but also because expertise and facilities are readily available. Many developing countries lack such a capacity or may not give the problems to be solved sufficiently high priority because of other pressing needs, particularly of an operational nature. When making country requests for assistance, Governments often are concerned with immediately visible needs and may not take into account unforeseen or potential needs. Preparation of designs and guidelines for research, or of training manuals and the development of innovative approaches are examples of activities which can be carried out more efficaciously at the intercountry level so that they can benefit several countries in one or several regions, or all developing countries.

20. There is much variety in the nature and magnitude of population problems encountered by developing countries, yet they still need constant exchange of knowledge and experience for their common benefit. Intercountry programmes are a particularly useful mechanism for reviewing, synthesizing and sharing experience gained by countries both in the same and in different regions. Through conferences, seminars, study tours, publications, clearing-houses and other channels of information, policy makers, administrators, researchers and teachers can benefit from developments in other countries and carry out their responsibilities more effectively. Such programmes also play a vital role in promoting technical co-operation among developing countries.

21. Intercountry population activities executed by the various substantive organizations in the United Nations system with UNFPA support, especially regional activities, allow for an integrated approach which combines population components with aspects of these organizations' regular activities. Examples of such integrated approaches in-

clude the linking of family planning with maternal and child health, immunization and other elements of primary health care, promotion of population education within formal and informal education programmes and the study of demographic problems in the context of general and sectoral economic and social development planning.

22. While recognizing that the technical and managerial capability of developing countries in the fields of population is constantly improving, it still remains a fact that inputs at the intercountry level will be required for some time to come to strengthen national infrastructures and to build up the countries' capability to become self-reliant.

IV. Some accomplishments of intercountry activities

23. Many intercountry activities supported by UNFPA over the years have contributed significantly to country programmes. They have promoted awareness of concepts and approaches subsequently adopted by national authorities, and have helped develop such approaches. A few illustrations of such accomplishments follow.

24. Intercountry activities have been vital in backstopping country projects by making possible the training of country cadres, have provided technical information and lent technical support to project development and implementation. The six regional and interregional demographic centres supported by UNFPA are important examples. The centres were established to train cadres of professional demographers and population experts in developing countries qualified to plan and carry out population studies for use in economic and social planning and in other vital areas of national development, as well as to assist demographers in carrying out research. Each year, approximately 200 students from the developing world participate in one or two-year courses at these centres; to date, over 1500 students have been trained. The centres also provide research opportunities for the teaching staff. Some of them offer training support for the organization of courses, seminars and workshops at national universities.

25. Significant contributions have also been made at the intercountry level in data collection and demographic research. UNFPA has thus helped standardize and simplify census procedures, test and develop new techniques for obtaining vital statistics and explore new methods in data collection to improve the administration of family planning services. Some 65 countries have been assisted through regional or interregional advisory services in census taking or census-related operations. Cross-national comparative research on various demographic and related factors has been supported, greatly contributing to the understanding of demographic processes and encouraging further research at the national level.

26. UNFPA has supported various schemes providing a framework for multi-country undertakings designed for the development and maintenance of international standards in the field of population, while also servicing the needs of individual countries. For example, some 31 developing countries are presently participating in the World Fertility Survey through large-scale national representative sample surveys aimed at determining the levels, trends and attitudes related to fertility and family

planning. Another 15 to 20 developing countries will, in the near future, participate in this programme, and some 20 developed countries are planning to participate at their own expense. Some 30 African countries, of which 17 have never taken a population census, are participating in the African Census Programme in which regional advisors have been playing a crucial role in solving problems related to standards, comparability, methods, language, data processing and programmes objectives. Nearly 25 countries have carried out studies of their laws relevant to population issues according to the guidelines and direction of the international Law and Population Programme; this has resulted in comprehensive publications on population and law, and sometimes in important legislative actions.

27. Co-operation between countries, particularly at the regional level, has contributed to developing concepts and approaches which might not otherwise have been promoted, or only much later. For example, an Asian regional workshop on population education was followed by a series of national workshops and/or seminars in the Philippines, Malaysia and Indonesia, and the Governments of Bangladesh, the Republic of Korea and Sri Lanka started national population education projects largely as a result of such meetings. A regional seminar on population education in Africa, designed to conceptualize population education in the African context, resulted in assistance requests to UNFPA in the area of population education from nine countries which were then provided with technical follow-up support by regional personnel.

28. Under a regional project in Asia and the Pacific a series of regional and national seminars on workers' education was carried out and it has led to the design and backstopping of some 15 UNFPA-financed country projects in this area, in Bangladesh, India, Nepal, the Philippines, Republic of Korea and Sri Lanka, with the full participation of labour ministries, trade unions, managements and co-operatives.

29. Within the framework of a UNFPA-financed global project a demographic-economic model has been developed and applied in four developing countries (one in each continent). In one country, Brazil, the model is being applied for the formulation of the next National Development Plan and a multi-disciplinary team has been established at a national research institute for modelling work on a more permanent basis. This illustrates how a global project can contribute towards institution-building and staff training at the country level.

30. An intercountry study which involved the development of a research design and methodology for the identification of major problem areas in family planning administration resulted in the application of the research methodology by programmes in Indonesia, Malaysia, the Philippines, Republic of Korea and Singapore. Subsequently, based upon the findings of the study, regional training courses for senior family planning administrators, with technical backstopping from regional advisory services, were conducted in Malaysia and the Republic of Korea. Research centres in Brazil, Ethiopia, India, Indonesia, Iran, the Republic of Korea, Thailand and Yugoslavia have also utilized intercountry funds for studies of the behavioural aspects of family planning in their own setting.

31. The intercountry mechanism of subcontracts with national institutes has been utilized to promote national studies on the use of folk media in family planning programmes. In more than 20 countries in Africa, Asia and the Pacific and Latin America, technical support in communication was made available through regional advisers who provided skills not yet available at the country level, and who were able to train national cadres.

32. Conceptualization of population education and preparation of prototype material and source books at global and regional levels have helped to clarify, develop and apply new ideas and directions in national programme development, in the co-ordination of programmes across various sectors, in the promotion of approaches to population education, such as self-instructional materials, and in research designed to improve population education and communication activities for health workers, educational planners, agricultural specialists and others.

33. These are but a few examples of the contributions that intercountry activities have made both in terms of providing much needed technical support to countries and in pioneering new directions that are of benefit to programmes in developing countries.

V. Constraints in intercountry approaches

34. The experience gained with intercountry activities has reinforced UNFPA's belief that such activities should remain an essential element in its assistance programme. However, the Fund is aware of certain constraints in intercountry approaches. For example, it is very difficult to strike a proper balance between, on the one hand, efforts to improve the "state of the art" through the development of new approaches and concepts and, on the other hand, efforts to promote the adoption and application in developing countries of existing techniques and knowledge. There is no easy answer to this problem and the Fund has to be particularly careful, in establishing priorities and planning the allocation of its resources at the intercountry level, not to foster only the continuous exploration of innovative approaches but also to support efforts at applying existing technical know-how to meet the countries' immediate needs.

35. Many of the population problems of developing countries cannot be solved by short-term approaches, and simple solutions with little technical sophistication may not be accpetable to many countries. But efforts should be made to avoid solutions which require technology and infrastructure not available in the large majority of developing countries. Methodological advances have recently been made in the direction of technical simplification, and these efforts should be continued through intercountry research and training programmes.

36. From an administrative point of view, application of research findings, new methodologies and results of experimentation with innovative approaches is sometimes hampered by limited dissemination of the findings to the countries and the individuals for whom they are meant. Language barriers may in many cases be a contributing factor since such materials usually are made available in only one or a few of the major official languages of the international organizations concerned. Sometimes application in

developing countries is constrained by a lack of trained and experienced personnel or financial resources. More research and experimentation at the country level, taking into account prevailing constraints in the application of findings, might be more fruitful in certain situations. In any case, intercountry research projects should have provisions for adequate dissemination and translation of findings, for appropriate training of personnel and for local institution-building to assure follow-up action at the country level.

37. It is fully recognized that the main purpose of UNFPA-supported intercountry programmes is to serve the developing countries, but sometimes insufficient attention is given in the design and planning of programmes to the practical needs of the countries. At the moment, there is, however, no firmly established, widely accepted mechanism for the identification of country needs at the intercountry level. UNFPA will explore improved mechanisms for regular consultations between the countries, the executing organizations and the Fund, to co-ordinate the approaches to meeting such needs and to identify priority areas. Increased attention will be given to ensuring follow-up action at the country level, sometimes to be promoted through, or implemented with, the technical support of intercountry activities.

38. The potential for multi-agency collaboration at the intercountry level is frequently insufficiently exploited and this results in overlapping or in isolated activities; the latter creates gaps in coverage when one or more appropriate agencies are not involved. International organizations or units within them may be highly experienced and knowledgeable in one substantive sector, but there is often the need to develop a broader approach which would also encompass other sectors and disciplines. It may be necessary to establish regional mechanisms for co-ordinating intercountry activities and for promoting more integrated programmes addressed to problems common to countries in the area.

39. UNFPA has already taken the initiative in this regard through its attempt to restructure its assistance programme to regional advisory services. There is general agreement between the Fund and its executing organizations that the current arrangement of regional advisory teams should be streamlined. This issue has been the subject of discussion at two regular meetings of the IACC. At an *ad hoc* inter-agency working group meeting in Santiago, Chile, an assessment of the needs for advisory services in the Latin America and Caribbean region was made, and an agreement was reached, subsequently endorsed by the IACC, to establish, on an experimental basis for a period of two years, a co-ordination group of all regional advisers on population in Latin America and the Caribbean, supported by a UNFPA liaison officer to be stationed at the headquarters of the Economic Commission for Latin America. It was further agreed that consultations should take place in the other regions to assess their needs for advisory services, with the view to developing, in due course, multi-disciplinary arrangements appropriate to each region, taking into account the experience gained in the experimental programme in the Latin America and Caribbean region.

40. While fully aware of the importance of intercountry activities in the UNFPA assistance programme and recognizing that there is much that can and needs to be done

at the intercountry level, the Executive Director believes that a more co-ordinated and integrated approach should be adopted in making future allocations in this regard. It is with this in mind that the suggestions about priority areas of intercountry support are outlined below, to provide guidance for future UNFPA support and for determining the degree to which UNFPA resources should be devoted to activities at the intercountry level.

VI. Suggested areas for UNFPA support

41. The following sections deal with the main programme areas of UNFPA support at the intercountry level, namely: basic data collection, population dynamics, population policies, family planning and communications and education.[9] In each area, the main types of activities UNFPA has been supporting are briefly outlined.[10] Subsequently, in each area the types of activities that require continued support, since they derive from the principles and criteria for selecting intercountry activities as noted by the Governing Council,[11] are identified. Because in almost every case the perceived needs extend beyond what UNFPA can support, the Executive Director has attempted to specify the Fund's principal areas of concern among these needs in the foreseeable future and recommendations for priority areas of support are made for the Council's consideration.

42. It is important to bear in mind here that almost half of UNFPA's resources allocated to intercountry programmes have, so far, provided technical backstopping to country programmes, and that such backstopping is expected to continue and to consume a considerble portion of future resources available for intercountry programmes. Thus, while the recommendations in the subsequent sections are based to a large degree on perceived needs of developing countries in the area of population, the extent to which the recommended activities can be undertaken is limited by the demands ongoing country programmes have in terms of direct technical support at the intercountry level.

Basic data collection

43. Efforts to improve the quantity and quality of basic population data, which are needed for the formulation and implementation of population policies and economic and social development plans, have to be made mainly in the developing countries themselves. However, intercountry programmes can make important contributions to building up data collection systems through improving methodolgy and through training of personnel for population censuses, vital statistics, civil registration and population-related sample surveys.

[9] See footnote [6].
[10] For details, see UNFPA paper "Summary of UNFPA-supported activities", 1977, (mimeographed).
[11] DP/263, paragraphs 19 and 20.

44. The African Census Programme and the World Fertility Survey are two of the largest ongoing UNFPA-supported schemes at the intercountry level. They have contributed greatly to developing and strengthening the capability of developing countries in basic population data collection. In the areas of vital statistics and civil registration regional advisers provide backstopping to national counterparts and also assist by convening regional expert meetings to promote improvement of population statistics. Regional and interregional advisers have contributed substantially to the improvement of national capabilities in census and other data collection operations by helping train national cadres. As a part of continuing efforts to develop better data processing systems, computer software has been developed at the global level to expedite the processing of censuses and other population data through small computers in developing countries.

45. Methodolgoical research is needed to improve the reliability of vital rates. This should include experimentation with various forms of estimation such as the use of subnational registration areas as bases for national estimates. Pilot studies are needed to improve civil registration under various conditions. The methodology must be improved for strengthening national capabilities for population surveys which would provide demographic and related socio-economic information essential for the formulation of population policies in the framework of development planning. The methodology for integrated population-related data gathering schemes should be developed through linking census programmes and population surveys with other types of data collection.

46. Survey design and methodology need to be developed particularly to measure the dimensions, causes and effects of international and internal migratory movements. There is also a need to develop concepts and methods to enumerate, identify and classify diverse population groups such as nomads, unemployed, underemployed, women working in their homes and self-employed.

47. It is recommended that UNFPA should in future mainly support the following activities: Assistance in census operations should be concentrated mainly on support of training programmes. Support to the World Fertility Survey should be continued until the present programme of surveys has been completed in 1982, and further support may be limited to methodological improvements based upon the experience gained and to the funding of advisory services to countries through the United Nations. Since Governments are increasingly concerned about the problems of population redistribution and in view of the serious deficiency which exists with regard to internal and international migration statistics, measures should be supported at the intercountry level to promote and improve data collection on the volume, types and motivation for migration. To this end an intercountry scheme similar to but more limited in scope than the World Fertility Survey might be established and supported through which guidelines, advisory services, preparation of manuals and training of personnel may be provided. In all areas of data collection support should be given to the dissemination of knowledge about methodological advances, to the promotion of exchange of experience between countries and to the preparation of teaching and training materials.

Population dynamics

48. Intercountry activities supported by UNFPA in population dynamics have covered a broad spectrum. They included research on mortality trends; the interrelations between population growth, employment and migration; studies of population and environment in selected situations; the effects of population growth on education; and various issues concerning agriculture, food and population change. Support has also been provided for the development of demographic and economic models, notably the BACHUE model of the ILO.

49. Substantial UNFPA support has been provided to the regional demographic centres for the training of personnel in developing countries in population-related research, including the processing and analysis of data. The centres have played an important role in providing basic training in demography and related subjects and in research, thus contributing significantly to building up the capability of developing countries to deal with population dynamics.

50. While national and sub-national planning is a process which should take place at the country level, there are a number of areas in which intercountry activities can effectively assist planning, notably the development of methodology. Countries need assistance for preparing periodic national impact reports that examine the effects of population trends on major socio-economic variables and the demographic effects of changes in the socio-economic structure. Work on national impact studies will be greatly enhanced by methodological and conceptual research on a global or regional scale so as to assist the design of such studies and to deal with difficult implementation issues such as the articulation, specification and measurement of interactions between population and socio-economic variables at both micro and macro levels.

51. Methodologies need to be improved for integrating population data into general and specific development planning. The application of such improved methodologies should be promoted through training programmes and seminars for key personnel in central and sectoral planning units. However, because an integrated body of knowledge on population and development does not yet exist, training in this area has to remain experimental for some time to come. Studies are required of the organizational structures and activities of government development planning units to identify where population data can best be integrated in the planning process. Provisions should be made to give countries assistance in establishing or strengthening population units in national planning offices.

52. In the area of population dynamics, it is recommended that UNFPA concentrate support mainly on the following: Research programmes currently receiving UNFPA support should be consolidated by placing emphasis on the most urgent issues concerning population dynamics and development planning. An International Review Group on Social Science Research and Population and Development has been funded by UNFPA along with several other donors to provide an overview of what is known in this area and what are the major gaps in knowledge. After the Review Group has completed its work a revision and consolidation of UNFPA supported research activities

should be undertaken and priorities established. Until that time, recommendations are made only with regard to demographic training and modelling work.

53. While intercountry training courses on basic demography and population and development will no doubt be required for some time to come, UNFPA support to the regional demographic centres and programmes should not be indefinite, even if the needs for continuation of such support vary from region to region. On the basis of the recent UNFPA evaluation of the centres, it is recommended that support of the International Institute for Population Studies (IIPS) in the Asia and the Pacific region be phased out gradually. The training and research needs in the region should be met increasingly at the country level, and provisions should be made for an adequate fellowship programme so that especially the smaller countries of the region can obtain the required training at institutions capable of providing it. Support to the Latin American Demographic Centre (CELADE) should be continued for the time being, but efforts should be made to encourage decentralization of basic training courses to countries, while more specialized training may be retained at the regional level. The two centres of Sub-Saharan Africa, the Regional Institute for Population Studies (RIPS) in Accra and the Institut de Formation et de Recherche Démographiques (IFORD) in Yaoundé, should receive increased support so that they can expand training, research and backstopping substantially, while the Cairo Demographic Centre should continue to be supported at the present level to enable it to service mainly the needs of the Arab States.[12]

54. Training at all of the regional demographic centres should be broadened and greater attention should be paid to social sciences in general and to issues of population and development planning in particular as well as to the analysis of demographic data needed for improving the formulation and implementation of population policies. Continued support should also be given for the inclusion of basic population courses and the consideration of population issues related to development in various other regional and global training programmes, such as regional development centres and statistical programmes.

55. Future UNFPA support to the development and use of models should be limited to the incorporation of demographic factors into broad development models and to population-focused models for national application.

Population policies

56. Intercountry activities in the area of population policies include efforts to identify alternative policies for meeting various demographic goals and to promote greater understanding of the policy formulation process, particularly the role of research; studies of the impact of population policies; and assessment of the effect, if any, upon population trends of policies not specifically intended to influence population factors.

---

[12] In DP/FPA/8/Add.9 recommendations are made concerning support to the United Nations-Romanian Demographic Centre for the next two years.

57. UNFPA-supported intercountry activities in this area included workshops and seminars, mainly regional ones to familiarize policy makers with the importance of demographic variables and of population policies in development. For example, studies have been undertaken on the social welfare aspects of family planning; on social security and population factors, with emphasis on the effects of different family allowance schemes; and on the environmental and population dimensions of human settlements. Advisory services have provided technical support for the development and implementation of population policies in a number of countries.

58. A comprehensive project to develop greater understanding of cultural values as they relate to population policies and programmes received UNFPA support. The project is expected to yield useful training materials. A regional population policy research project in Latin America known as the PISPAL project is also funded in part by UNFPA. A central unit formerly linked with CELADE has been charged with planning and developing multi-disciplinary research projects on the interrelations between socio-economic and demographic variables in the context of the formulation of population policies.

59. Given the importance of fertility as a population variable, considerable attention still needs to be directed to clarifying the determinants of fertility. Intercountry methodological research and comparative studies are needed to test the current research hypothesis that income distribution has significant effects on fertility, particularly as it changes over time, and how fertility is affected by the role and status of women. Although it was once believed to be an important element in fertility decline, questions are now being raised about the effects of a decline in infant and child mortality; further research is needed in this area, particularly in Africa. Further work is also needed to determine the extent to which children in different societies are considered important for security in old age, and the extent to which they fulfill this expectation. Concern with the determinants of fertility relates both to countries which desire to decrease and to those which want to increase their populations.

60. Intercountry programmes are needed for monitoring and research concerning alternative population policies and their possible adaptation to differing political, social or economic settings. Countries which have undergone significant fertility declines and other important population changes have to be studied to identify the underlying policy variables. Conceptual and methodological research is needed at global and regional levels to promote studies which would yield better understanding of different cultural, religious and ethnic perceptions of population policies and programmes and of how the family and the individual are motivated with regard to fertility, migration and other demographic phenomena. Such studies could contribute considerably to improving communication with family groups and individuals for the formulation and implementation of population policies.

61. International and internal migration are regarded as increasingly important problems by many Governments, particularly in the Middle East, Africa and Latin America. Greater attention must, therefore, be given to human resources planning as a way of giving greater rationality to the movement of persons both across and within

national borders. Research is needed on resources distribution and human settlements; this should include the interrelationships between industrialization, desertification, deforestation, desalinization, and land development on the one hand, and population factors on the other. Methodological and conceptual research is also needed concerning the demographic and socio-economic impact of migration on both the departure and arrival areas, and the motivations behind the migrants' decision to move. The impact of rural and urban development policies and of programmes in the area of population dynamics should be investigated, documented and disseminated to assist countries in developing programmes most suited to their needs.

62. In the area of population policies, it is recommended that UNFPA concentrate mainly on research and training activities which should be consolidated to focus on the major population issues of immediate concern to developing countries as outlined above. Conceptual and methodological research at the intercountry level should be supported to assist countries in assessing the impact of various policy packages, which should include not only population policies but also socio-economic policies not having explicit population objectives.

63. In terms of support to training in this area, UNFPA should focus on supporting programmes designed to create greater awareness and better understanding among researchers, policy planners and decision-makers on the role of research in population policy formulation and implementation. Courses or workshops should be supported which provide training for policy makers and planners who are in the best position to take population factors and relevant research findings into account.

64. Further recommendations for future support of activities in this area will be made when the conclusions of the International Review Group mentioned earlier are available.

Family planning

65. UNFPA support of intercountry programmes in the area of family planning has made contributions in essentially three aspects: human resources development, research and delivery of services.

66. In human resources development, UNFPA has assisted the development of training and education programmes and materials for health workers, including medical students and traditional birth attendants, through support of teachers training, fellowships, seminars, workshops, special courses and circulation and development of teaching materials.

67. As to research, epidemiological studies on maternal and child mortality and morbidity related to fertility trends and patterns, which have been supported over a number of years, are being completed. New operational research has emerged, for instance, on the high risk factors in reproduction, which will help develop more effective service strategies. Other research includes studies on the behaviour of adolescents, abortion, sterilization, the integration of nutrition aspects and the epidemiology of infertility in some African countries.

68. Considerable gains have been made in the expansion of family planning services but intercountry activities countinue to be urgently needed to strengthen already existing programmes, to explore alternative delivery approaches and to develop new and adapt existing contraceptive technology.

69. In recent years, considerable stress has been put on the delivery of family planning services in the framework of maternal and child health care programmes, and on improved programme management and administration. Activities in support of services have also received attention, particularly the development of methodologies for collection of services statistics and utilization of statistical data as a tool for monitoring and evaluating family planning programmes.

70. Among the needs which have to be met in the future are: the simplification of service statistics and record keeping; improvement of evaluation methods and their application; development of simplified methods of administration and financial management; improvement of supply lines; management of information systems for the training of health workers at various levels; improvement of the delivery of services to various special groups such as organized labour, migrants, youth and newly married couples.

71. Increasing emphasis has recently been placed on providing family planning services through community-based approaches, both inside and outside the national health system. The delivery of family planning services through this approach should involve existing programmes and institutions in areas such as functional education and literacy, agricultural and rural development, social security schemes and trade unions. Effective back-up support will be needed from a health system which includes community services as envisaged by the primary health care approach. Studies are needed to increase the understanding of what motivates communities to adopt family planning practices and to determine how community operated programmes can be established.

72. Research to identify the most effective and acceptable community based approaches to family planning should be encouraged, developed and analyzed through intercountry activities, and the various social, cultural, political and economic situations should be taken into account. In such studies, particular attention should be given to improving programme performance through new approaches to management, particularly at the village level. Studies are needed on how to overcome the lack of coverage and acceptability of existing family health services.

73. In the studies mentioned above, particular attention should be given at global and regional levels to problems of management and such issues as the following: How should programmes be monitored and evaluated; how is co-operation and co-ordination between different groups maintained; and how are workers to be trained and sustained in their efforts? Based upon the findings of such intercountry studies, guidelines should be developed for their application at the country level and for the development and implementation of training schemes for community based workers and the related training of teachers.

74. Continued attention should be given to developing effective, easily administered,

inexpensive and safe methods of contraception for use in developing countries, particularly where the contraceptives delivery points are moving from clinics to community-based programmes. Clinical and epidemiological research on methods of contraception, including the development of improved or new methods, should be expanded in the developing world. Greater resources for such research should be made available and should also include the testing and adaptation of traditional as well as modern methods.

75. In the field of family planning it is recommended that UNFPA should support the following activities: High priority should be on operational research, so as to reinforce ongoing programmes and to advance knowledge of new approaches; coverage should thus be expanded and resources for promoting family planning used more effectively. Studies which assess the conditions for success or failure of ongoing integrated maternal and child health family planning programmes should be supported, as well as studies designed to formulate and implement community-based approaches to family planning, with built-in evaluations after a reasonable period of experimentation. Research to be supported should assist programme planners in assessing the real and perceived needs of the members of different communities, in relating family planning activities effectively to such other social programmes as education, civic involvement, family economics, food, nutrition, and employment.

76. As country programmes adopt and utilize improved family planning schemes and countries become self-sufficient in basic training, the regional and interregional training programmes should become more specialized in character and probably decrease in intensity, volume and cost. However, one area where action has not been commensurate with needs is health education, and considerable intercountry support of training in this area will be required.

77. Substantial support should also be provided for research in family planning technology. This should include the adaptation of current methodologies, development of new contraceptives and the prevention and treatment of infertility and sterility. For this purpose, research facilities in developing countries should be strengthened particularly through grants, advisory services and through research and training at regional or global levels. The WHO Special Programme of Research, Training and Development of Human Reproduction and other appropriate international programmes should be utilized for this area of research. In accordance with the Fund's general policy to support applied and operational rather than basic or fundamental research, it is recommended that the Fund give priority to the development and improvement of family planning technology and practices.

Communication and education

78. The success of population policies and programmes depends to a large extent upon the understanding of the relevance of population factors and related issues in decision-making at individual, family, community and national levels. The Fund has, therefore, supported intercountry programmes which promote the involvement of as wide a

population as possible in census taking, registration of vital events, family planning and migration schemes. Various types of intercountry support of communication and education programmes have been provided including regional advisory services, the preparation of prototype materials, source-books and teaching materials, training of educators and the development of support communication strategies. Support has been provided within the context of sex education, population education, family life education, worker's and health education both formal and informal, and particular stress has been on existing institutions and channels in direct contact with the widest population groups. One specific example is an innovative scheme to mobilize community-level communication channels for population education and communication and their integration with modern mass media. Support was given to an International Study on the Conceptualization and Methodology of Population Education (ISCOMPE) which surveyed population related education activities around the world to broaden understanding of the nature and users of such activities in different cultural settings. A comprehensive programme to promote and develop national population education, information, research and communciations within the framework of rural development was also supported.

79. The promotion of population education and communication activities at the sectoral level has been very successful. On the other hand, experiments with intersectoral activities have brought out the advantages of integrated education and communication strategies in support of all population activities; they deserve to be developed further to complement sectoral approaches.

80. Special attention should be given to those intercountry activities which will help develop the appropriate modes of delivery and content for different audiences, with due account of relevant behavioural factors. The regional and interregional activities should promote training of educators, develop national training schemes for personnel in various development programmes, and establish the methodology for evaluation of population communication and education efforts.

81. Another need which can be met at the intercountry level is to make research on population communications and education more readily available and disseminated more widely for the benefit of country programmes. Through various types of intercountry activities the application of communications and education research findings should be promoted in the planning and execution of population policies and programmes.

82. In the area of communication and education it is recommended that UNFPA concentrate future support at the intercountry level mainly on efforts to promote information exchange in all types of programmes. More emphasis should be put on application of intersectoral communication and education approaches, and regional advisory services should be made available to assist in the development of specific country materials. Training for such application should also be assisted where appropriate, at the intercountry level. The development of prototype materials, sourcebooks and teacher-training hand books should continue to receive support.

83. Support to intercountry clearinghouses should be continued since they complement activities at national levels by focusing principally on exchange of technical information, the transfer of skills and experiences and on new ideas and approaches. Regional activities serve as a focal point for information exchange within regions and can provide a natural mechanism for sorting out and tailoring relevant information from other countries and regions to national activities in a particular region.

VII. Conclusions

84. Despite some constraints in programming, intercountry activities are a vital area which UNFPA must support to carry out its mandate and its primary responsibilities. In general they complement activities in countries and do not compete with them. Most UNFPA-supported intercountry activities cannot be carried out by or in individual countries, or at least not without becoming very costly and less effective.

85. The review undertaken of the intercountry activities financed by UNFPA in the past and at present suggests that future UNFPA support should, to a larger extent, go to major areas of needs, and that a consolidation of activities would be desirable. The impact of the Fund's efforts could be strengthened by concentrating on fewer but major intercountry programmes in areas of common concern to a number of developing countries as expressed in their own priorities for national action or derived from the basic population needs exercises. The objective of each programme or project and its relevance to the needs of developing countries should be clearly identified. Interdisciplinary approaches should be encouraged and, in this context, collaboration between two or more executing organizations should be promoted. In each case the most suitable implementing agency should be selected within or outside the United Nations system. Support for some of the training programmes, including the regional training centres, should continue over a number of years, in view of continuing demand. In research, however, it is suggested that some time limit be established for UNFPA support to specific projects. UNFPA-supported research activities should be concentrated on innovative and advanced approaches which are expected to have important policy implications in the developing countries in the near future.

86. As appropriate, programmes should be planned for five years and UNFPA commitments should be made for the same period, in line with the approach followed in major country programmes. All major intercountry programmes exceeding $1 million might be submitted for approval by the Governing Council as are all large-scale country programmes. This could be done on a rotating basis by selecting programme proposals in one or a few sectors or areas for consideration at each session of the Council. Interim measures, such as pre-project funding, could be adopted at the beginning of the cycle to avoid any adverse effects on ongoing activities. Such an arrangement would not only permit systematic, long-range planning of UNFPA intercountry support, but would also provide an opportunity for Council members to become more familiar with the nature of UNFPA-supported intercountry activities.

87. In the present paper, the Executive Director has made various recommendations on

the major programme areas of support in the coming years. At this time, it is not possible to indicate the magnitude of the funds required. Since 1975, UNFPA has provided intercountry support at an overall level below the ceiling established by the Governing Council, which was the absolute amount allocated in 1975. It is recommended that, in the future, this ceiling be replaced by a limit determined as a percentage of total programme resources. To some extent, the existence of the present ceiling has hampered programming and acted as a static influence because of a tendency to apply the overall ceiling proportionately to each programme area and each organization's activities. More flexibility is needed to bring about a more dynamic approach. The frequent lack of clarity about the borderline between country and intercountry activities also makes flexibility necessary. Since the main objective of intercountry activities is to support and strengthen population programmes at the country level, it seems justified to link the level of support at the intercountry level to the overall trend in UNFPA resources development by introducing limits in percentage rather than in absolute terms.

88. In view of prospective inflationary trends and other cost increases, it is clear that unless the current ceiling of resources for intercountry activities, which is expressed in an absolute amount, is replaced by a ceiling set as a percentage level of total programme resources, diminishing room will be left for funding research and the exploration of innovative approaches required for the strengthening and development of population programmes in countries. Under the present conditions new types of activities or increased support to ongoing activities such as demographic training and contraceptive research could only be undertaken if and when support to current programmes is reduced or phased out. However, in order not to cause any discontinuity or loss of momentum, the phasing out of UNFPA support to ongoing activities has to be a gradual process.

89. Around 60 per cent of the Fund's resources allocated in the past for intercountry programmes provides training of personnel and technical backstopping of country programmes which will undoubtedly require support, at least at the same level, in the future. In addition, there are certain intercountry programmes to which the Fund is committed for some time to come, such as the regional and interregional demographic centres and the block allocations for fellowships through the United Nations, which fulfill essential needs of developing countries. Thus, in recognition of these realities and of the fact that certain problems in the population fields have to be tackled through cross-national efforts, a flexible and adequate percentage level ceiling for future intercountry support should be established to ensure a balanced and dynamic approach in UNFPA's total assistance programme.

90. it is suggested that total UNFPA support to intercountry activities, as defined in this report, should not exceed 30 per cent of total programme allocations. Efforts should be made to reduce it eventually to 25 per cent.[13] This will mean a substantial

---

[13] It should be borne in mind that the range mentioned here refers to percentages of annual allocations. In view of the generally higher implementation ratio of intercountry programmes than of country programmes, year-end intercountry expenditures are usually a somewhat higher percentage of total programme expenditures than the allocation percentage. In 1975 intercountry allocations amounted to 36.2 per cent of all pro-

reduction from the 1975 level which was over one-third of all allocations and at the same time establish a goal for a reduction from the current (1976 and 1977) level of around 30 per cent. Establishment of the suggested range would also permit some, though only very limited, growth of UNFPA-supported intercountry activities in the near future.

91. The Executive Director is convinced that a very strong case exists for continuation of UNFPA support at the intercountry level and is confident that the Governing Council will become more aware of the importance of such support when it would begin to review and approve major intercountry programmes in the future, as proposed earlier in this paper. In addition to the priority areas of support outlined above, intensified and regular consultations with competent organizations and experts would further ensure that the Fund's intercountry resources will be deployed to fill the most critical gaps. While fully appreciating the desirability of giving increasing emphasis to country programmes, the Executive Director believes that the imposition of a tighter ceiling than proposed above for intercountry support would be detrimental to the development of important areas of support, particularly those of an innovative character, and reduce the Fund's overall programming flexibility.

VIII. Recommendation

92. The Governing Council may:

(a) *Take note* of the Executive Director's report on UNFPA support to intercountry activities;

(b) *Request* the Executive Director, in consultation with the international organizations concerned, to continue his efforts to streamline and consolidate regional, interregional and global activities supported by UNFPA;

(c) *Approve,* subject to comments made by members of the Council, the Executive Director's recommendations made in this report about the major programme areas of future UNFPA support, the types of intercountry programmes which should be approved by the Governing Council, and the level of future support; and

(d) *Request* the Executive Director to report periodically on the application by UNFPA of the proposed priority system for intercountry activities.

[The UNDP Governing Council, at its session in June 1978, approved the Executive Director's initiative to establish an experimental mechanism for co-ordinating intercountry activities and for promoting more integrated programmes addressed to problems common to the countries in the respective geographical areas and encouraged

Footnote[13] *continued.*

gramme allocations, while intercountry expenditures were 39.4 per cent of all programme expenditures. In 1976 the percentages were 28.2 and 30.2 respectively. In 1977, intercountry allocations constituted 30.7 per cent of all programme allocations and expenditures are estimated at around 31 per cent of total programme expenditures.

further efforts of this kind; urged the Executive Director, in consultation with the international organizations concerned, to co-ordinate approaches by organizations of needs and to continue his efforts to streamline regional, interregional and global activities supported by UNFPA; and requested the Executive Director to submit to the Council cost estimates for intercountry activities, as well as suggested priorities at levels of financing equal to 20, 25 and 30 per cent of projected 1982 resources. It also agreed that the Fund should continue the trend towards providing an increasing proportion of UNFPA resources to country programmes.]

INDEX

A

absorptive capacity 73, 138
academic community, role of 80-81
ACC *see* United Nations Administrative
    Committee on Co-ordination
acceptor characteristics *see* fertility trends, factors
    affecting
access to family planning services
    as a human right 200-202
    laws related to 202, 203
    see also population programmes, delivery of;
        contraceptives: community-based distribution
        of *and* governments permitting access to;
        villages, reaching out to
acculturation 162
action programmes *see* population programmes;
    family planning
actual costs of experts' salaries 241
administration of programmes *see* management
    of programmes
Administrative Committee on Co-ordination *see*
    United Nations Administrative Committee on
    Co-ordination
adolescents *see* youth and population
adult education *see* extension programmes
Advisory Board, Review Committee of UNFPA
    10-12
Advisory Committee on the Application of Science
    and Technology to Development   xviii, 33
advisory services   xix, xx, xxi, 238-240
Africa   xxii, xxv-xxvi, 60, 156, 158, 159, 160, 161,
    165, 171, 182-183, 184, 186, 198, 235, 255,
    257, 260
African Census Programme 63
age at marriage 202, 203
age composition of populations *see* children in
    population, proportion of; aged population
    groups
aged population groups 227, 228
agencies *see* executing agencies of UNFPA; United
    Nations Fund for Population Activities:
    United Nations agencies, relationships with
    and infrastructure support to agencies;
    co-ordination, interagency; bilateral agencies
agricultural development *see* food and population;
    rural development and population; population

and development, relationship between
aid *see* international assistance
allocation of financial resources *see* United
    Nations Fund for Population Activities:
    priorities for allocation of resources;
    population programmes: appraising proposed
analysis of data *see* data collection
annualized funding system 240
appraising programme proposals *see* population
    programmes: appraising proposed
approval authority of UNDP Governing Council
    on UNFPA expenditures 240
    see also United Nations Development
    Programme: Governing Council
Arab nations (often referred to as Middle Eastern
    or Western Asian nations) 117, 156, 159,
    160, 161, 183
Asia and the Pacific   83, 109, 124, 157, 158, 159,
    160, 164, 165, 171, 172, 174, 175, 182, 184,
    185, 215, 242, 257, 260
Asian Population Conference, first (1963)   xvi-xvii
assessment of programmes *see* monitoring of
    programmes; evaluation of programmes
assimilation, cultural 162
assistance: international; multilateral; etc. *see*
    international assistance; multilateral assistance;
    etc.
assistance requests *see* requests to UNFPA
attitudes, personal *see* family planning:
    socio-cultural factors affecting
audio-visual materials *see* education and
    communication components of population
    programmes
awareness of population problems, creating
    44-59, 122, 265

B

BACHUE models 191
balance of payments (foreign exchange status)
    of a country 263
Bangladesh 193
basic data collection *see* data collection
basic needs assessments *see* population needs,
    assessments of countries'
basic needs population and development approach
    144-145, 146, 167

G

H

I

S

V